In April 1985, Michael Wild suggested to the German publisher Alex Hinrichsen that he translate Baedeker's *Indien* into English. The title had appeared only once, in German (1914), but he felt sure that there would also be an English readership eager to acquire it.

Alex found the notion *verführerisch* (seductive!) and sold Michael a copy at half price, on the understanding that he would receive the translation and then publish it.

Five years later, the duly completed English translation of *Indien* was sent to Germany, only to come up against a problem: another publisher had in the meantime taken over the firm Baedeker and stipulated that they wanted the name to represent only the modern gazetteer-type of guide. Reprints or translations of the 'old' Baedekers were henceforth forbidden.

In recent times, however, the name Baedeker has become the property of the present owners of the Karl Baedeker house, (Mairdumont GmbH, Ostfildern), who have generously given the go-ahead for Michael's translation to be published. And so here it is, though, sadly, without the maps, plans and line drawings. The reader will however find all the original text faithfully presented, with the page numbering closely observed.

INDIA

Baedeker's *INDIEN,* (in the English translation © by Michael Wild), is reproduced here by kind permission of the Karl Baedeker Verlag

Published by The Red Scar Press
33 Longmeadow Lane, Natland LA9 7QZ
email: mrw33@tiscali.co.uk
in May 2013

ISBN 978-0-9565289-6-4

INDIEN

Handbook for Travellers

by

Karl Baedeker

With 22 maps, 33 plans and 8 diagrams

LEIPSIC

KARL BAEDEKER, PUBLISHER

1914

COMPARATIVE TABLES

Money:
Indian rupees
(See p. XVII)

Rupees	Annas	*M.*	Pf.
-	1	-	8½
-	4	-	34
-	8	-	68
-	12	1	02
1	-	1	36
2	-	2	72
3	-	4	08
4	-	5	44
5	-	6	80
6	-	8	16
7	-	9	52
8	-	10	88
9	-	12	24
10	-	13	60
11	-	14	96
12	-	16	32
13	-	17	68
14	-	19	04
15	-	20	40
16	-	21	76
17	-	23	12
18	-	24	48
19	-	25	84
20	-	27	20

Straits dollar (see p.282)

$	ct.	*M.*	Pf.
-	25	-	60
-	50	1	20
-	75	1	80
1	-	2	40
2	-	4	80
3	-	7	20
4	-	9	60
5	-	12	-
10	-	24	-

Distances:
(see p. XVIII)

Engl. miles	km.	Engl. miles	km.
1	1·61	100	160·93
2	3·22	150	241·40
3	4·83	200	321·86
4	6·44	250	402·33
5	8·05	300	482·79
6	9·65	350	563·26
7	11·27	400	643·76
8	12·87	450	724·22
9	14·48	500	804·66
10	16·09	550	885·13
11	17·70	600	965·59
12	19·31	650	1055·01
13	20·92	700	1126·52
14	22·53	750	1206·99
15	24·13	800	1287·35
16	25·74	850	1367·92
17	27·35	900	1448·38
18	28·96	950	1528·85
19	30·67	1000	1609·31
20	32·18	1100	1770·25
21	33·70	1200	1931·18
22	35·40		
23	37·01	Km.	Engl.M
24	38·62	1	0·62
25	40·23	2	1·24
26	41·83	3	1·86
27	43·44	4	2·48
28	45·05	5	3·10
29	46·66	6	3·73
30	48·28	7	4·35
40	64·37	8	4·97
50	80·47	9	5·59
60	96·56	10	6·21
70	112·65	11	6·83
80	128·74	20	12·42

PREFACE

The present travel guide, first proposed by Dr. *H. Wiegand* (†1901), Managing Director of North-German Lloyd, was originally intended to comprise south and east Asia in one volume. The problem of doing justice to such an extensive subject in a single book indicated that it would be advisable to restrict the area covered to southern Asia, especially since, even here, only the most important tourist routes could be dealt with. A manuscript by Prof. Dr. *Georg Wegener* forms the basis for this work. He has travelled the area repeatedly, especially for the sake of this book, and, latterly in 1911, in the retinue of His Royal Highness the Crown Prince. The data for the Practical Advice given in the Introduction come from Dr. *A. Faller* of Lenzkirch, who also knows India from extensive travels there and, in particular, from *W. v. Köppen,* former Secretary at the German Consulate in Bombay, now in Antwerp, who possesses many years' experience and who also worked on the section dealing with the Hindustani language. The descriptions of the collections of north Indian antiquities are by Dr. *J. Ph. Vogel,* of the Archaelogical Survey of India; they will be valued all the more, since there are as yet no catalogues for the major museums of Calcutta, Lahore etc. The Editor is much beholden to the *German Consuls* and other residents in the country for reading the proofs, particularly those sections devoted to Colombo, Madras, Bombay, Agra, Delhi, Calcutta, Penang, Singapore, Batavia, etc. When forming his opinions about the Indian people, their culture and art, the reader will find the excellent account by Prof. Dr. *Richard Garbe* of Tübingen most welcome.

Apart from the two general maps of India proper and Indo-China, taken from Wagner & Debes' atlas, all the maps and plans have been drawn specially for this volume from the best sources available.

The spelling of place names, which varies in almost all publications, is based chiefly upon the Imperial Gazetteer mentioned on p. LXXI. Where they differ markedly from the spelling in railway timetables, the variant is given. To spell according to German pronunciation e.g. Dschaipur, Tschitorgar, Lacknau, instead of Jaipur, Chitorgarh and Lucknow (as seen on the maps) would hamper rather than help the reader. Many forms which match the German orthography, such as Haiderabad, Darjiling (instead of Hyderabad, Darjeeling etc.) are found in English books also.

Total consistency is not the intention here. It is assumed that the peculiarities of English pronunciation are already known (to the German traveller). A few detailed points should perhaps be made: *ch* sounds like (German) tsch; *j* is similar to dsch; *ai* or *ay* like eh; *e* and *ee* like the German *i; ow* like au; *u* like a short flat a; *y* between two consonants like ai, between two vowels like j, at the end of a word like i. The accentuation of syllables varies as much as spelling. So, for instance, Bombay is pronounced bombé and bómbeh, Mádura is also pronounced madúra. In general one should give fairly equal emphasis to all syllables. More obvious variants are given an acute accent in the text of the handbook, e.g. Trincomalée, Mátale, while the circumflex, without reference to emphasis, is intended to denote only the length of the vowel. See p.310 for the orthography of place names on the Dutch island of Java.

The Editor is always grateful for comments which readers kindly send him, especially when these are based on actual travel experiences. The first edition of a book, whose task is to report innumerable details of every kind, is unlikely to be free from omissions and errors. It need hardly be reiterated that any commercial advertisements are excluded from Baedeker's handbooks.

The abbreviations used here correspond to those in the Editor's other handbooks.

With the prices given for hotels, P. denotes Pension (the price per day inclusive of room); Rm. room, Bd. beds [Translator's addition], B. breakfast, L. lunch or tiffin, D. dinner (the main meal in the evening).

For units of length and area the usual abbreviations apply: m metre, cm centimetre, km kilometre, sq m square metre, sq km square kilometre; a are, ha hectare; SM denotes the international sea mile, M. the English mile (see p. XVIII).

Directions: N., n. = north, northern; S., s. = south, southern; E., e. = east, eastern; W., w. = west, western.

Money: *M* = Mark; £ = pound sterling; sh. = shilling; fl. = Dutch guilder; R. = rupee, a = anna, p = pic (see p. XVIII); ct. = cent; $ = dollar (see p. XVIII).

The days of the week are denoted thus: Su, M, T, W, Th, F, S.

CONTENTS

India

Burma

The Malayan Peninsula

Siam

Java

[Because it has not been possible to include the original maps in this volume, a brief selection is listed here, to give the reader an idea of the complexity of producing a guide to such a large area.]

General map of *India* (1:10,000,000) in the pocket in the rear cover. *The Suez Canal, The Red Sea, Ceylon, Environs of Delhi, Darjeeling, Mandalay, Straits of Singapore, General Map of the Malayan Peninsula, Sumatra,Java.*

Town plans, to various scales, were given of all the main tourist cities, along with plans of such attractions as the Taj Mahal at Agra. There was a panorama of the Himalayas from Darjeeling.

Practical Information

The following remarks apply chiefly to Ceylon and the Indian subcontinent, but are also useful for travel in Burma and the Malayan peninsula. For information about travel on the Dutch island of Java, see p.308.

Among the non-European countries, India is one where travel is comparatively straightforward. Excellent steamer connections are available for the return journey by sea (3 weeks each way). The whole country is covered by an extensive network of railways, and even if, because of the vast distances to be covered, journeys of 30 hours or more are unavoidable, they are generally easier to bear than in Europe. All the places worth a visit are either on a railway line or can be quickly reached from one. The officials, especially the station masters, are instructed to give every assistance and advice to the travelling public, and they carry out this task in truly exemplary fashion. Accommodation is provided even in the more remote districts. While, up to 10 years ago, it was still regarded as out of the question to travel through India without a native servant, travelling conditions are now so far developed that one can manage on one's own, if one has a sufficient knowledge of English and is already used to foreign travel. Thanks to the rapid progress of popular education, one finds the occasional English-speaking native almost everywhere, especially in southern India, and anyone who has, during the long sea voyage, taken a little trouble to assimilate a few words of Hindustani (see p.XXVIII), will hardly ever run into difficulties. The people are neither hostile to strangers nor importunate, and far less likely to beg, than is the case, for instance, in Egypt. Public safety is guaranteed. Every native knows that any attack upon a European is punished severely, and that the culprit very rarely remains undetected. The carrying of weapons is therefore unnecessary. One gets by everywhere (in normal times) with a calm and assured demeanour. It is only when very incautious travellers leave their things lying about for all to see, that minor pilfering occurs.

1. Travelling expenses. Travelling Time. Itinerary. Equipment. Travelling Companions. Servants.

The expense of the journey depends, as everywhere else, upon the traveller's demands and needs, but the European way of life has a lower limit beneath which one cannot go. If one travels first class on steamers and trains, stays only in the best hotels and is accompanied by a servant, the monthly outlay must be budgeted at not less than 1200*M.* The customary four months spent in Ceylon and Hindustan would therefore come to 5000*M.* In connection with the time spent abroad, the return steamer fare is of no small consequence; in the case of a longer stay the total expenditure is proportionately less. On land the daily expense, including journeys by rail and carriage can, on average, be covered by 30-40*M.* The cost is lower if one uses the perfectly good second class on our German steamers, or travels with cheaper shipping lines, stays where possible in more modest hotels, travels without a servant and (by day, see p.XXI) uses the second class on trains. One will then manage on two-thirds of the sum mentioned.

The letter of credit must be issued by a banking house which is directly connected to one of the big Anglo-Indian 'Exchange Banks' (*National Bank of India Ltd.; Chartered Bank of India, Australia & China; Hongkong and Shanghai Banking Corporation Ltd.)* or the *German-Asiatic Bank,* and, to avoid losses in exchange, should be made out in English pounds only (see p.XVII). Very convenient are the increasingly popular universal letters of credit, which allow the user a completely free choice of route, and permit the withdrawal of money without complicated documentation. This letter of credit has to be in two parts: a letter of introduction with the holder's signature, and a special letter in which the amount of credit is given. One should keep both parts separate or send one on ahead *poste restante*. Since banks will pay only on presentation of both parts together, one is protected against misuse by unauthorised persons if one letter is lost. The letters of credit and credit notes issued by *Thos. Cook & Son,* London E.C., Ludgate Circus, are also to be recommended. There are branches in all the more important places, but these unfortunately, up to the present, have been manned by English-speaking staff only. One should always arrange one's affairs so that one can reach one's next destination with sufficient cash in hand. Indian festivals frequently last for several days; the more important ones are also observed as bank holidays, when no payments are made. Only Cook's branches are open then, and willing to help, generally for a few hours in the morning. – One is advised against taking German banknotes; even in the Consulates there is hardly any opportunity to change them.

The best time for travelling is December, January, February and the first half of March. Admittedly, it is in October, after the rainy season, that Nature unfolds her fullest splendour and luxuriance and, only a little later, displays already the results of the drought, which give the landscape an air of wintry repose. But October is still too hot for travelling, nor is India really accessible from Europe so early on, since one would be exposed to possible heat-stroke during the voyage through the Red Sea. One will hardly be able to start the journey before the first half of November. In Ceylon and southern India the first signs of the monsoon make themselves felt (p.10) until the middle of December, but the accompanying storms and downpours are seldom a hindrance for long at a time. In any case one can reckon from December onward upon continuous dry, fine weather and bearable daytime temperatures, not higher than at home in a hot summer. At heights of 1000m. or more above sea level and in northern India, the nights can be bitterly cold, with hoar-frost even. The heat sets in towards the end of March, sometimes earlier; from then on, temperatures of 40°C are no rarity. The government officials leave the cities of the plains and go to the resorts in the mountains.

Itinerary. – Not counting the sea voyage, 2½-3 months suffice in Ceylon and India proper for a reasonable assimilation of the wealth of wonderful impressions which Nature and people have to offer. The traveller who has less time at his disposal should limit his visit to northern India, the main seat of Indian culture and history. Ceylon, with its tropical nature and the ruined buildings of its splendid past, will seem to many a traveller a rewarding goal in itself. The longer the journey, the more one must guard against exhaustion, and see to it that one has sufficient rest-days, which are best spent in the hill stations, such as Kandy (p.35), Mount Abû (p.140), Darjeeling (p.232) or Matheran near Bombay (p.105) etc.

One should start with Ceylon, where 2 weeks should be devoted to *Colombo* (p.25), *Kandy* (p.35), *Nuwara Eliya* (p. 46) and *Anuradhapura* (p.56).

Southern India can be covered in 10 days at the most: *Madura* (p.74) 1 day; *Trichinopoly* (p.77) or *Tanjore* (p.79) 1 day; *Madras* (p.81) 1 day; *Hyderabad* (p. 112) 2 days; *Bijapur* (p.105) 1 day; the remaining time is taken up by the long rail journeys. If one wishes to add *Bangalore* (p.94) and *Mysore* (p.98) to the itinerary, then a further 5 days will be required. – The stay in *Bombay* (p.121) should be allocated at least 3 days, while the excursion to *Ellora* (p.118) takes 2.

In northern India the following time shoud be allowed: *Ahmedabad* (p.132) 1 day; *Mount Abû* (p.139) 1 day; *Chitorgarh-Udaipur* (p.144) 2-3 days; *Jaipur* (p.147) 2 days; *Delhi* (p.176) 3 days, to be visited in all events before Agra, or it will not make the impression which it merits; *Agra* (p.161) 3 days, if possible when the moon is full (Taj Mahal!); *Gwalior* (p.158) 1 day; *Benares* (p.221) 2 days; *Lucknow* (p.214) 1 day, not essential; *Calcutta* (p.237) 3 days; *Darjeeling* (p.232) 4 days; in addition about 10 days of rail travel. The return journey from Delhi via *Amritsar* (p.195) to *Lahore* (p.198) and *Peshawar* (p.206) requires a week and may seem to many travellers dearly purchased because of the lengthy rail travel and the cold nights.

One should allow a week for the journey from Calcutta to Bombay or Colombo back to the steamer on which one is to travel home. The sea journey to Colombo is preferable to the 3-day rail journey.

Recommended is the trip from Calcutta to Burma (about 14 days required), where a visit to *Rangoon,* the boat journey on the *Irrawaddy* and the town of *Mandalay* are the most rewarding (see p.256). – To return home from there, one travels from Rangoon to Colombo.

For travel on the *Malayan Peninsula* see p.281. – For *Siam*, the journey from Singapore to Bangkok suffices: return trip 12-14 days (see p.299). For *Java* at least 3 weeks should be allowed, see p.305.

One's equipment must be more carefully considered than for the usual journeys in the Near East. One must take into account the alternation of heat and cold here (p.XIII), the special travelling conditions in India, the long rail journeys, the often inadequate accommodation and also the social customs of the English, which are more or less standard to everyone. The following hints to gentlemen will give ladies at least a clue as to how they should best equip themselves according to custom and needs.

In general, the following are sufficient for gentlemen: two light-weight European summer suits and a thick autumn or winter suit (to be packed in one's hand luggage on railway journeys, to facilitate rapid changing); a light-weight dinner jacket for dinner on board ship and in the better hotels; a particularly light-weight suit for the journey through the Red Sea and the stay in Colombo; a summer overcoat; a warm overcoat and a good travelling rug for northern India and sea voyages, also a light-weight dust coat for railway travel. If one needs to extend one's wardrobe while in India, this should be done exclusively at good European firms in the major cities. The local tailors, particularly the so-called "Cheap Jacks" set up in hotels or nearby, demand the same or higher prices as the former for much inferior workmanship. If need be, one can get them to make up suits of raw silk in Colombo or Bombay (average price 35R.; give the tailor a well-fitting suit as a pattern, and the service will be better than if the customer's measurements were taken, however thoroughly). For those who wish to attend social gatherings, tails are obligatory. A frock-coat is required only at receptions by the Viceroy, governors etc. One can go visiting in any suit apart from white, which on the Indian mainland is usually worn only by officials of lower rank, or as military uniform. Nor is it a suitable colour to wear for travelling, because of the dirty state of the railways.

One should keep to the same linen and underclothing as one wears at home during a hot summer; if necessary, one can purchase very light-weight items in Colombo or Bombay. In the daytime, comfortable shirts (also coloured and other types) are worn, usually with soft double collars and self-knotted ties; with the dinner jacket in the evening only a fine white shirt and simple stiff collar with a black necktie are worn. One's supply of underclothing must last for at least 3 weeks without the need to have washing done, not to mention that in the hands of the native washermen (dhobies), many items of clothing become unserviceable after being washed only twice. (See also p.XXVIII). For night attire the so-called *pyjamas* are usual and, on trains, almost indispensable. Here, as in the smaller hotels and Dak bungalows (see p.XXIV) one should take at least half a dozen towels and a few sheets, since one very often comes across dirty bed linen. Under no circumstances should a woollen belt be forgotten, which is needed in bed also.

Good footwear is essential. One should equip oneself with two pairs of sound brown lace-up boots, a pair of canvas shoes for the sea voyages and for Ceylon, and patent leather shoes to wear with one's suit at social gatherings.

The indispensable tropical hat (*sola topi*) should be purchased either in a good German store for tropical equipment e.g. Dingeldey & Werres (Berlin W9, Potsdamer Strasse 127-128), where, apart from English products, German ones are to be had, or in transit through Port Saïd (p.4), thus avoiding the inconvenience of having to convey it thus far. Good English cork helmets may be purchased for 16-18 shillings, pith hats for 12-14 shillings. The German prices are similar, if somewhat lower. One should always select a better quality helmet, since the cheaper ones rapidly fade. In the morning and evening one wears a light felt or straw hat or a cap.

In addition, the usual small items, such as slippers, cap, binoculars, pocket thermometer, aluminium drinking beaker, knife with a corkscrew, electric torch, a pair of spectacles with tinted lenses for bright sunlight, a pocket compass and similar articles.

One should get one's family doctor to make up a small medicine chest, containing the following: quinine in pill form, potassium permanganate or similar substance as an additive to water used for rinsing the mouth; aloetic pills for chronic constipation; a laxative for diahrrhoea, some opium (see p.XXVII); bandages for external injuries, mercury chloride pastilles and iodoform as disinfectant; lanolin; an eyebath etc.; a small clinical thermometer whose use should be explained by the doctor.

Above all, one should not forget to take ample reading-matter, especially if one is not used or disposed to read English books.

Finally, one will have to equip oneself with bedding in a furnishing shop in Colombo (or Bombay), both for night travel by train (where it is unnecessary only in carriages on certain main lines) and for occasional use in poor accommodation (see p.XXIV). One needs at least a thickly padded quilt (*razai*) as underlay, a lighter blanket or plaid as top cover, and a pillow, all of which can be properly stowed away in the laundry bag or bedding roll. Whoever wishes for greater comfort, travelling of course with a servant, can take a complete bed with him, following the example of Europeans living in India. This consists of a good mattress of the same length and width as the couch in the train, a decent blanket and several pillows with the requisite linen. Many take their own wash-basin with them, since the basins on the trains are often really dirty, and unusable for reasons of hygiene (in any case one should wash one's face only with water which one causes to flow from the tap directly on to one's hand or sponge). These extra items of course greatly increase the quantity of luggage.

Photographic articles, fresh films and plates may be purchased in any of the larger tourist centres, but only in English sizes, for which one should be prepared. For developing one pays 1½-2R. per dozen. One should be cautious when handing over exposed films for development by natives, and it is best to make a trial first.

Good travelling companions increase one's pleasure and, as an alternative to reading, help one to bear the monotony of rail travel and the bleak evenings spent in hotels. In contrast to the convenience offered by the tours which a wide variety of travel bureaux arrange nowadays, is the disadvantage of being tied to one's travelling companions even if one finds them uncongenial, and to a fixed programme. In any case such tours, provided that one has sufficient command of the English language and previous experience of travelling, are no cheaper than going about in one's own chosen party of two or three people, where in any case the cost of coach journeys and a servant are shared out.

It is pleasant, but by no means essential, to have an English-speaking native servant (*boy;* Hindustani *chokra* or *naukra)* who packs, unpacks and guards the cases, sees to their handing in and recovery on trains, makes up the bed on night journeys and provides room service in hotels. In dealings with porters, drivers, launderers and other people he acts as interpreter and also helps to effect savings. On the other hand, one has to resign oneself to the fact that he receives fairly high commission from the shopkeepers, which one has to pay on top of one's purchases. The Madrassi make the best servants. Of course they must be able to speak the major Indian languages. There are even a few who can speak some German, but one should not rely upon being able to obtain one of these. One should not engage a servant purely by virtue of the certificates he proffers (Hindust. Chîtîs), which are often forged, but use the mediation of the manager of a European hotel or Cook's office (p.XII – gratis). After engaging a servant, one should take possession of his references and keep them under lock and key, to protect oneself from his possible breaking of his contract by absconding. The usual rates are 35-45R. per month. The servant provides his own food, except that he is to be paid a small amount towards this when on a steamer. All his other expenses for the journey fall to the traveller, these normally including the return journey to the place where the servant was hired; third class railway fares are however low (see p.XXI). It is customary to make him a gift of about 10R. in advance for a new suit, and, when visiting places at higher altitudes, to buy him a blanket. At the end of the tour a tip is generally given in recognition of the fact that one was satisfied. All in all the servant will thus receive some 250-300*M.* for the 10-week round trip, an amount which is excellent value for 2 people.

2. Coinage. Weights and Measures. Passport and Customs Regulations, Post and Telegraph Offices. Newspapers.

The Indian coin is the rupee, formerly of pure silver (Sanskrit rûpjakam, silver). To counter the severe currency fluctuations between English and Indian money, the value of 15R. was fixed at 1 pound sterling (£) in 1899. This rate applies however only to gold; English banknotes are subject to the rate of sight-bills. If one reckons, as in the money table before the title page, that £1 averages 20*M.*40Pf., then the value of the rupee in German money is 1*M.*36Pf., so 100R. = 136*M.*; in reality, the owner of a credit note to the value of 100R. will seldom have to pay less than 137*M.*, sometimes over 140*M.*, where this is issued in German currency.

The rupee is divided into 16 *annas*, the anna into 4 *pice,*and this again into 3 *pies*; 1a. therefore is worth 12 pies. The 2, 4 and 8 anna pieces are struck in silver, the 1 anna piece in nickel, and the ½, ¼ and 1/12 anna pieces in copper (which the natives call 'paulie', 'chaulie' and 'adha rupio'). The only gold coin in circulation is the English sovereign (£1), but the minting of Indian gold coins is presently being considered. Banknotes appear in denominations of 5, 10, 20, 50, 100, 500 and 1000 rupees, which are issued in Madras, Bombay and Calcutta, and are subject to small deductions outside the presidency for which they are primarily valid.

In Ceylon the rupee is divided into 100 *cents.* The 1R., 50, 25 and 10 ct. coins are minted in silver, the 5cts. in nickel (square coins, rounded at the corners), and the 1, ½ and ¼ ct. in copper. The banknotes of Ceylon, in denominations of 1000, 100, 50, 10 and 5R. are valid only on the island, not on the mainland.

Large amounts are issued in *lakhs* and in *crore*: 1 lakh = 100,000 rupees, approx. £6666/13/4d or 136,000*M.* 1 crore = 10 mill. rupees.

Burma uses the Indian currency. – On the Malayan Peninsula the *Straits dollar* is valid, whose value, in contrast to the Eastern Asiatic dollar (which fluctuates) is also fixed in relation to English money (see pp.282-283).

Outside the main towns one should ensure that one has an abundant reserve of small coins, since there is scarcely ever an opportunity to change money.

Weights and measures are according to the English system. Length: 1 Engl. foot to 12 inches = 0.3048m.; 1m = 3.28 Engl. feet (3 feet 3 inches 47/20 lines); 1 Engl. statute mile = 1.609km., the English (international) sea mile = 1.855km. – Area: 1 Engl. acre = 4046sq.m. or 40.46 a, 1 ha = 2.471 acres; 1 square mile (640 acres) = 2.589 sq.km.; 1 sq.km. = 247.1 acres. – Weights: 1 Engl. standard pound to 16 ounces (abbr. oz) = 453.6g.; the following older Indian names are generally still used in the conveyance of luggage by rail 1 *maund* = 37.3242kg.; 1 *ser* or *seer* = 1 kg. (formerly 0.935kg.). The value of silver and gold articles is reckoned by the *tola* = 11.66g., likewise the weight of letters, printed matter etc. for British-Indian inland mails.

In this book, all measures of length, height and area are converted into metres. Only for railway routes have the distances in the timetables been kept in English miles. The table before the title page will suffice for converting miles to kilometres.

Temperatures are given in Centigrade (Celsius). The English thermometer, on the Fahrenheit scale, places our freezing point at 32° and our boiling point at 212°, from which the following table is derived, for the conversion of medium-range temperatures:

Fahrenheit →	Centigrade	Centigrade →	Fahrenheit
+40	+4.44	+5	+41
50	10	10	50
60	15·56	15	59
70	21·11	20	68
80	26·67	25	77
90	32·22	30	86
100	37·78	35	95
110	43·33	40	104
120	48·89	45	113
130	54·44	50	122

A passport is not, in itself, necessary in India, since a visiting card suffices as proof of identity at post-offices and for officials of lower rank, but it is of importance in dealings with banks and consulates, which can only grant protection to nationals who can prove their identity beyond question. – The German General Consulate for India is at *Calcutta,* moving to *Simla* during the summer; in conjunction with it there is an elective Consulate, which remains in Calcutta all the year round. Besides these there is a professional Consulate in *Bombay.* Of the elective Consulates, the following concern the tourist: on the Indian mainland those at *Madras* and *Karachi;* in Ceylon, the one in *Colombo;* in Burma, the one in *Rangoon.* In the Straits Settlement the Consul General has his seat in *Singapore;* there is an elective Consulate in *Penang* (Georgetown). For Siam, *Bangkok* is the seat of the German General Consulate, and for Java *Batavia.*

Customs. – Luggage is examined only superficially on arrival in Ceylon, but more closely on the Indian mainland. Before disembarkation one must fill in a form, in which the number of pieces of luggage and their contents are to be described. Otherwise, one is asked virtually only about weapons and parts of weapons, on which there is a high duty; weapons must be exactly described, with factory number etc. Penalties for false information are high. Europeans are not subjected to bodily searches. Part of the duty paid on weapons, photographic equipment etc. is refunded if these articles are re-exported within a year; one should be careful to retain the receipts for duty paid (agents do whatever is required). – One is not recommended to take cigars with one.

Fairly cheap Manila and Dutch cigars are available in India, and the better ones of south Indian origin are quite tolerable and very cheap.

Post and telegraph offices. – Postage from British India: within the World Postal Union, letters of 1 oz. or 28.34gr. cost 2½a., postcards 1a., printed matter ½a. per 2oz.; letters within India and Ceylon up to 1 tola (p.XVIII) ½a., at greater weights 1a. for every 10 tola, postcards ½a., printed matter ½a. for every 10 tola. Registration fee 2a. – From Ceylon: letters within the World Postal Union, 15cts. For 1oz., every additional oz. 9cts., postcards 6cts., printed matter 3cts. per 2oz; to England and the colonies letters 6cts. per oz., postcards 6cts., likewise printed matter 2cts. per 2 oz. Registration fee 10cts.

Telegrams to Germany and the rest of Europe (except Russia and Turkey): 1R.8a. per word (from Ceylon 1R.55cts.). – Between the Indian mainland and Ceylon: 12 words 1R, each additional word 2a. (10cts.). – On the Indian mainland: 12 words normally 6a.; each additional word ½a., express telegrams 1R. for 12 words, each additional word 2a. – In Ceylon: 10 words 25cts., and 5cts. for every two words additionally.

On money orders one pays: on the Indian mainland 8a. for every 50R., thus 1R. for 100R.; in Ceylon 10cts. for every 10R., then 4cts. for every 25R. additionally, thus 6R. for 500, 7R. for 600R.

The Indian newspapers with the widest circulation are the *Times of India* (printed in Bombay) and the *Pioneer* (printed in Allahabad). They are sold almost everywhere at stations. One will find German newspapers nowhere except in German clubs; one should therefore have them sent on under wrapper. The weekend edition of the Kölnische Zeitung, for instance, costs 3*M.* quarterly if sent in this manner. As addresses (for letters also) one should use either the German Consulates (p.XIX) or the agencies of *Thos. Cook & Son* (p.XII), which will forward one's mail.

3. Means of Communication.

The best railway timetables are *Newman's Indian Bradshaw, Indian Railway Traveller's Guide* and *Indian ABC Railway Guide,* which may be had at all the larger stations for 8a. and 6a. Since the timetables are frequently changed, one should see that one always has the latest monthly edition. – The hours are reckoned, as in Italy and France, up to 24. (20.30 is thus 8.30 p.m.) Indian Standard Time is calculated at the 80th degree of longitude and is 4hrs 21min ahead of Central European time, but it applies only to railways. Local time deviates from it not inconsiderably, being, for example, 23min ahead in Calcutta and 9min ahead in Madras, while Bombay is 39min behind standard time.

The Indian railways, totalling some 32,000 miles or 51,000km., built largely by private companies, deserve the praise which is customarily bestowed upon them, if somewhat too lavishly. The whole concern gives one an impression of great safety. The trains travel slowly, even expresses rarely exceeding 50km. per hr. The timetable is however fairly rigidly adhered to on the main lines; on the small branch lines, one must arm oneself with patience. The fares are rather lower than in Germany. In the first class, up to a distance of 300 miles, they correspond to German fares; at greater distances there is a reduction to ⅔ of the extra amount; 1½ *maund* (p.XVIII) = approx. 56kg. of luggage travel free. The 2nd cl. fare is half that of the 1st, with 30 *seers* = 30kg. of free luggage. The 3rd cl. (suitable only for the boy) costs 1/7 of the 1st cl. fare.

As with us, the deposit of luggage may only occur after the ticket has been purchased, but it must be settled 1hr. before the train departs. It is advisable to verify that one's luggage is correctly labelled. Large quantities of hand luggage are allowed, and even medium-sized cases are often taken by their owners into the passenger coaches. This liberality naturally assumes that patience be exercised in the face of one's fellow travellers' demands for space.

One is recommended to secure one's tickets from the agencies of *Thos. Cook & Son* (p.XII). One can thereby avoid having to jostle about at the often dirty ticket counters, and one also enjoys the advantage of the above-mentioned reduction for distances over 300 miles, even if one breaks one's journey. Luggage handed in can be delivered, if one so wishes, at intermediate stations. Cook's interpreters are to be found at all the more important stations throughout India, Ceylon and Burma. Before commencing a lengthy journey, one should request the station master the previous day for a sleeping berth, which can only be guaranteed in this way. One pays a small fee and finds one's berth indicated on the train by a reservation ticket.

The carriages are very broad and have double roofs which overhang at the sides as protection against the sun,. They are equipped with electric ventilation and lighting. The windows often have 3-4 different means of closure (light glass, dull glass, wire mesh and wooden blinds) which one can alternate at will. The first-class compartments have leather upholstered seats along the side where the windows are, rather too wide for comfortable sitting; above them, a sleeping cushion strapped up lengthways in the day-time, and a broad aisle down the middle. They accommodate 8 people but, except in an emergency, are given to only 4. Next to the compartment is a spacious toilet with washing facilities (p.XVI) and, on some fast and luxury trains, even a bath. The second class is not greatly different from the first; the compartments are larger and more crowded. In the daytime, they can be used by Europeans who are content with more simple accommodation, although one finds oneself sitting next to half-castes (p.69) and better-class (though not always very clean) natives. To use the second class by night is out of the question for the European. – There are no sleeping cars as such. The first-class passenger who gives notice in good time receives a long sleeping-cushion for himself alone, on which his bedding (p.XVI) may be spread out.

Dining-cars form part of the train on a few major lines only. Meals are mostly taken in Refreshment Rooms at main stations, where the appropriate stops are made: early morning tea *(chota hazri)*, as a rule between 6 and 7, *breakfast* about 9, *tiffin* between 12 and 1 o'clock, both for 1R.8a., *dinner* at 7 to 8 o'clock for 2R. The guard generally inquires beforehand and issues meal tickets. There is no charge for advance orders made by telegraph. The meals leave a good deal to be desired, by European standards, although they have improved in the last few years.

It is up to the passenger to see that he gets off at the right point when his destination is reached. Larger towns have several stations, and one must consult the information in one's itinerary. If only two stations are named, *city* and *cantonment,* the latter (European quarter) is almost always the correct one for the hotels. On the arrival of the train, porters (*Coolie!* Fee 2-4a., or 1a. for a small article) can always be found; in the more popular tourist places carriages are available to convey one to one's hotel. In the remoter places it is sufficient to send a telegram to the station master, who will then arrange a conveyance or accommodation in guest rooms or in the waiting room at the station, or, if need be, even a seat in a railway carriage. The civility of station masters deserves a special accolade of approval.

Electric trams are found in most of the larger towns. They are rarely used by the resident Europeans and then usually only where there are special first-class compartments. The stranger may however quite well make occasional use of them; regular use is to be avoided, for reason of hygiene.

Carriages, cars, mounts, litters. – The usual means of conveyance in towns and on excursions are horse-drawn carriages, differing greatly in type from each other (Hindust. *tikka-gharri*, hired carriage). The fares are relatively high, the tariffs, where they exist, often vaguely set down. One must always agree the price beforehand, otherwise tiresome disputes are sure to occur. Of the European carriages, the so-called *Victoria* is the most popular. Among Indian carriages, which one has to depend upon especially for excursions, the so-called *Tonga* is pre-eminent, a two-wheeled back-to-back two-horse vehicle for 4 persons including the driver. They go quickly, on the open road mostly at a gallop, with frequent changes of horses on lengthy trips, and they are appreciably cheaper than the European carriages. If one does not fear the uncomfortable seat and the violent bumping, then they may also be used in towns.

For overland touring, *motor cars* may be hired in some cities, especially Colombo, Bombay, Delhi and Agra. The prices are high.

Mounts and litters for ladies are usual virtually only in the hill resorts. The Indian litter is intended exclusively for lying down, though there are chairs also. – The east-Asian *rickshaw*, a two-wheeled handcart pulled by coolies is found in India only in Ceylon and Madras, but is more frequent in Indo-China.

In a few Indian royal cities, for example Jaipur (p.147), Gwalior (p.158) and Udaipur (p.145) one may have the opportunity to ride on an *elephant,* at a high price or in exchange for a very generous tip. Mounting and dismounting is admittedly complicated, and not everyone finds the swaying seat pleasant, up on these great animals.

4. Accommodation and Fare.

The hotels do not match the standards of furnishing and cuisine which one is accustomed to find in Europe. The prices are therefore more modest in scale. Apart from a few large cities, only full Pension is offered, calculated in days from the hour of one's arrival. Part of a day is reckoned as a whole one, but any meals missed are deducted if claimed for. Service is exclusively by natives. Sometimes these people are forbidden to enter the room without permission from the traveller or his servant. Clothes and shoes are cleaned only superficially, but one should not expect much greater efforts from one's own servant. During busy periods it is advisable to reserve one's rooms in advance by telegraph. It is usual to pay the coolies directly, for fetching and carrying one's luggage.

As first-class hotels (more or less in the European sense) one can in fact name only the Galle Face Hotel in Colombo and the Taj Mahal Hotel in Bombay. Of similar standard in Ceylon may be mentioned the Grand Oriental Hotel in Colombo and the Mount Lavinia Hotel near that city, Queen's Hotel in Kandy, and Raffles Hotel and the Hôtel de l'Europe in Singapore. First class, by Indian standards, are the better hotels in Agra, Delhi, Calcutta (here hardly worthy of the former capital), Lucknow and a few other towns, as well as the hill stations. Comfortable public reception rooms are rare, electric lighting is a recent innovation. The guest rooms are often very spartan in their furnishing, being linked to the so-called toilet-cum-bathroom, a dark closet with rough cement walls. In place of the bath there is mostly a low tin tub, 100 by 60cm. in size, and a huge earthenware jug filled with water, from which one pours water over oneself with the aid of a small tin basin. Hot water is provided only very sparingly. A simple commode completes the fittings. One should always remove the doorkey.

The price for Pension accommodation is 8-13R. The first meal *(chota hazri),* consisting of tea, buttered toast and bananas, is brought to one's room between 6 and 7 by the room-boy, who asks when one wishes to take one's bath. Breakfast proper, consisting of eggs, meat etc., occurs between 8 and 10, lunch (tiffin) between 1 and 2 o'clock, and the dinner usually at 7.30 p.m. A good selection of wines is normally available, but the prices are understandably high. Even the better-known brands of mineral water are dear, as is German beer, which is sold bottled. One will soon adopt the habit of drinking whisky and soda (see p.XXVII). – Refreshments are served to non-residents at the bar or on the terrace.

There are also a number of second-class hotels, under European management, run on similar lines to those mentioned above, but their furnishing and cuisine are of an even lower standard. Pension 6-8R.

The third class of hotel is made up of establishments which are run by natives, but which look to a European clientele. A small number of them are good, but one often finds soiled and torn bed linen, and no proper covers. The bedstead, being only of solid wood, lacks either straps or elastic supports. In these circumstances it is imperative to take one's own bedding with one (p.XVI). It hardly needs to be said that the remaining furniture is limited to barest essentials. Doors do not always lock properly. All these things are annoyances which must be cheerfully borne. Pension 5-7R.

Dak bungalows. – In all the more important places visited by European travellers the government has set up *dak bungalows* (bungalows for short). These mostly contain 2-6 rooms (each with 2 simple bedsteads and very thin mattresses, with adjoining dark toilet and bathroom). A few bungalows, especially in Ceylon and on the Malayan peninsula, are comparable or even superior to the third-class hotels, but others would scarcely serve the most modest of requirements. Neither bedding nor pillows nor towels are provided. The travelling accessories mentioned on p.XVI are indispensable here also. The rate per day is normally fixed at 1R., but one can book only 24 hours' lodging in the first instance, a longer stay being permitted only if there is sufficient room for new arrivals also. Use of the bed is included in the daily rate; only in the rare cases where bed linen is provided does one pay a small charge for this. Food is available on demand but this, apart from a few honourable exceptions, is of very poor quality. The prices of meals are listed and are commensurate with those served in station refreshment rooms. One will generally prefer the latter, e.g. in Madura, Trichinopoly, Tanjore and Bijapur. Advance booking does not ensure places in the bungalows, for these go to those who arrive first. Nevertheless, one is recommended to telegraph beforehand as a precautionary measure.

Tips are expected everywhere. One may reward the services of one's waiter, room-boy, the *bhisti* who fetches water and sees to the bath, and the *sweeper,* who does the dirtiest but most necessary work in the toilet. In the country, particularly in the bungalow, the cook will often also present himself. 1-2 annas gratuity per day should suffice for each person.

5. Guides and Daily Programme.

The traveller who keeps to the main tourist circuits will, in using this handbook, seldom need any other guide, such as is naturally required in the remoter regions. There are very few really good guides for the whole of India who possess a certain amount of education and reliable knowledge of the subject. The explanations and romantic stories given by inferior guides are worthless. Immediately upon arriving at one's hotel one should engage the manager in conversation regarding the hire of carriages, agreeing there and then upon the fares to be paid. One should enquire about visits to places of special interest, since for many monuments and palaces regulations are in force, although these have recently been simplified. To show the way, a boy from the hotel or the driver will suffice. In temples and other public buildings local guides offer their services, and one engages one of these as a rule, if only to escape further molestation.

One should go out of doors only before 11 a.m. or after 3.30 p.m., remaining indoors during the interim. From 5 p.m. one need no longer wear one's tropical hat (see p.XV). The sun sets at approximately 6 p.m. The visitor who wishes to become acquainted with the interesting life of the people can safely wander about on foot, with the aid of our town plans, even through the native quarters, except during times of political upheaval, and religious festivals (e.g. the Mohammedan Moharram and Ramadan days, and some Hindu festivals which are akin to carnivals). One must however respect the feelings of the natives, act strictly according to instructions when visiting temples and mosques, and behave always in a considerate fashion. As is well-known, shoes must be removed as one enters a mosque, though one can usually keep the slippers, which one wears in their stead, tied over one's shoes, and then it is simply a case of guarding against the slippers becoming detached too soon. In Hindu and Jaina temples, the holy place is not to be entered. The Parsees' prayer houses are utterly prohibited to the European. In Mohammedan districts, one must also refrain from photographing women or entering cemeteries.

Apart from in a few major places, the evenings are boring. Dinner ends at 8 or 8.30 p.m. There is no kind of evening entertainment. The hotels mostly lie some distance from the native town, preventing a stroll to the latter. One will watch a performance of dancing girls *(nautch)* only once. The illumination in the smaller hotels and bungalows is often so pitiful, that even reading and writing are rendered almost impossible. At 10 p.m. at the latest, silence reigns everywhere. So, early to bed and early to rise!

6. Shopping.

The usual dealers in curiosities offer rubbish in the main; they assume that every foreigner has no idea about bartering, and they proportion their demands accordingly. Almost everywhere there are, however, honest dealers, where one is served properly, and with the advice of European experts. Recommendations from couriers and hotel employees always result in commission being added to the price. If one wishes to buy gold and silver articles, carpets, woven fabrics, embroidered items or carved ivory pieces, one should go exclusively to specialist shops. Mounted and unmounted jewels, especially rubies, can be acquired at reasonable prices only by the connoisseur. The better-known silversmiths and goldsmiths work almost only to firm orders, and have no shops. For better quality bazaar goods one pays: 80% pure silver 1½-1¾R. per tola (p.XVIII), so-called "jungle craftsmanship" more expensive still; 22 carat gold, 25-30R. per tola. One should insist upon a receipt with exact details of the weight and purity. If the dealer refuses to give this, the purchaser should then break off the transaction; one is usually dealing with 45% silver or 9 carat gold; most likely, even, the article originated in Pforzheim! [A busy manufacturing town in S. Germany, handling gold- and silverware. The equivalent to this remark might be "Made in Birmingham". Tr.] Larger pieces one should have valued by a "chapwallah", people of irreproachable integrity who however hardly ever understand English, so that one needs an interpreter when dealing with them. Finely-wrought and –patterned pieces of work in copper and brass can best be found on the sales counters of the Schools of Art.

In the case of wood and ivory carvings, it is important that only flawless materials are used, so that one can be sure they will not split. One can guard against imitation ivory by letting a droplet of oil fall on to the article: if the ivory is genuine, the oil can be wiped off, leaving no trace; if not, it immediately penetrates the material. All kinds of antique articles, and weapons in particular, are mass-produced in Indian factories.

Cooks are the most reliable agents for shipping items back to Europe.

7. Medical Precautions.

The large majority of travellers will get to know India only in the winter months. One can live very much as one does at home, by dressing according to the suggestions on p.XIV, paying particular heed to good protective headgear (that is, avoiding going out bare-headed even for a short walk between 8 a.m. and 5 p.m.), and by avoiding long walks, or any walking whatsoever around midday. The wise traveller will hardly need to be reminded about moderation in eating and drinking. One should never, under any circumstances, touch ordinary water, not even in mountainous areas. One should slake one's thirst with the well-known mineral waters, which admittedly are expensive, or with the thoroughly unexceptionable Indian soda water, whose stale taste may be improved by a tiny sprinkling of table salt or a small quantity of whisky. Whisky and soda, enjoyed in moderation, may be regarded as the cheapest and most wholesome drink, and is everywhere available. Strong spirits are particularly harmful in the tropics.

One should ensure regularity of the bowel and sufficient sleep. Stomach disorders must not be neglected. A powerful laxative usually cures diahrrhoea; if this fails, one should consult the doctor and not hamper his treatment by self-administered opium. If diahrrhoea and fever occur together, one should contact the doctor immediately.

In areas where fever is prevalent, beds are protected by nets against mosquitoes (malaria!); they are provided even in the bungalows. They are not however always in good repair, and cautious travellers will take their own with them.

During outbreaks of cholera, one should enjoy drinks of freshly uncorked water only, and take soda water with one, for cleaning the teeth. (See also pp.XV-XVI). The plague is less infectious to Europeans. Since it is however very widespread one should, as far as possible, avoid direct contact with natives. Smallpox is more serious, for it occurs in a particularly dangerous form. The best protection is to renew one's vaccination before beginning one's journey. Many Europeans have already fallen victim to disease because they neglected to take these precautions.

Whoever journeys through India in the hotter months, or remains there longer than a quarter-year will accommodate himself to the habits of the Europeans resident in that land, closely observe the medical rules and suggestions, bathe daily, refrain from so much as a drop of alcohol before sunset, etc.

One should have one's linen washed in steam laundries wherever possible, despite the high prices. If one uses the services of native washermen (p.XV) one runs the risk of contracting the contagious if harmless inflammation of the skin known as ringworm (Hindust. *dhobie itch)*, for which medicine can be obtained from chemists.

8. Hindustani Phrases for Travellers.

Hindustani is the most widespread language of communication in British India (see p.XLIII). If one travels without a servant, one will frequently find oneself having to issue orders or instructions to people to whom even the gibberish English spoken by the natives is foreign. A brief compilation of the more important words and expressions will therefore be welcome. One only needs to jabber away and fill in the gaps with English words. The mere indication of what one wants by a few nouns and imperative verb forms usually leads to surprisingly rapid results. Anyone who desires to gain a rather greater facility in the language should use A. Seidel's Hindustani Grammar (Vienna, publ. Hartleben; 2 *M.*), Thimm's "Hindustani self-taught" (London, E. Marlborough & Co.; 2sh.) or Rodger's "How to speak Hindustani". One should however not expect to reach an understanding of the native's spoken word without serious study and long practice.

Pronunciation. – While we are concerned elsewhere in the text with geographical names or other terms which are normally extant in their English forms, the following compilation uses the circumflex (^) to denote long vowels. [See my added notes at the beginning of the Glossary. Tr.]

GRAMMAR NOTES

Masculine nouns remain unchanged in the plural, except that those ending in *â* change that letter to *ê: mard*: the man, men; but *kuttâ* the dog, *kuttê* the dogs. The plural of feminine nouns ends in *en*, but those ending in *î* add *ân: aurat* the woman, *auratên* the women; but *bêtì* the daughter, *bêtîân* the daughters. – Genitive and Dative are formed by the prepositions *ka* (of) and *ko* (to, at), which are placed after the noun, e.g. *âdmî* person, *âdmî kâ* of the p., *âdmî kô* to the p. The other prepositions also stand after the noun e.g. *bungalow mên* in the house; *bâg kê pâs* at the garden. The verb has its place always at the end of the sentence: the horse is fine = horse fine is *gôrrâ acchâ hai.*

Pronouns. Personal pronouns are found in the verb conjugation table below: instead of *tû* ('you', only for subordinates), one usually employs the plural form *tum.*

Possessive words:

my	*mêrâ*	our	*hamârâ*
your	*têrâ*	your (plural)	*tumhârâ*
his, her	*uskâ*	their	*unkâ*

Numerals.

1	ek	12	bâra	50	pachâs
2	do	13	têra	60	sâtt (hardly different from sât, 7)
3	tîn	14	chauda	70	sattar
4	câr	15	pandra	80	assi
5	pâmc	16	sola	90	nauve
6	chah	17	satra	100	sau, sai
7	sât	18	atara	200	do sau
8	âth	19	unîs	1000	hazâr
9	nau	20	bîs	100,000	lâk
10	das	30	tîs		
11	igâra	40	châlis		

The difficult numerals for 21, 22 etc. can be replaced by 20 + 1, *bîs par êk,* 20 + 2 , *bîs par do*…. 40 + 7, *châlis par sât,* etc.

Conjugation of the auxiliary verb 'to be' *hona*

Present: I am *main hûn* — we are *ham hain*
you are *tum hai* — you are *tum hô*
he, she, it is *wû hai* — they are *wê hain*

Past: I, (you, he) was *main (tum, wû) tâ*
We (you, they) were *ham (tum, wê) tê*

Future: I shall be etc. (*main (hoûngâ) hûngâ*
The forms in (*tum (hoêgâ) hôgâ*
brackets are (*wû (") "*
regularly pro- (*ham (hoêngê) hôngê*
duced from the (*tum (hoêgê) hôgê*
stem, *hûnga* etc.(hoêngê) *hôngê*

Imperative: be *hô;* Participle: being *hôtâ*

LIST OF WORDS

[Translator's note: the romanisation of Hindu has to follow phonetic principles; the Germans transliterate the words in one way, the English rather differently. Anyone wishing to know more about pronunciation is advised to turn to one of the many manuals of Hindustani. For the rest, I have rearranged the English meanings in alphabetical order.]

able: be able *sakna;* can you speak English? *tum amgresi bat bolna sakte?*
and *aur, evam*
annoyance, annoyed *gussa* (n.&adj.)
answer *jabab.* Tell the servant I am waiting for an - . *Sahib ka naukar ko bolo: hamara sahib ka salam; javab mangta hai* (i.e. tell the master's servant: our master sends his greetings; an answer is requested).
arm *basu*
arrive *pahumcna*
arrival *amad, pahumc*
ask *puchna*
away! off! *chalo!*
bad *kharab*
banana *kela*
barber *hajjam;* to shave *hajjamat karna*
bath *gusl, gosel*
beard *darhi*
bed: bedstead *palang;* sheet *jadar;* bed cover *kammel*
bill *bil*
bird *ciriya*
black *kala*
blacksmith *lohar*
blood *lahu*
blue *nila, nil*
boat (small) *nao*
boot *sapat* (see 'shoe')
bottle *botal*
bread *roti*
breakfast *hazri*
bridge *pul*
brush *burush*
butter *makkhan, maska*
buy *kharidna*
cake *metai*
calf *bachra*
candle, lamp *batti*
car *garri;* cab *tikka garri*
careful *karbardar*
carpet *farch, galicha*
case *sanduk, baks* (box)
chair *kursi*
change (money) *churda dena;* money-changer *sarraf*
cheap *sasta*
cheese *panir*
chest of drawers *biru*
chicken: cockerel *murg(a);* hen *murgi*
cigar *churut* (cheroot)
clean *saf;* to clean *saf karna;* clean my boots (clothes) properly *mere sapa (kapre) baraber saf karo*
clock: o'clock *baje* (bell chime) what is the time? *kitne baje hain?*

close to *ke nasdik*
closet: where is the - ? *kackos kiddar hai?*
clothes *kapre* (plur.)
cobbler *motchi*
coffee *kafi*
cold *thanda*
collar *kalar;* coat collar *gireban*
comb *kangi*
cook *mistri*
crocodile *magar*
cup *pyala*
cupboard *almari*
curry *tarkari*
curtain *parda*
cut *katna*
day *din*
dear (price) *mahamga;* very - *bahut mahamga*
depart *bida hona*
departure *kutch*
dinner *kana*
dirty *maila*
distant *ke dur*
do *karna;* do! *karo!*
doctor (European) *daktar sahib;* (general) *hakim, tabib*
dog *kutta*
door *darvasa;* door lock *kufl*
drawers *pajama, saldrarz*
drink *pina*
drive *hankna;* drive quickly! *jaldi hanko!*
driver *garriban;* (cab-) *garrivala*
dry (adj.) *sukka;* to dry *sukkana*
duck *batak*
ear *kan*
eat, food *khana*
egg *anda*
elephant *hathi*
empty *kali*
enough: I have enough *mere pas bas hai*
evening *sam;* in the evening *sam ko* (also = in the afternoon)
extinguish, put out *bujana;* put out! *bujao!*
eye *amkh*
fan *panka*
fetch, bring *lana*
fever *tap*
finger *ungli*
fire *ag*
fish *machli*
foot *pamv*
for, for it *ke vaste*
forget *bhulna;* do not forget! *bhulo matt!*
fork *kanta*
from *ka, ke*
fruit *phal, banana*
full *bara*
furniture *baman*
give *dena*
glass *chicha;* (drinking -) *gilas*
go *jana, calna*
good *accha;* very good *bahut accha*
goose *hans*
green *hara*
greeting: the usual greeting is *salam* (i.e. peace) for Good Morning, Farewell, etc.
groom *malna*
guide *rabar, ranuma*
to guide *ranumai karna*
gun *banduk*
hair *bal*
hand *bath*
handkerchief *rumal*
harbour *bandar*
hard *sukket, sacht*
hat, helmet *topi;* tropical hat *sola topi*
have: is usually expressed by *pas* (with) and *hai* (is), e.g. *meere pas paissa hai* (money is with me = I have money)

head *sir*
healthy *tandurust;* health *tandurusti*
hear *sunna;* listen! *suno!*
heavy *bari*
here *gaham*
horse *ghora*
hour *ghanta;* ½hr *adha ghanta* ¼hr *pao ghanta*
house *ghar, bungalow* (Engl. for *bangla,* see p.XXIV)
house servant (room cleaner) *hamal* (really 'porter')
how? *kaise?*
how much, how big? *kitana*
how many rupees does it cost? *kitne rupie hain?*
ice *baraf, barf*
ill *bimar;* illness *bimari*
immediately *ekk dam*
in *men* (word order, see p.XXIX)
in front of *ke samne*
ink *syahi*
inkwell *davat*
interpreter *mutjarim*
journey *safar*
jug *ghara*
key *cabi*
knife *churi*
know *janna;* do you know? *tumko malum hai?*
large *bara*
later *ke piche*
lay, put down *rakhna;* put down! *rakho!*
lazy *sust*
laziness *susti*
left *daua hat;* to the left *daua hat ko, baen*
leg *tang*
letter *citthi*
light (weight) *halka;* (easy) *asan*
light (lamp etc.) *jalana*
lighting *krochni, nur*
linen (dirty, for washing) *maile kapre* (see also 'wash')
little: a little *tora;* too little *kamta;* That is 1 rupee too little *ek rupia kamt I hai*
lock *kufl lagana*
luggage *asbab*
luncheon *tiffin*
maidservant *aya*
make *banana;* make! *banau!*
man *mard* (see 'person')
mango *am*
master *sahib* (pron. sab);
Mr N. *N. sahib*
matches *dyasalai, machis*
mattress *gadela*
meat *gocht*
meat (roast) *kebab*
medicine *dava*
milk *dudh*
mirror *aina*
money *paissa, paisse* (plur.)
monkey *bandar*
moon *chand*
more *aur*
morning *savera*
mosquito *macchar*
mosquito net *macchardan*
mouth *mung*
much *bahut;* so much *itna;* how much? *kitna;* as much as *yitna;* too much *jasti;* that is much too much *bahut jasti hai*
mustard *rai*
neck, throat *gala*
neckerchief *kgalaband*
night *rat;* at night *rat ko*
night attire *pajama*
no *nahi, ne;* (emphatic) *matt!*
noon *dopahar;* at noon *pahar din*
nose *nak*
not *nahim;* do not hit! *matt maro!*

open *kholna;* open! *kolo!*
open (adj.) *kokhi*
order (food etc.) *mangana*
over, above it *keupar*
overcoat *labada*
pain *dard*
paper *kagaz*
payment *ada;* to pay *ada karna*
pen(-holder) *qalam*
pencil *pemsil*
pepper *mirch*
person *admi*
pig *suar*
pillow, cushion *takya*
poor *garib*
porter *kuli* (coolie)
post office *dakghar*
potato *alu*
poultry *murgi*
price *dam;* what is the price? *kya dam? kitna dam?* what does 1hr (by carriage) cost? *ek ghanta ke vaste kya dam hai?*
quick(-ly) *jaldi;* hurry! *jaldi karo!*
railway *rel ki sarakh*
rain *baris*
red *lal*
rice (boiled) *bhat*
rich *daulatmand*
rider *savar;* to ride *savar hona* (i.e. 'be a rider')
right (direction) *sidahat;* to the right *sida hat ko, dahine*
river *nodi*
room *kamra*
rug (travelling) *kammal*
saddle *sin*
salt *namak*
scissors *kainchi*
sea, ocean *samudr*
see, look *dekhna*
servant, boy *naukar, naukra*
shade, shadow *saya*
sheep *ber*
ship *jahoz*
shirt *gamiz*
shoe, shoes, boot *juti*
shoot (at) *goli chalana (par)*
show *dikhana*
shut *band karna;* shut (the window)! *(kirki) band karo!*
silent: be silent! *cup rau!*
sleep *sona*
slow(-ly) *ahista*
small *chota*
smoke *duan;* to smoke tobacco *tambaku pina* (= drink tobacco)
snake *sanp*
so (like that) *aissa, vaissa*
soap *sabun*
soda water *soda;* a – (with ice) without whisky *kali (baraf) soda* (i.e. 'an empty (ice) soda)
soft *naram*
soup *sorba*
speak *bolna;* speak! *bolo!* I wish to – to the manager: *manager sahib ko mera salam do* (i.e. give the manager my greetings); we do not speak Hindu: *hamko hindustani bat malum nahin hai*
spoon *cammac*
station (railway) *stesan*
steamer *agbot*
stocking, stockings *mosa, motcha*
stop! *karre karo, karre raho!*
straight on *age sidha*
street *rasta*
sugar *chini*
suit *kapra, kapre*
sun *suraj* (see also 'shade')
supper *rat ka khana*
table *mez*
tail-coat *kurti*
tailor *darzi*
take *lena;* take! *lo!*

take away *ledchana;* take away! *ledchao!*
tea *cay*
telegram *tar ki chabar*
tell: tell the driver to go to - *kotchvani ko bolo: - ko jau*
there *udar*
is anyone there? *koi hai?*
therefore *isvaste*
thirst *pyas;* I am very thirsty *main bahut pyasa hun*
ticket *tikat, tikit*
tidy, clean *barabar*
tiger *bag*
time: see 'clock'
tobacco *tambaku:* see also 'smoke'
today *aj;* also *aj (ke) din*
tomorrow *kal* (also = yesterday: the appropriate meaning is made clear by the tense of the verb used)
day after tomorrow *parsun* (also 'the day before yesterday', depending on the tense used)
towel *taulia*
town, city *sahr*
trousers *pantalun, patlun*
turn round *phirna;* turn round! *phiro!*
under, beneath it *ke niche*
very *bahut* (usually pron. *bot)*
village *gamv*
vinegar *sirka*
waistcoat *kamar, vaskit*
wait *pratiksa karna*
wake *jagana;* wake us tomorrow at 6 o'clock! *hamko kall che baje fajr ko jagao!*
walking stick *lati, chari*
warm *garam, garm*
wash *dhona*
wash-basin *bartan*
washerman *dhobi* (see also 'linen')
watch, pocket watch *garyal* (see also 'clock')
water *pani;* drinking-water *pine ka pani*
way *rah*
well *kua*
when? *kab?*
where, whither? *kiddar?*
where is the hotel? *hotel kahan hai?*
where is my servant? *mera naukar kiddar hai?*
white *safed*
why? *kisvaste?*
window *khirki*
wine *charab*
wish, want *chana*
I wish to eat: *main kana chata hun*
woman (general term) *aurat*
wife *joru*
'woman' as title: 'Mrs N' – *N. memsahib*
wood *jangal*
word, speech *bat*
wound *sachm*
wounded *sachmi*
write *likhna*
yellow *pila*
yes *ham*
yesterday, see 'tomorrow'
young *javan*

Concerning India's social customs, her art and culture

by *Richard Garbe.*

An incomparable treasury of ever-changing impressions awaits the traveller to India. The variety of the landscape is determined by the size of the country and the varying altitudes met with, by the climate and other natural conditions. More striking, however, is the diversity shown by the people in their external appearance and way of life, in their languages, cultures and religions. While it is mainly true to say that practically all Indians have black or dark brown hair and almost always dark brown eyes, yet their complexions range through all imaginable shades, from the pure black of the people of Andaman and the southern Indian races, to the ivory teint of the women from Kashmir and the light brown of the upper castes of northern India, which last is hardly distinguishable from the complexion of the southern European. Brown predominates in the most varied gradations, but grey is also strongly represented here. Although the intermingling of different races has long since ceased in India, it nonetheless produced a welter of ethnic types in prehistoric times, which ethnologists can categorise only by distinguishing between seven main skin varieties. The latter are not strictly defined, but merge imperceptibly into one another.

Of all the natives of India, the Parsees occupy the highest place in the range of ethnic character. These, numbering 100,000, reside as well-to-do business people on the west coast of India, mainly in Bombay and Baroda, with only about 7000 in other coastal towns, such as Surat, Baroch and Karachi. They are powerfully built with a yellow complexion and a full, fleshy face, often bearing pronounced Semitic features, which can perhaps be traced back to Jewish interbreeding from the time of the Exile. They readily adopt European culture. While the women entirely retain their national costume (which is light, tastefully coloured and often rich) with its shawl hanging down from the top of the head and framing the face, the menfolk have often exchanged their white cotton attire for European dress; but they wear the coat buttoned right up to the neck and, without exception, wear also the black or dark brown headgear which resembles a brimless top-hat with the upper part rounded off at the rear. European headgear is the last thing an Oriental will adapt to, and then only with reluctance, even if in other respects he has assumed European dress and habits.

As their name suggests, the Parsees derive from Persia, being the descendants of Persian refugees who, sorely oppressed by the Arab conquerors of the Sasanian empire, found a new home in India in the year 717, where they might be permitted to live in peace according to their beliefs and customs. They adopted Gujerati as their everyday language (p.XLII). Even today they adhere to their religion founded by Zarathustra (Zoroaster), whose etherealised conception of divinity belongs to the purest and noblest form of belief ever produced by human religious speculation.This cult, which reaches its zenith in the veneration of light and fire, forms a wholesome contrast to the rather repellent modern forms of the Hindu religion; partly, because in Parseeism the destruction of harmful creatures is an act of piety, whereas for the Hindus it represents a crime. Parseeism rests on such a solid ethnic basis and has so properly fathomed the role of man on earth, that it can satisfy the religious needs of civilised men even today, some three millennia after its foundation. Its very essence lies in the observance of purity in thought, word and deed. Some years ago, a Parsee proudly drew the attention of a meeting in Bombay to the fact that none of their religious communities in India contained criminals, beggars or prostitutes.

Among the customs of the Parsees, the only one which attracts the notice of the traveller, if he does not come into closer contact with them, is their method (repugnant to our way of thinking) of disposing of their dead. This has however a religious basis: according to Parsee teaching, everything dead is impure and may therefore not be brought into contact with earth or fire, which are both pure and holy. Corpses may thus be neither buried nor cremated, but are laid out in enclosed places (in Bombay in the Towers of Silence, p.128) for the vultures to pick at, after which the bones are allowed to rot in the baking sun and the rain.

Parseeism has been treated separately here because, as a religion that originated outside India, it does not fit into the description of Indian religions which follows.

Of the body of the Indian people about one fifth are Mohammedans, mainly descendants of those central Asian tribes given to Islam, who since the beginning of the 11th century directed their raids and attacks at India, spreading terror and alarm through the land for centuries. Only in the second half of the 17th century, however, under the mastery of the grim Aurangzeb, did forced conversions of Hindus to Islam occur.

The powerful increase in the number of Mohammedans, which has been noticeable since that time, and which has surpassed by more than four times the growth of the remaining population of India over the last few decades, can be attributed not nearly so much to religious conversions, as to the results of a more powerful natural propagation on the part of the former. Mohammedan girls are married at a maturer age than the Hindus and thus are healthier and more fertile. Besides, the Mohammedans are not subject to the complex marriage laws which so often render it impossible for Hindus to marry off their daughters, especially the ban upon the remarrying of widows. Nor should one underestimate the greater prosperity generally found among Mohammedans, and their better standard of living. As meat-eaters, the Indian Mohammedans are, on average, stronger than the Hindus, and far superior in energy, efficiency and personal courage. Since they are, moreover, bound together by community spirit, they constitute a much greater power than the Hindus, who outnumber them more than three times, and whose sympathies do not extend beyond their own caste or stem, (see pp.XLIV-XLV). – despite the nationalist movement, which is now permeating the better educated circles throughout India. If English rule (rich in blessings and justice as it is) were to come to an end in India today, this unlikely disaster would result tomorrow in the tyrannising of the Hindus by the Mohammedans all over again.

The Hindus make up more than two thirds of the total population. The traveller will only exceptionally come into contact with the upper classes; in the lower orders, he will be bound to remark those disagreeable traits of untruthfulness, unreliability and avarice. Vanity and ingratitude are also genuine Indian attributes. However, these are balanced in the Hindu by estimable qualities: a contented acceptance of the frugality of daily life, a marked feeling for the family, stoic endurance of misfortune and, in the better classes, a steady and earnest spirit, which is not to be shaken even by the most surprising occurrences. Whoever occupies himself with Indian antiquity in the wider sense of the word, will find this remarkable people typified by a wonderful mixture of contradictory features. Alongside deep religious faith and the most perfect devotion to God stand a freedom and boldness of speculation which do not shrink back from any inference, however negative; hand in hand with ascetic stoicism, for whose sake no self-abnegation is too great, no self-inflicted pain too hard, goes an insatiable desire for worldly pleasures and the sensuality of the abyss; the most ingenious and brilliant ideas go with hair-splitting casuistry, ridiculous pedantry and the pursuit of endless, silly drivel; artistic good taste and a pronounced feeling for the noble turn of phrase, for beauty and delicacy of form, are coupled to wild, dissolute fancies that run headlong to immoderate excess; along with soft, dreamy sentimentality there is practical, calculating worldly wisdom. In these and in other unbalanced contrasts one begins to sense the effects of disastrous interbreeding, wherein Hinduism has its origins, a mingling of the noble blood of the Aryans, who entered the country from the north-west in dim antiquity, with the savage blood of the resident barbaric tribes. The European will never fully understand the Indian psyche, nor indeed that of the Oriental in general. One must always be prepared for the fact that the instincts inherited from savage times will break out again, sometimes where one would least expect them. The author of this introduction recently made the acquaintance of an Indian educated in Europe, who had broken with Hindu prejudices and who, politically, had extreme radical views. However, the first thing that this man hoped to see reinstated after the overthrow of English rule in his homeland (an event much desired by him) was – suttee.

The mode of dress of the Indians is extraordinarily diverse and not subject to the demands of fashion. The men of the lowest classes wear only a grey loin-cloth, whilst the better classes clothe themselves picturesquely in all conceivable colours. On their heads they mostly wear a turban, artistically wound around the head, usually red or white, but also yellow, green or any other colour. Also, one may see small embroidered caps without peak or brim; the waiters who serve at the European's table wear headgear shaped like an inverted soup plate. The upper part of the body is clad in a toga-like garment which falls in graceful folds over the knee, and is often worn with a jacket which buttons up to the neck. Pointed shoes are worn on the feet, sometimes with short stockings; the lower part of the leg is left uncovered even in the colder regions and in winter. Only the Mohammedans always wear tight-fitting trousers. Female attire is usually in two parts only: a little coat covering the upper part of the body to below the breast, with short tight sleeves but rarely any back portion; and a large cloth (sari) wrapped round the whole body and sometimes over the head also. In addition, every Indian woman, except widows, will wear as much jewellery as her means permit. She wears rings on fingers and toes, jangling bracelets round wrists and ankles, necklaces, earrings, ornaments in her hair, hanging down over forehead and temples and, almost without exception, a splendid nose-ring; these are often supplemented by a kind of round gold brooch set with pearls and attached to one of the two nostrils. The taste for jewels and adornment is to be found in the earliest literature of India.

The Hindus have a simple way of life. They eat fish, vegetables, chiefly rice and pulse, milk and a little liquid butter. Spirituous drinks, eggs and meat are forbidden, with the exception of meat from goat or sheep, which has formed part of a sacrifice. This is eaten only occasionally, however, and by men. The male and female members of a family take their meals apart, the men eating first and receiving the better food. Only on her wedding day may the wife sit down to the meal with her husband. This curious custom of eating separately goes back not only to Indian antiquity but to the primeval Indo-Germanic era, according to evidence from the Greeks, German tribes, Slavs and Armenians, but it has been preserved to the present day only in the conservative land of India.

The native dwellings are generally humble by European standards. Indian cities and towns, with the exception of the European quarters, are cramped and crowded, the houses small and poorly furnished, even when their owners are quite prosperous, and the inner rooms are angular, stuffy and dirty. The number of mud hovels, in which whole families have to live, is quite considerable in the towns and much greater in the villages; they are often so faultily constructed that they simply disintegrate and collapse during the wet season. Prosperous families still often adhere to the principle of a patriarchal domestic and economic co-operative going back over several generations. Under the leadership of the head of the family, whose job it is to make decisions on all matters of importance, one often finds married sons with their wives and children, and even more distant relatives, living together. This joint family system is likewise a relic of primeval Indo-Germanic times.

The most characteristic portion of the Indian house is the *zenana,* the secluded women's quarter, like a prison in smaller houses, and clear testimony to the oppressed and undignified status of the female sex. Even today, women are mostly kept in total ignorance. According to the 1901 census, only 17½% of the girls in Calcutta (where education has made the most progress) learnt to read and write, as opposed to 37% of the male population; in Hyderabad this figure sinks to 3% for the whole population and ⅓% for girls. It is thus hardly to be wondered at if the interests of the Indian women relate almost only to externals, and if their pastimes are childish ones. Although polygamy is still permitted, in civil and religious law, it has become a rarity among the middle classes. The wife of the head of the family, who, according to the remarks above, must often attend to the needs of a large number of inmates, is doubtless glad to receive high esteem within her own circle; but she is nearly as much subject to the stern demands of etiquette as the other women. The female members of a family which sets some store by itself need the family head's special permission to step out of doors or visit women friends. When they leave the house, they are conveyed in a carriage into which no stranger's eye may penetrate, or are carried, supine, in a palanquin, which resembles a tightly locked box. The widow's lot is a sad one indeed. Even though, towards the end of 1829, the then viceroy Lord William Bentinck passed in judicial council the law banning the immolation of widows (suttee), the fate of a widow in an orthodox Hindu household is still the source of perpetual misery and wretchedness. Kept at a distance from all the pleasures of life, she is sentenced to go about with her head shaved, devoid of jewellery, eating but once a day, shunning all appetising food, observing numerous days of fasting – all as punishment for the fact that she must have been a wicked woman in a former life (p.L), who disturbed the married bliss of others! The worst circumstance in all this is the deep-rooted custom of child marriages, according to which girls are wed at an immature age, sometimes in the first few years of their lives and, even if they have not yet moved into their future husband's house, can nonetheless be widowed if he dies.

There is an extraordinary variety of languages, which only partly coincide with ethnic frontiers. Four main groups can be distinguished:

i) the Tibetan-Burmese group in the Himalayan regions and Indo-China;

ii) the Dravidian group which comprises the languages spoken by the people of southern India in the Deccan. To this belong several cultural and literary languages, particularly *Kanarese* in the west, *Malayalam* south of that on the Malabar coast, *Tamil,* spoken on the Coromandel coast and far inland, and in the northern half of Ceylon, and *Telugu* in the north-east portions of the Deccan, along with the unwritten languages of *Gond, Kondh, Oraon* and other wild races.

iii) The Colaric group, whose languages are spoken by the virtually uncultured tribes of central India, particularly in the Vindhya Range, the

Mundari, Santal, Kurku, Savara etc. – The ethnological differences between the tribes of the second and third groups are disputed by competent specialists, but linguistic variations indubitably exist. Certainly the forefathers of the savage tribes speaking in Colaric and Dravidian tongues inhabited the whole of India proper at the dawn of history. It is they of whom we must think when the Aryan conquerors referred, in the oldest literary annals, to the 'godless aborigines with their incomprehensible speech' and, graphically, dubbed then 'black-skins', whom they, the conquerors, partly drove out and partly subjected and enslaved.

iv) The Aryan or Indo-Germanic group, which is especially meant when one is speaking about Indian languages. In the forefront is *Sanskrit*, whose old form, old Indian or Vedan Sanskrit, found in the Vedas, can be distinguished from the Sanskrit proper which is the 'language of art and scholarship', in which 'classic' Sanskrit literature is written, and which is still used today for scientific and literary purposes, partly too as a useful *lingua franca* in this polyglot land. The literature preserved in this language is copious, and some of it is very valuable. As the vernacular used by the people, Sanskrit remained active until the 6th century B.C. at the latest. The *Prakrit dialects* of the people post-date Sanskrit, but they had already begun to form earlier. *Pali* may be included with these, the church language of the Buddhists in Ceylon and Indo-China, which has produced a rich and extraordinarily valuable literature. The 'new Indian' languages or dialects developed in literature out of the Prakrit dialects from the 12th century A.D., in as much as they are of Aryan origin, in the same way that the Romanic languages evolved from vulgar Latin. Seven sub-divisions are usually named: *Punjabi, Sindhi, Gujerati, Marathi, Hindi, Bengali* and *Oriya;* but others also deserve mention, such as *Assami, Nepalese, Kashmiri, Multani* etc. Within these languages there are an immense number of dialects, which might in part be described as languages in their own right, as well as dialect variants at a lower level.

One gains an idea of the unprecedented diversity of languages in India on learning that Sir George Grierson, the most important English Hindologist and distinguished director of the Linguistic Survey of India, discovered in the Punjab alone 20 languages and 87 dialects, in Assam 54 languages and 120 dialects, in Lower Bengal 60 languages and 124 dialects, the majority if which had no Aryan origin at all. The same scholar tells of the household of a Bengali acquaintance in which no fewer than 13 different dialects were spoken, of which 4 were actually languages proper. Every member of the household used his own dialect and yet was understood by all the others. This is of course possible where languages and dialects share common origins (in this case Aryan). On the whole, though, the modern Aryan languages of India are not so closely related that people living in different linguistic areas can easily understand one another. The development of a general language of communication therefore became a positive necessity. India's *lingua franca*, in general usage alongside the local languages, at least in the towns, and adequate for all the traveller's practical needs, is Hindustani, a hybrid language which developed in the camps of the Mohammedan conquerors and gradually spread from there across the entire north and west parts of the sub-continent and further, even into Burma and East Africa. Hindustani is a Hindi dialect leavened with a large number of Arab and Persian expressions. The form of the language current with the Mohammedans, and characterised by a large number of foreign infusions and the use of Persian script, is known as *Urdu.* In recent times Portuguese elements have penetrated into Hindustani, such as kamra (room), sabun (soap), padri ('father' in the sense of 'priest, missionary') and, since the establishment of British rule, numerous English words, often quaintly distorted.

Even greater diversity is found in Indian society. Here we find the phenomenon which, more than anything else, is the hall-mark of Indian social life, namely the caste divisions. In the earliest literature of India we learn of a dividing of society which, as it developed, surpassed in its harshness any class distinctions elsewhere or at any time. This division started with the formation of a separate priestly class which, even in earliest antiquity, claimed the right to offer sacrifices in a manner pleasing to the gods and, through this accomplishment, gained wealth, honour and influence. When the Aryans pushed further eastwards from their traditional dwellings in the Indus valley and the Punjab, the priests (*Brahmas*) fought for and won recognition as the highest class (this being alluded to in obscure sagas) and, also, precedence over rulers and warriors.

The latter then formed a second caste under the title *Kshatriyas.* The remaining people, who worked in agriculture, trades and crafts, composed the third caste, the *Vaishyas.* Only these three Aryan castes shared in the religious privileges and in the middle class community, whilst the entire non-Aryan original population were banished into a fourth caste, deeply despised, dubbed *Sudras* (peasants and labourers), and condemned to an existence utterly devoid of rights and privileges. According to Brahman teaching, the Sudras' sole task in life was to serve the Aryan castes, and the followers of Brahma in particular. It is obvious that this caste system had come into being largely by priestly influence and thereafter strove to strengthen the power of the Brahmans; for whenever the individual classes are sharply divided from one another in a community where religion is of supreme importance, it is an easy matter for a priest to set one against another, at will.

We find the above-mentioned four castes (which over the years were ever more rigorously divided from one another by Brahman legislation) everywhere in the literature of India, and we tend to think of them whenever mention is made of the Indian caste system. It is remarkable, though, that these four distinctions had almost completely disappeared from social life when the Buddha appeared (i.e. in the 6th century B.C.), so that only the Brahman caste survived from the former division of the people. In place of the remaining three there have arisen, without violent revolution, a vast number of new castes, which however are just as sharply divided from each other, as the old ones were. Some scholars therefore take the view that the present social division of India was chiefly predominant under the old Brahman state, and that the separation into four castes had never had any practical significance, but was merely a fiction dreamed up by the priests. This view is easy to refute, but one must admit that the idea of the four castes has long outlived their real existence.

Among the Hindus of today there are 3000 castes which will have nothing to do with each other, and do not intermarry. Various factors have contributed to this unparalleled splitting-up of the people. Many of the castes are of ethnic origin. When original settlers, who sometimes are still half-nomadic, convert to Brahmanism and assume its higher culture and religion, such as happens incessantly even today, a caste emerges from the old tribal society. Religious brotherhoods, in which India has been rich from time immemorial, are generally also separate castes. When members of a caste change their dwelling and settle permanently in another part of India, a new caste is formed, because they are no longer regarded as being of equal birth by their old friends, on account of the changes in their way of life, which such a move must cause.

The acceptance of new rituals has the same effect. The chief reason for the enormous number of castes lies, however, in the fact that every single profession has become a caste. Here, a whole scale of upper and lower castes is differentiated: at the bottom, though still above the impure and despised *pariahs* (outcasts) whose contact everyone shuns, are the hunters, fishermen, leather-workers and weavers. At the top are the goldsmiths, the bankers, the clerks (*Kayasthas*), who push their way into positions of office, the warlike *Rajputs,* and above all the others are, of course, the *Brahmans.* This hierarchy is subject to variation in different parts of India and has become an extremely complex system, because of the manifold diet prohibitions, purification laws and other customs, which strike one as now refined, now offensive.

The individual professions are so sharply divided from one another by the caste laws, that communal eating and drinking is permitted only within the same guild or craft, and marriage is forbidden between people who belong to different trades. The cobblers, tanners, tailors, potters, gardeners, washermen, barbers etc. all live in their own separate worlds. This disintegrating tendency has not even reached its end, but is constantly progressing still; for every division of labour means the appearance of a new caste, indeed one of the latter may arise through the slightest deviation from traditional methods of practising one's trade. In Cuttack, in the most southerly territory of Bengal, for example, potters who turn their wheel while seated, and produce small pots, do not marry those who stand at the wheel and make large pots. In another part of India, marriage is forbidden between those fisherfolk who make nets with the mesh from right to left and those who do this from left to right.

One must not ignore the fact that the caste system has certain virtues, in the handing down of a trade, for which the Hindu is prepared from childhood onwards, and in the solid cohesiveness of the guilds. This is shown by the Hindu's high degree of skill, producing good, careful work even with the most primitive tools, and by the flourishing of Indian handicrafts, although this is now largely fading out again. The caste also protects its members from financial exploitation and unfair competition, and it supports impoverished members. These benefits are however small compared to the serious harm which the caste system does to social life in India. It has rightly been said that "the Hindu has no fatherland, but only a caste". Most Hindus regard all fellow countrymen outside their caste with almost total indifference, and they rarely ask after who governs them, provided that they are allowed to practise their time-honoured religious and civil customs, and are not required to pay too many taxes. The caste hierarchy is therefore chiefly to blame for the fact that India has been easy prey to foreign invaders from the earliest times, and even today it offers the strongest support to English rule.

It is a strange thing that the Brahmans (who have long since ceased to be exclusively priests and scholars, but earn their living partly as farmers, soldiers, herdsmen, cooks etc.) also fall into no fewer than ten different castes with 1886 sub-divisions; and it is precisely established between which groups communal eating and marriage may occur and between which they may not. Even the Indian Mohammedans have assumed some caste rules and prejudices, which seem to spread there in the air like an infectious poison. Castes occur in Ceylon also, not only in those Tamils in the northern half of the island who adhere to Brahmanism, but also in the Sinhalese in the south, although Buddhism, which the majority of these profess, rejects the notion of castes.

In the major trading centres in India, in which European influence is felt, the caste system cannot endure in all its old rigidity: one artificial barrier after another falls away, English justice and law recognises no privileges, either among Brahmans or any other higher caste. Modern methods of transport, such as railways and trams, which are greatly used by the native population, make physical contact inevitable among people who used to shun it in fear. Modern philanthropic efforts at reform contribute, if without all too great success, to the removal of caste prejudices.

Things are however quite different in the interior of the country, e.g. in such a fortress of Hinduism as Benares, and particularly in the villages remote from the main routes. There the caste laws hold sway with undiminished vigour, and expulsion from the caste is, for the Hindu, still a threatening spectre, which keeps him in fear throughout his life. This punishment is meted out by a committee which constitutes the local executive of the caste, and mainly for the following misdemeanours: abandoning the religion or neglecting the prescribed rituals; enjoying forbidden food or dishes prepared by members of a lower caste; journeying to foreign countries and thereby offending against dietary laws; for lewd behaviour on the part of a female family member and (generally, at least) for intercourse with women from a lower caste or a foreign race. In many cases this punishment is synonymous with the miscreant's life-long banishment from home.

Anyone who is expelled from his caste is deserted by his nearest relations (in strictly orthodox regions), and is scarcely able to satisfy the most basic necessities of life; for nobody may enter his house, and tradesmen in the country refuse to do him any service. Nor will such an unfortunate be taken into another caste; the only choice left to him, if he has the strength, is to put his entire life on a new footing, and convert to Christianity or Islam. Such a step is normally rendered impossible, however, by his deep-seated views, his customary way of life and his religious convictions. Atonement can be made for most offences against the caste laws, it is true, but since the former consists of giving a festival for the caste, with generous presents to all of its local members, only the well-to-do have any hope of being accepted back.

What enormous significance religion has in the life of the Indian people even today, is indicated to the traveller by the great number of holy shrines and the rituals constantly being practised at them. Hindu cities are thronged with temples, idols, altars and symbols, and the countryside likewise abounds in holy trees, small chapels, heaps of stones and other objects of religious significance. Whoever is interested in India's spiritual life must, above all, be informed about religion, which here plays by far the most important role.

Since the preponderant forms of religion today come mostly from ancient times, and are only intelligible in the context where they belong, a brief survey of Indian religious history is now necessary. Firstly, however, a word must be said about the foreign religions in India. According to the 1911 census, there are 3,876,000 *Christians* in India, of whom ½ million are Europeans and Eurasians (half-castes); almost ⅔ of the entire Christian population is found in the province of Madras. 66,623,000 *Mohammedans* were counted, *Parsees* as mentioned above, only 21,000 *Jews,* including 3000 dwelling in Aden. The small number of Jews, which increases only naturally (and virtually not at all since their immigration), is attributed to the fact that India, because of its tribes of artful businessmen and its low wages, possesses little attraction for foreign Jews.

Of the indigent religions, *Brahmanism,* including the Sikhs, accounts for 220,600,000 adherents. Of *Buddhists* there are 100 million in Burma, over 2 million in Ceylon and about 400,000 on the mainland of India proper, principally in the Himalayan regions. It has recently transpired that Buddhism has not been so completely wiped out in India as was previously thought, but that it is still fairly widespread, in a garbled and veiled form, among the lower orders in Bengal. In several Buddhist countries, such as Japan, Burma and Ceylon, efforts are being made, not without success, to bring Buddhism back into currency in its native land. The closely related religion of the Jains numbers 1,248,000 followers. Besides this, 10,295,000 are designated Animists. In the history of religion, Animism is regarded as the primitive form of faith in which not gods but spirits are worshipped, which are thought of either as hovering about freely or dwelling within an object. When the census gives a certain number for the followers of this kind of religion, it could lead to misunderstanding; for Animist notions are extraordinarily widespread among the faithful of the other religions, especially among the lower orders. At the census, only those rough racial groups were included among the Animists, who observe this belief without regarding themselves as adherents to one of the great religious communities, and which, more especially, know nothing of Brahmanism and its system of castes.

Indian religious history begins with the Vedan religion whose sources are mainly the old collections, termed *Rigveda* and *Atharveda.* We have precise knowledge about the location of the most ancient dwelling places of the Aryan Indians: they lay on the banks of the Indus and in the Punjab. As regards period, one can however only make a rough estimate. H.Jacobi and an Indian scholar, B.G.Tilak, using astronomical data, independently of one another and yet simultaneously calculated the cultural era, which confronts us in the songs of the Rigveda, as spanning the time between approximately 4500 (4000) B.C. and 2500 B.C., the writing of the songs falling in the second half of this period. This date is thoroughly likely, even if eminent expert scholars have spoken out against it, in favour of the previous dating (1500-1200 B.C.). The Rigveda, whose songs were composed by priests mainly for ritual use, offers the higher religious images; the Arthveda, with its magic and spellbinding songs, offers the lower popular views, which are rooted in belief in a host of demons and in fear of their harmful influence. Most of the gods addressed in the Rigveda are personified forces of Nature, especially phenomena of light and air; above these, however, stand divinities with moral qualities, and looked upon as the noble protectors and lords of the world's natural and moral course, the *Adityas,* with *Varuna* at their head. The chief role is however played by the figure of *Indra,* represented in strongly human terms and entwined in a rich mythology, who developed from a god of storms to the god of war and to the national god himself of the Vedan Indians. In all the later phases of Indian religion, Indra has nominally remained the king of the gods, but is now only of little significance there.

One of the most celebrated godlike figures of the Veda is the god of fire *Agni,* the real priest-god, since all divine ritual was united around the sacrificial altar in ancient times. Another god often named is *Soma,* the divine and holy drink identified with the moon, which is obtained from a lactiferous plant and possesses strong intoxicating qualities. Ancient Vedan religion did not yet know the doctrine of transmigration of souls; instead, one hoped for eternal life in Heaven in communion with gods and ancestors as the reward for a pious life. Sometimes heavenly joy was seen in a spiritual sense, usually however as an improved continuation of one's earthly life. The concept of Hell occurs but rarely in the Veda; in later times, which know a larger number of hells, it is given preferential status, particularly in Buddhism. The Vedan religion numbers only a few followers in India today. They are called *Agnihotri* ('Bringers of the daily fire sacrifice').

The eastward penetration by the Aryan Indians, and the seizure of the so-called 'middle land' which reaches in the east to the confluence of the Ganges and the Jumna, brought about a major change in living conditions and in religious views. Brahmanism developed in this region, although one cannot determine exactly when. The only certainty is that it must have occurred gradually, and several centuries before the appearance of the Buddha. Characteristic of this period is the formation of the caste structure and the supremacy of the Brahmans, who not only demanded to be regarded as 'gods on earth', but contrived to acquire control of temporal matters as well. Hand in hand with this went the artificial development of holy service, about which we learn from copious writings. The old Vedan gods were, it is true, still revered in the main. But the sacrificial rites, already quite widespread at the time of the Rigveda, became much more complex. The ceremonies grew in number and extent; more and more priests were required for their expert performance, and the costs of putting them on rose to unheard-of heights. The sacrifices were not acts of gratitude or atonement, but merely the means of attaining one's every wish. Whoever possessed the means to satisfy the avidity of the Brahmans could wring anything from the gods through the sacrifices offered up by them. Suddenly a new idea emerged, which was to have fundamental significance for the entire further development of religious life in India. This was the belief in *metempsychosis* or the transmigration of souls, whose origin is not completely clear. Instead of the joyous expectation of a life of eternal bliss in Heaven, came the conviction that every individual repeatedly entered new existences after death, in which he received rewards for previous merit and punishment for previous wrongdoing. There is neither undeserved happiness nor undeserved misfortune according to this creed, which has given the Indians an astonishing capacity to bear suffering.

Since its first inception, the dogma of metempsychosis has been regarded in India as wholly natural, and which only the representatives of crass materialism have ever doubted. It forms the basis of all later Indian religions and still rules people's hearts today, even in those Indians who have enjoyed a European education. From the very beginning, the belief had an oppressive effect, and produced a paralysing sense of insecurity. The Indian's life was darkened by the conviction that one passes continually through human, animal and plant forms, experiencing more pain than joy in every existence, repeatedly tasting the terrors of death, and being even occasionally condemned to a sojourn in Hell. Nor was this conviction balanced by the consoling prospect that one might reach Heaven by one's own deserts; for even the inhabitants of Heaven stand, according to the doctrine of metempsychosis, in the cycle of existences *(samsara)* and must descend again to lower forms of life when the power granted by previous merit is exhausted. Thus the two doctrines are closely allied: that of eternal migration and that of the power of action *(karman)* with its all-determining after-effect.

Another concept, of a more theological-philosophical kind, is characteristic of Brahmanism. Already towards the end of the old Vedan era people had begun to put an impersonal god, under various designations, in first place in the divine order. Now, considerations about the strong powers ascribed to the religious song and the magic spell *(brahman)* led to an intensification of this concept. The powers, which seemed greater than those of the gods and of Nature, were regarded as being at one with the first cause of all existence, with the eternal, infinite force which created and maintains the world. Thus Brahman became world-soul, became the great One 'next to whom there is no other'. In the face of this one imperishable, indivisible and immutable Person, the world of phenomena, with its constantly recurring cycle of birth and death dwindled away to a phantom *(maya)*. One can only arrive at a recognition of Brahman, the uniquely true being, by finding it in the depths of one's own soul, for the innermost being of each one of us, the soul, the *Atman,* is identical with Brahman: not part of, not an emanation of, Brahman, but the whole, indivisible Person. This teaching was first delivered in diverse images and allegories in the world-famous literature class of the Upanishads, whose most important material it constitutes. It was then further developed and substantiated in the later *Vedanta* system, which is still the truly orthodox philosophy of Brahmanism.

When one had reached the conviction that only transitory joy was to be gained from all one's sacrifices, but not release from the necessity of constant rebirth and recurring death, one sought, along different paths, a means of redemption from the torment of an earthly existence which endlessly renewed itself, and believed that this means was to be found in the realisation of the true essence of things, which is veiled from common gaze; just as one believed one had discovered the root cause of the cycle of existence in 'unknowledge', i.e. ignorance, the view of the world that is inborn, but wrong in empirical terms. Ignorance decreases the desire to act, which binds Man to his existence; and, on the other hand, the successful struggle against sensual desire hastens one's entry into the realm of awareness. Brahmanism (and likewise Buddhism in its original form) is dominated by the idea that redemption from earthly existence can be attained only along the paths of awareness, and the redeeming state of awareness is readily accessible only if one renounces the world. The oldest form of redeeming awareness is offered by the doctrine of identity of the Upanishads (mentioned above), the doctrine of the absolute unity of the individual soul (which is only seemingly an individual soul) with the world soul. In this is included the realisation of the all-embracing unity of Brahman and of the illusory nature of the world of phenomena. In the ensuing era, other avenues of inquiry asserted themselves, finding salvation in a different realisation; but they always pursued the aim of abolishing the dogma of cyclical existence. Above all, one should mention the positively atheist *Sankhya* system, Buddha's starting-point when he founded his doctrine. This is dualist and recognises two uncreated principles which exist from eternity to eternity, yet which differ in their inmost essence: matter which is in a constant state of flux; and an infinite multitude of individual souls, which are eternally immutable. The releasing awareness consists, according to this, in the sharp distinction of soul from matter. All the systems of Brahman philosophy, too numerous to be mentioned here, still form the topic of zealous study in the circle of Indian scholars (the *Pundits)* and in the high schools in which, especially in Benares (pp.221-22), native learning is fostered.

The great spiritual movement which is briefly dealt with here and whose moving force was the need for salvation, brought about a phenomenon very characteristic of India down to the present day: the hordes of *ascetics,* who strive towards the highest degree of salvation by renouncing all earthly possessions, all worldly joys, preferring the forest solitudes and, not infrequently, inflicting upon themselves the most unspeakable torments. – The number of teachers and ascetic communities wandering about the land clad as beggars was particularly large in the 6th century B.C., when Buddha, the saviour, was expected, and when many aspired to the dignity of the Buddha. The merit for having lifted the doctrine of salvation out of the circle of philosophers and ascetics, and having placed it among the people, is to be awarded to the founders of Buddhism and the Jain religion.

The founder of Buddhism was born in the town of Kapilavatthu, not far from the Nepalese border, son of a prosperous tribal chief of the *Sakya* people. His name was *Siddhartha,* but he is often called by his family surname *Gautama;* the honorary title *Buddha* means ‘the Enlightened’. Until his thirtieth year, he enjoyed the opulent life of the Indian aristocrat, married and had a son. Then, one day, the feeling seized him that all earthly things were abject; he left his family and, as a beggar, went out into the ‘homeless’ state. Instruction from Brahman teachers and six years of practising a hard, ascetic life, brought him no satisfaction. Only when he had given up fasting and mortification did he believe that he had attained enlightenment while sitting under a fig tree one night (p.228). Since that decisive turning-point in his life, the Buddha worked unceasingly as a teacher until his death, wandering about in the land, accompanied by his pupils. His enormous success is to be attributed to the power of his personality, his engaging demeanour and his popular methods of teaching. He died, aged 80, in 477 B.C. at Kusinara in his homeland, where he was buried with princely honours.

Buddha based his teachings upon the conviction that mortal existence consists of nothing but suffering, sharing this pessimistic view with Brahman philosophy, but bringing it to bear much more resolutely. Already in his first sermon, given outside Benares at the place which is now called Sarnath (p.226), he clothed his views in the shape of the 'four holy truths' of suffering, of the genesis of suffering, of the removal of suffering and of the path which leads to the latter. These 'four truths' state: 1. constant suffering dominates the whole world; 2. the cause of suffering is 'thirst', i.e. the desire for power and the will to live; 3. the suppression of desires and of the will to live raises our existence and removes suffering; 4. the way to the removal of suffering is perfect inner purification and strict moral living and striving. The second 'truth' is completed by the formula of the 'causal nexus of genesis' (not easily comprehended), about which one need only say here that 'ignorance' stands at the beginning of the causal progression which, according to old Buddhism, simply meant ignorance of the four holy truths. It can therefore be seen that, even for Buddha, the final cause of all suffering was the power of deception, which hides from Man the true essence of the world process. Just as the Buddha agreed with Brahmanism in its belief in cyclical existence and in the power of the deed (with its after-effects and demands for retribution), so was salvation dependent from him upon a recognition of the four sublime verities and of the causal link of which he taught. Additionally, however, came the highest moral demands: according to Buddha's teaching, one cannot realise one's aim without total self-sacrifice to the wellbeing of one's fellow creatures, without pardoning the wrongs one suffers from others, or without loving one's enemy. The haven of peace, where the saved soul finds its salvation from the oceans of Samsara which are whipped up by the storms of passion (p.L), - that haven is the state of *Nirvana.* Although Buddha, according to the entire context of his teaching, can only have understood, by that concept, the snuffing-out of existence, he never uttered this idea (taking a tolerant attitude towards human weakness), but instead expressly demanded of his followers a renunciation of knowledge about the existence or non-existence of the rescued soul. Every individual must bring about his salvation by his own efforts, for there is no higher power which might help him to do this, or forgive him his sins. Doubtless the Buddha, enslaved by the views of his people and his age, believed in the gods, demi-gods and demons of popular religion; but, for him, these were transitory spirits banished to the Samsara, and much lower in staus than a man who had attained the highest goal. He denied the existence of a real god, and only in later phases of Buddhism did supernatural beings appear, which could be designated as gods. Thus, original Buddhism possessed no actual rites, although the later form acquired some of these, in which temple buildings, festivals, adoration of relics and pilgrimages played a major role.

Buddha's flock was an order of begging monks *(bhikku),* who, upon entry, renounced all possessions and their caste, broke all family ties and accepted the obligation of perfect chastity and abstinence. The return to temporal life was however left open to them. Anyone who entered the order had to have his beard and the hair of his head shaved off, and to adopt saffron robes. Apart from these, and the begging-bowl, he was allowed to possess only those articles of clothing and utensils most necessary for daily use. Alongside the monks were to be found in Buddhism from the earliest times lay disciples *(upasaka),* who believed in the truths of Buddha's word, but remained with their family and worldly occupation and in possession of their goods, without taking a vow. These lay disciples saw to the modest needs of the religious community, beginning already in the Buddha's lifetime to build for it monastic houses *(vihara)* with provision stores, meeting rooms and refectories. This led to the institution of real monasteries, which acquired growing significance in all Buddhist countries in the course of time.

Since Buddha had not appointed a successor by the time he died, it was inevitable that differences of opinion and splits should appear among the body of his followers. The spread of Buddhism across the greater part of Asia, because it adopted everywhere the popular religions already established, led later on to the most diverse changes in dogma and custom, so that it presents a different image with every nation that professes it. Of these changes, mention can only be made of those essential to an understanding of the phenomena which will meet the traveller's eye in Ceylon, Burma and the Himalayas.

The era of the greatest flourishing of Buddhism in India was the middle of the 3rd century B.C., when King *Ashoka* (Asoka in Pali) converted to it, elevated it to the state religion and advanced it with untiring zeal in his enormous kingdom. To the moral earnestness with which Ashoka devoted himself to this task, his religious edicts still testify today, preserved on columns and rocks and exhorting one to show respect and obedience to one's parents and superiors, consideration to inferiors, to uphold truth, show tolerance towards those of other beliefs, to spare animals etc. Ashoka's son *Mahinda* took Buddhism to Ceylon around 250 B.C., where the religion has preserved its original character, at least in its outward form, more faithfully than in any other land. Even the oldest sources, written in the Pali language, about the Buddha's life and teaching, originated in Ceylon. Much has however changed there also. Once, there were only monks and laymen. As in the other Buddhist countries, the development of ritual and monastic life produced priests of different degrees of rank from the monkhood in Ceylon also. Monastic life is however not limited here to the numerous monasteries; there are, still today, many simple monastic huts (individual cells) built in the ancient style, and scattered over the entire southern half of the island. The monasteries are linked to temple grounds, in which are usually set up a number of statues of the Buddha, his favourite disciples and even Brahman gods (who count as Buddha's servants and worshippers). The images of Buddha portray the prophet either standing (i.e. preaching), sitting (i.e. meditating) or lying down (i.e. in a state of Nirvana), and they vary between ten times life-size and a mere finger's length. In the preaching hall, sometimes in the open air also, the decoratively clad believers gather in the evening with lanterns lit and gifts of flowers. Sometimes there are fireworks and music. Every time the Buddha's name is mentioned in the sermon, the entire assembly cries 'sadhu' (good!). In the cities of Ceylon, especially Colombo and Kandy, there are large, many-storeyed monasteries, fitted out in European fashion with capital and land possessions, where the monks do not live on alms, but have their own food prepared for them. The most famous holy place on the island is the 'Temple of the Holy Tooth' in Kandy (p.37).

The moral and spiritual state of the Buddhist priesthood has declined in Ceylon also. Poor people regard monasteries as welfare institutions for their sons, and hand the latter over at about eight years old as novices to a monk for education and training. Ordination follows nowadays, as in Buddha's time, when the postulant reaches the age of twenty, and according to the original ritual. With the exception of a few seriously active scholars, the monks lead an indolent, monotonous existence, begging, doing domestic work, showing reverence to images of the Buddha and mechanically reading and learning by heart the holy texts. Only very few nowadays apply themselves to a life of irreproachable conduct, and thus the influence of the monks, even, is but small upon the religious life of the laity, as exemplified by the fact that the Sinhalese show little regard for one of the first commandments of Buddhism, namely the sparing of living things. The number of monks in Ceylon is decreasing; the 1891 census numbered 9598, that of 1901 only 7331.

In Burma, where Buddhism did not gain a firm hold until probably 450 A.D., the circumstances are very much the same, except that the hierarchical system in Burma is further developed, and the holy buildings afford a different aspect from those in Ceylon. In their layout, they are so like the wooden temples of Nepal, that one deduces that the Burmese style originated there, or directly from the country whence the Nepalese style came, i.e. China. Burmese monasteries and temples are almost always built of wood (excellent, durable teak), and adorned with rich, artistically executed carvings. They are built on columns and consist of only one floor, above which the roof rises steeply, running out to points at each end. The monasteries are usually sited in the middle of large gardens and contain only two rooms, the meeting-room for the monks and the temple hall, which is filled with images of Buddha. A colossal statue of Buddha generaly occupies the central position. Particular hallmarks of the Burmese landscape are however the so-called *Dagabas* (wrongly written *Dagoba*, distorted into *Pagoda),* with which the entire country is sprinkled. The erection of a Dagaba is regarded as a highly meritorious act, and it is the sincere wish of every monk. They are reliquary monuments but, since relics of the Buddha are not available in such enormous quantities, they mostly contain only statues of Buddha, fragments of religious text and models of holy buildings, or similar things. They are the true holy places of the people. The most famous is the Shwe-Dagon-Pagoda in Rangoon (p.259), which is surrounded by innumerable holy buildings, and which is a veritable museum of Buddhist art, and a much-visited place of pilgrimage (by people from other Buddhist lands also).

The Buddhist population of Burma takes the religion more seriously than its counterpart in Ceylon; the monks there are also more respected because, for centuries, they have done great service to popular education. In a Burmese village, the monastery will also be the elementary school. 20% of the population can read and write, which is an extraordinarily high level of education by Asian standards (cf.pp.XL-XLI). The monks of today admittedly do not match up to the old ideals, not even in Burma any more, as is evidenced by their unconcealed aspirations for money and property. If a monk is however expelled from the order for scandalous conduct, he is outlawed and exposed to the hatred and scorn of the whole community.

This portrayal of Burmese Buddhism would be very incomplete without mention being made of the old Animist popular religion of the country, which lives on there in a very widespread form, being often only barely hidden by the rituals of Buddhism. Under the appellation *Nat* innumerable demons, spirits and familiars are worshipped throughout the whole country, whose malevolence one is concerned to appease, and whose favour one strives to gain: the spirits of natural phenomena and of rivers, mountains, rocks, forests and trees, the protective spirits of individual places, of races, families and individuals, and also the souls of the dead. This worship can even be called the religion of the lower social strata, and the Buddhist monks themselves take an indulgent view of it.

Quite different in character from 'southern' is the northern form of Buddhism, in the Himalayan states of Bhutan, Sikkim, Nepal and Ladakh, to which it penetrated from Tibet in a form which resembles a caricature of the original Buddhist religion. Buddhism reached Tibet in the 7th century A.D., already in a totally degenerate state, after the Brahman gods had been assimilated into it as defenders of the church against the world of demons. Additionally, there was a confused magical theory, wherein mystical formulae for the attainment of supernatural powers and all kinds of other possible desires loomed large. About 100 years later the church of the Lamas ('priests') had been founded in Tibet with the absorbtion of local beliefs in spirits, (the so-called *Bon* religion) and of the traditions of the *Shamans* (magical priests) who exerted considerable influence upon the people. This church, with its rigid hierarchical organisation, developed into a complete church-state. Virtually nothing has remained of the ethical component of Buddhism. The ritual has become alienated in ridiculous fashion. Prayer banners are erected, on which the holy prayers flutter in the wind, and so-called prayer wheels are rotated, which are filled with written or printed petitions, so that the same rewards may be obtained, as if one were to recite the prayers equally often. On all the paths in the foothills of the Himalayas, one can see simple natives, however heavy their burdens, keeping little metal wheels constantly turning in their hands, while incessantly murmuring the same four-word formula (cf.pp.233-35).

The Jain religion is commonly found in the north-west, western and southern India (cf.p.XLVIII). It was founded by the Buddha's older companion (who was however no match for him in intellectual importance nor in nobility of sentiment), who is generally called by his honorary name *Mahavira* ('the great hero') or *Jina* ('the victor'), in the very region where Buddha also lived and taught. Jainism is so similar to Buddhism in doctrine and custom, that the Jains were for a long time regarded as a Buddhist sect. The main doctrinal differences consist in the fact that they recognise the substantial existence of the soul, which the Buddha denied, and that they regard the state of the soul released from the cycle of existences as a conscious, peaceful survival in the heaven of the Jina. There the soul, which equates with awareness, wins back its true and essential self, which it forfeited by migrating from one body to another, and enjoys this for eternity. Further, the Jains attach great value to the asceticism rejected by Buddha, and even regard voluntary death by starvation to be a distinguished action; they do not acknowledge the benevolent tolerance towards members of other persuasions, which was such an outstanding characteristic of the Buddha; nor do they make such a sharp distinction between monks and laity, but allow the latter to participate in the running of the community. In their consideration for the animal world the Jains are, if anything, more scrupulous than the Buddhists (cf.pp.127,133). In other respects both religions show a remarkable parallelism in their ritual development; even with the Jains we find the division into schools; they too have their synods, their monasteries, their splendid temples and, with the exception of a lower order, they practise iconolatry before the numerous staues set up in the temples, which represent the 24 *Jinas* or *Tirthankars* ('discoverers of fords'), i.e. Mahavira and his 23 reputed predecessors, of whom the last, Parshvanatha (250 years before Mahavira) seems to have had an historical existence. – The Jains escaped the Brahman persecution, which did such mischief to Buddhism in India, because they made all kinds of concessions to the former, and lived quiet, unobtrusive lives without doing active missionary work. While Buddhism became a world religion, the Jain sect remained however limited to India.

Brahmanism, which for a long time lost heavily to the spread of Buddhism, though allowing itself to be little influenced by the latter, developed into a complex and rather strange form, which we call Hinduism. The most important sources in this field are the two great epics *Mahabharata* and *Ramayana*, and the literature of the *Puranas*.

Already in pre-Buddhist times, the neutral concept of Brahman (p.L) had been transformed by simple personification of the notion (which was beyond people's capacity to grasp) into a male god, *Brahman*. This god, in peremptory fashion, was awarded first place in the divine order along with *Vishnu*, an old sun-god, and *Shiva,* a development of the Vedan storm-god Rudra, Brahman being regarded as the creator, Vishnu the preserver and Shiva the destroyer. Many old Vedan gods were also now retained, but altered in significance and lower in status. Added to these were all kinds of new deities, called into existence by the worship of Vishnu and Shiva, and placed in relationship to these. The senior god in this religious scale, Brahman, never had a widespread following and soon retreated completely into the background before his two more popular companions (cf.p.144).

The pictorial representation of the Hindu gods has often verged upon the grotesque, in that they have been equipped with the limbs of animals and other attributes. Vishnu is usually portrayed with a blue body and four arms, in whose hands he carries a club, a shell, a discus and a lotus flower. The pictures of Shiva have one or five heads; in the first instance, a third eye is fixed to the forehead and the hair of the head is bound in a strong plait pointing upwards. A necklace of skulls and other attributes of cruelty symbolise the terrible side of his nature, which is however balanced by kindlier qualities. Of the lower deities, which are new accretions to Hinduism, the traveller is most likely to see depictions of *Ganesa,* the god of knowledge, and the monkey-god *Hanuman.* Ganesa, with an elephant's head symbolising wisdom, usually sits upon a rat, for the rat can penetrate into the most remote hiding-places. Much more common are pictures of the deified monkey Hanuman, in whom we can see a relic of pre-Aryan animal worship. Hanuman is regarded as the special protective god of the rural population and of agriculture; his image is therefore to be found in almost every village. Objects of Nature-worship are, among many others, cows, snakes and innumerable holy trees.

Expressly monotheistic tendencies are to be found in Hinduism. This is shown by the grouping of the three main gods into the triune *Trimurti,* represented by one body with three heads, and the union of Vishnu and Shiva into the one god *Harihara* (Hari = Vishnu, Hara = Shiva), the worship of whom is widespread in the Deccan. Besides this, the striving towards monotheism is demonstrated by the fact that, for a long time, Hindus have worshipped either Vishnu or Shiva as the highest (often as the only) god, and accordingly the two large groups of *Vaishnavas* (Vishnus) and *Shaivas* (Shivites) have formed, of which each is divided into very many sub-sections. All these sects believe in the immortality of the soul and regard salvation as a conscious and happy after-life in the presence of God.

Vishnuism has its followers chiefly among the upper classes of the Hindus, and it is of a milder and kindlier nature than Shivism (more widespread among the lower orders), which inclines to ascetic excess and orgiastic debauchery, occupying itself with witchcraft and sorcery, and making altogether a much coarser impression. These things are practised in Shivism because of its veneration for the *linga* or phallus as symbol of Shiva's creative power, to be found in innumerable depictions all over India, and because of the disgusting rituals which are practised in the service of his gruesome wife. In antiquity, goddesses had no part to play. Under Hinduism, this has however changed. Each of the three principal deities has a wife: Brahman's is *Sarasvati,* the goddess of oratory and erudition, Vishnu's is called *Lakshmi*, the goddess of beauty and happiness, and Shiva's wife is venerated in many temples as *Durga,* though she is also called *Parvati, Uma, Kali* etc. This goddess, who appears in pictures as a fury, receives blood sacrifices, originally of humans, but now mostly goats or sheep, and very occasionally buffaloes. The goddesses are considered to be the *Shakti,* i.e. force, energy, the creative potency of their husbands, and their cult has developed particularly with the Shivites, who have subordinated the other Shaktis to Shiva's Shakti. Those Hindus who especially devote themselves to the service of Shakti, doing this partly in secret amid lascivious and immoral acts, bear the name of *Shaktas,* and form a sub-division of the Shivites.

Vishnuism is split into the two main branches, Krishnaism and Ramaism. Some worship Vishnu in the form of *Krishna,* the others in that of *Rama.* Both originated from the old monotheistic tribal communities whose god – Krishna and Rama – began as a human hero, elevated first to tribal hero and later to god. When Brahmanism succeeded in absorbing these two religious communities, it created out of Krishna and Rama (by using the convenient theory of the repeated incarnation of Vishnu – avatara) two outward forms in which the god appeared on earth. However rarely, in the history of religion, the so-called euhemeristic explanation of myths (which traces belief in gods back to grateful memories of distinguished men) proves to be right, it is often proved so in India. In the Hindu religion, virtually all of the numerous founders of sects have been deified after their death.

Krishnaism is older than Ramaism and more widespread in India, down to the present day; but Ramaism is deeper and more etherealised, numbering its adherents among the better educated classes of the Hindus, who are imbued with a tendency towards contemplation and philosophy, while Krishnaism dominates the more pleasure-loving middle class. The spread of Krishnaism has been especially aided by the popular veneration of the Krishna child, but also by the sensual and erotic element which pervades the old sagas about the life of the young Krishna among the shepherdesses and which, laced with theological speculation, has led to excesses rivalling those found in the Shivite sects. Ramaism is divided into a further two sects which feud violently with one another, while entertaining kindlier sentiments towards their common adversaries, which is also the case elsewhere in the world. In their theological views both Ramaitic schools, the southern and the northern, diverge over the fact that the first embraces the 'cat doctrine', while the latter professes the 'monkey doctrine'. According to the cat doctrine, God (Rama) saves men just as the cat adopts its young, i.e. without assistance and without Man's free will. According to the monkey doctrine, Man, if he is to be saved, must strive towards God and cling to him, as a monkey clings to its mother.

The two great religious communities of the Krishnaites and the Ramaites were not always rigorously separated from one another, but exhibited many variations and transitions during their development. Common to both, and thus a feature of Vishnuism as a whole, is the strong emphasis upon the love of God *(bhakti)* which, in its first traces, is already detectable in earliest antiquity, and therefore is wrongly attributed to Christian influence. The traveller will do well to bear in mind the higher concepts still alive in Hinduism, whenever he feels disgusted by the coarse polytheism and riotous fetishism of the masses. Whoever judges the present-day religion of the Hindus only by the idolatry which he sees practised in the temples, will be guilty of an unjust and one-sided view.

Of the Vishnu sectarian leaders of more recent times, who partly broke away from the basic principles of Brahmanism, without however renouncing their connection with it, one can mention here only the most famous, whose names are still adopted by their followers in India today. There are the Ramaites *Ramanuja* (12th century), *Ramananda* (14th century) and his pupil *Kabir*, who accepted Christian and Mohammedan teachings and waged war upon all idolatry; and the Krishnaites *Shaitanya* and *Vallabhasharya*, whose influence comes at the beginning of the 16th century. The latter admittedly scarcely merits mention alongside the other genuinely pious sectarian leaders, since his teaching aims at sensual pleasure, and can be held chiefly responsible for the excesses mentioned above.

An outward sign which immediately strikes the observer is the coloured schismatic mark, consisting of lines and dots, which all Hindus have painted or branded on their forehead, in order to give public expression to their adherence to this or that religious community. With the Vishnus, the lines run vertically, with the Shivites horizontally.

Of the modern reform movements one should principally mention the religion of the Sikhs, which numbers over 2 million followers in the Punjab (cf.p.195). The sect was founded by a Hindu from the warrior caste, called *Nanak* (1469-1538), with the aim of bringing about a union of Hindus and Mohammedans, - which the open-minded Mohammedan Emperor Akbar (1542-1605; p.162) also strove towards, by founding a new faith and cult, which however died with him. Nanak, strongly influenced by Kabir (see above, p.LXI), proclaimed the oneness of God and the equality of all men before God, while rejecting idolatry, pilgrimages and all magic trickery, along with the caste system and the claims of the Brahmans. However appealing this faith is, with its pure moral code, it had but little effect upon the life of the Sikhs, who for a long time constituted a separate state and led a wild existence as brigands. The political and social conditions in the Punjab have caused this religion, which basically offered nothing innovative, to enjoy a success which on the whole can only be described as superficial.

The 'union of God' *(Brahmo Samaj),* founded by Ram Mohun Roy (1772-1833), aroused a good deal of attention in Europe. This is a philanthropic sect, which strives after greater human happiness through contact with the great religions, but which rejects any special ritual. The founder used the pantheist ideas of the Upanishads (p.LI) as his starting point, but was, in the course of time, more and more strongly influenced by Christianity, which also exerted a very progressive effect upon the sect's further stages of development, in dogmatic, moral and social respects. In the Sunday meditations of the Brahmo Samaj, extracts are read from the Bible, along with those from the Veda, the Avesta (holy scripture of the Parsees), and the Koran. The sect numbers about 200 communities and, according to the census of 1901, a total of 4050 members; the communities are therefore only very small, and the whole movement has, as might be expected, remained limited to India's intelligentsia.

Much greater prominence is enjoyed by the 'union of Aryans' *(Arya Samaj)* founded in Bombay in 1875 by Dayanand Sarasvati, and which numbers over 100,000 members, living chiefly in north-west India. This sect also rejects idolatry, confesses a doctrine of pure monotheism and seeks an improvement in social conditions. It regards the only manifestation of God as being found in the Vedas which, for this purpose, are interpreted (in good faith) in an utterly unscientific and fantastic manner.

The spiritualistic mumbo-jumbo of the Theosophical Society of Madras deserves no place in this Introduction; for the confusion which has been caused in many troubled heads by Madame Blavatsky, Colonel Olcott and their successors, is not a specifically Indian phenomenon.

HISTORY OF ART

In the realm of the pictorial arts, the Indians' achievements frequently show more originality and imagination than beauty of form; only in their architecture have they produced anything truly great and admirable. Architecture occupies in India such a dominant position over the other arts, that painting and carvings have been created merely as decorative ingredients in buildings; separate sculptures have been set up almost exclusively for religious purposes, and not as independent works of art in their own right. Like the whole of life in India, art also stands under the domination of religion: the history of Indian architecture is therefore almost totally concerned with religious edifices.

Painting is the least developed of the arts, remaining on a naïve level. The Indians seem to find perspective particularly difficult. The attempts of Emperor Akbar in the 16th century to elevate Indian painting had no permanent success. From much earlier times, however, the remains of the frescoes in the caves at *Ajanta* (p.154) are worthy of note. Along with those at *Bagh* in the state of Gwalior they represent all that remains of ancient Indian painting. These frescoes date from the 2nd to the 7th century A.D., and seem, upon comparison with later painting, to have marked the apogee of Indian art. They portray, sometimes in lively fashion, scenes from the life and former existences of the Buddha, and also scenes from the temporal life of the Indian people. The oldest of these paintings are those which deal with Buddhist legends and were intended to uplift the beholder. – The modern miniature paintings meet with much approbation, especially those done on ivory. Since however they are principally but repetitions of those same images, they really belong to the field of handicraft, which itself has gained notable success in the most varied of ways through attractiveness of form, shining colours and neat work.

India is rich in the plastic works of art. Among these one cannot of course count the Brahman idols as examples in the artistic sense, with their multiplication of limbs and animal parts, grotesquely wrought. Only where human figures are portrayed without such deformities, do they possess beauty of facial expression, form and attitude. What however remains disturbing and often repellent is the lack of power, the Oriental sensuality, rigidity and ponderousness and, in the female form, a fleshiness that is all too vulgarly carnal (that is, when all these features are genuinely Indian and not influenced by foreign art).

Buddhist sculpture makes a nobler and more natural impression upon the observer; here, too, the beginnings of the art go back far in time, as in the case of architecture (p.LXV), although there may have been crude Brahmanist idols even earlier on. The lions on the columns (lat) erected in many places by King Ashoka, following Persian models, originate from the middle of the 3rd century B.C. The sculptures on the stone enclosures of the *Temple of Buddha-Gaya* (p.228), the *Stupa of Bharhut* (in the central Indian state of Nagod) and on the gateways before the great *Stupa of Sanchi* (p.157) date in all probability from the 2nd century B.C. From the 2nd century A.D. we have – to mention only the most important from the point of view of art history – the stone reliefs on the enclosure of the former *Stupa of Amaravati* (p.88). Only fragments have remained at Buddha-Gaya, the rich and very interesting reliefs at Bharhut now adorn the museum in Calcutta (p.245), the equally significant reliefs of Sanchi are still in their original location; the ruins of Amaravati, where Indian sculpture reached its highest level, are now in the British Museum in London and in the museum at Madras (p.85).

All these sculptures are, like the paintings of Ajanta, partly depictions of Buddha and saints, partly lifelike portrayals of scenes from the Buddha's former existences, which have been identified with well-known events in the literature of Buddhist legends, and scenes from daily life, which are of great importance for the cultural history of the country.

In composition it is possible to detect Grecian as well as Persian influences, which therefore penetrated not only the Ganges basin in the first centuries before and after Christ's birth but, at the time the Stupa of Amaravati was erected, reached to the far south of India. Indian coins from the north-west bearing the images of Greek gods (Zeus, Athene, Nike etc.) have been known about for a long time. More recent discoveries and excavations have brought to light abundant quantities of sculpture, which show Graeco-Roman influence, before and after the beginning of our chronology, which is much stronger than had been supposed. In *Mathura* (Muttra, p.173), a place where Buddhist and Brahman antiquities have been discovered, a Heracles throttling the Nemean lion, and a Silenus were found. Chiefly, however, one is concerned with the enormous numbers of Buddhist works of art of the old *Gandhara land* (p.207), and the expeditions to Turkestan have shown that this art was not limited to its country of origin, but found its way to central Asia also, to Turfan and Khotan. The Gandhara artworks are mainly still *in situ;* but hundreds of them have been taken to the museums of Calcutta, Lahore, Lucknow, Peshawar, London, Berlin (Ethnographical Museum), Paris and into smaller collections. The best items come from the era between 100 B.C. and 300 A.D. This art is an offshoot of Hellenistic art. Just as the capitals of columns carry acanthus leaves entwined, and figures from Greek mythology are utilised in architectural ornamentation, so we find statues of Buddha resembling Apollo, in Greek garb rich with folds. That Buddhism allowed itself to be so strongly influenced by this foreign art is explained by its cosmopolitanism, which burst out of the strict confines of India. Much smaller, indeed virtually undetectable, is the influence exerted by Greece upon the older Brahman works of art. Certainly the national, Indian, form of Brahmanism, as it outdistanced Buddhism in India, also withdrew at an early stage from the artistic influences coming from abroad.

Indian architecture consisted originally of wooden buildings, as in Burma, China and Japan, and these developed fairly slowly over the years before stone began to be used. The oldest Indian stone monuments are very clearly, both in their construction and ornamentation, imitations of wooden models. We have also the positive testimony of the Greek Megasthenes, who spent the years 302-288 B.C. as envoy of Seleukos Nikator at the court of King Chandragupta in Pataliputra (p.288), that the ramparts of that city were made of wood, and provided with openings, i.e. loopholes, for archers. The transition from the use of wood to that of stone in building must have occurred a considerable time before the erection of the oldest buildings still preserved: this we deduce from the assurance evident in the handling of the material. Foreign influences seem to have had little or no effect upon the construction of the older buildings, but Grecian ornament was very widely copied in India, as is evidenced by the numerous 'Indo-Corinthian' columns.

The first builders in India were the Buddhists, as has already been indicated. They always strove after a greater simplicity of style than the followers of Brahmanism who, as time went on, yielded increasingly to their inclination towards pompousness and affectation in this field. The oldest Buddhist structures are the *stupas* (p.LXIV), i.e. memorials and reliquary monuments, which were erected in large numbers in India and, with the spread of Buddhism, in neighbouring lands also, doubtless during the course of the millennium following the 3rd century B.C. These stupas, of which many are preserved, if in a badly damaged state, are shaped like a hemisphere or bell (with a surrounding terrace). On the top is a square structure crowned with a shade, the Indian symbol of dominance, and surrounded by stone trellis-work. Along with the stupas, mention must be made of the famous Buddhist rock excavations, which divide into *Shaityas* or temples, and *Viharas* or monks' cells, sometimes forming an amalgamation of temple and monastery.

The Buddhist Shaitya buildings are very similar in construction to Christian basilicas. Next to a wide nave run two aisles separated by columns. The roof is in the form of a barrel vault, the apse semi-circular. The latter contains a reliquary monument in the shape of a stupa with a roof like a shade. The most famous example of such a rock temple is the great temple at Karli (p.103), dating from the 1st c. B.C.

The building of grotto temples was also adopted by Brahmanism. Sometimes the rock excavations of Buddhist and Brahman origin lie close together, e.g. in *Ellora* (p.118), where this type of building was practised extensively and with great artistry. The rock grottoes of Ellora, which sometimes are superposed in several storeys, forming a town in their own right, originated from the period between the 4th to the 12th century A.D., the latter century being probably also the period of the mighty Brahmanist rock temples at *Elephanta* near Bombay (p.129).

Just as these buildings were produced by hollowing out the rock, so free-standing temples were hewn out of big blocks or left open in the rock, and in this way marvellous structures were wrought from a single piece of stone. The most famous example of the latter type is the Kailasa ('mountain of the gods') near Ellora, dating from the 8th century (p.120). This temple, which arouses astonishment in every visitor, stands in a large courtyard which was produced by chiselling away the rock from above and, in the fashion of the temples of southern India, it displays on its outside surfaces a rich collection of figures and ornaments. It has never yet been explained how it came about that a temple, built in the pure southern style, should be so far north. One assumes in this case that there was a definite family of architectural styles, which one comes across far away from the point of origin of this particular style. Such an assumption would apply to other temples and it is doubtless true that the fame of outstanding temple buildings was carried all over India by pilgrims, and that princes, on hearing about them and wanting also to erect a temple, often summoned their architects from remote districts.

Following Fergusson, the original expert on Indian architecture, five Brahmanist styles may be discerned: the *north Indian* or *Indo-Aryan*, the *Deccanese* or *Shalukya* style, the *south Indian* or *Dravidian*, the *Nepalese* and the *Kashmiri*. The well-known archaeologist Cunningham added a sixth to these, which he calls the *Gupta style*, because it was in its prime in the 4th and 5th centuries A.D., when northern India was ruled by the Gupta dynasty.

Of the buildings erected in this style about a dozen have been traced in the south of the United Provinces and neighbouring districts. Its characteristic features are a flat roof without towers, the extending of the upper connecting portions of the gateways beyond the vertical supports, statues of the Ganges and the Jumna on both sides of the entry gate, columns with massive square capitals, on which two lions stand back to back with a tree between them, and the projecting of the architrave of the pillared hall in the shape of a cornice running around the building.

The most important feature of the north Indian or Indo-Aryan style is the bulging tower, shaped like a bee-hive, which rises above the Cella, the space containing the sacred image. The Cella is square in form: the tower has curved surfaces bent slightly upwards and crowned with a strong notched disc, on which a pinnacle is set. There is no surfeit of sculptures, as is so characteristic in temples in the southern style. The material is usually hewn stone, but some brick temples have come to light. The best-known temples in this style are those of *Bhuvanesvar* at Orissa (p.90) and *Khajraho* (p.158). The most beautiful emanate from the period from 950 to 1200, some of the temples at Orissa being placed by Fergusson as early as the 7th century.

An off-shoot of the Indo-Aryan style is the Jain style in western India, which was earlier assumed to have developed in union with the Buddhist open-air temples (no longer preserved). Many examples of temples were built in the Jain style – by the Hindus also – throughout Rajputana, Malva and Gujerat. It flourished in the 11th-13th centuries, and again in the 15th century. It is characterised by pillared halls supporting domes, which in their most famous models, such as the white marble temples on Mount Abu and at Nagda near Udaipur (p.145), along with numerous shrines in Gujerat, are of surpassing beauty.

The so-called Shalukya style deviates rather more from the Indo-Aryan, and it is therefore regarded as a separate style. It takes its name from an ancient dynasty of the Deccan (p.111) and is widespread in central Deccan or, as Burgess more precisely puts it, in Hyderabad, in the central provinces, Berar and the districts of the Bombay presidency, where Marathi and Kanarese are spoken. This style marks a transition between the characteristic forms of the north and those of the south. Of the oldest temples in its sphere, some possess towers that are utterly north Indian, while others are closely related to the south Indian style, showing very rich plastic ornamentation. The plan of the buildings is usually star-shaped, the roof being a pyramid. The columns are massive, often round and having projecting capitals. Not infrequently, a central hall is surrounded by three temple rooms. These buildings generally date from the 12th and 13th centuries.

The southern Indian or Dravidian style, whose derivation from the art of wooden building is particularly clearly recognisable, is prevalent in the greater portion of the Dravidian linguistic area. It seems to have come into being in the 6th or 7th century, and has undergone many variations in the course of time, not always for the better. The later examples of this group of styles are overloaded with gods, humans, animals and all kinds of ornaments in a thoroughly confusing fashion. The Cella of the Dravidian temples forms an oblong, together with a vestibule. Above it rises a pyramidal tower of several storeys bearing a round or polygonal dome. The larger temples are surrounded by one or more forecourts with splendid gateways (*gopura*) surmounted by towers, which are especially typical of the courtyards of the Dravidian temples. One frequently comes across temples of enormous dimensions in southern India, that at *Srirangam* (p.78) being the largest in the whole country. The best example of Dravidian style is the temple of Tanjur (p.80), built around 1000 A.D., after which one might select those at *Madura* (p.74), *Shilambaram* (p.81), *Kumbakonam* (p.81) and that of *Ramesvaram* (p.77).

Styles with a more local currency are the Nepalese and the Kashmiri, both of which arose under outside influences. The Nepalese style is merely an off-shoot of the Chinese one, from which it differs by a slighter curving of the roof, whose edges turn back, as is well-known. The massive roof, supported by short wooden pillars is also, in Nepal, the most characteristic part of the temple, and one which chiefly attracts the observer's attention. Usually two or three such roofs are built on top of one another. In the narrow valley of Nepal proper, there are said to be over 2000 temples, most of them in the capital Katmandu. The oldest buildings in Nepal are Buddhist stupas, whose origins may well date back to the 3rd century B.C. The Indo-Chinese temples, just described, date only from the period beginning 1500 A.D. Remarkably, Jain temples in the Nepalese style are to be found in southern Kanara on the Malabar coast, and these pose the same enigma as does, in a reverse sense, the southern Indian style of the Kailasa near Ellora (p.LXVI).

The Kashmiri style, which is restricted to the valley of Kashmir and the Salt Range district in the Punjab (p.205), points to Greek style in its fluted columns, which are remarkably similar to the late Doric period. The other characteristic features of this style are the two-tiered pyramid-shaped roof, and the arch over the entrance gate which is shaped like a clover leaf. The temples are generally small but sometimes surrounded by large forecourts. Those buildings which have been preserved date approximately from the period 700-1200. Best-known is the Temple of the Sun at Martanda, east of Islamabad, and erected about 750.

From the year 1200 onwards, Indian architecture was enriched by a new element of extraordinary beauty and fruitfulness, namely the Mohammedan style which was brought to India from Persia. That the chief features of the Mohammedan buildings of India are domes and arches (especially *pointed* arches), as is the case in the mosques in other lands where Islam has penetrated, can be explained by the fact that this style spread from Baghdad over the entire Mohammedan world. It did not however remain a unified style in India, but developed, under the influence of the native Indian style of building (at various times and in various parts of the country, where Mohammedan dynasties were founded), into so many different forms, that Fergusson differentiates no fewer than 13 and Burgess 10 off-shoots of the Indo-Mohammedan style. Limitations of space do not permit one to go into further detail here. Up to the beginning of the 17th century the Hindus, who were employed by the Mohammedan overlords as artists and craftsmen, put the stamp of their own method of construction and working upon their buildings, except that they had to exclude from their ornamentation the depiction of living things, as prohibited by Islam. Many parts of individual mosques are almost purely Hindu in style, which is the more understandable, since the oldest mosques in India were built from materials taken from destroyed Hindu and Jain temples. The remains of the great mosque, completed in Old Delhi around the year 1300 by Ala-ud-din, are a particularly distinctive example of this. According to an inscription, 1200 pillars from 27 destroyed temples were used in its construction. Pairs of these artistically carved columns are always found positioned with one above the other, and the majority of them are still preserved today, although every sculpture that portrays godlike and animal forms has been mutilated, the heads having been struck off the figures.

The finest Mohammedan structures, mainly mosques (masjid) and mausoleums, date from the time of the Mogul dynasty (16th and 17th centuries), and are to be found in *Delhi* (pp.180-3), *Agra* (pp.164-7), *Fatepur Sikri* (p.170) and *Ahmedabad* (p.132). The latter-named town is also rich in splendid buildings from earlier times. The architecture of the Mogul era is characterised by a rejection of the influence of Hindu style and a return instead to a pure Persian style, whose chief features are towering domes, tall façades with huge pointed arches and slender minarets. The Mohammedan buildings at *Bijapur* (p.105), dating from 1557-1686, are quite free from Hindu influences. Emperor *Akbar* (1556-1605) admittedly caused many buildings to be executed in mixed styles, when he was inclined towards Hinduism, but he did build in pure Persian style also, e.g. the mausoleum of his father Humayun near Delhi (p.186). With Akbar's death, Hindu admixtures disappeared. His successor *Jehangir* (1605-27) erected his buildings in Lahore in Persian style, and *Shah Jehan* (1628-58), the greatest builder of the Indian world, ennobled this style in such a way that his most famous creations, the Jama Masjid in Delhi (p.183), the Moti Masjid (p.163) and, above all, the incomparable Taj Mahal (p.167), the mausoleum of his favourite wife in Agra, belong among the finest buildings ever made on earth.

The Mohammedan architecture of India differs from that of the Mediterranean countries perhaps most obviously (when manifesting the zenith of its art) in the extravagant use of white marble, in the precious ornamentation of the latter by inlaying it with coloured stone mosaics, and in the artistic marble filigree work of bars and windows, which may be admired in the astonishing delicacy of the outside windows and the wall of the cenotaph in the Taj at Agra, and the windows of older buildings of magnificence at Ahmedabad, such as the mosque of Sidi Saiyid and the mausoleum of Rani Sipri. As Fergusson remarks, such windows of marble filigree would produce almost total darkness in the interior of a building in our climate. In India, however, they serve to subdue in pleasant fashion the otherwise unbearably blinding light in a building made entirely of white marble.

Since this Introduction aims to offer the traveller an understanding of the characteristic features of Indian culture, it omits mention of European institutions and methods which the English have introduced into administration, higher education and other branches of India's political and economic life, and have adapted to the actual conditions in the country; nor does it refer to the activities of the Christian missions.

Bibliography.

We have picked out only a selection, especially the more recent major works on the subject.

General descriptions.

The whole area covered by this handbook is dealt with in a scientific and geographical manner in *Wilhelm Sievers'* "Asia" (2nd ed. Leipsic and Vienna 1904, 15*M*) and *Elisée Reclus*, Nouvelle Géographie Universelle, vol. VIII: L'Inde et l'Indo-Chine (Paris 1883, 30fr.).

India.

A general survey in a popular presentation is *H. Gehring's* "India, the old land of wonders and its inhabitants" (2 vols illustr. 2nd ed. Leipsic 1910, 15*M.*) An excellent geography is *Sir Thomas H. Holdich's* "India" (London 1904, 7s.6d.). *Sir Bampfylde Fuller's* "The Empire of India" (London 1913, 7s.6d) is a good compendium of the political and economic situation; *Sir John Strachey's* "India, its administration and progress" is a concise and comprehensive description of the nature of English rule. *The Imperial Gazetteer of India* is a detailed geographical lexicon prepared for the government (26 vols, Oxford 1907-9, 6s. each; atlas with 64 maps and plans, 15s.). The first four volumes give a general description of the country, a history of India, an economic introduction and a description of the English administration. *Charles Joppen's* Historical Atlas of India (London 1907, 3s.) describes, with 26 clear maps and accompanying text, the complex territorial history of the country since antiquity.

Of the numerous recent travel books we would mention the following: *Richard Garbe* "Indian Travel Sketches" (Berlin 1889, 8½*M.*). *P. Deussen* "Memories of India" (Kiel & Leipsic 1904, 5*M.*). *Moritz Schanz* "Eastwards by Rail" (2 vols, Hamburg 1897, 10*M.* – the first volume covers India, Burma, Ceylon, Straits Settlements, Java and Siam).*J. Dahlmann, S.J.*, "Journeys in India" (2 vols, Freiburg/Breisgau 1908 18*M.*, covering also China, Cambodia, Japan, Siam and Burma). *H.Zache* "Through India to the forbidden land of Nepal" (Leipsic 1903, 10*M.*). *Ernst von Hesse-Wartegg* "India and its Princely Courts" (Stuttgart 1906, 12*M.*). *O. Kauffmann*, "From India's Jungles" (2 vols, Leipsic 1911, 20*M.*: descriptions of Nature and hunting experiences). The most detailed guide is *Murray's* "Handbook for India, Burma and Ceylon" (9th ed. London 1913, 20s.); *Eustace Reynolds-Ball*, "The Tourist's India" (London 1907, 10s.6d.) gives useful advice in a pleasant form.

For information about individual cities: *H.C.Fanshawe*, "Delhi, Past and Present" (London 1902, 8s.), *Gordon R.Hearn*, "The Seven Cities of Delhi" (London 1906, 10s.6d.), *E.B.Havell*, "Agra and the Taj" (London 1904, 5s.); "Benares the Sacred City" (2nd ed. London 1911, 6s.6d.), *Miss K.Blechynden*, "Calcutta, Past and Present" (London, 1905, 7s.6d.).

The classical work on architecture is *James Fergusson's* "History of Indian and Eastern Architecture" (2nd ed. 2 vols. London 1910, 42s.) *Vincent A. Smith's* "A History of Fine Art in India and Ceylon" (Oxford 1911, 63s.) offers a comprehensive account of the important sculptures and paintings. Other important works on the history of art are *E.B.Havell's* "The Ideals of Indian Art" (London, 1911, 15s.), "Indian Architecture, its Psychology, Structure and History" (London 1913, 30s.) and "Indian Sculpture and Painting" (London, 1908, 63s.). Finally, the eminent publications of the *Archaeological Survey of India* (to be had in Germany from Otto Harrassowitz or Karl W.Hiersemann in Leipsic, or Friedländer & Son in Berlin).

Lord Roberts (cf.p.242) "Forty-one Years in India" (London 1897, translated into German by Ritter v.Borosini, 2 vols, Berlin 1904, 15*M.*) gives a vivid picture of the Indian uprising of 1856-57 and the struggles against Afghanistan in 1878-80.

Of *Rudyard Kipling's* Indian stories, the novel "Kim" (1901, German version by the publishing house Vita in Berlin-Charlottenburg, 6*M.*) provides a gripping introduction to the life and thought of the Indian people. His "Jungle Book" (London 1894), the "Plain Tales from the Hills" (London 1888, German version in Reclam's Universalbibliothek), "Under the Deodars" (London 1888, cf.p.194) and others, mirror English life in India.

For works about the Himalayas, see p.236.

Ceylon.

Ernst Haeckel, "Indian Despatches" (1882; 5th ed. Berlin 1909, 16*M.*); *K. Guenther,* "Introduction to the Tropics" (Leipsic 1911, 4*M*80); *E.Schmidt*, "Ceylon" (Berlin 1897, 6*M.*). The classic work among English books is *Sir J.Emerson Tennent's* "History and Topography of Ceylon" (London 1859, 50s.). A detailed and richly illustrated account is to be found in *Henry W.Cave's* "The Book of Ceylon" (new ed., London 1912, 121s.). The same author reports on the old ruined sites in "The Ruined cities of Ceylon" (4th imp., London 1907; 12s.), to be had in German also under the title "Baudenkmäler aus ältester Zeit in Ceylon" (Berlin 1901, 12*M.*). Of more practical use are *John C.Willis'* "Ceylon, a Handbook for the Resident and Traveller" (London 1907, 5s.) and the annual "Ceylon Handbook and Directory" by *Ferguson.*

Burma.

Sir J.George Scott, "Burma, a Handbook of Practical, Commercial and Political Information" (illustr.; 2nd imp. London 1911; 10s.6d.) encompasses a wealth of geographical, historical, economic and other information in a concise but very readable form. *Jos. Dautremer's* "Une colonie modèle, la Birmanie sous le régime britannique" (Paris 1912, 6fr.) gives a general picture. The country and people are described by *V.C.Scott O'Connor's* "The Silken East, a Record of Life and Travel in Burma" (2 vols with 400 illustr., London 1904) and *R.Talbot Kelly's* "Burma painted and described" (London 1905, 20s.; with 75 attractive illustr. from water colours). *V.C.Scott O'Connor's* "Mandalay and other Cities of the Past in Burma" (with 235 illustr., London 1907, 21s.) gives detailed descr. of Mandalay, Ava, Pagan, Prome and other historic sites. *Shway Yoe* (Sir J.George Scott, see above), "The Burman, his Life and Notions" (3rd imp. London 1910, 10s.6d.) is the main classic account of life in Burma. Similarly *Max & Bertha Ferrars'* "Burma" (with 455 illustr., 2nd imp, London 1901, 30s.) is chiefly devoted to depicting the life of the natives. Finally, the *Imperial Gazetteer of India* (see p.LXXI above) contains sections on Burma.

The Malayan Peninsula.

Sir Frank Swettenham's (cf.p.286) "British Malaya (illustr. London 1906, 16s.) and *Arnold Wright & Thomas H.Reid's* "The Malay Peninsula" (illustr. London 1912, 10s.6d.) are accounts of the development of the peninsula under British influence. German travel books incl. *A.Preyer's* "Indo-Malayan Expeditions" (Leipsic 1903, 5½*M.*; applies also to Java) and *Wilh.Wolff's* "In the Malayan Jungle and Tin Mountains" (Berlin 1909, 5*M.*). *C.W.Harrison's* "Illustrated Guide to the Federated Malay States" (London 1910, 3s.6d.) is a detailed guide-book.

Siam.

W.A.Graham's "Siam, a Handbook of Practical, Commercial and Political Information" (illustr. 2nd ed. London 1912, 10s.6d.), similar to Scott's "Handbook for Burma", see above. *P.A.Thompson's* "Lotus Land" (illustr. London 1906, 16s.) gives a good overall picture of the southern portion of the country. A famous travel book, somewhat older, is *Carl Bock's* "In the Realm of the White Elephant" (German by F.M.Schröter; Leipsic 1885, 8*M.*). *E.Young's* "The Kingdom of the Yellow Robe" (3rd ed London 1907) contains entertaining sketches on habits and customs. *Dilock's* "Prince of Siam, Agriculture in Siam" (Leipsic 1908, 6*M.*) gives accurate agricultural and economic information.

Java.

The chief geographical work, concerned especially with the volcanic nature of the country, is *Franz Junghuhn's* (p.323) "Java, its form, flora and inner structure" (German by J.K.Hasskarl; 3 vols, Leipsic 1854-7). A good survey is to be found in *A.Cabaton's* "Les Indes Néerlandaises" (Paris 1910, 8fr.) Among recent travel books: *Ernst Haeckel's* "Letters from the Malayan Archipelago" (2nd ed. Leipsic 1909, 6*M*.); *J.Giesenhagen's* "In Java and Sumatra, Expeditions & Journeys of Exploration in the Land of the Malays" (Leipsic 1901, 10*M*.). Also *G.Haberlandt's* "A Botanical Journey through the Tropics, Pictures of the Indo-Malayan Vegetation and Travel Sketches" (2nd ed. Leipsic 1910, 11*M*60) and *H.Morin* "Beneath the Tropical Sun, Expeditions in Java, Sumatra & Ceylon" (Munich 1910, 8½M.)

Route 1. From Europe to India by Sea.

Distances and travelling times: to *Port Saîd,* at the entrance to the Suez Canal, from Marseilles, 1510 SM., 5 days; from Genoa 1446 SM., 5 days; from Naples 1110 SM, 4 days; from Brindisi 930 SM., 3 days; from Trieste 1313 SM., 4 days.; - from Port Saïd to *Aden* 1395 SM., 5-6 days; - from Aden to *Bombay* 1664 SM., 4-5 days; from Aden to *Colombo* 2093 SM., 6 days. – The best survey of the shipping lines is to be found in the German State Timetable under no. 696-707. - → Since the steamers are usually fully booked up during the main tourist season, one should reserve one's passage as early as possible. First-comers obtain the best cabins, and this is true for the return journey from India. For especially good cabin accommodation one often pays increased prices, whereas the less popular internal cabins are charged at reduced rates. Return tickets are generally valid for a return journey on competitors' ships, where an adjustment to the price is accordingly made upwards or downwards. Detailed information may be had from the agencies of the various companies, who should be asked to send their latest timetable and 'Passengers' Handbook'.

For German travellers, the most important steamers are those of the *North German Lloyd* (Bremen: agencies in all the larger German towns), which leave every fortnight for Eastern Asia, and every month for Australia. Most travellers will save themselves the 14-day voyage via Gibraltar, and join their ship instead at *Genoa* or Naples. Luggage sent on in advance must arrive at the North German Lloyd company's office (Vico S.Antonio 11) 2 days before the departure from Genoa (express baggage takes 8-10 days from North Germany and 6-8 days from South Germany). It must be labelled 'in transito'. The voyage from Genoa to *Colombo* takes 17 days and costs 1080*M.* for 1st class and 675*M.* for 2nd class; from Colombo via Penang to *Singapore* 7 days, fare 247 rupees 50 cts., and 181 rupees 50 cts. respectively; in Singapore there are connections for Bangkok (p.299) and Java (p.311).

Austrian Lloyd (Trieste; general agency in Berlin, Unter den Linden 47) runs a rapid service to *Bombay* from Trieste twice a month (14 days; fare in English currency £33.6s. - £39.6. for 1st class, and £23.6s. for 2nd class); also, a rapid service to Shanghai once a month, calling at *Colombo* (17 days; £35 & £28) and then continuing via Penang and Singapore. The following English companies charge similar prices to those of North German Lloyd: P & O *(Peninsular & Oriental Steam Navigation Company,* 122 Leadenhall St., London E.C.; agent in

Hamburg: Herm.Binder, Spitaler Str. 11) which goes once a week via Gibraltar and Marseilles to Bombay, and once a fortnight to Colombo; and the *Orient Line of Royal Mail Steamships* (London; agents in Hamburg: Suhr & Classen), which goes once a fortnight to Colombo via Gibraltar, Toulon and Naples. – Other English companies: *Anchor Line* (Glasgow) which calls only at Gibraltar on the outward trip and only at Marseilles on the homeward; *Ellerman Line, Bibby Line* etc. (information from Thomas Cook & Son, London E.C.)

The Dutch company *Stoomvaart Maatschappij Nederland* (Amsterdam; agent in Berlin: Karl Senft, Unter den Linden 70) also calls at *Genoa* with its fortnightly steamers from Amsterdam to Batavia: travelling time from Genoa to *Colombo* 17 days, fares 920*M.* for 1st class, 600*M.* for 2nd class, return fares 1380*M.* and 900*M.*; from Colombo to *Singapore* 6 days, fares 335 and 200*M.*; from Singapore to Batavia 2 days, fares 105 and 60*M.* (Genoa to Batavia 1375, 815*M.*; return within 2 years 2065, 1225*M.)*.

French *Messageries Maritimes* (Paris, Rue Vignon 1; agent in Hamburg: Eug.Cellier, Dovenfleet 21): fortnightly from *Marseilles* to Colombo and monthly via Bombay to Colombo for 1200fr. 1st cl. and 900fr. 2nd cl.

Italian company *Marittima Italiana* (Genoa, see p.3): monthly from *Genoa* via Naples and Messina to Bombay in 16 days.

Japanese line *Nippon Yusen Kaisha* (agent in Hamburg: Paul Günther, Mattentwiete 1), fortnightly from Antwerp via London & Marseilles to Colombo, Singapore etc.

From Berlin to Marseilles the fast train takes 35 hrs via Paris. 32 via Belfort, 32 via Geneva; fare: 135*M*60, 87*M*60 Pf., via Geneva 141*M*70, 90*M*50 Pf.

Marseilles. – Hotels: *Gr.-H. du Louvre & de la Paix, Rue de Noailles 3, 200 Rm; *Gr.-H. Noailles & Métropole (prop. Bilmaier, German), Rue de Noailles 22-24, 140 Rm; *Grand Hôtel (prop. Rueck, German) also Rue de Noailles, near the former, 90 Rm; *Regina-Hot., Place Sadi-Carnot, 250 Rm; *H. de Russie & d'Angleterre, Boulevard d'Athènes 31, near the main railway sta., 60 Rm – Second class: H. de Genève, Rue des Templiers 3, near the port; H. du Petit Louvre, Rue Cannebière 16-18.

Marseilles, with 550,000 inhabitants, is the second largest city and the most important sea-port in France. Fine panorama from the loftily situated church of Notre-Dame de la Garde, to which a funicular rises from the S. side of the inner harbour. – Steamer agencies: Messageries Maritimes, 16 Rue Cannebière; P & O Company, 18 Rue Colbert. Embarkation of Messageries steamers 1 hr. before sailing at the earliest (either 11 a.m. or 4 p.m.)

From Berlin to Genoa, the fast train takes 27hrs. via the St Gotthard and 29hrs. over the Brenner Pass; fares: 125*M.*, 80*M*80 Pf. and 126*M*60, 83*M*70 Pf.

Genoa. – Hotels: *Gr.-H. Miramare, Via Pagano Doria, to the west of and above the main sta (Stazione Piazza Principe), elegant Swiss establishment, 280 beds from 6fr.; Gr.-H. de Gênes, Piazza Deferrari, H. Bristol, Via Venti Settembre, Eden Palace Hot., Via Serra 6 (quiet), the latter three far from the sta. and port; Gr.-H. Savoy above the Piazza Acquaverde, near the sta. More modest: H. Victoria, Piazza Annunziata, H-P. Smith, Piazza Caricamento, both good.

Cabs: one-horse to the port 1fr., at night 1½. 2-horse 1½, at night 2fr., cases 20c. each.

Genoa, with its 272,000 inhabitants, is Italy's premier commercial city and strongly fortified. Drive through the palace-lined Via Balbi, Via Cairoli and Via Garibaldi, then take the funicular from the Piazza Zecca to the Forte Castellaccio. – North German Lloyd office (Leupold Fratelli), Via Garibaldi 5; office of the Marittima Italiana provisionally at Via Balbi 40. Steamers moor at the Ponte Federico Guglielmo or nearby; in the latter instance, rowing-boat 30c., at night 60c. per person, luggage 50c. per 50kg.

From Berlin to Naples: fast train over the Brenner 46hrs., over the Gotthard 44hrs.; fares 154*M*10, 100*M*70 Pf. and 166*M,* 107*M.* One day's sea journey from Genoa is:

Naples. – Hotels: *Bertolini's Palace Hotel, *H. Bristol, *Parker's H., *Gr. Eden H., these being in elevated positions on the Corso Vitt.Emanuele; *H. Excelsior, *Grand Hôtel, by the sea; H.Hassler, German; all some distance from sta. and port.

Cab to the harbour: 1-horse 1fr., 2-horse, 2fr., from midnight 1fr.30, 2fr.50., cases 20c. apiece, hand luggage 10c.

Naples, Italy's most populous city with 600,000 inhabitants, can boast of one of the most beautiful situations in the world. On a short visit one should take the funicular to S.Martino (view) and walk along the Via Tasso or Strada Nova di Posilipo. – North German Lloyd office (Aselmeyer & Co.) Via Agostino Depretis 49-53. The steamers anchor near the Immacolatella: North German Lloyd conveys passengers aboard in its own tender; rowing-boat 1-1½fr. with luggage.

From Berlin to Trieste the fast train takes 22hrs. via Mühldorf-Salzburg or Munich-Salzburg; fares 109*M*50, 65*M*20, 41*M*40Pf.

Trieste. – Hotels: *Excelsior Palace Hot., 220 Rm from 4kr., near the Lloyd offices and port; H.de la Ville, at the port; Volpich all'Aquila Nera, near the port. – Cab to the harbour, 1kr., by night 1kr.60h., cases 40h. apiece.

Trieste is Austria's main sea-port with 183,000 inhab. – Austrian Lloyd office in the Lloyd Palace, Piazza Grande. Steamers tie up at the Molo.

The voyage to Port Saïd (cf. Baedeker's "Mediterranean") follows the Calabrian coast south of Naples and past the Lipari Islands (Stromboli Volcano), through the Straits of Messina, where one joins the route of the steamers coming from Marseilles through the Straits of Bonifazio (between Corsica and Sardinia), then round the southern tip of Calabria. Etna's mighty pyramid disappears from view only after a considerable time. After 2 days, the mountain ranges of Crete come into view. The colourful splendour of the sunsets increases as one proceeds southwards. At night, the phosphorescence of the sea (p.13) adds to the charm of the journey. Of the Egyptian coast the light at Damiette is the first thing to be seen, by night. Fort Jemil emerges on the low line of dunes that separates Lake Menzaleh (p.6) from the sea, and then the lighthouse at Port Saïd. The coast itself is not visible until one is already close inshore in water made opaque by the Nile.

The entrance to the harbour is protected by two massive breakwaters. The western one (Jetée Est) is 2000m. long. To the right, near the southern end of the western breakwater, a statue of Ferdinand de Lesseps (p.5), almost 7m. tall, stands on a 10m. high base. On dry land is the Phare, the 53m. high lighthouse.

Port Saïd. – The ship anchors near the Customs House (Douane). Disembarkation, without luggage, ½fr.

HOTELS: Eastern Exchange Hotel, Rue Sultan Osman, English with 100 Rm, lifts and garden, P. 13s.-18s.; Savoy Hotel (German manager), corner of Quai François-Joseph and Rue el-Tegara, with 63 Rm., restaurant and bar. P.11s.-13s; Hôt.Continental (prop. Simonini Bros.), Rue el-Tegara, 56 Rm, P.10-11s.; Casino Palace Hotel (same prop.), on the north beach by the breakwater, with 45 Rm, bathing place and garden, P.10-14s.; Hôt. De la Poste (prop. Albrand), Rue du Nil.

CABS: per journey 2½ piastres, to the sta. 4, to el-Raswa (steamer landing on Lake Menzaleh, p.6) 6pi; per hr. 10pi.

TRAMS: from the port westwards through the town and the Arab quarter to the cemetery, from the Greek church to the sta. and to el-Raswa.

BANKS: *Deutsche Orientbank*, Boul.Eugénie; *Crédit Lyonnais, National Bank of Egypt, Anglo-Egyptian Bank,* all three in the Rue du Nil. – The mixture of Egyptian, English and French currency is burdensome at Port Saïd (1 shilling = 5 piastres, 1fr. = 4 piastres). German marks are also accepted (1 *M* = 1s., 50Pf. 6pi).

POST OFFICES: Egyptian, Rue du Nil; French, Boul.Eugénie.

TELEGRAPH: Egyptian, Rue el-Tegara; English: Eastern Telegraph Co, for abroad only, Quai François-Joseph.

CONSULATES: Germany, *L.Rickmers,* Rue du Nil 26; France, *Meyerier,* Boul.Eugénie; Gt. Britain, *E.C.Blech*; Austria-Hungary, *A.v.Probizer,* Quai François-Joseph; Italy, *Tritoni,* at the Italian School.

TRAVEL BUREAU: *Thos.Cook & Son,* Quai François-Joseph. – SHIPPING AGENCIES: *North German Lloyd,* W.H.Müller & Co., Boul.Eugénie 10; *Austrian Lloyd,* represented by Cook. *Messageries Maritimes*, Wohrer, *Marittima Italiana,* Cav. Giulio de Castro, both also on the Quai François-Joseph.

Port Saïd, capital of the Egyptian province of the same name, owes its foundation to the Suez Canal. The rapidly increasing population numbered 50,000 in 1907, of whom 1,000 were Europeans of all nations, the remainder being a colourful mixture of Arabs, Berbers and Negroes. The town itself is of no interest except for the numerous shops offering all kinds of Oriental objects. Whoever has not yet acquired a tropical helmet (p.XV) should do so here, as this headgear is pleasant during the journey through the Red Sea, and necessary when visiting Aden (see p.10). We recommend Simon Arzt's shop.

The harbour of 230 hectares has a depth of 9-11m., which is maintained by laborious dredging. The inner harbour of 89 hectares comprises the main basin *(Bassin Ismaïl)* with three adjoining basins for loading and unloading cargo: commercial port *(Bassin du Commerce),* arsenal *(Bassin de l'Arsenal)* – the imposing Canal Company building is situated between these two – and the *Bassin Chérif,* with the splendid establishment erected by Prince Henry of the Netherlands (†1879), now a barracks and military depot of the English government and Lloyd's signal station (Marconi station). Beyond this, the coal port *(Bassin des Chalands charbonniers),* the *Bassin Abbas Hilmi* or *Africa Basin,* with the quarantine establishment and the new petroleum port (Bassin à pétrole).

Railway from Port Saïd (sta. in the SW quarter of the town) to *Cairo* (238km; fast train 4-4½ hrs.) See Baedeker's "Egypt". – At (77km.) *Ismailia* (p.6) the track to Suez branches off: Port Saïd-Suez 172km. in 3½-4¾hrs. for 74 piastres (about 19fr.) Suez has the following stations: *Arbaeen* (Arbain) for the new district in the NW; then, on the one side, *Rue Colmar* for the town of Suez and, on the other, the sta. *Terre-plein* (Port Taufik) on an island forming a port, and linked to the mainland by a 3km.-long stone causeway.

The Suez Canal, constructed in 1859-69 to the designs of the Frenchman Ferd.de Lesseps, by a limited company with the assistance of the viceroys Saïd and Ismaïl, has reopened the ancient trade-route through the Red Sea to southern Asia, which had fallen into disuse after the discovery of the passage round the Cape of Good Hope. It is now one of the world's most important steamer routes. 161km. long, it is 80-135m. wide and 11m. deep. Construction costs ran to approx.380 million marks, with an additional 14 million for the widening work commenced in 1899. It is owned by the Compagnie Universelle du Canal Maritime de Suez (The Suez Canal Company). The English government is the largest shareholder, having purchased the Egyptian government's 177,000 shares for £4 million in 1875. The number of ships passing through the Canal was 4969 in 1911, of which 3089 sailed under the English flag, 667 under the German, 284 Dutch, 232 French, 180 Austrian, 87 Italian, 80 Japanese etc. Since the introduction of electric lighting and the broadening of the navigation channel, the passage now takes only 15-22hrs., although steamers may travel at full speed only in the large Bitter Lakes, as their powerful wash would cause damage to the embankments. The dues for postal and freight shipping are 6fr.25c. per ton and 10fr. for each adult passenger. Distances are marked at 5km intervals on the east bank, the passing places for large steamers being marked 'Gare du Nord' and 'Gare du Sud' (North and South stations).

The first section passes through the shallow *Lake Menzaleh,* which is 2500sq.km in area, and which has been drained to the east of the Canal. The lake is populated by flocks of pelicans and silver herons and even flamingoes. Along the west side runs the railway (see p.5). At the southern end of the lake, the Canal cuts through the (44km) isthmus *El-Kantara* ('the bridge'), over which led the ancient caravan route from Syria to Egypt. In the adjoining *Lake Balah* the channel is enclosed by low banks. Further south, the 16m. high desert hills of *El-Gisr* ('the embankment') provided the most serious impediment to the construction of the Canal. During the period 1859-64, 20,000 Eyptian fellahin worked to break through the obstacle, until the introduction of machines. The cutting opens into the light-blue waters of *Lake Timsah* ('crocodile lake') where the channel is marked by piles. As his ship enters it, the traveller sees above, to the r., the viceroy's palace at *Ismaïlia.* This town, which lies among gardens (7000 inhab.) is the seat of the Canal administration and the station on the railway which here leaves the Canal to head for Cairo, 77km from Port Saïd. At (85km) *Tusun* r. the whitewashed dome of the tomb of a sheikh.

The Canal cuts through the rocky barrier of the so-called *Serapeum* (90km). The remains of memorial tablets discovered here remind one of the oldest attempt to connect the Red Sea and the Nile, in the era of the Persian King Darius (521-486 B.C.), who completed the waterway which the Egyptian King Necho (609-538 B.C.) had begun. Reaching a tall iron lighthouse, the Canal now enters the bluish-green waters of the *Bitter Lakes.* Above the low shores to the SW rises the chain of *Jebel Jenefeh* or *Jebel Ahmed Taher* ('jebel' being the Arabic for 'mountain'). At the end of the Great Bitter Lake, a second iron lighthouse. At *Esh-Shallufeh* (139km) the remains are preserved of another memorial tablet from Darius's time. At the 150km mark, the Canal reaches the northern, shallow part of the Gulf of Suez, where the channel is dredged. On the W. bank can be seen the workshops and magazines of the Suez Canal Company, and the town of:-

Suez, which now numbers 18,350 inhab. (2530 Europeans), but contains nothing remarkable for the traveller. Near the Rue Colmar railway sta. (p.5) is the Hôt. Bel-Air. – A stone causeway, 3km long, which also carries the railway, connects the mainland with the artificial port on the edge of deep water.

160km. *Port Taufik* (Hôt. Du Sinaï, near Terre-plein sta.) The main port, *Port Ibrahim,* with a special area for warships and dry-docks, opens to the SW and is protected by locks and banks. Steamers generally anchor a good distance before Port Ibrahim. There is a fine view of the mountains on both banks; to the SW, the step-shaped *Ataka Range* (831m), whose dark outline stands out clearly on the horizon at sunset.

The Gulf of Suez, 170SM in length, is the western of the two great inlets into which the Red Sea divides at the Sinaï peninsula (p.8). Like the Sea itself, it is dotted with numerous coral reefs, recognisable by the surf and the milky colouring of the water. The reefs are formed by the calcareous excretion from millions upon millions of colonies of molluscs found only in tropical seas. One differentiates between the reefs which line the coast and the atolls in open water (as a rule forming a curved line enclosing a lagoon). Coral debris washed up on the reefs causes low islands to be formed, to which plant seeds are carried by wind and current. The navigation channel is marked by buoys and lighthouses which are the responsibility of the Egyptian government as far as the Daedalus Reef (p.8), and then of the British-Indian government (each sending 4 Europeans, who are provided with food and water only every 3 months, to do this solitary and burdensome duty). However, the strong tides (difference between high and low water 2m. at Suez and at Bab el-Mandeb, but much less in the middle) can still be dangerous, as the occasional wreck seen during the voyage testifies. – Geologically, the Red Sea is regarded as a prehistoric inroad into the former Egyptian-Arab tableland ('Eritrean Trench'), which can be seen in the Gulf of Suez, especially to the W., by the horizontal upper edge of the barren Eyptian mountain slopes, partly rent by ravines. Since no rivers flow into the Sea, the salt content of the water rises to 41%, such as is found in no other sea, this being caused by the extreme evaporation (2.6m annually).

Soon after leaving Suez one catches sight, l. and 1½km inland, of the palm-girt oasis of the Springs of Moses, and r. the Zenobia lightship by the *Newport Reefs.* The Gulf broadens, but the reddish mountains on both sides remain in view, and are irradiated at sunset by a wonderful glow. 473m from the Newport Reefs, the 25m tall white stone lighthouse appears r. on cape *Ras Zaferaneh* (ras is Arabic for cape), whose light is visible for 14SM. Farther on r. rises the picturesque mountain range of *Jebel Gharib* (2000-2500m); in the foreground, the cape bearing the same name with a light on an iron frame, whose round white base serves the keeper as a dwelling. – To the l., the imposing Sinaï mountains, the most conspicuous of which are the serrated *Jebel Serbal* (2052m) and, to the S., the sugar-loaf of the *Jebel Umm Shomar* (2575m). In front of these, closely following the profile of the shore-line, is the undulating barren desert of *El-Kaa,* rising to 300m. In the foreground lies the lonely port of *Tor,* which serves as a quarantine station for the pilgrimages to Mecca. To the NW of Tor lies a small palm grove. Among the central group of the Sinaï range, one now briefly espies the summit of *Jebel Musa* (2292m; 'Mountain of Moses'), usually taken to be the Mount of the Covenant and, to its r., the *Jebel Katherin* (2606m). The Sinaï peninsula ends to the S. at the steep cape *Ras Mohammed* (30m). – On the r., the coast is now lined with a series of rocks and islands, of which the *Ashrafi Reef* bears a 43m high iron lighthouse with a revolving light, and the rugged island of *Shadwan* (370m high) with a flashing light.

After negotiating the 6.5km wide *Straits of Jubal,* the ship now enters the Red Sea proper. To the left one can look up the *Gulf of Akaba,* along which the 'Eritrean Trench' continues northwards towards the 'Syrian Trench' (Dead Sea, valley of the Jordan). Then the coast is lost to view on both sides. The Red Sea, without its northernmost gulfs, is 1080SM long and 120-190SM broad, reaching a depth of 2359m. The name comes from antiquity and is associated with the Homerite tribes ('Red'). The water is blue-green in colour. The hot climate is notorious, being made particularly unbearable by the extreme humidity of the air, owing to evaporation. The temperature often rises in August to over 40°C in the shade (danger of heat-stroke) but, during the main travelling season, October-May, it is often reduced in the northern part of the Sea by the prevailing N. wind to such an extent that it is easy to catch cold when returning from the tropics. In the southern third of the Sea, a powerful south wind is usually blowing during this time, which helps to make the heat more bearable, at least on the outward journey. In any case, the extreme heat seldom lasts more than 1-2 days during the winter voyage.

Of the islands and islets of the northern part of the Red Sea we mention: 80SM from Shadwan, the *Brothers,* two low coral islands with a lighthouse 21.6m high, whose light is visible for 12SM and, about 100SM further S., the once greatly feared *Daedalus Reef,* a submarine coral formation, marked by a girder-work lighthouse, 18.6m tall, whose light is seen for 14SM. From this point on, the steamer's course is free from islands for over 650SM. Around the latitude of 22° one can see, if the ship sets course down the western, Egyptian, coast, the *Jebel Soterba* (or *Jebel Ten,* 2220m); or, if a more easterly course along the Arab coast is pursued, one espies the walls and towers of the trading town of *Jidda* (20,000 inhab.), the port for *Mecca,* which lies some 80km inland. About 40-60,000 Mohammedan pilgrims land at Jidda each year, on their way to the prophet's birthplace.

The southern part of the Red Sea, from about the 18th degree of latitude onwards, again has copious numbers of islands and islets on both sides. Some distance from our ship's course, on the W. coast, lies *Port Sudan,* linked to Khartoum by a 578km-long railway through the desert, which has made it a new gateway to Anglo-Egyptian Sudan. Further on, also to the W., is the *Dahalak Archipelago,* beyond which, on the coast, is the Italian colony of *Eritrea* (Massowa). To port, one sights, around 15½°, the *Jebel Teïr* ('bird mountain'), a 270m high volcanic island which still emits sulphurous vapour, and at 15° the barren *Zebayir Islands,* with the mountain of the same name (230m). Far away, on the coast, the port of *Hodeida* (50,000 inhab.), whence a trade-route leads to the town of *Sana*, situated 150km inland at an altitude of 2210m., the main town of the fertile *Yemen,* which is only nominally dependent upon Turkey. At 14°, *Jebel Zukur* rises on the l., at 624m the highest island in the Red Sea. Further on, to the l. again, the strangely-formed islands of *Great and Little Hanish,* both of volcanic origin, the first being 600m high. Finally, the less prominent *Haycock Islands.*

Both coasts now come into view again. At 13⅓° of northern latitude, one can discern the once important town of *Mokha,* now decaying as a result of competition from Aden and Hodeida. Of its numerous mosques, the tallest with its minaret is a navigation mark visible at a great distance. The once famous (Mocca) coffee plantations lie some 80km inland.

The Sea now narrows at the Straits of Bab el-Mandeb ("Gate of Tears") which, only by recent exact survey and lighting, has ceased to be a peril to navigation. Between the foothills *Ras Siyan* to the W. and *Ras Bab el-Mandeb* to the E., the straits are only 14SM (25km) wide, being divided by the island of *Perim* into a narrow eastern passage and a 15km wide western passage. The island is 12 sq.km in area, volcanic, waterless, and fortified since 1857 by the English. It numbers 700 inhab.; the garrison, only 50 men strong, is relieved from Aden every 2 months. On the western route one sees the port, an ancient crater and the large coal stores of the Perim Coal Co.; the top-most point (65m) is crowned by a signal station of the London Lloyd Company for Marine Safety and Shipping Information, which telegraphs the names of passing ships to London.

On entering the Gulf of Aden (which forms the 125-180SM wide, 450SM long and up to 2700m deep western bight of the Indian Ocean, between the Arab states of Yemen and Hadramaut in the N. and the African peninsula of Somalia in the S.) the ship adopts a course almost due E. (each day now growing 23 mins. shorter). In winter, east winds are prevalent here, in summer strong west winds. These change in May and September (p.12). The average temperature from January to March is 20-26.7°C, which is a welcome relative coolness after the heat of the Red Sea; in April 26.7-30°, in May and September 29-35°. The remaining months are milder. The distance from Perim to Aden is 108SM. The Arab coast, a sandy plain with stark mountain ranges in the distance, remains generally in view.

From a long way off, three precipitous massifs are visible, projecting down to the shore at 15km intervals: *Jebel Amran* (225m), *Jebel Hassan* (371m) and *Jebel Shamsham* (552m). the latter, an ancient volcano with yellow-brown serrated slopes, forms the peninsula of Aden (54 sq.km) which, like Gibraltar, is linked to the mainland only by a low tongue of sand. The modern port, Steamer Point (p.11), lies in the western corner of the peninsula, facing *Tawahi* or *Tuai Bay*.Of the old town of Aden to the E., only a few rock fortifications are visible.

Aden. - The steamers of North German Lloyd usually anchor about 2km W. of Steamer Point, the rest in the inner harbour. The stop generally lasts only 4-8hrs. Traders come on board in considerable numbers (but one does better to purchase in the shops, p.11). 6hrs suffice for a brief visit ashore. One should ascertain the precise sailing time, since 2-3hrs are necessary just for the boat journey from and to the outermost anchorage; rowing boat ½R. per person, double fare after 9 p.m.: the tariff to be found at the pier, and an inspector is responsible for maintaining order. Indian currency (see p.XVII) is used in Aden, though German marks and English shillings are accepted in small transactions. – It is strictly forbidden to take photographs near the fortifications!

HOTELS: H.de l'Europe, H.de l'Univers, both in Prince of Wales Crescent. – An OMNIBUS leaves every ½hr. for the town of Aden (duration of journey 30 mins.; 1st cl. ½R.); CARRIAGE (covered one-horse 4-seater, called 'gharrries'), return fare 3R., incl. the 'tanks' or waterworks. GUIDE approx 1R. per hr.

POST & TELEGRAPH (Eastern Telegraph Co., closed Sundays) near the pier. For postal and telegraph rates, see p.XIX.

GERMAN CONSULATE (Prince of Wales Cresc.) provisionally administered by *C.E.L.Keppelhoff jun.,* also for Austria-Hungary and the Netherlands.

CHEMIST: *Cowasjee Dinshaw & Brothers*, W. of the Hôt.de l'Europe.

The CLIMATE is uncommonly hot. The mean annual temperature is 28°C, but rises much higher in the middle of the day. The sun's rays are particularly fierce in the bare rocky surroundings (tropical hat essential, dark glasses useful). One should beware the sudden drop in temperature after sunset. Rain falls only in short, violent downpours, though this rare phenomenon may be absent for years on end. The average annual precipitation is 76mm. The water is collected in cisterns (see below), supplemented by distilled sea water and, for the natives, a conduit of brackish water from the small oasis of Sheikh Othman.

The peninsula of *Aden* lat.12°46' N., long. 44°59' E.), part of the Bombay presidency, with a population (1911) of 46,165 Arabs, Somalis, Negroes, Indians, Persians, half-castes and whites (2000) and a garrison of one battalion of British, 1½ batt. of native infantry, 1/6 regt. of native cavalry, and 3 batteries of British siege-artillery (see p.72), takes its name from *Adana* of antiquity. The splendid arrangement of cisterns, dating back to the 6th c. (see below), testifies to its medieval importance. The discovery of the sea route round southern Africa caused the place to sink into oblivion. It was the English who realised again the excellence of its position and forced the Sultan of Lahj to cede it in 1839 (with, in 1905, an enlarged coastal strip of 23,000 sq.km) and fortified it strongly from 1850 onward. The opening of the Suez Canal has made Aden one of the most important stations in world trade (free port) and a major base for English maritime power. Numerous smaller steamers carry on trade with the neighbouring littorals of Arabia and Africa. Exported from here are: coffee, rubber, skins, furs, aloes, resin, ostrich feathers, pearls and tobacco (total annual value 51.5 million marks).

The town of *Steamer Point* consists of a modern beach road, the government buildings and the dirty Arab lanes of Tawahi. To the r. of the pier the telegraph office; to the l., in Prince of Wales Cresc., the consulates, business offices and shops, in which one may buy ostrich feathers, coral, shells etc. The public pleasure garden, despite considerable efforts, is not exactly a success.

The motor road to Aden (6km) goes E. along by Tawahi Bay. On the opposite side of the latter one remarks tent-shaped white pyramids of salt, which is extracted there from the sea water; the small windmills between them serve to pump the water into the evaporation pans. The road passes the village of *Maala* where the Arabs moor their sailing boats (dhows), then bears r. through a narrow cleft in the rock whose end is spanned by a masonry arch *(Main Pass).* At this point, the magnificent jagged crater opens to the E., on whose level floor stands the town of *Aden,* with its squat, whitewashed Arab houses and rectangular street layout, and its occasional umbrella acacias. In the centre, a large square for camel caravans. The cisterns (tanks) are hewn from the rock; the ravine which descends to them from Jebel Shamsham has been dammed, stepwise, to collect the rainwater. Of the 50 old basins, the English have restored 8 open and 5 closed ones, total capacity 36 mill.litres, most of which are however empty (see p.10). Below them are gardens which are tended with great effort. The old port of Aden is protected by the island of *Sira,* which has recently been linked to the mainland. – An alternative route back to the road to Steamer Point is via two tunnels of approx. 400m and 80m, bored through the tufa and continuing through a basin past the infantry barracks.

From Aden to Bombay 1664SM, 4-5 days: Austrian Lloyd, English P & O, French and Italian ships, see p.1. The coastline soon disappears and is not seen again until one reaches Bombay.

From Aden to Colombo, 2093SM, 6 days. On the second day the island of *Socotra* usually comes into view, 190SM E. of the Somalian coast (Cape Guardafui). Socotra has an area of 3580 sq.km and is under English sovereignty. If the ship passes it sufficiently closely one can see, at the E. and W. end, a line of hills about 250m high, descending in steps to the sea; in the centre of the island, picturesque, often cloud-capped mountains which culminate in Jebel Hagghier (1420m). There are a few settlements among cornfields and date palms on the small green coastal plains. The chief town is Tamridah. To the E. of this, Jebel Henlaf may be distinguished by the sand blowing from its slopes. The steep eastern cape is called Ras Badressa.

The ship now reaches the open Indian Ocean, whose north-western basin roughly as far as lat. 10°N., is known as the "Arabian Sea", and has an average depth of 3500m. The northern parts of the Ocean, the Arabian Sea and the Bay of Bengal (p.252) are subject to winds that change regularly every half-year, known as *monsoons* from the Arabic word 'mausim' (seasons). In winter the north-east monsoon prevails, a gentle, uniform and, because it originates on land, dry wind; in summer, the often turbulent and thoroughly wet south-west monsoon. The transitional months, April-June and September-November contain variable winds or total calm and, between lat. 6°1' and 19°8', violent tornadoes, which however, because we now have more precise knowledge about the paths they follow, can be avoided by shipping.

The north-easterly monsoon is the usual trade-wind in these latitudes, i.e. air currents streaming towards the Equator but deflected to the W. by the rotation of the Earth. It heralds a period of fine weather and pleasant sea voyages and, for coastal lands, a time of drought. In summer, the sun heats the land masses of southern Asia more strongly than the ocean at the Equator. To replace the rising air, the south-westerly monsoon comes in from the sea, reversing the trade-wind. The sky is clouded over, the air sultry, making sea travel, especially the voyage home against the heavy swell, very uncomfortable.

The interest of the journey is limited to observing the numerous other ships as they pass, signalling and greeting with their flags; the often superb cloud formations; the sunsets with their brilliant after-glow; the creatures in the ocean; and, at night, the phosphorescence of the sea, and the myriad stars in the sky.

Birds are rarely seen so far from land. Occasionally one may sight *whales*, more frequently the related *porpoises* (or dolphins) which like to accompany the ship with great leaps in the air, several kinds of *shark*, *flying fish* (exocoetus) which use their tails to accelerate them out of the water to a height of 5m over distances of 100m or more. Various species of *jellyfish* display pleasing hues. The drifting *seaweed* floats on the surface, thanks to the berry-shaped air bubbles which form in it. Microscopic *algae* tint the water, often for miles at a time, in dark-red or yellow-brown stripes. *Phosphorescence*, which is much stronger in the tropics than in the northern seas, is caused by various factors: some kinds of jellyfish develop a subdued, steady glow in the form of bands, dots and round shapes. The splendid, alternating bluish-green gleam of the wave edges, and other vigorously disturbed water, can be attributed to microscopic crustacea. Of similar origin is the rare phenomenon known as 'milky sea', whereby the entire surface of the water emits a uniform weak glow, even when the sky is quite dark.

One can place the constellations in the southern sky, observing the latter in the evening between their rising and culminating points, if one identifies the easily recognisable *Girdle of Orion* or *Jacob's Staff*, three bright stars of second magnitude close together in a straight line. To the l. of Orion is the reddish star *Betelgeuze* (Arab name like many of the following) r., at about the same distance, the bluish *Rigel*, both of the first magnitude. Between Rigel and Orion lies the bright spot that is the nebula of Orion, and if one produces a line through Orion's belt towards the horizon one finds, with a small deviation r., the brightest fixed star in the whole firmament, *Sirius*. By producing the line in the opposite direction, towards the zenith, and about 1½ times the distance of Sirius, one sees the reddish *Aldebaran* (1st magn.) A line drawn from Rigel to Betelgeuze and produced further will bring one to *Castor* (2nd magn,) and *Pollux* (1st magn.) If one connects Pollux and Sirius one finds, a little way below this line, *Procyon* (1st magn.). If one connects Rigel to Sirius and then turns r. at right-angles, one sees the twinkling *Canopus* (1st mag.) and, beyond, a broad glowing mass visible only on clear nights, the so-called Great Nebula, the brightest star nebula in the sky, after the Milky Way. The *Little Nebula* is beyond this, somewhat to the l. Both of these approach the comparatively starless celestial south pole at approx. 12°. Their counterpart is the dark *Coal Sack*, a starless spot in the Southern Cross which, as it were, opens up a view into the infinity of empty space. The *Southern Cross*, the most famous if not the most beautiful constellation in the southern sky, is visible from lat. 26°N.

onwards, that is to say already in the northern part of the Red Sea, but only from the early hours (2-4 a.m.) in winter. It resembles a distorted 4-pointed shape in which the fifth star (which would lie at the intersection) is missing. Only the southernmost star, 'Alpha Crucis' is of 1st magn.; one finds it by producing the line Sirius-Canopus to the r. for a similar distance at an angle of approx. 140°. If one continues the line Sirius-Canopus further to the l., at the same angle, one comes upon *Acharnar* (1st mag,) and, twice as far away, *Fomalhaut* (1st magn.) A little further on to the r. of the Cross, two beautiful stars are seen in close proximity, *Alpha and Beta Centauri.*

One does not see land again until passing the north-south submarine shelf upon which are the *Laccadives* and *Maldives,* flat coral islands belonging to the English, 15,000 and 30,000 inhab. respectively, who export coconut products, tortoise-shell and cowry shells.

The ships pass through the line of islands either by the Nine Degree Channel or the Eight Degree Channel, within sight of *Minicoy* (set between the two clusters of islands). The low-lying islands set on reefs seem, with their coconut palms and lighthouses, to be floating in the sea. The inner lagoon also comes into view.

About 270SM beyond Minicoy we are level with *Cape Comorin,* the southern tip of India; only on particularly clear days can one make out Conical Hill not far inland, or the more distant Mahindragiri (1500m).

The last stage to Colombo is another 150SM. The coconut palm groves on the flat coastline of Ceylon appear as a low, dark strip; above this, on clear days, the distant Central Ridge with the point of Adam's Peak becomes visible. On the sea one generally encounters native fishing fleets with their outrigger boats. This style of vessel, with its floating outrigger fixed parallel to the hull to prevent capsizing, is an invention of the Malays, which facilitated their enormous voyages of exploration from the eastern islands of Oceania to Madagascar (see p.282). The ship enters the port by its W. entrance. – *Colombo*, p.25.

Since ships usually take on coal now, travellers bound for more distant places also go ashore here (see p.34). The ship's baggage master will see to the despatch or storage of luggage.

CEYLON

Ceylon lies between lat. 5° 55' and 9° 51' N., and long. 81° 54' E., separated from the SE coast of India by Palk's Strait and the Gulf of Mannar. Between these two bodies of water, a series of small islands, rocks and sandbanks, the so-called *Adam's Bridge*, lead across to the mainland. Perhaps it is for this reason that Ceylon has been likened to a pear-shaped pearl fastened like a jewel to India's ear. Its area (65,600 sq.km) practically corresponds to that of the kingdom of Bavaria minus the Palatinate. Out of the flat land which comprises about ¾ of the island, the highlands tower up like the boss on a shield, in a wild, irregular and picturesque composition. The highest summits are *Pidarattallagalla* (2538m), *Kirilgalpota* (2387m) and *Totapella* (2351m). Most impressive, however, is the pyramid-shaped *Adam's Peak* (2241m; p.51). Some individual upland valleys and broad basins are embedded in this mountain labyrinth, e.g. the districts of *Kandy* (p.35), *Hatton* (p.44) and *Nuwara Eliya* (p.46). Of the rivers (the larger designated with the Hindu word "Ganga", the smaller with "Oya") only a few are even partially navigable. The most important is the *Mahawelliganga*, which rises between Pidarattallagalla and Adam's Peak, and flows to the E. coast. The fertile lowlands in the W. of the island lack natural harbours. The bay of *Galle* (p.32) is usable, and the harbour at *Colombo* has been artificially improved (p.27). The only harbour of excellence is that of *Trincomalee* on the rocky E. coast (p.65).

The mountains consist of ancient archaean slate, granite and gneiss, whose friable derivative, a brick-red clay or *laterite*, lends the soil a brilliant colour which stands out strongly against the green cloak of vegetation. The northern end of the island, broken up into islands and lagoons, is composed of Madrepore lime (coral), and of very recent origin. Coral reefs, sometimes attached by alluvial action to the mainland, also follow the W. coast southwards beyond Colombo. Ceylon's geological character corresponds to that of the Deccan peninsula (p.67). – Metals are found here scarcely at all. However, in the granulite and crystalline limestone of the S., W. and NW provinces, pure *graphite* is deposited in seams and pockets up to 1m deep, making Ceylon the most important producer of this material in the world (6.5

mill.cwt. annually). Hardly any other country can compete with Ceylon's abundance of *precious* and *semi-precious* gem-stones.

Most valuable of these are the *rubies,* whose red gleam is purer than that of Burmese rubies (p.278); perfect stones are however rare, fetching 300-800R. per carat. *Sapphires* are cheaper, especially the colourless "whites". Peculiar to Ceylon is the *star sapphire,* polished to a round shape with a six-fold radiance; only fine examples command high prices. Semi-precious stones include: *amethyst, topaze, turmaline, chrysoberyl* (cat's eye and alexandrite, the latter a bronze green colour in daylight and deep red in artificial light), *zircon, spinel, moonstone* (an orthoclase feldspar of pearly appearance, or a pronounced bluish gleam in its most valuable form; 75-100R. a piece), *garnet* and *beryl* (acqua marina). Only moonstone is found in solid rock, all the others among the riverbed pebbles in the districts of Balangoda (p.50), Rakwana and Ratnapura (p.33). Because of the rising tourist demand, foreign gems are also coming on the market in Ceylon (see p.XXVI).

The flora is that of the maritime tropical climate (mean temp.26·5°C in January, the coolest month, and 28·6° in April, the warmest). It is related to the vegetation of S. India, but enriched by foreign species from the rest of Asia and from Africa. About 10,000 sq.km of the island are cultivated. Most productive are the plains and the lower mountain slopes on the W. side, to which the SW monsoon (p.12) brings sufficient rain from April-May until Sept-Oct. (annual rainfall in Colombo 2237mm, in Kandy 2047, Hatton 3856). The NE monsoon, prevalent from Oct-Nov until Mar-Apr, is dryer; its humidity content benefits the E. coast almost exclusively (annual rainfall in Batticaloa 1372mm). 4/5 of the cultivated land is owned by natives who grow coconut and areca palms, bananas, tobacco, mangoes, breadfruit and, especially, rice in the marshy lowlands or on well-watered terraces on the lower slopes of the mountain range. The European plantations, on which the Tamils provide the labour, are highly developed (p.21); chief products are *caoutchouc* (1912 exports 6·6 mill.kg worth 52 mill.R.), *tea,* (developed since 1880 in place of the coffee plantations which were devastated by ergot), also *cocoa, cardamom, pepper, vanilla* and *cotton.* As a result of planting, the jungle, which formerly covered the W. and SW sides of the range, has been significantly reduced in area, but woodland is not sold beyond 1500m above sea level. On the E. slopes are mainly treeless areas of grass, called *patanas*. Thick jungle grows in the level N. (p.22).

A characteristic of the country is the rich variety of palm trees which thrive in half a dozen different types from the lowlands up to about 1000m. The most important is the *coconut palm* (cocos nucifera), mostly with a leaning trunk and broad feathery leaves hanging down. It loves sandy soil and the salty coastal air. The plantations (500 million trees) enclose the whole island in an almost unbroken ring. All parts of the tree are useful, the fruit (coconut oil and butter), the wood, fibre and leaves (sketches of these may be seen in the Colombo museum, see p.31).

The slender green *Areca palm* (Areca catechu), with its thin vertical trunk, surmounted by a small feathery crown on the green extremity of the trunk and whitish panicles, produces the areca nut which, mixed with lime and wrapped in the piper-betel leaf, provides the natives with a chewing material that colours their teeth red.

The splendid *Talypot palm* (Corypha umbraculifera) distinguishes itself from the rest by its giant leaves up to 6 sq.m in area, which serve the natives in many ways for house-building, as umbrellas and also, when cut into strips, as writing paper, (the writing being cut into the leaf and brought out by the use of ink; holy books in the temples, p.39); once, in its 60-70 year life, it puts out a cluster of blossoms 10m high or more and then, like the Agave, perishes.

The *Kitul palm* (Caryota urens) has double pinnate leaves which hang down untidily; a kind of wine (toddy) is made from the juices of the trunk.

An elegant variety is the *King's palm* (Oreodoxa regia) with a trunk which swells gently above the ground and is green beneath the crown. The tall *Palmyra* palm (borassus flabelliformia), with its dense and relatively small crown of fan-shaped leaves, the characteristic tree in southern India, is limited chiefly to the dry northern tip of the island.

[Baedeker's *Indien* carried sketches of palm trees etc. on pp.17-19. In order to preserve the pagination of the original text, some blank spaces have necessarily had to be inserted at this point.]

Similar to the palms are the *Pandanus* with its screw-shaped twisted stem and stilt-like roots, and the strangely flat *Ravenala,* like an open peacock's tail, which comes from Madagascar and is also called the 'traveller's tree', because drinking water collects in the hollows of its leaf-sheaths.

Other characteristic plants on the low ground are: *bamboo* (Dendrocalamus giganteus, p.43) which grows in splendid bushes to 30m and more; the *banana* (Musa sapientium) which, for a given area, produces 133 times more food than wheat and, in Ceylon, is found up to 1250m above sea-level; the luxuriant climber *Bougainvillia* with its bright blue flowers, which is grown especially in the gardens of the Europeans.

Typical fruit trees of particular interest are: both varieties of the *Breadfruit tree,* the common Artocarpus incisa with jagged leaves, and fruit which grow on the branches, and the Jak tree (Artocarpus integrifolia) with smooth-edged leaves, and fruits which hang down from the trunk; the densely crested deep-green Mango (Mangifera indica) whose fruits resemble upturned pears; the *Mangosteen tree* (Garcinia mangostana), likewise with deep-green, shining, somewhat larger leaves, whose orange-shaped fruit conceals a delicate snow-white flesh within a thick purple skin.

Attractive among the broad-leaf trees are: *Hibiscus poplar* (Thespesia populnea), the pinnate-leaved *Tamarind* (Tamarix indica), the *Tulip tree* (Liriodendron tulipifera), the flame-flowered *Spathodea* (Spathodea campanulata), one of the most splendid tropical flowering trees, the *Indian fig-tree* (Ficus indica), one of which will sprout into a small grove by putting out aerial roots and thus forming new trunks.

Related to the latter is the *Bo-tree* (Ficus religiosa), sacred to the Buddhists, with long spikes on its leaves, which is tended in temple gardens (see p.58).

Among forest trees of greater size are: the *Calophyllums* (Calophyllum tortuosum) with umbrella-shaped domes, also called *Quinia tree,* and the tree-shaped *Rhododendrons* (Rhododendron arboreum), related to our Alpine roses.

In recent times, the slender, fine-leaved Australian *Eucalyptus* has been introduced in many places. The *Lantana,* originally brought in as a decorative shrub, with its reddish-yellow flowers, has developed into an over-prolific weed which spreads everywhere as a companion to other plants. – The government maintains botanical gardens at various altitudes and in varying climatic conditions, which serve not only for scientific study but also for experiments with the acclimatisation of useful tropical plants, see pp. 34, 43, 49, 60.

The fauna is similar to that of India, but is less rich in its variety. The jungles in the N. and E. of the island are the most populous areas for wild animals. Recently, preserves and close seasons have been introduced (see p.24 for hunting). The proudest game beast is the *elephant* which however is rarely found with usable tusks. Although tigers are absent, one finds *panthers, bears, wild boar,* varieties of *monkeys, viverras* (lemurs, incl. the *mongoose*, which is immune to snake venom), the large *flying-fox,* winged *squirrels, stags* and *buffalo.* The Indian *zebu* and the *horse* are brought in as draught animals. Birds of interest include the *peacock* and, as a casual visitor during the NE monsoon, the *flamingo;* the *jungle fowl* (Gallus Lafayetti) is often heard but seldom seen. Among the reptiles are numerous *crocodiles* and *snakes,* the latter sometimes venomous, although they tend to flee away at the sound of a well-shod walker approaching. One is advised to wear tightly-buttoned leggings on walks through grass and jungle, as protection against ticks and the tiresome little leeches (Hirudo ceylonica). The rivers and pools are rich in fish, including *climbing perch* (Anabas scandens) which, with the help of the spines on their gill-covers, can also move about on land. In the sea there are *whales, dolphins, dugongs* and even *sharks.* According to local sources, *pearls* from Ceylon were prized as early as the 6th c.B.C.; Phoenicians, Greeks, Romans and Arabs all haggled for them. Since the 16th c., the Portuguese and Dutch dominated the pearl-fishing industry; now it is a government monopoly. The oyster banks (paars) lie off the NW coast of Ceylon, to the S. of the island Mannar. The yield varies: fishing for oysters often has to be suspended for years at a time. A London company which leased the rights in 1903 has had to buy itself out again after several profitable years (1905: £250,000) because the banks were quite exhausted. The government is doing its best to increase the yield over a period of years.

Pearls are formed inside the pearl oyster by secretions like gall-stones which enclose a foreign body, a grain of sand or the oyster's own excretion. The former, the round, so-called *Orient pearls,* are the most prized. The latter, known as *Seed Pearls,* are irregular in shape. Pearl-fishing is done in March and April, but only after a double inspection of the banks and the promise of a good yield. Many thousands of natives the come streaming in their boats from all the countries lining the Indian Ocean to *Marichchukkaddi,* the centre of the district and, afterwards, disperse equally rapidly. The oysters are brought in and auctioned immediately. The pearls are extracted by allowing the contents of the oyster to rot, there and then.

The population, according to the 1911 census, numbered 3,592,397 souls (1901: 3,565, 954), not counting seasonal workers and, apart from the Europeans, is composed chiefly of six different races, of whom the Sinhalese make up almost two thirds. The oldest race, one of the most ancient on Earth, are the remarkable Veddhas (i.e. hunters) who have recently formed the subject of special studies by E.Schmidt and P.& F.Sarrasin. They are small of stature, mainly dark brown with wavy hair, almost beardless, and they now are to be found only in the remote SE part of the island, the province of *Uva* (pop.in 1911: 5342). The so-called ‘village Veddhas’ have already settled down. The remainder, the ‘rock Veddhas’, live exclusively by hunting with trap and bow, carrying on a timid barter system with the Sinhalese, whereby they place some game or wild honey at the edge of the forest with a model of the object which they desire in return. – As yet still unexplained are the origins of the *Rodiyas* who often stand out because of their fine physique, but who are socially much despised. – The oldest cultured people of the island are the *Sinhalese* (1911: 2,676,230), said to be of Aryan descent. They are of medium height, bronzed, of delicate build with aquiline noses and long black hair, which can give the men a feminine appearance. Both sexes are extraordinarily handsome in youth. Their language “Elu” derives from Sanskrit. They are Buddhists (p.22) and possess ancient chronicles, such as the Mahawansa (p.22) and, in the Temple of the Holy Tooth at Kandy (p.37), one of the most famous pilgrimage places of the Buddhist world. – The *Tamils* or *Tamuls* (1911: 599,771) descend from the Dravidian peoples of southern India (p.69). They live partly as farmers in the northern provinces, partly as workers in the towns, sometimes also on European plantations, where they are prized as strong, willing workers. They are adherents to Hinduism, mainly of the dark Shivite cult, whose strange temples and idols are often encountered. The mark on their foreheads, daily renewed, is particularly noticeable (see p.LXI). – The *Moors* or *Moormen* (1911: 260,842) are Mohammedans from the Near East (p.22); they live as traders and moneylenders in the towns, and are easily recognised by their garb, particularly the woven cap. – Bearing the Dutch name of *Burghers* are the so-called Eurasians or half-castes from the marriages of Asian women with Europeans of Portuguese, Dutch or English origin (1911: 25,173). They are members of the Christian faith and speak English, but are not fully accepted by the pure whites. Among the better-class Burghers are many lawyers, judges and doctors, the rest being employed in office work for the Church, administration and commerce, partly also as craftsmen. – The *Malays* (11,870) are the descendants of former soldiers who were recruited by the English in Malacca. They are Mohammedans and make excellent policemen, prison warders and messengers. – Of the *Europeans* (5278), the English are by far the most numerous as government officials, planters, businessmen and industrialists.

History. The oldest name for the island, *Tambropani,* i.e. shining like copper, may have a connection with the colour of laterite (p.15). The Greeks, who came to know Ceylon since the campaigns of Alexander the Great, called it *Taprobane.* The classical literature of the Indians, e.g. the Ramayana epic, calls it *Lanka,* as do the natives today. The name *Singhala* (Europeanised to *Ceylon)* goes back to the Aryan invaders from N.India who, according to legend came to the island in 543 B.C. under their leader Singha (the lion). In the chronicles, the history of the Singhalese (Sinhalese) empire reached to the 3rd c.B.C. At that time, King Devanampiya Tissa (p.57) introduced the Buddhist religion. The Sinhalese settled in large numbers, chiefly on the N. plains. Theirs was an important civilisation based upon a magnificent irrigation system, whose splendid midpoint was the royal city of *Anuradhapura.* Vicissitudinous battles against the Tamils, who attacked from S.India (p.21) occupied the first millennium of our epoque. Gradually the Sinhalese retreated southwards. In 769 they moved their capital to *Polonnaruha*, in 1235 to *Dambadeniya,* and finally, around 1500, to the more easily defended *Kandy* in the uplands. Their irrigation works in the plains fell into ruin, the fertile fields became fever-infested wildernesses overgrown with jungle. On the coast, Arab-Indian half-castes had settled, seizing trade for themselves. Then, in 1506, the Portuguese came to Ceylon from Goa (p.102), founded a fortified settlement in 1517 at Colombo, and spread the Roman Catholic religion among the natives, who even today form the bulk of the 350,000 Christians. Despite fearful struggles, however, their mastery remained limited to a few coastal towns. The temporary union of Portugal with Spain brought the Dutch along, in the War of Independence of 1602. With the approval of the kings of Kandy, the latter drove out the

Portuguese, but then took over their possessions and monopolised foreign trade. In the interior of the country, the Dutch were no more able to exert political influence than the Portuguese had been. When the Netherlands were forced to an annexation with France in 1795, the fleet of the English East India Company put an end to their rule. In 1798 Ceylon was placed under British rule. The capture of Kandy in 1815 brought the Sinhalese kingdom to an end.

The Crown territory of Ceylon depends upon the Foreign Office in London for legislation and administration. The chief official is the royal *Governor,* usually nominated for 6 years at a time, who has three residences: in Colombo, Kandy and Nuwara Eliya. He is supported by the 5-member *Executive Council* and the *Legislative Council* of 17 members, including native representatives appointed by the Governor. The island is divided into 9 provinces, each administered by *Government Agents.* The three capitals, Colombo, Galle and Kandy, have their own municipal councils. Civil justice in the lowlands is still based on the code of law introduced by the Dutch.

As a tourist attraction, Ceylon is incomparable in many respects. In the lowlands and uplands, one becomes conversant with tropical Nature, both in the civilisation of the natives and Europeans, and in the jungle. *Colombo* (p.25) offers the peculiar charms of a tropical port. The villages and towns of the Sinhalese display the colourful way of life of tropical peoples. In *Kandy* (p.35) one gains insight into the world religion of Buddhism, The mighty ruins of *Anuradhapura* (p.56), *Polonnaruha* (p.65) etc. testify to a history which goes back for thousands of years. *Nuwara Eliya* (p.46) is one of the favourite hill stations in the tropics. The visit to *Adam's Peak* (p.51), which no vigorous mountain-walker will want to miss, may best be made between Kandy and Nuwara Eliya. Kandy is particularly suitable for a lengthy stay; in the lowlands, the uniform day and night temperatures, and the humid air, have a very enervating effect. The main travelling season falls in December, January, February and well into March (see p.XII).

The hotels in the main centres are among the best in Asia. The *Rest -houses,* or *Dak bungalows* (see p.XXIV) are, on average, better equipped than those on the Indian mainland, contain more rooms, with a dining-room, and offer good-quality accommodation. (B. 50-75cts., L. 1R., D. 1½R.).

The most important places are accessible by railway. On the major roads *coaches* ply, sometimes also post buses, both of which are however uncomfortable and often over-full.

Ceylon lends itself admirably to motor car travel. Cars may be hired in Colombo (p.25), Kandy and Nuwara Eliya (pp.35,46). They are generally good, the chauffeurs reliable, and petrol depots are found all over the island. The hire firms usually send their representatives with printed tariffs on board the North German Lloyd steamers when they dock. It is necessary to order in advance during the main tourist season, preferably through Cook (p.25). A day's journey is reckoned to be 90-100 English miles, or approx. 150km. The charge is 100R. per day. The following round-trip takes in the chief places of interest: 1st day from *Colombo* along the W. coast to: 82M. *Puttalam* (Rest-house); 2nd day: 46M. *Anuradhapura* (p.56); 3rd day: 66M. *Trincomalee* (p.65); 4th day: 73M. *Polonnaruha* (p.65); 5th day: 43M. *Dambulla* (p.55); 6th day: 45M. *Kandy* (p.35); 7th day: 48M. *Nuwara Eliya* (p.46); 8th day: via *Bandarawela* (p.51) and *Haputale* (p.50) to: 112M. *Ratnapura* (p.33); 9th day: 60M. *Colombo.* Since, according to this division of time, the stay in Anuradhapura, Kandy and Nuwara Eliya is very brief, one would do better to travel to the two latter places by railway and limit one's car travel to the N. part of the route: from Kandy via Dambulla, Polonnaruha, Trincomalee to Anuradhapura (4 days; if one intends to return to Colombo by rail, the amount to be paid for abandoning the car in mid-route must be precisely agreed beforehand). Night accommodation can everywhere be ordered in advance by telegraph.

For journeys to the interior, one should provide oneself at Colombo (at Freudenberg & Co., for instance) with a cheque book, in order to get money in the European hotels. Cook's circular notes can generally be used directly in hotels.

Small coin, see p.XVIII.

For hunting trips (see p.20) one hires in Colombo a native guide *(shikaree),* who, for 30-50R. daily, undertakes all the organising of the trip, incl. the following (according to how far away the hunting district is): tents and bedding (mosquito nets), provisions (without drinks, mineral water), and servants (cook, boy, etc.) One should insist on tinned food being purchased at the *International Stores* (p.26), through whom one can have one's arrangements made. The traveller must pay for the game licence, which the shikaree will obtain from the Government Agent. It covers only certain districts (which change from time to time), and the shikaree is made responsible for observing these restrictions. Each hunter is allowed to bag only a fixed amount of game (1 elephant, 2 buffalo etc.) Infringement of the hunting laws is severely punished.

Bibliography, see p.LXXII.

Route 2. COLOMBO

ARRIVAL. The steamer moors at one of the buoys, and hotel servants come on board, to whom one should entrust one's luggage. One is conveyed ashore in steam launches, rowing boats or native canoes: rate 35cts. (Engl. 6 pice) from 6 a.m. to 7 p.m.; at night 55cts. (Engl. 9p.); hand-luggage and chairs accompanied by their owner are conveyed gratis; larger items of luggage 10, 15, 25cts. One lands at the covered *Passenger Jetty,* close to the *Customs House.* Customs examination (see p.XIX) from 7.30 a.m. until 8 p.m. At night one may take only one article of hand-luggage. The rest must remain under lock and key at the Customs House, where one may also deposit superfluous items (50ct. per week per article). – The first rule for the new arrival: beware of sunstroke. If one still has no tropical hat, one should put one's shade up immediately.

Hotels (see p.XXIII; Oct-Mar. advance booking in writing advisable): *Galle Face Hotel, Galle Face Rd., 12min. by rickshaw from the landing place, open situation by the sea, 300Bd., airy rooms, sea-water swimming-pool, seaward-facing rooms preferable only when there is a sea breeze. The rooms in the annexe are cheaper in part, P. 15R. during the high season, cheaper for longer stays. There is often music and dancing in the evenings.

*Grand Oriental Hotel, abbr. to G.O.H., conveniently situated by the Jetty, very well spoken of, likewise of the 1st class, P. from 10R., rather cheaper after 3 days' stay, much-frequented verandah where dealers and tricksters are often to be found. – Bristol Hotel, York St., in the Fort district, less pretentious but equally comfortable and well spoken of, Rm from 2½, two-bedded from 4½R., B.2, L.2, D.3R., P. from 8R., families and businessmen by agreement; British India Hotel, Flagstaff St., in a pleasant position by the sea.. – *Mount Lavinia Gr. Hotel*, see p.32.

Transport (excellent roads). The most convenient form of transport is the East Asian rickshaw, introduced here in 1884, mostly pulled by Tamils (one briefly names one's destination): up to 10min. 10cts., ½hr. 25cts., waiting 10cts. per ½hr.; from 7.30 p.m. until 6 a.m., ⅓ more. For longer journeys, a carriage is however to be preferred: within the town 50cts. per ½hr., 1R. per hr, each extra hr. 50 cts.; ⅓ more between 7 p.m. and 6 a.m. There are also second-class carriages which are ¼- ⅓ cheaper. Outside the town of Colombo there are special prices which, for the usual trips, are displayed in the hotels, but should always be agreed beforehand (toll 60cts., payable by the passenger).

Motor Cars are recommended for lengthy excursions (see p24): *Ceylon Motor Co.,* Victoria Arcade (Thos. Cook & Son); *Walker, Sons & Co.Ltd.,* not far from the G.O.H.; *Arnold Motor Touring Co.,* 14-15 Victoria Arcade; *Morgan, Bulner & Co.,* by the jetty at the harbour.

Trams (10cts.; little used by European residents, though they have 1st cl. compartments, see p.XXII): from the Passenger Jetty through Fort and Pettah NE to Grand Pass (Victoria Bridge, p.29), SE to the suburb Borella.

Travel Agency: *Thos.Cook & Sons*, 1 Victoria Arcades, York St. – English-speaking guides (dark-blue coat with green revers) receive 50cts. for the 1st hr. and 25cts. for each additional hr.; they are required to show their pocket register on demand.

Shipping Lines and Agencies. *North German Lloyd* (p.1); represented by Freudenberg & Co. (p.26; telegr. address Nordlloyd): 3 times monthly to Europe, fortnightly to Penang-Singapore (p.1) – *Austrian Lloyd* (p.1), repr. by Darley, Butler & Co.: Shanghai Line once a month in both directions; Kobe Line every fortnight to Bombay and on via Karachi and Aden to Europe, in the other direction to Penang, Singapore etc., and Calcutta. – *Orient Line* (p.2): fortnightly via Suez to Naples etc. Also via Fremantle to Australia. – *British India S.N.C.;* fortnightly to Aden and Europe, also to Madras and Calcutta. – *Bibby Line:* twice a month to Rangoon (p.253). – The Dutch company *Nederland* (p.2), repr. by Aitken Spence & Co., 2 Prince St.: via Suez to Genoa etc. Also via Singapore to Java (p.311). – *Messageries Maritimes*, see p.2. – *Marittima Italiana* (p.2): once a month to Bombay, and to Penang, Singapore. Excursion round the island: *Ceylon Steamship Co.* (Walker Sons & Co., Main St.), every fortnight in both directions, major stopping places being Kankesanturai (Jaffna, p.64), Galle (p.32) Batticoloa (p.65) and Trincomalee (p.65).

Railway stations. Main station: *Maradana Junction* for the Kandy railway (p.34) and the coastal line, which has other stations in the town: *Fort, Slave Island, Kollupitiya* etc., see p.31. Timetables and information about dining cars and station restaurants may be found in the *Pocket Time and Fare Tables* (obtainable at stations, 10cts.).

Post and Telegraph, Queen St. See Introduction, p.XIX.

Banks: *Freudenberg & Co.*, 7 Prince St.; *National Bank of India,* York St.; *Chartered Bank of India, Mercantile Bank of India, Hongkong & Shanghai Bank,* all three in Queen St. – Doctors: Dr. *Castellani,* Galle Face Hotel; Dr. *Nell* (oculist), at Victoria Memorial Hospital, Alexandra Place. – CHEMISTS: *International Stores,* Chatham St.; *Colombo Apothecaries Co.,* Prince St.; *Cargills Ltd.,* York St., corner of Prince St.

Consulates: Germany: *R.Freudenberg,* 7 Prince St.; Austro-Hungary: *W.Freudenberg,* same address; Denmark: *E.Lütken*, Baillie St.; Netherlands: *J.Steiger*, Prince St.; Norway: *E.B.Creasy*, Baillie St.; Sweden: *W.W.Kenny*, Chatham St. Clubs: Deutscher Verein [German Club], p.30; *Colombo Club,* p.28; *Colombo Garden Club,* p.30.

Booksellers: *A.M.& T.Ferguson, H.W.Cave & Co.,* both in Queen St. and editors of several travel guidebooks about Ceylon.

Photographers: *Plâté & Co.*, at Galle Face Hotel (German); *Colonial Photographic Co.,* Victoria Arcades; *Colombo Apothecaries Co.* (also bookshop), Prince St. From all three one may purchase photographs and views of Ceylon, and one's photographic requirements. Darkrooms available.

Other shops: Travelling & hunting equipment, clothing: *Cargills Ltd.,* Chatham St., *Walter Sons & Co., Brown & Co.*, these latter for guns. – Gold and silver work, jewels (p.16), pearls, carved tortoiseshell, especially recommended in the arcades near the G.O.H. and York St.: *D.F.de Silva & Co.* and *Don Theodoris & Co.,* both in Chatham St. Besides products of the local native industry, one finds 'curios' from India, Burma, Japan, China etc.

For limited visits (1½ days): walk through the *Fort* quarter of the town (see below); take a rickshaw through *Pettah* to the N. parts of the town (pp.28-9) during the hours before sunset, when the blinding daylight softens and the deep colours of the landscape emerge strongly; view from the *Maligakanda reservoir* (p.29); *Museum* (p.30); evening in *Galle Face Road* (p.28).

One's delight in observing the colourful bustle of the natives never palls, with the varied aspects of their dwellings, markets and temples. – In the vicinity is *Mount Lavinia* (p.32), the most popular excursion; at the intermediate sta. *Dehiwala*, a Buddhist temple (p.32). Of greater importance is the *Kelani Temple* (p.32).

Colombo, the capital of Ceylon, winter residence of the Governor and the centre of trade, one of the most important places on the international trade route to East Asia and Australia, stretches out on the flat W. coast of the island, being 11.5km from N. to S., and 4.5km from W. to E. Nowhere can one gain a view of the whole town at once, since its bulk, consisting of the low houses of the natives, disappears beneath the palm trees. The old name *Kalambu*, by which it was mentioned in the 13th c. by the Arabian traveller Ibn Batuta, is connected either with the river *Kelani* (which enters the sea to the N.) or with the lake in the S. part of the old town ("kulam", pool). The nucleus of the European settlement is formed by the original fort which the Portuguese erected in 1517 on the rocky promontory by the sea, and which the Dutch continued to fortify from 1656 (see p.22). The inhabitants number 213,396 (1901: 158,093), mainly Sinhalese, then Tamils, Indo-Arabs, Malays, Parsees, half-castes (Burghers, pp.21-2). There are 5000 Europeans all told, of whom approx. 40 Germans form a respected colony.

The harbour, originally a poorly-protected roadstead, acquired its present-day importance through the construction of the three breakwaters, 1875-85, of which the S. is 1280m long, the NE 335m, the middle one (since its recent extension to afford better protection from the SW monsoon) 1600m. The two entrances are 300m wide. The southern breakwater (accessible from Gordon Gardens, p.28) provides a pretty walk and view. At its extremity is a low lighthouse whose red light is visible for 8SM. The harbour occupies an area of 200 hectares and contains more than 50 fixed mooring buoys. The previous depth of 9m is being dredged to 11m (like the Suez Canal) for over half of the harbour's area. On the E. side, large coal stacks, to the NE a dock for ship repairs. The number of steam and sailing ships in and out of port in 1911 was 3299, with 8,920,552 tons of cargo.

The quarter of the town which has arisen (with government and other public buildings, big business houses, banks etc.), since the English came here, upon the site of the dismantled fortifications, has kept the name Fort. Two broad streets covered with laterite macadam, partly lined with arcades and bearing the names York St. and Queen St., run through it southwards from the harbour. York St., which begins opposite the Jetty, is the chief commercial street, with an avenue of hibiscus poplars. On one side of it is a marble statue of *Queen Victoria* seated, erected in 1897 for her Jubilee (celebrating 60 years of rule), and the *Victoria Arcades* with many shops, agencies, refreshment rooms etc.; on the other side, the shopping arcades of the G.O.H. (p.25), whose reconstruction will be completed in 1914. Further on, the shops of jewellers and curio sellers. Three transverse streets, Prince Street, with the *German Consulate* and the *Public Library*, Baillie Street and Chatham Street link York St. with Queen St., which begins W. of the Passenger Jetty. In front, on the r., enclosed public gardens with a statue of the Governor *Sir Arthur Gordon*, l., the *Government Offices.* Behind Gordon Gardens r. stands *Queen's House,* the Governor's residence; by the garden gate opposite Prince St., a monument to Governor *E.Barnes* (1820-31). On the l., the *Post Office.* In the middle of the road, at the intersection with Chatham St., rises the square *Clock Tower & Lighthouse,* whose brilliant light is visible for 15SM. Nearby, some large banks and other business houses. At the S. end of the street, to the l., five large barrack blocks, r. the officers' quarters.

In Fort begins **Galle Face Road, which runs between the sea and the large grassy area known as *Galle Face,* and is one of the most splendid carriage drives in the world, possessed of an unforgettable magic at sunset. On its parallel road, the Galle Face Esplanade, l. the oval building of *Colombo Club*, then r. the large hotel already mentioned (p.25). Galle Face Road continues, always flanked by palms and other tropical trees, gardens and bungalows, to the suburb of *Kollupitiya* (abbr. to "Kolpetty" by the European residents), formerly, before the opening of Cinnamon Gardens (p.30), the most popular residential district of Colombo, now inhabited partly by well-to-do natives and burghers (pp.21-2), *Bambalapitiya* with some fasionable English bungalows, and *Wellawatta*, all three of which have stations on the coastal railway mentioned on p.31. Green Path (see also p.31) meets Galle Face Road at Kollupitiya.

To the E. of Prince St. (see above), one passes between the coal stacks to the S. of the harbour and a large, green field, and so reaches the Main Street of Pettah, the "black" (i.e. native) town, whose streets are lined with low houses and open-fronted shops, and constantly filled with a colourful human throng.

The market-place with the *Town Hall* lies on the E. edge of Pettah, on whose NE side abuts the St Paul's district. In Sea St., which runs N., one can view the large Hindu temple, a structure overloaded with strange decoration in the style (though not the proportions) of the great Dravidian temples of S. India (no admittance to the interior). To the E., *Wolfendhall Church* in a lofty position, built in Rococo style by the Dutch in 1749, with an ungainly dome over the crossing, from which one has a good panoramic view. Nearby, some other buildings of the Dutch era. – The road runs S. to the *Law Courts.*

The N. parts of the town break up into groups of huts. The Catholic cathedral of *Santa Lucia,* completed in 1904, is in the Roman style with a 46m high cupola. Further on, the large *St Thomas College,* a secondary school on the English model, with the Anglican cathedral of the same name, built in 1851. – To the N. of the harbour, the picturesque fishermen's district, Mutwal, extends as far as the *Kelani Ganga.* Before its estuary, the river forms a small lake, by which stands the villa "Whist Bungalow", made known by Ernst Haeckel's stay in 1881. From here, one goes inland to the busy *Victoria Bridge* and back along Ferguson's Rd., St Joseph St., Grand Pass Rd., etc. (tram, see p.25).

To the S. of Pettah stretches *Freshwater Lake, a lagoon furnished with sweet water by an inlet from the river Kelani. The shores of the lake are distinguished by the luxuriance of their vegetation, and the adjacent parts of the town are extremely picturesque. A walk or rickshaw drive around the lake is well repaid. From Galle Face Esplanade, a bridge leads to *Slave Island.* If one follows the main road (called Union Place), turning NE, at the S. tip of the lake, into Darley Rd., then into Forbes Rd., then across Mardana Rd., one reaches – after passing a large Buddhist *dagaba* l. – the Maligakanda Reservoir (tell the rickshaw coolie "Water Tanks"). Ascend the hill (approx. 30m above sea-level) from the SE side. Beyond the entrance r. is the administrative building (ask the assistant inspector or watchman for permission to enter). The reservoir, which is supplied with excellent drinking water by a 40km-long acqueduct, is covered with grass. From the top, splendid *view over the thick palm plantations, in which the town almost disappears. One can find one's bearings best from the Clock Tower and Lighthouse at Fort (WNW), Santa Lucia cathedral (to the N.), Galle Face Hotel (WSW) and the large prison to the SE. To the r. of the Lighthouse, the large Law Courts building. The broad dome of Wolfendhall Church is glimpsed only partially between the trees. One makes out numerous churches, mosques with their half moon, and white-painted dagabas. There is usually a clear view of the Central Ridge (Adam's Peak, 64km away) in the morning and evening.

The district to the SE. of Freshwater Lake is largely built on the area covered by the former *Cinnamon Gardens,* on which the government had the monopoly from the entry of the Dutch until 1832. The name has remained, though the original gardens have given way to public parks and leafy streets. In the N. part is Victoria Park (tell the rickshaw coolie "Cinnamon Gardens"), a circular lawn with a carriageway around it, called Edinburgh Crescent on the W. side and Albert Crescent on the E. In Edinburgh Crescent, among others, is the magnificent bungalow *Siriniwesa* of Consul Freudenberg, the club-house of the *Deutscher Verein* and, opposite, the sports field of the *Colombo Garden Club*. In the S. part of the park, the Museum; in front of this, a statue of Governor *Sir William Gregory* (1871-77).

The *Museum, opened in 1877, offers a superb survey of Ceylon's culture from the Middle Ages to modern times, with its geology and fauna. Open weekdays (10 a.m. to 6 p.m., except Fridays); Sundays and Christian festivals, 3-6 p.m.

The ground floor contains the *ethnological & archaeological collections* (printed guide, 1R.).

A. (from the entrance l., last room). Gallery of stone monuments from the ruined sites of Anuradhapura, Polonnaruha etc. In the centre, the three most important pieces: the *Yapahu window,* a pierced block of gneiss of excellent workmanship, from the 13th or 14th c.; the **Polonnaruha lion,* from a single block of stone,according to the Sinhalese inscription from the time of King Nissanka Malla (1187-96), whose throne it supported; the *Medagoda pillar* (province of Sabaragamuwa), richly carved, resting on a lion, likewise one block of stone. On the E. wall: the *Naga Stone*, portraying the nine-headed cobra, from Anuradhapura. Beneath the S. window: casts of a moonstone (p.58) and the giant statue of Parakrama Bahu (p.66).

B. Gallery of bronzes. *1st cabinet:* bronze stands, drinking vessels, *2nd & 3rd cabinets:* figures of Shiva and Parvati (pp.LIX-LX). *4th cabinet:* spoons, plates and jewellery. *5th cabinet:* images of the Buddha in bronze, copper and gold. Note especially the statue of Buddha in the upper part of the cabinet. *6th cabinet:* tripods, statues of Parvati; that of Bodhisattva Maittaeya (i.e. the loving Bodhisattva, see p.248) is beautiful. *7th & 8th cabinets:* various household utensils. *9th cabinet:* Chandeswar, the worshipper of Shiva. *10th-14th cabinets:* various items. Note the sun-god Suriya in cabinet 11. *15th cabinet:* Shiva as Nataraya, i.e. lord of the universe, the best bronze in the collection. – S. verandah: a heavy Portuguese copper cannon, lost in Colombo harbour in 1613, and dredged up again in 1888, - N. verandah: gravestones from the Portuguese and Dutch eras.

C. Central Hall (by the entrance): *17th-20th cabinets:* old Portuguese and Dutch firearms and swords; Sinhalese daggers and knives, some with ivory and silver filigree work on the handles. *16th & 21st cabinets:* carved ivory, some pieces to Dutch patterns. On the staircase two splendid old pieces of Dutch furniture in nadun wood: a brass-bound chest and a wall cupboard.

Room D: products from the inhabitants of the Maldives (p.14). Note models of boats and lacquer-work; *26th cabinet:* old pieces of pottery from Anuradhapura, Polonnaruha and Sigiriya (pp.56, 65, 64 resp.) *27th cabinet:* modern Sinhalese pottery. *28th & 29th cabinets:* masks, costumes, musical instruments used at magical and diabolical dances. *31st cabinet:* fishing and transport: models illustrating pearl-fishing (p.20). *23rd cabinet:* the coconut palm in its astonishingly versatile applications. Models illustrating the preparation of arrack. *24th cabinet:* products from the palmyra palm (p.18).

Room E (last room to the r. of the entrance). *34th & 35th cabinets:* Sinhalese domestic utensils and various toys. *36th cabinet:* models of a chieftain (Mudaliyar) from the lowlands, and a Sinhalese bride, 18th c. *38th cabinet:* models of a Kandy chieftain and Buddhist priest with begging bowl (cf.p.297). *39th-41st cabinets:* products of the goldsmith's art, Indian, Sinhalese, Moorish. Particularly delicate is the work by Tamils from Jaffna; Sinhalese Navaratna rings with the nine most-prized gems. Silver model of the casket in which the sacred tooth of Buddha is preserved (p.38). *42nd cabinet:* coins found in Ceylon, the oldest being Roman. *43rd cabinet:* materials and implements for the preparation of betel (p.17). *45th cabinet:* model of a Veddha man and woman (p.21). *46th & 47th cabinets:* metal work, incl. old Dutch and Sinhalese tobacco tins, spittoons; Sinhalese water clocks (copper bowls with a small opening and markings on the inside, by which one could read off the time according to the rising water; in the large bowl, the water reaches the topmost mark in 48min, i.e. in 2hrs. by ancient Sinhalese reckoning); in the 47th cabinet also old Sinhalese and Tamil records on palm leaves. From the ceiling hang Sinhalese brass lamps.

Back to the central hall and up the stairs, whose walls are decorated with imitations of the wall paintings at Sigiri (p.64), to the:-

Upper floor. *Scientific Collections.*

In the W. part, the mineral and geological collections. Of especial note: in cabinet 2, crystalline limestone formations; in cabinet 4, gems; in cabinet 5, mica; cabinet 6, graphite, with examples of its use. The cabinets in the middle of the room contain the combinations of sulphur found in Ceylon: oxides, silicates, phosphates, precious and semi-precious stones. – In the E. part, the zoological collection, in which is represented almost every kind of mammal, bird, reptile and insect found in Ceylon.

An annexe contains the library which, apart from numerous Sinhalese and Tamil palm-leaf mss. (see p.39), boasts the entire literature about Ceylon in 12,000 volumes. The reading-room is open at 6.30-10 a.m. and 3-5 p.m. In the garden, an unusually well-fashioned moonstone with a double portrayal of the Sri-pada (p.53).

S. of Albert Crescent, on *Torrington Place*, is the large Race Course (r.). – From Edinburgh Crescent, *Green Path* goes W. to Galle Face Rd. (p.28).

EXCURSIONS. Mount Lavinia, 8M: since the distance is too far for rickshaws, and the journey by car or railway (½hr. from Fort sta.; 50cts.) loses much of its charm, one should take a carriage (1-1¼hrs; 10R. return for 3 passengers). Along Galle Face Rd., by the coast, through the suburbs (see p.28) of *Kollupitiya, Bambalapitiya & Wellawatta,* then across the Kirilapane canal (town boundary). The tropical coconut palm forest and the colourful community life of the Sinhalese will astonish the newcomer.

7M. *Dehiwala.* Not far from the sta. and best visited on the return journey, a *Buddhist temple,* by no means among the largest of its kind, but very typical and nicely situated, with a dagaba (p.57) rising picturesquely among palms, and a well-preserved hall, whose modern wall-paintings demonstrate the punishment of wickedness and the reward of virtue; inside, figures of Buddha (tip 1R., no more!) On the way to the temple one sees small girls occupied in lace-making, which the Dutch introduced. Many beggars: one should have a stock of small coins. – Beyond Dehiwala the road bears r.

Mount Lavinia is a country house, built in 1824 by Governor E.Barnes and named after his wife, now **Mount Lavinia Grand Hotel* (Rm. from 2½, with two Bd. from 5R., B.2½, L.2½R., famous for its fish dishes, D.3, P. from 7R.) Its position on the rock above the sea, with a view of the palm-girt coastline, is romantic. The sandy beach is suitable for bathing, since a reef, lying almost 1½km distant, keeps the sharks away.

The coastal railway (Colombo-Matara, 98M.) continues via *Kalutara* (26M., p.33) and numerous insignificant places to (72M.) Galle (New Oriental Hot.), the former chief port of Ceylon, which has only recently been overtaken by Colombo, with 40,187 inhab.; English, Dutch reformed and Catholic churches. Then on (90M.) to *Weligama,* pleasantly situated, and *Matara,* with 13,000 inhab. on the *Nil Ganga,* over which a bridge leads to the former Dutch fort.

Kelaniya, station for the Kandy railway (p.34) is also best visited by carriage (1hr.; 10R. return). To *Victoria Bridge* (see p.29). Continue upstream on the r. bank of the *Kelani Ganga,* then bear l. to the Sinhalese village of *Kelaniya.* Pleasant drive along by the river through the tropical forest, where the life of the natives is even more primitive than on the way to Mount Lavinia. The village is surrounded by tea and rubber plantations. In a side-street is the Kelani temple, much visited by pilgrims, and whose original foundation can be traced back to the earliest era of Buddhism (p.22). The temple has been much rebuilt and is better preserved than the one at Kandy (p.37). A large outdoor staircase leads to a triumphal gateway with ancient sculptures. In the courtyard l., ruins of a more recent temple, partly European in style, whose completion was however obstructed by the priests. The temple buildings proper consist of two new buildings and a large architectural *dagaba* (p.57), with the imbedded relics from an ancient shrine, last repaired in 1301 A.D. In the courtyard, a sacred Bo-tree (p.19). The *first temple*, straight ahead, contains: grotesque representations of Buddha and other holy men, with effective, strictly stylised, wall-paintings of Buddhist legends; in the glass case by the rear wall a figure of Buddha in alabaster from Burma, among other items; in an adjoining room, under glass, a recumbent Buddha entering the state of Nirvana; on the long wooden table in front of this, offerings are placed, blossoms from the areca and talypot palms, the suriya tree and lotus flowers. In the *second temple,* further back: numerous votive offerings and works of art; in the vestibule on an altar, a large and very stylised "Sri-pada" (p.53) with a horoscope circle in the middle. All around are *priests' dwellings* and *small temples* to the Hindu gods Vishnu, Shiva and, with the elephant's head, Ganesa.

The narrow-gauge *Kelani Valley Line* goes from Colombo (Maradana Junc. p.26) up the Kelani valley through plantations of cinnamon, palms and other vegetation, past several Sinhalese villages in 3¼hrs. to (47M) *Yatiyantota.* – The most important intermediate station: 37M. *Avisawella* (good Rest-house), at the confluence of the Kelani Ganga and the *Sitamaka Oya,* which latter bears the name of an old town destroyed by the Portuguese. From Avisawella, a branch-line (27M., in 1hr. 40min) to:-

Ratnapura (33m; Rest-house), chief place of the province *Sabaragama,* with 4,500 inhab., surrounded by tea and rubber plantations, on the *Kalu Ganga,* whose deposits are a major source of gems. The former Dutch fort above the town, now seat of the administrative and judicial authorities, offers a splendid view of Adam's Peak (p.51) and other summits of the upland massif. Equally fine is the view from *Kaluganga Bridge* (p.51) and from Circular Road. In the streets of the town one's attention is caught by the Moors (p.21), occupied in polishing gem-stones. Pure stones are rare; one is hardly safer here, from being sold worthless examples, than one is with the small dealers in Colombo (cf.p.XXVI).

At Ratnapura the Kalu Ganga becomes navigable. Boats for carrying passengers generally consist of two hollowed-out tree-trunks linked together by a roofed-over platform of boards. When the water-level permits, the trip downstream is very enjoyable, partly over rapids, through luxuriant tropical vegetation, in which human dwellings are lost to view: one day's journey to *Kalutara* (p.32), leaving it at nightfall; arrangements may be made through the Rest-house manager at Ratnapura (15-20R. with 4-5R. tip for the rowers); provisions necessary.

Route 3. From Colombo to Kandy.

74M. Main Line, (built 1855-60, single-track) in 3-4¾hrs., for 6R. 1st cl., 1R. 2nd cl., return 9R., 6R., valid for 17 days (or 2 months, if purchased at Cook's); for dining and sleeping cars, and sta. restaurants, see the Pocket Timetables (p.26); the carriages are protected from the sun by double roofs. – Or one uses the excellent *Main Road* (built 1821-31, *cars* p.24), but the railway journey is finer. – Do not forget warm clothing (cf.p.XIV).

The excursion to Kandy may be made, in any case, during a one-day docking at Colombo, by going up on the early train and returning by the afternoon or evening one (in the former case one admittedly has only 2¾hrs. for Kandy itself, so that the lovely ride through the tropical landscape is the main attraction). One should allow at least 1 hr. for disembarkation and travel to the sta. at Colombo.

Maradana Junction (see p.26). On the morning train sit on the l., since the sun is still low in the sky and blinds one on the r. On the second part of the journey one has the finer views to the r. The railway crosses the Kelani Ganga, passing *Kelaniya* (3M.) and its temple, see p.32. Soon the main road appears on the r., following the railway most of the way.

The *journey through the richly cultivated plain is of great charm. Extensive paddy-fields, where rice is grown, coconut palm-woods and the other typical flora of the tropical lowlands (see pp. 16ff.) Here and there, small villages and single farms. Of the animals, one is particularly aware of grey water-buffalo, upon whose backs delicate white herons search for parasites. We mention only the more noteworthy stations. – 16M. *Henaratgoda* (11m above sea-level; Rest-house at the sta.), with approx. 5000 inhab.; 20min NW, a *botanical garden* opened in 1876, the most important one for useful plants which thrive in the humid plain, especially for S.American rubber trees, which are now being introduced and acclimatised here.

Beyond (22M.) *Veyengoda* (18m), the first stop for fast trains, the railway begins to ascend. Sporadic chains of hills come into view. Short tunnel. – 34M. *Ambepussa* (55m). Then across the *Maha Oya* and up its valley, which bears the name "Valley of the Shadow of Death", since the entire area up to the foot of the mountains is infested with fever. Soon, ahead and r., the double summit of Alagalla Rock appears (p.35).

40M. *Polgahawela* (73m), junction for the northern line Anuradhapura-Jaffna (p.54). Near the sta., a prettily situated Rest-house. In the vicinity, cocoa plantations.

53M. *Rambukkana* (95m). The train takes on a second locomotive. The track ascends (1 in 45 on average), up along the E. wall of the beautiful *Dekanda Valley,* hugging the irregular slope in numerous curves, and passing through 10 short tunnels.

The *view r. is magnificent; on well-watered terraces on the slopes, the native rice-fields; beyond the valley, the picturesque summits of the uplands, some with striking shapes, e.g. *Camel Rock,* resembling a castle ruin on a precipitous rocky cone, and *Bible Rock,* like a thick book. The flora of the uplands begins to mingle with that of the tropical lowlands. The railway line follows the steep granite wall of *Alagalla Rock* (1034m), about 300m above the abyss: *Sensation Rock,* from which the last king of Kandy reputedly had his prisoners thrown. Approaching Kadugannawa, one looks across at the sharp turns of the road which reaches the Kandy heights by the same pass as the railway. A column at the top of the pass r. commemorates the completion of the road.

65M. *Kadugannawa* (518m).

70M. *Peradeniya Junction* (473m), for the line to Nuwara Eliya-Bandarawala, see p.44 – The line Kandy-Matale turns NE, crossing the Mahawelliganga by an iron bridge (p.15). 71M. *Peradeniya* (473m), 10min from the entrance to *Peradeniya Gardens* (p.42): travellers who have only one day to devote to Kandy alight here and, after visiting the gardens, continue by carriage to Kandy (carriages and rickshaws according to the Kandy tariff, see below).

74M. *Kandy.* For continuation of the railway, see p.55.

Kandy.

The STATION (188m) lies approx. 1km from the lake; hotel servants and conveyances, also public transport, meet the trains.

HOTELS (heavily booked-up by visitors from Colombo at Christmas, so prior bookings necessary well in advance): *Queen's Hotel, in the best position at the NE corner of the lake, well spoken of, attractive double rooms with toilet and writing-room. Rm. from 2½R., P. from 9R., victorias available for excursions; *Hot.Suisse, prettily sited on the S. side of the lake, with villa annexe and garden, 50Rm., P. 6-11R.; *Florence Hotel, bungalow group beneath coconut palms, quiet, 32 Bd., P. 8R., (7R. from the 8th day, 6R. for stays of 30 days or more). – Second class: Empire Hotel, in Victoria Esplanade, 10Rm, P. 5R.; Oriental & Occidental Hotel, Ward St., 10Rm., P. 6R., cheaper for longer stays. – Less suitable for Europeans: King's Hotel, in the native town, at the intersection of King's and Castle St.; Rm. 1½, two-bedded 2½, P. 6R.

TRANSPORT. Rickshaws: short distances 10cts., first and second ½hr. 25cts. each, every further ½hr. 10cts., at night 15, 30, 15cts. – Carriages: one-horse, first and second ½hr. 60cts. each, the next hr. 60cts., each additional hr. 30cts.; two-horse, half as much again; rather higher prices at night. – Motor cars may be ordered through Cook.

POST & TELEGRAPH, at Government Office in the W. portion of Ward St., see p.36. – TRAVEL AGENCY: *Thos.Cook & Son.*

BANKS: *National Bank of India, Mercantile Bank of India.* – SHOPS, mainly branches of the Colombo firms mentioned on p.26; native metal- and woodwork at *Kandy Industrial School;* also in the small *Museum* near the Audience Chamber (p.40). – DOCTOR: *Dr Hay*, Queen's Hotel, - CHEMIST: *Miller & Co.*

FOR A LIMITED VISIT (1½ days): walk round the lake, visit the Maligawa Temple and the Audience Chamber, 1½-2hrs.; Lady Horton's Walk, 1¼hrs.; drive to Peradeniya and through the Botanical Gardens, 2hrs. – In summer one can attend the big Buddhist *Perehera* festival, which is celebrated at new moon, June-July, in honour of the birth of Vishnu. For 5 days, the casket with the sacred tooth of Buddha (p.38) and other holy objects are carried through the town in a great procession, decorated elephants playing the main part. 9 further days are filled with dancing and various ceremonies (at which the old chieftains' costumes and so on may be seen), partly in the town and partly by the river.

Kandy, 1500-1815 capital of the Sinhalese empire (p.22), whose degenerate kingdom was brought to an end by the English, and now capital of Central Province, with 30,148 inhab. (1901: 26,381) lies in the central part of an upland area, on average 505m above sea-level, around which the Mahawelliganga flows. The flora of Ceylon manifests itself here in its richest development. In addition to the purely tropical lowland vegetation, which still thrives here, one finds that of the mountains. The landscape is uncommonly charming. The climate is splendid, with 25°C annual mean temperature and about 192 days of rain; the air is fragrant and mild in the evening, and generally refreshingly cool at night, to a body spoilt by tropical heat. Half of the inhabitants are Sinhalese, whose habits and customs have been kept very much alive. There are however few old buildings still in existence, since Kandy was repeatedly razed to the ground in the struggles against the Portuguese, Dutch and English. There are 400 Europeans, with several churches of Anglican and Presbyterian denomination, and a Roman Catholic cathedral.

From the sta., one reaches the civil hospital and the police barracks, then, past the *Market Hall* (with the large Bogambra Prison to the E. behind it), into Ward St., the main business street. Here, l., the *Government Office* with the *Post Office.* Further along, r., the *Victoria Commemoration Building* of the Planters' Association of Ceylon (erected 1897-1900) with a small library etc., and the *Kandy Club.* At the S. end of Ward St. lies Queen's Hotel, beyond which *Trincomalee St.* goes off to the l., the main street of the native town, which however has nothing of interest to offer, compared to Pettah at Colombo.

The central attraction, both of town and immediate environs, is *Kandy Lake, surrounded by delightful promenades, and created by the last Sinhalese king, who caused this part of the Kandy valley to be inundated by the erection of a large dam. The lake is 1100m in length and, in its main basin, which contains a romantic islet with the ruins of a royal pavilion, is 300m wide. The dam, on the W. side, is approx. 200m long and, at its S. end, has a spill-stone to channel off the lake water, which forms a small cataract and is used by the natives for bathing, especially in the mornings. A road called the *Bund* follows the S. shore of the lake, lined on the side facing the lake with a fine old stone balustrade, as is the dam itself. Victoria Esplanade, next to the Bund, (with a statue of Governor H. Ward, 1855-60, a mounted statue as memorial to the Boer War, a *music pavilion* in Kandyan carved wood – concerts Sunday & Thursday evenings – and a *fountain* recalling the Prince of Wales's visit in 1875), is particularly noted for its superb flowering trees (spathodeas, p.19). – At the E. end of the Bund and Esplanade, r., built out into the lake, the *United Services Library* (open 9 a.m. to 6 p.m.), probably a former royal bath house; l., on the E. side of Palace Sq., the famous Temple of the Tooth, or:-

**Dalada Maligawa*, recognisable from a distance by its venerable grey battlements and the squat octagonal corner tower with its bent pointed roof (octagon, p.39), is otherwise plain and, to our way of thinking, neglected both within and without, although one of the holiest Buddhist places of pilgrimage, being visited by pilgrims from the whole of S. and E. Asia. Its foundation dates back to the 14th c. The present building was erected at the beginning of the 18th c. and, until 1815, formed part of the royal palace. The main entrance is a large *gateway* with two candelabra in front. On the wall on either side, two old elephant reliefs. One should take one of the many guides who importune for custom (1R.) and keep small change ready for the many beggars. At 5.30 and 9.30 a.m., and 6.30 p.m. (lit), there are services which one is free to attend, since Buddhists do not know sectarian hatred. Whoever is able to overlook the lack of outward veneration and the poverty of the proceedings, will feel a sympathy with the unique poesy of this gentle flower-cult.

Across the palace moat, which is enclosed by picturesque masonry and which (r.) still contains water inhabited by many turtles, one passes through a second *gateway* covered with sculptures of Buddhist-Hindu legends, and then reaches a narrow forecourt. On the wall in front, an old carving from Anuradhapura. To the l., the Audience Chamber (p.39), r. upstairs to the:-

TEMPLE OF THE TOOTH itself, with a narrow arcaded vestibule, on whose rear wall 15 paintings depict, in graphic, popular style the punishments of Hell: drunkards and opium-smokers are fed fire by demons; adulterers are transfixed on spiny tree-trunks; felling of the holy fig-tree is punished by being cut to pieces; those who have killed animals are torn apart by wild beasts; disobedient wives are pecked to pieces by parrots; murderers, thieves, usurers, spoilt children, disrespectful members of the lower castes and temple robbers suffer similar terrible punishments.

A beautifully ornamented door leads to the rectangular inner court, which is surrounded by open pillared arcades, and in whose centre is the little reliquary temple (see below). In the entrance wing of the arcade, during divine service, bowls of flowers are offered to the Tooth, especially the strongly scented blossom of the temple tree (Plumieria acutifolia). Here also are the musical instruments for the rite. L., the holy spring, where the priests purify themselves for the service, a small dagaba (p.57), whose gilding was subscribed for by pilgrims from Cambodia, and a locked chest, containing the adornment for the elephants in the Perahera (p.36); the other treasures are in the Treasury, to the r., where all kinds of votive offerings are exhibited, including a Buddha of crystal and silver-work; the small staircase in the corner leads to the Octagon (p.39). In the r. wing of the arcade, a votive tablet announces in English and Burmese the charitable gift of a splendid new case for the Sacred Tooth, and its delivery here by 1200 pilgrims from Burma in 1899.

The two-storey *reliquary temple,* in the middle of the courtyard, is completely covered with carvings and garishly colourful paintings on allegorical and legendary themes. Access through the centre door; in the vestibule r. the narrow stairs to the upper floor. From this vestibule, a door of gilded bronze encrusted with ivory carvings leads into the small centre room, which the holy chamber adjoins. One may enter the latter only without one's shoes, but from the door one has a general view: on the silver table in front, the priest spreads out the flower offerings; up on the ceiling, a golden lotus flower; behind a gilded iron grille, on a richly decorated, but noticeably dirty silver table, the *Karanduwa,* the sumptuous shrine which contains the relic. One makes an offering of some flowers and a coin (1R. at the most) on the priest's silver plate.

The Karanduwa is made of gilded silver, festooned with precious jewels, its centre piece forming a peacock with emeralds, rubies and sapphires. Within it, enclosed in seven gold, jewel-studded capsules, the so-called *Sacred Tooth* (Dalada) is kept, a brownish piece of ivory almost 4cm long and over 1cm thick, which is regarded as the Buddha's left upper eye-tooth, but is more like a wild boar's fang than a human tooth. The relic came from NW India (see p.89), was demonstrably in Anuradhapura after 300 A.D. (p.60) and was then taken, because of the Tamil wars, to Polonnaruha (p.65), Dambadeniya and Yapaku; in 1315 it passed briefly to the S. Indians and in 1560 was lost to the Portuguese, who publicly had the relic burnt in Goa by the archbishop, but the priests maintain that they rescued the true Tooth. Since 1566 it has been shown at major festivals.

The Octagon (Sinh. *Pattirippuwa),* to which the small staircase, (see above), leads from the SW. corner of the temple courtyard, contains on its upper floor the *Oriental Library,* with valuable Buddhist mss. on talypot leaves (p.17), of which the oldest is estimated to be 800 years old, partly in metal, partly in lacquer bindings. On request, the priestly librarian will write some Sinhalese characters on a palm leaf (1R.; any contribution to the library is placed in the collecting box). From the outer gallery of the Octagon, a pretty view of the lake.

The Old Palace, in Palace Square, dates back to about 1600, and is now the Government Agent's private residence. In front, an old fountain with carved wooden pillars. One is admitted only to the **Audience Chamber* (either from the temple forecourt or from Kacheri Rd.) which is used for public law sittings. The rectangular wooden columns are richly carved, especially those on the N. side; the motif of hanging banana blossom has been used copiously on the capitals. – The modern building to the E. is the *Kacheri,* seat of the Revenue Office.

Opposite the Old Palace and on the N. side of Victoria Esplanade, enclosed by a picturesque old wall, is the temple area of two Hindu divinities. Within this, on the N. side, the sanctuary *(Dewale)* of the god *Nata,* taken to be Shiva; on the S. the goddess of chastity *Pattini,* who protects one from smallpox. The garden also contains three dagabas with Buddhist relics and several Bo-trees (p.19). At full-moon it is decorated with lanterns and flowers and crowded with supplicants. A recently restored gate on the N. side constitutes the main entrance, which is decorated with images of the protective deities. – To the N., opposite this gate, a staircase in several flights with open arcading leads to the *Maha-Vishnu-Dewale,* the temple of Vishnu, whose image is displayed between 6 and 9 a.m. The Bo-tree in the temple courtyard is said to be an offshoot of the one at Anuradhapura (p.58). – *St Paul's Church,* near the Nata-Pattini temple enclosure, dates from 1853; the teak carvings with ebony and ivory inlays on pulpit and altar are good modern examples of Sinhalese craftsmanship.

Opposite St Paul's on the N. side, the entrance to *Governor's Park,* which contains many fine trees, incl. Amherstia nobilis with red blossoms (like chestnut), and the candle tree, whose fruit resembles wax candles hanging from the trunk. The *King's Pavilion* (1834) is the Governor's residence, standing in its own grounds, which may however be visited when the Governor is absent, on presentation of a ticket (obtainable from hotels or the Town Hall).

Mention must also be made of the Buddhist *Asgiriya Monastery*, to the NW of the native town: at the junction of Hill St. and Brownrigg St. cross the railway, then 6-8min in a westerly direction. The temple contains the largest statue of Buddha in Kandy, also figures of Hindu gods (when closed, tip). – To N. and S., the barracks of the English garrison.

WALKS. – Avoid the hottest hours of the day (or have a rickshaw on hand, p.35), also shun darkness, and stay on clearly defined paths, since one will be troubled by snakes, leeches (p.20) and clinging seeds from plants if one goes through grass or undergrowth. Carriageways are marked "Drive", footpaths and rickshaw paths "Walk". – One often has an opportunity to observe monkeys.

Victoria Drive, which encircles the lake (1hr. on foot) offers an uninterrupted succession of charming views of the shores, decked out in the most abundant and diverse vegetation, as well as of the wooded heights. Go E. from the United Services Library (p.37). Beyond Kacheri Rd., the *Kandyan Art Museum* l., of little importance (open 11-5; also sells genuine Kandy craftwork). Further on, l., a large terrace with remains of old buildings, called *King's Barn,* in an effective setting. At the SE end of the lake, among spathodea, tulip-trees and others, the courts of *Kandy Tennis Club.* Then, l., the hotels mentioned on p.35. Further on one catches sight, l. on a platforn, of the Buddhist monastery *Malwatte Vihara,* beyond a polygonal bathing pool with a brick surround. About 30 monks live here under the jurisdiction of an abbot. Inside, 16 monolithic columns support a wooden roof made from enormous trunks. Victoria Drive ends at the dam (p.36). – More time is required for the equally beautiful road which goes round the lake, somewhat higher up. Follow *Malabar St.,* then the road to Ampitiya, turning r. at the tennis courts into *Gregory Rd.,* which leads past a mineral water factory and, beyond this, up a grassy path l., by an ancient water basin called the King's Bath.

The ascent of Upper Lake Rd., to the *waterworks reservoir* (1hr. return) is also pretty. The vegetation around the little lake is marvellously rich. View over the town and the northern mountain area.

*Lady Horton's Walk & Drive is the most famous of the roads laid out by various governors, and mostly named after their ladies, and one of the most beautiful mountain walks at Kandy (1½hrs.) It begins in Governor's Park (p.39), where it rises to the r. by the private grounds, and is provided with signposts and seats. It passes repeatedly through splendid primeval jungle, which admittedly contains some artificial plantations. From *Eastern Redoubt* a fine view of the lake, the town and the Temple of the Tooth. Higher up, from two seats, view into the distant Dumbara valley with the Mahawelliganga and the mountains beyond which, although of average height, combine the wilder shapes of the high mountains with the vegetation of the tropics. (The dominant double summit is Hunysgeria, 1521m). – Of the subsidiary paths the most rewarding is *Gregory's Path* which leads to two summit viewpoints (25min). One may return along *Lady McCarthy's Drive* and *Malabar St.,* instead of Lady Horton's Walk.

Lewella Ferry and Gangarama Temple (2hrs. return): from Badulla Rd., the NE continuation of Malabar St., turn off l. at the sign "Lewella Ferry 1 mile": Lady Anderson's Drive then, r., Lewella Rd. The road is very busy. ½hr. *Lewella Ferry,* by which one crosses to the l. bank of the fast-flowing *Mahawelliganga* (5cts.) Then another ½hr. upwards to *Gangarama Temple* (Gangarama: river god), one of Ceylon's numerous rock temples. In front, six images of idols carved out of the rock. 18 monolithic columns support the outer verandah. The brightly painted but dark interior contains, at the rear, a 7m-long statue of Buddha, also carved from the rock. The usual dagaba and holy fig-tree.

The *Roman Catholic Seminary,* a giant red building with crenellations, on the road to Ampitiya, stands in its own gardens, which give splendid views over the Mahawelliganga valley.

To visit the Elephant Garden, 3km N., one takes a rickshaw (1½R.: "to the elephants"; 1½hrs. there and back, incl. visit). From the N. end of Trincomalee St. (p.36), along by the railway, then beneath it, and on along the W. side of it to the bridge over the *Mahawelliganga,* where there is a police station. To the r. of this, the *Elephant Garden.* Boys show the way. The 3-4 animals belong to a private Sinhalese gentleman who keeps them as a sign of affluence, and makes them available for temple festivities. Between 2 and 3 p.m. one finds them bathing. The keepers get them to perform small tricks and to adopt suitable poses for the camera (tip 1R.)

The excursion to Peradeniya Gardens (4M, 6½km SW) is made either by carriage or rickshaw (approx. ½hr.) or from the railway halt (p.35) on foot. It is advisable to set out early. Carriages are admitted to the main paths of the gardens. The round trip takes about 1hr., the extremely pleasurable circuit on foot 3-4hrs. Opposite the entrance is a government Rest-house (entrance 50cts.) where one can order breakfast for one's return.

The **Botanical Gardens of Peradeniya (*pera*: the guava; *deniya*: area), the most beautiful among the numerous gardens of this type in S. and E. Asia, competing with Buitenzorg in Java (p.318) in scientific importance, covers an area of 150 acres (60 ha), washed on three sides by the Mahawelliganga. Situated at an altitude of 479m above sea-level on the moist W. slopes of the mountain range, it produces a superb abundance of tropical flora, being particularly rich in lianas, palms, bamboo, pandanus, orchids, ferns and giant broadleaf trees. The garden was first established in 1821 for the observation of the native vegetation, but later was also used for experiments in acclimatising useful plants from other tropical countries. The professional staff comprises seven persons who are engaged in the production of a comprehensive "Flora of Ceylon" (the section on phanerogams was completed by Sir Joseph Hooker in 1900; that on ferns, mosses and fungi is in preparation). The Director is F.Macmillan. A special laboratory equipped on modern lines is available for scholars. There are some 3000 visitors per annum. Entrance free. One inscribes one's name in the visitors' book, in the *Lodge,* to the r. after the entrance.

Outside the entrance l., a group of Assam rubber trees (*Ficus elastica),* with strange roots; on the triangular lawn, a mahogany from the Honduras *Swietenia mahagoni).*

Passing the Lodge, one reaches a group of palm-trees, comprising 50-60 different species, incl. areca, date, corozo, sago and oil palms. Walking around this oval-shaped group, one notices, to the l. near Lake Rd. (p.44) a bush, *Napoleona imperiatis*, whose blossoms resemble an imperial crown; near this, an *Amherstia nobilis,* then a Durian *(Durio cibethinus),* the producer of the evil-smelling but tasty civet. Crossing Main Central Drive (p.43), one follows Liana Drive, lined with profuse garlands of lianas, mainly of the climbing palm variety *Calamus,* which provides the material for cane chairs. Leave the carriage by the round pool ("tank") which is enlivened by a fountain, and contains Egyptian *papyrus, lotus flowers* and other water plants. Continue on foot S. to the spice section ("spices"), which includes nutmeg *(Myristica fragrans).* Returning, note l. the insect-eating plants *(Nepenthes)* and, on the trees, the large-leaved Mexican creeper *Monstera deliciosa.* N. of the round pond a charming *flower garden* with its *Octagon Conservatory,* for plants which prefer the shade; beneath the palms nearby, the graceful *Chrysalidocarpus lutescens* from Mauritius. Of particular interest is the *orchid house,* N. of the round pond, where the drive continues round a curve.

By the Mahawelliganga there is a pretty view E. to Hantane Peak. The drive follows the river bank N. To the l., the *Nurseries,* for the cultivation of useful and ornamental plants, then *Palmyra Avenue*, whose palms are about 30 years old. Further on, Oreodoxa Avenue, containing 60-year-old Cuban King's palms, now being replaced by cabbage trees *(Oreodoxa oleracca).* On the l., the *Experimental Plots*, where cocoa, coffee, cardamom, banana, mulberry, vanilla, cocaine plants and sugar are grown. Further down the avenue, giant *bamboos.* In the treetops by the river one sees flocks of large bats, so-called flying foxes *(Pteropus medius),* which sleep in the daytime, hanging from the branches. The drive passes round the *Arboretum,* a large plantation of trees occupying the whole N. part of the peninsula. (Just before the NW curve of the Mahawelliganga, a ferry crosses to the *Experimental Station* on the opposite bank, where experiments are made with useful plants for the Ceylonese plantations). The drive S. along by the river offers excellent views, such as "Bridge View", towards the railway bridge (p.35).

We turn l. along West Road to the centre of the gardens, the *Great Circle,* a large expanse of lawn surrounded by magnificent tropical trees, the centre of which is bisected by Main Central Drive and its N. continuation, *Royal Palm Avenue*, planted in 1898. Of the trees, one's eye is particularly taken by the S.African *Spathodea campanulata* with its scarlet blossom. Some trees were planted by royal visitors, e.g. a Flamboyant *(Poinciana regia)* in 1899 by Princess Henry of Prussia, a Bo-tree in 1875 by the (later) King Edward VII of England, and an *Amherstia nobilis* (1898, by Prince Henry of Prussia). On the E. side of the Circle, one can see *Thwaites' Memorial* built in the Kandy style to commemorate the Director of the gardens from 1849 to 1880.

From *Main Central Drive,* to the S. of the Circle, Bat Drive runs NE. to the *Fernery,* laid out in 1861, and the Rose Garden; to the W., along Museum Rd., the *Museum of Economic Botany* (note the collection of Ceylon timbers), the adjoining *Entomological Museum* (insects: silk-spinners, carpenter bees, mimetic creatures etc.), *Herbarium, Library* and *Scientific Laboratory.* Near the latter, a cannonball tree *(Couroupita guianensis),* bearing fruit 6-12cm in size, which was planted in 1901 by the present King George.

Back to Main Drive, on whose W. side extends the *Great Lawn* in the style of an English park, and W. into Monument Rd., at the end of which stands a monument to *Gardner* (Director of the gardens, 1844-

49). Before this, turn off r. and, curving N. at first, continue to West River Drive, with a pleasant view downstream to Gangaruwa Hill. West River Drive continues S. to the lake, which contains beautiful water-plants (incl. *Victoria regia* from Brazil) and is surrounded by clusters of bamboo. To the l., the giant bamboo *(Dendrocalamus giganteus)* from Burma, which here attains the rare height of approx. 37m and girth of 30cm. From Lake Road (see below), *Talypot Avenue* heads S., a splendid drive planted in 1885, ending in a loop, in the middle of which is a classified collection of palms. R., a collection of bamboos and pandanus. One follows the path Hill Walk N. to *Herbaceous Ground,* a collection of herbs and low brushwood, then back to the lake and so along *Lake Road* to the entrance once more.

Route 4. From Kandy to Nuwara Eliya.
Adam's Peak.

65M. Railway in 6hrs. for 7R.16, 4R.82cts. Return tickets 1½ times the single fare, valid 17 days. – The sta. for Adam's Peak is *Hatton,* p.45. Nuwara Eliya is on a branch-line, for which *Nanuoya* is the junc., p.45; if there is no connection, telegraph for a carriage to Nanuoya through Cook or the Coach Office at Nuwara Eliya (tariff p.46). One is recommended to use a motor car for the return journey from the uplands via Haputale-Ratnapura (2 days), see p.24.

From Kandy to *Peradeniya Junction* 4M., see p.35. The main line from Colombo, which one rejoins here, slowly ascends the *Mahawelliganga valley.* At the third sta. (21M.) *Nawalapitiya* (583m), there are no more paddy-fields and soon no more palm trees. Tea plantations, which in the last few decades have gained an extraordinary foothold on the W. and S. slopes of the range, have almost ousted the jungle on both sides of the railway line. The latter crosses the river on a 50m arched bridge, then continues up a side valley. Steep gradient. Two tunnels, between which a beautiful waterfall is espied, l.

28M. *Galboda* (787m), centre of the Galboda tea-growing district. The railway returns to the Mahawelli valley. R., views open up towards the district near Nawalapitiya, then the lower Kelani valley and, in clear weather, the sea.

34M. *Watawala* (987m). The upper Mahawelli valley is one of the rainiest areas on the island (see p.16). The railway is constantly being reconstructed because of landslides, which are not uncommon after torrential rain during the SW. monsoon.

42M. *Hatton* (1262m; refreshments at the sta.; Hot. Adam's Peak, 3min from the sta. on a hillock, 32 Rm. from 2½R., B. 2¼, L. 2, D. 3, P. from 8R., room heating 50cts., very passable), with 1450 inhab., railhead for the tea-growing districts of Dickoya and Maskeliya, and a popular resort before the opening of the railway to Nuwara Eliya and the removal of the jungle. For the road to Laxapana and the ascent of Adam's Peak, see p.51.

The railway curves E., and descends through the 559m long Poolbank tunnel into the *Kotmale Oya* valley, the main feeder of the Mahawelliganga. To the r., the mountain ranges, then l., more than 100m below, the foaming Kotmale. Beyond (45M) *Kotagala* (1230m) there are some particularly striking views of the river valley and the Dimbula tea-growing district, of the broad *St Clair's Falls* and, behind these, the Great West Chain, rising to 2210m, on the edge of the upland valley of Nuwara Eliya. Through a tunnel to (49M) *Talawakele Halt* (1198m), then over the river Kotmale. Adam's Peak appears to the SW. The line ascends in tight curves. After Holyroad tunnel the so-called "Sodawater-bottle bend", a hairpin 1km long, whose upper end is 27m above the tunnel exit, at a direct distance of only 60m.

54M. *Watagoda* (1342m). To the r., splendid *views of Dimbula district, the river Kotmale (sighted in various different places) and the mountain chain, out of which Adam's Peak rises to its full stature. The railway has been boldly engineered along the face of the mountain. After a final large curve, the train reaches:-

62M. *Nanuoya* (1613m; Refreshment room at the sta., also accommodation, if need be), picturesquely situated by the wooded ravine which rises towards the upland valley of Nuwara Eliya.. Travellers to the latter leave the main line (pp.50-1) and board the train on the narrow-gauge…

Udapussalawa Line (Nanuoya-Ragalla), whereby one reaches Nuwara Eliya in 50min; max. gradient 1:25·87 (Gotthard rly 1:38·5); sharpest curves 25m radius. To begin with the railway follows the old road and the little river that foams among the rocks (splendid tree-ferns), always ascending until it crosses the river in a broad arc, passes Gregory's Lake and so reaches the sta. at (6½M) *Nuwara Eliya* (1890m).

Three more stations follow: 12M. *Kandapolla*, where the branch line reaches its highest point at 1970m.; 16M. *Brookside*, at only 1519m; 19M. *Ragalla*, the terminus, at 1819m.

Nuwara Eliya.

HOTELS (during the "season" which lasts from the end of December until May, accommodation is much in demand, and especially at Christmas and in the month of February; advance booking necessary): *Grand Hotel, in a good position near Scandal Corner (p.47), Rm. from 3R., with 2 Bd from 5R., B. 2¼, L. 2, D. 3, P. 8-9R., excellent cuisine, good service; *New Keena Hotel, also conveniently situated near the United Club, well run. Smaller: *St Andrew's Hotel (German prop. A.Humbert), not far from the golf links, Rm.3, with 2 Bd. 5R., B.75cts., L. 2½, D. 3½R., P. from 8R. if one's stay is longer than 3 days. – The guest-house Carlton Ho. is much praised, with 8 Rm., P. 5-6R. per day, 150R. per month. – Room heating is reckoned separately. – Excellent drinking-water.

TRANSPORT. – Rickshaw, with one or two coolies (two always necessary in the hilly environs): first hr. 50cts. and 75cts., each successive hr. 25cts. & 37½cts; with 2 coolies: to *Nanuoya* 1R.75 (descent also with one coolie, 1R.25); to *Rambodda Pass* 1.50, around *Moon Plains* or the lake, 2R. – Carriage: one-horse: first hr. 1.50, second hr. 1R., each successive hr. 75cts., half-day, i.e. 6.30 a.m. to noon, or noon to 7 p.m., 3.50; all day, 6.30 a.m. to 7 p.m., 6.50. Two-horse: first hr. 2R., second hr. 1.50, each succ.hr.1R., ½ day 6, all day 10R., outside the locality 1R. per mile; to *Nanuoya* 1-3 pers. 5R., 4-5 pers. 8R., each extra pers. 2R.; to *Rambodda Pass* and back, 3.50, 1.50; round *Moon Plains*, round the lake or to *Mahagastota* and ret., also 3.50, 1.50; to the Botanical Gdns at *Hakgalla*, 3 pers. 6R.; price always incl. 1hr's stay (at Hakgalla 2hrs), longer stays 1R. per hr. – Motor cars, preferable for lengthy journeys, see p.24.

POST & TELEGRAPH, see p.47. – BANK: *National Bank of India*, a red building near the Post Office and bridge. – DOCTORS: *Dr A.P.Day; Dr G.W.van Twest,* doctor at the well-appointed government hospital. – CHEMISTS: *Cargill's Pharmacy*, N. of the National Bank; *St Louis Pharmacy*. – SHOPS: *Cargill's Ltd.*, near the Bank and Post Office, for equipment and sporting gear; *Nuwara Eliya Apothecaries Co.* –

PHOTOGRAPHERS and photographic requisites: *Plâté & Co.* (p.26), near New Keena Hotel.

TRAVEL AGENCY: *Thos.Cook & Son*, for carriages and motor cars.

CLUBS (on longer stays, an introduction from the Consul or Banker is useful): *Hill Club*, nicely situated near the Grand Hotel, daily fee 1R.; *United Club* by the Race Course, with library, cricket pitch, croquet lawns, golf course and tennis courts, weekly fee 10, monthly fee 11R.; *Nuwara Eliya Golf Club*, weekly fee 5R., green fee 5R.; *Ceylon Fishing Club*, see the Honorary Secretary in the Kacheri about the rules, *Football & Hockey Club*, etc.

FOR A LIMITED VISIT (1½-2 days): walks to Single Tree Hill and Rambodda Pass (latter also by carriage); drive to the Botanical Gdns at Hakgalla; climb Pidarattallagalla. – Day trip to *World's End* (p.50): morning on foot or by rickshaw to Nanuoya, railway to Pattipola, then walk, 8hrs. return.

Nuwara Eliya ("open place in a clearing"), abbr. by the English to *Nurellia*, one of Asia's best-loved resorts, lies at an altitude of approx. 1890m in an upland valley 1-2½km wide and inclining gently from NW to SE. It is surrounded by the gently rounded gneiss summits of the highest mountains in Ceylon which, however, apart from Pidarattallagalla stand only a few hundred metres above it. The flat, partly marshy valley-floor was once the playground of elephants and other big game. The first European, Dr Davy, came here in 1819. Ten years later, Governor E.Barnes (p.28) designated the place as a centre of recuperation for English soldiers. The mean annual temperature is 14.4°C, rainfall 2444mm. The driest months are January, February (during which the thermometer often approaches zero), March and April. Frequent mist and cloud make the winter evenings bitingly cold (a fire is often indispensable), but a comparison with the European spring is not quite apt. The extremes of temperature are greater than at home, and a tropical hat is obligatory around noon. As with all tropical hill stations, it is the stimulating fresh air, reminding Europeans of home, that makes up the chief attraction of Nuwara Eliya; the traveller passing through, having just left Europe, will be less charmed by this. The place is most busy with visitors in winter and spring. For the remainder of the year, only a hundred Europeans and a few thousand natives remain up here.

The European dwellings, known as cottages or bungalows, lie mainly hidden in gardens all around, at the foot of the mountain slopes. Only in the middle of the valley is a relatively built-up area, formed by the *National Bank*, the *Police Station* and, S. of the Market, the *Post Office*, along with some other houses. *Trinity Church* is to the SE near the sta. To the NW, on the road to Rambodda Pass (p.48), the green Golf Links (r.) which are famous throughout the East, and l. the Governor's Residence, *Queen's Cottage*, hidden away behind trees and bushes. The busiest place for traffic is the intersection called *Scandal Corner*. To the S. of this, on the r. bank of the Nanu Oya, the *Race*

Course with golf course, polo field and other sports grounds, and the buildings of the United Club. *Gregory's Lake* was made by damming up the stream (dam, 15m high), and was called after the governor of that name. To the N. of the undulating *Moon Plains* is a second artificial lake, *Barrack Plains Reservoir* (dam 30m high).

The mountain slopes are still mainly covered with jungle, since clearing for tea estates (which latter have already reached here) is now no longer allowed (see p.16). Because of its altitude and humidity, the forest has a character all its own. The leaves are dark in colour, mostly leathery, tough and shiny, the trunks gnarled, the bark covered in lichens and mosses. Commonest are the calophyllums (p.19), whose fresh leaves with their red tones remind one of blossom, and rhododendrons, which grow into trees 3-4m high. One also finds imported eucalyptus, acacias and wattles.

WALKS & EXCURSIONS. – To Single Tree Hill, only on foot, 1½-2hrs. return (do not set out too late in the afternoon, as the return is difficult after the rapid onset of darkness). About 300m S. of Scandal Corner, on the way to *St Agatha's School*, one follows the signpost (r.) "One Tree Hill" (further on, a second one: "To Single Tree"), and reaches a tea plantation (r., a high waterfall on the mountain). Follow zigzag paths up through the plantations to the saddle of the ridge which forms the S. boundary of the Nuwara Eliya valley. Here, l. up the terraced hillside planted with tea as far as a few scattered trees, where the *view is open on both sides: NNE, the bare summit of Pidarattallagalla with a cross on the top; N., at one's feet, the Nuwara Eliya valley, l. the main cluster of houses, in the middle the green expanse of the Golf Links, r. the playing fields and Gregory's Lake, with Moon Plains beyond; SE, the twin peaks of Hakgalla Rock (p.49), in the distance the uplands of Uva (p.51) and, in the foreground far r., the road and railway to Nanuoya; to S. and W. one looks out across the tea-growing districts of Pandaloya, Dimbula and Dickoya to the picturesque mountain chain, out of which rises, approx. 35km away, the sharp pyramid of Adam's Peak. – The view from the trigonometrical point on the actual summit (good path SE in 10min) is rather hampered by vegetation.

Another walk on the S. side of the valley leads to *Lady's Waterfall*, a set of rapids in the Nanu Oya below Gregory's Lake: on the far side of the playing fields turn r. to Blackpool Bridge, from there up the l. bank or r. bank (prettier), 1½-2hrs. return.

To Rambodda Pass, at the NW end of the upland valley: about 5km, 1hr. on foot, carriage, see p.46. Easy road on the r. bank of the Nanu Oya past the Golf Links (r.) and Queen's Cottage (l.), ascending slowly. About half-way (l.) a small Buddhist temple with a dagaba. On through tea estates, with a beautiful forest of calophyllums above. The view from the top of the pass (about 2000m) is famous, and especially delightful at sunset: W., the Kotmale valley, the plantations of Pandaloya, Dimbula and Dickoya and Adam's Peak; E., the valley of Nuwara Eliya with the romantic Rock of Hakgalla (p.49) in the background. The good road permits one to return even after nightfall.

Pidaratallagalla (Engl. abbr. *Pedro*; 2538m), the highest mountain in Ceylon, can be climbed by paths (1½-2hrs.) that are mostly easy, but in several places severely fissured. The name means "matmakers' mountain" from the rushes growing at its foot, which are used in basketwork. Since the mist, which lies early in the valley, surrounds the summit in the daytime, one should set out while it is still dark, with guide and lantern, which the hotel can provide. One can dispense with a guide by day.

The path branches, beyond National Bank and a small bridge, r. down Cross St., at the end of which is a signpost marked "To Pedro". Ascend through the wood which, about halfway up, takes on a decidedly high-altitude appearance: the trees become lower, and creepers, mosses and lichens increase.

The summit is bare, the highest point marked by a round cairn with a flagpole in the form of a cross. The *view is magnificent, and the play of the clouds in the valley most attractive. The sea is visible to W. and E. To the E., Namunukula dominates the landscape; to the SW., Adam's Peak (both p.51).

The excursion to Hakgalla (6½M SE) requires a carriage (p.46), 2½-3hrs. return. The road follows the S. shore of Gregory's Lake, crosses the outlet of the Nanu Oya, rises to the watershed and gradually descends through a gully overgrown with rhododendrons and ferns to a spot where the valley broadens and, l., one sees a small shrine of the partly Tamil uplanders (approx. 5km from Nuwara Eliya). Beyond a second tree-filled gully, a surprising *view opens up of the approx. 40km-wide basin between the Pidarattallagalla group and the heights of Badulla (p.51), which collects the waters of a few E. tributaries of the Mahawelliganga; rising suddenly near the road, the twin summits of the *Rock of Hakgalla* (2100m); further on, r., the long Haputale ridge (p.50); straight ahead, E., Namunukula (p.51) and the grassy expanses of the patanas (p.16), which make the shape of the mountain stand out as if in relief; far below, terraced paddy-fields; to the SE, the white roofs of the former Boer camp (p.51). – an avenue of Casuarinas (with leafless branches) leads to the entrance of the gardens.

Hakgalla Experimental Gardens (1650m above sea-level), the second largest botanical gardens on the island, cover 226 hectares, of which only one seventh is cultivated. Sited on the borderline between upland and lowland climates, it is used for acclimatisation experiments with foreign, also European, useful plants. The use of the natural milieu and the existing forest gives the gardens great appeal. At the administrative building, outside which the carriage stops, one finds native keepers who act as guides (tip 1R.) Do not miss the pretty forest garden with its labyrinthine paths, the area around the pond and the picnic place, which latter offers the finest panorama. Scholars may stay at the administration buildings (1R. per day).

The road continues to Badulla (37M from Nuwara Eliya; by carriage 7-9hrs., approx. 40R.): 13M from Nuwara Eliya, *Wilson's Bungalow* (good Rest-house) and the village *Welimada;* one descends, crossing the *Uma Oya* by a lattice bridge, then ascends again; 26M *Etampitiya* (1055m; Rest-house, order lunch in advance); on an eminence (1200m), a Buddhist dagaba and an abandoned Sinhalese fort from pre-English times; then down to Badulla (p.51).

From (*Nuwara Eliya)* Nanuoya to Badulla. – Railway to *Bandarawela,* 32M, in 3¼hrs., for 3R.96, 2R.61cts.: from there to *Badulla,* 18M, main road, post in 3hrs.

Nanuoya, see p.45. – The railway ascends in a luxuriant green rocky valley via (9M) *Ambawela* (1848m) to (11M) *Pattipola* (1903m; Rest-house), starting-point for the excursion to World's End.

One asks the station master for a coolie as bearer and guide. The path passes through splendid jungle to *Horton Plains,* rich in game, a plateau rising slowly S. about 35km from Hakgalla and then dropping abruptly to the lowland plain. The forest contains many Nillu trees, the favourite food of wild elephants. Now and again there are stretches of patanas. In about 2½hrs. one reaches the *Government Rest-house* (2200m), where one can find good food (also quarters for the night), provided written notice is sent several days ahead. From here, continuing through the jungle, it is about ¾hr. to *World's End, where one suddenly stands before a sheer drop of some 1500m, unsurpassed in its steepness anywhere on earth. The view over the lowlands of S. Ceylon is overwhelmingly magnificent. The little house (Atkinson Bungalow), seen immediately below, is only 685m above sea-level. The transition from sub-tropical to tropical vegetation is clearly perceived. There is a second "World's End" ¼hr., to the NE. – One can return, firstly by an easy path through grassland to the edge of the plateau, then by descending steeply through thick forest to Ohiya (see below).

A tunnel cuts through the watershed between the W. and E. headwaters of the Mahawelliganga. At its exit, an astonishing view of the mountainous country of the province Uva. – 15M. *Ohiya* (1799m), also a starting-point for World's End (shorter but steeper path).

25M. *Haputale* (1452m; good Rest-house), centre of a tea-growing district, with 500 inhab.; near the station a splendid view, similar to the one from World's End: to the E. over the undulating grassy patanas (p.16), above which float picturesque cloud-formations during the NW monsoon; to S. and SE over the blue mass of jungle far below, extending to the sea; to the W., the mighty shapes of the edge of the high mountains.

From Haputale to Ratnapura, 51M, a most rewarding car drive (see p.24). The road descends in tight bends along the abrupt mountainside, with splendid views over the dusky blue lowlands to the sea, quite steeply to (8M) *Haldumulla* (1023; simple Rest-house). Then, less steeply, through tea and occasional coffee plantations, past pretty villages. Rice cultivation begins, and one sees areca and kitul palms once more. – 16M. *Belihuloya* (570m; good Rest-house) by a rushing torrent in a basin, open to the W., that possesses tropical vegetation in wonderful abundance. Finally, across the *Welawa Ganga*. – 24M. *Balangoda* (522m; excellently equipped Rest-house). The fertility of the soil increases, as does the number of settlements. Several fine views back over the low foothills to the serrated mountain peaks. The marshy banks of the *Weganga*, which the road follows closely for a while, are alive with buffalo and herons, parrots, kingfishers and monkeys. Here and there one sees pits where gems are extracted. At (40M) *Pelmadulla* Rest-house), the landscape becomes flatter and more open. Finally, across an iron suspension bridge over the *Kalu Ganga*. – 51M. *Ratnapura* p.33.

At *Diyatalawa* (1331m) is the summer camp for English troops; during the Boer War, 5000 prisoners were kept here in barracks. – 32M. *Bandarawela* (1230m; good Rest-house), with 1450 inhab., popular hill station, and rly terminus.

The post road, winding and partly hewn out of the rock, descends to the well-watered valley of the *Badulla Oya,* above which one sights, to the E., the steep Namunukula (2036), to (18M):-

Badulla (638m; good, roomy Rest-house), capital of the province *Uva*, with 6500 inhab., English and R.C. churches, a large hospital and Buddhist and Hindu temples. The cemetery by the English church contains, among others, the grave of a Mrs Wilson who died in 1817, and whose tombstone is tightly enwrapped in the aerial roots of an Indian fig-tree. Outside the town, many tea estates, paddy-fields, jaks, mangoes, fig-trees and palms. The Race Course goes round a small lake. In the vicinity, a pleasure (formerly botanical) garden. Pretty excursion to *Dunhinda Falls* (10km, with guide).

Adam's Peak.

This excursion takes 2-2½ days, either from Kandy or Nuwara Eliya. Best seasons: October and December to March. From the rly. sta. *Hatton* (p.45) a mail coach leaves after the arrival of the important trains, approx. 2 p.m., for *Laxapana* (in 2hrs., return seat 14R.) Return the next day at 3 p.m., staying in Hatton. Pleasanter, and no more expensive for 3 people, is to have one's own car (27R. return) with which one can connect with the afternoon train for Nuwara Eliya the next day. For both methods of travel, one should reserve by telegraph at least one day in advance, with the hotel manager or with Pates Livery Stables at Hatton. The actual ascent (4hrs. up, 3½ down) is no more exacting for mountain walkers free from vertigo, than ordinary Alpine walking. One must have stout walking shoes or boots; one will also appreciate leggings, a change of underclothing and a warm coat or rug for the summit; for night ascents, a cap is useful; for day ascents, a pith helmet, everything else being provided by the landlord at Laxapana, to whom one should also telegraph one's arrival time: guide (3R.), coolies with lanterns as bearers (1R.50 each), lights (50cts.), a bamboo cane as a walking-stick (may be loaned, 25cts.), and provisions (tea, toast, eggs, 1R.25cts.)

Adam's Peak (2241m), a steep gneiss pyramid, wooded to the summit, rising alone out of one of the mountain chains in the SW of the Ceylon uplands, is admittedly not the highest (p.15), but because of its striking shape, visible over great distances, has been the most famous mountain on the island from time immemorial. A mark in the rock at its summit (similar to the Rosstrappe in the Harz mountains) has endowed it with a religious significance and made it a place of pilgrimage for the faithful of three religions: the Buddhists see in it the footprint of Buddha who, after propagating his teaching left the island again from this spot; the Hindus connect it with Shiva or Vishnu; the Mohammedans attribute the mark to Adam, whom the archangel set down here after his expulsion from Paradise. The mountain is mentioned as a holy place in the Mahawansa chronicle (p.21) around 150 B.C. by its Sinhalese name *Samanala.* The legend about Adam is pre-Mohammedan, mentioned already in a Coptic ms. of the 4th c. A.D. Ceylonese sources of the 13th c. report a new access route to the summit. The Venetian *Marco Polo,* who called at Ceylon in 1293, reports that the mountain was only climbable with the help of fixed chains. The Arab *Ibn Batuta,* who was on the summit in 1340, saw both the chains and the rock steps, which still exist.

From Hatton to Laxapana, 14M., excellent road. First through the valley of a tributary of the Kelani Ganga (p.32) down to *Dickoya,* a bustling place among excellently managed tea estates. Adam's Peak is glimpsed only once more. Then in a romantic ravine over the water-course and descending in cleverly engineered curves to the E. edge of the main valley to (6M) the *bridge over the Kelani Ganga.* Beyond the bridge, in *Norwood,* change of horses and carriages for the mail coach. Now uphill again and, with ever more superb views of the Peak to the r., on through prosperous tea plantations to (12M) *Maskeliya,* another lively place. 2M further on, the little town of:-

Laxapana (about 1250m), where *Peak View Hotel* offers very decent accommodation for 10 pers. and food (Rm. 1½, with 2 Bd. 3½, B. 2¼, L. 2, D. 3R.; "Peak arrangements", see p.51). One should have an early dinner and retire immediately. One is woken at midnight, and the march begins at 1 a.m. One should ascertain that everything carried by the bearers is protected from the wet.

The ascent (4hrs.) begins on a good bridle-path, which winds upwards through the plantations towards Maskeliya and, beyond an iron bridge, continues on the r. bank. After 1¾hrs., one reaches the narrow and bad pilgrim path, which often only the guide can make out. A few giant blocks of gneiss, towering like roofs, serve exhausted pilgrims as shelter in bad weather. After a further ½hr., at the foot of the mountain-face upon which sits the summit pyramid, one crosses the ravine of the stream *Sita Gangula,* full of tree ferns. Now begins the most difficult part of the ascent, over loose pebbles and tree roots in the virgin forest. One should take great care where one places one's feet, and allow the guide to assist. The place where, after 1hr., one reaches the top of the rock-face, is called *Indikatupana* and is marked by Rest-houses (ambalams) for pilgrims. The summit pyramid is surrounded by a thick profusion of myrtle, laurel, magnolias, rhododendrons etc., which protect one from giddiness on ascent and descent. In many places, irregular steps are cut in the rock and, in the steepest places, iron rails or chains are fixed. After ¾hr. appears a small pool r. ("Adam's Tears"), from which the coolies fetch fresh water for making tea. Immediately below the summit, 10min higher, a few hovels offer protection from rain and cold, and the opportunity to change one's underclothing. A small flight of steps leads to the very top.

The summit is a small area of about 25 paces in an irregular square, and surrounded by a low whitewashed wall. In the N. corner, four small bells hang on frames; in the S., the pilgrims' path from Ratnapura ends here (see below). In the centre, a 4m-high (approx.) mass of rock juts out, upon which (beneath an open pavilion) is visible the holy footprint, the *Sri-pada* of the Buddhists. The impression in the rock is 1·62m long and 0·74-0·79m wide; an added stone edging and weak painting-in of the shape support the fancy; it is a left foot, the toes facing the onlooker, and extending a little beyond the protective railing; a slight rise, where the ball of the foot should make a depression, proves that the artifice of Man has assisted but little. Priests and guardians are up here mostly only from January to April. The ancient shrine is open to everyone. The faithful offer blossoms, fruit incense, etc. – The **view, if the sunrise is unobscured, is of indescribable magnificence. As soon as the sun comes up, one can often see, to the W., the famous shadow of the summit, which stands out in the form of a gigantic triangle on the fine morning vapour. One seems to hover like a bird over the white ocean of mist which covers the depths. All around, a fantastic labyrinth of jagged mountain chains and fertile valleys. Pidarattallagalla rises out of the mighty mountain group to E. and NE. (p.48). To the ESE the group to which belong Horton Plains (p.50). To the W., one can make out the long coastal strip, to the WNW Colombo, to the ENE, far below, Laxapana; to the SE, the coastal lagoons of Hambantota (p.65).

The descent in daylight discovers new delights, but is rather exhausting. In any case, one should not begin too late, so as to avoid the midday heat.

The descent to Ratnapura (p.33) is advisable only for strong walkers who are quite free from giddiness (8-10hrs.) On the way one passes 5 government Rest-houses, of which *Palabathara,* not quite half-way, is the most important. Here, and 2hrs. further on at *Gillemala,* are Buddhist temples and tame elephants.

Route 5. From Colombo or Kandy to Anuradhapura.

Railway from Colombo or Kandy. – From Colombo: 127M, (*Main Line* to Polgahawela Junc.: from there, *Northern Line)* in 6⅓-6⅔hrs., for 10R.20, 6R.80cts. In the dining car of the morning train breakfast is served (2R.) as far as Polgahawela; for continuation and for the afternoon train one should provide one's own refreshments. Since the route remains in the lowlands, one does not need warmer clothing. – On the rail journey from Kandy, one often has a long stop at Polgahawela. The car drive via Dambulla is more rewarding (see p.55).

From Colombo to *Polgahawela Junc.* (see p.34). change coaches. Because of the sun, sit on the l. in the morning and r. in the afternoon. The following distances are given from Polgahawela.

The Northern Line runs through open, flat country which is dotted with occasional rocky heights, like islands. This area was once the main territory of the Sinhalese people until the Tamils invaded and, by neglecting the irrigation works, allowed it to revert to a wilderness (p.22). The energy of the English, their road-building and railways, their restoration of the old tanks and regulation of the water-courses, - all this is helping the progression towards winning back the culture of this country. In jungle clearings, villages, rice-fields and other plantations are coming into being.

13M. *Kurunagalla,* capital of the NW. province, with 7800 inhab., surrounded by cocoa, rubber, tea and coconut palm plantations. In the vicinity, numerous graphite mines.

The region becomes lonely, the stations further apart, the settlements hidden in the bushes. The palmyra is seen more frequently than at Colombo (p.18). Beyond (19M) *Wellawa,* the land is quite flat, a single primeval jungle, in which millions of white and coloured butterflies swarm during the daylight hours. The line often crosses water-courses incl., before (26M) *Ganewatta,* the *Dederu Oya.* The telegraph wires are fixed to iron poles, since the wooden ones are destroyed by white ants. – 40M. *Maha,* 47M. *Ambanpola,* 53M. *Galgamuwa.* Cow pastures, rice-fields, banana and maize plantations, tanks and a few coconut palms announce the proximity of human settlements. – Before (72M) *Talawa,* the line crosses the *Kala Oya* (r. a sawmill). Finally over the *Malwatte Oya* to (81M) *Anuradhapura* (p.56).

From Kandy by road via Damballa. - 86M, railway to *Matale*, 21M, in 1hr., for 1R.44cts, 96cts.; from there with the Trincomalee Post (p.64) to *Dambulla,* 28¾M in 4½hrs. for 6R. (Reserve seats in advance). On to

Anuradhapura, 45M, no Post connection; one resorts to the car, which one takes in Kandy (p.24). The road from Kandy to Matale goes over the beautiful *Matale* or *Balkaduwa Pass.*

The continuation of the railway mentioned on p.35 crosses the *Mahawelliganga* by an iron bridge after *Mahayava* on the edge of Kandy, skirts *Katugastota* and two unimportant stations, and reaches the terminus at:-

Matale (368m; good Rest-house), town of 5400 inhab., with a large bazaar, English chuch etc., starting-point for the Post to Trincomalee, which connects with the early train (p.64).

2M to the N., on the l. of the road, and in jungle, the rock temple of *Alu Vihara,* containing wall paintings of the kind described on p.38. Extensive view from the top of the rock.

The road to Dambulla (29M) descends through tea, cocoa and rubber estates and rice-fields. Approx. half-way it touches *Nalanda,* with a prettily situated Rest-house. Approaching Dambulla, one sees the long form of the dark temple rock.

Dambulla (good Rest-house) is famous for its five rock temples (dedicated for 2 millennia to the service of Buddha) which were constructed by the Sinhalese King Walagum Bahu (p.57), who had taken refuge here during the Tamil overlordship. If warned in advance, the keeper of the Rest-house arranges a guide and asks the priest to have the keys ready.

A stepped path leads up to the temples in 20-25min (170m, approx. 30m below the summit); fine view over the plains to the N. (NE, the rock of Sigiriya, see p.64) and the uplands to the S. One enters the forecourt through a rough brick gateway and sees, immediately r., a long inscription recalling King Siri Nissanka (1192 A.D.) A wall 18m high, in front of which a wooden gallery runs along above the drop, forms the outside face of the cave temples. The first temple, *Deva Raja Vihara* or "temple of the prince-god", contains among other things, a statue of the recumbent Buddha, 14m long and carved out of the rock, at whose head is a much-revered wooden figure of Vishnu, proof of the way in which Hinduism and Buddhism have become intermingled in Ceylon through the ages; Buddhist painting on the ceiling. The second temple, *Maha Vihara* or "large monastery", 50m long, 15m wide, 7m high at the front but only 1.4m at the back, owes its adornment especially to King Siri Nissanka. The rock roof is covered in material which is painted with religious and historical pictures. On the l., a giant dagaba surrounded by seated Buddhas, partly beneath cobra-shaped baldaquins. In the rock floor nearby, a water basin used for consecration, in which drips from the rock collect. The temple contains 53 statues, incl. l. behind the dagaba, that of King Walagum Bahu. The wall-paintings include: opposite the entrance, King Dutthagamini's fight with the Tamil conqueror Ellala (p.61); in a niche in the rock at the E. end, the landing of the Indian prince Wijayo, legendary founder of the Sinhalese empire; and the introduction of Buddhism to Ceylon; on the S. side, not far from the niche, the king Kirti Siri Nissanka. The three other temples also contain numerous statues, but are of less interest.

From Dambulla to Anuradhapura, the road passes at first through rice-fields, then almost completely through thick jungle rich in game, past a very few small Tamil villages. It crosses the *Mirisgoni Oya,* leaves the Trincomalee road to the r. (p.64) and, with a distant view r. of the rock of Rittigala (794m), reaches the (13M) Rest-house *Kekirawa.* Continue via (20½M) *Maradankawala,* (26¾M), *Tirappane* (Rest-house) to (30¾M) *Galkulam,* where the great S.-N. road continues towards Mihintale (p.62) and, l., a secondary road branches off to (45M) *Anuradhapura.*

Anuradhapura.

STATION 2km to the E. of the town: carriage (reserve in advance by telegraph) 1R.; if one uses it further, immediately, one pays the hourly tariff. On the journey one catches sight of two green hills: l. the Ruanwelli Dagaba (p.59), r. the Abhayagirya Dagaba (p.61). Beyond the bridge across the Malwatte Oya one reaches, at the so-called Brazen Palace, the "Via Sacra", into which one turns, see p.59.

HOTELS (rooms should be booked in advance by telegraph with pre-paid reply; busiest time for visitors, Dec. to March): Anuradhapura Hot., near the Botanical Gdns (p.60), about 15 Rm., mostly twin-bedded, the best on the first floor, 2½R., good cuisine; Govt. Rest-house, 100m r. from the *Via Sacra;* in the garden a paved pillared courtyard has been excavated, to which stairs lead up, and a handsome large granite trough.

CARRIAGES. One-horse (1st & 2nd cl., latter ¼ cheaper): within the town boundary ½hr. 50cts., 1hr. 1R., each successive hr. 25cts., 6hrs. 2R., all day 4R.; outside the town, 50cts. per mile. Two-horse, half as much again. From 7.30 p.m. to 6 a.m. prices rise by ⅓. – POST OMNIBUS to Trincomalee (see p.63) in 6½hrs.; uncomfortable bus: 8 seats, only light hand-luggage permitted; fare 20R., for native servants 10R. (The manager of Anuradhapura Hotel, in front of which the omnibus stops at 1 p.m., issues tickets); departure from the sta. 1½hrs. after the arrival of the morning train from Colombo. There is an opportunity for snacks at intermediate sta.

Native GUIDES receive 1½R. for half a day, 3R. for a whole day.

FOR LIMITED VISITS (1½-2 days): two perambulations, *Inner Circular* and *Outer Circular Road*, see p.58, and excursion to *Mihintale* (p.62), all three half a day each. The inner circuit may be done on foot also (3-4hrs.), but not advisable on the day of one's arrival when one is still tired from the railway journey. The circuit of the outer road takes about 2hrs., but the distances here are too great for walkers. – At full moon the ruins are picturesquely thronged with pilgrims, men and women neatly dressed, monks in saffron robes; they prostrate themselves at the shrines, say their prayers, make offerings of flowers etc. The main time of pilgrimage falls in June and July.

Anuradhapura (90m), the oldest royal seat of the Sinhalese, the holy city of Buddhism, now reawakening through the restoration of the old tanks after more than a thousand years of desolation, is the capital of the North-Central province and seat of the Government Agent, with 4,700 (mainly Tamil) inhab., and English and R.C. churches. Since the opening of the railway, the number of Buddhist pilgrims has increased, as has the number of inhabitants. An enormous quantity of ruined buildings, some of giant dimensions, manifest Anuradhapura's former glory and richness, and make it one of the most remarkable ruined cities on Earth.

The name ("Anuradha town") is said to hark back to a legendary warrior of the first Sinhalese conquerors (p.22). The historical era begins with the introduction of Buddhism, under King *Devanampiya Tissa* in the 3rd c. B.C., who accorded the missionary Mahinda (p.LIV) and his companions a generous reception. He apportioned a palace to the monks and, for the rainy season, the hill of Mihintale (p.63). The marking-off of the area for the sacred Bo-tree (p.58) and the construction of the Thuparama Dagaba (p.60) also belong to that era. With the prosperity of the city grew the covetousness of the Tamils making inroads from S .India (p.22). The bold king *Dutthagamini* (161-137 B.C.), who drove back the enemy, adorned his liberated capital with new buildings, of which the Ruanwelli Dagaba (p.59) and the Brazen Palace (p.59) were acclaimed by the chroniclers to be wonders of the world. Among his successors, *Walagum Bahu* (104-77 B.C.) attained particular eminence, building the enormous *Abhayagirya Dagaba* after 15 years of dispossession by the Tamils (p.55). Alternating glory and decline fill the next centuries. Even the Buddhist religion was at times in peril. Under the influence of the newly strengthened Brahmanism (see p.XLIX), it seems, king *Maha Sen* (275-302 A.D.), the last scion of the Lion dynasty (p.22), had many temples destroyed but later, since he could not break down the resistance of the people, reconstructed them in even greater splendour than before, adding the Jetawanarama Dagaba (p.62). Besides this, he laid out numerous lakes, particularly that of Minneriya (p.65). At the end of his reign, the tooth of Buddha (p.38) was brought from N. India to Anuradhapura (p.89), to save it from the Brahmans, and the first temple was built for it. The Chinese monk Fa Hien, who visited the city in the year 404, has given us an excellent description of it. Envoys were exchanged with Rome (Ptolemy mentions the city as Anurogrammum Regia). A good deal of quarrelling about succession filled the 5th c. In 846, the seat of government was transferred to Polonnaruha (p.65). Only once more, under *Parakrama Bahu I* (The Great, 1164-97; see p.66) was Anuradhapura cleared of the encroaching jungle. Then the holy city was subject to a steady and continual decline, remaining just a place of pilgrimage. Only since 1827 have European travellers brought it back to some prominence.

At present, the scientific investigations are being led by *H.C.P.Bell,* the Archaeological Commissioner.

The ruins cover an area of more than 4 sq.km, much of which is still hidden by jungle. Only a part has been cleared, largely at government expense. The Buddhist natives are also participating in the restoration of individual buildings. Most important are the *dagabas,* consisting of a square stone base upon which stands a bell-shaped massive structure rising to a point. They served as repositories for relics of Buddha and they assume at Anuradhapura, in part at least, the most mighty dimensions known to the Buddhist world. There are numerous *pillared halls,* formerly roofed over, artistic bathing-pools called *pokunas,* also individual carved pieces such as *stone troughs* of purpose unknown; *stone slabs,* like sarcophagi; and so-called *moonstones,* semi-circular slabs, richly ornamented, before the steps of the entrance gates. The dagabas are essentially brick stuctures. For the carvings, granite from the neighbourhood has been used. The buildings display little variation, architecturally speaking; their noble simplicity and tasteful execution do not, however, fail to make an impression. – Two drives, *Inner Circular Road* and *Outer Circular Road,* enclose an inner area and a northern outer area.

The inner area now resembles a superb English park with solitary trees and extensive lawns, across which the numerous ruins are spread. The centre is occupied by the Precinct of Great Sanctity, not far from the intersection of *Ayton Rd.* (from the sta.), *Puttalam Rd.* (running W., see p.60) and the *Via Sacra* (see below).

Maha Vihara, a walled-in enclosure of the holy Bo-tree. The entrance gate, an ugly modern structure, the result of native attempts at restoration, arches over a beautiful old moonstone with incised decoration (in the outer curve, elephant, horse, buffalo, lion; in the inner one, the holy goose; lotus blossom in between). The hard granite material shows minimal wear even after 2000 years of being walked on. The garden is filled with holy fig-trees and palms. Immediately r., a large fig-tree, among whose branches a splendid palmyra palm is growing out. The treetops are peopled by monkeys. In the interior of the garden, stairs lead to the triple whitewashed *Terrace of the Holy Bo-tree.* The string-boards bear peculiar ornamentation: the railing issues from the jaws of a mythological beast; effigies of sentinels (called Dvarpal) are arched over by the nine-headed holy naga snake. The holy tree (Ficus religiosa, p.19) itself looks rather woebegone. According to chronicle, it was planted here as an offshoot of the holy tree of Buddha Gaya (p.229) in 245 B.C., and revered on the same spot through all the subsequent centuries. Since the Bo-tree propagates itself by means of aerial roots, its constant self-renewal down to the present time is quite possible, botanically speaking. Its discarded leaves are sold by the priest (1R. suffices).

At the Maha Vihara, the Sacred Road (Via Sacra), shaded by beautiful trees, debouches from the N. This cuts through the N. part of the inner ruined area and, for the last 2000 years, has been the road along which pilgrims approach the holy tree. Immediately to the r., beyond Ayton Rd., (p.58), a strange forest of pillars, ruins of the so-called Brazen Palace, a building designed for the priesthood.

The Brazen Palace (Sinh. Lohapasada*),* erected by Dutthagamini (who was so fond of building, p.57), rose, if one can believe the Mahawansa chronicle, upon 1600 granite columns clad with brass plates, to a height of nine storeys, and was roofed over with copper. No less magnificent was the adornment of the interior with silver, gold and gems. The high priest's throne was of ivory, and the vessels in which the monks washed their hands and feet, of gold. After being destroyed several times, the palace was renewed again by Parakrama Bahu (p.57). The pillars (coarse-cut monoliths) are arranged in 40 rows, on average 3½m tall, forming a square with a side of more than 60m. The corner pillars are twice as massive as the others. The columns increase in strength towards the centre also, so that one can deduce that the entire building was pyramid-shaped, the chief load being in the centre (cf.p.171). – On the N. side of the Brazen Palace, the road to Trincomalee via Mihintale branches off eastwards (see pp.62-3).

On the Via Sacra, beyond the road on which the Rest-house lies, a white-painted pavilion, l., indicates the entrance to the:-

Ruanwelli Dagaba, the mighty victory monument of Dutthagamini (p.57), completed in 140 B.C., destroyed for the last time by the Tamils in 1214 A.D., but still over 60m tall and 115m broad, presently being restored thanks to contributions from pilgrims, to which one may add a small sum. Through a restored gateway, then past a large round pokuna on the r. (p.58) and through a second gate, one reaches the base upon which the round masonry structure towers up. It was originally covered in its entirety with shining white plaster. Around it stood a circle of elephant figures with genuine ivory tusks. The upper stage of the base has a frieze depicting lions. Near the NE. corner of the outer enclosure is an enormous monolithic granite column. On the S. side, five standing stone effigies and one seated, making a strangely serious impression upon the beholder; the largest figure is said to represent Dutthagamini himself. Altars are positioned at the four points of the compass, the best preserved being on the W. side. In the wall decoration one can make out a nine-headed naga. The interior of the building contains relics of Buddha, golden images and other treasures, which were only accessible by a secret passage.

Opposite, on the E. side of the road, one sees a seat, shaped like a sarcophagus, on two pillars where, according to legend, King Dutthagamini died within sight of his works. – A few steps to the SE a well-preserved and beautifully carved *urinal,* to which a small flight of steps leads (the pictures on the horizontal slab give a clue to the reconstruction of the strange groups of columns which one often encounters in Anurahapura).

About 500m N., the *Inner Circular Road,* which one should take, branches off l. from the Via Sacra. To the r., a large stone basin. Near this, a block of stone with a funnel-shaped depression, which is regarded as a receptacle for dyeing priests' garments. To the l., noticeable on account of its brightness visible at a great distance, the white:-

Thuparama Dagaba, the oldest and holiest Buddhist monument in Ceylon, in which was preserved the Buddha's left jawbone. According to Fergusson, it is probably the oldest preserved structure in all India. It foundation dates back to King Devanampiya Tissa (p.57). The restoration was carried out by native priests in the middle of the 19th c. The building is 19m high, and is surrounded by three rows of beautifully carved monolithic columns, the inner row 7m tall, the outer 4m. Its circumference measures some 250 paces. – The ruined buildings nearby to the SE are the remains of the first Palace of the Tooth *(Dalada Maligawa,* see p.38), built by King Sri Meghavarna. – On the W. side of the dagaba, one sees fine capitals lying in the grass.

The Inner Circular road turns S. and, further on, climbs the retaining wall of the great lake *Bassa Kulam* ("kulam" is Tamil for "pool"), in which crocodiles live. To the l., numerous pillared halls in ruins and a view of the Ruanwelli and Abhayagirya dagabas (pp.59, 61). The road passes through the E. part of the modern town, then along a causeway between two lakes to Puttalam Road. The lakes belong to a group of water basins arranged in a stepped formation, fed by the Tissa Wewa and used by the population for bathing and washing. – The continuation of Inner Circular Road leads into the *Experimental Garden*, which contains some fine pandanus trees.

We follow Puttalam Rd. W. and cross the small canal, which brings water to the topmost of the basins mentioned above. Immediately beyond the whitewashed *Jail,* a road forks r. to the *Miriswetti Dagaba* which was restored at the expense of a Siamese prince. It was an expiatory temple, erected by Dutthagamini, because he had eaten egg-fruit without putting aside the priest's portion. The chapel on the W. side has fine carvings. About 75m to the W., one sees 62 large columns (37 well maintained), presumably of a priestly dwelling in the style of the Brazen Palace. – One can return along Puttalam Rd., eastwards through the town bazaar to the Via Sacra (p.58; 10min).

The following walk is also recommended, taking about 1hr. Go W. along Puttalam Rd., and, branching l. about 6min past the Jail, continue to the E. bund of the large lake called Tissa Wewa ("wewa" is Sinhalese for "pool"), and thence along the wall for about 20min to the rock temple:-

Isurumuniya, an odd place dating from the reign of King Devanampiya Tissa (approx. 300 B.C.) On the outer walls of the upper terrace, 15 low reliefs have been chiselled out of the rock; noteworthy, on the S. wall, a group of 3 women, a man and a servant; nearby, 3 seated men, grotesquely formed; on the N. wall 3 figures, of which one plays a musical instrument etc. The stone gate, too, is beautiful. There are various modern additions, incl. the temple building itself, which a priest will unlock. The figure of Buddha within, 1½m high, is old, but freshly painted. On the E. side of the rock, a flight of steps leads to the top, on which an imitation of the Sri-pada (p.53) has recently been cut.

The paved way to the E. of the rock temple joins the Kurunagalla road, which one follows northwards. On the l., an excavated hill, the so-called *Tomb of Ellala*, the Tamil king who was beaten by Dutthagamini, and the ruins of the so-called *Peacock Palace,* with pretty carvings. At a three-armed signpost one reaches Ayton Rd. (p.58), to the W. of Maha Vihara.

The *Outer Circular Road* (carriage, see p.56), begins just a few mins E. of the Rest-house in Trincomalee Rd. (p.59), where a signpost gives direction. Soon one sees, r., the ruins of a base, with the recently re-erected parts of a fine stone balustrade. To the l., the:-

Abhayagirya Dagaba, an extremely effective structure, erected in 89 B.C. by Walagum Bahu (p.57) as a monument to his victory over the Tamils. It original height of 123m matched that of the dome of St Peter's in Rome, without the lantern, and competed with the pyramids at Gizeh (pyramid of Cheops now 137m, originally 146; third pyramid 62, formerly 66m). To execute it now with our modern technical aids would occupy a team of 500 workmen for 6-7 years. Destroyed and ruinous, the structure was threatened with total collapse, until the English began their restoration work. The present height of the dome above the platform is 70m, with a diameter of 99m at its base. The altars at the four compass points are larger than those of the Ruanwell Dagaba and, in part, of very fine workmanship, e.g. the naga stone on the W. side. One should take one's time over the ascent, which is extremely rewarding but somewhat arduous: on the E. side to the r. of the altar, one makes one's way over piles of broken brick up to the restored wall; then, inside, up 92 steps to the upper platform, above which rises the truncated spire. The *panorama is wonderful, especially in the evening light: in the foreground, rice-fields, large and small lakes, roads, with innumerable dagabas sprinkled all about; in the background, the limitless jungle with isolated rock towers so typical of N. Ceylon; to the E., the rock of Mihintale (p.63).

The road continues N. for 2km and then bears W. Here, r., the great *Kuttam pokuna,* a fine double bathing-pool more than 40m long and 15m wide (the E. side of the first pool is restored). Further r. and l. in the jungle a number of old sculptures, incl, l., a large *seated Buddha,* a strange sight beneath the trees. The road skirts round the mighty *Jetawanarama Dagaba*, from the end of King Maha Sen's reign (p.57), with a lower diameter of 93m, and as yet undisturbed by excavation work. Then follows, r., a vihara, *Maha Sen's Pavilion,* with a superb *moonstone (p.57) at the foot of the steps: the best example of these chiselled granite slabs. Everywhere in the forest, groups of stone pillars appear, of which a particularly large example is described by the local people as an elephant stall. Curving to the S., the road passes the so-called *stone canoe*, a giant granite trough. The small pavilion in the middle of the curve is an attempt at reconstruction. To the r., a pillared hall, called the *Queen's Pavilion* and, further on, the *Tomb of Dutthagamini* (p.57).

The Outer Circular Road then describes a wide arc around the W. end of the ruined city without however offering any more objects of particular interest. It is therefore usual to return by the road branching off to the l., a few min. beyond Dutthagamini's Tomb. To the l., in the forest, a dilapidated *pokuna* of especially large dimensions, then, l., the *Lankarama Dagaba*, then again, to the r., *King Ellala's Chapel* and the Thuparama Dagaba (p.60).

The *excursion to Mihintale (8M, carriage 8R.) is recommended, whose holy remains, much overgrown by jungle, possess a fantastic charm. The road (p.59; suitable also for cyclists in fine weather) follows the bund of the extensive lake Nuwara Wewa, then through thick jungle past numerous ant-hills. After about 1hr. the carriage halts at the *Mihintale Rest-house,* where one can order a meal for one's return from the hill.

Continue on foot along the road for about 4min to its intersection with the N-S. road (p.56). Follow the signpost r. towards Matale, walk through the hamlet of Mihintale and, after about 3min, take the path which branches l. Cross a small wooden bridge, continue through the forest for 6-7min, and then the lowest flight of the *granite staircase is reached, which leads up to the 300m-high:-

Rock of Mihintale *(Mihintale Kanda):* a magnificent spectacle among the wildernesses of the primeval jungle. The staircase has 1840 steps in four flights, and narrows towards the top. Above the third flight, a narrow path leads off l. to an old conduit and a large stone trough. The long, uppermost flight is partly hewn out of the rock. Approx. half-way up, a path branches off r., which leads to a rock pool known as *Naga Pokuna* after the relief, 2·13m high and 1·83m broad, of a five-headed naga snake on the back wall. Higher up, near the staircase r., an inscription in the rock, presumably from the 3rd c. B.C. At the top of the staircase, passing a small gatehouse, one reaches a rocky platform on which stands the *Ambustella Dagaba* amid rocks and coconut palms, the burial place of Mahinda, son of Ashoka (p.70), the first Buddhist missionary in Ceylon (†267 B.C.) The sacred goose is to be seen carved on the octagonal pillars which surround the dagaba. The broken stone statue on the S. side is regarded as that of King Devanampiya Tissa (see p57). There are some unfinished cave dwellings cut out of the rock. Obliquely across from the spot where one entered the flat space, a path goes off down to the l. through a gully full of banana trees, and rather difficult to negotiate. At the end of it, an iron ladder descends to the so-called *Mahinda's Couch,* a granite slab beneath an arch of rock, where one has an extensive view out over the jungle; the caves immediately below this spot, in which live innumerable bats, were formerly occupied by Buddhist settlers. Return to the plateau and ascend further to the highest point, which is crowned by the recently restored *Maha Seya Dagaba.* Pilgrims hang prayer banners on the branches of trees all around. The view is obscured by trees but, on the SE side, not far from a small figure of Buddha, one can walk, firstly over grass, then over dark granite bulges, to a more open place, where one has an outlook towards Anuradhapura, as well as a good view of the dagaba. – Return to the Rest-house by the same route.

The road goes to Mihintale through low jungle, in which one sees tribes of monkeys now and again, onwards via *Horuwapotama* and *Pankulam* to *Trincomalee* (p.65; 66M from Anuradhapura): post omnibus, see p.56.

The continuation of the Northern Line (Anuradhapura-Kankesanturai) passes through limitless jungle. 16M Madawachchi, junc. for the new rly to *Manaar* and over Adam's Bridge (see p.73). Beyond (82M) Paranthan the rly crosses by a causeway the narrowest part of the lagoon between the northernmost parts of Ceylon and the main island, the so-called *Elephant* Pass (halt). The landscape now changes in character. Plantations of palmyra and coconut palms are now seen. Scattered rice-fields. 105M. *Kodikamam,* sta. for *Point Pedro* (10½M), the most northerly town in Ceylon, with 3000 inhab., and a large market.

119M. *Jaffna* (govt. Rest-house), once the most important Dutch settlement in Ceylon, now capital of the Northern Province, with 40,539 inhab., an old Dutch fort, a Dutch-built church of 1706 (tombstones), Anglican and R.C. churches and many missions, of which the American one, founded in 1824, is the most important. The surroundings are excellently cultivated: palms, vegetables, tobacco.

130M. *Kankesanturai,* small port, at which the coastal steamers briefly call (p.26), in both directions, once a fortnight.

Route 6. From Dambulla to Trincomalee.

68M Post-automobile (from Matale) in 19hrs., departing in the afternoon, arriving the next morning, uncomfortable conveyance (cf.p.54). – Off the road lie the remarkable ruined sites of *Sigirya* and *Polonnaruha,* the latter a favourite destination, thanks to the motor car. Boots advisable as protection against ticks; for Sigiriya one should carry provisions, for Polonnaruha carbolic soap for washing, mosquito-nets and quinine (for fever). One should warn the Rest-house by letter of one's arrival. Best travelling-time: mid-January to mid-March.

From Dambulla until the division of the roads to Anuradhapura and Trincomalee, see p.56. The latter road passes almost entirely through splendid forest, rich in wild-life.

6M. *Inamaluwa,* where, r., an unpaved track branches off to *Sigirya* (5½M, unfit for motor vehicles, 1½-2hrs.' walk). The village (very simple Rest-house, no food) lies near the remarkable rock fortress of Sigirya which the royal parricide Kasyapa built during the war of succession (p.57) in 479-497 A.D. The path (it is desirable to engage a guide) passes the original wewa, at whose NW corner the rock towers up for 120m. The ruins cover about 750 sq.m and are largely covered by forest. To the S., W., and N. they are enclosed by moat and rampart, the rock providing shelter to the E. At the SW foot of the latter, the beautiful Audience Hall. Staircases, whose remnants survive, gave access to the rock gallery leading to the summit. Nowadays, one climbs up by iron ladders. From below one can see, beneath a rock overhang, splendidly preserved frescoes painted on the smooth cave wall. They are supposed to represent a procession of Kasyapa's wives with their maidservants and offerings. The summit is terraced in steps. The foundations of the palace and fortress can still be made out, with those of the covered walk which runs round the edge of the rock. In the centre of the site is a cistern (pokuna). The brick walls are of a later period.

15M. *Habarane* (good Rest-house), at the intersection of the road from Maradankawela (p56.; 15M) to Polonnaruha (see below).

The road runs from Habarane through jungle via (31M from Dambulla) *Alut Oya* (Rest-h.), then past the crocodile-infested *Lake Kanthalai* (Rest-h.; 43½M), and via *Tampalakam* (Rest-h.) to:-

68M. *Trincomalee* (good Rest-house), abbr. to "Trinco", a town of 11,000 inhab., with one of the best natural harbours in the world, but which is devoid of a fertile hinterland. It is commercially unimportant, formerly strongly fortified and a naval station. The Esplanade by the harbour runs to the former *Admiralty House* and E. to the Government Agent's residence by the open sea. On the rocky promontory to the N., *Fort Frederick* (dismantled); on the summit behind, *(Saami Rock),* once stood a Hindu temple, destroyed by the Portuguese in 1622.

Post-automobile to Anuradhapura (see p.56), dep. 6.35 a.m.

Trincomalee is visited once a fortnight by the coastal steamer (see p.26). The excursion round Koddiyar Bay, into which the Mahawelliganga flows from the S., is beautiful. The chief place on the E. coast, 100M S. of Trincomalee, is Batticoloa, capital of Eastern Province, with 10,000 inhab., and an old fort. The steamer calls also at *Hambantota, Matara* and *Galle* on the S. coast.

From Habarane (see above) to Polonnaruha, 17M, new carriageway, finally (2M before the objective) past *Minneriya* and *Minneriya Tank*, the latter a lake 30km in circumference, and an almost 50m-high bund to retain it, built by the Sinhalese King Maha Sen (275-302) amid a splendid tropical landscape. Minneriya is the residence of an engineer of the Public Works Dept., and his officials.

Polonnaruha, now called Topare (new Rest-house) was, from the 8th to the middle of the 13th c., the residence of the Sinhalese kings (see p.57), and it retains structures from that period which compete in importance with those at Anuradhapura. The city reached its apogee under Parakrama Bahu (1164-97), who united all of Ceylon beneath his sceptre.

The ruins, which in modern times have been partly freed from their jungle covering, stretch to the NE of the lake Topa Wewa, partly along the shore, partly northwards from there in a line almost 6km long. From the Rest-house one first reaches the remains of the pillars of the great *Audience Chamber,* then the *Kotuwa* or fort, and the *Pattiripuwa*, a rectangular building 23m long by 11m. About 5min to the N. of this, the beautiful *Dalada Maligawa,* or Temple of the Sacred Tooth (see p.37) with remarkable pillars, and the *Thuparama,* a large, elegantly arranged building, rectangular, with a smaller, square structure on top. Opposite the NE corner of the Thuparama, on a raised platform, the *Wata Dagaba* or Round Relic House, a circular brick structure with fine reliefs on the pedestal (figures of men and lions) with a balustrade above; four staircases with Dvarpals (p.58) lead upwards; on the S. side, a fine moonstone (p.58); in the interior, remains of a dagaba and seated Buddha. To the N., the *Attha Dage* or House of the Eight Relics, with a well-produced frieze in relief (dancers and tam-tam players), and a monolith (8·5m long, 1·5m wide and 0·75m thick), which, according to the inscription, was brought hither from Mihintale in the reign of King Nissanka (p.55). NE from the Wata Dagaba, the *Sat-mahal-prasada,* a pyramid-shaped stepped structure, of whose seven storeys six are preserved; to the W. of this the *Bana Salawa* or "preaching hall" witb antique decoration. – A forest path leads in 10min NE to a *Temple of Vishnu,* of similar layout to the Thuparama, but smaller.

Outside the northern town walls, which to the W. abut on the lake, one reaches (by going N. for 10min, twice crossing a water-course), the *Rankot* or gold-spired *Dagaba,* which is over 60m high and 55m broad, from Parakrama Bahu's time, with eight chapels added later. 5min further on, the *Jetawanarama,* the most massive structure in Polonnaruha, over 45m long and 25m tall, with Hindu decoration; to the E., the main entrance, between mighty polygonal columns. To the N. of this, the smaller *Kiri Dagaba,* over 30m high and 20m in diameter. – Further to the NE, the *Gal Vihara* or rock temple, with three colossal figures hewn from the granite: Buddha's favourite pupil Ananda (7m high) between a seated (5m high) and recumbent (14m) Buddha; in the rock chamber an altar and a seated Buddha. The last ruin in this direction, 10min further on, is the *Demala Maha Saya,* from the top of which one has a fine view.

Finally, one should visit, 15-20min outside the S. town-walls, and almost at the end of Topa Wewa, one of Polonnaruha's chief attractions, the so-called *Statue of Parakrama Bahu,* hewn out of the rock, 3.5m tall, with a dignified bearded countenance.

INDIA.

The peninsula or sub-continent of *India,* together with the adjacent areas in the NW, N. and E., forms the British Indian Empire which, along with the vassal states ruled by the native princes, occupies an area of 4,860,000 sq.km, with a population of 315 million. This state is therefore eight times the area of Germany, with almost five times the population. Contained by the bordering mountains of the Iranian uplands, the Himalayas and the mountain chains on the Burmese frontier, it consists in the N. central region of lowlands, and, in the S., of a tableland. This latter, the Deccan plateau, broadly speaking, is a dismembered land mass of ancient rock (archaean gneiss, slate and old sedimentary rocks), which in the Delhi region reaches almost to the Himalayas, and juts out to the S. as a peninsula. This peninsular area, the *Deccan* (p.100) in the narrower sense, overlaid in the NW by basaltic trap, is primarily a rocky, arid plateau rising from E. to W., from 350 to 950m above sea-level, and fertile only in the valleys and deltas of the eastward-flowing rivers, and in the so-called "black soil" regions. Its W. edge, rising to 2700m, falls away sharply to a rich, tropical coastal strip. The N. part of the Deccan plateau, *Central India,* is similarly formed. It rises to a height of 1720m in the *Aravalli Chain* to the W., to 879m in the *Vindhya Mountains* (p.157), and to 500m in the basaltic *Malwa Plateau.* – The N. Indian lowlands, or Hindustan, are formed from the recent alluvial deposits of the *Indus, Ganges* and *Brahmaputra;* steppes occur in the Indus valley, taking on a desert character, even towards the SE. *(Thar*, p.142). In the valleys of the other two rivers, one finds uniformly flat land, rich and fertile, with fields and orchards. The *Himalaya Range*, with its primeval forests and snowy peaks exceeding 8000m, offers scenery of unsurpassed magnificence.

The climate, 26·7°C on average, is tropical but, in the continental NW it ranges between 48·3° in the warmest month and 9·8° in the coolest (Peshawar). In summer, the damp SW monsoon and rainy season prevail (except in the NW Punjab), in winter the dry NE monsoon, which brings rain only to the E. edge of the Deccan. The highest annual rainfall occurs in the Khasi Hills in Assam (12,400mm), the Himalayas (Darjeeling 3050mm), and the W. edge of the Deccan peninsula (Bombay 1890mm), the lowest being in the middle Indus valley (p.209; only 12-13cm).

The flora varies greatly in the uplands and lowlands, the S. and the N. The Deccan and the lower Ganges and Brahmaputra valleys have tropical vegetation. Dry vegetation predominates on the *Deccan plateau:* sparse, often thorny woodland and bushes. The palmyra is the characteristic palm here (p.18). Despite a variety of fertile soils, permanent cultivation is possible only near rivers, and then mainly grassland. Millet and wheat are the main crops. The chief Indian cotton-growing area lies between lat.15 and lat.22. On the *W. slopes* of the *Deccan* and at the mouths of the *Ganges* and *Brahmaputra,* the moist warm climate brings about a luxuriance of vegetation that reminds one of W. Ceylon. Mangroves are found in the coastal marshes, coconut palms in the plains, banyan figs, tamarinds, mangoes and bamboo. The staple crop is rice. The mountain forests provide teak, sandalwood and ironwood, also rubber and pepper. The other regions have sub-tropical vegetation. The plains around the *Indus* display the types of vegetation found in steppe and desert, and the flora has a Near Eastern influence about it. The date palm is characteristic here. Wheat is the chief crop. There are almost no forests. The middle *Ganges valley* is mainly park-like in character, and filled with orchards. Downstream, as far as Lucknow, wheat is the chief cereal, but millet, sugar cane, leguminous plants and poppies (for opium) are grown. The *Himalayas* bring together all the different zones of vegetation. Between 1600 and 3000m, one finds oak, elm, hornbeam, maple, barberry, box-tree and roses. Higher up, conifers predominate. In the E. Himalayas, the influence of Chinese vegetation is seen in the magnolia, abele, etc. Above the tree-line (approx. 4000m), the Alpine flora begins. Higher still, there are only mosses and lichens. – In most of India, agriculture is dependent upon the abundance of the monsoon rains. Insufficient rainfall leads to poor harvests and famine, against which the English government is trying to fight, by extending the irrigation system.

The fauna is very rich in variety and quantity. The Near Eastern *dromedary* is to be found everywhere in the Indus basin and W. Rajputana; lions, once common here, are said to occur now only in Kathiawar. In the upper Himalayas one finds *yaks, antelope, wild sheep, goats* and *bears.* On the forested lower slopes of the Himalayas in Assam, Coorg, Mysore and Travancore there are wild *elephants.* The *rhinoceros* occurs in the forests on the Burmese frontier. Here too, and in the primeval forests of the Deccan, are the *gaur* (Bos gaurus) and the *wild buffalo* (Bos bubalus). The tame humped ox or *zebu* (Bos indicus) is used as a draught animal and is sacred to the Hindus. Among beasts of prey, the dreaded *royal tiger* (Felis bengalensis) is found in the deserts all over India; likewise the *leopard* (Felis pardus) whose relative, the *cheetah,* is tamed and used for hunting. There are also *wolves, hyenas* and swarms of *jackals.* Particularly numerous are *monkeys* (esp. the Hanuman, p.133) and *bats* (esp. flying foxes, p.43). There is a great variety of birds, esp. birds of prey. In the rivers of N. India lives the narrow-snouted *crocodile* (Gavialis gangeticus). The dolphin is to be found far up the Ganges. Among poisonous snakes, the dangerous *cobra* or spectacled snake (Naia tripudians) is found all over India; it is often displayed by conjurors.

Population. – Remnants of the enigmatic original settlers linger on in the wooded mountains of the Deccan (p.93) and in the Himalayas. The Dravidians also in S. Deccan (60 mill.), to whom belong especially the *Tamils* and *Telugu* (see p.XLI), have scarcely been touched by any European influences. Their enormous temples at *Madura* (p.74), *Trichinopoly* (p.77), *Srirangam* (p.78) etc. are full of life. At markets and festivals one sees the people practising their strange customs, and also conjurors, snake-charmers, etc. The Hindus (p.XXXVIII) originate from a mixture of the original natives with Mongolian immigrants in the NE, (Mongolian-Dravidian race, esp. in Bengal) and the Caucasian Aryans from the NW, (Indo-Aryan race, see p.XLIX). Their temples are less sumptuous than those of the Dravidians, but the throng of believers in the chief centres of pilgrimage, such as *Benares* (p.223) or *Allahabad* (p.212), is much greater and more colourful. The Mohammedans (p.XXXVII) penetrated from the Near East, bringing their culture with them. In their outward appearance they stand out on account of their dignified demeanour and their typical Islamic sense of pride. India owes a debt to the splendid dynasty of the Moguls (pp.162,178) for the abundance of magnificent monuments, among which those at *Agra* and *Delhi* rank among the noblest artistic creations (see pp.LXIX-LXX). The *Parsees* form smaller religious communities (p.XXXVI), as do the *Jains* (p.LVII), and *Sikhs* (p.LXI). One comes across yellow-skinned Mongols in the Himalayas (p.LVII). Of the native *Christians* (see p.XLVII), about ⅔ are Roman Catholics. Among the Christians of European origin, the so-called *Eurasians* predominate (half-castes, descendants of Europeans and Indian women).

In addition to what landscape, people and native art have to offer, there are the considerable cultural achievements of the English, which the traveller will repeatedly encounter. In the major cities of Calcutta, Bombay and Madras, there are public buildings on a grand scale. The businessmen's and officials' bungalows, set in parks and gardens, often astonish the beholder because of their elegant settings. The bustle in the ports never ceases to amaze the observer. The railway network, which covers the entire country, has a total length of over 50,000 km. No less important are the canals and irrigation schemes. The system of justice protects every inhabitant's life and property. There are all kinds of welfare services. Education is being made available to an increasingly wide number of natives, though, at the same time, it is also raising their aspirations and beginning to fill them with ideas of an independent Indian nation.

As far as history is concerned, a few remarks will suffice. Since the country, before English rule, was broken up into innumerable principalities, which, in the N., were only occasionally united into one realm (esp. under the Moguls), the present text must dispense with exact details. The arrival of *Buddha* (†477 B.C.), the founder of the religion named after him (see p.LII), marks the first solid point in Indian history. *Alexander the Great* penetrated across the Indus in 326 B.C. His Syrian successors, the *Seleucids*, made a treaty with King Ashoka (272-231; see p.LIV), who ruled over the country between Indus and Ganges, and elevated Buddhism to the state religion. The Greek Bactrian King *Menander* extended his kingdom around the middle of the 2nd c. B.C., as far as the Jumna. King *Kanisha's* conversion (around 125-150 A.D.) caused Buddhism to develop further (see pp.174, 207). In the 7th c. began the incursions by the *Mohammedans*, first Arab caliphs, then Turkish and Persian conquerors, among whom *Mahmud of Ghazni* (997-1030) and *Mohammed Ghori* (1186-1206) especially stand out. The latter's general, Kutb-ud-din, founded in 1206 his own kingdom with *Delhi* as its capital, which lasted through four generations of sovereigns until 1526 (see pp.177-8). Mohammedan princes ruled also in *Multan* (p.209; 1206-1591), in *Jaunpur* (p.213; 1394-1493), in *Ahmedabad* (p.132; 1394-1572), in *Golkonda* (p.114; 1512-1687), in *Bijapur* (p.105; 1490-1686) and many other places. Finally, the Mongols came on the scene and, after several forays, founded the empire of the Grand Moguls in 1526 in Agra and Delhi (cf. pp.162&178) which, at the peak of its prosperity, comprised all of northern and central India.

The first Europeans to gain a foothold in India were the *Portuguese* (1498), who had to give way, at the beginning of the 17th c., to the *Dutch* (cf.p.22). The English then came on the scene as rivals (p.83), their East India Company soon acquiring considerable significance. The *French* won Pondicherry on the E. coast in 1674 (p.81) whence, towards the middle of the 18th c., they tried to found a Franco-Indian colonial empire. In the meantime, the Grand Moguls' empire had fallen into decay. Their governors and tributary princes made themselves independent: thus the Nizam of Hyderabad (p.112), the Nawab of Oudh (p.215) and the Sikhs in Lahore (p.199); but, above all, the Hindu *Mahrattas*, who founded in the NW Deccan the princedoms of Poona (p.102), Nagpur (p.155), Indore (p.156), Gwalior (p.158) and Baroda (p.131), and extended their attacks as far as Delhi; while the English, under the future *Lord Clive* (who had already distinguished himself in 1751 when defending Arcot in S. India), won Calcutta and, at the battle of Plassey (p.250) brought Bengal under their sovereignty in 1757. Family disputes among the princes of Poona led to intervention by both the European major powers even in the realm of the Mahrattas. Most of the Indian princes, but especially the sultan *Hyder Ali* of Mysore, whom the Hindu overlords had driven out in 1759, allied themselves with the French. Only through the energies of the governor-general Warren Hastings (1774-85) was the East India Company saved. The governor-general *Lord Cornwallis* (1786-93) was victorious over Hyder Ali's son *Tippoo Sahib*, and made him yield up half his empire. During Bonaparte's Egyptian campaign in 1799, excitement mounted again. By skilful diplomacy, governor-general the *Marquess Wellesley* (1798-1805) was able to isolate Tippoo Sahib. General Harris took by storm the fortress at Seringapatam (pp.96-7), on which occasion Tippoo lost his life while fighting valiantly (1799). In two further wars (1802-4 & 1817-18), the subjection of the Mahrattas was completed, while General Lake took Delhi in the N. in 1803. Thus, in competition with other powers in India, the English took the prize, although people still did not believe in their lasting supremacy. Disputes with the N. frontier tribes resulted in new wars (against the wishes of the East India Company) which caused the English-held territory to increase constantly. In three wars (1824-26, 1852 & 1885-86), *Burma* was subjugated; *Sindh* was taken in 1843 (p.210) and, in two wars against the *Sikhs* (1845 and 1848-49), in which the Afghans took part, the *Punjab* was incorporated and, in 1856, the territory of *Oudh* (p.215). Then, in 1857, occurred the terrible *mutiny* by the majority of the native troops (p.179), after whose suppression the East India Company was dissolved, and rule passed to the English crown. At the Durbar in Allahabad on the 1st of November 1858, a general amnesty was announced, the existing native states were to be preserved under British sovereignty, and universal protection under the law was promised, regardless of religion. On the 1st of January 1877, at the Great Durbar in Delhi, the solemn proclamation of the British-Indian Empire was made in the presence of all the Indian princes.

At the head of government is the *Secretary of State for India*, in England, with whom the Council of India is co-ordinated. The government representative in India is the *Governor-General of India*, generally known by the title of *Viceroy*; he resides in Delhi in the winter, and Simla in the summer. He is supported by the *Executive Council* and *Legislative Council*. The empire is divided into 8 large and

5 small provinces, the latter again into districts, of which every 4-6 are combined into divisions. The large provinces are: the two old presidencies, *Bombay* (19,627,000 inhab.) and *Madras* (14,405,000); then, under lieutenant-governors, *Bengal* (52,668,000), the *United Provinces* (Agra-Oudh; 47,182,000), the *Punjab* (19,974,000), *Burma* (12,115,000), *Eastern Bengal* and *Assam* (34,018,000) and, under a Chief Commissioner, the *Central Provinces* with *Berar* (13,976,000). The smaller provinces *(North-West Frontier Province, British Baluchistan, Coorg, Ajmer-Merwara* and the *Andaman Is.)* are designated as local governments. – The native states occupy about one-third of the country; they number 693, of which 591 are tiny. The most important states, dealing directly with the Indian government are, in order of princely seniority: *Hyderabad* (214,179 sq.km; 13,374,000 inhab.), *Baroda* (20,975 sq.km; 2,032,000 inhab.), *Mysore* (76,257; 5,806,000), *Kashmir and Jammu* (209,552; 3,158,000); also *Nepal* (140,000; 5 mill.), with its own independent government. The other states are grouped under agents to the Governor-General: *Central India Agency, Rajputana Agency, Baluchistan Agency,* and are also partly answerable to the local governments. The British Government's representatives working with the princes have the rank of *Resident, Political Agent, Commissioner,* etc., according to the importance of the state.

The British-Indian Army comprises, together with the Aden garrison (p.11), 120,000 infantrymen, 25,300 cavalry, 10,400 artillery, 6000 engineers and 5000 service corps etc., 213,280 men in all. Of these, the *British troops* number 52 infantry battalions (each with 29 officers, 2 warrant offrs, 45 sergeants and 957 men); 9 regiments of cavalry (each with 29 offrs, 2 W.O.'s, 53 serg. and 543 men); 11 batteries of horse artillery (5 offrs and 157 men), 45 field batteries (5 offrs, 157 men), 8 mountain batteries, 28 fortress garrison batteries. *Native troops:* 133 infantry battalions (each with 12-14 British offrs, 16 native offrs, 812-896 men); 39⅛ cavalry regts. (10-14 Brit., 16-17 native offrs., 608 men), 10 mountain batteries, 1 fortress garrison battery. The army is divided into two portions, each containing 5 divisions. The Northern Army has 29 Brit. and 73 native infantry battalions, 6 Brit. and 23 native regts. of cavalry; artillery: 7 horse batteries, 22 field batteries, 8 mountain batteries and 14 fortress batteries of European soldiers, 4 mountain batteries of native soldiers. Also the reservists, reckoned at 400 offrs. and 35,000 men; the troops belonging to the native princes, with 750 offrs and 20,250 men; and the volunteers (Europeans and Eurasians), with 1400 offrs and 35,700 men.

Bibliography, see p.LXXI.

Route 7. From Colombo via Tuticorin. Madura.

Tanjore to Madras.

From Colombo to Tuticorin, 136SM. Steamers of the *British India Steam Navigation Co.* daily, except Sunday, 6 p.m. (vice versa from Tuticorin, 5 p.m.) in 15hrs., for 21R.½a. – From Tuticorin to Madras 443M, *South India Rly*, fast train ("Boat Mail") in 22hrs., for 27R.15a, 14R., 4R. 1a. – Through tickets from Colombo to Madras: 1st cl. 48¾R., 1st cl. steamer and 2nd cl. train, 35R., 2nd cl. 24½R., 3rd cl. for the boy 7¼R. All fast trains carry a dining-car.

After the opening of the rly line from *Madawachchi* (p.64) over Adam's Bridge to *Madura* (see pp.76-77), scheduled for the beginning of 1914, the main traffic will be by this route.

Crossing of the Gulf of Manaar, see p.15.

Arrival outside *Tuticorin* at about 8 a.m. The steamer anchors about 5km offshore because of the shallow water. A steam launch connects with the jetty: ¾hr., 2R. per person, native servant ½R. more. The coolies, who convey the luggage to the *Customs House,* receive 2-4a., which one's servant pays. One fills in a form about the contents of one's trunks (2a. stamp duty; for weapons, see Introduction p.XIX), registers one's luggage for the railway and goes on the harbour line to the sta. at:-

Tuticorin. Breakfast will be ready at the sta. rest. if previously ordered. HOTEL: British India Hotel, opp. the sta., P. 3-4½R. There is also a Dak bungalow (see p.XXIV).

Tuticorin, in fact *Tutticudi,* on the flat coast E. of Cape Comorin, with 28,000 inhab., incl. many Christians, carries on a vigorous trade, esp. with Ceylon. Cotton, coffee, spices and cattle are exported. If one walks through the town (guide 1R.) one can see some Hindu temples, of which more splendid examples are to be found elsewhere. At the sta. there is a grove of palmyra palms.

The railway (Tuticorin-Madura, fast train in 4½-5hrs.) at first crosses a sandy plain, then passes through a rocky district. The W. coastal mountains catch most of the rain. In contrast to Ceylon's tropical luxuriance, the ground here is made to yield only through toilsome irrigation from innumerable pools which fill in the rainy season. In places, however, agriculture is practised very intensively, and the population (Tamils, p.69) is dense. One sees enormous rice- and crop-fields, also cotton plantations and bush-covered fields with cattle, goats, sheep and buffalo, or arid land, upon which the sugar-yielding palmyra will however grow. The villages, with their dust-coloured clay huts, lie in scanty groves or are quite devoid of shade. Occasional gneiss ridges rise like islands from the plain, sometimes bearing fortifications or shrines. In the fields also one notices numerous holy objects: under large trees, stones with cobras chiselled into them, suggesting ancient tree- and snake-worship, horses hewn from stone, small chapels etc. Shortly before Madura, r., the rock (with rock temple) and the Teppakulam (pool) of *Tiruparankundram.*

99M. **Madura**. – ACCOMMODATION (see p.XXV) at the sta. rest. (Rm. 3R. daily; purchase ticket at the luggage office); cheaper and quieter, 2min beyond the rly line, the Dak bungalow (Bd. 1R.) – CARRIAGES at the sta.: landau or brougham, 2-horse 6, one-horse 3R. per day, 4, 3½, 2R. per half day. GUIDES: 3R. per day, plus tip. The Great Temple is not open to guides of low caste. Europeans are permitted everywhere but the inner chambers of the temple. One should engage a Brahman guide at the entrance, recognisable by his cord, and give him a few copper coins in advance, to placate the beggars; one should keep on one's person some silver for offerings and tips in the temple. It is well worth visiting the temple in the evening, when it is illuminated for the service.

Madura (133m), a town of 134,130 inhab., on the river *Vaigai,* surrounded by rice-fields and deciduous trees, with cotton trade and some industries (fine muslin, shot with gold thread, metalwork, wood-carvings), traces its foundation back to the 5th c. B.C. Pliny already knew Madura as the capital of the *Pandyan Empire,* with which the Romans traded (rich hoards of Roman coins have been found here); Augustus exchanged envoys with the Pandyas. In the 9th c. A.D., the Pandyas had indecisive fights with the Sinhalese (p.22). Later, Madura belonged to the empires of Chola (p.79) and Vijayanagar (p.101), but remained a centre of Hindu culture in S. India. It reached a new high point in the 17th c., especially under Prince *Tirumala Naik* (1623-59). The splendid buildings at Madura date from that time. It has been English since 1783.

In the centre of the town, about 1km E. of the sta., and within a 19m-high enclosing wall, whose red and white painted stripes are typical of the Shivite shrines, is the:-

***Great Temple*, the most fantastic Hindu temple in all India (p.LXVIII), 260m long, 230 broad, built almost entirely by Tirumala. It is dedicated to *Shiva* (p.LVIII), called *Sundareswara* here (sundara, beautiful; ishvara, highest being), and the "fish-eyed" goddess *Minakshi.* The perimeter wall has nine mighty gate towers (characteristic of Dravidian temples), called *gompurams,* with a many-storeyed pyramidal structure surmounting the lower section which contains the entry arch. They are completely covered with mythological sculptures, often painted over in bright, garish colours. The wooden gates are richly carved. The temple area is filled with a confusing mass of edifices; besides the two main temples (vimana), with their gilded gopurams and baroque decorative carvings, there are several small temples (mantapam), priests' dwellings, etc.

Through the main entrance, one enters the *Hall of the Eight Lakshmis,* named after the figures of the gods of wealth, which support the roof, and busy with traders. In the next Hall, one usually finds the colourfully painted *Temple Elephants.* A brass gate with lampholders leads into the gloomy passage of a gopuram, after which there is a mantapam. The large S. courtyard contains the *Potramarai,* a pond full of mud and weeds, from which, as legend has it, golden lilies sprang at the dedication of the temple, as adornment for the lingam of Shiva. The water is regarded as holy. Penitents and holy zebu cows populate the pool-side steps. Beneath the arcades which run round the court, and which are decorated with legendary paintings, scholars elucidate the holy scriptures. From the S. and E. arcades, there are picturesque views of the gopurams of both the main temples, and a few other gate towers. The *Sundareswara vimana* and the *Minakshi vimana* are enclosed by special courts, the inner halls being debarred to strangers. In the E. vestibule of the Sundareswara Temple, one sees the wagons and articles used in the processions of the divine images, the former being partly of gold and silver work and covered with tinsel. In exchange for a handsome tip, one is shown the temple treasure here also. – There is then a succession of large and small, light and dark passages and halls, whose pillars, mainly monolithic and wrought from solid granite, represent fantastic forms from Indian mythology; particularly often one sees the *Yali* ("lion of the south"), a fabulous beast rearing up, with an S-shaped stick in its jaws. The weird painting accentuates the bizarre impression made upon the beholder, as for example in the portrayal of a dancing contest between Shiva and the dark goddess of death, Kali (p.LX). The artistic effect of the sculptures is destroyed by the lime-wash which is renewed from time to time by charities. – The NE corner is occupied by the so-called Thousand Pillars Hall, built in 1550, an essential part of almost all the larger Dravidian temples, with 985 pillars and a built-in Minakshi shrine. The pillars are all of differing, sometimes extraordinary, work. The general artistic impression is but slight. Worthy of attention is the statue of the "goddess of education". – The *large gopuram* in the middle of the E. side is 46m high.

Opposite the E. entrance lies the *Pudu Mantapam,* now usually called Tirumala's Choultry, a splendid hall, formerly open on all sides, 101·5m long, 32m wide, with over-ornately carved pillars, built 1623-45 as a reception room for the image of Shiva, which was brought here every year for ten days, to return the temple visits of the prince. One of the sculptures in the centre corridor, beneath a baldaquin, represents Tirumala. It is said that in later years, when Tirumala threatened, as a result of the successes of the Jesuit missionary Robert de Nobili (1605-56), to shrug off the influence of his own priests, the latter lured him into the holy of holies and immured him there, announcing to the people that their pious king had gone to Heaven. The Hall provides a temporary resting-place for images of idols, and serves as a bazaar.

About 1km NE of the Great Temple is **Tirumala's Palace*, one of India's finest and noblest buildings, now fitted out as a centre for justice and administration. Around a magnificent courtyard (64m long, 43 wide) run massive pillared arcades with Hindu decoration. The 12m-tall pillars are clad in stucco (chunam, p.86). In the octagonal Throne Room, which is crowned with an 18m-high dome, the law sittings take place. The former Audience Chamber, 37m long and 21 high, resembles a Gothic church aisle. View from the roof, best in the evening.

One takes a carriage to the **Teppakulam*, 5km E. of the sta., a holy pool 365m square. The enclosing wall, with steps for the bathers and grotesque sculptures, consists of granite painted red and white (Shiva's colours). In the pool, an artificial garden islet with the tall, whitewashed *Mausoleum of Tirumala* at its centre. Boats are available for trips to this. Every year, in January or February, a festival of lanterns takes place, at which the temple idols are conveyed around the pool on a raft.

Next to the pool, the little *Temple of Marcammas* with many dolls on the roof, votive gifts from women who wish to have children and spend the night here after bathing in the pool. – On the return journey, one sees a large example of a *Banyan tree,* whose top is 50-60m in diameter, which is regarded as holy by the people.

The following evening excursion is recommended. Cross the River Vaigai (which is lined with coconut palm woods) by the large modern bridge. To the E., a *temple to Vishnu* is seen in the river, to the W., a *temple to Shiva,* to which the idol of the Great Temple is brought in July. Continue past the Tamkam, a strange building, half Moorish in style, now the dwelling of the English tax collector, and past a variety of shrines amid tanks and rice-fields. In the distance, 8km NE, the *Elephant Rock,* with temple to Vishnu.

Madura is the junc. for the branch-line to Mandapam and Danushcody, which is connected by a direct steam ferry to the Northern Line of Ceylon (see p.73). The rly follows the mainly waterless *Vaigai* until (67M) *Ramnad* and, on the peninsula of the same name, reaches at *Mandapam* the extremity of the mainland. It crosses the *Pamban Channel,* which resulted from an inroad of the sea in 1480, by viaducts and, at the deepest point left open for shipping, over an iron bridge constructed by the Scherzar Co. of America.

95M. *Pamban*, at the W. end of the island of that name; 102M. *Ramesvaram,* main place on the island, with a famous temple (see below); 112M. Danushcody, on the E. side of the island which is linked by a submerged sandbank (the so-called *Adam's Bridge)* to the island of *Manaar*. The distance is 25M. The steam ferry, which conveys the train across in 1¼hrs., runs along the N. or S. side of the shoal, depending on the direction of the monsoon (p.12), landing at *Talaimanaar*. – 162M. *Manaar*, at the SE end of the island, whence the railway reaches the Northern Line of Ceylon by way of a viaduct (p.64).

Ramesvaram is one of the holiest places of pilgrimage for the Hindu, and is said to have been founded by Rama during his crossing to Lanka (p.22), at which the monkeys of Hanuman levelled the way for him. The **Temple,* situated on the shore, dates from the 16th-17th c. and, in its layout and the mastery of its stone-masonry, is perhaps the most perfect example of Dravidian style (p.LXVIII). The temple grounds cover an area of 304 X 198m; the gopuram over the entrance is 30m high; the pillared halls total 1200m in length and give an impression of grandeur.

The name *Adam's Bridge* comes from the Mohammedans; according to their legend, Adam was driven at this point out of paradise (Ceylon).

The railway to Madras (fast train in 4½hrs. to Trichinopoly) crosses the watershed between the Vaigai and the Cauveri (p.96). Not far from Madura, r., the Elephant Rock p.76). The scenery becomes more mountainous and charming, but remains parched outside the artificially irrigated fields. Coconut palms, palmyras and date palms. L., in the distance, the *Palni Hills*, in which lies the English hill station of *Kodaikanal* (2200m). – 137M. *Dindigul* (sta. rest.) with 25,000 inhab. and picturesque rock fortifications, for a long time a stronghold of the princes of Madura, but English since 1792.

195M. **Trichinopoly**. – Station: *Trichinopoly Junction* (at the Cantonment, p.78), for the rly to Erode, which has a second sta. at *Trichinopoly Fort,* see p.91.

ACCOMMODATION at the sta. rest. at Junction Station (Rm. 3R.; 20min from the sta. is a Dak bungalow, not good, and a fair distance from the rock temple. – CARRIAGE at the sta.: 1½-3R. for ½ day. – GUIDE at the sta.: 1½R. for ½ day. – 4hrs. suffice for the sights mentioned below.

Trichinopoly (more properly *Tirutchinapalli),* near the apex of the 150km-long delta of the *Cauveri*, on the r. bank of its S. arm, district capital with 122,000 inhab. (15,000 Christians, 13,500 Mohammedans) and some silk and cotton-weaving mills, is the seat of a Jesuit mission (already founded in 1623), and of English and German Protestant missions. The town consists of the European *Cantonment,* with a garrison of 1½ infantry regts., and the *Fort,* inhabited by the natives, whose now dismantled fortifications were much fought over in the wars of the French and English in the 18th c.

Inside the Fort, the picturesque **Rock of Trichinopoly* rises 63m above the town, beyond a large *Teppakulam* (p.74), which contains an islet with a pretty mantapam. One ascends a covered staircase of 290 steps painted in red and white stripes between strange idols to the half-way point, where there is a large *Temple of Shiva* with two gilded domes. Access to the interior is not permitted. Opposite, a large Nandi bull, entirely covered in silver. From here, an open-air path, partly made from steps cut in the rock, leads to the graceful *Temple of Ganesa,* at the summit. There is a splendid view of the town with its temples, palaces, gardens and luxuriant green landscape, out of which rise other rocky pinnacles. To the SW, beyond the pool, the Neo-Gothic Jesuit church. To the S., a mosque; in the distance, the angular church tower of the Portuguese Goa Mission, and the romantic "Golden Rock". To the SE, another mosque with a white dome. To the E., in clear conditions, one can make out the great temple at Tanjore. To the N., the broad sandy bed of the River Cauveri with its 27km-long wooded island of Sriringam.

The Cauveri is one of the rivers sacred to the Hindu. From the bridge, over which the road to Srirangam crosses to the l. bank, one views the holy *bathing-places,* with their broad stone steps, upon which a colourful and busy throng collects in the mornings. The road continues mostly through forest.

The town of *Sriringam*, with 23,000 inhab., (virtually all Hindus), is famous for its temple to Vishnu, the most extensive in India. Near the handsome arched bridge over the arm of the river in front of the temple are bathing-places, those upstream for men, downstream for women; on one shore, the Brahmans bathe, on the other, the members of the lower castes.

The ***Temple of Vishnu* existed already in the 10th c., according to individual inscriptions, but the present structure was begun only in 1700 and gradually extended. It forms a rectangle, 936 X 768m, and has seven enclosing walls with 15 gopurams. The main entrance is in the form of the 15½m-high and 30½m-deep substructure of an incomplete gopuram, with enormous stone slabs at the entrance (the door lintel is 9m long and 2½m wide) and on the roof. From above, a good general view of the temple area. The outermost wall encloses a bazaar and accommodation for pilgrims. In the courtyards of the second and third enclosure live the Brahmans who look after the temple. The succeeding courtyards are reserved for holy objects. The fourth contains, among other things, a so-called *Thousand-pillared Hall*, 137m long, 39 wide, with 940 pillars, of which the outer ones portray horsemen killing tigers with spears, while the inner pillars have only banana capitals (p.39). From the roof of the hall there is a view over the three innermost courtyards (not open to strangers). The *vimana* (see p.75) with its rich gilding stands at the centre. There is an annual 10-day major festival, usually in December or January, with an enormous influx of the faithful. At other times the temple is always busy with priests, pilgrims, the sick and crippled, conjurors, elephants etc.

About 20min E. of the Temple of Vishnu lies the *Temple of Jambukeshwara*, dedicated to Shiva. It is 100 years older, smaller, rather neglected and less visited by the faithful, but artistically more important. Its priests are currently devoting large sums of money to its restoration.

To one side of the street, the guide will indicate also a small *Temple to Kali,* with grotesque painted figures. Here, low, dark-skinned castes worship a blood cult.

The railway (Trichinopoly-Tanjore, fast train in 1¼-2hrs.) passes through the fertile, populous and well-cultivated Cauveri delta. On the l., the temple of *Tiruverumbur.* Finally, l., the great pagoda of Tanjore appears above the trees.

226M. **Tanjore.** – Station: *Tanjore Junction,* for the branch via *Tiruvallur* to *Negapatam.*

ACCOMMODATION (see p.XXV) at the sta. rest., and the Dak bungalow near the "Little Fort". – A stay of 3hrs. will suffice: carriage 2, bullock cart 1R. for ½ day; guide 2R. (not essential if the carriage is used); luggage is left at the sta. (2a. per item).

Tanjore, a town of 57,870 inhab., is the seat of ancient Indian scholarly study and of several missions (the converted are mainly pariahs). The dexterity of the craftsmen is famous, who produce worked articles of copper and silver, as well as carved models of temples from pith. Musical instruments are manufactured here, and silk is woven etc. In the 10th & 11th c., Tanjore was the centre of the *Chola Empire*, which was at times the supreme power in S. India, even conquering Ceylon under King Rajaraja I (985-1012) and sending out fleets against Java. Around 1670 it became the chief place of a small Mahratta state which comprised the Cauveri delta, and remained the reservation of the Raja after the rest of the country had passed to the English in the 18th c. The town is very extensive. The Brahmans inhabit the N. part, the Europeans the

SE. The objects of interest are to be found in the Fort, which consists of the Large Fort and the Little Fort, forming part of it, with picturesquely ruined fortifications.

In the Little Fort is the **Brihadiswaraswami Temple* which, with its unity of plan, surpasses almost all other Dravidian temples. According to the inscriptions, its foundation dates back to Rajaraja I (p.79), but the present structure is of a later date. A 27m-high gopuram forms the entrance; in niches to l. and r., statues of the god of war Subrahmanya riding on a peacock, and the elephant-headed god Ganesa (p.LIX). A passage and a second gopuram lead into an inner courtyard, 244m long and 126m broad. In front, beneath a richly sculpted pillared hall, a 4m-high and 5m-long *Nandi bull* of black granite, the symbol of Shiva. The arcades on the W. and N. sides of the courtyard contain 108 niches with granite lingams. The *vimana*, in the centre of the courtyard and forbidden to non-Hindus, rises in two storeys, surmounted by a 60m-high, generously proportioned *pyramidal tower, crowned by a dome-shaped monolith (estimated to weigh 8000kg), which is said to have been dragged up here on a mile-long ramp. Distinguished for the delicacy of its wall construction and its carved decoration is the rather younger, elegant **Temple of Subrahmanya* in the NW corner of the courtyard. In its whitewashed interior are kept the tawdry idols for the processions.

The NW corner of the Fort contains the holy *Sivagangai Tank* within an enclosing wall. NE from here, the *Schwartz Mission Church*, named after the Evangelical missionary *Chr. Friedr. Schwartz* from Neumark, who was active here from 1778 to 1798 and is said, by putting in a good word with the English on behalf of his pupil, *Raja Sarabhoji*, to have saved the latter's throne. A marble relief by Flaxman shows the grateful prince at the missionary's death-bed, whose career in God's service is likened by the inscription to that of an apostle.

One visits also the *Palace of the Princesses,* a rambling complex of courts, houses and towers in the Saracen style, erected around 1550, latterly the residence of the surviving wives of the Raja (who died in 1855), and sadly dilapidated.

Of particular note within: the two ceremonial halls, *Maratha Hall* and *Naik Hall* (statue of Sarabhoji by the English sculptor Fr. L. Chantrey); the *Armoury*, with some fine guns; the *Library*, comprising 22,000 volumes, with famous Sanskrit mss. (no. 1 in the catalogue is an illuminated manuscript of the Rigveda, executed in 1838 with meticulous care).

The railway (Tanjore-Madras, fast train in 11½-12hrs.) touches on: 250M. *Kumbakonam* (sta. rest.; Dak bungalow, no staff, 1M from the sta.), lively town of 60,000 inhab., in the richest part of the Cauveri delta, one of the oldest in S. India,, with temples in Dravidian style (p.LXVIII), and the *Mahamagham Tank* which, according to popular belief, receives water from the Ganges every

12 years, and is then visited by hordes of bathing pilgrims (the last occasion being 1909).

292M. *Chidambaram* or *Chillambaram*, with 20,000 inhab., and famous temples of Shiva (p.LXVIII). – 316M. *Cuddalore*, a town of 52,200 inhab. with two stations: Old Town and New Town.

345M. *Villupuram* (sta. rest.)

Branch-lines from Villupuram: NW to Katpadi, see p.91; - E. (24M in 2hrs.) to Pondicherry (Gr.-H. d'Europe, H. de Paris & Londres, P. 3-5R.), capital of the remnant of the former French colonial empire in India, with 48,450 inhab., founded in 1674 by the Franco-Indian Company, in Dutch hands from 1693 to 1697, and often taken by the English during the 18th c. The European quarter is clean and welcoming, if somewhat lifeless. Steamer connection: Calcutta-Colombo (*Mess. Mar.,* fortnightly), Rangoon-Negapatam *(B.J.S.C.,* weekly), Madras-Singapore *(B.J.S.C.,* fortnightly). – The "Etablissements français dans l'Inde" now consist of Pondicherry, Karikal and Yanaon on the E. coast, Mahé on the W. coast and Chandernagore (p.229), comprising a total of 509 sq.km, with 282,000 inhab.

409M. *Chingleput* (sta. rest.; Dak bungalow, staffed, near the sta.), with 10,000 inhab., and a house of correction founded in 1881 for young delinquents, junction of a connecting line to Arkonam (p.91).

On the Chingleput-Arkonam line *(S. I. Rly)* lies, 22M from Chingleput and 18M from Arkonam), *Conjeeveram* (actually Kanchipuram, i.e. the golden city), an ancient seat of Buddhism, now one of the Hindus' holy cities, with 46,000 inhab. and a picturesque *Temple of Ekambaranatha* (i.e. Shiva), which developed gradually from small beginnings to an extensive group of gopurams, vimanas, pillared halls and bathing tanks (the largest gopuram is 57m high). In Little Conjeeveram, ¾hr. from the sta., a *Temple of Vishnu* with fine carvings, esp. in the Hall of a Hundred Pillars.

From Chingleput to the *Seven Pagodas* at Mahabalipur (p.87) 38km; carriage road to Sadras Bridge 29km, then boat, 6hrs. in all.

From Chingleput to Madras, travelling time 1½hrs. Last stops: *Saidapet* (p.86). *Kodambakam* and *Chetput.*

443M. *Madras*: Egmore Station and Beach station, see below.

Route 8. Madras.

STATIONS. S. India Railway (p.7): *Egmore Station* (sta. rest.), nearest to the hotels and the European residential quarter; terminus: *Beach Sta.*, at the port. Madras & S. Mahratta Rly (Routes 11, 12): *Central Station* and, for the coastal rly to Calcutta (East Coast Railway, Route 9): *Rayapuram Sta.* or *Beach Sta.*, where one connects with the S. India Rly. – By sea, one lands at the *Port.* Jolly-boats (1R.), or masulah boats, convey passengers and luggage ashore. Port dues for luggage: minimum 4a., for 1 ton, 1R.

Hotels (only of medium quality; see p.XXIII). In the European quarter: H. Connemara, Mount Rd., 45 Rm., B. 8a., L.2R., D.3R., P. from 8R.; H. d'Angelis, also in Mount Rd., with rest., cake shop and garden; H. Spencer, 152 Mount Rd., 35 Rm., P. from 8R.; Buckingham H., Westcott's Rd; Elphinstone H., Mount Rd.; Victoria H., Commander-in-Chief Rd.; Langham H., Mount Rd.; Castle H., close to the Madras Club, with a large, shady garden, 23 Rm. from 6R. to 10R.10a., out of season 1-2R. cheaper. By the beach, N. of St Thomé, 1hr. from Egmore Sta.: Marine H.

Carriages (indispensable for greater distances): ½ day (6-12 noon, 12-6 p.m. or 6-12 midnight), 1st cl. 2R.8a., 2nd cl. 1R.4a., all day (6 a.m. to 6 p.m.) 5R., 2R.8a. They may usually be hired at the main stations, e.g. Egmore, otherwise through firms of carters (incl. *Madras Stables Co.,* Mount Rd.) where one is well served for little extra outlay.

Trams (max. distance for 1½a.): from Egmore Sta., every 5min via Central Sta. to the Customs House at the port; branch to Mount Rd., Royapettah, St Thomé, Mylapur and Pursavakam.

Travel agencies: *Carl Simon Sons*, Esplanade; Binny & Co., Armenian St.

Steamer lines & agencies: *British India S.N.Co.,* agents Binny & Co., once a week to Calcutta and Bombay, calling in at coastal ports, or direct to Rangoon (p.253), every fortnight to Penang and Singapore in the one direction, and London in the other; *Austrian Lloyd,* agents Volkart Bros., Armenian St., once a month to Calcutta and Colombo. Agencies: *North German Lloyd,* Carl Simon Sons, Broadway; *P.&O.S.N.Co.,* Best & Co.Ltd., *Bibby Line,* Walker & Co., 2nd Line Beach 3; *Messageries Maritimes,* Volkart Bros.

Post & Telegraph: *General Post Office* at the port (7 a.m. to 6 p.m.) Branch post offices in the town, one in Mount Rd. One should, where possible, post one's mail oneself, since errand boys are liable to purloin letters for the sake of the stamps.

Banks. *Madras Bank; National Bank of India.*

Consulates. Germany: Consul *M.Miersch*, c/o Carl Simon sons, Broadway. Austria: Consul *E.Steiner.*

Clubs: *Madras Club,* Mount Rd., with rooms reminiscent of a palace; *Adyar Club,* in the suburb of Adyar (p.86). Introduction through a member is necessary. There is no German club here.

Shops, all in Mount Rd. Bookshops: *Higginbotham's Ltd., Cambridge & Co.* - Photographers: *Wiehle & Klein* (German); *Del Tufo; Willie Burke.* – Stores: *Spencer & Co., Wrenn, Bennett & Co.,* etc. – Opticians: *P.Orr & Sons; Lawrence & Mays.* – Jewellers: *Orr & Sons; T.R.Tawker & Sons.* – Equipment for the traveller: *Spencer & Co.* – Tailors: *Smith & Andree; Moses & Co.; Oakes & Co.* – Curiosities, embroidery, silverware: *Daday Khan; E.Lekragh & Co.; Chelleram Gianchand; Kilmatrai & Co.* – Newspapers: *Madras Mail; Madras Times; Madras Standard; The Hindu.*

The climate is hot. The mean temperature fluctuates between 24 and 34°C. The main rainy period, subject however to many interruptions, occurs during the NE monsoon (p.12). – Doctors: Surgeon Major *Clarence Smith,* Mount Rd., and the officers of the *Indian Medical Service.* Dentists: *C.F.Badcock,* Egmore; *Eaton Bros., A.A.Mix.* – Chemists: *W.E.Smith & Co.Ltd, R.Maclure,* both in Mount Rd. – Hospitals: *General Hospital,* with 500 beds for Europeans and for natives, *Ophthalmic Hospital; Maternity Hospital.*

For a limited visit (1 day): morning: museum, Victoria Technical Institute, School of Arts, High Court, the port and fort, returning via the Island. Afternoon: SW down Mount Rd. to St George's Cathedral and the Horticultural Gdns, then E. along Cathedral Rd. to St Thomé and the marina (aquarium), returning N. The most important thing is to gain an impression of the town and its traditional Anglo-Indian life, which flourishes still on an apparently aristocratic scale.

Madras, the third largest city in India, seat of the Presidency of Madras, of a supreme court and many places of learning, stretches for almost 15km along the sandy Coromandel Coast (so dangerous to shipping), and covers an area of 75 sq.km. The meandering course of the *River Cooum* divides the city into a N. and S. half, both intersected by the *Buckingham Canal* (p.88). Madras is the oldest settlement of significance of the former East India Company, founded in 1639. Disputes with the neighbouring native princes and the ambitions of the French (p.81) did not favour its development. The French governor La Bourdonnais took the town in 1746, but English rule was re-established by the treaty of Aix-La-Chapelle (1748), and Lord Clive's energetic intervention (p.71) assured their superiority along the Coromandel Coast also. The city numbered 518,660 inhab. in 1911, of whom 54,000 were Mohammedans and 40,000 Christians. Trade is on the increase. Imports consist mainly of English cotton goods and yarn, metals, railway material, oil, machines, items of apparel etc., metal products, chemicals and drugs, drinks, spirits and food, to a total value (1908-9) of 126,243,000R. Exports include hides and skins, grain and pulse, cotton, seeds, coffee, tea, woven cotton goods and yarns, coconut fibre, oil, spices, comestibles etc. to a total value (1908-9) of 186,558,600R. Industry plays no major part here.

The oldest part of the city, the cramped *Black Town* by the port, originally the native dwelling quarter, is now called George Town, and is the business quarter with the large offices and banks, consulates and Customs House, and a colourful and busy district. The port replacd the open roadstead in 1875, and has been considerably improved during the course of the last decade. The new NE breakwater now provides sufficient protection against cyclones. – To the N., beyond the sta. of the coastal rly (p.88) is the fishing quarter *Rayapuram.*

To the S. of George Town, and opening on to the sea, is the Esplanade, at whose NE corner rises the High Court Building, a massive and impressive edifice built (1888-92) by Brassington and Irwin in a hybrid Hindu-

Mohammedan style, with a central tower, 50m high and serving as *lighthouse* (white double flashing light of 18,000 candlepower, visible 20SM distant). The great west door of the Court is kept shut, access being through side doors. The interior layout is appropriate to the climate. Opening from a labyrinthine number of gloomy corridors are airy little rooms and some larger court-rooms, which are decorated with carvings and which receive their light through coloured windows. The sittings are open. – To the S., opposite, the old:-

Fort St George, the point of departure for Lord Clive's victorious campaign in S. India (1758). It contains the barracks of the European garrison, some government offices, the first evangelical church in India *(St Mary's,* dedicated in 1680 and containing a monument to the missionary Schwartz, p.80) and the *Arsenal* with a collection of historic weapons of little importance. – North Beach Rd., on the seaward side of the fort, continues S., becoming the Marina (p.86).

To the SW of the fort, the *Island*, enclosed by arms of the River Cooum, with gardens and sports grounds (Gymkhana Club). In the main road, a statue of Governor Thom.Munro (1820-27) by Chantrey. On the S. bank of the river is Governor's Park.

The road to the W. of the fort goes past the *Memorial Hall*, in the style of a Greek temple, with meeting rooms for religious and social purposes, built to commemorate the fortunate preservation of the Presidency of Madras during the military revolt of 1857. At the fine *General Hospital* (p.82) the road turns W.; passing *Central Station*, it crosses Buckingham Canal and skirts the *People's Park*, which stretches between the Canal and the suburb of *Vepery*. At the front of the Park is *Moore Market,* a modern Mohammedan arcaded market-hall, and the *Victoria Public Hall* for concerts, gatherings, etc. Further on, the *School of Arts*, an institution founded in 1850, now run by the State for the furtherance of Indian crafts (wood-carving, carpet-weaving, work with copper and precious metals, etc.); and the church of *St Andrew's* with a tower 54m high.

The European town with its villas and gardens and large hotels extends to the S. of *Egmore Station*, known as "Egmore", as far as the River Cooum, then beyond this as "Nangambakam" to Long Tank.

In Egmore is Pantheon Rd., the main thoroughfare. In this is the *Police Commissioner's Office,* the *Maternity Hospital* and a fine ensemble of buildings, comprising the Museum, a theatre, the Victoria Technical Institute and Connemara Library.

The Museum, with art and applied art collections, cultural and natural history exhibits, was founded in 1846 and contains principally objects from S. India. Director: Dr Henderson. Entry free from 7 a.m. to 5 p.m., except Friday, and the first Saturday afternoon in each month, which is reserved for native women. There are explanatory notices everywhere.

In the S. wing, the *art & ethnographic collection.* A staircase on which stand two modern carved thrones from the Delhi Exhibition of 1903, leads to a vestibule with fine views of Indian *temples* and interesting old *bronze figures.* From here, along a gloomy passage to the main hall, with *works of applied art.* Noteworthy is the so-called “Bidri ware”, metal utensils inlaid with silver wire from the town of *Bidar* in the state of Hyderabad, fine ivory carvings from *Vizagapatam*, pith carvings (p.79), objects of wood and brass, and painted and printed native textiles. A small room at the foot of the stairs contains more textiles of the same kind, and wooden blocks for printing. In the corresponding room opp., a collection of fine old Indian *weapons.* – A corridor leads to the splendid room that houses the *Connemara Library* (founded in 1896; Connemara was a governor of Madras), with reading niches containing richly ornamented book cabinets (catalogue from the attendant); also, the marble statue of Lord Cornwallis (p.71) by the English sculptor Fr. L. Chantrey stands here, having formerly been in Fort St George.

A second corridor gives access to the *Zoological Collection.* In the first room, some living birds and snakes; then stuffed animals and skeletons. On the walls, photographs of the capture and utilisation of elephants. R. and l. of these rooms, a valuable *Archaeological Collection* of old pieces of temple sculpture, esp. from Amaravati (p.88). Next to the Zoological Collection is the *Mineralogical* and, above this, on the upper floor, a *herbarium* with an “economic collection”of useful products.

The Victoria Technical Institute contains a display of S. Indian handicrafts for sale: daily, except Tues., 7.30 a.m. – 6 p.m., entrance free. (No sale on Sun.)

Two bridges, Anderson’s Bridge and Commander-in-Chief’s Bridge, connect Egmore with the district of Nangambakam, whose numerous (often palatial) European bungalows with their gardens on a princely scale give that part of the town its special quality. The long Mount Road is the main thoroughfare with the most splendid shops and major hotels. At the intersection with the road from Commander-in-Chief’s Bridge is a memorial to *General Neile*, who fell at the Relief of Lucknow. To the S., and opposite, the extensive gardens and buildings of the *Madras Club.* The NE continuation of Mount Rd. passes *Government House.* Outside the entrance to the park, a *statue of the King-Emperor Edward VII*, by the English sculptor Wade. The interior of Government Ho., with many pictures of former governors, is open to the public only when the family is not in residence. – Continue via the Island (p.84) to the fort.

At the SW end of Mount Rd. rises *St George’s Cathedral,* completed in 1816, within a large enclosed area and with a massive pillared portico. The interior is noteworthy on account of the way it has been adapted to the climatic conditions; stucco ("chunam") resembling marble (a favourite method of covering walls in S. India), is a well-known feature of buildings in Madras; many tomb monuments. Further on, the *Horticultural Gardens* with the Victoria Regia Pool. – The meteorological *Observatory,* in the NW of Nangambakam, gives Standard (Railway) Time for the whole of India (80° 14' 19·5" long. E. of Greenwich; 4hrs.21min ahead of Central European Time).

The favourite evening promenade is the Marina, which stretches S. of the fort from the Cooum estuary 3km southwards along the ocean shore. The beach is unusually level, the surf quite remarkably powerful, so that only the flexible "masulah boats", sewn together with coconut fibre, and the natives' small catamarans can negotiate it. At the beginning of the Marina, r., the astonishing *Senate House*, built 1874-79. In front of this, beneath a baldaquin, a *statue of the Queen-Empress Victoria* by Ward, 1887. The Aquarium is open daily, except Friday, 7-11 and 1-6 (entrance in the morning 1a., afternoon ½a., Wed. 4a.; the last Monday of the month is reserved for native women). Further, to the r., *Chepauk Palace*, of the nawabs of Karnatik, deposed by the English in 1801. The last nawab died in 1855, after which the Palace was restored in Moorish style and became the offices of the Revenue Board. Its park is of no interest. Next, the poky native suburb of *Triplicane.* – The Marina ends at the suburb of *St Thomé* and the R. C. cathedral of the same name, in which is revered the tomb of the apostle St Thomas who, according to the legend, came in slavery to India. The later Indian Christians traced their origin back to him ("Thomas Christians"). S. of St Thomé is the estuary of the broad River Adyar.

The S. continuation of Mount Rd. goes past Long Tank to *Saidapet*, with a railway halt (p.81), an agricultural college and a model farm, then crosses the *River Adyar* by means of Marmalong Bridge, built in 1726, to *Guindy,* where the Governor of Madras has a country residence, and where the race-course is. *St Thomas's Little Mount* (67m), E. of Guindy, where St Thomas the Apostle is said to have been martyred, is surmounted by a 16th c. Armenian church.

3km further E., near Elphinstone Bridge, are the buildings of the *Theosophical Society* (p.LXII), whose aims include, among other things, the improving of social conditions in India..

The excursion to the Seven Pagodas, one of the most remarkable of India's ruined sites, on the coast 35M south of Madras and peacefully secluded from the world, may be arranged with a travel agency (p.82) or undertaken simply with a well-versed boy in 2-2½ days, either via *Chingleput* (p.81) or on the *Buckingham Canal* (in the latter instance, according to the direction of the monsoon, an 8-17hr. boat journey may be made from Guindy). The traveller takes his own provisions and bedding.

One lands at Mahabalipuram (or *Mahavellipur),* where there is an unstaffed Rest-house. The village lies on a 2-3km-broad spit of land between the Canal and the ocean. The ruins stretch out along the rock-strewn granite ridge, which runs N-S down the centre of the island.

The oldest structures, dating in all probability from the 7thc. A.D., are the so-called *Seven Pagodas,* to the S. of the southern end of the ridge, in deep, fine sand: five small rock temples in the Dravidian style ("the five raths") and a superbly carved elephant and a less effective lion. Up on the ridge, and of more recent origin, a group of similar *rock temples*, some completed on the outside only, others with lively reliefs in their interior, which are still to some extent used by the villagers for religious services.

On the E. side of the ridge, at the point where the rock wall is cleft in two, is a remarkable and enormous relief, 9m high and 27m long, to which the name *Arjuna's Penance* has been given, from the figure of a penitent on the S. half of the rock. The relief depicts a wealth of figures: gods, men, mighty elephants, monkeys, lions, tigers, birds, snakes, and a penitential tom-cat surrounded by rats; the four-armed chief figure is taken to be Shiva; in the cleft hovers the deity Vasuki, with a seven-headed snake baldaquin above (the broken upper portion of the figure was found in the rubble); beneath, her daughter Ulipi, with a smaller snake baldaquin. The figures of the Buddha and his five disciples seem to form the centrepiece of the representations, which Dr Hunter sees as the introduction of Buddhism or the symbolising of peaceableness towards man and beast.

To the E., close to the sea, among another group of more recent ruins (8th c.), lie two smaller temples, one being built of masonry in the early Dravidian style, usually called the *Temple of the Sea:*the main pinnacle (18m) above the vimana is beautiful in shape; the low, former entry gopuram was later altered into a chapel. In the vimana is a black marble lingam with a recumbent Vishnu behind.

To the N., near the village, a piece of granite sculpture portraying a *family of monkeys*, surprisingly true-to-life. – 1hr. to the N. of Mahabalipur, on the Buckingham Canal (by boat from Madras), behind a tangle of palms, is the so-called *Tiger Cave*, a hollowed-out granite hump, around whose opening are nine fantastic tigers' heads.

Route 9. From Madras to Calcutta.

1032M. *Madras & S. Mahratta Rly* as far as Waltair, then by the *Bengal Nagpur Rly:* through fast train, connecting with the main line from Tuticorin, in 39½hrs, for 91R., 44R.4a., 13R.7a. – Steamer connections, p.82.

Madras (Central or Rayapuram Sta.), see p.81. – The railway crosses the hot, humid depression (80km wide, on average) between the lower edge of the NE Deccan (p.67) and the flat, almost harbourless, coast of the Bay of Bengal. Only occasionally does a lone outlier of the mountains advance to the sea. The coastal lagoons are connected by canals, for inland shipping, esp. the *Buckingham Canal*, built in the 19th c., which extends 320km N and 100km S. of Madras. Everywhere, the traveller sees paddy-fields and palms. The richest and most civilised settlements are to be found on the deltas of the large rivers which flow out of the W. Deccan and through the Eastern Ghats (p.100) to the sea. There is little on the journey to interest the tourist. We will name only a selection of the more important stations.

86M. *Gudur* (4hrs' journey from Madras; sta. rest.), junc. for the connecting line from Renigunta (p.101). – 110M. *Nellore*, town of 32,000 inhab. on the r. bank of the *Penner*; 131M. *Bitragunta* (sta. rest.); 182M. *Ongole* (sta. rest.); 222M. *Bapatha* (sta. rest.) – 268M. *Bezwada* (8hrs.' journey from Gudur; sta. rest.), junc. for the lines from Guntakal (p.101) and Hyderabad (p.115), town of 24,200 inhab. on the l. bank of the broad *Krishna* or *Kistna*, which forms a delta won by irrigation channels for cotton-growing (900 sq.km); 20M SW of Bezwada, on the r. bank of the Krishna, the village *Amaravati* with the remains of a Buddhist stupa (p.LXIV), whose reliefs were taken in 1840 to the museums at Madras and Calcutta.

305M. *Ellore* (sta. rest.), town of 33,500 inhab., in the marshy area by the freshwater *Lake Colair* or *Kolar*, which can swell to 250 sq.km, but dries out now and again in the hot season. – 361M. *Rajamundry* (4hrs.' journey from Bezwada; sta. rest.), town of 36,000 inhab., on the l. bank of the *Godavery,* whose delta has been excellently cultivated with rice (3000 sq.km) by means of irrigation. – 392M. *Samalkot* (sta. rest.), linked by a branch line to the port of *Coronada.* 426M. *Tuni* (sta. rest.) – 485M. *Waltair* (3½hrs.' journey from Rajamundry, 22 from Madras; sta. rest.), junc. for a branch line to the port *Vizagapatam,* which numbers 40,000 inhab. and carries on a not inconsiderable trade. – 522M. *Vizianagram* (sta. rest.), with 37,000 inhab., residence of a rajah, whose small territory is under British administration. – 594M. *Naupada*, sta. for the branch line to *Parla Kimedi*, where another rajah resides; 656M. *Berhampur* (sta. rest.). Then past *Ganjam*, perhaps the capital of the ancient kingdom of *Kalinga*, which stretched along the coast as far as the mouth of the

Ganges, and played a part in the history of Buddhism. R., the extensive lagoon, *Chilka Lake*.

747M. *Khurda Road* (29hrs.' journey from Madras, another 10 to Calcutta; sta. rest.), station for the branch to Puri (28M, 1½hrs.), the most famous place of pilgrimage for the Hindu after Benares (p.221). Rich countryside with rice fields, palms, lotus pools.

Puri. – The spacious *station* lies in the N. part of the town. About 1km from it, in the English quarter by the coast, is the Seaside Hotel (limited and expensive) and the small Dak bungalow (book in advance, one brings one's own provisions). Carriage at the sta.

Puri, probably the Buddhist *Dantapura* where, for eight centuries, the holy tooth of Buddha was kept (p.38), is the holy city of the *Jagannath,* i.e. lords of the world, the most pleasant embodiment of Vishnu, to worship whom more than 100,000 pilgrims swarm in from all parts of India for the 24 great festivals, all differences of caste being ignored. The cramped town consists largely of pilgrim accommodation. The permanent population is put at 32,000, that of the priests (pandas) at 3000, of whom however many are itinerant preachers. The owner of the temple and head of the brotherhood of priests is the mediatised Rajah of Khurda who, in deference to the god, styles himself as a mere temple sweeper.

The *Jagannath Temple*, founded as long ago as the second half of the 12th c., lies on an eminence in the middle of the town. It occupies an area of 198 X 192 sq.m, surrounded by a wall 6-9m high and surmounted by pinnacles, above which rises the 59m-high conical main tower (visible from far off), with the mystical wheel (p.227) and the banner of Vishnu at the top. Access is strictly forbidden to non-Hindus. Outside the main gate, on the E. side, is a 10m-high monolithic column from Konarak (p.90). From the roof of a nearby house, one has a good general view of the site. In the outer courtyard is the temple kitchen, from which pilgrims are fed with holy rice. The inner court, shut off by a second wall, contains the main temple with the sacrificial hall, the large pillared hall for music and the dance by the nautch maidens (bayaderes), the audience hall, and the holy of holies. The latter, (beneath the tower), houses the misshapen wooden images of the Jagannath, his brother Balabhadra and his sister Subhadra, along with 120 smaller objects of piety, in which the god is worshipped in various forms.

From the N. gate, a broad street lined with stalls and pilgrim houses leads to the so-called *Country House of Jagannath,* almost 2km distant, where the idols are dragged by thousands of pilgrims on heavy decorated floats at the main festival in June or July. The Jagannath float, the largest, measures 9m square, is almost 15m high and has 16 wheels of 2m diameter. Beforehand, the idols are washed and remain hidden for 14 days to heal the "fever" which they supposedly catch from this, i.e. they are freshly painted. – From here one visits the pool of the holy giant turtles, the largest being 1½m in length.

The traveller is recommended to undertake the excursion to the so-called *Black Pagoda* at Konarak, 21M E. of Puri, near the coast, a demanding day's trip (16hrs. return; one uses a palanquin or litter, 16R.) There are remains of a temple of the sun, built in the 13th c., and reckoned to be one of the major works of Hindu art. The outside wall encloses a courtyard approx. 150 X 95m. The temple is richly adorned with sculpture, of which the most important is the E. gate. Near this, a small square building which, to judge by its sculptures, was intended for music and dancing.

The railway then skirts *Bhuvaneshwar*, a major centre of the worship of Shiva, with numerous temples (p.LXVII), among which the great Lingaraj Temple of the 12th c. reminds the observer of the temple art at Tanjore (p.80); 4M to the W., the *Khandagiri* and *Udayagiri Hills*, with cave temples and monasteries which in part date from the 2nd c. B.C. (Hathi Gumpha) and are still inhabited by Jain monks. Even a fleeting visit (incl. the temple at Bhuvaneshwar) cannot be made in less than 7-8hrs. (take provisions).

777M. *Cuttack* (sta. rest.), town of 51,300 inhab., with an old fort (Kataka), also the main centre of the small tributary states of the *Orissa District*, which extends W. as far as the hilly part of Lower Bengal (62,779 sq.km, with 5 mill. inhab., who have their own language, Oriya, see p.XLII). The town lies on the r. bank of the broad *Mahanadi River* (which the railway crosses), navigable for steamships. The river delta, together with the adjacent estuary plain of the *Brahmani*, constitutes an enormous rice-field, out of which a handful of palm plantations rise.

887M. *Balasore* (sta. rest.), town of 20,880 inhab. on the r. bank of the *Burhabulang*, once with Dutch, Danish and English trading stations; an English possession since 1803. – 959M. Kharagpur (sta. rest.), where the Madras Railway meets the railway from Bombay, see p.155.

1030M. *Howrah-Calcutta*, see p.237.

Route 10. From Madras to Calicut. Ootacamund.

413M., Madras & S. Mahratta Rly: night fast train in 16½hrs., for 29R.15a., 15R., 4R.7a.6p. – The line is of interest to the visitor only from Ootacamund: branch-line from *Podanur* to *Mettupalaiyam* (through carriages from Madras); then narrow-gauge rly. Luggage, incl. larger items of hand-luggage, can be booked through to Ootacamund. The traveller who visits Nuwara Eliya (p.46) or Darjeeling (p.232) can leave out Ootacamund, since in the winter season, the best travelling time for S. India, the place is almost deserted.

Departure from *Madras Central Station* (p.81). – 26M. *Trivalur* or *Tiravallur*, with a temple to Shiva and four to Vishnu. The fast train takes 1hr. from Madras to Arkonam.

43M. *Arkonam* (sta. rest., B.1, L.1½R., if ordered in advance, otherwise 1½ and 2R.), junction for Bombay (p.100) and a branch to Chingleput (p.81). – The fast train takes another 3hrs. to Jalarpet: 65M. *Walajah Road*, sta. for Ranipet. – 81M. *Katpadi* (sta. rest.), junc. for the lines via *Vellore*, with 45,000 inhab. and a temple of Shiva; and *Tiruvannamalai* to Villupuram (p.81); via *Pakala* to Renigunta (p.,101).

132M. *Jalarpet* (sta. rest.), junc. for Bangalore (p.94). – Fast train to Erode in 4hrs.; the most important intermediate stop is (207M.) *Salem* (sta. rest.), district capital with 59,200 inhab., S. of the *Shevaroy Hills*.

243M. *Erode* (sta. rest.; good sleeping accommodation), an old town of 15,000 inhab., junc. for a branch-line from Trichinopoly (p.77; 87M in 4¾-5hrs.) – In another 2½hrs., the fast train reaches:-

302M. *Podanur* (sta. rest.; good sleeping accommodation), junc. for the branch-line to Mettapalaiyam (Ootacamund), see below.

The main line continues W. The fast train takes 5hrs. to (414M) *Calicut*, with 78,400 inhab., on the *Malabar Coast*, formerly capital of a Mohammedan empire, where the Portuguese landed in 1498 under Vasco de Gama and founded a trading-post in 1513. The town was laid waste in 1789 by Tippoo Sahib, but was rebuilt from 1792 onwards. The solid cotton material used in bookbinding, and known as calico, took its name from Calicut, whence it first found its way to Europe. – The railway continues N. along the coast via Cannanore to the old trading town of *Mangalore* (44,000 inhab.)

From Podanur to Ootacamund. – S. Indian Rly to *Mettupalaiyam*, 26M in 1¼hrs., then by the Nilgiri Hills Rly to *Ootacamund*, 29M in 5hrs., 1st cl. at the front of the train, with viewing platform; larger items of hand-luggage are not permitted in the carriages of the N.H.Rly.

In Podanur, the carriages destined for Mettupalaiyam are detached from the train. The railway goes via *Coimbatore* N. towards the Nilgiri Hills, which rise like walls. The plain, covered with palmyra and date palms, partly resembles steppe. – 328M (from Madras) *Mettupalaiyam* (480m; sta. rest.), terminus of the Madras railway and point of departure for the:-

Hill Railway. The *Nilgiri* (blue) *Hills* comprise an almost isolated upland area with steep declivities furrowed by ghats (p.104). 5M. *Kallar*, where the cog railway begins (the locomotive behind the train). As one enters the ghat, there are coffee and tea plantations. The line is boldly engineered. Several tunnels, and halts for water. At (14M) *Runnymede* (1406m) one can see the railway line 300m higher up on the steep edge. – 17M. *Coonoor* (1860m), a small health resort. On across a grassy terrain recently planted with eucalyptus trees. – 18M. *Wellington Barracks*, the English troops' hill station.

29M. **Ootacamund.** – HOTELS incl. Shoreham Hot., a family hotel prettily situated on a hill not far from Charing Cross, Coonoor Rd., P. 7R.(single Rms only out of season, P. 5R.); Royal Hot., Government Gdn Rd., 10 Rm., P. 7-10R. (out of season 5-8R.) RICKSHAW, with 2 coolies, expensive; no tariff.

Ootacamund, in the Engl.abbr. *Ooty,* the most important hill station in S. India, 2250m above sea-level, is the summer residence of the Governor of Madras, with many European villas and gardens. It lies in a broad, undulating upland valley which opens to the W., between two arms of the Dodabetta (2730m), the highest point of the Nilgiri Hills. The mean annual temperature is 14°C. One should beware the coldness of the nights, contrasting with the strong sunlight by day. There is an active social life here during the season (April-September). The most important public buildings are *St Stephen's Church,* the *Municipal Offices,* the *Post Office,* the *Bank* and the *Nilgiri Library.* To the S. of these, the *Market,* a *native bazaar,* the Parade Ground and some playing fields, separated to the W. from an artificially dammed *lake* (2200m) by a causeway planted with willows. *Lake Road,* which encircles the lake, is the thoroughfare frequented by polite society. Of great beauty are the deep clarity of the sky and the rich vegetation, created principally by the introduction of foreign trees and shrubs.

To the N., above the other houses, is *Government House*, which is open from early morning until evening. The large trees come from Europe, Japan and, especially, Australia: for instance, the splendid Acacia melanoxylon and the giant Eucalyptus on the E. edge of the garden. On the terraces, beds filled with rich European flowers. - ½hr. NE, above the Botan.Gdn., on the slope of the Dodabetta, the *Cinchona Plantation,* inaugurated in 1861, is the first successful attempt, after many setbacks, to introduce the Peruvian cinchona tree. Fine view.

10min from the guest houses (l. up the road after the exit), a small settlement of the *Toda*, one of the enigmatic original races which have remained in the Nilgiri district.

The total number of the Toda is no more than 600-700. Their settlements ("mand") always consist just of a few wooden huts, shaped like half barrels, with palm straw roofs. The people are well-formed, having good heads of hair and almost European features (aquiline nose). They wear a cloak shaped like a himation. They live from buffalo breeding (Bos bubalus). In every village is a holy *milk house*; the priest performs the sacred ritual of milking. In some villages one finds also a conical *temple* with a bronze idol in the form of a buffalo bell; an enclosed cattle-pound belongs to the temple. Polyandry is prevalent: several brothers may marry the same woman. The Toda are proof against Christianity. At Ootacamund they are avaricious, being accustomed to visits from strangers.

From Ootacamund to Nanjangud (p.100), a 3-day arduous journey by bullock-cart (40-45R.); one must take food, drink, bedding and mosquito net. One rests at noon (10-4). Night quarters in the Dak bungalows *Sigur* and *Goondloped.* The whole area is rich in game (see below).

Route 11. From Madras to Bangalore and Mysore.

To Bangalore: 219M. *Madras & S. Mahratta Rly* in 10½hrs. for 20R.9a., 10R.4a., 2R.14a.; from Bangalore to Mysore: 86M. Narrow-gauge rly (*Mysore State Rly*, not bearing comparison, in its standard of amenity, with the major Anglo-Indian railways) in 6-8hrs. for 8R.1a., 3R.9a., 1R.2a. – From Bombay via Guntakal to Bangalore (744M), fast train in 33½hrs., see p.101.

Bangalore and Mysore are the two capital towns of the native state of Mysore, which extends over the S. triangle of the Deccan plateau (see p.72). At the collapse of the Great Mogul empire (p.179) in the 18th c., the Brahman ruling family reassumed its independence, but was supplanted in 1759 by *Hyder Ali,* the Mohammedan commander-in-chief of their troops. Hyder and his fanatical son *Tippoo Sahib* extended the empire and entered the Anglo-French struggle for the domination of India on the side of the French (pp.70-1). After stubborn resistance to the English, Tippoo lost both his throne and his life during the storming of his capital Seringapatam (pp.96-7) in 1799. The English restored the old dynasty in the areas reduced to their present extent. In 1830 they annexed Mysore; but, in 1880, they handed government back to the princes, with some restrictions.

The best travelling time, because of the continuous fine weather and the cool mornings and evenings, is in December and January.

Those who wish to hunt need a *Licence for the Pursuit of Game*, obtainable from the District Authority (cf.p.94). Elephants, bison (doubtless the largest bovine on earth), sambur and axis deer, muntjak, cauchill, colsum etc.

are found only in the primeval forests of the Western Ghats. Everywhere there are tigers, panthers, wild boar, gazelles (Gazella Bennetti), blackbuck (Antelope cervicapra), hares, snipe, quail, jungle fowl, all kinds of birds of prey, etc. The best hunting season is April (at the beginning of the first growth of grass).

From *Madras* (Central Station) to (132M) *Jalarpet,* where the line to Calicut branches off, see p.91. The line ascends the S. plateau of the Deccan (p.100), with its broad, arid, partly forested or cultivated plains and low, strangely-shaped chains of hills and rock outcrops. In particular, a kind of millet (ragi) is grown and, where irrigation is plentiful, rice.

176M. *Bowringpet* (850m), situated in the state of Mysore, and junction for the branch-line to Marikuppam.

The railway to Marikuppam (10M) passes through the *Kolar Gold Fields*, the richest in India, known to the natives for a long time, and exploited in modern fashion in 1880. The annual yield is over £2¼ mill. The state of Mysore, which itself has an interest in this, has installed a long conveyor system, powered by electricity, from the Cauveri Falls (p.96) to here. The gold is extracted from veins of quartz. At the sta. *Nine Reefs* begins the appallingly dreary mining town with its limitless rows of coolie huts, low office buildings and engine houses. Powerful stamping mills, driven by electricity, reduce the quartz to dust, from which mercury baths remove the gold. The penultimate sta. is *Champion Reef,* the more welcoming European settlement with gardens, among enormous waste heaps of pulverised quartz. One can only visit the gold fields by introduction, since accommodation and food are not otherwise to be had.

219M. **Bangalore**. – STATION: *Cantonment* for the European Civil & Military Station; second sta. *City* (sta. rest.) 2M further, for the native town and the lines to Mysore (p.96), Guntakal (p.101) and Hubli (p.101).

HOTELS: Cubbon Hotel, High Ground, Cubbon Rd., not far from the Residency, West End Hot., High Ground, near the Race Course, both tolerably good, 7-10R, the rooms being mainly bungalows surrounded by gardens). More modest: Albert Victoria Hot., Brigade Rd.; Central Hot., Infantry Rd.

CARRIAGES: *Hackney carriages:* one-horse, for the 1st hr. or the first 3 miles 1R., 2nd cl. 12a., each successive hr. or mile: 6 or 3a.; two-horse, twice the above rate. Unless an arrangement is made, the tariff is reckoned by time. One is advised to drive, if longer distances are involved.

POST OFFICE; TELEGRAPH OFFICE, Old Museum Rd.

BANK: *Bank of Madras,* Old Museum Rd., opp. the telegraph office, 11-3, Saturday 11-2 p.m.

HOSPITALS: *Victoria Hospital; Bowring Civil Hospital; Lady Curzon's Hospital for Women and Children.*

BOOKSELLERS: *Higginbotham's Ltd.,* South Parade Ground. – PHOTOGRAPHER: *Wiele* (German). – GENERAL OUTFITTERS: Spencer & Co. Export & Import: *E.F.H.Wiele* (German), also for information about arrangements for hunting (p.93). All to be found on the S. side of the General Parade Ground.

CLUB: *United Service Club*, 27 Residency Rd.

ROUND TRIP (with stops, 2-3hrs.): through Cubbon Park to the Museum, then along the S. side of the Parade Ground, thence to Lal Bagh and back via Fort, Pettah, past the Residency, and to the Maharajah's Palace.

Bangalore (950m), the second residence of the Maharajah of Mysore, with 189,500 inhab., has a mean temperature of 24·5°C and, being regarded as very healthy, is therefore a favoured dwelling-place among English pensioners, as well as being a summer resort (the season begins in July). The town is rather more extensive in layout than Madras, surrounded by reservoir tanks, and possessing good roads and splendid gardens. It is divided into the European *Civil & Military Station* (previously called *Cantonment)* to the NE, and the *City* to the SW. The European station, with a 35 sq.km district to the E., is under British government and jurisdiction. The garrison comprises, by way of European troops, a regiment of infantry, one of cavalry and three field batteries; and, of native troops, two regts. of infantry, one of cavalry, etc. The city consists of the *Pettah* (native town) and its surroundings. Bangalore is a major centre for Indian missions and education, and has numerous churches.

The Maharajah's Palace, N. of the Cantonment station, is situated in a splendid and spacious English park. The building was executed in the style of Windsor Castle, with some Hindu additions. A N. wing in the Hindu style contains the rooms for the Maharani (i.e. princess). The interior of the Palace (open during the absence of the Maharajah, by permission of the government, information at one's hotel), is furnished in a predominantly European style. The large Durbar Hall, with its tall white columns supporting Gothic arches, is impressive.

Between the European and the native quarters extends Cubbon Park, laid out by the British Commissioner Sir Marc Cubbon (1834-61). On the NW edge of the park are the *Public Offices of the State of Mysore*, built 1861-68, painted red and with pillared halls in the European classical style. In front of this, an *equestrian statue of Cubbon.* In the SE part of the park, the Government Museum, founded in 1865, a small building also in classical style (open 7 a.m. to 5.30 p.m., except Sunday). On the lower floor, an archaeological collection, incl. a beautiful black stone tablet with Persian verses from the palace of Tippoo Sahib (destroyed in 1871) in the Fort mentioned below (translation next to the stone); in the main room, a geological collection. On the upper floor, zoology is represented. There is also a library with books on India. – The *General Parade Ground*, over 3km in length, is the largest square of its kind in India. It is surrounded by a busy carriage rd.

¾hr. SW is the attractive Botanical Gdn., called *Lal Bagh* by the people (i.e. "red garden"). The park comes down from Hyder Ali's time. There is also a small menagery. – From here one can reach the Fort, to the NW, which no longer serves any military purpose, with walls and round towers from Hyder Ali's first period of rule. Adjacent to its N. side is the Pettah, the oldest part of Bangalore, a cramped and noisy native quarter, inhabited almost exclusively by Hindus. The chief industries are silk- and cotton-weaving, lace-making and the working of gold.

The main street, which passes through Fort and Pettah in a NE direction, leads past the *Central Jail*, where good carpets of Persian and Turkish design are made, to the *Race Course*, and the *Residency,* seat of the British Resident (who, apart from the territory of Bangalore, administers the province of Coorg, annexed in 1834, and lying on the W. frontier of the state of Mysore), and then to the Cantonment Station.

The narrow-gauge rly to Mysore forms the S. end of the S. Mahratta Rly, which reaches Bangalore from Poona (p.102) via Londa-Hubli, a distance of 625M. The region is, during the dry season, a stark wilderness: rocks roasted by the sun, and jungle, the hiding-place of the panther. – 46M. *Maddur* (sta. rest.), starting-point for the excursion to the *Falls of the River Cauveri* (worth seeing even in the dry season), the most important water-course in the S. Deccan which, at Sivasamudram (48km S. of Maddur), finds its way valley-wards from the plateau through the Eastern Ghats (cf.p.77).

The excursion requires 2 days: daily tonga service in 4½hrs., 5R. per seat; private tonga 12R., to be ordered 12hrs. beforehand from the station-master. One is advised to take every precaution against fever. Good road. Finally over a fine old stone bridge to the 5km-long island of *Heggwa,* enclosed by the Cauveri. On the S. point of the island lies:-

Sivasamudram or *Shivasamudram* (i.e. Lake of Shiva). Accommodation at the Dak bungalow, provisions and bedding to be brought: better at the Inspection Bungalow where, however, one will only be received after a written request for permission from the Superintendent Engineer of the Cauveri Power Station. At this point, the Cauveri flows N. Its two arms form a succession of rapids and falls, totalling 160m vertical descent. The main fall of the W. arm, the *Gangani Chakki,* ¾hr. from Sivasamudram, is 500m broad and 120 high, with a horseshoe fall in the middle, often compared to Niagara. The fall of the E. arm is called *Bhar Chakki.* During the dry season, both falls break into many branches. The water-power of the Gangani Chakki is estimated at 200,000 h.p. (similar to Trollhättan in Sweden), and 12,000 h.p. in the dry season. To exploit this power, the *Cauveri Electric Power Station* was erected in 1900-02 at a cost of £340,000, providing 4000 h.p. to the stamping mills of the Kolar Gold Fields (p.94), as well as the electricity to illuminate Bangalore. A dam complex at the S. tip of the island permits, during the dry season, all the water in the river to be diverted along the W. arm. Beyond Maddur, the line approaches the Cauveri. The wilderness gives way to intensive cultivation of the soil.

77M. *Seringapatam* (in fact Srirangapathana; 735m), former capital of Mysore, numbering 150,000 inhab. under Hyder Ali and Tippoo Sahib, and stormed by the English in 1799. Because of the danger of fever, it was vacated again by the English forces as early as 1809, and now has barely 10,000 inhab. As one of the great memorials of British India, it merits a visit (see below; do not spend the night here). At the station, a Handbook for Visitors to Seringapatam is for sale (1R.), which deals in detail with the battles.

The town lies on an island in the Cauveri, 5km long and 1½km wide. The sta. is at the W. end of the island in the former Fort, close to the large *Temple of Sri Rangam* (i.e. Vishnu), dating, it seems, from the 9th c., after which the town is named. There is an attractive view from the ancient stone *Peripattan Bridge*, which conveys the road from Mysore to the island, and contains an acqueduct below the carriageway. Near the bridge, a *Hindu temple*. Numerous monkeys, regarded as holy.

Outside the E. gate of the Fort, near the N. arm of the Cauveri, lies the garden Darya Daulat Bagh, the favourite seat of Tippoo Sahib, reminding one of the gardens of the Taj Mahal at Agra (p.167). Within its pleasantly cool interior, the small palace contains low, gloomy rooms, which are but poor imitations of the halls at Agra and Delhi. The wall painting in the outer arcade, crudely restored from memory after the originals destroyed around 1850, depict on the one hand the defeat of the English by Hyder Ali with the assistance of the French (1780) and, on the other, scenes from the lives of Indian princes. – 40min from there, near the E. end of the island, in the middle of a thickly wooded garden, the Mausoleum of Hyder Ali and his wife, in which the English also buried Tippoo Sahib with military honours, after his heroic death in 1799: on a platform, a square white building with dome and surrounding arcade, whose pillars are of polished black hornblende; a mosque nearby. The three tombstones within are covered with richly embroidered silk palls. The religious services are presided over by Moslems of dignified appearance.

The country beyond Seringapatam bears traces of increasingly rich cultivation and careful irrigation. Between the rectangular rice-fields, clumps of date and coconut palms are seen, as well as extensive orchards. – 86M. *Mysore.*

Mysore.

Station 20min from the Fort; carriage meets the train. HOTELS: Gordon Hot., Church St., to the E. of Curzon Park, managed by a Parsee, moderate, 4R. – At the N. edge of the town, a Dak bungalow on the rd. to Seringapatam, 20min from the Fort.

CARRIAGES are provided by the hotel; prices as in Bangalore (p.94). – The excursion to *Seringapatam* (see above, 15km, shady rd.) takes ½ day by carriage.

POST & TELEGRAPH OFFICE: N. of the Fort, by the bell-tower. – DOCTOR: *T.J.McGann,* palace doctor. – HOSPITAL, supported by the Maharajah. – SHOPS: run almost exclusively by natives.

FOR A LIMITED VISIT: Fort and Maharajah's Palace, Zoological Gdns and Royal Stables, Elephant Lines; Chamundi Hill.

Mysore, since 1800 the actual capital of the princes of Mysore, with 71,300 inhab. (mainly Hindus; few Europeans), lies on an undulating upland without river, but among dammed-up lakes in a richly cultivated area, dominated by Chamundi Hill to the SE. In contrast to Bangalore with its important English settlement, Mysore appears as an expressly Indian royal residence on a grand scale. The Maharajah is one of the wealthiest Indian princes.

At the centre stands the Fort, an irregular oblong of sides 400-660m, surrounded by an old rampart and moat. The circuit is a rewarding one, and takes approx. ¾hr, The Fort contains the offices of the royal household and, on the W. side of a spacious square, the superb:-

Palace of the Maharajah which, after the fire of 1897, has been entirely reconstructed by native artists and craftsmen under the direction of English architects, in imitation of the old Mogul buildings (pp.164,180). The building material is reddish porphyry from Chamundi Hill, and a bluish-green stone, which matches it very well. An abundance of small decorative carving, displaying a rare richness and variety of motifs, is scattered over the entire building, which is several storeys high.

To the r. and l. of the entrance are low halls with stocky, richly sculpted stone columns. Moorish arches enclose small round domed ceilings with lotus flower motifs in polished stucco. One enters a polygonal courtyard, around which similar arcades run on all floors. The sculptures in Hindu style on the architraves of the pillars are executed in an astonishingly lively manner. To one side of the courtyard lies a red hall, several storeys high, with a glass roof bearing peacock motifs. The main floor contains, among other splendid rooms, the Desahara Hall, on the side towards the square, its polished white marble covered with tasteful flower decoration in pietra dura. The Indian scenes on the magnificently carved door-frames are charming: human figures strolling and making music in the forest, stags among the foliage, etc. The Hall projects towards the palace sq. as a portico shaped like a baldaquin. At the 10-day Desahara Festival the Maharajah appears before the people on the balcony, amid celebrations every year in September or October, recalling the heights of former glory. The throne, famous since the 17th c., is said to have been a present from the Emperor Aurangzeb. Another hall contains a wonderful coffered ceiling of dark wood, and doors with panels and frames of embossed silver or ivory work.

To the N. of the Fort stretches the modern Curzon Park, named in memory of the visit of the viceroy Lord Curzon. In the middle, an equestrian statue of the previous prince, now deceased. The long market halls on the W. side are the *Lansdowne Bazaars* where one can find, among other things, jewellery, worked in fine gold plate, which is so characteristic of Mysore. From the S. end of the bazaar, one turns W. to *Jagan Mohan Palace*, a curious complex built of worthless materials in the worst fairground style, erected by the previous maharajah "to entertain his European guests". NW of this, *Gordon Park*, with the Public Offices and other municipal buildings.

10min to the E. of the Fort is the *Pleasure Palace* in a park which also contains a maze. S. of this, the extensive *Zoological Gardens* (open 7-11, 3-5, except Sunday), with llamas, giraffes, monkeys, bears, ostriches, wild boar, various types of felines, esp. some splendid tigers. To the E. of the Pleasure Palace, the *Royal Stables*, with hundreds of horses of various breeds, among them the State horse, a snow-white stallion.

In the *Elephant Lines*, a large garden 10min S. of the Fort, 50 or so elephants are kept, which the Prince requires in order to display his oriental magnificence. The same purpose is served by the sacred white bullocks which are accommodated nearby, and the State camels.

3km to the SE, the holy *Chamundi Hill rises 300m above the town, an isolated 4km-long porphyry rock, on which Chamundi, a grim and gloomy personification of the goddess of death, Kali, is venerated. The ascent takes 1½hrs. A road leads along the causeway between the large dammed lakes Dod Kere and Gobli Kere, past coconut plantations and the race course, as far as the beginning of the pilgrims' path, which ascends the NW side of the hill in an almost uninterrupted succession of rock-cut steps, (very exacting in the heat of the day; one should opt for the morning hours!) A longer route is by the good road, up which one can drive (many curves), on the NE side of the hill, (returning down the pilgrims' path).

At the lower point of access to the pilgrim path (750m) is a small shrine. One passes through the gateway, beyond which the steps begin. They are of uniform width, hewn in the rock, enclosed by a parapet painted red and white (p.74) and provided with a few open resting halls. One ascends between large outcrops of rock, with which the hill is strewn. Halfway up, the massive black *Nandin Bull* (875m), 5·2m high and carved out of one piece of rock, surpassing in size the one at Tanjore (p.80). After another steep, but then gentler climb, one reaches the *village of Chamundi* (1043m) near which, on a small plateau, lie the two great temples, *Chamundishvari* and *Mahabalishvari*. The former is the main temple; the enormous gopuram is crowned with a gilded protuberance with golden horns. Around the temples runs a broad festal way, on which stand the processional carriages. There is a superb *view of the upland plateau of

Mysore, the town and its environs, inhabited and cultivated to a considerable distance; forests to the SW; to the S, the Nilgiri Hills, abrupt and fantastic in formation. – 300m N. of the village, on the highest point of the hill (1065m), there is a Dak bungalow.

The rly continues S. to (101M) *Nanjangud* (Dak bungalow, 20min from the sta.), a place of pilgrimage with a large temple where, at the end of March, a holy cart festival is held, with many visitors. – To *Ootacamund*, see p.93.

Route 12. From Madras to Bombay.

794M. *Madras & S. Mahratta Rly* to Raichur; from then on, the *Great Indian Peninsula Railway:* the through fast train ("Bombay Mail" or "Madras Mail" in the opp. direction) takes 32hrs., departure in the evening; fares from Madras to Bombay 68R.6a., 34R.4a., 11R.8a.6p., with 120lb, 60lb and 30lb of free luggage. Passengers and (until 1½hrs. before departure) luggage can also be booked at the Office of the Madras Railway, 186 Mount Rd. – Meals at the station restaurants, see p.XXII.

In the chief travelling season, the mail trains are so crowded that one can only be sure of a seat at intermediate stations by warning the station master 24hrs. in advance of departure. Travellers wishing to make the splendid journey down through the Bore Ghat (p.104) to Bombay by day, spend the night at *Poona* (p.102). For shorter distances, one may use the slower trains (known as "passengers").

At *Madras* (Central Station) one can have dinner before the departure of the Bombay Mail. The station for this is, in fact:-

43M. *Arkonam* (sta. rest.; 30min stop; also good night-quarters), junction for the Madras-Calicut line (Route 10), and for a branch-line to Chingleput (p.81).

The fast train takes 10hrs. from Arkonam to Guntakal. At (60M) *Nagari,* the train leaves the flat Coromandel coastal strip and ascends towards the *Eastern Ghats,* the edge of the Deccan plateau advancing towards us in a series of frequently scored mountain precipices.

The plateau of the Deccan (p.67), the upland area of the Indian subcontinent, rising gradually from E. to W., largely resembles a gently undulating, sometimes quite level, plain which, in the S. and E., tends to be punctuated by fantastic granite debris, and in the NW by basaltic tufa. On the isolated rock summits are castles and holy buildings. The small amount of rainfall and the sparse settlement lend the landscape a desert-like appearance in the dry season. Where larger areas have been won by cultivation, the latter is extensive rather than intensive. Nonetheless, the black "cotton soil", which in the SE part of the Deccan extends as far as the state of Hyderabad, provides, in the vicinity of rivers, among the best yields in India. In addition, millet, wheat, maize, pulse and linseed are grown. At these higher altitudes, the temperatures are less oppressive than on the coastal lowlands; beware the rapid cooling-off at night!

84M. *Renigunta* (sta. rest.), intersection with the Pakala-Gudur line (p.91, 88). – 162M. *Cuddapah* (sta. rest.); 228M. *Tadpatri* (sta. rest.); 258M. *Gooty* (sta. rest.).

276M. *Guntakal* (sta. rest.; the Bombay Mail makes a 15min breakfast stop), junction for three lines of the S. Mahratta Railway (change coaches): NE to *Bezwada* (p.88; 279M., in 15hrs.); - W. via *Bellary*, *Hospet* (to the N. of this, the ruins of the Hindu royal city of *Vijayanagar* which for more than two centuries stood up to the Mohammedan attacks, until it was conquered and destroyed in 1565), *Gadag* (branch-line Gadag-Bijapur-Hotgi, 173M in 12hrs., see p.102) to *Hubli* (p.102; 160M in 11½hrs.); - S., the line to *Bangalore*, important for its access from Bombay (p.93; 174M, fast train in 12¾hrs., for 16R.8a., 7R.6a.); intermediate stations: 63M. *Dharmavaram* (sta. rest.; p.91), 112M. *Hindupur* (sta. rest.) with pilgrimage temple, 152M. *Dodbellapur* (4hrs. to the E. of this, the mountain fortress of *Nandidrug*, stormed by the English in 1791).

From Guntakal to Dhond, the fast train takes 13hrs. – 308M. *Adoni*, a very old town with a large cotton market and weaving-mills. Between Adoni and (325M) *Kosgi*, the line passes through some particularly strange granite formations. At 334M, one crosses the *Tungabhadra*, a tributary of the *Kistna* and, with it, the border of the state of Hyderabad (p.111).

351M. *Raichur* (sta. rest.; 28min stop for breakfast; Dak bungalow in the town), 22,000 inhab., formerly capital of the sultanate of Bijapur (p.106), with a citadel on a 100m-high rock and an old city wall, like most of the towns in this area, which was much fought over in the disputes of the princes of the Deccan.

The rly crosses, by a bridge 1175m long, the broad, rock-strewn and sandy bed of the *Kistna*, whose water divides into a maze of unnavigable channels, as is the case with all the rivers of the central Deccan. Uniform culture of the soil depends no longer on irrigation, but upon rainfall. Scarcely a spot of black soil remains unused. Trees are rare.

418M. *Wadi* (427m; sta. rest.; 20min stop), junc. For the line to Hyderabad (p.112).

The line now enters the region of volcanic tufa which, in the NW parts of the Deccan, overlay the archaean basement. The brownish-grey rubble announces itself as a basaltic product by its softened polygonal shapes. A few small chains of hills show the smoothness of the surface of the tufa covering.

425M. *Shahabad*; 441M. *Gulbarga*, from 1347 to 1514 the seat of the Mohammedan ruling class, the Bahmani. – 502M. *Hotgi* (sta. rest., 10min stop for tiffin; no night accommodation), junc. for the line to Bijapur (p.105).

511M. *Sholapur* (509m; Dak bungalow), town of 61,300 inhab., already in the Presidency of Bombay. Its environs are richly cultivated. – 560M. *Barsi Road* (sta. rest.) – 610M. *Diksal* (sta. rest.)

627M. *Dhond* (sta. rest.; 30min stop for dinner), junc. for the connecting line via Ahmednagar and Lakh to Manmad (p.154; 146M in 5¾-6½hrs.) – After another 2hrs., the fast train reaches:-

675M. *Poona* (564m; sta. rest., 20min stop; hotels: Taj-Mahal, National Hot., both at sta., Connaught Hot., good, Club Hot., Napier Hot., Poona Hot., Royal Hot.) town of 158,850 inhab., 1714-1817 residence of the *Peshwa*, the most important Mahratta rulers (p.70), now headquarters of the English troops of the Bombay Government, and the Governor's summer residence. It lies at the confluence of the rivers *Mutha* and *Mula*, which then flow into the Bay of Bengal. The European part of the town, by the sta., is distinguished by its splendid gardens and bungalows. 2min to the N., on the r. bank of the Mula, is the excellently kept *Bund Garden* and, beyond the high Fitzgerald Bridge, the extensive *Deccan College*, an Anglo-Indian centre for learning. To the W. of the European town, on the r. bank of the Mutha, lies the native quarter *(City)*, whose houses often bear old wooden carvings and quaint wall-paintings, which are generally renewed at the time of wedding celebrations. Only ruins remain of the Palace of the Peshwa. – To the S. of the City, 1hr. from the sta., rises the *Hill of Parvati*, famous throughout India, surmounted by a large temple to the goddess (p.LX) with a partly gilded dome, and several other temples.

From Poona to Bangalore (p.94), the *Madras & S. Mahratta Rly,* 626M in 32hrs., of no interest for tourists. The most important intermediate stations: 69M. *Wathar*, stop for the much-visited pilgrimage town and upland health resort of Mahalabeshwar (1430m; also accessible by car from Poona, 75R.); - 160M. *Miraj*, junc. for a branch-line to *Kolhapur*, capital of the native state of the same name; - 278M. *Londa*, junc. for the branch-line to Castle Rock, see below; - 334M. *Hubli*, junc. for the line via *Gadag* to *Guntakal*, see p.101.

The branch-line from Londa is continued at (16M) *Castle Rock* by the Portuguese Rly to (71M) *Porto de Mormugao*, whence a small steamer goes to *Panjim* or *Villanova de Goa*, capital of the Portuguese possession of Goa, which was founded in 1510 by Affonso de Albuquerque and flourished up to the end of the 17th c. The luxuriant and fertile coastal strip which, 35-80km wide, stretches along at the foot of the Deccan (p.67), and called *Konkan*, N. to Bombay, and *Malabar* to the S., was once the chief centre of trading with the Occident. Goa now comprises only 3370 sq.km, with 475,000 inhab. (of which ⅔ are R.C. Hindus, few Europeans). Panjim has been the seat of government since 1753. A road, 8km long, goes E. to Old Goa or *Goa Velha*, the old capital, now in ruins, with dilapidated monasteries and churches, of which Bom Jesus contains the grave of *St Francis Xavier*, apostle of the Indies (†1552), and the governor's palace, now in ruins. From Villanova de Goa there is a steamer connection to Bombay etc.

The railway (fast train Poona-Bombay, 6-7hrs.) crosses the Mutha and skirts (676M) *Kirkee* where, in 1817, the 3600-man strong English army gained the last decisive victory over the Mahrattas, though outnumbered seven to one; r., the big artillery garrison of the Bombay Presidency, where 4 regts. of field artillery are stationed.

709M. *Karli*, known for the *Karli Caves* in the rock face, 6-7km NE (¼hr. S. of the sta., the lesser *Bhaja Caves*). Since Karli is served by only a few trains, the next sta., (714M) *Lanauli*, is a more suitable point of departure for the visit to the temple: 12km; by carriage, which the station-master will book (3R.), if warned in advance, or by bicycle, 3hrs. return. One should order a meal at the sta. rest. for one's return.

Crossing the line behind the sta., one follows the military road up the broad valley, next along a short bridle path then, after ¾hr., one takes the carriageway ("Tonga Rd.") which branches off l., curving round to reach the rock face (if the weather is cool, one may climb up on foot, ¼hr.); otherwise, litters are available; one should get a coolie to bring up the bicycle.

The **Cave Temple of Karli*, the oldest and most beautiful Buddhist structure of its kind in India, dates from the 1st or 2nd c.B.C. (see p.LXVI). It later served the rites of Shiva and is now owned by the government, which has had a small shrine for Hindu pilgrims erected outside. A watchman opens the outer gate and gives information (tip, 4a.-½R.) To the l. of the entrance, a hexagonal pillar *(Sina Stambha)*, with 4 lions on the capital. From the outer hall, whose external wall is partly destroyed, three doors lead to the interior of the temple through a horseshoe arch blocked by an old wooden lattice gate: a triple-aisled hall, 39m long, 11 wide and 13 high, with a semi-circular E. end, in which stands a large dagaba. The pillars, 2 r. and l. of the entrance, and 15 pairs down the length of the hall, are hexagonal. The capitals of the series of pillars each bear two kneeling elephants, on which men and women ride, facing into the central aisle, and figures of horses facing the side aisles. The 5th pillar on the l. depicts, on the E. side of its capital, the Buddhist wheel of life (p.227). The centre pillar r. has 16 faces, with a richer capital on which, at the front, a dragon is depicted in relief. The vaulting above the centre aisle, blackened by sacrificial smoke, is divided into sections by teak ribs. Above the centre-piece of the dagaba, which contained the relics, are the remains of a peculiar wooden protective roof (called *Ti*, see p.254). The seven pillars in the semicircle behind the dagaba are of simple design. – Adjacent to the temple, on both sides, and hewn on the r. out of the rock, 3 storeys high, are the *viharas*, low rectangular cells accessible by stairs.

The railway reaches the W. edge of the Deccan plateau which forms the watershed between the Bay of Bengal and the Arabian Sea, the latter no further than 35km distant, in direct line. – 716M. *Khandala* (621m; Hot.: Glendale Hot., Khandala Hot., Hamilton Hot.) highest point of the railway and favourite summer resort of the people of Bombay, with a splendid view down to the sea.

Directly after Khandala, the **Bore Ghat* commences, one of the steep ravines created by atmospheric action, which cut through the W. edge of the Deccan plateau *(Western Ghats)*. The railway, built 1855-63, negotiates the Ghat at an average gradient of 1:37 (steepest gradient on the Gotthard Rly 1:38.5), with 26 tunnels, enormous embankments and viaducts (duration of the journey 1 hr.) At first the railway follows the W. side of the valley (sit on the r.) Splendid view of the deep ravine, which is covered in fern and brushwood, and wild mountain precipices with their romantic summits, spikes, towers and castle formations, and their clearly seen stratification and rich vegetation. During the rainy season, dozens of magnificent waterfalls hang, as it were, on the rock walls. Further, through a tunnel in the narrow mountain ridge to the W. of the ravine and then along, high above *Campoli Valley*, with a glorious view into the distance W.

At the *Reversing Station* (411m) the locomotive moves to the other end of the train, which now continues in the opp. direction, as is the practice elsewhere in India, to avoid the use of spiral tunnels (cf.p.153). There is a brief view l. Then the rly crosses again to the E. side of the ridge which, in the meantime, has become lower. There is a further view into the ravine, r. The temperature rises rapidly. Beyond the last tunnel, the line descends the ridge of the mountain until:-

732M. *Karjat* (61m, sta. rest.), where it reaches the coastal plain. The slopes of the Deccan tower above. The vegetation is tropical: bamboo, bananas, numerous palms etc.; the native huts are flimsily built. During the dry season the land admittedly becomes extremely arid even here, but it is possible to visualise the rich abundance of water in the SW monsoon season, at the sight of the enclosing walls of the paddy fields and the lotus ponds.

740M. *Neral*, halting-place for the mountain railway (13M) to the popular hill resort of *Matheran* (750m; Rugby Hot., 45 Rm., P. 6R.; Granville Hot.), visited by hordes of people from Bombay on Sundays.

– The line describes a wide arc to the N., round the *Bay of Bombay*; the picturesque hills to the W., which one approaches, lie on its E. edge.

760M. *Kalyan* (sta. rest.), junc. for the line to Calcutta (Route 17), the former capital of the Konkan (p.103), where Greek and Roman trading ships landed in antiquity. – The railway skirts (r.) the *Ulhas*, whose twin mouths enclose the island *Salsette*, and crosses the broad S. arm, which is subject to tidal action. – 773M. *Thana,* on the E. shore of the island Salsette, mentioned by Marco Polo in the 13th c. as the capital of a kingdom, and point of departure for the Kanhari Caves (p.130). The train passes between low, steep hills and S. across the coastal marshland to (784M) *Kurla*, finally across a causeway over the narrow strait to Bombay Island, past the stations *Parel, Byculla, Mazagon* etc. (the fast train does not stop at these) to:-

794M. *Bombay, Victoria Terminus.* (p.121).

Route 13. From Hotgi to Bijapur.

58M. *Madras & S. Mahratta Rly* (line from Hotgi to Gadag, p.101) in 4hrs., for 5R.9a., 2R. 7a., 9a.9p.; only the morning train (mixed mail) carries 1st & 2nd cl., the others only 3rd but, if warned 3 days in advance, the station-master will add on a first-class compartment. – The fast train from Madras has no connection to Bijapur; since there is no accommodation of any kind to be had in Hotgi, one should continue on to Sholapur (p.102), returning to Hotgi the next morning on the train from Bombay.

Hotgi, see p.101. – The intermediate stations are unimportant. As one approaches Bijapur, the mighty dome of Gol Gumbaz comes into view, near to which lies the sta., E. of the city walls. Tongas meet the trains (1R.) The road into the town passes through a gap in the walls.

Bijapur. – ACCOMMODATION: Dak bungalow, ½hr. from the sta, 6 Rm. at 1R. per night, ½R. by day (see p.XXV). – TONGA for a whole day 2R. GUIDES: indispensable; they only speak inadequate English, however.

FOR A LIMITED VISIT (1 day): early morning walk from the Dak bungalow to the tomb of Ali II, then by carriage to Gol Gumbaz, back via Jama Masjid, Mithar Mahal and Asar Mahal (pp.107-8) to the Dak bungalow; afternoon (about 3 p.m.) by carriage through the bazaar to Haidar Burj, Chand Baoli, Sherza Burj (Malik-i-Maidan), Fathe Gate, Ibrahim Rauza, Taj Baoli (pp.110-11), the Citadel (p.108). By following this sequence, one sees the E. town in the morning and the W. town in the evening, both in the best light, and one can rest during the hottest hours. One is however recommended to devote more than one day to Bijapur.

Bijapur (600m; Sanskr. Vijayapur, victory city), capital of a district in the Bombay Presidency, with 24,000 inhab. (28% Mohamm., 70% Hindu) and a bustling market, lies on a gently undulating upland of central Deccan, in a treeless situation, which appears terribly arid and barren during the dry season. From 1489 to 1686 it was the capital of a Mohammedan sultanate under the *Adil Shah* dynasty (founder *Yusuf Khan*, an adventurous son of the Turkish sultan Murad II, †1510; his more important successors: *Ali I,* 1558-79; *Ibrahim II*, 1580-1626; *Mohammed*, 1626-56), was conquered in 1686 by the Grand Mogul Aurangzeb (p.178), fell to the Mahrattas at the beginning of the 18th c. and in 1818 to the English, who left it in the hands of a native prince until 1853. In its heyday, Bijapur is said to have had almost 1 mill. inhabitants and a circumference of 45km. Huge mosques and palaces in a generous style all of its own, but influenced by Persian art, still bear testimony to the glories of the sultanate of the Adil Shah, and make Bijapur one of India's finest show-pieces.

The old city wall has a perimeter of 10km, with 5 main gateways in the form of bastions, and 96 projecting semi-circular towers; the moat in front of it is partly hewn out of the rock. Only a portion of the area is inhabited, the remainder being covered in ruins, partly excavated and partly romantically overgrown by Indian fig thistle. The main street, joined by the road from the sta., passes through the town from E. to W. More or less in the middle of the town, and to the N. of the main street, lies the *Dak bungalow*, with the Citadel to the S. of it, where most of the English officials live. The native quarters stretch to the W., both inside and outside the walls.

Near the road to the sta., **Gol Gumbaz* rises on a low platform, the mausoleum of Mohammed Adil Shah, a giant stone cube 62m square and 40m high, crowned by a dome 44m in diameter and surrounded by four 7-storeyed corner towers, with an outer gallery round the top, which projects almost 4m. The building's size and beauty are best seen as a whole from a distance where, dominating its surroundings, it appears in ever-changing and delightful forms as the sun moves round. In the interior also, which is entered from the S. side, the beholder can only gradually become aware of the considerable spaciousness of dimension, since one has no yardstick with which to measure such simple architecture, and signs of age, such as flaws in the materials, affect one's first impression. The floor area measures 41·28m square (1704 sq.m; the Pantheon in Rome 1471 sq.m). The dome rises 54m above the floor and has an inner diameter of 38m. A technical masterpiece, it rests half on the outer walls and half on arches which spring from the walls, 17m up, leaving a circular centre opening of 29·6m diameter, through which one can look upwards into the vault. The gravestones of Mohammed and his family on the great platform beneath the dome are cenotaphs (the sarcophagi with the bones are in the vault beneath, which is accessible from the W side).

It is worth ascending to the galleries (staircase from the interior of the building in the tower to the l. of the entrance). One first reaches the outer gallery, which provides a splendid *view over the ruined town. A visitor susceptible to giddiness would do better to view this from the roof. To the W., the mosque belonging with Gol Gumbaz, in the distance the tower Haidar Burj with its spiral staircase (p.110); rather nearer than this, the flat bulk of Ali II's uncompleted grave (p.109); in front of the latter, the Dak bungalow; to the WSW, most impressive, the two domes and minarets of Ibrahim Rauza (p.110); nearer, to the SW, the numerous buildings of the Citadel; to the SSW, the Jama Masjid; the city walls are also visible in many places. – One then enters, inside the dome, the inner gallery which runs round above the arches. Although this gallery seems purely ornamental from below, it is in fact more than 3m wide. The balustrade around the central opening is low. The vault conveys softly spoken words from one side to the other, where they are still clearly audible.

The former music room above the entrance gate (Nakka Khana, see p.106) has been fitted out as a small local museum.

S. of Gol Gumbaz, one crosses the E-W. main street (p.106), reaching its parallel street, which runs W. to the Jama Masjid, and E. to *Allahpur Gate*. Not far to the S. of the latter, lying on the next bastion set in the walls, is the *Mustafabad Gun*, an old cannon made from iron rings welded together, and almost 4m long.

The **Jama Masjid* ("Great Mosque"), begun by Ali I Adil Shah and continued by his successors, is distinguished by its harmonious proportions. The entrance, from the N., leads firstly into the outer courtyard. Here one removes one's shoes or is offered a pair of socks to slip over them. The courtyard, with a basin in the middle for ritual ablutions, is 101m long and 34 wide, with arcades on both sides; its E. wall is missing. On the W. side is the mosque, 101m wide, and 78 long, with a dome. Near the central entrance, a stone chain, wrought out of a single block, hangs down from the cornice. The interior of the mosque, which is grave and solemn in aspect, is divided by rows of pillars into 9 aisles and 5 transepts, with a flattish cupola over each rectangle so formed. The main dome is in the centre, where 4 pillars are missing, measures 15·5m in diameter and is built in a similar way to the (later) dome of Gol Gumbaz. It is unlit, and therefore makes its effect only from the outside. The floor, made of "chunam" (p.86), is patterned in black lines like prayer mats. In the centre of the W. wall behind a curtain (which is drawn aside on request), the splendid *Mihrab* (prayer-niche), whose decoration, with inscriptions, medallions and metaphorical images (buildings, censers, book alcoves, flower vases) dates back to the time of Mohammed Adil Shah.

The road continues W. to the **Mihar Mahal*, a slender three-storeyed gatehouse which, on account of the richness of its Hindu-Mohammedan decoration, puts entirely in the shade the mosque to which it belongs. – To the N. of this, the Asar Mahal ("Palace of the Relics"), built as a law court around 1646 by Mohammed Adil Shah, later converted into a holy place, which is still said to contain a hair from the Prophet's beard. The large pool in front of the hall is fed from the underground water-course, built c.1650, which comes from the Begam Tank in the S. part of the town. The E. part of the building is occupied by an 18m-long, 11m-wide hall, open to the E., whose wooden ceiling, supported by 4 massive teak pillars, was once painted. The W. portion of the buildings contains, among other things, on the upper floor a hall 25m long and 8m wide, in which some valuable old carpets are exhibited; a balcony, whose ceiling was once gilded, projects into the E. hall; the doors, with the remains of ivory inlay, open l. into a (locked) reliquary chamber, r. into two former state-rooms, with badly damaged wall-paintings. A viaduct of which some pillars are still standing, used to connect the palace to the Citadel (see below). – Further to the W., the S. gate of the Citadel, through which one returns to the Dak bungalow, postponing a closer view until the second visit.

The former Citadel, to the S. of the main road (p.106), is still largely surrounded by walls and moats and encloses a number of renovated buildings, which form an artistic ensemble with their courtyards full of greenery, and their leafy gardens. All these are now used for administration and dwellings for officials. The settlement on this site dates back to the pre-Mohammedan era, as the appropriated older pieces of architecture testify. A broad road bisects it from N. to S.

On the E. side of the road (l.) an *Old Mosque*, composed of building materials from former Jain temples; beyond this, to the E., the *Adalat Mahal,* the former court of justice. Further, opp. the Gagan Mahal (p.109), the *Anand Mahal* ("Palace of Pleasure"), the splendid former seraglio, built in 1589 by Ibrahim II, now in a sad state of disrepair; the façade incomplete. High above, on an E. bastion, the *Chinch Diddi Mosque.* The flat arch, which boldly spans the road, belonged to the viaduct of the Asar Mahal, mentioned above. Opposite the Granary (see below) stands the delightful *Mekka Masjid*, in a courtyard surrounded by a high wall with two heavy, ancient minarets, a miniature mosque of grey stone, with pretty arabesques, built in 1669, perhaps for the womenfolk of the palace. Of the gates to the Citadel, only the S. one remains.

Back to the buildings along the W. side of the road. Here, near the S. gate, the *Mosque of Karim ud-din,* adapted from a Hindu temple. The outer entry gate, which one negotiates through a turnstile, is a former mantapam (p.75); the inner gate, decorated with carvings, is Mohammedan; the mosque, with its pillars showing great diversity of style (which have been brought up to the same height by additional pieces), and its flat roof surmounting it in the middle, reminds one of the first Mohammedan buildings at Ahmedabad (p.134). The palace beyond it is called *Chini Mahal* by the people, because of the many fragments of porcelain which were found here. The adjacent arcaded courtyard to the N., usually called the Granary, was presumably the quarters for the bodyguards. At the W. wall of the Citadel rises the tower *Sat Manzli*, formerly 7 storeys high (hence the name), now only 5 storeys. The small building N. of the Granary, on the road, has been converted into the English Church. The last large building on the W. side of the road is the *Gagan Mahal*, the former audience hall, built in 1561, with a splendid (now free-standing) façade, of whose three 15m-tall arches the centre one has a span of 18m; above, a gallery for the womenfolk of the Court. It is here that Aurangzeb is said to have accepted the submission of the last Adil Shah, who appeared before him in silver chains. – A few old cannon and stone cannon-balls are still lying about, at the N. exit from the Citadel.

To the N. of the main road (p.106) and W. from the Dak bungalow lies the monument or **Rauza of Ali II*, which remained uncompleted at the death of the ruler in 1672. On a high platform rises the square structure which, with a side of 65m surpasses even Gol Gumbaz, each side possessing seven elegantly executed pointed arches. Inside, a double arched aisle surrounds the central space with the cenotaph, above which a dome was doubtless intended.

The main road runs W. from the *Post Office*, beyond which the recently restored pretty *Bokhari Mosque* merits attention on account of its delicately executed cornice, and on to a point where the five roads from the main gates of the city meet together. One goes straight on to Fatke Gate (p.110), SW to Mekka Gate (p.111), NW to Shahapur Gate, SE to Fath Gate and NE to Bahmani Gate.

We take the road NW, which passes through the *bazaar* of the native quarter, and reach in about 6min the remarkable tower, 18m tall, known as Haidar Burj after its builder, a general of Ibrahim II (1583), also called *Upari Burj* (upper tower) from its situation. It is oval in plan, with an external staircase, broad enough even for visitors prone to giddiness, At the top, two old cannon wrought from iron staves put together lengthwise with iron hoops round them (the larger is 9m long and has a calibre of 30cm), and a pleasant view. – The strange flat walls with three pinnacles (Idgah) S. of the Haidar Burj are taken to be the remains of an old mosque.

200m to the NW, near *Shahapur Gate*, is the second largest and most beautiful of the rock-hewn cisterns of Bijapur, the Chand Baoli ("baoli", also pron. "bauri" here, means "well", cf.p.137). A fine arch spans the entrance; a flight of stone steps leads downwards. On the high walls on the other sides hang scoops. The water is better than that of the Taj Baoli (p.111). The women who come to fetch water, with a jug at the hip or on their head, and wearing colourful garments, are a pleasant sight in this picturesque setting.

Following the city walls S. one comes upon the Sherza Burj, built, according to the inscription, in 1671, and named after the two quaint stone lions (sherza = lion). On the bastion, which projects to a considerable degree, lies a cannon, over 4m long, called *Malik-i-Maidan* ("lord of the battlefield"), a fine piece of casting with a shining finish and inscriptions, of which one gives the year of manufacture (1549), the other having been added after the conquest of Bijapur by Aurangzeb. The mouth is shaped into the head of a monster, crushing elephants in its teeth. The large calibre (68cm) shows that the gun was intended only for firing grape-shot at short range. – further to the S., *Fatke Gate*, then *Zohrapur Gate*. – From here, one passes through the outer town for 10min, to the:-

**Ibrahim Rauza*, the monument to Ibrahim II, modest in size but delicately proportioned and distinguished by the splendid richness of its decoration. One goes along an avenue, then through a tall entrance gate, and so enters the square courtyard, in which the mausoleum rises on a platform on the E. side, with its attendant mosque on the W.; a water-basin between the two buildings. The *Mosque* opens in five beautiful arches; above these, a richly ornamented cornice, from which stone chains hang down (cf.p.107); at the top, a balustrade and slender minaret. The *Mausoleum* is two-storeyed with a (restored) pillared passage round it, whose sumptuously carved ceiling contains verses from the Koran (the letters formerly gilded) on a blue background with flower designs forming a decorative frame. The perforated stone slabs in the window openings, with marvellous patterns, partly Arabic characters, rank among the most perfect examples of craftsmanship of this kind in India. Above the richly adorned cornice, a parapet, lace-like in its delicacy, runs round the flat roof, with slender minarets at the corners. The dome rises at the centre, whose substructure supports another 4 minarets on each side. Four teak doors lead into the inner pillared hall, whose central area (12m square) contains the tombstones of Ibrahim and his family; the flat ceiling is a single slab of moulded stone. A staircase in the wall leads up to the similarly decorated space beneath the dome. The whole complex is extraordinarily atmospheric, and the view from the roof in the evening light is splendid.

S. of Zohrapur Gate is Mekka gate, now closed and used as a school. – One returns to the town proper through a gap in the walls N. of Mekka Gate, reaching, to the SE, the largest cistern in Bijapur, the *Taj Baoli* ("Taj" means "crown"), built around 1620. The pointed Moorish arch at the entrance (on the N. side) has a span of 10m; the high retaining walls are simply jointed. The dirty green surface of the water measures 68m square. – To the E. of the Taj Baoli lie the *Two Sisters*, two very similar domed monuments in a walled courtyard. They are now inhabited by officials, and therefore not accessible to the visitor.

On returning to the Dak bungalow, one should also visit the *Zanjiri Mosque* to the W. of the Citadel. This was built in 1587 by Ibrahim II in honour of his wife Malika Jaham Begam, and has a richly adorned façade and recently restored minarets at the corners. – A fine tomb to the S. of the Langar Bazaar has likewise been restored.

From Bijapur to Gadag (p.101; 115M), the following intermediate sta. are worthy of mention: 57M. *Bagakot*, town of 19,000 inhab., with silk and cotton mills; 73M. *Badami*, an insignificant village but, in the 7th-8th c., capital of the kings of the Chalukya dynasty, with cave temples and well-preserved small temples to Shiva from that era (cf.p.LXVII).

Route 14. The railways of the State of Hyderabad.

The State of Hyderabad, officially called *The Nizam's Dominions*, after the title "nizam" of its Mohammedan rulers, is India's largest native state (p.72), with Mohammedans making up one-tenth of the population, Hindus almost nine-tenths, and 16,000 native and 8000 European Christians. It occupies an upland position, on average 380m above sea-level, consisting of tufa in the NW (p.100) and archaean rock in the SE. Wheat and cotton are grown in the NW, which is peopled by races speaking Aryan (Mahrattas); in the SE are extensive rice-fields, irrigated from artificial lakes. The inhab. *(Telugu)* speak Dravidian tongues. At the collapse of the Bahmani Empire (1347-1526), the land passed in 1512 to the Mohammedan royal race of Kutb Shahi, with its seat at Golkonda (p.114), which was reduced by Aurangzeb (p.178) in 1687. The viceroys of the Grand Moguls moved their residence to *Hyderabad.* In 1713, the Grand Mogul appointed the commander *Asaf Jah* as "Nizam-ul-Mulk" (viceroy), the latter becoming independent in 1720 and founder of the present dynasty. In the Franco-British wars in the 18th c., the Nizams were on the side of the English, who protected them against annihilation by the Mahrattas. Even in the Indian Mutiny of 1857, they were loyal to the English, thereby preventing the annexation of S. India by the rebels. Thanks to this policy they have, among the Indian princes, preserved the greatest degree of independence. Their jurisdiction over the natives knows almost no limits.

14a. From Wadi via Hyderabad to Bezwada

(Madras, Calcutta)

338M. Nizam's Guaranteed State Railway in 18hrs. for 31R.11a., 10R.9a., 3R.14a.; to Hyderabad in 4¾hrs, for 10R.13a., 3R.10a., 1R.8a.

Wadi (sta. rest.), see p.101. – Monotonous landscape: fields, fallow land, scattered trees, more rarely low woods; now and again outcrops of rock tower up, often fortified. – 44M. *Tandur* (sta. rest.) – 100M. *Lingampalli*, so-called after the many natural stone columns which remind one of the lingam (p.LIX). The rly continues through a region of fantastic granite formations which extend for 60km, far beyond Hyderabad: jagged low chains of hills, solitary summits, oddly-formed blocks of debris, often resembling buildings. Finally, the train passes to the W. of the 21 sq.km large reservoir *Hussein Sagar* and enters:-

111M. **Hyderabad**. – STATION (rest.) in the suburb Chadar Ghat, almost 3km N. of the city. – HOT.: Montgomery Hot., by the sta., branch of the hotel in Secunderabad mentioned on p.115, 9 Rm., P. 6-7 R. – CARRIAGES per hr., 1st cl. 1R., 2nd cl. 12a.; per day, 9 and 4½R. respectively. Hotel conveyances are dearer. – *Bank of Bengal.*

Tickets for admission to the *Nizam's Palace* and for *Golkonda* may be obtained by calling on the First Assistant of the English Resident, or the Nizam's Chief Adjutant. Personal recommendations can also be useful elsewhere in Hyderabad.

Hyderabad, capital of the state of that name, with 500,600 inhab., India's 4th largest city, founded 1589 by the kings of Golkonda, lies in a very verdant situation on the r. bank of the *Musi* (a tributary of the Kistna), linked by several bridges to the suburb *Chadar Ghat*. The Mohammedans dominate, not so much in numbers (189,000, as against 243,000 Hindus), as through their influence, giving the city an expressly Mohammedan character. Nonetheless, one sees types and costumes of the most varied Indian and Asian races: Arabs, Turks, Afghans, Persians, people from Zanzibar, from Bokhara, Rajputs, Sikhs, Mahrattas, Parsees, Madrassis etc. The native Mohammedans are recognised by their trousers, and turbans ending as scarves; the most aristocratic classes carry valuable and ornate weapons. Moslem women wear veils. The city's chief attraction lies in the strange, colourful animation permeating its streets and bazaars. Famous are the cotton and silk materials with a gold pattern, which are manufactured here ('mashru' or 'sufi').

The suburb Chadar Ghat, on the l. bank of the river, contains the dwellings of the Europeans and the higher officials, the race course, the polo ground (Fateh Maidan), a large *public garden* and, 1½km SE of the sta., the British Residence, built in 1800-7 in the Greek style and surrounded by a splendid park which, since an attack in 1857, has been enclosed within a solid wall. – S. of this *Oliphant Bridge* leads to the NE corner of the city. One should however head for the middle bridge, *Afzal Bridge*, which leads into the city's main street.

The city of Hyderabad is enclosed by a wall 11km long, with bastions. Near the bridge is the beautiful *Afzal-Ganj Mosque*, with 4 tall minarets. The broad main street, named after it, bisects the city from N. to S. The flat-roofed houses are adorned with pretty decoration, carvings and often grotesque wall-paintings. Not far from the gate, l., is the Palace of Sir Salar Jang, the former prime minister (1853-83) and co-regent, who administered the state in a fashion much admired, though he admittedly acquired great wealth for himself. It was thanks to him that Hyderabad remained neutral in 1857. The outwardly plain palace contains several courtyards, gardens, pavilions, stables etc. The living quarters are grouped around a water basin surrounded by a peristyle, from which rooms open off, furnished with a strange but now faded splendour. In one room the Chini Khana, a quantity of Chinese porcelain is let into the walls; another contains valuable old weapons; a series of rooms, fitted out in the European style, house some valuable mechanical toys, such as singing birds, moving dolls and so on.

Further S., beyond a high-arched gate, appears the 55m-tall Char Minar (i.e. "four towers"), arching over the intersection of the N-S. and W-E. main streets: a particularly characteristic edifice for Hyderabad. Built in 1591, restored around 1880, it possesses several galleries and slender corner towers, and was formerly a centre of learning. Arches give access to the streets on the other three sides also. – To the S., nearby, is the Mekka Mosque, the city's chief mosque, built in 1614, a solid structure 68m long, 55 wide, 17 tall, with 4 minarets and 2 domes; from the outer court, a good view of the Char Minar. The interior contains the graves of the Nizams and is accessible only to Mohammedans.

A narrow st. leads SW to the Chaumala, the Nizam's Palace (for entry, see p.112), an extensive complex with three courtyards in succession, spectacular but in many respects tasteless and, since the prince resides mostly in the Sirdar villa in the E. suburb of Malakpet, also in a state of neglect. Two of the courtyards are surrounded by pillared arcades in white stucco, in the Italian style; in the middle, marble basins with fountains. On the S. side of the main courtyard is the reception hall for Europeans and, next to it, a room for the English Resident; on the N. side, the reception room for natives, a semi-circular hall. The living rooms with the harem are not shown. The courtyards are full of servants, noble horses, elephants etc.

20min S. of Hyderabad, the *Falaknama* ("view of Heaven") rises impressively on a hill, a former ministerial palace, built by a French architect in Renaissance style and fitted out magnificently in the European manner, since 1897 in the possession of the Nizam. From the terrace, one has a fine *view of the city amid its lakes and gardens, with the ruins of Golkonda in the distance to the NW and, all around, the wild and rocky landscape. Of the tanks, *Mir Alam*, ½hr. W. of Falaknama, has a circumference of 13km; the cost of the 1000m-long granite dam ran to 2¼ mill. marks.

10km W. of the suburb Chadar Ghat lies the old ruined fortress of *Golkonda* on the l. bank of the river. It was formerly the residence and chief citadel of the Kutb Shahi (p.111), whose brilliant royal court and rich hoard of diamonds made the name Golkonda synonymous with the idea of fabulous wealth. The ruined site is surrounded by mighty granite walls with 87 bastions, on which the old cannon are still lying. The doors of the E. gate, by which one enters, are armed with iron spikes against attacks with elephants. In the W. part of the fortified town, the *Citadel* towers up on an isolated rock 107m above the plain, and still serving as a state prison. From the entry gate, where the sentry will demand to see one's permission (p.112), one ascends through a three-fold ring of fortifications to the royal palace, where one has a broad *panorama from the stone throne on the roof. – One also visits the *Domed Tombs of the Kutb Shahi,* which lie in an impressive setting to the NW, outside the city wall, 18 in all, surrounded by gardens. Between the city ramparts and the garden wall is the tomb of Abdullah Kutb Shah (1635-72). To the N., outside the garden wall, the tomb of Mohammed Kuli Kutb Shah (1580-1612), founder of Hyderabad, and his wife, Hayat Baksh Begam (†1617), 55m high. The beautifully chiselled sarcophagi are mostly of black basalt or syenite. The tomb of the last Kutb Shah, Abu'l Hassan, who ended his days as a prisoner of Aurangzeb in the fortress of Daulatabad (p.117), was built only as far as the beginning of the dome.

The railway returns along the W. shore of the Hussein Sagar (p.112), curving round the N. end of the lake, into which a broad promontory projects, with the race course. It is more rewarding to go by carriage (¾hr.) along the road to the E. end of the lake, used as a corso in the evening. The country houses along the avenue belong partly to Europeans and partly to officers and officials serving the Nizam.

121M. **Secunderabad**. – rly from Hyderabad ¼hr.; *Station* (rest.) to the E. of the town. – HOT.: Montgomery Hot., 43 Oxford Rd., 5min drive from the sta., 9 Rm., P. 6-7R.)

Secunderabad (558m) or *Sikanderabad*, founded at the beginning of the 19th c. and named after the then Nizam Sikander (Alexander), is the chief town of the 49 sq.km British cantonment in the state of Hyderabad, and HQ of the 9 divisional commands of the Indian army. The strong garrison consists (with Bolaram, see below) of 2 European battalions, 6 regts. of native infantry, one European and 2 native cavalry regts., 1 horse-drawn and 3 motorised batteries, sappers, engineers, service corps etc. Like all British garrisons, Secunderabad possesses good roads, public parks, bungalows in gardens, sports fields, clubs, some shops and a large *Parade Ground*, on which one may observe quaint and picturesque military drill (elephant battery). – Railway to Manmad, see below.

202M. *Kazipet*, sta. for *Hanamcondah*, 3km N., capital from the 5th -12th c. of the Hindu kingdom of *Telingana*, with the ruins of a so-called thousand-pillar temple built in 1163 in the Chalukya style (p.LXVII). – 208M. *Warangal* (sta. rest.), a second capital of the same empire, junc. for the railway (under construction) to Balharsbah-Warora (p.155); 3½km S., the old fort with 4 free-standing, decorated, so-called "Kirti Stambha", which one assumes to be wooden imitations of the gates at Sanchi (p.157).

261M. *Dornakal* (sta. rest.), junc. for a branch-line (16M) to the coal mines of *Singareni* near *Yellandu*. – Shortly before (328M) *Kondapalli*, the rly leaves the State of Hyderabad and the plateau of the Deccan and reaches the coastal plain which forms part of the Presidency of Madras.

338M. *Bezwada* (p.88), junc. for Madras-Calcutta.

14b. From Hyderabad to Manmad (Bombay).

391M. Narrow-gauge rly *(The Nizam's Guaranteed State Railway)* in 22-24hrs. for 24R.11a., 12R.4a.; to Aurangabad (sta. for Ellora, see p.118) in 18-20hrs., for 20R.3a., 10R.2a.

From Hyderabad to (6M) *Secunderabad*, see p.115. – 14M. *Bolaram*, a garrison suburb of Secunderabad. Monotonous landscape, esp. during the dry season.

Beyond (105M) *Indore* (sta. rest.), the rly crosses the *Godavery* (pp.88,154), and continues up its valley to (174M) *Nander*. The character of the landscape is still determined by the Deccan granite. Near (193M) *Purna* begins the region of basaltic tufa (p.100).

281M. *Jalna* (sta. rest.), town of 20,270 inhab., ruined castle and high-yield fruit orchards.

321M. *Aurangabad* (663m; sta. rest.. good; Dak bungalow in the town, 3km N. of the sta., also good), the second town of the State of Hyderabad, with 37,000 inhab., some trade, a cotton-spinning mill and ancient crafts (lace and embroidery done with silver and gold thread), not far from the l., that is to say E., bank of the *Ganda*, a tributary of the Godavery. Between the station and the town are to be found, on both banks, the barracks of the garrison (one cavalry and 2 infantry regiments under the command of English officers). The town was in its prime during the reign of Auranzeb (p.178), who resided here as viceroy from 1635, also as Grand Mogul until 1670, and gave it its present name. The ruins that are preserved today lend credence to the tradition that Aurangabad once numbered 200,000 inhab. The modern town lies to the E. of the old town. Of particular interest is the *Makbara* or monument of the Rabia Durani, Aurangzeb's wife or daughter, a small and abortive copy of the Taj Mahal (p.167), set amidst gardens. The tomb itself, surrounded by pierced marble screens is, according to strict Mohammedan orthodoxy, covered only with grass. The unimportant mosque *Jama Masjid* predates Aurangzeb's time (nearby, a massive old Indian fig-tree). Likewise, the beautiful old *Mecca Gate* and bridge. On the steep bank of the Ganda lies the *Pan Chakki* or monument, in coloured marble, to Baba Shah Muzaffar, Aurangzeb's father; the adjacent garden contains two stone water-basins, the one towards the river being 49m long and 24 wide, on a vaulted substructure.

.The railway crosses the Ganda. To the r. one glimpses the chain of the *Jalna Hills* (the late Buddhist cave temples on the slope towards Aurangabad are not worthy of a visit).

328M. *Daulatabad* (sta. rest.), originally called *Deogiri*, and capital of the last Hindu kings of the Deccan (1187-1318), was forced by hunger to yield to Ala-ud-din in 1294 (p.178). Since 1318 it was in the permanent possession of the rulers of Delhi; in 1339 it was chosen by Mohammed Tughlak (p.178) as the stronghold for his conquests of S. India and renamed (Daulatabad = "fortunate city"); and, later, it was also the dwelling, from time to time, of Shah Jehan and Aurangzeb. The now insignificant town (730m) lies 2km to the N. of the station at the E.

foot of the abrupt rock (911m), the highest point of the Jalna Hills, and surmounted by the formerly impregnable fortress. This repays a visit: one approaches by 5 gates, of which the first two are defended by iron spikes against attack by elephants. Beyond the fourth gate, l., a small mosque, with the 64m-high *Chand Minar*, erected in 1445, serving both as minaret and victory tower (cf.p.189). Beyond the fifth gate, r., the *Chini Mahal* or china palace, named after its earlier wall covering. A winding path leads up, partly through a dark tunnel, to the *Fortress* itself, with rock walls hewn vertically, and ditches. The top is levelled and enclosed by walls. There is a view E. to Aurangabad and N. to Khuldabad in the Ellora direction (p.118).

As the journey continues, there is a fine view of the fortress of Daulatabad. Half-way to Manmad, the rly crosses the *Sina*, a tributary of the Godavery, leaves the State of Hyderabad and, after a 2hr. journey from Daulatabad, reaches:-

391M. *Manmad*, on the Bombay-Gwalior-Delhi line, see p.154.

**Excursion to Ellora.* – The cave temples of Ellora are the most remarkable in India but, because they lie away from the main tourist routes, are less often visited. The traveller who arrives in the afternoon from Hyderabad will spend the night at *Aurangabad* (p.116) and order, from the Mail Contractor, a tonga for the following morning to Ellora (25km; 4hrs.) From Bombay (cf.p.130), one descends at Daulatabad sta. (p.117), where the station master will book a tonga, if wired in advance: 2½hrs, to Ellora, return fare 10R., with a night's lodging approx. 2R. more. – At Ellora there is a staffed *Dak bungalow,* quite tolerable during the main travel season, and also a *Rest-house* belonging to the Nizam. For the use of this, permission is granted by the Private Secretary to His Excellency the Minister at Hyderabad (request may be made by telegraph). Both types of accommodation are now staffed, whereas one previously had to bring supplies from the station restaurants of Aurangabad or Daulatabad.

The road ascends steeply from Daulatabad in the pass between the main ridge of the Jalna Hills and the fortress rock. 12km *Khuldabad* or *Roza* (833m), a village of 2800 inhab., with extensive old enclosing ramparts and many monuments incl., in the courtyard of a large mosque, the simple grave of the Grand Mogul Aurangzeb (†1707), also that of his son Alam Shah (†1712), and that of the founder of the State of Hyderabad, Asaf Jah (†1748) etc. – 3km beyond Khuldabad, one reaches the *Dak bungalow* mentioned above. One descends the steep slope on foot for 10-15min and finds, on both sides of the road, to the E. of the tree-fringed village *Ellora*, the famous:-

***Cave Temples of Ellora*, hewn out of the tufa. To the l., by the road, the Kailasa Temple (p.120). In the small house nearby are Brahman guides, of whom one should be engaged, if only to avoid further importunities. (They can scarcely speak English). – There are about 1000 such cave systems in India, mainly in the NW Deccan (pp.103,154). They date from various periods, mostly from the 1st millennium A.D., serving as monasteries and temples at the same time. The oldest and by far the most numerous are of Buddhist origin. Later, Brahmans and Jains followed their example. The Ellora Caves belong to all three religions, whose development may be followed in the building styles. From an artistic point of view, they are to some extent equalled by others, but the general impression is one of unsurpassed magnificence. cf.p.LXVI. – One takes the path which leads along the bottom, l., and begins at:-

The BUDDHIST CAVES (1-12), whose construction dates back to 350-750 A.D. A distinction is made between the so-called *viharas*, i.e. groups of monks' cells with a room for communal devotions, and *chaityas*, i.e. temples for divine worship, and for the setting up of the reliquary, usually in the form of a dagaba or stupa. Here, 11 viharas are grouped from S. to N. around a chaitya.

No.1. The oldest vihara, in accord with the original form of Buddhism, i.e. denying actual divinity, is quite simple. – The development from this to a richer style of ornamentation, under the influence of the revitalised Brahman religion with its rites appealing to the senses, is shown in no.2, with vestibule and beautiful columns and, even more, no.3, with sculpted pillars and a giant figure of the Buddha. – No.4 almost totally destroyed. The vihara no.5, called *Mahavara* (or *Dhervara* in older descriptions), 17·6 X 35·5m in extent, contains a main hall with two rows of 10 columns; the low centre aisle is lined with two long stone benches. – Of similar size and type are caves 6-9, all of them viharas.

No.10 is the chaitya, called *Visvakarma*, from the end of the 6th c., with a pillared vestibule and elegantly decorated façade, two storeys high. The inner chamber measures 26 X 13m with vaulting 10m high, which rests on 28 short pillars and, as in the case of the temple at Karli (p.103), is divided by ribs; at the rear, the dagaba, over 8m high, in front of which is a seated Buddha surrounded by mythical figures, all hewn out of the tufa itself. The 3-storeyed vihara, no.11, bears the name *Do-Thal*, i.e. two floors (the third was discovered only in 1876), with a forecourt 14 X 31m in size, leading to a verandah 27m long, 2m wide and 2·5 high; above this, two more verandahs, each 31m long; behind these are the inner chambers.

The vihara no.12, **Tin Thal*, i.e. 3 storeys, made around 700-750 A.D., shows Buddhism at the peak of its artistic development, but also, through its contact with the spirit of Brahmanism, nearing its decline. From the forecourt, 14 X 33m, a staircase leads to a massive hall, 35 X 13m, with 24 pillars in 3 rows, and 6 cells at the sides; beyond this, a smaller hall, 12 X 11m, with 6 pillars. The second floor contains a verandah, 35 X 3·5m, with 8 pillars, and a splendid hall, 36m long, with 24 pillars in 3 rows. Most splendid is the hall on the third floor, 35 X 19·5m in area and 4m high, with 40 pillars in 5 rows, probably the finest of the Ellora Caves. The rich, figurative decoration to be seen everywhere here shows the Buddha and Buddhist saints in various incarnations.

The BRAHMAN CAVES (13-29) probably date from the 7th to the beginning of the 9th c. They differ from the Hindu caves both in layout and in their richer adornment, which expresses the weird demonology of the cults of Shiva and Vishnu. The Kailas temple in the centre is regarded as a marvel of ancient Indian architecture.

No.13 is inferior. – No.14, *Ravana-ka-Khai*, i.e. Ravan's cave, is 26m deep, with vestibule and central hall; at the rear, a free-standing reliquary shrine. The sculptures represent: on the S. wall, Shiva killing the demon buffalo, playing chess with his wife Parvati, dancing etc.; on the N. wall, Vishnu with Lakshmi as a bear; in the outer passage on the S. side one can see, along with diabolical skeletons and Ganesa with the elephant's head, the seven chief goddesses with their symbols: Chamundi with the owl, Indrani with the elephant, Varahni with the bear, Lakshmi with the gryphon-like Garuda, Kaumari with the peacock, Maheshwari with the buffalo and Brahmi with the goose. – By way of a stepped path cut in the rock, one reaches no.15, the *Das Avatara*, i.e. temple of Vishnu's "ten incarnations". The forecourt surrounds a shrine to Shiva. The 29m-long hall on the lower floor has 14 pillars, and the 28 X 33m hall on the upper floor possesses 44. The sculpture is similar to that in the previous cave: on the N. wall, Shiva's wedding with Parvati; on the S. wall, Vishnu on a five-headed snake, as dwarf, as man-lion etc.; particularly gruesome is a Shiva with a chain of skulls, tearing apart one sacrifice with his trident and sucking the blood from another, etc.; the lingam appears frequently. On the other side of the road is:-

16. The **Kailas Temple* (Kailasa being the name of the mountain of the gods in Trans-Himalaya), hewn entirely from the rock in 730-55, with all its details, as a free-standing building, 47 X 84m in area and 33m high: it forms a giant monolith. One can only marvel at the builders' technical assurance, even if Fergusson does remark, in this connection, that it was less expensive to produce such a structure out of the easily-worked tufa, than to build one from masonry. The façade fronts towards the slope; the figures of Vishnu, Shiva and other gods are chiselled out of the wall. The pyramidal shape of the gatehouse reminds one of the gopurams of S. India, which however belong to a later era (cf.p.74). The courtyard has been dug out to a considerable depth. From the entrance gate, a rock bridge, from which one catches sight of two giant stone

elephants in the courtyard r. and l., leads over to the shrine at the front *(mantapam)* which encloses a Nandi bull. Crossing a second rock bridge, one reaches the *Temple* proper, which also stands on a high, massive substructure (33m broad, 50 long, 29 tall). R. and l. in the courtyard, two 15m-high stone columns, beautifully wrought. Stairs lead to the upper floor where, through the vestibule, one enters the 16·7 X 17·4m main hall. 16 pillars divide the space into a broad centre aisle and two side aisles. To the E. is the entrance to the dark cell (vimana) for the holy lingam, guarded r. and l. by river deities. From the outer aisles of the hall one reaches an open ambulatory, adjacent to which are 5 chapels with images of gods. The mouldings, niches and columns throughout the temple display an extraordinary wealth of delicate ornament. The N., E. & S. sides of the courtyard are lined with splendid galleries, with richly carved pillars and huge images of gods in a style both melancholy and visionary. The 3-storeyed hall by the S. gallery was perhaps intended for priests' dwellings. – Also forming part of the Kailas Temple, and above the W. part of the N. gallery, where a spiral staircase ascends, is no.17, the *Lankeshwara*, temple of the "lord of Lanka" (cf.p.22), i.e. Rama, a hall of 37 X 18m with 27 pillars decorated in a great variety of styles. No.23, the *Rameshwara*, with portraits of Shiva, 25. the *Khumbarvada*, with depiction of the sun-god on a seven-horse chariot, and *28. the *Dumar Lena* or *Sita's Chavadi*, by a rocky ravine into which a waterfall shoots. The majestic main hall is about 45 sq.m in area and 6m high, with 16 pillars and an ante-room (containing a lingam), reminding one of the rather smaller Elephanta Cave (p.130), and probably post-dating the latter.

The five JAIN CAVES (30-34), a few min N. of the last Brahman ones, probably originated in the 9th or 10th c. and, in contrast to the older cave complexes, are not linked to any monastic quarters. Façades, walls and pilasters carry the overdone pictorial decoration so characteristic of Jain architecture (p.136).

One should visit no. 30, the *Indra Sabha* (Indra's banqueting hall), two-storeyed, with smaller caves hollowed out all around it. Through the forecourt, which contains a small shrine with statues of Tirthankar, a stone elephant and a fallen pillar, 9m long, one enters the bare lower hall (22 X 17m). Then up to the upper hall (24 X 17m), with 12 fine columns and many Tirthankar cells all around. The reliquary chest contains a statue of Mahavira. A portrayal of Indra in the verandah is regarded as one of the best pieces of sculpture at Ellora. – No.31, the *Jagannath Sabha*, is also two-storeyed.

Near the handsome village of Ellora, another pretty Hindu temple from the 2nd half of the 18th c., is worthy of mention.

Route 15. Bombay

ARRIVAL. – By sea (cf.p.XIX): the P & O steamers moor at the new *Ballard Pier* at the entrance to Alexandra Dock, where trains wait for Delhi, Calcutta and Madras; others, e.g. the steamers of Austrian Lloyd, anchor outside *Prince's Dock,* whose shallow depth permits entry only for 1-1½hrs. at high tide (passengers are conveyed ashore in small launches). Travellers intending to continue immediately by rail are given priority. Heavy luggage is taken to the various customs examination points in the docks, where one must be present at the inspection. – Stations: *Victoria Terminus* (sta. rest.), for the Great Indian Peninsula Rly (routes 12, 17, 18); *Colaba Station* and *Church Gate Station,* for the Bombay-Baroda Rly (route 16), the latter being 10min drive from the hotels, and recommended to departing travellers who prefer to choose their seat at leisure; at Church Gate Sta., which is nearest to the hotels, the trains stop for a few minutes only; natives who live by Malabar Hill or Cumballa Hill board the train at *Grant Rd. Sta.* The Baroda line also has the stations *Marine Lines* and *Charny Rd.*, to serve local and suburban traffic.

Hotels: *Taj Mahal Palace Hotel (cf.p.167), at the S. end of the port, built at the expense of the rich Parsee Tata, with over 400 Rm., well appointed, good cuisine, P.10-15R. – Majestic Hotel, between Wodehouse Rd. and Colaba Causeway (p.126), 96 Rm., P. from Oct. to Mar. 8-9, Apr-Sep. 6-7R.; Watson's Esplanade Hotel, Esplanade Rd., with verandahs on the various floors all around; Great Western Hotel, Apollo St., P. from 8R.; Pyrke's Apollo Rest. & Hot., corner of Colaba Causeway and Lansdowne Rd. – RESTAURANT: W.B.Green & Co., or Apollo Bunder Rest., near the Taj Mahal Hotel, with an excellent grill room, beer on tap and regular evening concerts, meeting-point for Germans. – CAFÉ & PASTRY COOK: *Cornaglia,* Esplanade Rd., opp. the Esplanade Hot., very busy.

Carriages. One-horse: ½-day (5hrs.) 4R., all day (10hrs.) 6R.; *taxi-cabs,* cheap for short distances. – *Trams:* from the Depot, two lines through the suburb Fort, then N. through the native town.

Sea-bathing: two bathing-places, one at Back Bay (the N. one for Europeans), the other by the open sea near Mahalakshmi Battery.

Travel agency: *Thos. Cook & Son,* 13 Esplanade Rd., also representing North German Lloyd.

Steamship lines & agencies: *Peninsular & Oriental Co.*, 3 Rampart Row West, once weekly to Europe; *Austrian Lloyd,* 50 Church Gate St., 2-3 times a month to Europe, twice to Colombo (cf.p.1); *Marittima Italiana* (p.2), Elphinstone Circle, in the building of the Alliance Bank of Simla, once a month to Europe; *British India Steam Navigation Co.*, 2-3 times a week to Karachi (p.210).

Post & Telegraph Offices. *General Post Office,* near Victoria Terminus; *Telegraph,* at the corner of Esplanade and Church Gate St.

Banks. *National Bank of India*, Esplanade Rd.; *Hongkong & Shanghai Banking Corp.*, 47 Church Gate St.; *Chartered Bank of India, Australia & China,* Esplanade Rd.; *Mercantile Bank of India* etc.

Consulates, found mostly in the part of the town S. of the Apollo Bunder (p.126). Germany: *Dr Heyer,* near the Saluting Battery; (residence, Cumballa Hill, p.129).

Clubs (admission only by introduction): *German Club*, Kennedy Sea Face, not far from Marine Line Sta. (p.121); *Royal Yacht Club,* by the port; *Bombay Club,* Esplanade Rd.; *Gymkhana Club,* Esplanade Rd.; *Byculla Club* (p.127), the most select club in the suburb Byculla.

Shops. Bookshops: *Thacker & Co., Combridge & Co.,* both in Esplanade Rd. – European & tropical clothing, travel equipment (cf.p.XIV): *Asquith & Lord, Ltd.,* opp. the clock tower; *Hoar & Co.*, next to Cook's office (p.121); *Whiteaway, Laidlaw & Co., Evans Fraser & Co.* and *Army & Navy Stores,* all in Esplanade Rd. – In the native bazaars one can find, in particular, carvings in sandalwood, black wood and tortoise-shell, Bombay boxes (famous inlay work), vessels of copper and brass, embroidery and embossed silver (the latter esp. in Meadow St. and Hummum St. Reputable dealers are: *Framji Muncherji* at M.Madon & Co., 16 Meadow St.

Newspapers: *Times of India* (p.127); *Bombay Gazette, Advocate of India.*

The climate, influenced by the sea, is warm and humid, without the extreme variations found in the interior. The mean annual temperature is 25-27°C. The most pleasant months are November to March. The wet season occurs during the SW monsoon, June-Sept. The plague is limited almost exclusively to the native city (p.127). – DOCTOR: *Dr Alph.Mayr,* Roosevelt Ho., opp. the Taj Mahal Hot. – CHEMIST: *Kemp & Co.,* several branches, incl. the Taj Mahal Hotel, and in Elphinstone Circle. – HOSPITAL for Europeans: *St George's Hospital.*

For a limited visit (2 days). Walk through the Fort quarter (pp.124-5), *Elphinstone Circle* with the Town Hall, *Hornby Rd.* and *Esplanade Rd.* (p.125), the public buildings from outside (pp.125-6); view from *Rajabai Tower* (p.125); evening visit to the *Apollo Bunder* (p.126). Tour of the *native city* (pp.127-8) and trip to *Malabar Hill* (best done exclusively in a carriage, outward via Queen's Rd., return via the native quarter), the the *Towers of Silence*, for which tickets may be obtained at one's hotel or as indicated on p.125, and the *Walkeshwar Temple* (p.129). - Those who prefer to forgo the discomforts of the visits to Karli (p.103) and Ellora (p.118), should not omit the trip to the island of *Elephanta* (p.129): by the motor boat belonging to Cook's travel bureau, 1½-2hrs. (5R. per person); also by sailing boat from the Apollo Bunder, if the wind is favourable (4½-6hrs. 3-5R., irrespective of the number of passengers). Tinted spectacles will be found convenient against the blinding light during the crossing.

Bombay, capital of the Presidency of the same name, with 979,500 inhab., the most important trading and industrial centre in India after Calcutta, seat of one of the supreme courts, and possessing many educational establishments, is situated at 18° 55' lat.N. and 72° 84' E., on the S. tip of an island 17km long and, on average, 4km wide, forming an excellent harbour with the mainland opposite. Foreign trade, which in total value is about 1/5 less than that of Calcutta, is on the increase: exports rose from 431mill.R. in 1905-6 to 598mill.R. in 1910-11; imports from 395mill.R. in 1905-6 to 478mill.R. in 1910-11. The chief articles for export are raw cotton, seeds (sesame, cotton, castor-oil, mowra seeds), cotton yarn and material, opium, wheat and flour, skins and hides; imports are cotton goods and yarn, iron and steel, railway material, machines, copper and brass, silk, small iron trade ware, petroleum, woollen goods, food-stuffs etc. The English shipping lines make up 70% of the maritime traffic. The German, Austrian, French, Italian, Japanese etc. lines lag far behind. Among the industrial concerns, the cotton-spinning and -weaving mills are the most important, the number of factories having more than trebled since 1881. There are also some woollen mills, silk factories etc. Crafts are represented by work in precious metals, pottery, embroidery etc. – As the English fleet's main base in the Indian Ocean, the port is defended by several forts, both on islands and on shore. The shore garrison consists of 3 companies of English artillery, one English and one native infantry regt.

Its magnificent position, the splendour of its public buildings, its dense flow of traffic and the colourful bustle of its natives make Bombay one of the most beautiful and remarkable cities in the world. The name originates from the shrine of the goddess Mumba (p.124), and acquired its European form perhaps in imitation of the Portuguese "Bom Bahia" (good bay). The island passed in 1661 from the Portuguese, who had been here since 1534, as Catherine of Braganza's dowry, to Charles II of England, who made it over to the East India Co. in 1668. The latter founded the present city in 1672, moving its headquarters in 1700 from Surat to this safer place, which soon began to flourish rapidly (1744: 70,000 inhab.; 1780: 113,000; 1812: over 200,000; 1836: 236,000; but the figures fluctuate, partly because of the mortality rate during epidemics, partly because of a high immigration rate during famines in the Deccan). The city's constitution, introduced by governor Mountstuart Elphinstone (1820-27), aroused an interest in the common good, even among the richer natives. Around 1850, the city already numbered 550,000 inhab. The introduction of the cotton-spinning industry (1854), the mail-steamer connection with Europe (1855), the railways (1864), the rise in Indian exported cotton during the American Civil War (1861-65), the opening of the Suez Canal (1869) – all benefited Bombay to a high degree. After a drop during the plague years 1896-99, the population rose again in 1901 to 776,000, of whom 45,000 were Christians (12,270 Europeans), 508,000 Hindus, 156,000 Mohammedans, 46,000 Parsees (p.XXXVI) and 14,000 Jains (p.LVII). By 1906, the population numbered 977,800. The Parsee wholesale merchants, industrialists, ship-owners and bankers occupy leading positions here, and generously deck out "their city" with splendid buildings, and centres of learning and welfare.

The Fort quarter makes up the heart of the city, with the public offices, centre of the wholesale trade and European business houses. It comprises not only the old town by the harbour, walled until 1863, but also the more slender new town which has arisen since then by the shallow Back Bay to the W. Hornby Rd. and Esplanade Rd., which follow the former line of the walls, separate both parts.

To the N. of the Fort rises *Victoria Terminus Station* on the site of the old Mumba devi shrine, a spectacular structure in Venetian Gothic style, reflecting the importance of Bombay as the chief gateway to the British-Indian empire. It was built in 1888-97 by F.W.Stevens. The 450m-long main front faces W., with projecting wings and a tall dome above the central portion. – As one leaves it, one sees the *Municipal Offices* to the r., in Market Rd. (p.127), built in 1884-93, with tower and dome 78m high; to one's l., Hornby Rd., (see below), and several streets leading to the centre of the old town.

The middle of the latter incorporates Elphinstone Circle. In the gardens are statues of the governor-generals *Lord Cornwallis* (p.71) and *Marquess Wellesley* (p.71). To the W., in Church Gate St., *St Thomas's Cathedral*, the main church in Bombay (though plain in appearance), founded in 1718 with a tower from 1833 and numerous monuments within. To the E., the *Town Hall*, built 1821-35; on the upper floor, a large banqueting room with statues of governor Elphinstone and other benefactors of the city, incl. the Parsee Sir Jamsetji Jijibhoy (1783-1859), whose name is frequently found in Bombay; and the library of the Asiatic Society (about 100,000 vols.) – To the E., behind the Town Hall, by the harbour, the former *Castle*, now an arsenal, with a clock tower from which a time-ball falls at 1 p.m., and the *Mint*.

Along the edge of the harbour, N. of *Ballard Pier* (p.121), stretch magnificent quays and docks to a distance of over 4km. Immediately N. is the new *Alexandra Dock* which encloses some 20 hectares, then *Victoria Dock* (10ha.), *Prince's Dock* (12ha.) etc. – S. of the Castle, the *Government Dockyard*, laid out in 1736, containing repair shops and dry docks within its 80ha. Further on, the Royal Yacht Club, p.126.

The broad Hornby Rd., which starts at Victoria Terminus (see above), is one of the chief traffic arteries of the elegant business quarter. Among the houses on the E. side, whose irregularities remind one of the course followed by the original defensive walls, *Jamsetji Jijibhoy's Benevolent Institution* is worthy of mention, where tickets are issued for the Towers of Silence (p.128). The road joins Esplanade Rd. and broadens out into an elongated triangular space, whose centre is taken up by the *Frere* or *Floral Fountain.* The continuation of Church Gate St. (p.124), which crosses this open place from E. to W., passes between the large *Telegraph Office* and *Public Works Offices* across Mayo Rd. to the *station*, already mentioned (p.121). Near this, the headquarters of the *Bombay, Baroda & Central India Railway Co.* by F.W.Stevens, with many domed turrets and a 49m-high central tower. – Not far away, at the corner of Mayo Rd. and Esplanade Rd., a marble statue of *Queen Victoria* by the English sculptor Mathew Noble, placed here in 1872, mainly at the expense of the Maharaja of Baroda.

The above-mentioned buildings belong to the group of palaces erected in 1870-80, which stretch S. between Esplanade Rd. on the one hand, and Mayo Rd. and Esplanade on the other. Executed chiefly in English or Venetian/Oriental Gothic styles, and surrounded by fine gardens, they make an uncommonly splendid ensemble. Nearest the square is the *Bombay Club*; behind this, in a side street, the massive *High Court*, 170m long, with a rectangular central tower 50m high. Between the *National Bank of India* and Esplanade Hotel (p.121) lies a park, behind whose high treetops one may catch sight of Sir Gilbert Scott's university buildings: the *Library*, with the slender 80m-tall *Rajabai Clock-tower* (entrance on the 1st floor, 2a.; awkward spiral staircase with 248 steps; view well described), and the elegant *University Hall*, one third of whose costs were borne by the Parsee Sir Cowasji Jehangir (entrance on the N. side). The university is an examining body, which stands at the head of all the institutes of higher education in the Presidency of Bombay. To the SW, behind Esplanade Hotel, the impressive *Government Secretariat* of the Presidency, with a main façade 135m long, facing W., and a central tower 52m high.

Esplanade Rd. debouches into an open place, adorned with an *equestrian statue of the Prince of Wales*, later King Edward VII, by J.E.Böhm, erected in 1875-76 and paid for by Sir Albert Sassoon, a relative of the Rothschilds and head of one of the most important banking houses in Asia. On the r., next to the Army & Navy Stores, the *Sassoon Mechanics' Institute*, founded by the same family, with a library of literature and technical books. Next, the extensive *Elphinstone College*, a high school endowed chiefly by rich Parsees for the instruction of natives in "western sciences", and the university *Examination Hall*, at present under construction. – In the large grassy semi-circle, a *Museum* of arts and crafts is being built. In front of this, a statue of King George V as Prince of Wales, in admiral's uniform. The large *Royal Alfred Sailors' Home*, endowed by the Maharaja of Baroda, was opened in 1876.

Further E., by the harbour, the Apollo Bunder, a platform projecting out from the shore, with views of the harbour, busy with shipping; the islands, mentioned on p.130; and, in the distance, the mountains on the mainland. This spot is particularly populous in the evening, when there is music in the gardens of the adjacent *Royal Yacht Club* (p.122). It is intended to erect a marble hall to commemorate George V's landing here in 1911 (cf.p.184). The impressive bulk of the *Taj Mahal Hotel* (p.121) with its 70m-high dome, is one of the most conspicuous buildings in the town.

The S. part of the Esplanade, to the W. of the Museum square, is also busy with strollers and carriages in the evenings. A military band is frequently to be found playing at this time of day in the Band Stand, to the S. of the so-called Oval. Between the railway and the shore there is a well-kept beach promenade, offering a splendid *stroll in the early morning, with a view of Malabar Hill, and in the evening, when the sun, as it sinks into the sea, gilds palaces and treetops. At both times of day, one may observe Mohammedans and Parsees here at prayer, the former facing towards Mecca, the latter moistening their hands and faces at the water's edge, the women often in flame-red garments, which shine like dots of fire on the bright shore.

Colaba Causeway, S. of Museum Sq., (see above) passes the *Tramway Depot*, then the huge cotton stores *(Cotton Green)* and the Cotton Exchange, continuing to the peninsula of Colaba, which stretches more than 3km into the sea. L. of Colaba Rd., a series of artificial harbour basins (incl *Sassoon's Dock*, cut out of the solid rock, the oldest in India; now serving military purposes). To the r., *Colaba Sta.* (p.121), officers' dwellings and the barracks of the English infantry regt.; the *St John's* or *Afghan Memorial Church,* built in 1858 (in memory of the English soldiers who fell in the campaigns of 1838-42). To the l., the *Observatory* and an old lighthouse. The road ends at a former cemetery for Europeans. There is a shore battery at the S. extremity *(Colaba Point).* – 2km further out to sea, *Prongs Lighthouse*, connected to the shore by a row of reefs which are dry at low tide.

From Victoria Terminus, Market Rd. leads past the Municipal Offices (p.124), the imposing *Times of India* building and, further on and set back, on the l., *Jamsetji Jijibhoy's School of Art*, then on to *Crawford Market*, a large market hall for all kinds of foods. The main building, with its clock tower, contains the fruit and vegetable section; inside, an attractive drinking-fountain. One is recommended to make one's visit in the morning. – In Esplanade Cross Rd stands *St Xavier's College*, to the W., at the junction with Esplanade Rd., still run by

German Jesuits. Also here, the *New Elphinstone High School* for the education of natives, and the barracks of the native regt. Esplanade Cross Rd. forms the boundary between the Fort quarter and the:-

*Native City, usually called *Bazaar*. Its streets and alleyways teem with the most varied forms of life. The houses are up to five floors high, decorated with paint and carvings, the courtyards surrounded by galleries. The Hindu temples stand out, on account of their lurid colours. All the ethnic types of India and the neighbouring lands swarm around the bazaars and craftsmen's stalls: Hindus, Mahrattas, Parsees, Jews, Arabs, even Persians and occasional Afghans (see p.122). The chief bazaar streets are *Kalbadavi Rd.*, the continuation of Esplanade Rd. (p.125), and Shaik Memon St. which connects with Market Rd. and, to the E. of the former, *Abdul Rahman St.* In Shaik Memon St. are the *Jama Masjid*, the main mosque, built in 1802, and the large *Mumbadevi Tank*, with a modern temple, built to replace Bombay's oldest shrine (cf.p.124; Mumba or Maha Amba, i.e. great mother). The street continues, not far from the R.C. cathedral of *Nossa Senhora da Esperança*), to the remarkable animal sanctuary *Panjra Pol*, in whose spacious courtyards old and sick pets, cattle, horses, dogs, birds etc. are fed to their wretched deaths at the expense of rich Jains, since the Jain religion forbids their being killed (cf.p.LVIII). – In Bellasis Rd. is the *Byculla Club* (p.122), with a large park. Opposite it, on the S. side of the road, the *Arab Stables* (horse mkt., sales in the mornings).

The N. suburbs of Byculla, *Mazagon* and, esp., *Parel*, further N., are the centres of the cotton-spinning mills and other factories. Not far from Byculla Sta. (p.105) is a large public park, *Victoria Gdns* (known to native drivers as *Rhani-ka bagh*), with the *Victoria & Albert Museum*, a collection of the country's raw products and manufactured goods (entrance free, Sundays 7-10, 2-6, otherwise 10.30 a.m. to 5.30 p.m., except Wednesdays).

The native city is bounded on the W. by the beautiful Queen's Rd., which runs from Church Gate Sta. (p.125) alongside the Baroda & Central Indian Rly towards Malabar Hill, very busy in the evening with the motor cars and splendid horse-drawn carriages of the rich Europeans and Parsees who live by Malabar Hill. Not far to the N. of *Marine Lines Sta.,* it skirts the *Hindu Burning Ground* (called *Sonapur* by the natives), a long-drawn-out narrow area for the cremation of Hindus. The funeral pyres, for which valuable wood is occasionally used, are built up behind perforated iron plates; the burning of the corpses takes about 2hrs. (The visit is scarcely a rewarding experience; entrance free, with possession of a ticket, which may be had at one's hotel). To the l., the *German Club* and the *gymkhanas* (sports fields) of the Parsees, Mohammedans and Hindus. On the r., the European and Mohammedan Burial Grounds. – Beyond *Charny Rd. Sta.*, the road adopts the name Lamington Rd., crosses the railway line, beyond the *Royal Opera House*, by means of the new *Sandhurst Bridge* and, at *Wilson College*, a school for native boys, becomes Malabar Hill Rd. (p.129). The newly-built *Hughes Rd.*, branching off r. at Sandhurst Bridge, leads to the Towers of Silence and Cumballa Hill, see below and p.129.

On the high ridge, which stretches out above the SW corner of Bombay Island between Back Bay and the ocean, called *Cumballa Hill* at its N. end (88m; see p.129), and **Malabar Hill* (85m) at its S. end, rich Europeans and natives have settled, with sumptuous villas and superb palm gardens. The trip can best be done by carriage along Queen's Rd. (see above), across Sandhurst Bridge into Hughes Rd., ascending by way of Gibbs' Rd.

Gibbs' Rd. runs along the E. slope of Malabar Hill and offers excellent views. Above the road, wild rocky outcrops and circling vultures betray the position of the famous **Towers of Silence*, in which the Parsees, in solemn cortège, place the bodies of their dead for the vultures to destroy (cf.p.XXXVII). The area measures 30 hectares, the towers being invisible from the outside. Visiting hours, with the exception of one day per month, 7-8.30 a.m., 2-4.30 p.m. A dignified demeanour is expected. Smoking forbidden.

The carriage stops in the forecourt, which is shaded by trees. One gives the attendant the entrance ticket (p.125), and ascends the high white flight of stairs. At the top, a Parsee clad in white takes charge of the guided tour. The plateau is still partly wild and overgrown with trees and bushes. Potted plants line the paths. The *towers*, three larger, two smaller, are low retaining walls, circular in shape and painted white (the largest 24m in diameter). The vultures can be seen sitting on the edges of the walls and in the branches of the trees all around. Neither mourners nor priests are permitted within the towers; only those bearing the corpse may enter. The layout is however shown in a model: three concentric rings of pits, in which the naked bodies are placed (the outer one for men, the middle one for women and the inner one for children); at the centre, a shaft for the bones left by the vultures, to dry in the sun and then decay in the rain. The resulting water is filtered through charcoal and channelled into the sea.

The *view embraces both seas, being esp. fine to the E., from the platform of the *Temple of the Holy Fire* (interior not accessible).

Gibbs' Rd. leads upwards, partly on stone arches, S. to Ridge Rd. which runs along the ridge. To the l., one glimpses the pointed domed tower of the Hindu *Babulnath Temple*. To one's r. is the *Municipal Waterworks* (cf.p.130), installed in 1892, whose reservoirs are roofed over, to keep the water cool. There is a superb **view from the so-called *Hanging Gardens,* also to the l. of the road, over the beautiful crescent of Back Bay to the public buildings in Fort (p.124; to the r., the dome of the Taj Mahal Hotel) and further, across the harbour to the island Elephanta and the mountains on the mainland: one of the most splendid townscapes on earth. Next to the Hanging Gdns are the courts and grounds of the Ladies' Gymkhana Club. The road reaches the summit of the ridge. The view is obstructed by villas. Beyond the intersection with (l.) *Malabar Hill Rd.*, which returns along Back Bay to Queen's Rd. (cf.p.128), and (r.) Harkness Rd., one should descend from the carriage and follow the narrow, winding Banganga Cross Lane to the old Brahman shrine of **Walkeshwar*, whose foundation dates back to the 9th c. The name signifies "Lord of the Sand" because Rama (p.LX) shaped a lingam from sand here, during his journey to Lanka (p.22). The holy pool is surrounded by temple and houses. The colourful activity of the pilgrims, beggars in orange garb, ascetics in clothes covered with ashes, etc., reminds one of Benares. One should walk round the pool on the W. side and climb the steps E. to Walkeshwar Rd., to which point one should instruct the carriage to go. – The S. tip of the peninsula is occupied by the Governor's Park (no admittance).

The transverse Harkness Rd. (see above) runs down to Napean Sea Rd., which follows the W. slope of Malabar Hill to Gowalia Tank Rd. The latter separates the two hills and continues N. along Cumballa Hill as Warden Rd. Here, too, one finds elegant country houses and gardens everywhere. Passing *Mahalakshmi Battery*, one reaches *Mahalakshmi Temple*, in a romantic setting by the shore, whence one returns through the Native City.

The excursion to Elephanta (cf.p.122) offers one the opportunity to see one of the most famous, if not the most important, rock temples in India. Distance 5-6M. Pleasant trip across the harbour, past *Butcher's Island*, upon which a wireless telegraphy station towers up.

The rocky island *Elephanta*, which owes its name to a stone elephant formerly situated here, is 11-12 sq.km in size, completely covered in jungle, and reaching 173m at its highest point. One lands on the N. side, ascending by an easy stepped path to the *Cave Temple,* which lies not quite half-way up. At the bungalow by the entrance, where refreshments may be purchased, one pays 4a. to the guardian and receives a printed description. The temple probably originated in the middle of the 8th c., and is connected with the Dumar Lena cave at Ellora (p.120), though smaller than the latter, but superior from the architectural and pictorial point of view. With its 26 pillars, of which 8 have been destroyed, and all of its carvings, it is hewn out of the natural rock and about 5m high. The original entrance was on the E. side. Opposite, in a shrine open on 4 sides, with large carved gatekeepers (dvarpal, p58), is the Shiva Lingam. The sculptures on the walls depict Shiva's doings as the destroyer and recreator of things (cf.p.LVIII). The main piece at the N. entrance, the colossal three-headed "trimurti", portrays the trinity of Brahma (in the centre), Vishnu (r., with lotus flower) and Shiva (l.) Near the temple there are courtyards and chambers with similar adornment hewn from the rock.

Much simpler are the Kanhari Caves on the island of Salsette, a Buddhist monastic foundation of the 2nd-9th c., 3M E. of *Borivli* (p.131), 6M W. of *Thana* (p.105). One should set out early, in order to profit from the cool morning hours., The monks' cells, (more than 100 of them), either hewn from the rock or made by enlarging natural holes in it, extend up the hillside to six floors. The large chaitya (p.LXVI) is 26m long, 12m wide and has 34 columns. – 2-3M to the S., *Vihar Lake* and *Tulsi Lake* (artificial), constructed in the 2nd half of the 19th c., to provide Bombay with water.

The extremely interesting *trip to Ellora (p.117) can if necessary be done in 40hrs.: by the afternoon fast train via Manmad (p.154; long stay) in 10hrs. to *Daulatabad* (p.116), returning the next evening by the night train. It is more rewarding to devote 3-4 days, incl. the fortress at Daulatabad, spending the night at Ellora and breaking the return journey at *Nasik* (p.154).

Route 16. From Bombay via Ahmedabad, Jaipur and Alwar to Delhi.

849M. *Bombay, Baroda & Central Indian Rly*: fast train in 37hrs., for 62R.7a., 31R.4a., 8R.10a.; from Bombay to *Ahmedabad* in 11¾-12½hrs., for 28R.12a., 14R., 3R.6a.; from Ahmedabad to *Ajmer* in 13½-15½hrs., for 19R.1a., 9R.9a., 2R.14a.; from Ajmer to *Jaipur* in 4¾hrs., for 5R.7a., 2R.10a., 9a. – During the main travelling season there is a luxury train, with sleeping and dining cars, twice a month from Bombay as far as Agra (p.161); the train travels at night, stopping by day at *Ahmedabad, Ajmer* (whence it branches off to *Chitorgarh* and *Udaipur), Jaipur* and *Delhi*; the journey takes 9 days; 1st cl. 220R., incl. food but not drinks (3rd cl. for servants, no food, 19R.):

information from Cook & Son (p.121), where tickets may be obtained for other trains, permitting the journey to be broken at will.

Stations at Bombay, see p.121. – The railway passes between the native city and Cumballa Hill N. along Bombay Island (p.122), crossing, beyond *Mahim* (10M), over a broad causeway to *Salsette Island* (p.105). 11M. *Bandra*, a European residential quarter of Bombay, full of villas and lapped about by the sea. The railway continues along the W. coast. – 18M. *Goregaon*; 2½M to the SE, the *Jogeshwar Caves*, one of the greatest Brahman rock temples; 20M. *Malad*; 22M. *Borivli*, the most convenient point of departure for the visit to Kanhari Caves (p.130). – 23M. *Bhayandar*. – Then across an iron bridge 3km long over *Bassein Creek*, the N. arm of the estuary of the River Ulhas (p.105); on both sides, an extensive view, l. to the distant ancient walls of the former Portuguese trading town *Bassein*, for which *Bassein Rd.* (29M) is the sta. The railway closely follows the coast. Lush tropical landscape; to the W., the sea; to the E., the mountains. – 39M. *Virar*, 58M. *Palghar*. – 109M. *Daman Road*, sta. for the trading town *Daman*, still in Portuguese hands, 11km to the W. on a silted-up estuary. – Beyond (123M) *Bulsar* lies the old town *Navsari* (fast trains do not stop), with 21,000 inhab., incl. around 5000 Parsees, in whose history it has played a part since 1142. – 167M. *Surat* (sta. rest.), junc. for the Tapti Valley Rly to *Jalgaon* (p.154), formerly India's most prosperous commercial town, where Portuguese, Dutch, French and English had trading posts. In 1797 it still possessed 800,000 inhab., but has long since been outstripped by Bombay, though still numberng 114,900 inhab., whose chief occupations are cotton-growing, spinning and carvings in sandalwood.

The railway crosses the *River Tapti* and, beyond (198M) *Anklesvar Junc.*, the *Narbada* also, by means of an iron bridge 1400m long (p.157); to the l., a fine view of the old commercial town of Broach (203½M), in fact Bharotsh, with 43,000 inhab., a major exporting town for cotton, in the province *Gujerat*, which stretches from the Gulf of Cambay, into which the Narbada flows, N. to the Rann of Cutch (p.139). The province is extremely fertile, excellently cultivated and, with its various native states, covers 266,700 sq.km, with over 270,000 inhab.

247M. *Baroda* (sta. rest.; Guest House Hotel, 9 Rm., P.6R., tolerable), capital of a princedom founded at the beginning of the 18th c. by the Mahratta general Damaji Gaikwar; although the princedom is only of medium size, it numbers, as far as independence is concerned, among five privileged states (cf.p.72). The town has 99,350 inhab. and lies on the E. bank of the little river Vishvamitri. Noteworthy: *Baroda College* near the sta., numerous Hindu temples, a few pretty fountains; the palace of *Nazar Bagh*, where the crown jewels (valued at 60 mill.R.) are kept; two splendid cannon of silver and gold; the modern *Lakshmi Vilas Palace* or *Raj Mahal;* the elephant park *(Hathie Bagh)* and the *Library*, endowed by the Maharaja. Several bridges connect the town to the European *Camp*, where the British Resident lives, and a British native regt. is garrisoned. The Maharaja resides at the *Makarpura Palace*, 6-7km S. of Baroda.

From Baroda, a railway (not used by fast trains) goes via *Godhra* (see below) and *Rutlam*, connecting here with the line from Ajmer to Chitorgarh (p.144), to *Nagda*, 185M; thence via *Kotah*, capital of a native state, to *Bharatpur* (p.153) and *Muttra* (p.173), 341M. – From Nagda, a branch-line (35M) to Ujjain, one of the 7 holy cities of the Hindus, by the *River Sipra*; thence to Bhopal (p.157).

The journey (another 2hrs. to Ahmedabad; in all, 10hrs. by fast train from Bombay) is attractive throughout. The last stopping points for fast trains are: 269M. *Anand*, junc. for branch-lines SW to the ancient port of *Cambay*, on the gulf of the same name, and NE to Godhra (see above); - 280¾M. *Nadiad*; 291¾M. *Mehmadabad*. Soon, the chimneys of the cotton-spinning mills of (309M) *Ahmedabad* come into view, junc. for the narrow-gauge line to Delhi (change carriages), see p.139.

Ahmedabad.

HOTELS: Grand Hot., in the Mirzapur quarter (p.135), 12 Rm., P.7, out of season 6R.; Empire Hot., at the N. entrance of the Bhadr (p.135), 15 Rm., same prices, both good; sta. rest. with Rm., B.1½, L.1½, D.2R. – Passengers on the luxury train use their own sleeping-car, see p.131.

POST OFFICE, SE of the Bhadr. TELEGRAPH OFFICE, in the Bhadr.

CARRIAGES, at the sta.: per hr. 1R., successive hrs. 12a. each, per day 6R. – GUIDES, also at the sta., 2R. per day. – Dark glasses are essential against the blinding sunlight.

FOR A LIMITED VISIT (1 day). Within the town: *Jama Masjid* (p.133), the *Queens' Tombs* (p.134), *Ranee Sipri's Mosque* (p.134); through the *Triple-arched Gate* to the citadel, *Bhadr* (p.135), here past Admed Shah's ancient mosque to *Sabarmati Bridge* (p.138; view); then back to the *Sidi Saiyid Mosque* (p.135), to the *Ranee Rupavati Mosque* (p.135) and the Mosque of *Muhafiz Khan* (p.136), whose minarets were the only ones in the whole town to survive the earthquake of 1819 without damage. Outside the town: the *Jain Temple of Hathi Singh* (p.136), the subterranean system of wells near *Asarva* (p.137), *Lake Kankariya* (p.137), and the *mosque and funeral monument of Shah Alam* (p.137). Ours is by no means an exhaustive description of all that is worth seeing here; many other mosques will repay a visit. For the rest, one should devote a second day to the excursion to *Sarkhej* (p.138). – The typical Indian street scenes are fascinating. The natives differ, in their dress and the colour of their skin, markedly from those of the S. Indian types. The women go about heavily veiled, the upper part of the body bare between the belt and the breast, which is covered by a short jacket. One occasionally encounters Hindu wedding processions, in which the couple's entire domestic utensils are carried on display; the young people are often still only children. The Jains' love of animals is often manifested in the attractive feeding-places (like dove-cotes) for birds and squirrels. The trees inside and outside the town are populated by monkeys, which often behave in an audacious fashion. The grey hanuman (Semnopithecus entellus) is the holy monkey of the Indian folk epic (cf.p.77). In the trees one also sees the nests of weaver birds, and the so-called flying foxes (cf.p.43).

Ahmedabad (53m), the second largest city in the Bombay Presidency, on the l. bank of the *Sabarmati* (500-550m wide, generally with little water in it) owes its name to the sultan *Ahmed Shah* of Gujerat (1411-43), who probably built the citadel at the older Hindu town of Karnavati. His successors, of whom *Mahmud Shah Bigarah* (1459-1511) was the most important, ruled until 1572. An astonishing abundance of splendid buildings still bears witness today to the glory of that epoque. The city continued to flourish during the Grand Moguls' rule (1572-1707); the number of its inhabitants reached about 900,000. With the Mahratta wars of the 18th c. its decline set in, this giving way to a new impetus, due particularly to the cotton industry since the British occupation (1818).

Ahmedabad is one of the most remarkable cities in India. Among its 215,800 people, more than 70% of whom are Hindus, there are prominent groups of Mohammedans (38,200) and Jains (15,500), the latter being rich merchants and moneylenders. There is no European population here. The traditional crafts are still practised: gold and silken articles, lace-making, jewellery, wood-carving, delicate mosaic work and, more recently, carpet-weaving.

At the *station* rise two minarets, 30m high, the survivors of a mosque now destroyed. Kalapur Gate is the usual point of entry to the town, enclosed by a low, thick wall and strengthened by round towers, but without a moat. One then follows the main street which passes close to *Sakar Khan's Mosque*, built in 1450-60. The houses, mostly of two storeys, display an uncommonly rich variety of imaginative wood and stone decoration in the form of pilasters, cornices, window frames and domes. Family life has its place on the open ground floor. – Roughly in the middle of the town is the **Jama Masjid*, the chief mosque, founded in 1423 by Ahmed Shah. One enters the forecourt from the N. side, up some steps and through a nondescript pillared gateway while, on the S. side, long flights of steps and a beautiful vestibule of 8 pillars – some taken from older buildings – give access. The *forecourt* measures 85 X 69m, and is surrounded on 3 sides by arcades; in the centre, the well of purification. The *Mosque*, on the W. side of the court, displays that peculiar mixture of Saracen and Hindu styles, which can be explained by the Mohammedan conquerors' use of native labour, this being characteristic of Ahmedabad. It is 63m wide, 30·5 deep, 14 tall in the centre aisle and 9·5 and 6·7 in the side aisles, with 15 domes supported by 12 pillars, 252 slender columns and 60 wall pilasters. During the 1819 earthquake, the minarets flanking the main entrance lost their upper portions. The domes are formed in the Hindu manner with stone rings set one above the other and narrowing as they rise, these being richly decorated with sculptures, esp. in the centre aisle. All 5 aisles lead to prayer niches (mihrab) in the rear wall, also rich in carvings in coloured marble. The baldaquin for the courtyard (Muluk Khana) is supported on slender columns and enclosed by pierced stone screens.

If one leaves the courtyard of the mosque by the E. gate, one comes face to face with *Ahmed Shah's Funeral Monument* or Rauza, which occupies the middle of the adjacent courtyard. The building, a square with sides of 27m, consists of an 11m-high domed space at the centre and four corner chambers, connected by pillared halls. The domed area contains the tombs of Ahmed Shah, his son and grandson, the W. and E. pillared halls containing the tombs of two other sultans – all delicately carved in marble and covered with brocade. Note also the exquisitely pierced window tracery in the corner chambers.

The E. exit from the courtyard leads into the street, on whose opposite side decaying steps ascend between the houses to the 3m higher **Burial-place of the Queens* (Rani ka Hajira), a kind of cemetery 37m square. The courtyard is surrounded by arcades divided by a marble wall, with richly pierced window screens, into an inner and outer ambulatory. The tombstones are marble with carved decoration. The chief tomb, of white marble, is, according to a Persian inscription, that of the wife of Mohammed Shah II. Nearby, a black marble tomb, similarly executed. The ladies' pets are said to be buried in the smaller graves between the tombs.

Backing on to the road leading S., near Astodiya Gate (p.137), l., is *Ranee Sipri's Mosque*, reached by going up a few steps. The building, completed in 1514 and ranked by Fergusson alongside the Erechtheion and the noblest Gothic churches for its delicacy and beauty, is executed in red sandstone. It is only 15m wide and 6m deep, with 6 domes, barely 6m high, and two minarets of 15m. The rich ornamentation of the architrave, the pillars, the interiors of the domes etc. displays the finest workmanship. On the other side of the courtyard is the attendant *Funeral Monument* or *Rauza*, a square pillared structure of side 12m, with a 10m-high dome, also distinguished by the delicacy of its decoration, esp. in the pierced screens surrounding the tomb.

In the SE part of the town, the following are worth a mention here: *Dastur Khan's Masjid*, completed in 1463 (a square courtyard with sides 30m long, surrounded by vaulted pillared halls with domes, doubled on the W. side, where the mosque stands), and the *Mosque of Mohammed Ghaus Gwaliari*, built 1560 (not in the style of Ahmedabad, but that of the mosque at Jaunpur).

To the W. of the Jama Masjid, at the end of the main street, one passes through the triumphal arch *Tin Darwaza*, built by Ahmed Shah, and possessing 3 arches, 7·35m high, to the forecourt of the:-

Bhadr, or Citadel, by building which, in 1411, Ahmed Shah secured his possession of the town. To the l. of the entrance, the noble *Palace of the Azam Khan*, of 1636, now a prison. In the SW corner, the *Old Mosque of Ahmed Shah*, erected in 1414 chiefly from portions of Hindu temples, 47·7m long, 16·46 deep, with 152 pillars, 10 domes and a layout similar to that of the main mosque (p.133), decaying since the Mahratta rule, now under government ownership. The S. gate of the Citadel leads into Victoria Gardens (p.138). – The buildings of the N. part of the Citadel are given over to administrative purposes and the Telegraph Office. The NE corner is occupied by the former *Mosque of Sidi Saiyid*, of the 15-16th c., now restored. The building is 21m long, 11 deep, with 4 pillars in front and 8 within, and open to the front; the splendid *stone tracery in the eleven pointed windows is famous, depicting an astonishing abundance of the most diverse motifs, esp. in the second and third window of the rear wall (the effect is even more beautiful when viewed from outside).

In the *Mirzapur* quarter, N. of the Citadel, special attention should be paid to the *Ranee Rupavati Masjid, that is, *Queen's Mosque*. It dates from the end of the 15th or beginning of the 16th c., and differs from the other mosques in the town by its blending of the Saracen arch and the Hindu entablature into a unified effect, further enhanced by the pretty garden in front of it. The rich ornamentation in red sandstone is of the finest workmanship. The façade, 41·4m wide, opens in a main entrance at the centre, framed by the minarets, whose tops fell down in 1819, and two subsidiary entrances between balconied windows on each side. The interior is 28·5m wide and 11 deep. 36 columns support the high central dome and the lower side domes. The prayer niches (mihrab) are in white marble. Obliquely opposite the mosque, on a low platform 12m square, is the funeral monument or *Rauza* of *Ranee Rupavati,* with 20 pillars outside and 12 within, a high central dome and 4 lower ones at the corners; the interior almost completely destroyed.

The *Mosque of Muhafiz Khan*, 5min to the N., near the Delhi Gate, and from the late 15th c., is the best preserved of all the mosques in the town. The small building, erected by a high dignitary of Sultan Mahmud Shah Bigarah, opens in 3 entrances of equal height, above which attractive balconies are fixed; the minarets at the l. and r. corners display rich craftsmanship. The interior, 14·3m wide, 7·5 deep, has 8 columns; only the centre aisle is vaulted with domes, the side aisles having flat roofs. – To the SE, the Hindu temple *Svami Narayana,* completed in 1850, an octagonal domed structure; and the *Animal Sanctuary,* frequently mentioned in the older travel descriptions (cf.p.127), now little used.

Outside the city walls. – To the N., 5min beyond the Delhi Gate, stands, r., the modern:-

**Great Jain Temple*, built at the expense of the merchant *Seth Hathi Singh,* completed in 1848, an ostentatious edifice entirely in white marble. The long arcaded building, which borders the temple area along the road, is the pilgrims' quarters. In the *outer court*, a bathing-place for pilgrims and a large model of Girnar Mountain (p.139). The inner court, which one may enter only without shoes, or with socks pulled on over them, is in the shape of a rectangle 38·5m wide and 49 long. It is surrounded by arched arcades, surmounted by 52 small pointed domes; in the cells beneath these stand alabaster figures of the 24 holy Tirthankars (p.LVIII), which recur in other places (they are, in contrast to the figures of Buddha, always portrayed naked; each has its particular emblem). In the centre, the *Temple* rises on a high plinth, to whose vestibule a flight of steps leads up. It consists of a pillared hall in front, 11m square, crowned by a dome, a closed hall 7·5m square, and the holy of holies, a rectangle 6·7m wide and 1·8 deep, containing the image of the Tirthankar Dharmanatha. Floors, door frames and the rear walls behind the sacred images are of polished coloured marble. The services, which one may freely attend, resemble the Buddhist rite. The ascent to the roof offers a general view of the building's astonishingly rich amount of sculpture.

1-1¼km to the NW, near the bank of the Sabarmati, lies the Mosque of Bibi Achut Kuki, in a large walled courtyard, completed in 1472, one of the finest examples of the blending of Saracen and Hindu styles, with a richly carved façade and 36 elegant pillars supporting a high central dome and two subsidiary ones. Opp., the usual *Funeral Monument*, a pretty domed pavilion with 32 pillars.

To the N. of the town, 1500m E. of the Great Jain Temple, near the houses of *Asarva*, are two remarkable groups of wells, such as are frequently found in the Gujerat area, and called "Wav" or "Baoli". One of these, *Mata Bhavani Wav,* dates from the Hindu era, probably the 11th c. Far more splendid is the later **Dada or Bai Harir's Wav*, whose completion is dated by inscription at 1499-1500. The entrance is beneath a 12-columned domed pavilion, whence a flight of steps with several landings and pillared chambers, 65-70m in total length, leads down to the well shafts. The niches in the side walls are adorned with sculptures, the richest being before the penultimate octagonal shaft. The last shaft, 14m below ground-level, is round and has, at its lower end, a circle of relief depicting geese, parrots, elephants etc. It is connected to a bucket wheel which provides water for the nearby gardens. Near the octagonal shaft, one may regain ground-level by means of spiral staircases. From time to time, the guide lends a welcome hand on stairs and ledges. – Nearby, the *mosque and funeral monument* of the same name, both neglected.

To the SE of the town, 1km outside Rayapur and Astodiya Gates, is *Kankariya Lake*, laid out in 1451, one of India's greatest ornamental pools, a polygon of 34 sides with circumference of almost 2km., surrounded by stone steps and with an island in the middle, which once bore a palace and is accessible by a bridge causeway. The sluice on the E. side is decorated with attractive sculptures. The shady, tree-lined walks in the vicinity are inhabited by numerous monkeys. The guide calls them over with "how, how". They take the proffered food from one's hand and are very importunate.

Also, outside Astodiya Gate, and 1500m SW of Kankariya Lake, is the **Tomb and Mosque of Shah Alam*, a holy man and teacher of the sultans (†1475). The grounds cover more than 2 hectares. One passes through 3 gateways to the spacious inner court with the *fountain of purification* at the front in the centre, a *reception hall* for great festivals, to the l. in the NE corner; the holy man's tomb in the SE corner; and the Mosque on the W. side. The building which houses the tomb or *dargah*, with a large central dome surrounded by lower ones, and possessing large, beautiful windows filled with stone tracery and a vestibule on the W. side, was completed around 1485. Within, a soft twilight reigns. A double ambulatory surrounds the central space, being enclosed by a richly pierced stone balustrade with three lattice-work doors in brass.

Above the grave, a baldaquin, supported by pillars inlaid with mother-of-pearl. The *Mosque*, a spacious hall in simple style, 16m wide and 35 long, is of a later era, and the two minarets, 30m tall, were completed in 1620. Beneath its forecourt is a covered cistern, towards the fountain of purification, which one may enter through a low wicket gate in the SE corner (resounding echo across the dark surface of the water; 40 sq.m). A *second monument*, of similar design to that of Shah Alam, but simpler, to the S. and opp. the Mosque, contains the graves of the holy man's relatives; upon that of his brother (in the centre) one remarks a black stone bearing the prophet's footprint, which is said to have come from Mecca; the brass lattice-work doors bear unusually beautiful engraving. – One should return NW via *Beherampur*, where the fine *Tomb of Abu Turab* (†1597) may be visited, an open, domed structure resting on 32 pillars, and 12·5m square. Inside *Jamalpur Gate*, where one re-enters the town, one sees, to one's r., *Haibat Khan's Mosque*, the second oldest in the town and built from the ruins of a Hindu temple.

Finally, near *Victoria Gardens,* to the S. of the Citadel (p.135), one should pay a visit to Sabarmati Bridge, rebuilt in iron to replace an earlier bridge destroyed by a flood in 1875. From here, an extremely picturesque *view of the deeply-cut river-bed and the W. side of the town. Hordes of natives in colourful garb wash their clothes, bring their cattle to drink or bathe in the narrow channels; on the dry places, little plots of vegetables are laid out, which their owners tend with great enthusiasm. One should stop the carriage before the bridge (to avoid paying the toll of 8a.!)

The excursion to the ruins of Sarkhej is rewarding, on the r. bank of the river, 10km SW of Sabarmati Bridge. The road, lined with tamarinds, goes past the massive *Mausoleum of the brothers Azam and Muazzam Khan*, built around 1457.

Sarkhej was a magnificent park of the sultans Mohammed Shah (1443-51) and Mahmud Shah Bigarah (p.133), arranged round an artificial lake, 260m long and 213 broad. The most important buildings are on the E. shore of the lake. With their slender pillars, their domes rising above a rectilinear entablature and the richly pierced stonework of the walls, they display the native style of the mid-15th c., scarcely affected by Saracen influences in its most elegant development. Entering through the gateway, one has, to one's l., the Mausoleum of *Mahmud Shah Bigarah,* with that of his wife *Bibi Rajbai* adjoining, beyond a portico facing the lake. To the r., on a low plinth whose main entrance is indicated by a graceful domed pavilion, rises the superb Mausoleum of *Shaikh Ahmed Ganj Baksh,* teacher of the founder of the dynasty (†1445) and renowned for his piety; the building forms a square of side 32m with a large main dome and rows of smaller domes around it, resting on 150 single and double pillars. Further to the N., one reaches the forecourt of the *Mosque*, whose simple pillared façade lines its N. side. It measures 45 by 20m and has 120 pillars supporting two rows of 5 domes each. The terrace above, by the domes, provides a fine panoramic view out over this desolate landscape, frequented only by marabous, parrots and monkeys.

The main line continues W. from Ahmedabad, crosses the Sabarmati (313¼M, sta. of the same name), and reaches its terminus at (350M) *Viramgam*, town of 23,000 inhab. with important cotton trade, and junc. for several branch-lines, incl. one to the peninsula *Kathiawar*, which is washed to the SE by the Gulf of Cambay (p.132), to the W. by the ocean and, to the NW, by the *Rann of Cutch*, an extensive lagoon formed by the sinking of the land, which is filled with sea-water only during the SW monsoon.

The peninsula Kathiawar is divided into 187 native princedoms and has preserved many features of cultural interest, esp. remarkable being the two main religious centres of the Jains: in the SE, near Palitana, the sacred mountain *Satrunjaya*, whose summit is crowned by temples dating from the 11th c. down to the present; and, to the W. of this, near the rly sta. of Junagarh, the granite Mount Girnar (1120m), also bearing many temples.

From Ahmedabad to Ajmer, 306M, narrow gauge rly (fast train, see p.131). – The line branches from the main line at *Sabarmati* sta. (see above), heading N. Monkeys, gazelles and jackals are often seen. – 326M. *Kalol*, 353M. *Mehsana*, both junc. for several branch-lines in N. Gujerat. – 374M. *Sidhpur*, on the River Sarasvati; 393M. *Palanpur* (sta. rest.), junc. for Deesa. The rly crosses the border of *Sirohi*, the SW state in the Rajputana district (p.141).

425M. *Abu Road* (sta. rest., with sleeping quarters and bath; a Dak bungalow, 1½km from the sta.), or *Kharari*, town of 6600 inhab., point of departure for the 1½ day excursion (scenically and, on account of the ancient Jain temple, extremely rewarding) to:-

*MOUNT ABU (in fact Ar-budha, mount of wisdom), which rises from the plain as a massive, isolated granite block. – From the sta. by the *mail tonga* (twice daily, 4R., with 4 changes of horse, ascent in 2½hrs., descent in 2, much used by natives). A party of passengers would do well to hire their own *tonga*, usually available at the sta., though it is expedient to order in advance, 10-12R. or 19R. return;

luggage cart (ekka) 4½R., but it is better to leave heavier items behind. For the return, rickshaws may be hired at the top, 6R.

Accommodation at Mount Abu: Dak bungalow, where the mail tonga halts; 10min further on, the pleasantly positioned Hotel Rajputana (owned by a Parsee; several bungalows, 30 Rm., P.6R., modest but quite good). – For the visit to the *Delwara Temples*, the hoteliers obtain from the Magistrate of Abu written permission, on which rules of behaviour are printed (visiting time, 12-6 p.m.) They also provide rickshaws or ponies (1R.) for those who are disinclined to walk; rickshaw to the *Achilgarh Temple* 4-5R.

The road (27km) leads NW across the plain, then over the bed of the *Banas*, and climbs through a magnificent ghat (p.104), with views of the wide valley; to the r., high up by the edge of the mountain, the white Achilgarh Temple (p.141). At this altitude, the cool temperature is noticeable. In sheltered spots, date palms are to be found. Many irrigated fields. The whole area is swarming with monkeys.

The small township of Mount Abu, (summer residence of the British Government Agent of Rajputana, with several palaces belonging to the princes of Rajputana, many European villas, church, schools and a military sanatorium), lies in the S. part of an undulating tableland rising towards the N., and surrounded by steep mountains which reach a height of 1726m. The chief feature of this landscape is the charming lake, *Nakhi Talao* (1149m), with a great variety of rock formations on its shores, and bushy islands.

Above the SE shore, the *Palace of the Maharaja of Jaipur* rises majestically. Pretty walk round the lake (40min), and also to the W. to **Sunset Point* (half an hour), at the foot of the W. mountains, which drop precipitously more than 1000m to the plain: view magnificent, esp. at sunset.

To the N. of the hotel one ascends a little at first, past the tennis courts and a bizarre rock formation, then downhill across the plateau, strewn with blocks of granite, (views, to the r., of the palaces of the Maharajas of *Alwar* and *Bikanir*, to the l., of the little white temple of *Arbuda Mata*, or mother of Abu.

Finally, one ascends again in ½hr. to the **Delwara Temples* (1193m), lying amid date-palms and cacti in a depression ('Dewalwara' means 'place of temples'). They date from the 11th-13th c. and are built entirely of marble brought here from a great distance.

The layout of the two main temples (the older, dedicated to the Tirthankar *Adinath*, 1032 A.D.; the second, dedicated to *Nemnath*, 1230) is the same as obtains at the temple built by Hathi Singh at Ahmedabad (p.136).

Through a vestibule, one enters the inner court which is surrounded by pillared halls with 52 Tirthankar cells behind lattice-work screens of brass. The temples themselves consist of a domed vestibule and holy of holies, open only to the front (entry forbidden). The imaginative richness of the marble sculptures is superb, the overall impression nonetheless harmonious. The third temple has less to offer. The fourth, on the other hand (without ambulatory), is worthy of attention. The fifth, to the NE on the other side of the road, is crude and insignificant.

The carriage road goes NE from Delwara to Achilgarh (1½hrs.), soon ascending, with a view to the W. of the plain, dotted with a few jagged hill chains. At the dividing of the ways, one bears r., reaching an upland valley with irrigated fields and water-scoops where, to the E., the white temple at Achilgarh appears.

One then reaches the holy pool *Mandakni Kund*, surrounded by date- palms and several ancient Hindu shrines: to the N., a marble statue of the archer Pramar, who wards off demons in the form of buffaloes; to the S., in a mango garden, a temple etc. From here, a rocky path leads in another ¼hr. to the height of Achilgarh (i.e. fortress of immobility).

One climbs up through ruined fortifications of the 14-15th c., past a holy pool, finally up picturesque flights of steps to the upper terraces, where the temple buildings stand (one discards one's shoes before entering). The temple has been much restored and is of little importance in itself, but there is a splendid view from its roof over the Banas valley to the Aravalli Mountains. Even finer is the view, taking in the temple of Achilgarh, from the rather higher summit to the r. (1380m; ¼hr.), with a ruined temple.

The railway remains in *Rajputana*, which is divided up into 20 native princely states, consisting in part of ancient Hindu dynasties and, in all, 330,318 sq.km, with over 10,530,000 inhabitants. The Rajputs (i.e. kings' sons) are a proud and warlike race, probably Aryan in origin, which made an inroad here from the N. in the 7-10th c. A.D. To the r., the *Aravalli Mountains* (p.67) are visible throughout this portion of the journey, with a wild, steep W. slope and an average height of 1040-1390m. During the winter months, the yellowish soil is bare, the air full of dust. The green fields along the dry river beds are watered from ground-water cisterns. Cacti, date-palms and numerous birds of prey lend the landscape a desert-like appearance.

528M. *Marwar* (sta. rest.), junc. for the branch to *Luni* (44m), where the railways from Hyderabad, Sindh and Phalera meet (fast train Karachi-Jaipur-Agra-Cawnpore-Calcutta, see p.210).

The second sta. on the Luni-Phalera line (p.147) is: 20M. *Jodhpur*, capital of the largest Rajput state (90,500 sq.km in area, with 2,057,000 inhab.), romantically situated in an arc at the foot of a rock crowned by the fortress with the Maharaja's palace. The town, linked by bullock tram to the sta., is surrounded by high walls, and contains several old patrician palaces and temples. – The next important intermediate sta. is (84M) *Merta Road*, junc. for a branch-line which crosses the E. part of the *Thar Desert* (p.67), via Bikaner to *Bhatinda* (p.192, 304km, no fast trains). Bikaner or *Bikanir,* situated in a desert oasis, is also the capital of a large Rajput state (60,350 sq.km, 700,900 inhab.) with 50,000 inhab., old walls and fortress, narrow streets, richly sculpted houses in sandstone etc. The Maharaja's new palace is situated above the town.

The railway to Ajmer-Jaipur enters, just before (582M) *Beawar*, the British province of *Ajmer-Merwara*, an enclave of 7021 sq.km with 501,400 inhab., in the middle of Rajputana.

615M. **Ajmer**. – ACCOMMODATION: sta. rest., with 4 Rm. at 1R., tiffin 1R.8a., L. 2R., quite good; Dak bungalow, close to the sta; Rajputana Hot., cheap, unremarkable. – CARRIAGES: 1st cl. 5R. per day, 3 per ½ day; 2nd cl. 3 and 2R. – GUIDE 2R. – For a limited visit, ½ day suffices. One should provide oneself with small change for the temples. The excursion to *Pushkar* (p.144) takes 3½-4hrs. ret.: tonga 5R.

Ajmer (pron. Adjmeer), one of the oldest capitals of Rajputana, taken several times since the 11th c. by Mohammedan princes, incorporated by Akbar (1556-1605) into the Grand Mogul Empire, at times a royal residence also under his successors Jehangir (1605-27) and Shah Jehan (1627-58), (cf.p.178), from 1756 in the hands of the Mahrattas, then from 1818 onwards British, with 68,200 inhab. (55,000 Hindus, 30,000 Mohammedans), with brisk trade and several native banks, Ajmer occupies a picturesque setting, surrounded by a wreath of jagged mountains, at the foot of the once fortified *Taragarh Rock* (838m) and, with its N. suburbs, extends as far as *Ana Sagar Lake*. The town itself is enclosed by a wall with 5 gates. The narrow, winding streets, with their many bazaars, teem with oriental life. The houses are flat-roofed and have balconies and graceful loggias.

To the NW of the sta. (480m) rises *Akbar's Palace*, a massive building with high octagonal bastions at its four corners, and a splendid entrance gate on the W. side. The former palace, within, was restored in 1906, and contains a collection of sculpture; nearby, a room with inscriptions. Fine panorama from the palace roof: to the N., the red Jain temple and the British Residency by Lake Ana Sagar; to the SW, Taragarh Rock, SE Mayo College and, S., the Queen Victoria Jubilee Tower. – Passing through several small streets, with the bazaars of the corn- and food-merchants, coppersmiths etc., one reaches, in the SW quarters, the:-

**Dargah Khwaja Sahib*, a group of courtyards and buildings surrounding the tomb of the holy man Muin-ud-din Chishti (†1235), revered by Hindus and Mohammedans alike. Ascending a flight of steps, where one has to don shoe-covers, one enters the first courtyard through a recently painted gateway with silver doors. Above the gate, a music gallery with two large kettle-drums. To the r. (W.), a long staircase leads up to the forecourt of *Akbar's Mosque,* a simple building. Continuing to the S., one passes through the tall and extremely slender arch of *Shah Jehangir Gate* into the second courtyard: the pavilion at its centre contains a bronze lamp donated by Akbar; the giant iron cauldrons to the r. and l. of this (called "big and little deg", the former able to hold 5000kg of rice, the latter 3000kg), serve, at festivals, for the preparation of food for pilgrims, of whom about 25,000 visit the shrine each year. In the third, innermost, courtyard one sees, to one's r. (W.), the delicate **Mosque of Shah Jehan,* built, together with its forecourt, entirely of white marble; to one's l. (E.), a domed building, also of white marble, containing the *tombs of the holy Muin-ud-din Chishti* and, in the W. and S. ante-chambers, those of his daughter and of a daughter of Shah Jehan, respectively. Of the three entrances (with silver doors), the E. one is the main gate, being surmounted by a baldaquin and offering a view of the holy man's silver coffin. The interior is barred to strangers. Note, in the E. forecourt, the railed-off tomb of the holy man's water-carrier. Adjoining the third courtyard to the s. is a fourth courtyard, planted with trees, from whose parapet one looks down into the steep rocky gully *Jalrah.* The picturesque flights of steps are busy with women, who fetch water from the rock pools below.

Return to the entrance of the Dargah, then l. up through the S. city gate *(Tirpolia Gate,* 521m) to Arhai-din-kha-Jhonpra's Mosque, set amid wild mountains. It was originally a Hindu temple, with slender columns and 5 domes, which was converted to a mosque "in 2½ days" by Mohammed Gori (hence the name). Under Sultan Altamsh (p.178), it received a five-arched façade. It has recently undergone some discreet restoration. The centre gate is 16·75m high, 6·7 wide, the lower side gates 4 and 3m wide; the pointed arches are constructed not of tapering stones, but instead display the practice of building up in horizontal layers (cf.p.189). Of especial merit is the surface decoration, among the finest of its kind in the canon of Mohammedan art.

From Tirpolia Gate issues the narrow carriage-road leading to the top of *Taragarh Rock* (p.142). The ascent (1hr.) is somewhat arduous. At the summit, a sanatorium for English soldiers, replacing the fortifications dismantled in 1832. Fine view.

The road to Lake Ana Sagar, in the NW quarter of the town, passes a modern *Jain temple*, whose interior is adorned with mirrors and scenes from Jain mythology done in quaint tinsel.

**Ana Sagar Lake* (843m above sea-level) is one of India's many beautiful reservoirs, and was laid out earlier than the town itself (12th c.) It dries out in the Spring, and is then cultivated. Along its SE shore stretches the "park of splendours", **Daulat Bagh,* one of Jehangir's creations, with a fine lakeside promenade built by Shah Jehan, and several pavilions, all in gleaming white marble and restored 1900-2. On the height to the N. one sees the *Residency,* winter seat of the British Government Agent and Chief Commissioner of Rajputana.

In the SE part of the town, Mayo College is worth a mention, an English school opened in 1885 for the sons of the princes and nobles of Rajputana. In front of the main buildings is a statue of the viceroy Lord Mayo (1868-72), at whose behest the college was established. Dotted about the park are the (sometimes) elegant dwellngs of the princes of Jaipur, Kotah, Alwar, Bikanir, Jodhpur, Udaipur etc.

There is an attractive drive (cf.p.142), past Ana Sagar Lake W., by a very winding road, over a ridge to *Pushkar*, (11.5km; 728m above sea-level), a Hindu place of pilgrimage, visited in Oct/Nov. by almost 100,000 pilgrims. The town, with 3800 inhab. and five large, modern temples in marble, lies in a deep depression in the ground by the lake of the same name, in whose muddy waters the pilgrims bathe. One temple is dedicated to Brahma who, elsewhere in India, is revered only in three insignificant shrines. Simple Dak bungalow on the shore.

The EXCURSION TO UDAIPUR, which takes one into a scenically rewarding area almost untouched by European tourists, requires 2½days, or 3½ if one includes Chitorgarh. Take the night train on the narrow-gauge railway Ajmer-Rutlam (p.132), 8¼hrs., for 9R.1a., 1st cl., to (115M):

Chitorgarh (412m; Dak bungalow, moderate, 1.5km from the sta.), station for the small town of *Chitor*, 2.5km to the NE, beyond the little river *Ghambir,* crossed by an old bridge with ten arches. The town, still walled, lies at the W. foot of a mountain ridge almost 5km long and scarcely 800m wide, which is crowned by the legendary fortress of **Chitorgarh* 565m), family seat of the princes of Udaipur. The origins of the fortress date back to the 8th c. It was at its peak in the 13-15th c.; in the 14-16th c. it was stormed four times by the Mohammedans, finally in 1567 by the Grand Mogul Akbar the Great. Comprehensive restoration in progress. The visit takes 3-4 hrs. (tonga, 4R., to be ordered from "first official Hakim" at the sta.)

A winding path leads upwards through 7 partly destroyed gates. Entrance tickets are issued outside the first of these, r. The last gate, called *Ram Pol*, near the N. corner of the walls, forms the entrance to the interior of the fortress, which is filled with the ruins of temples and palaces and many pools for catching rainwater. Among the various buildings, which are generally distinguished by their rich decorative carvings, the following merit particular mention: the 24m-high "tower of honour", *Kirti Stambha*, of the 12th or 13th c., dedicated to the Jain Tirthankar Adinath, whose image appears frequently in the carvings; the 37m-high "victory tower" **Jai Stambha*, one of the most perfect pieces of Hindu architecture, executed by prince Rana Kumbha in 1442-9 in yellow marble, completely covered inside and out with mythological scenes and decoration, and crowned with a dome, which offers a broad panorama; the *Temple of Kumbha* and his wife *Miran Bai*; and the *Singar Charri Temple*, built in 1448, with charming sculptural decoration.

From Chitorgarh W. to Udaipur, 69M, branch-line in 4½hrs. for 6R.8a., 3R.4a., 11a.6p.

Udaipur. – STATION almost 5km from the town: tonga 2½R. per day. – HOTELS: Udaipur Hot. (8 Rm., P.5R., quite decent), 1km outside the N. gate, not far from the British Residency. Entry to the Palace and use of the prince's rowing boats: if one fails to get permission for these from the hotel, one should write immediately to the prime minister, using the wording of the formula in the hotel register. GUIDES: 3R. per day, recommended. Strangers bearing letters of introduction, and who have previously announced their arrival, will be accommodated in the *Maharana's Guest House*, above Lake Fateh Sigar.

Udaipur (620m), residence of the Maharana of Udaipur, the present representative of the most ancient and eminent among the Hindu royal houses, and of many noble families, possessing 46,000 inhab. (63% Hindus, 20% Mohammedans, 10% Jains), extends along the slope of a hilly ridge running N. to S., whose W. edge is washed by Lake Pichola. The town is enclosed by a bastioned wall with 5 gates and, at some further distance, ringed by forts, of which *Eklingarh Fort*, to the S., particularly catches the eye. The style of the houses and layout of the streets, along with the appearance of the people (many still bearing weapons), provide a rare picture of Indian life unchanged by time.

From the N. gate, *Hathi Pol*, the main street passes by the *Jagannath Temple*, built in 1652 (cf.p.89), and continues to the *Maharana's Palace*, which crowns the ridge of the hill in an extremely romantic fashion. The whitewashed building, measuring 450m by 250, dates, in its oldest parts, from 1571, having been greatly extended during the ensuing centuries. The rooms in the N. wing have been preserved in their original furnishing and fittings and offer one an insight (such as can be gained almost nowhere else) into the traditional, almost medieval, domestic life of an Indian prince. The virtually windowless main building contains the women's quarters (the Zenana). The S. wing, recently refitted, is generally occupied by the prince in the afternoons. Also accommodated in the palace are the royal offices, the lawcourt and treasury. Adjacent to the S. are the *Sajjan Newas Gardens*, with a small collection of animals; further on, one reaches Lake Pichola. – The *Victoria Hall*, outside which is a statue of the Queen, contains a library and an unimportant museum.

**Lake Pichola*, a reservoir built at the end of the 14th c., 3·5km long and 2km wide, with many bays, and shores wooded partly with dark-coloured trees, is uncommonly delightful. It is commanded to the E. by the town with its walls, gates and royal palace. Many villas all around,. The architectural enclosure of the banks with bathing steps (ghats, p.223), dates from the end of the 16th c. The two islands, to the S. *Jagmandir* (with a palace and small mosque built at the beginning of the 17th c. for the Mogul prince Khurram, later Shah Jehan p.162) and, to the N., *Jagniwas*, with a palace from the early 18th c., surpass the Borromean Is. on Lake Maggiore, in Fergusson's opinion. Crossing the lake (only in the Maharana's boats, see p.145) is best done in the afternoon, because of the more favourable position of the sun, and usually begins at *Swaroop Sagar Lake*, the N. continuation of Lake Pichola. The further S. one proceeds, the more beautiful the scenery becomes. The view from Jagmandir Is. is especially fine in the evening. One lands at the S. end of Lake Pichola near the hunting lodge *Khas Odi*, where the wild boar are fed at sunset. The boat then continues to Sajjan Newas Gardens, but one can order the carriage to wait at Khas Odi.

A free morning is ideal for the drive NW to the royal pleasure gardens of *Sahailyan Ki-Bari*, with waterworks, and to *Lake Fateh Sagar*, laid out in 1900, or to the palace *Sujjangarh*, perched on the cone above Pichola to the N. (3hrs. return; carriage as far as the mountain, then on foot up the winding road), offering an overview of the Udaipur district (like a string of oases, with its lakes), and W. to the Aravalli Mountains.

Lying 1km N. of the sta. and surrounded by high walls, is the *Mahasati* or cremation ground of the ruling family, with beautiful halls of remembrance, in which the ashes are kept. – W. of this, by the river, the ruins of the old town of

Ahar. 12M N. of Udaipur, the ruined marble temples of *Eklingaji* and *Nagda* (p.LXVII), from the 12-14th c.

From Ajmer to Jaipur (84M; fast trains, see p.131). The most important intermediate stations: 633M. *Kishangarh*; 664M. *Phalera* or *Phulera*, junc. for branch-lines to Jodhpur and Bikanir (p.142), as well as the line to Rewari (p.152; 185M), which provides a short cut but is not used by fast trains. To the W., *Lake Sambhar*, over 200 sq.km in area, which however dries out in summer: its salt deposits bring in £584,000 annually to the British Government, from which it hands over fixed amounts to the states of Jaipur and Jodhpur. – 699M. *Jaipur*.

Jaipur.

STATION (rest.) 3km to the W. of the town. The lakes more or less dry out in the Spring.

HOTELS (run by natives): Kaisar-i-Hind, near the sta., 50 Rm., P. from Nov. to Mar. 7R., otherwise 6; Jaipur Hot. (Rustom's Family Hot.) 20min to the E., P.10R.; New Hotel, S. of the sta., 38 Rm., P.7-9, out of season 5-7R., is the hotel best spoken of now. The managers provide carriages (cf.p.154), riding animals, guides, and admission tickets to the Maharaja's Palace and Amber Palace.

CARRIAGES (official tariff at the town gate): 1st cl. 1R.4a. the first hr., 12a. the second hr., 8a. each succeeding hr., 3R. per ½ day, 5R.8a. all day; 2nd cl., 12a., 8a., 4a., 2R., 3R. respectively.

TELEGRAPH & POST.

SHOPS. Of the ancient native crafts, enamelling still flourishes (bright colours, "Jaipur red"); also the manufacture of brass goods and fantastically-shaped weapons with pretty metal inlay work, the cheaper ones being suitable for decorative use. A good selection may be seen, and bought cheaply, at the *School of Arts* (p.150), founded by the Maharaja. Also recommended are the shops of *S. Zoraster & Co., Allah Buksh & Co., Nu Bux, Khuda Bux & Co.* (cf.p.150), and the jewellers *Phul Chand* and *Sobhag Chand.* One is pestered by dealers in the hotels. Fleecing of travellers is particularly bad everywhere in Jaipur.

If time is limited (1-1½ days): morning excursion to *Amber* (p.150), afternoon in the Museum in the *Albert Hall* (p.148; open from early morning until dusk, but closed on Sun., 10-3), and the *Palace of the Maharaja*, with the Observatory, Stables and the *Tiger Cages* (p.150). The life in the streets is particularly charming to the eye. One should devote one's second afternoon to *Galta Pass* (p.151). – At Amber, one may well have the opportunity of an *elephant ride*, for which the Maharaja will make his animals available from Kala Mahadeo to the top, on request (arrangement made through the hotel manager, 10R.; higher demands are forbidden).

Jaipur (430m), seat of an ancient Hindu ruling family and capital of Rajputana, with 137,000 inhab. (69% Hindu, 25% Mohammedan, 5% Jain), many trades, weaving and dyeing mills, banks, etc., lies in a richly wooded plain with steep mountains immediately to N. and E., of whose fortresses the *Nehargarh* (600m) or "Tiger Fort", with a royal summer palace, is particularly prominent. The town was founded by the Maharaja *Jai Singh II* (1699-1743), distinguished as warrior, politician, law-maker and scholar, whose nickname "Sawai" (i.e. 1¼ men) passed down to his successors, and who found the old settlement of Amber (p.150) unsuited to the stimulation of trade and traffic. Just like the European residences of the 18th c., Jaipur differs from medieval towns in its regular plan and its spaciousness, without however thereby losing its Indian character. It covers an area of almost 8 sq.km, and is enclosed by a bastioned wall 6m high, with 7 large and strongly fortified gates.

The road from the sta. reaches the town proper at *Ajmer Gate*, outside which is the *Ram Newas public park*, 3ha. in extent (music on Mon. afternoons). On the E. side of the park, a menagery. To the S., the:-

Albert Hall, a brilliant building in Indo-Saracen style, built 1867-87, with the **Museum of Arts & Crafts,* one of India's finest and richest collections, which one is recommended to visit, preparatory to making any kind of purchases. There is a detailed description in the "Handbook to the Jeypore Museum" by T. Holbein Headley, 1895. (Opening times, see p.147)

Ascending the steps outside, one passes through the entrance hall, with its pictures of the princes of Jaipur, into the main hall, designed for lectures and exhibitions. Continue to the end of the corridor beyond, on the l., and then r. through a turnstile into the Museum, which houses more than 10,000 old and modern objects from all parts of India, Persia and other parts of the Orient. From the ante-room, one enters Room I (3 sections): damascened and chased weapons, swords, daggers, pistols and so-called chatris, which are set up at the funeral pyres of royal personages; gold and silver lace-work and weaving; vessels and jewellery inlaid with silver and enamel; embossed silver jewellery, salvers; vessels in chased brass; ivory and tortoiseshell work. – II. Main Room (5 sections): wood carvings, painted, gilded and lacquered toys; semi-precious gems in gold and silver settings; jewel-boxes; imitations of European antique and medieval work; native painting. Room III (3 sections): pottery in a wide variety of forms. Adjacent, the room with *stone carvings*, sculptured figures in marble and other types of stone, and the *Mythological Room*, with many Jain, Tirthankar (p.LVIII), Vishnu and Shiva figures, and Egyptian antiquities. The upper floor contains experiments, models and explanatory pictures for the instruction of the natives, who visit the collection in considerable numbers. There is also painting, embroidery, etc. of native origin. – From the roof, a fine view over the town and its surroundings.

The inner town is divided into 8 quarters (chaukris) by a 34m-wide main street, running W-E., and several 17m-wide transverse streets. The 9m-wide side streets also intersect at right angles. There are large, rectangular squares where streets also intersect at right angles. The private houses are given a reddish, raspberry-coloured wash, with white decoration and sometimes garish, grotesque figures. The open ground floors contain shops and workshops; the living rooms are on the upper floors, which are adorned with projecting bays, galleries and pavilions. The Maharaja's buildings stand out from the rest by being painted yellow.

There is a fairy-tale quality about the life and bustle in the streets: dealers and merchants in colourful costumes, horsemen garbed in white, carriages preceded by outriders, the Maharaja's riding elephants, camels piled high with goods, bullocks with brightly coloured horns etc. ; on the window-sills of the houses are monkeys, parrots and other creatures grown impertinent because of the Hindu reverence for them; in the squares, thousands of pigeons.

The **Maharaja's Palace* which, with its living quarters and offices, occupies an entire section of the town, is almost completely surrounded by walls and houses, making therefore no impression at all on the outside, except for the SE corner, where the five-storeyed *Hawa Mahal* ("Palace of the Winds") rises, built by Jai Singh II, in a superabundant, extravagant style, with more than 50 oriels instead of windows (on the opp. side of the street, the College, see p.150). *Tripolia Gate*, the main entrance (cf.p.150), is in the middle of the S. front. From the outer court, a rich brass door, opened only to the ruler, leads to the inner courts. The visitor is admitted through side doors. In the first court, the *Divan-i-Am* for public audiences; in the second court, the *Divan-i-Khas* for private audiences: both halls devoid of artistic interest and meanly fitted out. The entire central palace area is taken up by large gardens with many kinds of fountains, which play at religious festivals in March and August.

In the S. part rises the main palace, *Chandra Mahal,* 7 storeys high, with gallery and oriels, containing not only the reception rooms, but also the living quarters of the prince and his wives (no entry). Opp., to the N., a Hindu temple. Beyond this a large water-basin *(Tal Katora)* with many jets and, further on behind some rather dilapidated halls, the pool *Raja Malkatalao,* 40ha. in extent, in which crocodiles are kept (the keeper coaxes them to come and be fed). – In the SE part of the palace compound is the *Observatory *(Yantra),* built in 1718-34 by Jai Singh II, recently carefully restored, with enormous astronomical instruments executed in marble and precious metal, their purposes being described on tablets. The largest is the gnomon, a meridian wall rising to 27m (Dakshina Bhitti Yantra), with two quadrants of 14·93m radius to

W. and E., on which the shadow of the wall covers almost 4m every hr., so that its progress may be followed with the eye. (There are similar structures by Jai Singh at Benares, Muttra, Delhi and Ujjain). Next to the Observatory are the great *Royal Stables* with several hundred horses, fine carriages, elephants, camels and dogs.

Opp. the Palace of the Winds (p.149) to the E., stand the quaint little buildings of the *Maharaja's College*, a place of learning founded in 1845, and elevated to the status of high school in 1897, where natives are instructed in Hindustani, Persian and the rudiments of English. Further, an *Oriental College* for Arabic and Persian, and a *Sanskrit College*, are supported by the Maharaja.

Besides the *School of Arts*, for instruction in arts and crafts such as drawing, painting, chiselling and carving in marble and wood, pottery and metal-work (80 native students on average), most of the shops mentioned on p.147 lie in or near the street called Chaura Rasta which leads S. from the Tripolia Gate of the Palace. The stock for sale is generally found on the first floor, the workshops in courtyards surrounded by arcades, where one can watch the people at work (all done by hand). – At the S. end of Chaura Rasta, the Maharaja keeps a few magnificent *tigers in cages.*

The *excursion to Amber, the old capital, founded in the 10th c., requires 4-5hrs. (carriage to Kala Mahadeo, then on foot or by tonga). The road leads from *Zorawar Gate* along the E. foot of a rock wall. Rich villas on both sides, derelict gardens, tombs and Hindu chapels with lingam or naudi symbols and various idols, hedges of Indian fig and candle cacti. Numerous monkeys infest the trees. On the r., one sights the crocodile pool *Man Sagar,* with a dilapidated palace. After 1hr's drive, the carriage stops at the Hindu shrine of:-

Kala Mahadeo, where one has an hour's ascent to the fortress. To r. and l., walls ascend the ridges. One's entry authority is required at the gate. The road continues uphill to a second gate *(Ghati Gate)* and then along the E. shore of a reservoir. Magnificent *view (esp. in the morning light): to the W. the white palace at Amber, half-way up, and the red Jaigarh Fort above; to the E., also, battlemented walls, bastions and towers; to the N. the virtually deserted *town of Amber*, a muddle of ruined temples, palaces, houses and overgrown gardens, inhabited by a colourful fauna. – The path to the palace turns off l. at a refreshment room, past the N. end of the lake, and rises fairly steeply.

The **Palace of Amber* (435m), founded in 1600 by Man Singh (1590-1614), extended by Jai Singh I (†1668), and completed at the beginning of the 18th c. by Jai Singh II before his move to Jaipur, can be regarded, along with the Fort at Gwalior (p.159), as the most important building in Rajput art. The ruler's castle sits on a sub-structure of high defensive walls.

From the large forecourt, which one enters first, one ascends the steps l. to a second court, bordered on the l. by the superb hall of the *Divan-i-Am* (cf.p.164), with an open staircase and a double row of marble columns. A large open staircase (next to which, l., before a small temple of the goddess *Kali* (p.LX), a goat is sacrificed daily), leads through a massive gate with an image of Ganesa to a garden terrace. Here, l., the *Ruler's Palace,* with the "Divan-i-Khas", magnificent rooms and galleries. The walls in most of the rooms are covered, in their lower portion, with white marble, bearing flowers and butterflies in relief; above, brightly-coloured stucco decoration, with gold lines and innumerable pieces of mirror, reaching up across the ceiling also, with a very original effect. The windows are pierced marble slabs, the floors polished marble plates. The doors are of sandal-wood inlaid with ivory and mother-of-pearl. Dark stairs lead down to the marble baths with running water, which can be illuminated from beneath. The women's rooms on the upper floor are furnished like the prince's rooms, but even airier and more graceful in aspect; a soft comforting light penetrates the marble grilles at the windows. The flat roof is surrounded by marble balustrades and offers a splendid view of palace and town, the lake at its feet and mountains all around. Opp. the palace, a few rooms, similar in type, are shown. In the corner, r., a room with Indian landscape pictures.

The fortified walls continue up to the top of the mountain (587m), which is crowned by *Fort Jaigarh,* like a keystone, where the state trerasures were formerly kept.

The trip to *Galta Pass, to the E. of Jaipur, which should be undertaken in the morning, because of the light, takes 2-3hrs. One drives from the E. town gate *(Suraj Pol)* in ½hr. to the foot of the Pass, walking thence up a gentle gradient. At the top, the *Suraj Deora Temple* and a magnificent view back over the town, then E. into the Galta valley, by which one descends along a winding path. At the narrowest place, where a spring rises, are two holy bathing-pools between the rocks for pilgrims, and several Hindu temples. The gully swarms with pigeons and monkeys. Below, on the broader valley floor, are a few holy buildings resembling palaces (in a small shop one can buy food for the monkeys). Next to these, a fine orchard with parrots and wild peacocks. In the three domed pavilions of white marble, the ashes of several princes have been placed. Nearby, some simpler graves. Chiselled into the tombstones can be seen footprints, as a symbol of souls gone to Heaven.

From Jaipur, one can continue one's journey to Delhi or Agra.

From Jaippur to Delhi, 191M. Fast train in 7½hrs., for 14R.15a. – 705M. *Sanganer;* the town lies 5km to the SW of the sta., with a Jain temple, supposedly of the 10th c. – 755M. *Bandikui*, junc. for Agra, see p.153.

770M. *Raigarh*, first town on the territory of the small Rajput state of *Alwar,* comprising an area of 8132 sq.km and 828,487 inhab., of whom 74% are Hindus and 24% Mohammedans.

792M. *Alwar* (Dak bungalow near the sta.), also written *Ulwar,* state capital with 56,700 inhab. and a large cotton mill, picturesquely situated at the foot of some wooded rocky bluffs, surrounded by walls and moat, and dominated by an old *Fort,* set up high, and covering the NW side. The town is over 1km from the sta. Near the latter, the *Tomb of Fateh Jang,* an otherwise unknown man, from the year 1547, 19 sq.m in size, with a dome, and minarets at the 4 corners. In the market-place in the town, a *Jagannath Temple* (p.89) and, in the main street, an old tomb dating from 1393. The *Maharaja's Palace*, a group of buildings mainly from the time of Banni Singh (1824-57) contains, apart from the rooms used for functions, a library with valuable modern illustr. mss., an armoury with excellent old ceremonial swords, and the rich treasury (viewable only through introduction from the British Political Agent). The garden contains a small lake enclosed by white marble walls and small domed marble pavilions. On a plinth, the *Tomb of Bakhtawar Singh* (1791-1816), a magnificent two-storeyed structure with dome, terrace and corner pavilions, offering a splendid view. Also worthy of a visit are the *Maharaja's Royal Stables,* containing 500 horses, and the *cages of the hunting leopards.*

10km SW of Alwar is *Siliserh Tank*, laid out in 1844, which provides the town with water. A small palace on the shore.

After travelling for 1¼hrs., the train reaches the British province of *Punjab.* – 838M. *Rewari*, town of 27,000 inhab., junc. for the direct line from Phalera (p.147) and the line to *Hissar-Bhatinda-Ferozepore* (Lahore, p.209). – The line to Delhi descends to the plain, touches on (864M) *Garhi* and (870M) *Gurgaon*, crossing the last outliers of the Aravalli chain W. of Delhi and, cutting through the city wall, reaches the main sta. of (890M) *Delhi*, see p.176.

From Jaipur to Agra, 150M: Karachi-Calcutta Express (p.210) in 7¼hrs., semi-fast (day) train in 8½hrs., for 12R.5a., 6R.3a. – As far as (56M) *Bandikui,* see p.152; except for the night express, there is a change of carriages on all trains.

117M. *Bharatpur*, capital of a Rajput state (5100 sq.km; 627,000 inhab.), which arose at the collapse of the Grand Mogul Empire, and whose ruling house and half of the population belong to the Aryan race of *Jats.* The town has 43,000 inhab. The now dilapidated fortifications were attacked, unsuccessfully, by the English in 1805, but were stormed in 1827. – Bharatpur is the junc. for the railway from Nagda to Muttra, already mentioned on p.132 (see also p.173). – 134M. *Achnera* (p.173).

150m. *Agra* (Fort), see p.161; for the continuation to Tundla-Cawnpore, see pp. 175 & 211.

Route 17. From Bombay to Calcutta.

Two fast trains daily (Calcutta Mail): midday fast train (via *Nagpur*; shorter line but longer journey) in 42½hrs., for 91R.1a., 49R.9a., 15R.10a.; evening fast train (via *Jubbulpore)* in 37hrs., for 99R.1a., 49R.9a., 13R.7a. Also, once weekly, after the arrival of the P & O steamer at Bombay, a rather faster express mail train with only 36 1st cl. seats, to which travellers with direct tickets from Europe have priority. – All trains depart from *Victoria Terminus* (p.121), arriving at *Howrah,* opp. Calcutta (p.237). For amount of luggage conveyed free, see p.XXI. Travellers are advised to make early bookings for sleeping berths with the station-master at Victoria Terminus, or through Cooks. Meals in the dining-car: 16R. for the whole journey; individual prices: early morning tea 1R., tiffin 2R.8a., dinner 3R.8a. evening tea 12a. The station restaurants, where sufficient stops are allowed, are somewhat cheaper. There is also a direct fast train to *Lucknow* (p.214): via Bhusawal (p.154), Jhansi (p.157) and Cawnpore (cf.p.211), in 27¼hrs.

17a. Via Nagpur.

1221M. *Great Indian Peninsula Railway* to Nagpur, then the *Bengal-Nagpur Rly:* see above for fares and length of journey, etc.

From *Bombay* to (34M) *Kalyan,* see p.105. – The rly ascends NE through the *Thal Ghat, a pass much utilised by traders before the construction of the line, on the W. edge of the Deccan plateau *(Western Ghats,* p.104). From a scenic point of view, the route is hardly inferior to the Bore Ghat. Luxuriant vegetation, steep rock-faces and, in the wet season, numerous waterfalls. The ascent commences at (59M) *Vasind* (74m). At (75M) *Kasara,* we reach an altitude of 285m. 3 tunnels. Beyond the *Reversing Sta.,* where the locomotive is transferred to the rear of the train (cf.p.104), the line achieves its steepest gradient (1:37). 9 tunnels, numerous bridges and several viaducts, from which one enjoys splendid views down into the valley. – 85M. *Igatpuri* (583m., sta. rest.), at the top of the Ghat, favourite summer resort with the people of Bombay.

At (113M) *Deviali* or *Deolali,* where the fast train stops only by request, is a military station for the acclimatisation of European troops after their arrival or before their return home. - 117M. *Nasik.* A tram links the sta. with the town, 8km distant (Dak bungalow), lying on both banks of the *Godavery,* with 21,500 inhab. As the legendary refuge of *Rama* (p.LX), Nasik is one of the holy cities of the Hindus, visited annually by hordes of pilgrims. The larger part of the town, on the r. bank, is linked by a bridge constructed in 1897 to the part on the l. bank, this inhabited mostly by Brahmans, and containing the main temples. Both banks of the river are lined with stone steps, down which the pilgrims descend, to bathe in the holy water. The lively activity at the bathing-places, along with the curious temple buildings, remind one of Benares (p.221).

The country around Nasik is rich in rock temples, from the 3rd c.B.C. to the 6th A.D. Most important among these are the *Pandu Lena Caves,* 8km SW, on the main road to Bombay.

After a 5 hr. journey from Bombay, the train reaches (162M) *Manmad* (sta. rest.; accommodation in the Dak bungalow), junc. for the Hyderabad line (for Ellora, see p.117) and the connecting line from Dhond (p.102). - 204M. *Chalisgaon,* junc. for a branch-line to (35M) *Dhulia*, the chief place in the W. part of the Khandesh destrict (rich in cotton), 2km from the sta., with important cotton trade and industry, junc. for the Tapti Valley Rly to Surat (see p.131).

From Jalgaon one visits the Ajanta Caves, 60km S., over the border into the State of Hyderabad (2 days). The Mamlatdar (chief district official) of Jalgaon will provide a pony-cart (chukra), if warned several days in advance, and also arrange for permission to spend the night at the bungalow of *Fardapur*, the nearest settlement to the caves (5km). One takes one's own provisions and bedding. – The **Caves of Ajanta*, consisting of 24 monasteries (viharas) and 5 temples (chaityas), are hewn from the rocks of a ravine, at whose upper end a waterfall pours down. They date from the Buddhist era and are, almost without exception, older than those at Ellora (p.118); some date back as far as the 2nd c. B.C., the newest from the 5th c. A.D. The wall-paintings, in which Buddhist art shows itself almost superior to the then European style, are of particular interest. They mostly depict the Buddha's life and miracles; on others, battles, hunts, public processions and domestic scenes are portrayed, cf.p.LXIII.

276M. *Bhusawal* (214m; sta. rest., dinner 2R.8a.), town of 16,000 inhab., with large railway workshops employing 1500-2000 workers. In Bhusawal the two lines to Calcutta divide: E. via Nagpur (see below), NE via Jubbulpore (p.156).

The line via Nagpur to Calcutta (travelling time to Nagpur 9hrs.) crosses the mountainous land of *Berar,* part of the State of Hyderabad but entirely under British rule. It lies 400-1000m above sea-level, occupying 45,888 sq.km, and its central portion, watered by the *Purna* and its tributaries, belongs to the richest cotton-growing areas of India. The railway then enters the British-run Central Provinces. The flourishing towns are engaged in the cotton industry and trade. The main towns of Berar: 363M. *Akola* and *Amraoti*, connected by a branch-line to (413M) *Badnera*. – 480M. *Wardha*; branch-line to *Warora-Balharsbah*, which is to be continued to *Warangal* (p.115).

520M. *Nagpur* (sta. rest.), capital of the British Central Provinces, with 134,700 inhab., dominated by the fortified height of *Sitabaldi* (343m), and terminus of the Great Indian Peninsula Rly and first sta. on the Nagpur-Bengal Rly.

The Bengal Railway (fast train to Jharsuguda, 12¾hrs.) touches (529M) *Kampti*, a former important military cantonment, crosses the *Kanhan* and continues through fertile country, with plantations of cotton, wheat, millet and oil seed. Beyond the sta. (550M) *Bhandara Road*, which a branch-line links to the town of *Bhandara*, the line crosses the *Wainganga*. – 601M. *Gondia*, junc. for a few branch-lines, incl. one N. to Jubbulpore (p.156). – The W. part of the Central Provinces is bordered by thick jungle, in which live tigers and other large beasts of prey. The line climbs (tunnel) and passes through the small native states of *Khairagarh* (647M. *Dongargarh*, with sta. rest.) and *Nandgaon*. – 708M. *Raipur*, chief town in the division *Chattisgarh*, in the E. part of the Central Provinces. – 776M. *Bilaspur* (sta. rest.), a flourishing town of 19,000 inhab., junc. for a rly from *Katni* (p.156; 208M). – 858M. *Raigarh*, main town of the native state of the same name (3847 sq.km, 175,000 inhab.) – 900M. *Jharsuguda* (sta. rest., dinner 2R.8a.; branch to *Sambalpur*).

The fast train takes a further 11hrs. to cover the last section to Calcutta. The line crosses the river *Brahmani* and then passes through the hilly wooded country of S. Bengal. – 1008M. *Chakardarpur* (sta. rest.). – At (1050M) *Sini*, the line forks NE to Asansol (p.229), SE to Calcutta. The latter line crosses the river *Subarnarekha* and reaches, at (1149M) *Kharagpur* or *Khangpur*, the *Midnapur* rice-growing district, watered by numerous canals. The town of 33,000 inhab. is linked by a branch to Kharagpur, (8M), this being the junc. for the rly to Madras (Route 9). – One then crosses the *Rupnayaran*, which flows into the Hooghly or Hugli, the W. estuary branch of the Ganges. The rly reaches the Hooghly itself at *Ulubaria*, and accompanies it upstream.

1221M. *Howrah*, Calcutta's suburb on the r. bank, see p.239.

17b. Via Jubbulpore.

1349M. *Great Indian Peninsula Railway* to Jubbulpore, then *East Indian Rly:* for travelling times, fares, etc., see p.153.

From Bombay to (276M) Bhusuwal, see pp.153-4. From there to Jubbulpore, the fast train takes 10½hrs. – The railway crosses the *River Tapti* and follows its r. bank up the valley. – 310M. *Burhanpur* (260m), town of 33,000 inhab., with cotton trade; the old walls date from the 15th c., when the rulers of Khandesh had their seat here. – Onwards, through a depression in the *Satpura Range* to (353M) *Khandwa* (307m; sta. rest.), junc. for a narrow-gauge line via *Indore* (or *Indaur*, founded in 1767, now with 68,700 inhab., and capital of a Mahratta state of 24,000 sq.km in the Vindhya Range). Thence to Ujjain (p.132). – The rly enters the broad, fertile valley of the *Narbada* (which, next to the Indus, is the largest river in India flowing to the W. coast), but remains some distance away from its bank, only crossing several tributaries.

464M. *Itarsi* (330m; sta. rest.), where the rly branches off N. to Gwalior-Agra-Delhi (p.157) – 494M. *Sohagpur;* 505M. *Piparia,* the stop for the hill station *Pachmarhi*, 50km S. in the Mahadeo Hills, 1100m above sea-level; 536M. *Gadarwara;* 564M. *Narsinghpur.* On, across the Narbada. 606M. *Mirganj,* the stop for the Marble Rocks, a gorge on the Narbada.

616M. *Jubbulpore* (398m; Hotels: Commercial Hot., Jackson's Family Hot.) or *Jabalpur*, district capital with 100,600 inhab., ⅔ Hindu, lively corn and oil-seed trade, spinning and weaving mills, potteries, terminus of the East Indian Railway, also the junc. for a branch-line from Gondia (p.155).

The fast train takes 12hrs. from Jubbulpore to Gaya (p.228). – 673M. *Katni*, junc. for lines from Bilaspur (p.155) and Bina (p.157). The rly cuts through the E. heights of the Vindhya Range (p.67), then the native states of *Maihar* (712M., the capital of the same name, 603m above sea-level), and *Rewah.* The latter is 33,600 sq.km in size (more than ⅓ of it forest rich in game), with 1,327,000 inhab., 76% Hindu; 734M. *Satna.* Then on through the British United Provinces: 782M. *Manikpur,* junc for the line from Jhansi (p.158). The fast train for Calcutta passes Naini (in the direction of Allahabad, p.212) without stopping and, at (822M) *Chheoki,* reaches the line Delhi-Allahabad-Mughal-Sarai-Calcutta, see pp.213 & 227.

Route 18. From Bombay via Gwalior to Agra (Delhi)

Great Indian Peninsula Rly: to Agra, 835M, fast train (Punjab Express) in approx.24hrs., for 61R.9a., 30R.13a., 8R.4a.; to Delhi 957M. in 29½hrs, for 66R.4a., 33R.2a., 8R.12a.; for amount of luggage conveyed free, see p.XXI. Since the Punjab Express has only 32 1st cl. seats, it is necessary to book a berth in advance; cf.p.153. Meals in the dining-car: early morning tea 12a., with fruit 1R., tiffin 2R., afternoon tea 8a., dinner 3R. – The route is the most rapid link between Bombay and Delhi. However, Route 16 (via Ahmedabad-Jaipur) is to be more strongly recommended, because it allows a visit to Agra to be made *after* the visit to Delhi (cf.p.XIII); the trip to Gwalior may then be made from Agra.

From Bombay via *Bhusuwal* to (664M) *Itarsi*, where the rly to Calcutta via Jubbulpore diverges, see pp.154 & 156. – 476M. *Hoshangabad,* on the l. bank of the *Narbada,* which the line crosses. The river forms the frontier between the British Central Provinces and the native states of central India (148 of them, totalling a population of 8,510,000), whose princes are mainly descendants of the Mahrattas (Indore, Gwalior) or Afghans (Bhopal). – The line climbs through a picturesque ghat on the steep S. slopes of the *Vindhya Range*, and then continues downwards on an easy gradient to the *Malwa Plateau* (p.67).

521M. *Bhopal* (503m; sta. rest.), capital of a native state 17,869 sq.km in area, with a pop. of 1,050,000, mainly Hindus, amd governed by the Begum, a Mohammedan lady. The town (56,200 inhab.), surrounded by old walls, occupies a romantic situation on a slope overlooking two lakes.

From Bhopal, a branch-line (105M; travelling time 7hrs.) to *Ujjain* (p.132).

549M. *Sanchi* (fast trains do not stop; accommodation and food at the Dak bungalow, if booked in advance), at the foot of the *Sanchi Stupa, one of India's most ancient Buddhist monuments (p.LXIV). The stocky, hump-shaped structure is executed in sandstone and tiles, 17m tall and 37 in diameter. It is surrounded by a stone wall composed of massive blocks, with four gates at the compass points, whose architectural style is clearly in imitation of earlier wooden buildings (p.LXV). The gates are richly adorned with figures and reliefs. The oldest is the S. gate (around 140 B.C.), from which steps lead to the gallery. The W. gate has been restored.

555M. *Bhilsa* (471m). – 607M. *Bina,* junc. for branch-lines W. to *Baran* and *Kotah* (p.132), and E. to *Katni* (p.156). – 646M. *Lalitpur.*

702M. *Jhansi,* town of 55,700 inhab., in the British province of *Bundelkund,* picturesque, dominated by a fortress, formerly the capital of a small state, which the English occupied in 1853 after the death of the last prince (who was without an heir); his impetuous widow, the Ranee of Jhansi, joined the Mutiny in 1857 and, dressed in a man's clothing, was killed in battle at the storming of Gwalior.

From Jhansi, branch-lines via *Kalpi* to *Cawnpore* (p.211; 91M) and via *Harpalpur, Mahoba* and *Banda* to *Manikpur* (p.156, 181M). – About 35M S. of Mahoba lies the ruined village of *Khajurahu*, once capital of a kingdom, with many Hindu temples from the 9-11th c., of which the Kandariya Mahadeo, covered entirely with carvings, is among the most famous in India (p.LXVII).

718M. *Datia* (299m), main town of a still existing small princely state, not served by fast trains.

763M. **Gwalior**. – *Station* (rest.) 2-3km E. of the town. – A few minutes away, Gwalior Hotel (good), maintained by the Maharaja and run by a Swiss, 20 Rm., P.8-12R., out of season 6-8. (Extension under construction). The manager provides *carriages* (3R. per day) and permission to visit the Fortress, for which the Maharaja places an elephant at one's disposal (5R.), unless one prefers to go on foot; the mahut or driver waits with his animal at Alamgiri Gate (p.159; he, and the guide, should be given a tip of 2R. each).

Gwalior (208m), capital of the princely state of the same name (with an area of 64,830 sq.km and a pop. of 3,090,000, 75% Hindus), lies at the foot of a steep rocky ridge crowned by an ancient fortress, much fought over in the past. Of the changing dynasties, the *Kachvahas* (9th c. to the beginning of the 12th), and esp. the *Tomars* (1398-1518), were particular-ly prominent. During 1526-1761, Gwalior was part of the Grand Mogul Empire. The present dynasty (Hindu again) was founded in 1784 by the Mahratta leader Sindhia. In the Sepoy Mutiny of 1857, the Maharaja remained loyal to the English, while his troops rebelled and joined forces with the Ranee of Jhansi (see above). On the 19th of June 1858, the Fortress was taken by the English. – The town consists of two separate parts: *Old Gwalior*, NE of the Fortress, with 16,000 inhab., and *Lashkar*, the new town which has developed since 1810 from the tented camp (lashkar) of the Mahrattas, to the SE and S., with over 46,900 inhab.

The road from the sta. to the new town passes the Maharaja's *New Palace,* a sober building of 1876, fitted out in European style (the regal durbar hall is 46m long and 15-16 wide). Next to it, the stable for the Maharaja's horses and elephants. To the S., before the main façade of the Palace, is an old cannon. Through the park, one reaches *Victoria Gardens,* with a natural hist. Museum of little interest; thence to *Victoria College*, a modern building in the Hindu-Saracen style, and the large *Hospital.* Also worthy of mention are the *Temple of Sindhia's Mother*, as an example of the further development of Hindu style down to the present day (mid-19th c.) and, in the busy native quarter, a pretty modern *Market Hall.* The Maharaja's *Old Palace* now serves as offices.

The decaying old town of Gwalior preserves its character from the era of the Grand Moguls. The finest building, to the E., outside the town, is the *Tomb of Muhammed Ghaus,* 16th c., with a square main building, flat dome, arcade all round and 4 two-storeyed corner and gate pavilions; the walls consist entirely of stone tracery work; the holy man's marble sarcophagus inside is surrounded by a pavilion of pierced marble slabs. In the vicinity of the tomb are several lesser graves, incl. that of the singer *Tan Sen.* In the town, near the lower main entrance to the Fortress, the *Jama Masjid,* of the 17th c.

The **Fortress* (or Fort), 90m above the town, on a 3km-long sandstone rock, 200-850m wide, whose abrupt and sometimes overhanging walls are sculpted in places, is a splendid sight from far off across the plain. Its history dates back to the 6th c. A.D. The most important buildings are of the time of Man Singh (1486-1518), the penultimate and most influential representative of the Tomar dynasty. In the NE, the walls project to the foot of the rock, where *Alamgiri Gate,* built in 1660, forms the main entrance. With this, seven gates in all span the path up to the Fort. The second, *Badalgarh Pol,* with a pretty pointed arch, is 15th c. Beyond the 3rd gate, r., the ruin of a large palace from Man Singh's time *(Gujari Mahal),* with beautiful windows. Beyond the 5th gate, a small rock temple of the 9th c., which was dedicated to the Chatur Bhuj, i.e. the "four-armed" Vishnu. Further along, depictions in relief of the Mahadeo Shiva, and many lingams. Worthy of notice is the last gate but one (the 6th), *Hathi Pol,* 15th c. The way to the rocky plateau is dominated by the:-

**Palace of Man Singh,* linked to the Hathi Pol and the last gate. This was completed around 1500 and restored in 1881, with two main floors and basement, like the palace at Amber (p.150), but more fortified in appearance. The E. front, 91m long and 30 high, is strengthened by 4 semicircular towers surmounted by domed pavilions; the 49m-long S. front has 3 similar towers, with pierced breastwork. Coloured tiles with pictures of plants and animals, in green, blue and yellow, cover the surfaces of the walls within and without. The living quarters face in to the two courtyards, small and linked by winding stairs. The air is made foul by bats. – Adjacent, to the N., is the *Chit Mahal,* built by Man Singh's son, with pretty decoration. The palaces further N. are of no significance, being partly given over to military stores (no entry).

The two *Sas Bahu Temples,* which stand, 8-10min to the S. upon an E. projection of the Fortress rock, belong to an earlier period. The larger, built according to an inscription in 1092-93 and dedicated to Vishnu, is approx. 30m long, 19 wide and 22 high, with vestibules on its four sides and 4 massive pillars within. The smaller temple, similar in plan, lies right out on a kind of bastion, with a marvellous view. – From here, one proceeds SW, past the recently renovated *Suraj Kund,* the oldest reservoir for water in the Fortress (end of the 3rd c.), and, in 6-8min, to the *Teli Mandir,* a temple to Vishnu from the 10-11th c., which was dedicated to Shiva in the 15th c. The richly articulated and carved building, 18 sq.m in area, with a projecting entrance hall and flat top, at a height of 25m, reminds us of the gopurams of S. India. Pieces of masonry and carvings, found during restoration work in 1881-83, have been set out in the enclosure. The round tank, with a two-storeyed pavilion at its centre, is now empty of water.

Remarkable are the (mostly) giant-sized figures of Jain Tirthankars (p.LVIII) from the time of the Tomar dynasty (ca.1440-73), which were chiselled out of the living rock in five places, high up on the Fortress rock, defaced in part during the Grand Mogul rule, and later completed with painted stucco. One of the most important groups is to be found in the *Urwahi Valley,* access to which is by means of a gate in the Fortress wall, a little to the N. of the Suraj Kund (see above). Of the 22 figures, below which the path passes, the 17th represents Adinath with a bull at his feet; the 20th figure (whom it depicts is unclear) is 17m tall, its foot almost 3m long; the last is a seated Nemnath, with a shell at his feet. One can order the carriage to wait at the lower entrance to the valley, then drive through Lashkar to the group at the *SE edge of the Fortress rock;* but it is equally convenient to climb up there from the hotel (¼hr.) A row of 18 giant figures lines the steep rock face, which is overgrown with bushes and trees. Here and there are caves, inhabited by hermits. The total impression is strangely gripping.

Narrow-gauge railways connect Gwalior to the NE with *Bindh,* to the SW with *Sipri* and *Sabalgarh-Sheopur.*

The railway (from Gwalior to Agra, 2¼-3¾hrs.) passes over a monotonous plain. Beyond (786M) *Morena,* it crosses the *Kuwari* and, after (795M) *Hetampur* the more important *Chambal*, which forms the frontier between the State of Gwalior and the British "United Provinces". On both rivers are gorges formed into fantastic shapes by erosion, reminiscent of the loess formations in China; they are esp. prominent on the Chambal. – 804M. *Dholpur* (sta. rest.), capital of a small Rajput state.

835M. *Agra*, see p.161. – From Agra to *Delhi*, see p.173, via Tundla to Cawnpore, see p.211.

Route 19. Agra.

STATIONS: *Cantonment Junction,* for the rly Bombay-Gwalior-Muttra-Delhi (Routes 15, 17); *Fort Station,* between Fort and Jama Masjid, for the lines from Bombay via Jaipur (p.153) and from Tundla (p.175). The sta. *Idagah* lies on the connecting line between Cantonment Junc. and Fort Sta. – *City Station*, also for Tundla (Calcutta; see p.175).

Hotels (1½-3km from the stations): *Cecil Hotel, Mall Rd., new and comfortably furnished, open only from the end of Oct. to the end of Mar., Swiss proprietor, German spoken, 50 Rm., P.8-12R.; Laurie's Great Northern Hot., also aspiring to 1st class, quite good. P. from 7R.: Metropole Hot., Drummond Rd.; Savoy Hot.; Dak bungalow, W. of the Post Office, well spoken of.

Carriages: within the town limits, 2-horse landau 2R. per hr., 1-horse phaeton 1R. for the 1st hr., and 12a. for each succeeding one; ½ day 3½R., 3R., whole day 5R., 4R.; Taj Mahal and back 3R., 2R.; Itimad-ud-Daula 4R., 3R.; Sikandra 4R., 3R. Fatepur Sikri 16R., 12R., with overnight stay 24R., 18R. Carriages etc. can be ordered at *Hatum Buksh,* Gwalior Rd. The hotels charge higher prices but do not allow carriages hired elsewhere to drive up to them. – MOTOR CARS from *H.Pestonji & Co.,* opp. Laurie's Hotel, esp. recommended for Fatepur Sikri, approx. 40R. there and back.

GUIDE: 3R. per day, cf. p.XXV. There are also special guides for most of the places of interest.

POST: Main Office, Mall Rd., near the hotels. – TELEGRAPH: a few mins to the SE. – BANKS: *Bank of Bengal, Alliance Bank of Simla.* – CLUB: *Agra Club*, S. of the Post Office. – DOCTORS. the civilian surgeon at the English station.

Shops. Jewellery, embroidery using gold, silver and precious gems: *Alla Bux, Chutton Lal Jahori Bazaar,* both in the city; *Ganeshi Lal & Son,* Drummond Rd. near the Metropole Hot. (esp. good for thin silk fabrics shot through with gold, and Indian miniatures). – Soapstone and marble items, mosaics: *Nathooram,* Drummond Rd. – Photographic articles at *Raina & Co.,* in Perthapura. – Provisions at the *Agra Co-operated Stores.* – Carpets at the factory of *Otto Weylandt & Co.*, Geman prop., who is also happy to give information. One can watch the carpets being made. The knotwork is done mainly by boys.

For a limited visit (3 days). 1st day: *Fort,* with the Pearl Mosque and Palace of the Grand Moguls (p.163; all photography in the Fort is forbidden, as is the introduction of certain native guides), *Jama Masjid* (p.166); in the afternoon, the *Taj Mahal* (p.167; most beautiful in the evening light, though the morning is not unfavourable; quite lovely by moonlight, though the gardens are closed at 10 p.m., after which one may enter only with the Superintendent's permission; it goes without saying that the visitor is expected to behave decorously). – 2nd day: *Sikandra* (p.168); in the afternoon, the *Tomb of Itimad-ud-Daula* (p.166), second visit to the Taj Mahal. - 3rd day: excursion to *Fatepur Sikri* (pp.169-70): Motor car 40R., tonga 12R.

Agra (204m,) the older seat of the Grand Moguls (p.178), now the blossoming capital of a division of the British "United Provinces", with a pop. of 185,500, of whom 62% are Hindus and 20% Mohammedans, lies in a plain planted with crops and cotton, though dusty during the dry season, on the r. bank of the 40-70m-wide *Jumna* (or *Jamna*), which at this point curves sharply towards the E. Junction for several railway lines, it is an important cotton depot, also a centre for some cotton mills and ancient crafts. The powerful *Fort* overlooks the river. Two railway bridges, of which the N. one also serves pedestrians and vehicles, cross to the l. bank. The native quarter *(City),* lying N. and W. of the Fort, contains winding but well-kept streets busy with traffic. The *Cantonment,* with many gardens, extends to the S., containing most of the European dwellings, barracks and administrative buildings. – Agra possesses some buildings which rank not only among the noblest creations of Mohammedan architecture, but of architecture in general.

The name (from "agur", i.e. salt-pan) indicates salt-trading in the past. The town originally lay on the l. bank of the river. The first Grand Mogul, *Baber* (p.178), who conquered it in 1526, also took up residence there. The founder of the present town was his grandson *Jelala-ud-din Mohammed*, known as *Akbar*, i.e. *The Great* (1556-1605), whose powerful personality confronts us esp. in his other residence at Fatepur Sikri, nearby (p.170). He mounted the throne at the age of 13, and by the time he was 25 (1567), he had subjected the numerous separate states of N. India and incorporated the entire area into his empire. By good administration and the development of trade and agriculture, he raised the standard of living. By tolerating those of other religious persuasions, he tried to weld the various elements of the people together and, himself, took as his legitimate wives a Hindu prince's daughter and apparently also an Armenian or Portuguese Christian girl. He organised debates between the representatives of different faiths, and finally founded a latitudinarian cult (p.LXII). Numerous artists came to his court, also painters, whom he permitted (against Islamic law) to depict human figures. His original and powerful buildings, done in the red sandstone of the area, unite the forms of Hindu and Jain style with those of Mohammedan art. His son *Jehangir,* born at Sikri in 1569, who, as prince, bore the name *Selim* (cf.p.170), moved the residence to Lahore in 1618 (p.199). Just as the Italian renaissance was spreading through Europe at that time, Persian art made a breakthrough at the court of the Grand Mogul where, in any case, Persian was favoured as a language. Marble, dragged here from great distances, became the preferred building material. Massiveness of form gave way to simple elegance, esp. under *Shah Jehan* (1627-58), the first ten years of whose reign can be described as Agra's period of greatest glory. The walls of buildings were incrusted with pietra dura, likewise in the Persian style, and perhaps executed in part by Italian artists. Also, in his later residence at Delhi (cf.p.180), Jehan still showed favour to Agra, where he spent the last years of his life as a prisoner of state (1658-66). Then, Agra declined into a provincial town, being several times sacked in the wars of the 18th c., and passing in 1803 from the command of the Mahrattas into the possession of the English, who successfully defended the Fort against the mutineers in 1857. – The maintenance of the monuments and the laying out of the gardens around them is to Lord Curzon's credit.

The *Fort, with its sandstone walls 21m high, battlemented and strengthened by semicircular towers, and with its 10m-deep moat, describes a half-circle 2km in circuit, whose straight diameter faces towards the river. Surprisingly spectacular in aspect, it is worth driving all round it. The main entrance is *Delhi Gate*, on the W. side opp. Fort Station (p.161). A drawbridge crosses the moat. Through an outer bastion we reach the splendid inner gate, called *Hathi Pol* or Elephant Gate, after two stone elephants, destroyed by Aurangzeb, which stood to l. and r. on the pedestals (traces of the feet remain). The two huge octagonal gate towers are decorated with white sandstone and divided by a gallery, running round them, into two floors, the upper one with broad, tall lancet openings. Above the gateway, a gallery for the musicians who played for the arrival of the ruler or the reception of important guests. In the r. gate tower, a staircase goes up, which however may only be used by permission of the Station Staff Office (view of the Jama Masjid and, to the NE, on the other bank of the river, the Tomb of Itimad-ud-Daula; to the SE, the dome of the Taj Mahal).

Inside the Fort, which is partly built over with barracks, a path to the l. from the gate leads up in an arc to the E. entrance of the Pearl Mosque, while another, the original main path, bears r. and then l., and straight on to an open square; here, the mosque is on our l., and the palace of Shah Jehan to our r. The name of the square, *Mina Bazaar,* reminds us of the time when the town's merchants were allowed to offer their wares here.

The **Moti Masjid or *Pearl Mosque,* built at the Fort's highest point by Shah Jehan in 1648-55, may be regarded as one of the noblest places of worship in the Mohammedan world. The outside walls, enclosing a rectangle 72 X 57m, are simple and made of red sandstone. The principal gate is on the E. side; a double staircase of 49 steps leads up. As we enter through the low, vaulted gateway, the whole splendour of the building is unfolded. Everything is of white marble, without any decorative carving, but perfect in the harmony of its forms. The courtyard (47 X 48m) is bordered by arcades, partly open and partly closed, and paved with marble slabs; in the middle, the basin for ablutions. The Mosque itself, on the W. side, opens in seven arches. The Persian inscription, in black marble on the frieze, praises the building's beauty which, it says, is like that of a valuable pearl. The interior is only 17m deep, consisting of three transverse aisles, with three domes above the centre one. At the back wall, the prayer niche (mihrab) with the pulpit (mimbar). Behind the delicately pierced marble grilles, on the N. and S. sides, the women of the court attended the service. The mosaic floor bears a pattern resembling prayer mats.

The Palace of Shah Jehan, opp. the Mosque, to the S., is similar in plan to that ruler's later palace at Delhi (p.180). The buildings are grouped round three large courtyards.

The outer court, which we enter first, measures 150 X 112m and is bounded by arcades on three sides. On the E. side, the *Divan-i-Am opens off, a pillared hall 58·5m broad and 13·5 deep, built of sandstone with a white covering of stucco. Here, the ruler's public audiences were held (cf.pp.180-1). The throne stood against the E. wall in the raised niche (decorated in marble and pietra dura), whose access was from the Machhi Bhawan behind (see below; a narrow little flight of steps leads up). The pierced marble windows to r. and l. permitted the women to see what was going on in the hall. – The two-storeyed pavilion in Hindu style on the W. side of the arcaded court, called *Selimgarh,* is presumably the remnant of one of Jehangir's larger buildings (Selim, see p.162). – To the N., near the Divan-i-Am, one enters the *Inner Mina Bazaar,* a small courtyard with a delightful marble loggia for the women, when they personally wished to purchase finery and jewellery from the brocade and jewel dealers. Also worthy of our attention, near the *temple* added by the Hindu conquerors of the 18th c., are the fine bronze gates, which Akbar removed from Chitorgarh (p.145) as booty. They form the entrance to the Machhi Bhawan, but are generally shut. We therefore return to the Divan-i-Am and ascend the staircase mentioned above.

The Machhi Bhawan (pron. match-hi) is the second courtyard of the Palace, much smaller than the first, and mainly in ruins. The name ("fish place") seems to indicate that it once contained fish tanks, possibly also fountains and flower beds. It is enclosed by two-storeyed arcades. The small staircase finishes at the upper arcade, in whose NW corner Aurangzeb added a mosque for domestic use, the *Najina Masjid* ("Jewel Mosque"). We also visit a room which the guides claim to be Shah Jehan's prison, and the upper loggia by the Inner Mina Bazaar, and then reach a *terrace,* offering a magnificent view towards the Taj Mahal. A polished black stone block with a carved edge, known as Jehangir's throne, is supposed to have served at the nomination of prince Selim as heir to the throne (1603). Opposite, a white marble seat for the Grand Vizier. To the E., below the terrace, a cage in which animal fights were held. – Adjacent, to the S., is the *Divan-i-Khas, the private audience hall built in 1637, 20 X 10.4m in size, and thus smaller than the hall at Delhi (p.181) but, in its fashion, also a work of beauty and perfection. The material is white marble, and style and decoration are nobly simple. The marble slabs (dados) on the lower part of walls and pillars are decorated with flower reliefs. - To the E., on a projecting bastion, stands an octagonal pavilion in marble, **Sam man Burj,* i.e. Jasmine Tower. This charming structure was probably built by Jehangir for his favourite wife Nur Mahal (p.166; cf. Thom. Moore's poem "Lalla Rookh"). Later, her niece Mumtaz-i-Mahal lived there, who was Shah Jehan's favourite wife. The lowness of the marble parapet round the balcony can be explained by the oriental custom of sitting on the floor. – The unusual paving in the small court between the Divan-i-Khas and the Sam man Burj is reminiscent of *Pachisi,* a kind of board game popular at that time, for which the players liked to use children as living figures. The tiny *Mina Masjid* on the S. side of the courtyard was the imperial private mosque.

The third great court of the Palace, lying SW of the Divan-i-Khas, a square of side 85m, with a fountain in the middle, is called *Anguri Bagh*, i.e. court of grapes, probably because vines might have been planted here. Its E. side is bounded by the **Khas Mahal,* a marble structure of 1636, in whose splendid rooms lived the women of the harem; the two flanking pavilions, with gilded roofs and white marble courts in front, contained the bedchambers. The building's basement, to which a staircase leads down from the S. platform, served as a refuge during the intense heat of mid-summer. The *Shish Mahal*, in the NE corner of the Anguri court, with the baths for the harem (opened on demand), possesses mirror decoration similar to that in the palace at Amber (p.151). Three attractive rooms in the SE corner of the court are said to be *Shah Jehan's private apartments,* the E. one being an octagonal pavilion like the Jasmine Tower. According to the story handed down, Jehan died here within sight of Mumtaz-i-Mahal's tomb (cf.p.167), in the arms of his faithful daughter Jehanara (p.187). – Along the S. wall of Anguri court, behind railings, are kept the carved doors seized during the Afghan war of 1842. At that time, they were mistakenly regarded as old Indian temple doors removed by the Afghans in 1025, when in fact they are later Mohammedan work.

Continuing S., we reach the *Jehangiri Mahal, i.e. Jehangir's Palace, which however dates back in its essentials to Akbar. The stern, solid building in red sandstone, akin to the style of buildings at Fatepur Sikri (p.170), makes an arresting contrast to the sensuous elegance of Shah Jehan. The main front faces the outer court towards the river. We gain access through an ante-room, then on through a fine gate and a domed hall with carved ceiling, to the inner court, whose excellent Hindu decoration merits our attention. Of the rooms around the courtyard, the large hall on the N. side (19 X 11m) contains a stone roof with corbels in the manner of the Jain architecture at Mount Abu (p.139). On the roof, we see cisterns and several pavilions, esp. rich on the W. side. The outer front of the palace is also worthy of notice.

The S. bastion gate of the Fort *(Amar Sing's Gate)* is less important than Delhi Gate.

To the W. of Fort Station rises (pretty view from the footbridge over the railway line) the Jama Masjid, built by Shah Jehan in 1639-44 in honour of his daughter Jehanara, and providing the model for the large main mosque in Delhi, though smaller and simpler than the latter (cf.p.183). The substructure, on which it stands, is only 40 X 31m and 3m high. The domes sit directly on the roof without drums, and are decorated with a zigzag motif in sandstone and marble.

From the N. part of the City, the bridge already mentioned (p.162) crosses the River Jumna. On the l. bank, we follow the road of the mill-stone makers, past the goods depot of the East Indian Railway and, in 5min., reach, on the l., the entrance to the:-

**Tomb of Itimad-ud-Daula*, erected in 1622-28 by the empress Nur Mahal (p.165) to her father Mirza Ghiyas Beg, who was Jehangir's Grand Vizier and Treasurer (Itimad-ud-Daula). We pass through the garden in front and, by a pretty gate, enter the main garden which, with its lawns and decorative water channels, surrounds the monument. At the four corners of the garden wall are towers with pavilions made of red sandstone, and mosque-like structures on the long sides. The Tomb, entirely of marble, stands on a plinth and resembles, in shape, a single-storeyed garden pavilion of sides 21m, with round corner towers topped by pavilions, and a beautiful central pavilion, whose roof still displays the Hindu style, while Mohammedan styles predominate everywhere else. For the first time we find here the Persian type of decoration with inlays of coloured stone. The pierced marble windows are also notable. The central pavilion above contains the cenotaphs of Itimad and his wife, while the graves themselves are in the gloomy basement. – The W. garden gate, facing the river, is an attractive viewpoint.

A few other tombs are dotted along the bank of the river upstream: for instance, 10mins further on, the *Chini-ka-Rauza* or “Porcelain Tomb”, in which it is said the poet Afzal Khan (†1639) is buried. The tomb probably dates from Aurangzeb’s time, and is sadly neglected. It takes its name from the decoration in glazed tiles.

From the Fort and the Cantonment there are good roads leading, in 2½km to the E., by the Jumna, to the most splendid building in the entire canon of Mohammedan art, upon which warm praise has been lavished down the centuries:

The ***Taj Mahal,* tomb of Shah Jehan’s favourite wife Arjumand Banu (called *Mumtaz-i-Mahal,* i.e. the chosen one of the palace), who died in childbirth in 1629. She was a grand-daughter of Itimad-ud-Daula and niece of Nur Mahaol (p.166), and in 1612 became the wife of the future emperor, upon whom she exerted a considerable influence by virtue of her beauty and her nobility of sentiment. The building was begun in 1630 and completed in 1648. Its plan and elevation are reminiscent of the older Tomb of Humayun (p.186) and probably hark back to Persian master-builders; there is no authentic indication that western craftsmen had any hand in it. The grounds form a rectangle of approx. 567 X 305m in area, and consist of a forecourt 137m deep, a garden 288m square and the low terrace to the N., upon which stands the Mausoleum itself. The buildings are in an excellent state of preservation; the damage, which they suffered in the wars of the 18th c. and in 1857, has been repaired, and the entire complex restored to its original form.

The first court *(Taj Ganj),* which we now enter from the W., between rows of colonnades, is surrounded by magnificent buildings in red sandstone, containing the assembly rooms and guest quarters for pilgrims. In the middle of the N. side is the splendid *Main Gate* (giving access to the garden), a square sandstone structure 43m high, clad in white and coloured marble, with lofty gate recesses and smaller side niches. The central portion has, at the front and on the garden side, an upper part with eleven pretty little domes in the style of the Fort gates at Delhi. The four corner towers are crowned by pavilions. The l. wing contains a collection of old plans of Agra, photographs of the Taj since 1860, and experiments with pietra dura material. Superb view from the roof. – A few steps lead down into the garden. There is a breathtaking view, along the main avenue, of the marble domed Mausoleum rising in the distance, and reflecting in the clear water of the ornamental channels. The present growth of trees in the garden is, despite recent cutting-back, undoubtedly fuller than it was many years ago, a factor which impairs the general effect. At the intersection of the two main avenues is a marble platform with fountains and seats. At each end of the transverse avenue, an ornamental pavilion.

The N. end of the garden is shut off by the 1·2m-high paved terrace, which supports the main building. In the centre, the Mausoleum; r., a *meeting hall,* l. a **mosque,* both of great beauty, in red sandstone with marble inlay (from the interior of the mosque we have a magnificent view of the Mausoleum, which is seen here standing alone and divorced, as it were, from its surroundings).

The ***Mausoleum*, of white marble with bluish veins, and bearing noble pietra dura decoration and delicate bas-reliefs on its base, rises from a marble substructure, 50·5m high and 94·4m square, between four marble minarets, 41·75m high. Its plan is a square of side 56·7m, cut off at the corners. On all four sides, huge outer arches open at the centre, rising to a shallow point, with windows of similar shape next to them on two floors. The cornice is 32·92m above the ground. The large central dome, flanked by four smaller ones, is 26m in diameter and rises to a height of 65m, or 75m with its gilded spike. The general effect surpasses the imagination. The Mausoleum's simplicity of design, together with the splendour of its artistic execution combine into a marvel of art which competes, in its sublime beauty, with the temples of the Greeks, and the most famous cathedrals of medieval and renaissance times. The same harmony prevails within the building, where the octagonal central hall, vaulted with a 24m-high intermediate dome, contains the cenotaphs of Mumtaz Mahal and Shah Jehan. The solemn atmosphere is heightened by the subdued light which seeps in. Both cenotaphs, that of Mumtaz in the centre, a shining polished block of marble inlaid with floral mosaics and sayings from the Koran, and the rather larger cenotaph of Jehan to one side, are surrounded by alabaster screens pierced in a wonderfully delicate lace-like pattern. The silver doors, the priceless jewels and the carpets which covered the stones, were stolen in the 18th c. The guide draws attention to the remarkable acoustic inside the building. The sarcophagi, containing the couple's mortal remains, are shown in the basement.

The road to Sikandra (8km NW; for carriages, see p.161) leaves the old town of Agra by the Delhi Gate, in the former city walls, and passes by the central prison. It is the ancient Mogul highway to Lahore and still, in parts, marked with milestones (Kos-minar) at 4km intervals. On both sides there are numerous ruins, mostly of tombs. Half-way, there is a large open pillared hall with 4 corner pavilions and the octagonal domed tomb of a nephew of Itimad-ud-Daula (p.166). – The village of *Sikandra* takes its name from Sultan Sikandar of the Lodi dynasty (p.178), and it famous for the:-

**Tomb of Akbar*, one of the most important tombs in India, completed in 1613. It occupies the centre of a garden, 60 hectares in extent, surrounded by a battlemented wall. Four magnificent gates, 21m high, in red sandstone with white marble decoration, provide access. On the main gate, to the W., rise 4 recently restored marble minarets. From above, a fine view of the tomb and E. to Agra, SW to Fatepur Sikri where, on the horizon, the triumphal gate of the Jama Masjid may be seen (p.172). The garden lawns are interspersed with trees. Along the broad paths there are basins with fountains.

The *Tomb* differs from all the other Mogul graves by virtue of its unique layout, apparently pointing to ancient Indian models. The vaulted substructure, recently painted white, with open arches and tall entry gates, is 9m high and 94 sq.m in area. Above this rises a four-storeyed stepped building with numerous pavilions and arched halls on the terraces. The lowest floor is 57 sq.m in area, the uppermost 48 sq.m. Three storeys are built of red sandstone. The top one is of white marble and forms a kind of cemetery, whose outer walls are enhanced by 44 marble windows executed in the richest of geometrical patterns. Arcades surround the open inner space in which, on a low platform, stands Akbar's cenotaph, elegant but simple. The chiselled inscriptions proclaim the fundamentals of Akbar's free-thinking faith: "Allahu Akbar" (God is great) and "Jalla Jalalahu" (may his glory shine forth), together with the 99 holy names of the Creator. Into the pedestal nearby, the famous big diamond Koh-i-nor (i.e. mountain of light) is said to have been set: after a chequered career, it finally found its way into the English crown jewels. – The sarcophagus itself is placed immediately below the cenotaph in a subterranean vault, whose entrance is on the S. side of the basement. The simple tombstone, its head facing not towards Mecca, but to the rising sun, bears only the name; the valuable covering over it was a present from the viceroy Earl of Northbrook (1876). Members of the family repose in the other rooms.

To the E., outside the gardens, lies the beautifully ornamented *Kanch Mahal*, a country residence of Jehangir, recently renovated. – To the W., about 1km further along the road to Muttra, the *Bahradari*, a former palace of Sikandar Lodi (1495), now a branch of the Agra orphanage.

The *excursion to Fatepur Sikri (37km; good, shady road), is best done by motor car (cf.p.161; travelling time 1 hr.), but if one uses a fast tonga (3-3½hrs.), one still has time for a fleeting visit. Travellers wishing to spend the night here will find good accommodation and food in the new Dak bungalow, provided an advance booking is made.

The town of *Fatepur Sikri* (also Fatehpur or Fathpur), built in 1569-1602 by Akbar, owes its foundation to a meeting of the emperor with the holy sheik Selim Chisti at the village of Sikri, who promised him that an heir to the throne would be born after a victorious campaign. Fatepur means "victory town", and the prince (p.162) was named Selim. The buildings are powerful in style. Most date from the period up to 1587, but the emperor continued to show favour to the town, even after he had moved his residence back to Agra. Abandoned since Akbar's death, almost unaltered and kept in an excellent state, they offer us an incomparable view of the era and artistic tastes of the great builder. The following short description picks out only the most important buildings. The usual notes are generally not authentic, historically speaking.

The town forms an oblong 2700m long and 1350 broad. It is surrounded on three sides by high walls, with bastioned gates; to the NW it used to be protected by an artificial lake, now dried out. From *Agra Gate*, the road runs, r., up the long, low, rocky ridge, which the imperial palace crowns. The old gate *Naubat Khana* remains now to our l., the name meaning "music house", reminiscent of ceremonial receptions (cf.p.163). Passing the Dak bungalow, we reach the *Mint*, a building 70 X 73m with an inner courtyard enclosed by low arcades (brick arches, perhaps the first of their kind in India, cf.p.189). On the other side of the road, the prettily decorated little *Treasury*.

The general grouping of the buildings of the palace resembles the layout of the later palaces at Agra and Delhi. From NE to SW we can distinguish three main groups, of which the first has the Mahal-i-Khas at its centre, and the second the palace of Jodh Bai (p.171); the third is the Jama Masjid (p.172) with the great triumphal gate.

In the first group, we begin with the Divan-i-Am, a court 102 X 55m, bordered by arcades, with the public audience hall in the W. range; here, between beautifully pierced screens, the imperial throne. – We continue through the S. (short) side of the courtyard, then past the *Turkish Sultana's* so-called *Bath of Hakim* (i.e. of the doctors), whose size and decoration with stucco and paintings point to its more probable use by the emperor and his court, and we reach the *Daftar Khana* or archives, with a colonnade around it. – To the W. of the Divan-i-Am stretches the imperial private palace, the Mahal-i-Khas, whose buildings are grouped round two courtyards. The first court (64 X 67m), with a water-basin at its centre, is bordered by: the emperor's two-storeyed dwelling on the S. side, on whose roof a small pavilion is pointed out as his sleeping quarters (*Khwabgah*, i.e. house of dreams; inside, ornamental and metaphorical paintings, the latter including a trip by water and Buddhist scenes, redolent of Chinese models); to the NE, the so-called small *House of the Turkish Sultana,* surrounded by a verandah, covered inside and out with charming bas-relief decoration, and linked by a staircase to the bath mentioned above. A colonnade separates the first court from the second (called Pachisi, this name being explained by strips set in the pavement resembling a games board, cf.p.165). Its N. side is occupied by the *Divan-i-Khas,* the private audience hall, 13·15m square on the outside, 8·6m square within, with a famous, richly decorated centre column, whose giant corbel capital is linked by four bridges to the wall galleries. The *Ankh Michauli* is said to have been used for entertainments and games ("blind man's buff"), but was probably a treasury or archive. The baldaquin on the platform in front of it was supposedly for Akbar's Hindu astrologer *(yogi).*

On the W. side of the Pachisi court, the remarkable **Panch Mahal* rises in terraces, which possibly served the womenfolk of the court as an airy abode. There are five storeys. The ground-floor measures 23 X 18m, with 84 columns; the first floor has 56, the second 20, the third 12 columns; the fourth floor, about 14m above the ground, also supports a 4-pillared pavilion with dome, whose point rises a further 7m. Note the versatile design of the columns. If the supposition is correct, that such buildings hark back to ancient Indian models, then we have here a clue for the completion of the ruins of the so-called Brazen Palace at Anuradhapura (p.59). – The large, two-storeyed house to the SW, with verandahs on 3 sides, bears the name *Miriam's Kothi* and is claimed to be the dwelling of Bibi Miriam, the alleged Christian among Akbar's wives; it contains wall-paintings by Persian artists, possibly illustrations from Firdusi's Book of Kings, alas in very poor condition and recently covered with cheap varnish.

The main building in the second group, formerly linked to the Mahal-i-Khas by a covered way, is the palace known as Jod Bai's Mahal, the oldest in the entire complex, probably built for Akbar's Rajput wife Mariam Zamani, mother of Jehangir. Any suggestion of a connection with one of the latter's wives, who was a princess of Jodhpur, is erroneous. The building, with its main entrance on the E. side, and an open inner court, is almost pure Hindu style and simpler than the other women's palaces. A projecting pavilion with window grilles, called *Hawa Mahal,* i.e. palace of the winds, offered a view over the gardens to the former lake. To the W. of this, the adjoining ruined stables for horses and camels. – The two-storeyed palace to the NW, architecturally outstanding, is designated the **House of Rajah Birbal,* a Hindu favourite of Akbar and follower of his free-thinking religion, completed in 1572 according to the inscription. It contains four rooms below, with entrance halls N. and S. and, above, two rooms surmounted by domes and two open terraces. Note the rich reliefs, in the most varied patterns, inside and out. – To the N. of this point, the road descends l., towards the former lake, through the magnificent gate *Hathi Pol,* whose name (cf.p.163) derives from two now destroyed figures of elephants. After passing through the gate, we glimpse, to our r., ruins of reservoirs which served the palace; to our l., ruins of a large caravanserai; straight ahead, on an octagonal substructure, the tower *Hiran Minar,* like a minaret, whose round central portion is entirely covered with imitations of elephants' tusks. Its total height, together with the base, is 43m. There is a pretty view over the town from the upper platform, which is crowned by an octagonal pavilion.

To the SW of the royal palace, on a low rise, stands the *Jama Masjid,* begun in 1571 in honour of the holy man, Selim Chisti. It is one of the most superb complexes of its kind, 165m long, 126 wide, enclosed by a high battlemented sandstone wall, with two large gatehouses to E. and S., to which flights of steps lead up. The *Badshahi*, or *King's Gate*, on the E. side, was originally the main entrance. After new conquests in the N. Deccan, Akbar built the "High Gate" *(*Baland Darwaza)* in 1602, an immense triumphal gateway uniquely massive in effect, esp. when viewed from without. Its total height from the foot of the external steps is 54m, that of the gatehouse itself being 41m, and 40 wide. The outer structure, whose cut-off corners are arranged in three storeys, has a mighty gate opening, being half a hexagon with a diameter of 14m. The lower part of the gate itself is studded with decorated horseshoes which, it is claimed, were originally silver. The upper platform of the building is surmounted by 3 large and 13 small domed pavilions or kiosks which, since Akbar's time, have been characteristic of Mogul architecture. The rear of the gatehouse has three openings.

Next to the outer gates, r. and l., are entrances to the stairs leading to the upper platform: 123 steps in all; from the top, a broad panorama, to the NE as far as the Taj Mahal, to the NW to Bharatpur (p.153).

The court is 133 X 109m in size, enclosed by wide pillared halls, whose flat roofs are dotted with rows of small kiosks. Abutting all around on the rear walls of the halls are about 90 cells, intended, it seems, for the teachers and scholars observing Akbar's religious beliefs. The W. wall of the court contains the *Liwan,* or mosque proper, 88m long, incl. the wall, 17m deep and surmounted by three domes. It consists of the central portion, containing the portal and the 12 sq.m main room, with pillared halls on both sides, containing 2 smaller chapels with 5 cells on the N. short side and 5 more on the S.; above these latter, galleries for the womenfolk, the stairs to which lie outside. Walls and vaults are adorned mainly with decorative paintings, whose colours have largely faded. There is a legend attached to the child's grave to the W., behind the mosque: a little son of Selim Chisti went voluntarily to his death, because a prophecy made the birth of an heir to the throne dependent upon such a sacrifice.

In the N. part of the court stands the **Tomb of Selim Chisti,* built entirely of white marble in 1571, a veritable little jewel-box of oriental architecture, only 15 sq.m in size, with a low dome, a small ante-room and ambulatory, whose pierced walls produce a mysterious effect. The entrance doors are of ebony. The interior, which is barred to women, is partly decorated with stylised flower motifs. A baldaquin of ebony inlaid with mother-of-pearl covers the holy man's marble cenotaph: he is revered by Mohammedans and Hindus alike (the sarcophagus lies in the walled-up crypt). Women hopeful of being blessed with children plait colourful strips of cloth, from outside, in the openings in the marble walls. – Nearby, executed in red sandstone, the larger *Tomb of the Islam Khan,* a grandson of Selim Chisti, who was nawab (governor) of Bengal under Jehangir (†1604). The general plan is similar to that of the other tomb. The ambulatory walls are richly pierced here also. The base of the dome is covered by 9-10 kiosks on each of the four sides.

The present-day small town (7000 inhab.) occupies only the SW part of the area enclosed by the old walls.

Route 20. From Agra to Delhi.

Route 20a. Via Muttra (route Bombay-Gwalior-Agra-Delhi).

122M. *Great Indian Peninsula Rly:* fast train in 3hrs.50min, ord. train in 6¾-7½hrs., for 12R.7a., 5R.12a., 1R.15a. Quickest and most convenient connection.

Agra (Cantonment Junc., see p.161) – The line crosses the road to Sikandra (p.169) and heads NW. On our r., we see the W. gate of Akbar's Tomb which appears impressively among the treetops. The flat landscape is well cultivated and irrigated by canals.

33M. *Muttra Junction,* 3km S. of the town of the same name, lying on the line Agra Fort-Achnera-Hathras. Muttra (Dak bungalow), in fact *Mathura,* on the r. bank of the Jumna, and district capital with 60,000 inhab. and many temples, is reputed to be the birthplace of Krishna (p.LX), making this one of the religious centres of Hinduism, being visited every year by swarms of pilgrims. Along the river stretch the *ghats,* for ritual bathing (cf.p.223). Excavations have brought to light a wealth of Buddhist, Brahman and Jain sculptures and inscriptions, dating back to the times of the Indo-Scythian kings (1st & 2nd c. A.D.) Part of the find was sent to Calcutta (p.247). A good deal has been retained here to constitute a *Museum*, in the European quarter, S. of the native town, near the District Offices.

The Museum was founded in 1881 by F.S.Growse, and significantly enlarged during the last decade by the efforts of the honorary director Pandit Radha Krishna R.B. (illustr. catalogue by J.Ph.Vogel, 1910; 3R.8a.) The Buddhist sculptures date mainly from the era of the Indo-Scythian Kushan dynasty (p.207; Kanishka, Vasishka, Huvishka and Vasudeva). The school of sculpture, which then blossomed at Mathura is, although influenced by Graeco-Buddhist art from Gandara, basically a continuation of ancient Indian art from Bharhut and Sanchi (cf. pp.LXIV & 246).Characteristic of this are, in particular, the numerous columns of stone enclosures for Buddhist and Jain stupas. Peculiar to Mathura are the naked female figures, usually standing on dwarfs and holding the branch of a tree. Noteworthy: 2 columns from *Bhutesar* (cf.p.247), each bearing 3 reliefs relating to Buddha's former lives; C1. colossal statue of a *Yaksha* (?), one of the oldest statues in India, from the 2nd c. B.C., according to the Prakrit inscription; C2. *Bacchanalian double group,* markedly classical in character (cf.p.247); *statue of Kanishka* (minus head), with inscription; colossal statue of another Kushan king, likewise with inscription; Q13. sacrificial post or *yupa,* with Sanskrit inscription, set up during the time of King Vasishka by a Brahman; C13. Statue of a *Naga-* (snake)-*demon,* with inscription on the back, from the time of King Huvishka; A1. statuette of a *Bodhisattva* with a richly decorated nimbus, and two small kneeling figures at its feet, presumably the patrons, from the 5th c. A.D., according to the inscription.

The railway passes to the W. of the town, which however remains out of sight. – 53M. *Chata;* r., a large, fortress-like serai from the Grand Mogul era, with light-coloured battlemented walls and tall red gates. – 103M. *Faradabad.* To our l., the castle of *Tughlakabad* (p.191) comes into view upon an outlier of the Aravalli Mts.; the appropriate sta. (110M) lies 3½km SE. of Tughlakabad, near the village of *Badarpur.*

The railway passes through the extensive ruined area covered by ancient Delhi. At (114M) *Okhla,* the tall tower Kutb Minar (p.189) appears, l., in the distance; before (117M) *Nizam-ud-din,* r. and quite close at hand, Humayun's Tomb (p.186) and numerous other ruins; finally, r., above the walls and houses of Delhi, the brightly shining domes and minarets of the Jama Masjid (p.183) and, to its r., the tall battlemented gates of the Fort (p.180). Finally, the line goes along close by the W. city wall and, after a stop at (122M) *Delhi Sadr,* the station for the suburb *Sadr Bazaar,* cuts through the city wall and reaches *Delhi main sta.*, see p.176.

Route 20b. Via Tundla.

141M. *East Indian Rly.:* connecting line to Tundla (fast train Karachi-Jaipur-Agra-Calcutta, see p.210), from there to Delhi shared with the Calcutta-Kalka line; only a morning train from *Agra Fort* and an afternoon train from *Agra City* have direct connections at *Tundla* (Agra-Delhi 7¼ & 6¼hrs.), all others having a stop there of several hours.

Agra, see p.161. The trains depart either from City Sta., or Fort Sta. Both lines cross the Jumna on bridges 500m in length, and stop at *Jumna Bridge Sta.*, near the goods depot. To the r., we have a magnificent view of the Taj Mahal. Most trains then continue in ½hr. to 15M. *Tundla Junc.* (sta. rest.), where one changes to the train coming from Cawnpore (p.211).

The country between the Jumna in the W. and the Ganges in the E. (*Doab*, cf.p.192), through which the railway goes N., owes its present prosperity to the English Government, which has made the area tillable, (having been formerly covered in thick jungle) and, through canals, has provided water from both rivers for irrigation, esp. the 496km-long *Ganges Canal* which begins near Saharanpur (p.193) and ends at Cawnpore (p.211), with branches in all directions. The chief agricultural product here is wheat. There are numerous stations on the line, of which we name here only the more important ones. – 54M. *Hathras Junc.,* for the Central Indian Rly from Achnera-Muttra (p.173), on which lies the town *Hathras,* with 42,000 inhab. and a considerable trade in crops.

63M. **Aligarh**, junc. for a branch-line to Bareilly and Moradabad. The sta. lies between the old native quarter of *Koil* and the adjacent European quarter to the N. Together, both parts number 64,800 inhab., of whom 60% are Hindu and 39% Mohammedan. The fortress *Aligarh,* 2km further N., was first mentioned in the 12th c.; in the 18th c. it was in the possession of the Mahrattas, and in 1803 was stormed by the English.

The *Mohammedan Anglo-Oriental College* is growing in importance. This was founded in 1875 from private funds at the suggestion of the far-sighted Mohammedan Sir Saiyid Ahmad Khan. Extended in 1898, it is a kind of university with feeder schools, which combines instruction in English language and literature, mathematics, philosophy, history, Arabic, Persian, Sanskrit etc., with the nurture of the Islamic religion and erudition, thus granting the normally reserved Muslims access to the study of occidental learning. Its Principal is an Englishman; two of its professors are English, the rest being Mohammedans who graduated in England. It numbers about 500 students, incl. also Burmese, Persians & Africans. As with the Oxford & Cambridge colleges, they live in 5 imposing buildings and indulge in all kinds of physical sport. The annual budget is 1 mill. rupees, of which the State of Hyderabad contributes 24,000R. and the British Government 18,000R.

Route 21. Delhi

STATION (given as *Delhi Junction* in the timetables), with a good restaurant and some accommodation, serving all lines. Carriages and hotel representatives meet the trains. – The new *Kingsway Station,* out to the N., and the suburban stations, play no part in the more important rail traffic.

HOTELS: *Maiden's Metropolitan Hotel, good cuisine also, P. 8-10R.; *Cecil Hot.; (prop. Hotz, Swiss, German spoken), open only from the end of October to the end of March, 50 Rm., P. 8-12R.; Woodland Hotel, Civil & Military Hotel, both near Kashmir Gate, P. 6-7R.

CABS: 1st cl. 1R, per hr., each succeeding hr. 12a., all day 5R.; 2nd cl. 8a., 6a., 4R.2a. - Better but dearer are the carriages of the large hotels, e.g. at Maiden's: landau or phaeton, within the city confines, 2R. per hr., 1R. for each succeeding hr.; all day, phaeton 6, landau 7R.; excursion to Kutb Minar, phaeton 12R., landau 14.

GUIDES (cf.p.XXIII), at the hotels, dispensable, since special guides present themselves at the chief places of interest, most of whom speak some English.

POLICE: Hamilton Road.

TRAVEL AGENCY: *Thos. Cook & Son,* by Kashmir Gate. Party excursions by car in the surrounding country, 20-30R. per person.

POST & TELEGRAPH OFFICES to the E. of the station. The new *General Post Office* is near Kingsway Station (see above).

DOCTOR: the British Government Civil Surgeon.

CHEMIST: by Kashmir Gate, in the town.

SHOPS: (cf.p.XXVI). Famous are: jewellery and silver objects, carving in ivory, embroidery with silver and gold thread (already influenced by European patterns), woven muslin, painting of miniatures and the production of brass and copper articles. Most of these shops are to be found in or near Chandni Chauk (p.180). Jewellery from *Chota Lal and Semt Lal, Hurjeemal;* ivory carvings from *Fakir Chand and Rughnat Das,* Bara Dariba St.; embroidered silk (good quality) from *Kishen Chand and Manik Chand.* – There is a wide selection of various items, also carpets etc. at *Imre Schwaiger* (formerly Tellery), not far from Kashmir Gate (p.180).

PHOTOGRAPHY: *Sultan Ahmed Khan,* in the Fort, Lahore Gate (p.180); *Fakir Chand.*

FOR A LIMITED VISIT (2-3 days). Day I: *Fort* (p.180), *Jama Masjid* (p.183), *Kalan Masjid* (p.184), *Jain Temple* (p.183) and the road *Chandni Chauk* with Queen's Garden (p.180); p.m. walk along the Ridge (p.184).

Day II: drive by motor car through the ruined site of Ancient Delhi to *Firozabad* (p.185), *Purana Kila* (called Indarpat, p.185), *Humayun's Tomb* (p.186), *Nizam-ud-din's Tomb* (p.187); then on past Safdar Jang's monument to *Lalkot* (Kutb Minar, pp.188-9); back via *Tughlakabad* (p.191).

Delhi, more properly *Dehli* (252m), has been for almost 3000 years, as go-between for trade for the Punjab and the states bordering the Ganges, the focal point of culture and seat of government; in the 17-18th c., the famous seat of the Grand Moguls, then chosen in 1877 for the proclamation of the Indo-British Empire and, on the 12th December 1911, elevated to capital status in place of Calcutta (p.235). It has a pop. of 232,800 (40% Mohammedan, 55% Hindu), vigorous trade, ancient arts and crafts, and modern cotton, sugar and milling industries. It lies on lat. 28° 40' N., and long. 77° 12' E., on the r. bank of the *River Jumna* which at this point is 180-300m broad, and dotted with several islands. The city has changed its name and location 7 times during its history, partly because of devastating wars, and partly at the whim of its rulers. New Delhi (the *modern city* or *Shahjehanabad)* dates from the 17th c. It has a circumference of 9km and consists of the *Fort,* the former residence of the Grand Moguls, and the densely populated *native town,* with ten well-maintained roads and a jumble of narrow winding streets and blind alleys. The station lies in the N. part, and more or less to the SE of this is the splendid main mosque. The city walls, built in 1648 and strengthened and given a moat by British engineers, possess 7 gates, of which the most important are *Kashmir Gate* to the N., *Farash Khana Gate* to the W., *Ajmer Gate* to the SW, and *Delhi Gate* to the S. The river crossing, where the former bridge of boats was replaced in 1864 by a railway bridge 1km long, was protected by the fort *Selimgarh* (1546), now in ruins. Outside the N. city gate stretches the *Civil Station,* the older part to the E. of the Ridge (p.184), the newer to the W., with the *Viceroy's Residence.* The construction of a new European town is being planned to the SW of Shahjehanabad. *Ancient Delhi,* outside the city walls to the S., is an enormous tract of ruins, 14-15km long and 9-10km wide. Its mosques and superb tombs, with their numberless domes, arches and pillars, poking up between the trees or half-hidden in the brush, the mighty ruins of dilapidated city walls and the soaring victory tower of the Mohammedan conquerors (p.189) – all these present a marvellous picture of former power and magnificence.

The oldest settlement is supposed to date back well into the 2nd millennium B.C. Its name was *Indraprastha,* mentioned in the ancient national epic, the Mahabharata, as the royal seat of the Pandavas ("whites"), and alluded to by Ptolemy as *Indabara.* The name *Dilli* is said to have come from a prince of the 1st c. B.C. The Rajput prince (p.141) Anang Pal built the fortress of Lalkot (p.188) around 1050, which remained his seat and that of the succeeding Rajput dynasties until their last ruler, *Rai Pithura,* succumbed in 1193 to the army of the Sultan of Ghor. The Sultan's general. Kutb-ud-din, a former slave, made himself independent in 1206 and began the succession of Delhi's Mohammedan rulers. His son-in-law *Altamsh* (1214-36), the most important representative of the "Slave Dynasty", extended the empire over the whole of N. India, from the Indus in the W. to the mouths of the Ganges in the E. During the next centuries there followed four other dynasties, founded mostly by victorious generals. First, the *Khalji* (1290-1320), whose second ruler, *Ala-ud-din* (1295-1316), built the town of *Siri* (p.188), beat back the Moguls' attack and penetrated to the S. tip of India. Then the *Tughlak Shahi* (1320-1413). Among these, apart from *Ghiyas-ud-din Tughlak* (†1325), the builder of *Tughlakabad* (p.191), two rulers are worth an especial mention: the well-educated but whimsical *Mohammed Tughlak* (1325-51), who several times tried, with extreme cruelty, to move the population of his capital (even to the remote town Daulatabad, p.117), and the excellent governor *Firoz Shah* (1351-88), founder of Firozabad (p.185). During the rule of the last Tughlaks occurred (1398-99) the Mongol raid under *Timur-i-Leng* (i.e. Tamburlaine), who left the city and country in a state of utter desolation. New disputes over succession filled the final century of native dynasties, the *Saiyids* (1414-51) and *Lodis* (1451-1526).

With the Mongol conquest of 1526 by *Zahir-ud-din Baber* (†1531), of Timur's line, the rule of the Grand Moguls began, bringing the land a series of powerful princes, distinguished both in warfare and in the works of peace. Baber's son *Humayun* (1531-56) admittedly had to yield for a long time to the Afghans *Sher Shah* (1540-45) and *Islam Shah* (1545-54), only returning in victory towards the end of his life. His son Akbar (1556-1605; cf.p.162) built him a sumptuous tomb (p.186), but resided in Agra and Fatepur Sikri, occasionally Ajmer also (p.142). *Jehangir* (1605-27) was another ruler to shun Delhi (cf.p.162). Not until *Shah Jehan* (1627-58) was the residence set up again (1637) on the old historic site, and the new town built (named *Shahjehanabad* after him). Art reached the peak of perfection (cf.p.162). The splendid Imperial Palace and Great Mosque are his work, both of them magnificent in design, pure in architectural style and displaying the noblest taste in their rich adornment. The reputation of Jehan's brilliant court spread to the Occident and enticed many artists from there. Still preserved are several descriptions of Delhi and Agra by European travellers. The emperor was, however, not to enjoy a happy end to his life. His forceful son *Aurangzeb* (1658-1707) took advantage of his father's illness to seize power. He defeated his three brothers, who were also aspiring to the throne, and sent his father to

Agra as a prisoner of state (p.163). Warlike activity came once again to the fore, and Bijapur and Golkonda were conquered. Art went into a rapid decline, building work ceased and many sculptures from former times were destroyed in a fit of bigoted orthodox zeal. Harsh oppression of the Hindus replaced earlier tolerance. The Grand Mogul Empire began to crumble with the disputes about succession by Aurangzeb's sons and grandsons (*Shah Alam*, 1707-12; *Jehandur Shah,* 1712; *Farruksiyar,* 1713-19; *Mohammed Shah* 1719-48). The raid by the Persian *Nadir Shah,* who sacked the capital in 1739, and repeated advances by the Mahrattas (p.70) accelerated the decline *(Ahmed Shah,* 1748-54; *Alamgir II,* 1754-59; *Shah Alam II* 1759-1806). In 1803, Delhi fell into the hands of the English, who allowed the last Grand Moguls to retain their empty titles only *(Shah Akbar II,* 1806-37; *Bahadur Shah,* 1837-57).

Delhi played a large part in the military uprising or *Mutiny* of 1857. The revolt began at Meerut (p.193); from there, the mutinous regiments turned upon Delhi. On the 11th of May, the native troops here renounced their loyalty, murdered English officers and officials, seized all war materials and proclaimed the 90-year-old Bahadur as independent emperor. About 30,000 mutinous troops collected together in Delhi, the suppression of whom by the numerically much inferior English within the fortified city belongs among the most glorious acts of war in recent times. On the 7th of June, General *Barnard* moved up from the Punjab with 3000 men and 22 field-guns, beat the enemy to the N. of the town and took up position on the Ridge overlooking the plain. Here, the courageous band of soldiers stood its ground, strengthened by reinforcements, finally under General *Wilson,* against almost daily fanatical attacks by the troops occupying the town until, at the beginning of August, further reinforcements under General *Nicholson* arrived, raising their number to about 10,000, of whom more than half were native troops who had remained loyal. After some heavier artillery had been moved up, the bombardment began on the 7th of September of Mori Gate, Kashmir Gate and the Water Bastion. At the storming of the city on the 14th of September, General Nicholson brought the left wing of the English columns, only about 1000 men strong, up to Kashmir Gate and, despite the heaviest of fire from the defenders, forced a way through the breach, storming thence to the W., where he was mortally wounded at Kabul Gate. On the W. city wall and in the streets of the town the struggle continued until, on September the 20th, Lahore Gate and then the Fort fell into the hands of the English. The remnants of the defenders retreated to the S., with the Grand Mogul Bahadur, who was captured the next day in Humayun's Tomb (p.186). He died in Burma in 1862.

Not far from the hotels, the so-called *Ludlow Castle* in the Civil Station (p.177) catches the eye, with its blue walls and white battlements, HQ of the Delhi Club. In the road leading to Kashmir Gate are: to the E., *Kudsia Garden*, an 18th c. park with fine trees and picturesque building remains (the batteries which made the breach were sited here); to the W., *Nicholson Garden*, with a statue to the heroic general; his grave is in the cemetery opp., to the N.

Kashmir Gate has two passages and still bears signs of the breaching action. A tablet gives the names of the brave soldiers who dragged up the sacks of powder and met their deaths in the explosion. – We follow the road SE. To our l., *St James's Church,* completed in 1836 in the form of a Greek cross surmounted by a tall central dome; the former adornment above the dome (ball and cross, showing signs of the bombardment of 1857) stands on the ground next to the building. Further on, the *Telegraph & Post Offices* and a few European shops.

Beyond the railway crossing, we reach the Fort (see below) then, to the r., turn into the broad Queen's Road which, following the railway line, traverses the N. part of the city from side to side. On the far side of the road stretches the superb Queen's Garden, the "Hyde Park" of Delhi. To the S. of its central part lies the modern *Town Hall* with the *Delhi Institute,* assembly rooms, library and a small museum which includes, among other things, photographic views of the city taken in the days after the siege of 1857. In front, a *bronze statue of Queen Victoria.*

The 21m-broad Chandni Chauk or "Silver Street", always busy, which crosses the city from W. to E. (S. of the Town Hall), is Delhi's main traffic artery, with the most elegant shops for native arts and crafts. In the centre, near the Town Hall, a modern bell tower and, opp. to the S., the great *Caravanserai* established by Shah Jehan's daughter Jehanara (p.187). At the W. end of the road we see the *Fathpuri Mosque*, in red sandstone. The E. end of the road emerges into the extensive open area which divides city from Fort, opp. the latter's main entrance.

The **Fort*, the imperial palace built in 1628-58 by Shah Jehan on the model at Agra (p.163), constitutes a town in itself with its 16m-high crenellated walls of red sandstone, its numerous low towers and two projecting bastion gates. It measures almost 1km in length and 490m in width. At its transformation into a citadel, a large proportion of the old buildings inside the Fort had to make way for stores and barracks for the European garrison, but the preserved parts of the actual palace still testify to the fairy-tale splendour of the Grand Moguls' court, about which the French travellers Tavernier and Bernier reported, in approx. 1660 and 1669 respectively. At Lord Curzon's suggestion, the entire E.

side has recently been cleared and enclosed by railings. The gardens, also, have been restored to their original plan.

From *Lahore Gate,* to the W., a majestic, vaulted arcade (104m in length), leads to the forecourt, which itself was originally surrounded by arcades. Through the next, richly decorated gate, which served as a music room *(Naubat Khana)* for the reception of guests (cf.p.163), we reach the main courtyard and the **Divan-i-Am,* a pillared hall open on three sides, 30·5m long and 18·3 deep, for the daily public audiences, to which all subjects, regardless of rank, could bring their petitions before their sovereign. The columns, formerly covered in white stucco, support tall toothed arches; in the outer row they are coupled in pairs, and linked in fours in the corners to pillars. In the rear wall is the splendid niche, accessible only from the rear, where the famous jewel-encrusted throne stood, of which Tavernier gives a detailed description. The niche's decoration, with rich pietra dura mosaics on black marble, in the style of the work at Agra (p.162), is ascribed to the Frenchman Austin de Bordeaux who, during Shah Jehan's time, had been thrown ashore in India. The flowers, fruits and animals thus portrayed and, as *chef d'oeuvre,* Orpheus with his lyre, were made quite realistic, exploiting excellently the colours of the stones. They were recently restored by an Italian artist, when the picture of Orpheus, taken to London in 1857, returned to its old place. Beneath the throne niche was the Grand Vizier's seat.

Behind the Divan-i-Am, on the bank of the river (now greatly receded), lay the imperial dwellings and staterooms. The visit commences with the ***Divan-i-Khas* or private audience hall, open on all sides, of white marble, 27m X 20 in size, and restored in 1891. The pillars, large in girth, are adorned with splendid pietra dura mosaics and rich gold decoration, the ceiling is radiant with blue and gold. The whole effect is quite superb. One can understand the builder's pride, who announced in Persian script over the N. and S. entrances: "If there be a paradise on Earth, then it is here, then it is here, then it is here." A water-channel, partly covered, runs through the hall and through most of the palace. – To the N. of the Divan-i-Khas lies the *Hamman*, or imperial baths. The walls and floors of the 3 main rooms are of white marble decorated with pietra dura. The light descends from coloured windows above. Fountains and seats complete the impression of luxurious comfort. The bottoms of the water-basins are decorated in wave-like patterns. The small **Moti Masjid* or Pearl Mosque, adjoining on the W. side, was built in 1659 by Aurangzeb, of white and pearl-grey marble, with a courtyard 12·2 X 10·7m, a double-aisled hall and three gilded domes; the bronze door was given by Bahadur Shah. The area is enclosed by red sandstone walls.

The N. limit of the palace buildings is marked by the monumental gardens *Hayat Bakhsh,* recently restored. They measure approx. 183m square with, at the centre, a four-cornered basin, to which broad sandstone paths lead from S., E. and N., each containing a water-course. The basin is surrounded by decorative stone slabs and contains a small island palace *(Zafar Mahal).* At the end of the N. and S. paths are open marble halls: to the S., the *Bhadon Pavilion,* to the N., the *Sawan Pavilion,* with a marble basin and veil-like waterfall in front of niches which are designed to hold lamps. At the NE corner of the garden rises the tower *Shah Burj,* whence emanate the palace's water-courses; the (restored) chute is grooved, to make the water sparkle.

To the S. of the Divan-i-Khas lies the ***Khas Mahal,* or dwelling quarters of the emperor. In front, two small rooms and an open hall with fountains. The three main rooms are sumptuous, esp. the middle one, whose walls are clad in rich pietra dura work; in the N. wall is a famous pointed grille window; inscriptions praise God, who granted power to the rulers from Timur's race. From the E. room, a polygonal pavilion, the *Samman Burj,* juts out on a bastion, where we have a view of the river frontage of the Fort. To the S., adjacent to the centre room, is an open hall with fine windows and a richly decorated ceiling, whose faded colours make it look like an old carpet. – Further S., the women's palace or *Rang Mahal,* which takes its name ("painted palace") from its former decoration. It has a fountain in the middle. Also, the Small or *Mumtaz Mahal,* which now contains a small but valuable collection illustrating the history of Delhi, with items mainly from the times of the Grand Moguls.

Four *stone tablets with Sanskrit inscriptions* from the early Mohammedan era (13-14th c.), on which the Rajput dynasties (p.177) and the conquest of the town by the Mohammedans are alluded to. *Persian inscription by Mahmud Khan,* cook to the Grand Moguls Humayun, Akbar and Jehangir, who died at the age of 89 and had a family tomb built near Nizam-ud-din's Dargah (p.187). Remains of the elephant statues and elephant riders from Delhi Gate (see below). *Furniture, arms* and *fish standards* from the Grand Mogul era. 3 penned documents *(fermans)* from Akbar II (p.179). *Miniatures & sketches* from the Grand Mogul era: several portraits of Shah Jehan; the emperor and his court; a very fine picture of Bahadur Shah, son of Aurangzeb; picture of Jehangir's elephant. *Photographs & sketches* of the palace buildings etc. *Plans* of the city and Fort, since the first half of the 19th c. Fine collection of *coins* from the Rajput and Mohammedan dynasties. – Catalogue of the main collection by J.Ph.Vogel (new ed. by Gordon Sanderson), another for the coins by R.B.Whitehead, 1910.

The S. main gate of the Fort, known as *Delhi Gate*, is fortified in a similar fashion to the W. gate. The elephant sculptures r. and l. are copies of those formerly here, which Aurangzeb had destroyed. At both gates, there are steps up to the enclosing wall, where we have, in particular, a fine view of the Jama Masjid.

The broad open space to the S. of the Fort was once partly built up, and was only cleared after 1857 to provide a field of fire for the defence of the Fort. The delicate *Sonari* or Golden Mosque, built in 1751, however survived this clearing operation; past it runs the road *Faiz Bazaar,* towards Delhi Gate (p.185). To the SE, the *Daria Ganj* quarter with the barracks of the native infantry regiment, a military hospital and a number of European dwellings. – To the W. of the open space rises the:-

**Jama Masjid*, built in 1644-58 by Shah Jehan, the largest and, by virtue of its effective external design, the most outstanding mosque, still, in the Mohammedan world. It stands on a base 10m high and approx. 100m square, and is surrounded on 3 sides by open arcades of red sandstone, with pavilions at the corners. Magnificent flights of steps lead to the huge entrance gates, of which the E. one would formerly open its doors only to the Grand Mogul. The paved courtyard, with the fountain of purification at its centre, is bordered by arcades on the N. and S. sides. On the W. side, the Mosque itself, built of red sandstone with white marble inlay, framed on both sides by minarets 33m high, and surmounted by 3 large onion-shaped domes, whose snowy white marble is subtly broken up by black lines, and whose points are gilded. One must don over-shoes in order to enter. The interior is 60m wide, 27·5 deep; the decoration, incl. that of the prayer niche (mihrab) is simple and dignified.

In the NE corner of the courtyard, a few relics will be shown if a tip is offered: fine mss. from Mecca and Kerbala, a hair of the prophet's beard, his slipper, etc.

There is a splendid *view from the S. minaret (stairs in the S. gate of the courtyard), esp. in the evening light, because of the view of the Fort; to the r. of this, the Golden Mosque (see above), behind it among gardens the so-called Mosque of Jehan and the River Jumna. To the S. one can make out, within the Pahari quarter (set on a hill), the gloomy Black Mosque (p.184); beyond the city walls, to the SE, Firozabad (p.185) and, further, Purana Kila (p.185); beyond the latter again, rather to the l., the white dome of Humayun's Tomb (p.186); to the S., in the middle distance, the Tomb of Safdar Jang (p.188); on the skyline, the Kutb Minar (p.189) and, to its l., Tughlakabad (p.191). To the W. one has a view of the main part of the city, with the street Chauri Bazaar in the foreground. To the NW, close by, the vaulted roof of the Jain Temple, surmounted by three golden spires (see below); further off, the red Town Hall, with the Bell Tower in front (p.180). Beyond the city walls, the Ridge with its memorial (p.184). In clear weather it is said that one can make out the Himalayas, 200-250km distant.

In the narrow streets NW of the Jama Masjid, a remarkable *Jain Temple* is worthy of mention, dating from the 16-17th c. which, in contrast to the older Jain buildings, borrows its plan and style from Mogul architecture. Narrow steps and a prettily carved wooden gate lead into a courtyard surrounded by stucco arcades with double marble pillars. Behind this, a hall with a garishly painted dome and a beautifully carved portal. The interior, with 3 aisles, is rich and tastefully done; on an altar dais, a Tirthankar statue (p.LVIII) beneath an ivory baldaquin.

In the SW quarter of the city is the so-called Great or Black Mosque, among old houses: the *Kalan Masjid,* completed in 1386 and originally part of Firozabad (p.185), which perhaps extended as far as Chandni Chauk. The unadorned freestone building, in the strict style of its age, with its tall flight of outside steps, its scarped walls, 15 low domes and its minarets rising to a point at the top, is nonetheless impressive in its effect, which was perhaps once enhanced by a brilliant coating of stucco. The interior is a single pillared hall, 22 X 12·5m.

Excursions in the environs.

To the W. and NW of the Civil Station (p.179), a long-drawn-out rocky spine rises about 20m above the plain: the Ridge, well-known from the fighting of 1857. The road goes past the barracks of the native cavalry regt. Near the S. end of the Ridge, the *Mutiny Memorial* has stood since 1870, a pointed Gothic column of sandstone. To the N. of this, one of the two *Ashoka pillars* (p.LIV), more than 2200 years old, which Firoz Shah (p.178) brought to Delhi; it stood here in one of his palaces and was blown into 5 pieces in a gunpowder explosion in the 17th c. Re -erected in 1867 by the English Government, it is now 12m tall (cf.p.185).Further on, *Hindu Rao's House,* built in 1830 for a Mahratta of high birth, the so-called *Observatory* and the *Chauburji Mosque* (dating from Firoz Shah's time), of whose domes only one survives. These three buildings were the strongpoints of the English position in 1857.

Further to the N. along the Ridge rises *Flagstaff Tower,* also much alluded to, in connection with the siege.

The view of Delhi nestling in its bed of greenery is beautiful. Esp. prominent are the Jama Masjid and the Lahore Gate of the Fort and, in the foreground, the yellowish pointed dome of St James's Church. Far to the S., one can make out the Kutb Minar (p.189). To the E., below, the older part of the Civil Station with, in its midst, the so-called *Ludlow Castle* (p.179); to the W., the newer part with the *Viceroy's Residency* and *Circuit House,* in fine positions on a hill. Nearby, the quarters of the Governor of the Punjab. – 3-4km to the N. of Flagstaff Tower, on the r. bank of the Jumna, the splendid Durbars were held in 1877, 1903 & 1911, the first for the proclamation of Queen

Victoria as Empress, the second for King Edward VII and the third for King George V (both of the latter as Emperor of India). On all 3 occasions, the Indian princes appeared, with large retinues.

The vast ruin-covered area of Ancient Delhi is best visited in two separate excursions by motor car or carriage (cf.p.176); to cover all of it in one day would be quite exacting. Some points are also accessible by rail. Of the daunting number of monuments, only the most important have been selected.

Excursion 1. Firozabad, Purana Kila, the tombs of Humayun and Nizam-ud-din. - a 4hr. round trip by carriage, leaving by Delhi Gate, returning past Safdar Jang's Tomb to Ajmer Gate (cf.p.187). By rail (p.174), one needs about the same amount of time: one should take the train around noon to the halt *Nizam-ud-din* (p.187, 26mins' journey); from the waiting-room, on foot for 10min to the S. along the rly line, then l. across this to (r.) the ruined site near Nizam-ud-din's Tomb; then on along the carriage road to where the roads intersect and, beyond the main road, to Humayun's Tomb, 3hrs. return which, if need be, allows Purana Kila (see below) 1½km distant, to be included.

From *Delhi Gate* emanates the Grand Trunk Road, which goes to Muttra and Agra.. On the road branching off l. almost immediately, lie the ruins of the citadel of Firozabad, (the Delhi of the 14th c., cf.p.178), called the *Firoz Shah's Kotila*, and barely 500m outside the Gate. Within these ruins rises, from a dilapidated 3-storey building, the second of the two *pillars of King Ashoka,* brought here by Firoz Shah. It is a red sandstone monolith, 13m high, of which 1·25m is sunk into the ground, and 1m thick. The inscription refers to the introduction of Buddhism (p.70) and mentions, as contemporaries, the kings Antiochus Theus of Syria, Ptolemy Philadelphus of Egypt and Antigonus Gonatas of Macedonia (3rd c. B.C.). Close by, a ruined mosque.

The main road passes the (r.) prison and the (l.) beautiful gate *Lal Darwaza,* which probably belonged to Sher Shah's palace (p.178). Stretches of the road are lined with trees. There are many ruins in the fields and pastures on both sides. To the r., the railway, (cf. p.174).

About 3·5km from Delhi gate we have, on our l., the considerable ruins of *Purana Kila*, the citadel of the town built in 1534 by Humayun (p.178). In antiquity, this is where *Indraprastha* was allegedly situated (p.177), which the village name *Indarpat* would seem to suggest. The fortress, with its battlemented walls and mighty gates framed by semicircular towers, makes a most imposing sight. Only the SW gate is open. Passing through dirty village streets, we reach the **Kila Kona Mosque*, built in 1541 by Sher Shah of red sandstone with white marble decorative inlay. Of the three domes, only one survives. The noble proportions and the rich ornamentation which, in part, imitates the forms of Hindu wooden architecture, show pre-Mogul style in its finest development.

Barely 2km further on lie the two most notable ruined sites in this area, of which those to the l. of the road group around Humayun's Tomb, those to the r. around Nizam-ud-din's.

The road intersects with a carriageway, whose W. arm crosses the Jumna Canal (p.187), while the E. arm goes to Humayun's Tomb. We follow this direction and, at a sign-post, first turn r. to *Isa Khan's Tomb*, within a walled courtyard. The large octagonal building of 1545, with a fine dome and surrounding arcade, makes a strangely antiquated impression on the observer. Note the use of coloured glazed tiles. The entrance is on the S. side. Several cenotaphs within. To the W., the attendant small mosque, with 3 gates. – We return to the sign-post, then walk round a garden wall, whose corner pavilions are also decorated with glazed tiles (beyond, the dirty village *Arab Sarai* with its mud huts), and find ourselves outside the gate in the derelict retaining wall of Humayun's Tomb, which soars up in the middle of a spacious but overgrown park: a magnificent sight.

**Humayun's Tomb,* built by Emperor Akbar in his father's honour, completed in 1572, is the oldest of the 3 famous Grand Mogul mausoleums (pp.168, 204), simpler than the Taj Mahal (p.167), for which it provided the model, but equal to it in its splendid and dignified overall effect. It stands upon a huge red sandstone substructure, whose side surfaces are broken up by blind arches and gate openings. The octagonal main building, with gate openings 12m high, and a beautifully designed white marble dome (whose copper spire reaches a height of 43m above the platform), is surrounded by 4 corner pavilions, also octagonal in plan. The sandstone walls are encrusted with white marble. The main entrance is on the S. side. The first hall is decorated with stucco. The interior has lost its former adornment. In the centre, a simple marble cenotaph indicates the spot beneath which Humayun's sarcophagus stands in the vaults of the crypt. Apart from him, relatives and successors are buried in various places, along with eleven of their viziers and generals. In the NE adjacent room, his wife and sister.

On the N. and S. sides of the main buildings, stairs lead to the upper gallery, whence we have a splendid *view. To the W., a little to the l. of the gate in the enclosing wall, the Tomb of Isa Khan and the mosque at Nizam's Tomb; straight on in the distance beyond the gate, the white dome of Safdar Jang's Tomb (p.188). SW, on the main road, Khan Khanan's Tomb; on the skyline, the Kutb Minar towers up (p.189). To the S., beyond a rise in the ground, Tughlakabad (p.191) is visible. In the foreground to the SE, and still within the park, the pretty, so-called *Tomb of Humayun's Barber*; outside the park wall, the blue dome of *Fahim Khan's Tomb.* To E. and NE, the plain across which flows the Jumna. On the far bank, hidden in trees, the village *Patparganj,* where Lord Lake won the decisive victory over the Mahrattas on the 14th of Sept. 1803, thus delivering Delhi up to the English. To the N., in the middle distance, the fortress of Purana Kila (p.185); beyond, the Jama Masjid, to the r. of which are the tall gates of Delhi Fort (p.180), while l. the Memorial on the Ridge may be seen (p.184).

Return to the intersection (p.186) and continue W. across the narrow Jumna Canal. Here, to our l. on this side of the railway and overgrown by brushwood, is an utterly confused mass of decaying buildings, comprising some of the finest monuments of Indian art (guides offer their services, ½R). Passing between old tombs, we first come upon a deep cistern in the rock *(Badi),* into which divers will jump, for bakhshish, from about 15m. At the centre of this group of buildings is the delicate:-

**Dargah of Nizam-ud-din,* the tomb of a holy man (†1325), much revered by Hindus and Mohammedans, only 30 sq.m in size, built by Mohammed Tughlak, and given a dome and surrounding arcade during the time of Akbar the Great. The tombstone lies within a shrine in marble grille-work and covered by a wooden baldaquin with mother-of-pearl inlay. The stone itself is always covered with a pall. – The courtyard, partly enclosed by a balustrade, is bordered on the W. side by the imposing *Jamat Khana Mosque* of 1353, with a dome 16m in diameter and rich sculptural decoration. – In the S. part of the courtyard, three **Princes' Tombs* lie below ground, enclosed within marble screens most noble in style, and artistically and technically perfect. Without any kind of roofing, they are grouped from E. to W.: that of *Prince Mirza Jehangir* (†1821), son of Akbar II (p.179); that of the Grand Mogul *Mohammed Shah* (1719-48); and that of Shah Jehan's beautiful and pious daughter *Jehanara Begam* (†1681), who voluntarily shared her father's imprisonment after his dethroning (p.165) and lived afterwards in Delhi only for works of charity. The princess's tomb slab is filled with turf, according to her last wish, as the inscription on the tablet at the head of the tomb reports: "Do not erect a splendid monument to me: grass is the best covering for poor, waning Jehanara, pupil of the holy family Chisti" (p.170).

Note, in the vicinity of the courtyard: to the S., the tomb of the poet *Abal Hassan* or *Amir Khusran,* a friend of Jehanara, surrounded by old trees; to the E., the excellently preserved white marble **Chausath Khamba,* or "hall of 64 pillars" (counting the clusters of pillars on the outside twice and fourfold), with 35 domed vaults and 9 mainly beautifully carved sarcophagi of the family of Azam Khan, the loyal companion of Humayun; to the NE, the recently restored colourful Tomb of Azam Khan (†1556).

The carriage road crosses the rly line (r. to the halt, 10min) and, about 2.5km to the W., opp. Safdar Jang's Tomb, joins the road from Ajmer Gate, see below.

Excursion 2. Lalkot, with Kutb Minar & Tughlakabad.

A longish day's journey by carriage, better done by motor car (cf.p.176): from Ajmer Gate to Lalkot (the Kutb Minar) 15km. (9M or 11M by the milestones, but the counting does not start from the gate); from Lalkot to *Tughlakabad* 8km (5M); thence back to Delhi Gate 14km. The trip just to Lalkot can be done in a half-day. One would then visit Tughlakabad by rail: the sta. of the same name lies 3½km to the SE (p.174). – Near the Kutb Minar is a well- maintained *Dak bungalow,* where one can stay the night (accommodation and food to be ordered in advance by telegraph).

From *Ajmer Gate*, which is still covered by a small outwork for that purpose, the road crosses the railway, reaching the main road running past the inner city to the W. We follow this S., between gardens and clusters of houses. On the journey we glimpse, about 1½km from the Gate and on our l., the remarkable buildings of the *Observatory,* erected by Jai Singh of Jaipur around 1730 for Mohammed Shah (cf.p.149; the larger of the two gnomons is 17·28m high, recently restored by the Maharaja of Jaipur). – Beyond the 5th milestone we notice, also to our l., and at a greater distance, an effective group of several domed buildings from the time of the *Saiyids* and *Lodis* (p.178), 3 tombs and an attendant mosque.

At the 6th milestone (6.5km from the Gate), the carriage road from the Nizam ruins enters from the l. Opposite, in a pretty garden, the large *Tomb of Nawab Safdar Jang,* minister to Ahmed Shah and viceroy of Oudh (†1754, cf.p.215), a smaller imitation of Humayun's Tomb: over 18m square, with a marble dome 26m high, and inferior decoration with considerable use of gesso. Smaller domed tombs and insignificant ruins continue to line the road.

Beyond the 9th milestone (14.5km from the Gate), the road cuts through the N. rampart of the town *Jehanpanah*, built 1328 by Mohammed Tughlak, and connecting the rather older *Siri* (p.178) with Lalkot. The walls were torn down by Sher Shah in the 16th c. The position of Siri, also, is recognisable to our l. only by a few mounds of earth. Barely 1km further, l., the village *Begampur,* with a large, many-domed mosque of 1387. A bend in the road indicates the former line followed by the ramparts of the fortress of Lalkot, the oldest authenticated site of Ancient Delhi, founded around 1050 by the Rajput prince Anang Pal, re-fortified and extended in the last quarter of the 12th c. by Raj Pithura, and conquered in 1193 by Kutb-ud-din, who made the place his capital (cf.p.178). The fortifications are in a good state of repair, esp. on the W. side, 18m high, 9m thick, with breastworks and bastions. In the SE part of the fortress stand the oldest Mohammedan buildings in India, the remains of the mosque and the enormously tall minaret (Kutb Minar), a landmark for a great distance in every direction. Nearby, the Dak bungalow (p.188).

The **Mosque Kuwwat-ul-Islam*, i.e. "Power of Islam", begun in 1193 by Kutb-ud-din, continued by his successor Altamsh and completed around 1300 by Ala-ud-din, 46m wide and 53 long, occupies the site of a Hindu temple, whose pillars were used. The main entrance, to which some stone steps lead up, is on the E. side. The inner court is bordered at the front by a four-fold pillared hall with a dome at the centre and two at the corners, and by three-fold pillared halls to the r. and l., of red sandstone, but only partly preserved; the pillars, which support the flat roofs are similar, in the richness of their carved figures, to those in the temple at Mount Abu (p.141). The *chef d'oeuvre* is the façade of the mosque itself, on the W. side of the courtyard, with a noble centre arch 16m high and 6·7m broad, flanked by two lower side arches and splendidly executed bas-relief work, which is equalled in the whole of Mohammedan art only in the rather more recent mosque at Ajmer (p.143). Here also, the arches are built up from horizontally placed corbel stones, since the indigenous workers, who had to carry out the architectural concepts of the Mohammedan conquerors, were not conversant with the construction of vaulting with wedge-shaped stones. The interior of the mosque is in ruins. In the courtyard, before the centre arch, stands the remarkable *Iron Pillar,* set up here probably in the 4th c. A.D. It consists of a single piece of pure wrought iron (and therefore not susceptible to rust), over 7m long, of which 0·6m is set in the ground; its diameter is 0·4m at its base, and 0·3m at the capital (about 1m high). The clean-cut Sanskrit inscription describes it as the victory monument of a Chandra prince, but is undated. A later inscription contains the name of Anang Pal (p.188) and the date 1052.

The ***Kutb Minar*, set up by Kutb-ud-din, both as minaret and victory column, and completed by Altamsh, is one of the world's proudest monuments, and in a marvellous state of preservation. It is 72·54m in height (Victory Column in Berlin together with the figure of Victory, 61·5m), 14·64m in diameter at the bottom, and 2·74 at the top. Of the five storeys (which taper as they rise), the first three are of red sandstone, the lowest having round and square section vertical ribs, the second square-edged, and the third round ones. The two upper stages, struck by lightning in 1368 and entirely renewed, perhaps by Firoz Shah, are of white marble with layers of sandstone between, and smooth of surface. Each stage is terminated by a splendid balcony, running right round. On the three lower stages, the broad bands of inscription with verses from the Koran in elegant Arabic script make a very decorative effect. The pavilion which once crowned the column was dashed to the ground by an earthquake in 1803 and has been set up again at the bottom.

Inside the tower, a spiral staircase with 156, 78, 62, 41 and 42 steps leads upwards (379 in all). The *view, even from the balcony of the lowest storey, embraces the entire ruin-strewn site of Ancient Delhi and the present city, in which the white domes of the Jama Masjid are particularly prominent. In the middle distance, Safdar Jang's Tomb; NE, the white dome of Humayun's Tomb; to the r. of this, and rather closer, the Begampur Mosque and the tower of *Bedi Mandal,* then the light-coloured domes of the Tomb of the holy man *Roshan Chiraghi Delhi*, built in 1373. To the r. of the latter, and surrounded by trees, the village of Khirki with its mosque; in the distance, in the same direction, the Hindu *Kalika Temple* and, to its r. again, Tughlakabad, the dome of Tughlak Shah's Tomb and the fortress Adilabad. Close at hand, S. and W., the buildings mentioned below and the village Mahrauli, with domed tombs. – The view from the topmost platform is said, in clear conditions, to extend NE to the Ganges (100km) and the Himalayas (250km).

Of the buildings which Altamsh executed to extend the ground plan of the mosque, the lengthening of the mosque façade to N. and S. is worth mentioning, whereby the mosque reached a total length of more than 117m, both sides again having a tall arched opening in the middle, flanked by lower arches. In connection with this, he intended to lay out a larger court all round his predecessor's mosque, of which the SE corner would be occupied by the Kutb Minar. Only a few rows of pillars now remain, on the S. side and NE of the mosque's main entrance. A third outer court was added by Ala-ud-din at the beginning of the 16th c. on the E. side. Of this, only the S. enclosure remains, with the flat-domed entrance gate *Alai Darwaza* of 1310, whose delicately carved decoration reminds one of the Alhambra in Spain, though here it is in real stone, there only gesso. Outside the gate, to the l., is the pretty little domed tomb of the holy man *Imam Zamin* (†1537). – 120m N. of the Kutb Minar, Ala-ud-din began a second, even higher, victory column, the *Alai Minar*, which has a diameter of 30m at its base, and was planned to rise to a height of 150m; the building work broke off when it reached 26m. Also to be noted: outside the NW corner of the mosque, the *Tomb of Altamsh,* the oldest tomb of a sultan in India, barely 12m square and roofless, probably left incomplete in the period of wars after Altamsh's death; with beautifully carved decoration inside; - 3min to the SW of the Kutb Minar, by the ramparts of the fortress, and very effective in its simplicity, the large *Tomb of Adham Khan*, a half-brother of Akbar, whom the ruler struck down with his own hand because of a murder (1561); the antiquated octagonal building, with surrounding arcade, seems however to date back to the previous century.

2min further on, by the road to the village *Mahrauli*, a well, 25m deep and hewn out of the rock *(Gandak Baoli),* of 1532; a flight of steps leads down; here too are people willing to leap into the water from above, for bakhshish. – To the SE, the *Dargah of Kutb-ud-din Bakhtiar Kaki*, a Mohammedan holy man of Altamsh's time (†1235), with a marble mosque built in 1709 and the graves of the Grand Moguls Shah Alam II (†1806) and Shah Akbar II (†1837). – To the W. of the village, a large complex of cisterns from Altamsh's time, called *Hauz Shamsi* ("sun bath"); nearby the mosque *Aulia Masjid*, a red sandstone building said to date from the end of the 12th c.

The carriage road to Tughlakabad cuts through the remains of the E. rampart of Lalkot, descending then into the plain. On our l., we glimpse the mosque of *Khirki,* from the end of the 14th c., by the former S. rampart of Jehanpanah (p.188). The massive dark walls of Tughlakabad rise, with increasing impressiveness, out of the plain, with Tughlak's Tomb in front of them.

Tughlakabad, built on a low rocky hump by Giyas-ud-din Thughlak (1320-25), the warrior founder of the Tughlak dynasty (p.178), is shaped like a half hexagon, about 6km in circumference. The corbelled walls consist of regular layers of enormous dressed granite blocks, the largest measuring 4m long and almost 1m thick, with massive round towers and 13 gates. The 3 shorter sides, to NW, N. and NE, are bordered by a moat; the steeper long side to the SW, where the main entrance is, was protected by a reservoir, now full only during the rainy season. The interior of the fortress is in ruins.

To the S. of the main entrance rises a small pentagonal outwork (within a pool now converted into arable land), to which a long bridge-causeway leads across. It encloses the **Tomb of Tughlak,* who erected this solemn, impressive structure during his lifetime. The smooth walls, of red sandstone with white marble inlay, are corbelled like those of the fortress. Entry arches open on three sides, whose upper part is filled with marble filigree work. The white marble dome has a diameter of 10·5m. The three tombstones within show the places beneath which the builder, his wife and successor Mohammed are buried. – A smaller domed tomb in the E. corner of the main area is regarded as that of one of Tughlak's ministers. About 500m to the SE, opp. the S. frontage of Tughlakabad, past which runs the road to the railway sta. of the same name (cf.p.174), the fortress of *Adilabad* or *Muhammadabad* rises on a smaller rock. A side road leads to it. Fine view of Tughlakabad and, to the W., Lalkot.

Route 22. From Delhi via Umballa to Lahore.

310M. *East Indian Railway* via Karnal-Umballa (123M), then *North Western Rly:* Punjab Mail in 10hrs.; fares 27R.13a.6p., 13R.14a.9p., 3R.7a.9p.; meals in the station restaurants, cf.p.XXII. The older line via Saharanpur to Umballa (p.193) is 39M longer and has the disadvantage that only slow trains go as far as Saharanpur (4-5½hrs.), where one takes the fast train from Calcutta. Besides these, there is a shorter route *(Southern Punjab Rly)*, not however used by fast trains, via *Bhatinda,* passing through the native states of *Jind, Patiala & Faridkot,* joining the Lahore-Karachi line (p.209) beyond *Ferozepore* at *Raewind:* Delhi-Lahore, 296M, in 12hrs., same fares as above.

The excursion to NW India completes our general view of the country. In the Sikh state of *Amritsar* (p.195), we make the acquaintance of the strange religious cult of an admittedly small section of the Indian population, but one which in recent history has come into some prominence. On the *Khyber Pass,* and in the *bazaars* at *Peshawar* (p.207) we gain an insight into ancient Indian trading life, such as one can scarcely find in the vicinity of European culture. There is also much to remark upon in the landscape and agriculture of the Punjab along the foot of the Himalayas. The old Mogul town of *Lahore* (p.198) can however not rank alongside Delhi or Agra, and the railway journeys are very long (Punjabi fast trains: Delhi to Amritsar 10-14¼hrs., Amritsar to Peshawar 14-18½hrs,), and of course one has to use the same lines for the outward and return journeys (Peshawar-Saharanpur-Lucknow, 33¼hrs.)

The Punjab (or *Panjab,* both forms in common use), i.e. “land of five rivers”, takes its ancient name from the rivers: *Sutlej* (pron. sutledge; p.194), *Beas* (p.195), *Ravi* (p.205), *Chenab* (pron. chinab; p.205) and *Jhelum* (pron jeelum; p.205), which rise in the Himalayas, flow SW, gradually join up with one another and, as a single river called the *Panjnad,* flow into the Indus. Each area of land lying between two of these rivers is called *Doab*, i.e. “two river land”, *(Bist Jullundur Doab, Bari, Rechna, Chinhath, and Sind Sagar Doab,* the latter stretching to the Indus. The present British province (251,761 sq.km, 20,330,400 inhab.) in fact extends well outside the Punjab proper, in the W. up to and beyond the Indus, in the E. as far as the Jumna, and in the NW into the Himalayas, taking in 9 medium-sized and 25 small native states, (94,583 sq.km, 4,424,400 inhab.). It is essentially a plain built up from detritus carried down from the Himalaya range, sloping to the Thar desert in the SW (p.142). The broad rivers, which fill only in the rainy season (end of Dec. to beginning of Mar., end of June to mid-Sept., with the SW monsoon), frequently change their courses. The *climate* is definitely continental in character; in summer, scorching heat is the norm (heat-stroke often occurs), in Jan. and Feb. frequent frosts. There is also a considerable difference between day and night temperatures, so that the traveller is obliged here to take more precautions against heat and cold than elsewhere in India. The annual precipitation is adequate only in the foothills of the range; further S., it sinks rapidly to 25-30cm, so that *agriculture* is confined to the river margins and artificially irrigated areas. Thanks, however, to the installation of wells and canals, the tillable acreage is being constantly increased. Thus, the *Sirhind Canal* (opened in 1882 at a total cost of 40 mill.R.), to the E. of the Sutlej, has 700km of main waterway and 4335km of subsidiary channels. The *Chenab Canal*, constructed in 1884-92, has created out of a desert region an arable area of more than 6 mill. ha., with 25,000 inhab. A similar colony has sprung up since 1901 by the *Jhelum Canal*. The strip of land from Delhi to the Jelum, beyond Lahore, belongs to the most densely populated areas of India, whereas the district to its S. is one of the most sparsely populated. – The Punjab is the most ancient Aryan dwelling-place in India; the Aryans here exchanged their nomadic existence for one of cultivation, and created the religion and culture of Brahmanism, to which the majority of the Indian people still adhere. Since Alexander the Great, this territory has fallen prey to all the conquerors from the W. (cf.p.70). In the 16-17th c. it belonged to the Grand Mogul Empire, with Lahore as its capital. In the 18th c. it was ruled by the Sikhs (p.195). In 1846 it was conquered by the English. Its character as a land of passage is matched by the strong mixture of races, though Indo-Aryans predominate. As far as religion is concerned, there are 12 mill. Mohammedans, 10 mill. Hindus and 2 mill. Sikhs.

From Delhi via Karnal to Umballa (fast train in 3½hrs). – The rly leaves Delhi on the W. side, branches off, S. of the Ridge, from the Rajputana and Southern Punjab Rly, and heads N. – 44M. *Panipat*, an old town of 26,900 inhab., known in history by three decisive battles: the victory of Baber over Ibrahim Lodi in 1526, the victory of Akbar over Mohammed Adil Shah's army (nephew of Sher Shah, p.178), and that of the Afghan sultan Ahmed Shah Durrani over the Mahrattas in 1761. – 76M. *Karnal*, old town of 23,560 inhab., lying in the former bed of the Jumna, from which it is now 12km distant. – 123M. *Umballa*.

From Delhi via Saharanpur to Umballa (cf.p.192). – As far as (13M.) *Ghaziabad*, when the Oudh & Rohilkhand Rly via Hapur to Moradabad-Lucknow (p.211) branches off E., and the East Indian Rly to Tundla-Cawnpore-Allahabad (p.209) to the SE, see p.175. – 44M. Meerut *(Mirat;* Hot.: Empress Hot., Lytton Hot., Meerut Hot.), with 116,200 inhab. (51% Hindu, 43% Mohammedan), of whom 78,740 live in the old town and 39,389 in the Cantonments. Meerut is famous on account of the outbreak of the Mutiny on 10th May, 1857 (p.179). The garrison comprises 4 regts. of European & native infantry & cavalry, 2 horse-drawn and 2 motorised batteries. – 112M. *Saharanpur* (273m; sta. rest.), town of 66,254 inhab., more than half Mohammedans, on both banks of the *Dhamaula Nadi*, with large rly workshops, and junc. for the Oudh & Rohilkhand Rly from Moradabad-Lucknow (p.211), used by a fast train from Calcutta, to which the through carriages from Delhi are attached. To the N. of the plain, bordered in about 50km by the *Siwalik Hills* (1065m), the snowy peaks of the Himalayas appear. – Beyond (120M) *Sarsawa*, the line crosses the *Jumna* and enters the province of Punjab. The Himalayas remain visible. 162M. *Umballa*, also written *Amballa* or *Ambala*.

Umballa, with 80,100 inhab., has 2 stations: *Cantonment Sta.* (sta. rest.), junc. of the North Western and East Indian Railways (travellers, who are not sitting in a through carriage, need to change) and, 4M. further on, the *City Station.* The Cantonment possesses one of the strongest garrisons in India, comprising, by way of European troops, 3 regts. of infantry, one of cavalry and 2 horse-drawn batteries; of native troops there are 1 battalion of infantry and 2 regts. of cavalry. The native town has 28,200 inhab.

The continuation of the East Indian Railway proceeds N., with through carriages from Calcutta and Bombay, to (39M) *Kalka* (sta. rest., Lawrie's Hot.) at the foot of the Siwalik Hills, a spur of the Himalayas, where the narrow-gauge mountain rly begins (Simla State Rly): 70M in 6½-7hrs., for 18R., 10R.; max. gradient 3%, more than 100 tunnels; 36km *Barogh* (stop for breakfast).

Simla. – HOT. (consistently good); Grand Hot., only in summer; Cecil Hot., P.7-10R.; Carlton Hot., 42 Rm., P.7-10R., Corstorphen's Hot., P.7R.; Hot. Metropole etc. – *United Service Club.* – *Rickshaw:* in winter, carriage hire ½R. per day, additionally 2a. for each coolie up to 2hrs., 4a. up to 8hrs.

Simla, a British enclave in the Simla Hill States (under the rule of native princes), situated in the foothills of the Himalayas at an average altitude of 2150m, with an excellent climate (March 13°C, June 23°; Dec.-Feb. 7-10°, occasional frost and snow), is the summer residence of the Viceroy of India, as well as the Governor of the Province of Punjab and the Commander-in-Chief of the Indian Army, also of the German and Austro-Hungarian general consuls for India. During this time, a brilliant social life develops; the number of residents rises from approx. 14,000 to 30-40,000, incl. 3500 Europeans. The imposing government buildings, private bungalows, club-houses, sanatoria, hospitals and sports fields lie in magnificent surroundings. Among the rich vegetation, one notices in particular the graceful deodar cedars and, during their flowering time in February, the rhododendrons (Kipling's book "Under the Deodars" is set in Simla). In winter, the place is deserted and far less rewarding for the tourist than Darjeeling (p.232).

From Umballa to Amritsar, the fast train takes 5hrs.; the following distances are reckoned from Delhi (via Karnal). – 141M. *Rajpura*, town of 55,000 inhab., where a line branches off via Dhura to Bhatinda (p.192). – 194M. *Ludhiana,* town of 48,650 inhab., junc. for a branch-line to Ferozepur (p.209). – The rly crosses the largest of the "five rivers", the *Sutlej*, which originates in the holy Manasarovar Lake in Tibet. Then (202M) *Phillaur* (sta.

rest.) with an ancient Grand Mogul fortress (227M), *Jullundur*, old town of 676,700 inhab., almost ⅔ of them Mohammedan, consisting of the Cantonment and (230M) City. Beyond (250M) *Beas East Bank,* we cross the broad, flat bed of the *Beas* (the *Hyphasis* of the Greeks), which flows into the Sutlej, and to which Alexander the Great advanced (p.205). The mountains which descend sharply to the plain (on the r.) are covered with snow in winter.

278M. **Amritsar**. – *Sta. rest.* – HOTELS: Hot. Amritsar, New Court Rd, near the sta., opp. the Main Post Office, 15 Rm., P.7R., Cambridge Hot., pleasant, friendly hotel (non-alcoholic drinks only). – CARRIAGES: 1st hr. 1R., each succ. hr. ½R., all day (9hrs.) 5R. (2nd cl. carriage, half tariff). – BANKS: *National Bank of India, Commercial Bank of India.* DOCTOR & HOSPITAL at the English Civil Station. – SHOPS: carpets at *Davee Jahai Chumba Mull* (p.196), one of the largest carpet-makers in India, where the knotwork can also be observed; silverware and ivory carvings at the bazaars.

A half day's stop suffices. The main object of interest is the Golden Temple of the Sikhs, deserving of attention not only because of its situation, but also for its unusual religious rites. One enters it in cloth shoes (cf.p.196; tip 4a.) and accompanied by a policeman, whose directions must be obeyed. A dignified demeanour is expected; smoking forbidden. Cigarettes must be deposited outside; nor may one take a folding chair with one.

Amritsar, third largest town in the province Punjab, centre of a very flourishing trade with Afghanistan, Baluchistan, Bukhara, Kashmir, Tibet and Nepal, seat of several missions, schools and educational institutions, lies in a fertile strip, planted densely with trees, between the rivers Beas and Ravi, in such a deep hollow that the groundwater almost comes to the surface during the rainy season. The picturesque narrow streets, with their hosts of brightly-painted and richly carved houses, are full of curious life, in which we discern also the ethnic types of the neighbouring lands. The once important weaving of fine Kashmir shawls, produced from Tibetan goats' wool, has been on the decline for some decades now. It has been replaced by the manufacture of carpets. The pop. numbers 152,800, of whom 70,000 are Mohammedans, 65,000 Hindus and 17,800 Sikhs, the Golden Temple being the centre of the latters' religious cult.

The Sikhs are a reformed sect of Hinduism (p.LXI). The name means "scholar". The founder of the sect was the "guru" (teacher) *Nanak* (1469-1538), whose teachings were collected together into a holy book *(Granth)* by the fifth guru *Arjan* (1581-1606). Admission into the faith is by a kind of baptism, performed on or after one's 10th year. Rebelling against the cruel persecution by the Grand Moguls, the sect acquired military prowess and, organised by the tenth guru *Govind Singh* (1675-1708), on a theocratic basis, into a number of leagues *(misl),* seized the mastery of the whole of Punjab and Kashmir in the course of the 18th c. Finally, the leader of a misl, *Ranjit Singh,* elevated himself to the status of chief and ruled from 1801 to 1839 as a recognised maharaja, with his seat at Lahore (p.199). The disputes for succession after his death led to wars with the English in 1845-46 and 1848-49, and the annexation of the Punjab, while Kashmir became a vassal state under a successor of Ranjit Singh. In the Mutiny of 1857, the Sikhs remained loyal to the English, since when they have been a valued part of the British native troops. They are handsome people, of proud and commanding bearing, wearing a beard and yellow turban.

From the railway crossing, continuing straight on, we reach the modern *Hall Gate,* one of the town's twelve gates. The large red building, with two European-style marble figures on its façade, directly outside the gate on the r., is a *Serai* for the accommodation of caravans. We follow the straight, tree-lined main street of the town. The second house r. is Davee Jahai Chumba Mull's carpet factory, mentioned on p.195. Then, r., the gate of a small mosque, decorated with blue faïence tiles. Further on, near the end of the street, the municipal offices, an ugly bare brick building, whose gateway forms the entrance to the gardens of *Kaisar Bagh.* In the park, the *Saragarhi Memorial* (an open pavilion with tablets in English and Sikh, in front of which a priest recites prayers) commemorates the heroic defence of the frontier fort Saragarhi, against hordes of Afghans (100:1), by 21 men of the 36th Sikh Regiment, all of whom perished in the attack in 1898. On that same spot is a statue of the Queen-Empress *Victoria,* erected for her jubilee, to celebrate 50 years of rule, in 1887.

From Kaisar Bagh, we continue along the main street and, taking the r. fork, reach, in a few minutes, the:-

**COMPOUND of the GOLDEN TEMPLE, which is holy to Hindus also. This was founded in 1766, in place of an older Sikh shrine destroyed by the Afghans, and was made even more beautiful by Ranjit Singh. The total effect is extremely romantic, filled with the colourful bustle of pilgrims, dealers and priests, and yet kept clean and dignified. The *Bell Tower* next to the entrance, built in 1874 in English Gothic (!), offers a general view (tip; it is sufficient to climb only to the first floor). In the guardhouse r. one is given cloth overshoes for entry to the temple area, and a guide (cf.p.195).

The centre is occupied by the *holy pool* (Amrita saras, pool of immortality), laid out in 1577, which surrounds the Golden Temple. The pool measures 143 X 155m and is 5m deep, with stone steps for ritual bathing. Around it is a 9m-wide marble pavement with 84 public and private pilgrims' houses *(bungas)*, the latter partly in the possession of aristocratic Sikhs. Thus, in the NW corner, the bunga of the Sindhanvalia family; near the W. entrance, that of the Maharaja Sher Singh; others belong to the rajas of Patiala, Nabha, Jind, Kapurthala etc.; in some of these, special services are held, or food distributed to the needy. On the W. side of the pool, the marble pavement broadens out into a picturesque square. To the W., the *Akal Bunga* ("House of the Eternal One") with a gilded dome in which, in a gilded chest, various relics are kept, such as the sword of the guru Govind Singh (p.195), baptismal vessels and 3 old copies of the holy Granth (p.195), bound in gold and silver, of which one is carried daily in a solemn procession to the Temple at 3 a.m., being returned at 11 p.m. To the N., a marble pulpit and several banners. – To the E., the *Darshani Darwaza*, i.e. gate of adoration, leading to the Temple Bridge, with fantastically adorned vestibules r. and l. A gold inscription to the l. of the entrance commemorates a "wondrous" ball-lightning which ran through the Temple in 1877 without causing any damage. The doors are clad on the outside with gold, and on the inside with ivory. The ceiling of the gateway is decorated with gold and mirrors; on the r. wall, a commemorative tablet for the 35th Sikh Regiment, which distinguished itself in the Chitral campaign of 1895; nearby, a marble tablet with pietra dura decoration. The Temple treasure is housed on the upper floor of the gatehouse, but permission to view it is difficult to obtain. – The Temple Bridge, with a marble balustrade from Shah Jehangir's Tomb (p.204), and gilded lamps, is 5·5m wide and 69m long.

The **Golden Temple*, as the Europeans call it, or *Harmandar* or *Darbar Sahib* (i.e. house of God, or great audience chamber) as the natives call it, occupies the centre of the island (which is 20m square), itself having sides of 12·2m. The outer walls are beautifully articulated; two floors are of white marble inlaid with pietra dura; the upper part, with balustrade, rows of small domes and corner pavilions, as well as the central dome, is covered with embossed and gilded copper plates, whose inscriptions were taken from the holy Granth; a richly gilded oriel projects on the E. side. Of the 4 gates, only the N. one is open to visitors of other faiths. The interior is decorated with gold in an almost romantic and operatic manner without imagery, as befits the Sikh religion; at the level of the first floor, a gallery runs round. Strange, but of dignified simplicity, is the rite: the priest sits beneath the baldaquin in the middle of the hall, holding a white yak's tail whisk by a golden handle, and reads from the holy Granth, placed before him on silk cushions (cf.above); two musicians accompany his words. Of the 3 silver vessels on the carpet in front of the baldaquin, one contains pieces of sugar, which are offered to the stranger, another melted butter, the third the alms (silver, give 1-2R.); copper and cowrie coins are dropped on the carpet. – The steps outside at the SE corner of the Temple lead to the upper gallery and the roof, whose domed centre pavilion (Shish Mahal), richly adorned with gold and mirror glass, is regarded as the guru's residence.

On the E. side of the pool, a path leads through to the so-called *Guru Garden,* in whose SE corner rises the 40m-high *Baba Atl,* an octagonal building, four storeys high and surmounted by a two-storey tower with a pointed gilded dome, erected 1779-1832 in honour of a son of the 6th guru celebrated in Sikh legend. The wall-paintings on the lower floor depict the life of the first guru. Many penitents reside in the Guru Garden.

To the NW of the town is the Fort *Govindgarh,* erected by Ranjit Singh in 1805-9. To the N. of this lies the Cantonment.

Branch-lines link Amritsar to the NE with (67M) *Pathankot,* SE with *Patti.* On the latter line lies (14M) the little town of Tarn Taran, with a temple founded in 1768 and extended by Ranjit Singh, similar in plan to the one at Amritsar and also a religious centre in Sikh life (a 4hr. excursion by carriage, 6-8R.)

From Amritsar to Lahore, the fast train takes another hour. The last intermediate stop (307M) is *Lahore Cantonment East Sta.,* for the large military cantonment, in which the HQ of the 3rd division of the Northern Army is situated, with a garrison of 2 motorised batteries, 2 battalions of native infantry and 1 regt. of native cavalry. – 310M. *Lahore Junction,* the sta. for the town, see below.

Route 23. Lahore.

STATION (rest.), a fortress-like building to the NE of the European quarter and E. of the Old City. - HOTELS: Nedou's Hot., P.8R., Upper Mall Rd., ½hr, from the sta., P.8-10R., reasonable; Faletti's Hot., Egerton Rd. - CARRIAGES: 1st cl. 1R. per hr., ½R. each succ. hr., 4R. per day; 2nd cl. ½, ¼ ,3R.; to Shah Dara (p.204) or Shalimar (p.204), 1st cl. 2R., 2nd cl. 1R., waiting 8a., 4a. per hr., bridge toll at the two Ravi bridges 1R. each, return. - BANKS, on the Upper and Lower Mall: branches of the *National Bank of India, Bank of Bengal, Alliance Bank of Simla & Commercial Bank of India;* the *Punjab Banking Co.* has its head office at Lahore. - DOCTORS may be inquired after at the *Mayo Hospital* and at *Plomer's,* the chemists. - EUROPEAN SHOPS, photographic dealers, also tailors, shoemakers, barbers: in the European quarter. – NEWSPAPERS: Civil & Military Gazette, Tribune.

IF TIME IS RESTRICTED, a one-day stop will suffice: drive through the European quarter, visiting the Museum (p.199), then through the Old City; to visit the *Fort* (p.202), one needs to obtain permission from the Deputy Commissioner (information about this at one's hotel); excursion to Shalimar or Shah Dara (p.204).

Lahore (215m), government capital of the province of Punjab, seat of the Lieutenant Governor, with 228,700 inhab. (130,000 Mohammedans, 80,000 Hindus, 7000 Sikhs, 5000 Christians), not far from the l. bank of the *Ravi,* in a well-cultivated plain, dates its foundation back to Lava, a son of Rama (p.LX), but is first mentioned historically by Mohammedan writers (as "Lohawar"). Since its conquest by Mahmud of Ghazni in 1031, the town remained under Mohammedan rule. It reached its zenith during the Grand Mogul era, of whom *Akbar* resided here, 1584-98, and *Jehangir*, 1622-27. *Shah Jehan* and *Aurangzeb* also favoured the town. After its destruction by Nadir Shah (1739) and the Afghan sultan Ahmed Shah Durrani (1747), it rose to new prominence as capital of the Sikh empire under *Ranjit Singh* (p.195). In 1849 it became a British possession; in place of the suburbs devastated in the 18th c., a pleasant European quarter has sprung up, to the S. of the Old City. Lahore is the centre of numerous missions (American Presbyterian Mission since 1849, Church Missionary Society since 1867, Methodist Episcopal Mission since 1883).

The European Quarter *(Civil Station)*, distinguished, as everywhere in India, by its beautiful gardens and broad roads, consists of an older part, called *Anar Kali*, to the W., and the newer suburbs to the E.: *Maulakha,* near the sta., and *Donald Town.* The more recent public buildings were executed mostly in Indian styles adapted to modern needs. The main streets in the E. quarter are Empress Road which begins at the sta. and, branching from it, Davies Road. Both join Upper Mall Road, which crosses the entire Civil Station from NW to SE, and leads to the Cantonment (p.198). Not far from the junc. with Davies Rd., on the E. side, is the extensive *Punjab Chief's College,* an educational institution for the sons of native princes and dignitaries (cf.p.144), founded in 1888 at the suggestion of the Lieut. Governor, Sir Charles Aitchison. In the park gardens at the S. end of Empress Rd. stands *Government House,* a former mausoleum of the Grand Mogul era. On the other side of Upper Mall Rd. are *Lawrence Hall* and *Montgomery Hall,* erected in honour of the distinguished governors Lord (John) Lawrence (1853-59) and Sir Robert Montgomery (1859-65); their portraits, among others, hang in Montgomery Hall. Around the halls stretch *Lawrence Gardens,* with Indian and foreign trees, a zoological section (where water-birds are particularly well represented), and a section of useful plants. Further on is the intersection Charing Cross, with a statue of Queen Victoria. To the l., a statue of Lord Lawrence; then the large *Chief Court.* On the r., and set back, the Anglican *Cathedral of the Resurrection*, a brick building in English early Gothic style, completed in 1887. Outside the Telegraph Office, a statue of Edward VII. Continuing straight on, we reach the:-

**Central Museum*, an imposing modern building, also housing the *School of Arts.* It comprises of a *department of arts & crafts* in rooms B & C, an *archaeological section* in rooms D & E, and a *zoological section* in room F.

The archaeological collection is the most important, with its "Graeco-Buddhist" sculptures from the ancient land Gandhara (p.207), originating mostly from Hellenistic sculptors, who came to the land during the rule of the Graeco-Bactrian kings (p.70), and here created the typical image of the Buddha, using classical models, and depicting the life of the Master in countless reliefs (cf.pp.LXIV & 246). Apart from the first Monday in the month, the Museum is always open. Guide to the archaeological section by Percy Brown, 1908.

Section of arts & crafts: Room B: *fine miniatures,* mainly portraits: the Grand Moguls from 1500 to 1857, with their princes, ministers, governors etc.; in the middle, Sikh kings and other rulers of the Punjab from 1750 to 1849, with ministers and generals (the latter incl. Frenchmen and Italians); r., princes (elected & royal) of the Rajput dynasties in the W. Himalayan area (Jammu, Chamba, Kangra etc.) from the end of the 18th and beginning of the 19th c.; a depiction of Nagarkot, capital of Kangra, before the earthquake of 1905; portrait of the English traveller William Moorcroft, who perished in Bukhara in 1825. – Also here, and in Room C: old wood-carvings, musical instruments, clay figures by Indian workers, cloths and embroideries.

Archaeological section (Gandhara sculptures): Room D. In the centre of the room the *stupa from Sikri,* with classical motifs in its adornment (e.g. small Corinthian pillars between the panels) and 13 reliefs depicting aspects of the legend of Buddha, which Alfred Foucher (l'Art Gréco-Buddhique) explains thus: 1. Conversion of Yaksha Atavika; 2. Jataka of Dipankara, an earlier Buddha; 3. the divine king Indra visits Buddha in the cave at Indrasaila; 4. the gods require Buddha to proclaim his teaching; 5. Buddha preaching in the heaven of the 33 gods; 6. monastery scene, probably rthe election of Ananda to be a disciple of Buddha; 7. Buddha meets the grass-cutter Svastika; 8. the future Buddha waiting in the Tushita heaven; 9. Buddha and Vajrapani meeting the snake prince Kalika; 10. Buddha's first meditation under the rose-apple tree at the festival of the plough; 11. the courtesan Amrapali presenting a mango grove to Buddha and his followers; 12. a monkey offering Buddha a pot with palm wine; 13. the 4 guardians of the world presenting Buddha with golden pots.

There are reliefs and other carvings along the walls, grouped in 7 sections according to where they were found. Section A reliefs: I, 209. leaving the house (above: Buddha leaves his wife Yasodhara; below: he rides out of the town gate of Kapilavastu); 261. the nativity; II, 101. the hermit Asitadevala predicting the Buddha's future career; 538. the demonic horde of Mara, the Buddhist Satan; 567. leaving the house; III, 30. Buddha subduing a black snake; 543. Mara's demonic army; 600. Buddha taming the wild elephant which had been set upon him (cf.p.247); IV, 464. the disciples of the 3 Brahman Kasyapa brothers attempting to extinguish the flames of their fiery temple; V. 205. Return of the 7 princes with the relics of the Buddha; 234. dancers and musicians. – Section B: 2. Colossal statue of Buddha, 3. a Yaksha prince. – Section C, reliefs: 148. the bones of Buddha are brought to the town

Kusinagara; IV, 384 (r.), Buddha, on the way to the bodhi tree, receives a bundle of grass from the grass-cutter Svastika; (l.) he puts the grass down by the bodhi tree, from which the spirit of the tree steps, to worship him; 802. Buddha (r.) riding out of the gate of Kapilavastu, (l.) exchanging his clothes with those of a hunter; VI, 399. the 4 guardians of the world bringing golden pots to Buddha; VI, 143. Buddha's first sermon in the grove of gazelles near Benares; 376. Buddha's nirvana; 590. (above) Buddha meets a naked penitent, (centre) he defeats the black snake in the fiery temple of the Kasyapa brothers, (below) he shows the brothers the captured snake in his begging bowl; VIII, 61. Buddha meditating inside a temple; 390. depiction of a richly decorated temple; X, 1493. Bacchanalian scene; X!, 413. Riders on dromedaries. – Section D (principally finds from Sikri): II, 2058. 4 figures of Buddha with companions; 2114. Lotus motif; 2118. Torso with bearded head (Herakles type); IV, 2088. (above) Buddha being measured by a Brahman, (centre) conversion of the rope-dancer Ugrasena (?), (below) the boys Jaya and Vijaya offer Buddha a handful of dust; VII, 2169. Ananda and the Matangi girl; 2335. dream of Maya, the mother of Buddha; 2340. Buddha's leavetaking from his servant and his horse; VIII, 2100. Hariti, goddess of excess; IX, 2099. Buddha, fasting; XII, 1056. 8 Bodhisattva figures; XIV, 1060 & XV, 1022. Marriage to the Princess Yasodhara; XVI, 1227-30. Stone shades from stupas; XVII, 1625, the goddess Hariti, with a Kharoshthi inscrip. (late work); 1183. giants. – Section E. (also chiefly finds from Sikri): 1. richly decorated Bodhisattva figure; 941-1632, Corinthian capitals. – Section F (mainly finds from Dargai): III, 1155. Buddha (above) being measured by a Brahman, (below) visited by the snake king Elapatra; IV, 911. sermon in the grove of gazelles near Benares; V, 730. Robbers lying in wait for Buddha; 916. pedestal of a statue of Buddha with depiction of nirvana; VII, 865. headless female figure, the garments imaginatively done; VIII, 1137. 3 series of Buddha and Bodhisattva figures; IX, 1134 & X, 1135. the miracle of Sravasti; XIV-XVII. Casts of sculptures from Swat (originals at Calcutta, p246). – Section G: 7. figure of a Yavanani (called Athene); 25. Buddha figure with votive inscription.

Also on display here: a collection of *inscriptions* in Sanskrit, Prakrit, Tibetan, Arabic, Persian & Armenian; a Kharoshthi inscr. from Takht-i-Bahai, from the reign of the Indo-Parthian prince Gondopharus, mentioned in the legend of Thomas; a collection of *metal vessels* which, according to the inscr., were presented to a Buddhist monastery at Sibipura (now Shorkot in the Punjab), around 402 A.D. – The rich *coin collection,* esp. of the Indo-Bactrian dynasties, is shown to experts only. – Room E. Golden jewellery from Tor Dher in the Peshawar distr. also betraying Hellenistic influences. A copper statuette of Buddha from Fatepur in the Kangra distr., with inscr. from the end of the Gupta era (6th c. A.D.). – *Lamaist collecion:* Tibetan temple banners; esp. valuable is the one embroidered with the portrait of Padmasambhava, the Buddhist apostle of Tibet (bought for 1500R.); 2 painted flags with the "wheel of life" and scenes from the Buddha legend (r.: above, the birth; below, the 4 journeys, during which the Master encounters an old man, a sick man, a dead man and a monk; l., below, the illumination and first sermon; above, the nirvana and division of the relics).

The enormous gun *Zamzammah* (lion's roar), opp. the Market Hall, is said to have been used by the Afghan sultan Ahmed Shah Durrani in the battle at Panipat (p.193); popular belief ascribes the mastery of the Punjab to the owner of the gun (cf. R. Kipling's novel "Kim"). – To the W., beyond the Museum, stands the *Punjab Library,* in an old Mogul palace with 4 corner-domes; to the SW, the *Town Hall,* opened in 1890.

The road joins the Lower Mall, also called "Old Mall", the chief traffic artery of the W. part of the European town. The yellow-washed octagonal building near its S. end, with 8 corner towers and a low dome, is the *Tomb of Anar Kali,* a favourite wife of Emperor Akbar (the name is Persian, meaning "pomegranate blossom") who, according to hearsay, was condemned to death by being walled up because of an alleged relationship with his son Jehangir (Prince Selim, p.162). The building, erected in 1615 by Jehangir, with the richly carved marble cenotaph within, now serves as a government library. – To the N., Lower Mall passes *Government College* (site of Punjab University, founded in 1822), the *District Court House* and other public buildings, and leads to the SW gate *(Bhati Gate)* of the Old City.

The Old City (known simply as *City),* whose defences have been largely dismantled and converted into walks, has narrow, winding bazaar streets, interspersed with innumerable blind alleys, all teeming with picturesque native life. The tall, narrow houses, with their domed roofs, wooden galleries and balconies, are partly decorated with carvings. Of the mosques we mention: the small white *Sonahri Masjid* or Golden Mosque, near the W. end of the Kashmiri Bazaar, effectively sited at a fork in the street; dating from 1753, it has 3 gilded domes and a gilded minaret spire; and, further E., on an open place, the large *Mosque of Vizier Khan,* built in 1634 in the Persian style by one of Shah Jehan's governors, with 4 solid minarets, a tall centre arch and gleaming coloured faïence decoration in yellow mortar (kashi work).

We leave the City by *Delhi Gate,* following the walks round the NE side of the town, then the road along the N. wall of the Fort, where we have a view of the rear façade of the palace, covered with images in faïence (hunting scenes, mythological figures). We then reach, on the NW side of the Fort, the *Hathi Pol* or Elephant Gate, the entrance to the Fort. In front of it, r., a chapel dedicated to the memory of *Guru Arjan* (see p.195).

The **Fort*, on a low rise to the NW of the City, rebuilt by Emperor Akbar and adorned with splendid buildings both by him and his successors, lost most of its magnificence in the devastation of the 18th c., being largely requisitioned for barracks and other military purposes. Only in recent years has Lord Curzon brought about the restoration of the most important buildings.

At Hathi Pol, we are given a soldier as a guide. The former main gate, *Akbari Darwaza,* to the S. of this, with towers shaped like giant flowers, is now closed. Near the top of our climb, l., the *Moti Masjid* or Pearl Mosque, of white marble. The Persian inscr. over the entrance arch of its outer courtyard, in which occurs the date 1027 in Mohammedan reckoning (1617-18 A.D.), doubtless refers to the completion of the whole of the older palace. We continue past a pretty little marble hall, to the N. and upwards to the Shish Mahal, i.e. mirror palace, thus named for its colourful mirror and stucco decoration, from Shah Jehan's time. The buildings are grouped round a large court, with a shallow water-basin at its centre: to the N., the fine large *Main Hall,* with some subsidiary rooms whose windows offer, r., a view of the fortress walls; to the W., the small pavilion *Naulakha* (i.e. 9 lakhs, see p.XVIII), of white marble with exquisite pietra dura inlay, its roof in the style found in Bengal; the S. building contains a collection of weapons, with old implements of war, incl. weapons belonging to the guru Govind Singh (p.195).

East of the Shish Mahal is a group of buildings generally referred to as the Akbari Mahal, but which can only have been begun by Akbar. Most of them were erected by Shah Jehan and, according to an inscr. above the Hathi Pol, were completed in 1631-32. Of particular interest are the *Chhoti Khwab-gah* ("small bedchamber"), of white, blue-veined marble and, to the S., the *Divan-i-Am,* a large pillared hall of red sandstone (until recently used as a barracks and badly altered; against the rear wall is the throne, of yellowish-grey marble.). – Only little remains of *Jehangir's Palace,* the easternmost of the buildings.

To the W. of the Fort, on a tall base, stands the Jama or Badshahi Masjid, built by Aurangzeb. The front part of the walled enclosure, to the W. of Akbari Darwaza Gate (p.202), is occupied by the gardens known as *Hazuri Bagh* with, at their centre, the delicate two-storeyed pavilion *Barahdarri,* built by Ranjit Singh from the materials taken from the tombs at Shah Dara. A small gate, on whose upper floor relics of the prophet Mohammed and the first caliphs are preserved, leads to the mosque's tree-lined court. The prayer hall, with its large central gate, three white marble domes and four corner minarets, has remarkable external decoration: flowers and tendrils in white marble, standing out in relief against the red sandstone of the building. The interior, enttirely of marble, was used as an arsenal by Ranjit Singh, but was restored in 1856.

To the N. of the Hazuri Bagh, the Samadh rises on a two-storeyed battlemented substructure. This is Ranjit Singh's mausoleum, a fantastic white marble building of two floors, with a tall centre dome and many pavilions. The tomb inside, containing the prince's ashes, is shaped like a lotus flower; the 11 smaller blossoms around it commemorate 11 women who allowed themselves to be cremated with the corpse.

Excursion to Shalimar Gardens, 5km NE. (carriage, see p.198): beautiful drive on a good road, past numerous gardens and ancient buildings. Half-way, we see l. the gate (1635) of the *Gulabi Bagh* or rose garden, with colourful kashi decoration (p.202); to the r. and to one side, the *Tomb of Ali Murdan Khan,* a Persian who distinguished himself by laying out canals in the Punjab during the reign of Shah Jehan. Passing, l., the village *Baghbanpura,* we reach the entrance to the *Shalimar Gardens,* a creation of Shah Jehan, rising in three terraces. The once famous fountains, installed by Ali Murdan Khan, are now in a state of neglect, but the view from the park, with its dense clusters of mango trees, is nonetheless a pretty one. Note the many-coloured ceilings of the pavilions.

If time is short, we can dispense with the visit to the tombs at Shah Dara (6-7km NW; carriage, see p.198), since they have been robbed, for the most part, of their former brilliant adornment (cf.pp.197, 203). The road twice crosses the *Ravi* on bridges of boats, and finally, 1½km SE of Shah Dara sta. (p.205), crosses the North Western Rly. To our l., before the railway crossing, the ruins of the *Tomb of Nur Jehan,* Jehangir's favourite wife. Beyond the rly crossing, the domed tomb of her brother *Asaf Khan,* who died as governor of Lahore and, adjacent to the E., the *Tomb of Jehangir,* who died in the mountains in 1627, while returning from his summer residence. From the forecourt, we pass through a 28m-high arched gate into the garden, 15 ha. in extent, at whose centre stands the generously proportioned tomb, which was perhaps left incomplete. The materials used were red sandstone and marble. The substructure, with a fine entrance gate, four corner towers 28m tall and a restored balustrade, measures about 60m square. Within, the marble tombstone, decorated with pietra dura.

Route 24. From Lahore to Peshawar and the Khyber Pass.

From Lahore to Peshawar, 288M. *North Western Rly:* 2 fast trains (Punjab Mail) in 12-17hrs., for 26R.13a., 13R.8a.; this line also has a connection to Jamrud (12M; p.208). – For the excursion to the Khyber Pass, only 2 days in the week are possible (Tues. & Fri.), cf.p.206. The best months are February, March & April. In December & January, the temperature often falls below freezing point, even in the daytime. In summer, the air is hot and hazy. From August to October, there is heavy rainfall (danger of fever).

Attractive journey through the gently inclined alluvial plain of numerous Himalayan rivers, which rush like torrents towards the Indus, in broad beds filled with sandbanks. Thanks to artificial irrigation, the land is resplendent in its fertility. The railway first crosses both arms of the *Ravi,* then passes *Shah Dara* (5M); before this, to the r., Jehangir's Tomb (see p.204), 2km SE of the sta., near Shah Dara village. – 42M. *Gujranwala.* Town of 29,224 inhab., and Ranjit Singh's birthplace (p.195). – 52M. *Wazirabad* (sta. rest.)

From Wazirabad, there are branch-lines NE to (27M) *Sialkot,* town of 57,956 inhab., incl. a strong garrison, with the tomb of the first guru (p.195), to which a large Sikh pilgrimage is made each year; then over the frontier of the State of Kashmir to (52M) *Jammu,* town of 26,000 inhab., winter residence of the Maharaja of Kashmir, with many mosques; - SW, via (96M) *Lyallpur,* with cotton mills and iron works, to (232M) *Multan* (p.209).

On our r., the foothills of the Himalayas come into view, snow-covered only in winter. Further on, we cross the *Chenab.* – 71M. *Gujrat*, an old town with a fort, founded by Emperor Akbar. The victory over the Sikhs near Gujrat in 1849 finally brought the Punjab under British rule. – 82M. *Lala Musa* (sta. rest.), junc. for a branch-line (not used by fast trains) to Shershah-Multan (p.209; 357M). – The railway negotiates a maze of deep gullies in the basin of the *Jhelum* or *Jihlam* (p.192), the *Hydaspes* of the Greeks; it crosses the river, at which point a superb view of the Himalayas (in the vicinity of Pir Panjal Pass, 3470m) opens up to our r. We then reach the town of *Jhelum* (103M, 252m; sta. rest.), set on the r. bank of the river, not far from which, (about 30km SE), Alexander the Great crossed on May, 326, to the l. bank of the Hydaspes, and defeated King Porus.- We continue through the E. uplands of the *Salt Range*, a rough series of hills, distinguished by deposits of rock salt, and stretching W. across the Indus. – 180M. *Rawalpindi* (520m; sta. rest., several hotels), a modern town with 86,500 inhab. half of them Mohammedan, HQ in winter of the Northern Army, with a strong garrison (2 European & 2 native infantry regts., 1 European & 1 native cavalry regt., 1 mounted, 1 motorised and 1 mountain battery, fortress artillery etc.) It is a significant industrial centre and also the stop for the summer climatic station *Murree* (2291m), and for the road via Baramula to Kashmir.

The line passes through several more (unimportant) stops, where fast trains halt now and then and, at (242M) *Attock Bridge,* reaches the *Indus,* which forms the frontier between the Punjab and the North-West Frontier Province created in 1901 (p.72). The lattice bridge, fortified on both sides and carrying on its upper deck the railway, on its lower deck the main road, crosses the river (which, at this point, is only 200m wide but, because it is deep-cut, can often rise by 25-30m in flood), and offers us a superb view of the Himalayas; in the foreground r., posed romantically on a rocky promontory above the l. bank, stands *Fort Attock,* with a small British garrison, built by Emperor Akbar in 1581, to command the exit from the Kabul gorge (p.208) and the ancient crossing-point of the Indus.

The Indus (Sanskr. *Sindhu*, i.e. river), from which India takes its name, has its source (reached in 1907 by Sven Hedin) in Tibet, 5165m above sea-level, to the N. of the holy mountain *Kailasa,* at whose S. foot the Sutlej and Brahamaputra also rise. After following a NW course for almost 1000km through Ladakh and Kashmir to a point above *Bunji* (1410m), it turns sharply S. to cut through the W. Himalayas, descending rapidly over another 500km through deep gorges until it is 350m above sea-level at *Attock,* where it receives the Afghan waters of the Kabul River and, after breaking through the Salt Range (p.205), comes to the plain, where navigation can commence. The lowlands, which it then passes through, are one of India's driest regions. As with the Nile, only a narrow cultivated strip follows the river, beyond which the whole area resembles desert. Because of the channels made for the irrigation of the fields, the river steadily decreases in size until its confluence with the *Panjnad* (79m above sea-level; p.192), although it still surpasses the latter in volume of water. Shipping is insignificant. For the estuary delta, see p.210. With a total course of about 3200km, the Indus is the longest river in India, although its basin (960,000 sq.km) is inferior in size to that of the Ganges (p.222).

At (244M) *Khairabad,* on the r. bank of the Indus, there is another view back to the river and Attock. – 261M. *Naushahra,* with a strong garrison (1 Eur. & 4 native infantry regts., 2 native cavalry regts., 1 mountain battery), on both banks of the *Kabul River,* which are linked by a pontoon bridge and a rly bridge (branch-line to Dargai).

285M. **Peshawar**, station *City,* 288M. *Cantonment.*

HOTELS, in the Cantonment: Flashman's Hot., on the Mall, good, P.7R.; Dak bungalow, near the sta. – CARRIAGES: 1st cl. 1hr. 1R., each succ. hr. ½R., all day 4R.; 2nd cl. 12a., 6a., 3R. – Recommended dealers for caravan wares, esp. Bukhara and other carpets, are *Mull Chand & Sons, Safdar Ali* and *Haji Raman,* in the City.

The excursion to the Khyber Pass is permitted on Tue. and Fri. only, when the Khyber Rifles (p.208) occupy the Pass, to ensure the safety of caravan traffic. One must ask for the requisite permit at the *Political Agent's Office, Khyber-Peshawar,* and it will be sent to the hotel. The price of a *tonga* from Peshawar to Ali Masjid is fixed at 7R., but one is unlikely, even by haggling, to pay less than 10R. The distance is 33-34km., which is covered in about 3hrs. Fort Jamrud, half-way, must be passed by 11.30 a.m. at the latest. An early start is therefore strongly urged.

Peshawar (pron. Peshour; 360m above sea-level), capital of the Frontier Province, seat of the Chief Commissioner and of the Command of the 1st Division of the Northern Army, with 97,900 inhab. (¾ Mohammedan) and busy trade with caravans from Kabul, Bukhara, Yarkand etc., lies on the *Bara,* a tributary of the Kabul River, in a plain enclosed by mountains. To the N. and NW, the view embraces the foothills, rising one behind the other, of the

Himalayas, and the Hindu Kush, whose snowy peaks are visible when the air is clear; to the W., the Safed Koh range (p.207), with its low outliers to the S., stretching E. as far as Attock.

The European Cantonment, which possesses gardens and avenues, as is customary, shows the special character of the advanced frontier guard. The barracks of the Eur. Troops (2 regts. of infantry, 1 motorised battery) lie mainly to the N. and W., and behind them the barracks of the native troops (3 regts. of infantry, 1 of cavalry). – The native *City*, 3km to the E., is surrounded by a low clay wall, whose gates are shut at night, and which is riddled with narrow streets. The timber-framed houses generally have flat roofs with parapets, where the women and children dwell. There is busy, colourful life in the bazaars, where the ethnic types, costumes and wares from Afghanistan, the lands bordering the Oxus, Tibet and Central Asia, intermingle with those of India. There is a good general view of the town and its surroundings from the flat roof of the *Ghor Katri,* a former Buddhist monastery in the NE part of the town, now utilised as a caravanserai. A similar view may be had from the 28m-high tower of a clay-built fort, outside the town wall to the N.

The old Hindu name for the territory, of which Peshawar is now the centre, was Gandhara. Around the time of Christ's birth, nomadic tribes from Inner Asia settled here, of whose kings *(Kushan dynasty;* 1st-2nd c. A.D.) *Kanishka* (p.70), who embraced Buddhism, is the most important. Numerous monasteries and other religious buildings came into being. Further, the quantity of reliefs and statues excavated during the last few decades, portraying the Buddhist legend in Graeco-Roman artistic styles, bear testimony to the cultural efflorescence of the country at that time. The more ancient finds were transferred to Lahore (p.200). In 1907, a *Museum* was founded in Peshawar also, accommodated in the Victoria Memorial Hall, opp. Government House. The large ground floor room is used for durbar gatherings. The sculptures, mainly from the ruined monasteries at Sahri Bahlol and Takht-i-Bahai, are distributed below and in the galleries. Their arrangement, according to where they were found and what they represent, is very easy to follow: figures of Buddha and Bodhisattva, reliefs of the Buddha legend; besides classical decorative motifs we find some of Indian origin. Excellent guide by *Dr.D.B.Spooner*, director of the excavations. The more important later finds from Sahri Bahlol (1909-10), not yet listed in the guide, are: 2 colossal statues of Buddha (at the entrance); a female statue, richly bejewelled, doubtless a royal patroness of Buddha; a remarkable head, perhaps of a Buddhist prior; depiction in relief of the conversion of the robber Angulimala ("bunch of fingers"); reliefs with Jataka scenes, incl. the story of Maitrakanyaka; also, the *Bronze Reliquary of King Kanishka,* with cupids bearing garlands, seated figures of Buddha and a standing figure of the king, festooned with the sun-god and moon-god (the identity of Kanishka confirmed by a Kharoshthi inscr.) The relics found in the reliquary, purporting to be of Buddha, were presented by the Indian Government to the Buddhists in Burma (cf.p.273).

The **Excursion to the Khyber Pass* (cf.p.206), the narrow and winding cutting through the *Safed Koh Range,* used since antiquity, fortified by the Grand Moguls and much fought over in the Afghan wars of the 19th c., offers us an extremely remarkable insight into the trading life of Inner Asia. The caravans, which we encounter, come mainly from the countries bordering the Oxus (over the passes of the Hindu Kush and the Afghan capital Kabul, 290km from Peshawar). They often consist of hundreds of heavily laden camels, whose shaggy winter coats strike the observer as curious. The drivers are generally Afghans, tall, robust people, bold of expression, wrapped in sheepskins, with round leather caps on their heads.

At the entrance to the Pass, 17km or 1½hrs.' drive from Peshawar, stands Fort Jamrud (509m), a three-storeyed clay-built structure, to which one could also use the branch-line, if the train departure times were not so inconvenient. On the other side of the road, a large enclosed caravanserai with the Customs Post, where one must show one's permit, and the fortified barracks of the Khyber Rifles (an auxiliary corps under Brit. officers, formed by agreement with the predatory Afridi tribes). The Pass road begins to ascend, though with several dips, between dark, rocky walls, 180-300m high, behind which higher mountains tower, jagged and interspersed with caves. On rocky spurs to l. and r. we see small mud-built huts, to which zigzag paths lead up, some watch-towers and, at short intervals, double sentries of the Khyber Rifles. Finally, we follow a stream which flows off l. into a side valley. Continuing to ascend, and passing an Afridi village, we reach *Ali Masjid* (742m, 16.5km or 1½hrs.' drive from Jamrud), a small mosque and a caravanserai, dominated by a mountain peak surmounted by a crenellated fort. One is not usually permitted to proceed any further. It is the custom to give the horses 1hrs.' rest before the return journey, which must occur before 2.30 p.m. – The road worsens. The Pass narrows to a ravine. The last British post is *Landi Kotal* (1028m; 16km from Ali Masjid), whence the road descends steeply towards Afghanistan.

At *Dakka* (428m), at the NW end of the Pass, 53km from Jamrud, the road reaches the Kabul River, following it upstream to the W. – The river's E. valley-cutting down to the Indus, difficult of passage and joining the latter opp. Attock (pp.205-6), was the oldest route to India, even though most conquerors from the W., such as Timur Leng in 1397, Babar in 1519 and Nadir Shah in 1738, may have come over the Khyber Pass.

Route 25. From Lahore to Karachi.

784M. *North-Western Railway:* fast train in 24½hrs., for 58R.6a., 29R.3a., 9R.3a. – The route is of little importance to the tourist, the steamer connections from Karachi are limited and the rly journey via Luni to Bombay takes 48hrs., cf.p.210.

The line to Karachi branches off S. from the Amritsar-Delhi line (Route 22), follows along the W. side of the *Cantonment* (p.198) and reaches (25M) *Raewind* (sta. rest., where the line from *Ferozepore* joins it), a town founded by Firoz Shah (p.178), and large Brit. Cantonment, with 49,000 inhab. in all, junc. of the Delhi-Bhatinda-Lahore line (p.192) with those from Ludhiana (p.194) and Samasata (see below).

104M. *Montgomery,* 178M. *Khanewal,* junc. for the branch-line Wazirabad-Multan (p.205). – 207, 208M. Multan, two stations: *City & Cantonment* (123m; Dak bungalow, opp. the sta.), an old town with pop. of 99,200, half Mohammedan, half Hindu, referred to already in antiquity as Kasyapapura, several times destroyed; now, as the depot for the products of the Punjab, busy and flourishing. – 219M. *Sher Shah* (sta. rest.), on the l. bank of the Chenab (p.192), junc. for the branch-line from Lala Musa (see p.205), which crosses the river.

The line to Karachi remains on the l. bank of the Chenab and, after crossing the *Sutlej* (p.192), enters the territory of the native state *Bahawalpur* (41,000 sq.km; 721,000 mostly Mohammedan inhab.), with the (271M) capital of the same name (114m above sea-level); 279M. *Samasata,* junc. for the South Punjab Railway from Ferozepore and Bhatinda (p.192); 355M. *Khanpur* (sta. rest.)

Before (418M) *Reti* (sta. rest.) the rly reaches the province of *Sindh,* politically part of the Bombay Presidency, which stretches on both sides of the Indus to the ocean, and belongs to the driest parts of India (in some areas, only 12-13cm of rainfall per annum). Only 12-13% of the total area has been won by irrigation for farming, the remainder being chiefly scrubland, steppe or desert, occasional stretches being planted with forest. The population (3,208,000), whose language (p.XLII) is of Aryan origin but uses Arabic characters, practises stock-breeding on a considerable scale (camels, buffalo, sheep, goats, horses, bullocks). – 488M. *Rohri,* on a limestone rock on the l. bank of the Indus, linked by a magnificent rly bridge which crosses the fortified island *Bhakkur,* to the town of *Sukkur* on the r. bank. The construction of an enormous dam to increase the area of irrigation is being planned. The line to Kotri (following the r. bank) is not used by fast trains. – The main line cuts across the NW corner of the native state *Khairpur* (15,800 sq.km; pop. 200,000, mainly Mohammedans), touching the (504M) capital of the same name. 564M. *Pad Idan* (sta. rest.).

674M. Hyderabad (Dak bungalow), called *Hyderabad (Sindh),* to distinguish it from the Deccan capital of the same name (p.112), a town with pop. of 69,400, ⅓ Hindu, ⅔ Mohammedan, until 1844 residence of the Emir of Sindh, set on a rocky height, with vigorous trade and famous art and craft industries (gold & silver embroidery, weaving, gold & silver enamelling). The large Fort, separated by a moat from the town, contains the Arsenal of the province. – The estuarial delta of the Indus, which begins near Hyderabad, covers 8000 sq.km. The arms of the estuary stretch over 250km to the coast, but are quite shallow and unnavigable. The first, E., subsidiary arm branches off further up and comes out into the Rann of Cutch (p.139).

The line crosses to the r. bank of the Indus. 679M. *Kotri*, where the goods brought downstream by ship are transferred to the railway. – 731M. *Jungshahi*, the last stop for fast trains.

782, 784M. **Karachi**, stations *Cantonment & City.*

HOTELS: Paul's Hot., Bonus Rd., in the Cantonment near the sta.; Western Hot., Victoria Hot., all middling. – CARRIAGES: 1st cl. 1R. per hr., ½ day 3R., all day 5R.; 2nd cl. 12a., 2R.10a., 4R.2a. – TRAVEL OFFICE & DISPATCH: *Latham & Co.,* Bunder Rd.

Karachi or *Kurrachee,* cap. of the prov. Sindh, pop. 151,900 (85,000 Mohammedans, 65,000 Hindus, 8000 Christians, 2000 Parsees), only grew to its present importance since passing to British rule in 1843, esp. as an exporting port for wheat, oil-seed, cotton and other products of the irrigated districts of the W. Punjab (p.192). The total value of exports came to 200 mill.R. in 1910, that of imports, 130 mill.R.

The city has little to offer the tourist, although the *Zoological Gardens* rank among the best in India. The spacious *Port* was laid out in 1869-73 by extending the sand dunes and marshes, and is defended by 3 forts which lie on the *Manora Headland.* The entrance is marked by a lighthouse, 36m high. It is worthwhile to drive by carriage, just before sunset, to *Cliff House,* ¾hr, away, where the bathing-beach is.

Once a week, there is a direct connection to Bombay *(British India Steam Navigation Co.*, linking with the P & O steamers to Europe); once monthly, steamers of the *Messageries Maritimes* sail direct to Europe; apart from these, there is a coastal steamer to Bombay every fortnight, as well as a weekly steamer to the Persian Gulf. From Karachi to Calcutta (1572M) a fast train dep. daily, with sleeping accommodation and dining-car, in 82hrs.; via *Hyderabad (Sindh),* see above, *Khokhropar, Luni,* (branch to Marwara for connection to Bombay, cf.p.142), *Jodhpur* (p.142), *Phalera* (p.147), *Jaipur* (p.147), *Agra* (p.161), *Cawnpore, Allahabad,*etc.

Route 26. From Delhi via Lucknow to Benares (Calcutta).

From Delhi to Lucknow 311M: *East Indian Rly* as far as Cawnpore, 271M, fast train (Punjab-Calcutta Mail, with dining-car) in 8¼hrs., for 25R.7a., 12R.11a.; the fast train continues via Allahabad-Mughal Sarai (Benares) to Calcutta, cf.p.213. – *Oudh & Rohilkhand Rly* from Cawnpore to Lucknow, 46M in 1¼hrs., for 4R.5a., 2R.2a.6p. – From Lucknow to Benares 187M: *Oudh & Rohilkhand Rly*, fast train (Dehra Dun Mail and Naini Tal Mail) in 5¼hrs., for 17R.9a.6p., 8R.13a.3p.

From Delhi via *Ghaziabad* to *Tundla* (1213M; sta. rest.), where passengers from Agra (p.175) board the train, see p.193. – 149M. *Shikohabad* (branch-line to Farukhabad). – 183M. *Etawah*, town of 42,570 inhab.

270M. **Cawnpore.** – *Sta. rest.*. Hot.: Empress Hot. (prop. G. Vincent), near the Memorial Garden, 23 Rm., P. 7-12R., good cuisine; Civil & Military Hot., Victoria Hotel.

Cawnpore or *Kanpur* is a lively industrial and trading town on the r. bank of the *Ganges*, at the mouth of the large *Ganges Canal* (p.175), with 178,500 inhab. (144,000 Hindus, 47,000 Mohammedans, 4000 Christ-ians). It consists of the native quarter *(City),* the *Civil Station* to the N. towards the Ganges, with large cotton-spinning and –weaving mills and equally important tanneries etc., and the extensive *Cantonment,* to the E. towards the Ganges, with the barracks of the garrison. The *Memorial Garden,* between Civil Station and Cantonment, near the river bank, commemorates the terrible days of the Mutiny in 1857. The chapel stands on the site of the entrenchment, where about 400 European officers and squads of men under General Wheeler, with the same number of women and children, held out against Nana Sahib, the most important leader of the mutineers, from June 7th to 25th. Despite an agreement giving safe conduct, the defenders were treacherously mown down, for the most part. The remainder, with the women and chldren, were captured and, as General Havelock approached with the British relief forces, were brutally massacred. The corpses were flung down the well, which is now enclosed by a stone parapet and decorated with an angel of the Resurrection by Marochetti.

Cawnpore is the junc. for the Great Indian Peninsula Rly (section Jhansi-Kalpi, p.158; fast train, Bombay-Cawnpore, 26hrs.) and the Oudh & Rohilkhand Rly to Lucknow, see p.213.

The East Indian Rly continues along the r. bank of the Ganges, at some distance, via (317M) Fatepur to (fast train in 3½hrs.):-

389M. *Allahabad* (Laurie's Great Northern Hotel, a few min N. of the sta.), capital of the United Provinces (p.71), with pop. 171,600, 67% Hindu and 12% Mohammedan, considerable trade in corn and seeds, and numerous educational institutions and missions, on the l. bank of the *Jumna*, above its confluence with the *Ganges* which flows in a wide arc, to N. and E., round the peninsula over which the town spreads. The Hindu name for the town is *Prayag* (place of sacrifice) and it is one of their holiest cities; since time immemorial, it has attracted pilgrims in their hundreds of thousands, who do their ritual bathing where the two rivers meet. The present name dates from the Grand Mogul era, when Akbar built the Fort in 1575. In the 18th c. wars (p.70), it finally came into the possession of the Nawab of Oudh (p.215) then, in 1803, of the English, who held the Fort even during the 1857 Mutiny.

The sta. lies between the native quarter or *City* to the S., and the Eur. Quarter, *Canning Town*, to the N., to which are attached the *Cantonments*, NE and NW, as far as the Ganges. In the W. part of the City the *Khusru Bagh* is worthy of mention, a garden originally laid out by Jehangir, with the tomb of his eldest son, Khusru. Canning Town contains numerous public buildings. Near the sta., *All Saints' Cathedral,* the *Post & Telegraph Offices;* to the N., the *High Court* and the *Secretariat & Public Offices;* to the E., the *Roman Catholic Cathedral, Muir College* founded in 1872, with chemistry and physical laboratories), *Alfred Park* with the Thornhill & Magne Memorial and an imposing Victoria Monument, the new *Government House* etc. – Further to the SE, we reach the Fort, at the point where the Jumna discharges into the Ganges. Fine entrance gate. Within, a 15m-tall *Ashoka Pillar* (cf.p.LIV), the best-preserved example of its kind. The large *Arsenal,* which encloses the remains of a Mogul palace and, in a subterranean temple chamber, vestiges of an "immortal" banyan tree, may be viewed only by permission of the military authority, and accompanied by a soldier. – On the shore of the Ganges N. of the Fort, the pilgrims set up their camp (Magh Mela) in January, at the time of the great pilgrimages, whence they travel downstream in large numbers of boats to the bathing-place. Every 12 years (the next occasion will be 1918), a "Kumbla Mela" takes place, attended by over 1 million people.

Allahabad is the junc. for the Oudh & Rohilkhand Rly, which crosses the Ganges to the N. and then shares the lines via *Partabghar* to *Fyzabad* (p.213) and via *Janghai* to *Jaunpur* (p.213).

The line to Calcutta crosses the Jumna. The fast train (2¾hrs. to Mughal Sarai) passes (393M) *Naini* (direction for Jubbulpore, p.156) and *Chheoki* (Bombay-Calcutta Express, p.153), stopping only at: 445M. Mirzapur, pop. 32,400, with large carpet factories, on the r. bank of the Ganges, in whose vicinity the railway now remains. – 484M. *Mughal Sarai*, junc. for the line Jaharanpur-Lucknow-Benares (see below), with which one can travel to Benares (though only after a longish wait): 10M., 16km, in 25min, for 15a., 7a.6p.) – From Mughal Sarai to Calcutta, see p.227.

From Cawnpore via Lucknow to Benares, 243M, Oudh & Rohilkhand Rly (p.211). The line (fast train from Bombay, see p.153; another 1¼hrs. to Lucknow) passes through the NE Cantonment of Cawnpore and crosses the 2km-broad bed of the Ganges. 13M. *Unao*; then over the *Sai*. – 46M. *Lucknow* (p.214), where the branch-line joins the main line from Saharanpur.

From Saharanpur (p.193) to Lucknow, 322M, fast train in 10¼hrs., for 30R.3a., 15R.1a.6p. Most important stops: 33M. *Lhaksar*, junc. for a branch-line via (16M) *Hardwar*, pop. 25,000, on the r. bank of the Ganges, famous place of pilgrimage with an old Hindu temple, to (48M) *Dehra Dun* (700m), pop. 28,000, whence one can go by tonga via *Rajpur* to the hill station *Mussooree* (2000m). – 120M. *Moradabad* (60m; sta. rest.), pop. 81,100, on the r. bank of the *Ramganga*, well-known centre for engraved and enamelled brassware. – 137M. Rampur, pop. 74,300, capital of the native state of the same name (7090 sq.km, pop. 533,212) under a Mohammedan ruler (Nawab). – 176M. Bareilly or *Bareli* (52m; sta. rest.), town of 129,460 inhab., with important sugar refineries, capital of the administrative division *Rohilkhand*, and starting-point for the visit to the hill station *Naini Tal* (1950m; railway as far as *Kathgodam*, 66M in 4¼hrs.; then tonga service, 22M). – 220M. *Shahjehanpur* (47m; sta. rest.), town with pop. 71,700, founded in Shah Jehan's reign (p.178) by the Nawab Bahadur Khan. – 322M. *Lucknow* (p.214).

From Lucknow to Benares, fast train in 5¼hrs., for 17R.8a.6p., 8R.11a.3p. Intermediate stops: 48M. *Rai Bareli*, 107M. *Partabgarh* (p.212), 140M. *Janghai*; 187M. *Benares*, see p.221. – A second line, not used by fast trains, (199M), goes via *Fyzabad* and *Jaunpur*.

Fyzabad or *Faizabad*, a town with pop. 54,600, and important sugar refineries, was the residence, 1765-75, of the Nawabs of Oudh (p.215), and has preserved some buildings of that period. The next stop is *Ajodhya*, with pop. 21,000 on the l. bank of the Gogra. Hindus regard it as the ancient town of the same name, which was supposedly Rama's birthplace (p.LX), and praised for its splendour in the Ramayana epic. During the Grand Mogul era (16th to mid-18th c.), the governors of the province of Oudh resided here. – Jaunpur, with

42,000 inhab., on the site of an old Hindu town founded in 1359 by Firoz Shah (p.178), on both banks of the River Gumti, crossed by an imposing bridge from Emperor Akbar's era. The larger part of the town, on the l. bank, contains several notable mosques from the 14-15th c., and the Fort, dismantled in 1859. – The last stop before Benares is *Sarnath*, see p.226.

Route 27. Lucknow.

Lucknow lies at the junc. of numerous rly lines, which all meet at the main sta., *Lucknow Junction*, between City and Cantonment: to Cawnpore, to Moradabad, to Benares, to Fyzabad, see p.213. – A branch-line to Sitapur-Bareilly, which starts from Lucknow Junc. and cuts N. through the town, has on it the stations *Aish Bagh* and *Lucknow City*, of no consequence to the tourist.

HOTELS: *Wutzler's Royal Hot. (Swiss prop.), pleasant and in a pretty garden, P. from 7R.; Imperial Hot.; Civil & Military Hot.; Prince of Wales Hot. The 4 hotels all lie near one another in Abbot Rd., about 2km from the sta.

CARRIAGES: 1st cl. per hr. 12a., ½ day 2R.4a., all day 3½R.; 2nd cl. ½R., 1½R., 2R.

POST OFFICE, Hazratganj Rd., almost 1km from the hotels. – TELEGRAPH, Neill Rd.

BANKS: *Bank of Upper India, Allahabad Bank, Delhi & London Bank.*

DOCTORS may be inquired about in the hotels and *Peake Allen,* the chemist, opp. Government House. – HOSPITALS: *Balrampur Hosp., King's Hosp., Lady Dufferin Hosp.* (for women only).

SHOPS. Damascened metal ware (silver in a dark iron setting, called *bidri*), chased silverware (*sarais*), work with gold and silver wire, embroidered silk (*chikan*), brocades, open-work covers, clay figures of Indian types, lively in their conception: to be had (among other dealers) at *Rufener* (German), *Madann Mohan* (esp. embroidery), and in the sale rooms of the Prov. Museum (p.217). – Books, paper etc.: at the *Methodist Publishing House.* – Photography at *Moll* (German) and *Laurie.* – General outfitters: *Murray & Co.* Engl. tailors: *Anderson & Co.,* Hazratganj Rd.

The CLIMATE is very pleasant during the cool season (Oct.-Mar.); in April-June it is very hot; the rainy season is from mid-June to the beginning of Oct.

FOR A LIMITED VISIT (1 day, using a carriage): *Kaisar Bagh* (p.216); the ruins of the *Brit. Residency from 1857*, with its reminders of the terrible siege (p.218); the *Great Imambara* (p.218); *Hussainabad Park* and its environs (p.219); *Wingfield Park* (p.220) and the *Martinière* (p.219). – During Moharram, the first month of the Mohammedan lunar year (which, in 1911, began at almost the same time as the Christian year, but falls back 11 days per annum), grand illuminations are staged at the Hussainabad Imambar (p.219), paid for by an endowment from Mohammed Ali Shah (p.219); on the 6th evening of the illuminations, the garden is reserved exclusively for Europeans. – A good descr. of the town and the events of 1857 is contained in: "The Tourist's Guide to Lucknow" by Edw. H. Hilton, price 3R.

Lucknow or *Lakhnau* (37m), former capital of the Kingdom of Oudh, now second residence of the Governor of the United Provinces (pp.71 & 212), with pop. of 259,790 (150,000 Hindu; 100,000 Mohammedan; 7500 Christian, chiefly Europeans and Eurasians), lies on the r. bank of the navigable *Gumti*, which is 40-60m broad. It is linked to its suburb on the l. bank by 3 iron bridges and 2 railway bridges. With its suburbs and extensive parks, the town covers an area of 80 sq.km (i.e. almost a quarter more than Berlin). The W. part is occupied by the old town or *City*, whose densely-populated, dirty alleys and culs-de-sac have only recently been given light by being pierced by several broad streets. The new town or *Civil Station* stretches E. to the Gumti, with its public buildings, European bungalows and gardens, the hotels and European business houses. To the SE of the sta. is the large *Cantonment*, where 2 European infantry regts. and one Europ. Cavalry regt. with field artillery are garrisoned, along with another 2 infantry and 1 cavalry regt. of native troops. – Lucknow is one of the most popular abodes among the Europeans in India, and one of the centres of modern Indian ways and customs, where native drama, music and literature are fostered. The native population, esp. the Mohammedan element, is also enjoying a surge of prosperity. The main season is January and February. The great races which take place then are also attended by the Indian feudal nobility.

The dynasty of the Nawabs of Oudh originated from a race of governors, which made itself independent when the Grand Mogul Empire collapsed. The founder was the Persian *Saadat Khan*, to whom the province was given in 1732; his successor was *Safdar Jang* (1739-53, see p.188), who united Rohilkhand with Oudh. The 4th Nawab *Asaf-ud-Daula* (1775-97), moved the Residence to Lucknow, which up to then had been a small and insignificant place. He, along with the ensuing rulers, *Saadat Ali Khan* (1797-1814) and *Ghazi-ud-din Haidar* (1814-27), beautified the new town with spacious buildings, which display an original (even if, in its details, not entirely felicitous) development of Indian architecture under the European classical influence. The annexation by the English during the Mahratta wars bestowed the royal title upon the Nawabs in 1819, which they admittedly did little to honour. The fecklessness and immoderate extravagance of the kings *Nasir-ud-din Haidar* (1727-37), *Mohammed Ali Shah* (1837-42) and *Amjad Ali Shah* (1842-47) plunged the land into misery. The last king, *Wajid Ali Shah* (1847-56), was a degenerate libertine who usually went about dressed as a woman. Art also went into a deep decline. Crudeness of execution and poverty of material spoilt the effect of the ostentatiously magnificent proportions of the buildings. The occupation of the land by the Brit. Governor-general Lord

Dalhousie in 1856 put an end to this chaotic situation. Wajid Ali Shah died at Calcutta in 1887. However many blessings the annexation brought with it for the people, it was, nonetheless (since a large proportion of the British native army consisted of men from Oudh), a major cause of the Military Revolt or Mutiny of 1857, in which Lucknow, along with Delhi (p.179) played the most important part. *Sir Henry Lawrence,* well-versed in the ways of this land, and who had taken office as Chief Commissioner only just before the Meerut Mutiny (p.193), foresaw the danger, strengthened his Residence (p.216) and collected together inside the ramparts the European garrison (750 men), the few native troops who had remained loyal (479 men), 130 officers and 150 European volunteers, and the latters' wives and children: 2763 people in all. On the 30th of June began the attacks by the mutineers, whose numbers gradually rose to 40-50,000 men, and the bombardment, which stopped only at night. The most violent attempts to storm the Residence took place on July the 20th, August the 10th & 18th, and September the 5th. The besieged suffered terrible losses. As early as July the 2nd, Lawrence was mortally wounded and, on July the 21st, his successor, Major Banks. Sickness, brought on by the confined space, the burning heat and tropical rains, only increased the misery. The women competed with the men in faithful devotion to the task. A relief army of 3000 men under generals *Sir Henry Havelock* and *Sir James Outram,* which approached from Cawnpore via *Alam Bagh*, a fortified garden house 2km S. of the present rly sta., forced its way through to the Residence on Sept. the 25th, after hard street fighting. It too was hemmed in. Now, however, the line of defences could be extended as far as the river Gumti, and SE to the Chattar Manzil (p.217). Unfortunately, supplies of food were running low. It was not until the 12th of November that the Commander-in-Chief of the British Army, *Sir Colin Campbell* (later Lord Clyde) arrived at Alam Bagh with 4500 men, fighting his way forward on the 16th of November via Dilkusha (p.219) to the Sikander Bagh (p.220), within whose strong fortifications he was opposed by 2000 mutineers. With the aid of heavy artillery, it was possible to make a breach in the wall which, though only a few feet wide, permitted the death-defying British storming-party, with Scottish Highlanders at its head, to force its way inside. The battle raged on until the entire defence force had been mown down. After fresh engagements, the relief army reached the Kursheed Manzil (p.220) at 3 p.m. on the 17th of November, where Campbell met generals Havelock and Outram. Of all those who had been together in the Residence at the beginning of the siege, fewer than 1000 were still alive. From the 20th to the 30th of November Campbell, with his troops, conducted the women, children and the sick by the same route via Dilkusha, (where General Havelock succumbed to his exertions), and via Alam Bagh to Cawnpore and Allahabad, whence they were shipped to Calcutta. General Outram remained behind in the fortified position at Alam Bagh. The town was abandoned to the enemy and only finally retaken on March 9-15th, 1858, by Campbell. – The drama of Lucknow is the subject of numerous descriptions in poetry and prose, of which we mention here only the account by *Lord Roberts,* who fought under Campbell as a lieutenant (in "Forty-one years in India", see p.LXXII), and *Tennyson's* "Defence of Lucknow" (printed in Hilton's guide).

The most notable part of the town is the strip of land, 1-2km broad and almost 5km long, which borders the river Gumti to the NE of the Civil Station and City. The parks here are incomparably lovely, and compensate for the fact that the buildings are of less interest. – Banks Rd. leads NW to the Kaisar Bagh.

The *Kaisar Bagh,* built 1848-50 at a cost of 8 mill.R., huge in its proportions but executed with poor materials, was the palace of the last king of Oudh and scene of his orgies. The European-classical style mingles with Indian forms (the fish above the gates, to be found elsewhere also in Lucknow, are the emblem of the dynasty). Of the buildings which surround the pleasantly leafy courtyard, one now serves as lodging and meeting-place for the Talukdars, the province's feudal large-landed proprietors, who have also set up an educational institute for their sons, *Canning College* (recently moved to the l. bank of the river). The former college building, in front of the NE façade of the Kaisar Bagh, now contains the *Provincial Museum,* with scientific objects (esp. zoology) and products by artists and craftsmen, and a quite noteworthy collection of antiquities. Open daily, 7.30 a.m. to 3.30 p.m., except Friday.

ANTIQUITIES. – The large Room I is divided into two sections by a stone partition recently constructed from various different pieces: on the l., Buddhist sculpture, on the r. Jain, mainly from Muttra (p.173). – Room II, Brahman sculpture: Vishnu in his various incarnations (avatars); Shiva, sometimes seated with his wife Durga on the bull Nandin; the elephant-headed Ganesa and the warrior god Kartikeya or Skanda, with 6 faces; the goddess Durga or Parvati; the 8 mothers; 3 carvings from the Gupta era (p.247); 2 beautiful friezes and a stone horse, taken to be the memorial of a horse sacrifice (Sanskr. Asvamedha). – Room III, finds from the ruins of the old town *Sravasti* (p.220; now Maheth) and the neighbouring site of the grove *Jetavana* (now Saheth), the former partly Brahman (remarkable terracottas), the latter exclusively Buddhist. The grove Jetavana was famed as Buddha's favourite stopping-place, and is referred to in some inscriptions. – Room IV, finds from *Kusinagara* or *Kusinara* (now Kasia, in the United Provinces), the traditional place of Buddha's Nirvana. – Room V: Sanskr. inscr. on stone and copper plates, and a coin collection.

Further to the NE, the imposing mausoleum, *Saadat Ali Khan's Tomb,* next to the smaller one of his wife. It is not worth entering.

We continue along Neill Rd. NW, to the so-called *Small Chattar Manzil,* i.e. "shade palace", named thus from the gilded shade above the dome, from the beginning of the 19th c., now offices of the Registry and Agricultural Dept.

– Next to this, to the NW, the Lal Baradari, the large durbar hall and throne-room built by Saadat Ali Khan, now fitted out as the Public Library; the ochre wash is presumably intended to imitate the red sandstone of the buildings at Agra.

The red brick building nearby is the *Judicial Commissioner's Court.* – To the NE, between Strand Rd. and the river Gumti, the former royal palace, Farhat Baksh catches our eye (end of 18th c.); its imposing distant aspect much surpasses the view of it from close to. Inside, the copious library of the Civil Station is housed. Nearby, to the E., the fantastic Great Chattar Manzil, dating, like the small Chattar Manzil, from the first half of the 19th c., quite effective when seen from the river. Formerly the harem, it is now the HQ of the *United Service Club,* with a pretty ballroom. Fine view from the topmost roof, to which one may ascend on request.

The traveller's chief object of interest will be the **Ruins of the former British Residence,* set among gardens, the scene of the heroic English defence of 1857 against a fanatical enemy twenty times stronger. Small stone pillars indicate the course of the rampart thrown up by Lawrence. One must remember that what is today a comparatively open site was then surrounded by houses in a dangerous proximity. As we enter by the *Baillie Guard Gate,* shaded by splendid bougainvillias, we see to our r. the *Treasury & Banqueting Hall,* amid attractive foliage, which served as a hospital. To our l., *Dr Fayrer's House,* a major strongpoint in the defence of the gate, and the so-called *Begam Kothi,* in which are exhibited an instructive model of the buildings and fortifications, and pictures from that time. 44 steps lead down into the cellars, where the women and children had to remain in complete darkness, since the windows were sandbagged against bullets. There were similar underground refuges in other buildings also. Opp., to the N., stands the picturesque ruin of the *Residence*, a former palace of Saadat Ali Khan which was later handed over to the British Resident. The tower served the besieged force as an observation post and attracted heavy enemy fire; it was here that Lawrence was mortally wounded. To the N. of the Residence is the important *Redan Battery.* Other places connected with the defenders, often mentioned, are: *Innes' House* (to the NW), *Gubbin's Battery* (to the W.), *Sikh Square & the Brigade Mess* (to the S.) and, to the SE, the *Post Office.* In the *cemetery* next to the church nearly 2000 victims of those terrible days lie buried in the shade of the tall trees. There are moving inscriptions, such as that on Lawrence's grave, (the words chosen by himself): "He tried to do his duty".

We pass the *Iron Bridge*, built in 1844 and leading to the suburb on the l. bank, then cross the rly to Sitapur-Bareilly, and reach a low hill occupied by the Fort *Machchi Bhawan*, which was blown up before the siege began, on the grounds that it was untenable. Inside the former ramparts rises the *Great Imambara,* i.e. hall for the commemoration of the dead, begun by Asaf-ud-Daula in 1784, one of the few buildings in Lucknow to make a lasting impression upon the observer, with its massive gates, enormous flights of steps, 2 minarets etc. The innermost courtyard contains (tipping forbidden; hats to be removed in the inner rooms): on the r. the mosque with 3 domes; l., the Imambara proper, with a main hall measuring 80 X 44m, and octagonal minor halls. The astonishingly wide vaults were done in plaster moulding. In the ante-room is a silver pulpit; in the main hall, behind a silver grille, the builder's tomb. In the month of Moharram (p.214), the memory of Hussain is celebrated, grandson of the prophet Mohammed, who fell in 680 at the battle of Kerbela, and a large catafalque covered in tinsel is set up.

We leave the Fort area on the NW side by the imposing *Rumi Darwaza* or "Turkish Gate". On our l., as we leave, *Victoria Park,* laid out in 1887, and further on, to our r., Hussainabad Park, with splendid expanses of lawn and architectural ornamental pond, a creation of Mohammed Ali Shah, who bequeathed 3½ mill.R. for the maintenance of the park and the buildings mentioned below. The pool is surrounded by: a *clock tower* (to the E.) with carillon, built in 1881 out of the interest; to the W., the picturesque ruin of the uncompleted *Sat Khanda* ("seven-storey tower"); to the N., a large hall now designated as *Picture Gallery,* containing portraits of the rulers of Oudh, and works by European painters, except for the last picture (usually covered), by a native artist. There is a nice view of park and pond from the verandah. The buildings further N., with blue-white decoration, are remnants of the oldest Nawab palace *Daulat Khana,* from the end of the 18th c.

The *Small or Hussainabad Imambara* was built by Mohammed Ali Shah as a mausoleum for himself and his family. The forecourt, which we enter through a triple-arched gate, serves as bazaar. The garden behind it, with its long water-basins and the two mausoleums r. & l. within it, is a poor imitation of the Taj Mahal (p.167); at the rear, the Imambara itself, with gilded dome: everything, both inside and out, is decorated with tawdry and tasteless tinsel. – To the SW, effectively placed on a grassy plinth rising in steps, the Jama Masjid begun by the same king, with 3 domes and 2 minarets, well-proportioned, but in a sad state of decay.

We return to the S. of Victoria Park through Chauk Bazaar, the main trading street of the natives. The bird market *(Nakhas)* is of interest.

On a second circuit we can visit the SE part of the Civil Station, with splendid parks and reminders of the fighting of the relief army under Sir Colin Campbell (cf.p.216).

We follow Banks Rd. SE from the hotels, past *Government House,* and continue along Dilkusha Rd. Beyond the railway line we reach the picturesque ruins of Dilkusha Palace, formerly Saadat Ali Khan's country seat. The name means "heart's delight". There is a particularly beautiful view of the E. side from the flower garden. – 1km to the N. of here, and crossing the railway again, we reach:-

Martinière College, a strange and fantastic villa on a colossal scale, belonging formerly to the Frenchman Claude Martin (†1800), who used the riches which he had acquired in the service of the rulers of Oudh to found an educational institute for the sons of Europeans resident in India. The College was opened in 1840 and now has 200 pupils. The main front faces E., where a 37m-high column rises from a pool.

**Wingfield Park*, 1km to the NW, laid out around 1865 and over 30 ha. in extent, is a favourite walk for the Europeans. It possesses wide expanses of lawn, superb groups of trees, giant bamboos, palms, ferns, orchids, rose hedges and red gravel paths. The hall at its centre and the marble groups come from the Kaisar Bagh (pp.216-7).

Clyde Road describes an arc round the NE edge of Wingfield Park to some other notable places near the bank of the Gumti. First, the Sikander Bagh, a garden and summer retreat of the last king of Oudh, with a strong rampart, scene of the bloody struggle of the 16th of Nov. 1857 (cf.p.216). – To the W. of this, the Shah Najaf, the mausoleum of Ghazi-ud-din- Haidar and his family, maintained by a bequest from the king. Passing through the Lion Gates and several courts, we reach the low-domed mausoleum; the interior is filled with the usual tinsel; the king's monuments are of silver and gold; on the walls, paintings by native artists depict life at the royal court, elephant fights, cock-fighting, dancing etc. (In one of the pictures, the Frenchman Martin mentioned above, in English uniform). – On the river bank, the *Moti Mahal* or Pearl Palace, a little garden house of Saadat Ali Khan, painted blue and white. Opp., to the S., on the other side of the road, the *Kurshed Manzil,* built by the same ruler in the shape of a citadel but, in fact, a summer palace, where the besieged were united with the liberator Campbell on the 17th of Nov. 1857. Since 1876, it has been equipped as the girls' department of Martinière College.

Returning to our hotel, we also pass the *Hazratganj Imambara*, the rather neglected mausoleum of Amjad Ali Shah.

From Lucknow to Kalihar (p.251), 480M., Bengal & North Western Rly, in 28hrs.: 73M. *Gonda*, with 15,800 inhab., once the capital of a princely state, junc. for a branch-line via *Balrampur & Uskabazar to Gorakhpur* (196M; 10M NW of Balrampur is *Saheth Maheth,* with the ruins of the ancient town *Sravasti,* cf.p.217); - 91M. *Mankapur*, 169M. *Gorakhpur*, 281M. *Chupra* etc.

Route 28. Benares.

STATIONS: *Cantonment Station,* for all trains, i.e. of the Oudh & Rohilkhand Rly to Lucknow (p.213) and Mughal Sarai (p.227; Calcutta, Allahabad); the East Indian Rly to Calcutta and the Bengal & North Western Rly. The other stations, *City Sta. & Kashi Sta.* are of no importance to the tourist.

HOTELS: *Clark's Hot. (prop.C.V.Clark) P.7R., Hôt. de Paris (prop. Mohammed Jan & Sons, Indians), P.6R., decent, both 1½km NE of Cantonment Sta., in the Civil Station.

CARRIAGES: 1R. per hr., each succ. ½hr., ½R. – BOAT TRIP on the Ganges, along by the ghats (p.223) 3R. (The boats are fitted out for the purpose and provided with seats on deck); to Ramnagar (p.226) and return, 4R. – GUIDE indispensable, inquire of the hotel manager.

POST OFFICE & TELEGRAPH (in the centre). – *Bank of Bengal*, on the l. bank of the Barna. – *Doctor:* the Civil Surgeon. – *Chemist:* Lazarus & Co. – SHOPS (muslin shawls with gold thread): Cooperative Store (general merchants), Girdar Das and Hari Das. – *Photographer:* Saeed Bros.

FOR A LIMITED VISIT one needs 1 day. Unique, in its way, is the boat journey along by the *ghats* (see above; tinted spectacles are advised on account of the blinding light), esp. early in the morning when the ritual bathing occurs, from the Dasasamedh Ghat upstream to the Assi Ghat, then downstream to the Pahlvad Ghat and back again to the Manikarnika Ghat (travellers in a hurry will restrict themselves to the stretch between Tulsi Ghat and Panchganga Ghat: cf.pp.225-6). A stroll through the streets of the native town and visits to some of the *temples* will complete the impression, which the traveller will take with him, of this city sacred to the Hindus (pp.222-3; one should take an abundance of small coin for the priests and beggars). – Excursion to *Sarnath*, see p.226.

Benares (77m), on the l. bank of the *Ganges*, originally *Varanasi* and still called by its Sanskrit name *Kashi* by the Hindus, was a holy place already in prehistoric times. From the 6th c. B.C. to the 3rd A.D., it was a major centre of Buddhism (cf.p.226) and, since that time, has been a focal point for Hinduism as a whole and, as such, is holy to the Jains and Sikhs also. Conquered in 1194 by the Sultan of Ghor (cf.pp.177-8), Benares was later part of the Grand Mogul Empire, passed to Oudh in the 18th c. (p.215) and, after a short period of independence, came under English domination in 1775. Pilgrims stream from all over India to the holy city, about 1 mill. annually. They bathe in the Ganges, whose waters are said to be specially effective for washing away their sins at this point where the river, curving northwards, once more salutes its origins in the holy Himalayas. Old people gladly await their deaths in Benares, so that their bodily remains may be committed to the holy river after their cremation, thus assuring them of instant entry into Shiva's paradise. Brahman scholarliness is also zealously nurtured here. Several colleges are maintained at Benares by the British Government and by Indian princes, where the *Pundits* (p.LII) teach Sanskrit, grammar, literature, etc., and explain Brahman beliefs from old mss. The pop. amounts to 203,800, of whom 150,000 are Hindu, 52,600 Mohammedans and 1200 Christians.

The Ganges results from two feeder rivers on the S. side of the Himalayas, the *Bhagirathi,* with its source at 4495m above sea-level, and the *Jahnavi,* accepting the waters of the *Alaknanda* also, near the ancient temple of Deoprayag. At Hardwar (p.213) the river enters, at an altitude of 342m above sea-level, the ancient cultivated tract of the N. Indian plain, where it is fed by several tributaries. The most important of these is the *Jumna* (pp. 162, 177, 212), which runs parallel to it for almost the whole distance, forming with it the "two-river land" (Doab, p.175). The Ganges (2700km) is inferior in length to the Indus and Brahmaputra, but its basin of 1,060,000 sq.km surpasses those of the other two rivers in size. The volume of its water is so great that, at Benares, more than 1300km from its mouth, it is 450m broad and 10-20m deep, even in the dry season. It runs most strongly in Sept., reaching a width of 1km and a depth of 16-18m. Sprung from Shiva's head, according to legend, it is the Indians' most sacred river ("Mother Ganga"). For notes on its delta, see pp.251-2.

The *Cantonment,* NE of the sta., with a garrison of 2 companies of European infantry and a native infantry regt., and the *Civil Station,* which adjoins it to the N., with the government offices, have nothing of interest to offer the tourist. All the more remarkable, by contrast, is the:-

Native town *(City),* stretching E. from the sta. to the Ganges, and forming a crescent along the steep shore of the river. The labyrinthine confusion of narrow streets and alleys is filled with the strangest crowds of busy people, religious pilgrims (usually recognisable by their garments dyed with ochre), beggars and penitents (yogi). Amidst all these, holy bullocks wander about, to whom the pedestrian must give way; it is regarded as pleasing to the god to set free such animals in honour of Mahadeva (Shiva). The number of Hindu temples, excluding all the smaller shrines, is put at 1500, most of them recent and unimportant, since the older ones fell victim to the Mohammedan conquerors' fanatical zeal. Nor can the mosques, about 300 in number, rank alongside those of the Mohammedan rulers' seats. In the houses lining the alleys, we can see craftsmen producing embossed brassware, small idols, amulets etc.

Of the temples and mosques, but few are worth a visit. The ground-plan of the temples is nearly always the same. Arcades surround a rectangular courtyard. The central building, containing the idol or lingam, is usually surmounted by a towered structure, tapering and worked up in a variety of different ways, or covered by a dome.

The so-called *Golden Temple* attracts the most attention, lying in a narrow street not far from the Dasasamedh Ghat (p.224). The heavy, overloaded structure dates from the end of the 18th c. The court is here surrounded by 3 chapels with towered roofs, the middle one 15·5m high. The decoration and gilding of 2 of the towers was done in the early 19th c. at Ranjit Singh's expense (p.199). The temple is inaccessible to Europeans, but the guide will take the visitor to a place where he may look into the courtyard. – Immediately to the N. lies the covered *Gyan Bapi* or well of knowledge, always thronged with the faithful, drinking holy water handed to them by Brahmans. The sacrificial flowers decaying in it give off a repulsive smell. The so-called *Great Mosque of Aurangzeb,* whose enormous, dilapidated bulk lines the NW side of the square, was probably built by Akbar or Jehangir in place of older, Brahman temples. – We are taken on to the *Temple of Annapurna,* the goddess of wealth, in which holy peacocks and cows are kept. Through a small side gate we enter the arcaded walk, whence we see the courtyard and the temple. – Near the Assi Ghat (p.225) is the *Durga Temple,* named after the numerous Hanuman monkeys (p.133) which populate it, usually called Monkey Temple by the Europeans. The goddess Durga is one of the most horrific incarnations of Shiva's wife (p.LX). By the pillar in front of the entrance, a goat is sacrificed every day. The general plan is characteristic of the temples at Benares. The centre building consists of a pillared ante-chamber with adjoining vimana at the rear (p.75). The walls are covered with grotesque paintings. From a distance, we can see the image of Durga in relief, killing a demon with a tridental spear. The red colour of the temple, and the garments (spattered with what looks like blood) of the faithful offering red flowers, make a sombre impression. The begging of the priests is here esp. burdensome.

The view is wonderful of the 5km-long river frontage of the native town, along which stretch the **Ghats (i.e. gates), or bathing-places of the various Hindu sects, castes and nationalities, in an unbroken series, as far as the eye can see. Around the broad flights of steps (often 80-100 in number) down to the water, temples and smaller shrines and palaces cluster, mainly of the 18th & 19th c., differing greatly in style, often bizarre and lacking in plan, yet, in their entire effect, quite irresistible. The mighty river is a constant threat to its shore. Places which it has undermined collapse now and again, and subsided buildings are seen everywhere. Life is here at its busiest in the morning hours. Already at dawn, thousands of men and women come streaming on to the ghats to take their ritual baths, and watch the rising sun conquering the demonic mists. Brahmans and nobles in costly garments observe particular ceremonies, murmuring prayers the while. Simple people, clad only in loin-cloth, are less formal. In all solemnity, they stand in the river, sprinkling their heads and shoulders with water from the hollow of their hand or from small scooping vessels, or immerse themselves totally.

There are, in all, 47 ghats, of which the more important are mentioned below. Approx. mid-way is *Dasasamedh Ghat,*, convenient of access from the town and, for this reason, usually the point of departure for the boat (cf.p.221). It is supposed to mark the spot where Brahma made his great ten-horse sacrifice (dasa-asva-medha), and is one of the most grand and most visited bathing-places, even if it lacks the decorative background which larger buildings would provide; it has just a red temple to Shiva, with a tall towered roof.

Immediately next to it, going upstream, is *Sitala Ghat,* with a temple of Sitala, the protective goddess against skin diseases, extraordinarily busy with people. – The next bathing-place, *Illabhaj Ghat,* belongs to the inhabitants of the Deccan; in niches, we see figures representing the rivers Ganges, Sarasvati and Jumna, also the trinity Trimurti (p.LIX) and Vishnu as Narsingh ("lion man"). – *Munshi Ghat* is impressive, with large structures to protect the bank, and 3 enormous pillars, supporting balconies; part of this ghat is given over to the Mohammedans. – Less important are *Rana Ghat,* with the dilapidated palace of the Maharana of Udaipur, *Chausatti Ghat,* one of the oldest, etc. Here, as in many other places, we see many Brahmans who, as "sannyasi" or begging monks, have reached the highest state of earthly sanctity and, utterly renouncing the world, are preparing for paradise. – Further on, the small *Chauki Ghat* where, beneath an ancient holy fig-tree, the remains of a platform can still be seen, dating probably from the Buddhist era, and bearing images of snakes and other reliefs. Directly after this comes the *burning ghat* for the corpses from the S. part of the town, and *Kedarnath Ghat*, with large flights of steps and a temple to Shiva above (the Kedarnath Temple near the Himalayas is a major shrine of Shiva). – *Hanuman Ghat* is one of the most extensive of all, and very animated; above, a temple to the monkey god (p.LIX); to the N. of this, a small red chapel shows the site where, formerly, suttee was practised. – *Dandi Ghat* belongs to the ascetic sects of the Dandi Pants; here we see yogis in brownish ash-strewn garments undergoing all manner of self-inflicted torments. – *Shiwala Ghat* is artistically noteworthy, a well-preserved building of pale pink sandstone, formerly the palace of the Maharaja of Benares, now inhabited by 15-20 monks of the Kapila sect; the very busy steps are rounded off at the upstream end. – *Bachraj Ghat* belongs to the Jains (p.LVII); steep steps, crumbling above; at the top, a Jain temple beneath fine trees. – The imposing *Janki Ghat* is still quite new; at the top, 4 temples to Shiva with gilded spires. – After this follow: the brick quay of the municipal waterworks, with intake vents at various levels (those below water being marked with flags, to warn shipping); *Tulsi Ghat,* an attractive sandstone structure, well-preserved; *Lala Misr Ghat,* with white masonry and yellow corner towers; finally, *Assi Ghat,* the furthest upstream of all, much frequented but devoid of buildings, the steps made only of earth, below the inlet of the (generally dry) Assi stream. – On the return journey, there is a splendid *view of the river frontage of the town.

Going downstreram from Dasasamedh Ghat we first see, to our l., *Man Mandil Ghat*, impressive in its effect, esp. on account of the *Observatory of Jai Singh* (p.149), tall, magnificent and abutting on to the ghat, above, with an observatory on its roof (access from the rear). – At *Mir Ghat*, we see the smooth, sloping surface caused by the subsidence of a house into the river. – The *Nepali Ghat* is very beautiful; above, half concealed among tamarinds and holy fig-trees, a graceful temple in Nepalese style with rich wood-carvings, in part admittedly grotesquely obscene, perhaps satirical. – Further along, *Pari Jalsai Ghat,* the most important burning ghat for Hindu corpses, a picturesque building with fine arches, blackened by the smoke from the funeral pyres. – Passing a bathing-place for women we reach:-

**Manikarnika* or *Mankaranka Ghat*, where we should be sure to land. It is the holiest ghat of all, frequented by all pilgrims, esp. in November. The front-structures come down into the water, many of them having sunk. The priests, with their large sunshades, are a strange sight. At the top of the first flight of steps lies Manikarnika Pool, lined with stone steps, into which Mahadeva Shiva is said once to have thrown an earring (Manikarnika), and where flowers, cakes etc. are now offered. Next to the pool, a stone block with Vishnu's footprints. At the top of the second flight of steps, a temple to the elephant-headed Ganesa (p.LIX).

The magnificently laid-out *Sindhia Ghat,* built around 1830 by a prince of Gwalior (p.158), has been half destroyed by being hollowed away by the river, and is now a romantic ruin. Beyond this, *Baji Rao Ghat,* a large palace of the Maharaja of Gwalior. Then, the beautiful *Ghosla Ghat*, built by the Raja of Nagpur, and in a fine state of preservation, then *Ganesh Ghat*, built by the Peshwa of Poona, and *Ram*

Ghat, built by the Maharaja of Jaipur. The clumsy, giant recumbent figure (painted pink) of a legendary giant called *Bhima* is worshipped by childless women; the head, with its painted eyes and moustache, is extremely grotesque. Above, a Ram temple. – further along, *Chor Ghat* and *Nana Sahib Ghat*, the latter built by the rebel leader mentioned on p.211; his palace, lying to the rear, is now an apartment house.

Most effective is **Panchganga Ghat,* i.e. "five-river bath", named after the five great flights of steps leading up to the town. At the top, dominating the river vista of Benares, the so-called *Small Mosque of Aurangzeb*, built to humiliate the Hindus, in place of a former demolished temple to Shiva; it has two 45m-tall minarets, slender and already leaning precariously, which can be climbed by 131 awkward steps. From the top, there is a fine view out over the flat-roofed houses of the town, and over the Ganges, which is green on this side from waterweed, and a muddy yellow on the far side; in the distance to the N., the Dhamek Stupa at Sarnath is visible (see below).

We turn back, either here or at the next ghat but one: *Barma Ghat,* narrow but picturesque. – Of the last 4 ghats we mention *Gai Ghat* or "cow ghat", named after the many holy cows (colossal stone statue of a cow on one of the staircases), and *Pahlvad Ghat,* with large broad flights of steps, just before the railway bridge. To the N. of the latter, where the last ghat is, the little river *Barna* enters the Ganges.

4km to the SE, upstream from Benares, is the small town Ramnagar, on the r. bank of the Ganges, and residence of the Maharaja of Benares, who has certain rights of sovereignty here and in 2 districts further S., and who enjoys also considerable prestige among the Hindu population as a whole. The palace, like a fortress, and a temple richly adorned with carvings, date from the 18th c.

Sarnath, the place made holy by Buddha, 6km to the N. of Benares, is best visited by carriage (p.221), but railways go there also (the line mentioned on pp.213-4 and the NW line to Bhatni; travelling time from Cantonment Sta., 15-20min). The name is interpreted as Saranga natha, i.e. lord of the wild game. Here was the great game park where the Buddha began to preach after his enlightenment (p.229) and, through his unselfish intervention on behalf of a deer, won over the king of Benares. Only ruins now remain of the buildings erected in Buddha's honour. Esp. conspicuous is the *Dhamekh Stupa*, a tumulus-shaped stone structure, 33m high and with a diameter of 28m at its base, with a richly-carved plinth, dating from the Gupta era (p.248). Nearby, a modern *Jain temple.* 1½km to the S. of this, a second *stupa* 21m tall, in brick and surmounted by an octagonal tower, which Emperor Akbar built in 1588 in memory of a visit by his father Humayun.

A new *Museum,* built in the style of a Buddhist monastery, contains the finds yielded by the excavations of 1904-5 and 1906-8. A catalogue is being printed.

I. Main hall: **lion capital from an Ashoka pillar* (p.LIV), one of the finest pieces of sculpture in India (the remains of the pillar, whose inscr. contains an edict against schismatic monks and nuns in the Buddhist communities, were left where they were found). *Colossal statue of a Bodhisattva,* dedicated (according to the inscr.) by the Buddhist monk Bala in the 3rd year of Kanishka's reign (p.70); in style and material it belongs, like the statue mentioned on p.247, to the Mathura school of carving (p.173): it originally stood below the richly ornamented protective stone canopy, which is set up in the SW corner of the hall. On the wall behind the lion capital, a fine **Statue of Buddha* as preacher in the gazelle grove near Benares, from the Gupta era (p.247); on the base, between two gazelles, we see the mystical wheel which symbolises the all-embracing significance of the teachings. In the SE corner, an uncompleted *colossal relief of the eight-armed Shiva* as victor over the demons. Late work. – II. Statuette Gallery: Buddha, Bodhisattvas, Buddhist gods and goddesses. – III. Gallery of reliefs: scenes from the legend of Buddha, esp. the 4 main themes, birth, illumination (Bodhi), first sermon and death (nirvana), sometimes linked to the 4 subsidiary scenes (cf.p.248). Also, decorative reliefs: boys riding on gryphons, from the Gupta era. In the verandah, a fine architrave from the same period, portraying Kubera, the god of wealth, at each end, and scenes from the Jataka (cf.p.246) of Kshantivadin, the "preacher of patience". – IV. Gallery of terracottas, in the S. wing, which also contains the dwellings of the officials of the Archaeological Inspectorate.

Route 29. From Benares to Calcutta.

428 or 478M: *Oudh & Rohilkhand Rly* to Mughal Sarai, then *East Indian Rly*: through passenger train in 23½hrs. for 36R.4a., 18R.5a.12p.; for the Ambala Express (17¾hrs.) and the Bombay Mail (15hrs.), one changes at Mughal Sarai.

The line skirts Benares to the N., touches upon *Kashi Sta.*, crosses the Ganges and its high-water bed on the 1km-long Dufferin Bridge and, after about ½hr's journey, reaches (10M) *Mughal Sarai,* junc. for the main lines Delhi-Calcutta (Ambala Express), and Bombay-Jubbulpore-Calcutta (Bombay Mail), see pp.213 & 156.

The fast trains to Calcutta go to Asansol either N. via Bankipur-Kiul or S. via Gaya. Soon after we leave Mughal Sarai, the province of *Bengal* begins (Sanskr. Vangalam), comprising an area of 299,959 sq.km, with a pop. of 52,668,260 (incl. 25 mainly small native states in the N. and S. of the province). Of the inhab., 78% are Hindu, 17% Mohammedans; about 94% live on the land. Regular and plentiful rain, artificial irrigation and the fertile alluvial soil favour the cultivation of rice, maize, barley, wheat, oil-seed, millet, cotton, indigo, jute, hemp, tobacco, sugar-cane and poppies (for opium). The small-scale farming permits the best possible exploitation of the soil.

The most important stops on the northern line are: 68M. *Buxar* (sta. rest.), where the English secured a decisive victory in 1764 over the Nawab of Oudh, bringing Lower Bengal under their command. – 111M. *Arrah*, town of 46,000 inhab., famous in the Mutiny of 1857 for the courageous defence of a house outside the town by barely 100 English and Sikhs against more than 2000 mutinous sepoys. – The rly crosses the *Son*, shortly before the latter flows into the Ganges. – 138M. *Dinapore*; the town, 5km N. on the Ganges, has a pop. of 33,700, a small garrison and iron foundries.

114M. *Bankipur*, also on the Ganges, junc. for a branch-line to Gaya (57km; see below), suburb and seat of the government of Patna, with European dwellings and iron foundries. – 150M. *Patna,* capital of a division, after Calcutta the most populous town in Bengal, with 136,150 inhab. (incl. Bankipur), considerable trade and industry (carpet and brocade weaving, pottery etc.), centre for opium production, which is done under government supervision. Nearby lay the ancient Indian *Pataliputra*, the brilliant capital of King Chandragupta (the Sandrakottos of the Greeks, p.LXV).

Opp., on the l. shore of the Ganges, where it is joined by the *Gandak,* lies the town *Hajipur*, frequented by pilgrims, and a stop on the rly line from Lucknow via Gonda, Bhatni & Chupra to Katihar (cf.p.220).

170M. *Bukhtiarpur,* junc. for a branch-line via (18km) *Bihar*, regarded as the capital of the ancient kingdom of *Magadha,* to (33km) *Rajgir Kund.* – 197M. *Mokameh,* 218M. *Kiul,* junc. for branch-lines, esp. the line Mokameh-Kiul-Jamalpur-Sahibganj-Khana(p.229).–Burdwan(p.229)-Hooghly-Howrah (346M).

– 296M. *Madhupur,* junc. for the branch to (23M) *Giridih,* centre of the Karharbari coal-mining area. – 341M. *Sitarampur,* 347M. *Asansol,* see p.229.

By the southern line, the distance is less great, but the journey takes the same time. – 72M. *Sasaram*, town with 24,000 inhab., with the tombs of the Afghan ruler *Sher Shah* (p.178) and his father *Shah Suri,* the former at the W. end of the town, set in a small lake, and one of the most magnificent in India, of sublime beauty (a 2hr. stop suffices for the visit). – After crossing the *Son*, the train reaches the halt called *Sone East Bank*, junc. for the branch to the coal-mining area of (80M) *Daltonganj*.

136M. *Gaya,* junc. for the branch from Bankipur (see above). The town lies on the l. bank of the small Phalgu river, with a pop. of 70,400. It consists of the cramped and dirty Old Town, with its much-revered temple of the *Vishnupada* (Vishnu's footprint; pron. Bishnpad by the people), to the S. of the rly line; and the modern *Sahibganj,* where the officials and Europeans reside, to the N. of the rly.

7M to the S., by the Phalgu, is *Buddha Gaya*, the cradle of Buddhism, to which thousands of its adherents annually make pilgrimage from Ceylon, Burma, Sikkim etc. The village is populated by Hindus, and the guardian (mahant) is a Hindu. A low wall surrounds the tree-lined declivity in the ground, whose centre is occupied by the ancient *Temple of Buddha,* restored in 1881. On a two-storeyed substructure, about 7m high, the pyramid-shaped and many-storeyed main structure rises to 46m, flanked by 4 lower corner buildings, with the throne of Buddha in its gloomy central hall. Behind the temple, in a compound enclosed by King Ashoka (p.70), is a descendant of that holy bo-tree (cf.p.LII), beneath which the Buddha, after 7 years of inner conflict and continuous mortification is supposed to have received his enlightenment (Bodhi). The altar with its seated Buddha dates back before our timescale, but the decoration on it is from the latest era of Indian Buddhism (800-1200 A.D.)

At *Manpur*, a line branches off via Nawada to Kiul (p.228). – 214M. *Hazaribagh*, 242M. *Gomoh*, junc. for a line of the Bengal Nagpur Rly to *Kharagpur* (p.155). –262M. *Dhanbaid*, 286M. *Barakar*, 291M. *Sitarampur*.

297M. (via Bankipur 347M) *Asansol*, a thriving town with pop. of 15,000, important railway junc. and chief centre of the Bengali coal-mining industry near (308, 358M) *Raniganj*, which numbers 16,000 inhab. and also has important potteries and paper-mills. – 354M (404M) *Khana*, where the line from Mokameh joins (p.228); 362M (412M) *Burdwan*, ancient town with pop. 35,000. on the River Banka, residence of a titular maharaja; 400M (450M) *Magra*; 404M (454M) *Bandel*, junc. for a branch-line which crosses the *Hooghly* (p.239) and continues to Naihati (p.230). The line to Calcutta closely follows the river, busy with shipping, where bathing-places alternate with industrial plants and country houses standing in their own parks. – 405M (455M) *Hooghly*, a town with 29,300 inhab., founded by the Portuguese in 1537, stormed and destroyed in 1632 by the Grand Mogul's troops and, since 1651, in the hands of the English. Its attendant suburb *Chinsurah* (406, 456M) houses the offices of the authorities. – 408M (458M) *Chandernagore*, town of 25,000 inhab., French since 1688. Fast trains do not stop. – 425M (475M) *Lillooah*.

428M (478M) *Howrah*, see p.237.

Route 30. From Calcutta to Darjeeling.

379M. *Eastern Bengal State Rly,* main line to Damukdia in 3hrs.20min., steam ferry to Sara Ghat in 20min, narrow-gauge line to Silliguri in 8½hrs.; then the ascent by the *Darjeeling Himalayan Rly*, in 5¾hrs.: 19hrs. in all, for 49R.12a.6p., 24R.14a.3p., 8R.3a.9p., return ticket (within 14 days), 66R.6a., 33R.3a., 14R.6a.6p.; luggage 5R.11a. per maund (p.XVIII). If one uses the through fast train *(Darjeeling Mail)*, departing from Calcutta in the afternoon, dinner is taken on the steam ferry (2R.); early tea the next morning at Silliguri, breakfast at Kurseong, or in the sta. rests. at Tindharia and Kurseong. If the train is crowded, one should telegraph the station master at Sara Ghat for a berth also, for the night journey to Silliguri.

Warm clothes, top-coat and a rug are needed for Darjeeling, as well as for the mountain rly. Since only the smallest items of hand luggage are permitted on the latter, one should mark with the instruction "Wanted at Silliguri" the cases handed in at Calcutta, which will be required for the change of clothes before one begins the ascent. A dust-coat is also desirable for the rly journey, and spectacles to protect the eyes from the smuts in the open carriages of the mountain rly.

Calcutta (Sealdah Sta.), see p.237. – 5M. *Dum-Dum Junction* (p.251); the line approaches the Hooghly; 14M. *Barrackpur*, a villa suburb of Calcutta, with a country residence of the Viceroy, whose park contains, among other trees, an enormous banyan (p.245), (also, steamer connection to Calcutta); on the l., the Hooghly; 24M. *Naihati*, linked to Hooghly by a branch-line on the r. bank of the river (p.229); 28M. *Kanchrapara*. – 46M. *Ranaghat*, first stop for the Darjeeling Mail, junc. for the line to Katihar (p.251) and a branch-line to Bangaon (p.251). – Monotonous journey through the luxuriant green depression; 58M. *Bogoola*, 84M. *Choodanga*. – 103M. *Poradaha*, second stop for fast trains, junc. for the line to *Goalundo* (150M from Calcutta), with steamer connection to *Naraingani*, whence a railway goes to the town *Dacca* (90,000 inhab.), important in the 16-17th c., and recently flourishing once more.

At (120M) *Damukdia Ghat* (20m) the line reaches the 3-4km-wide *Ganges*, formerly the boundary between the now re-united provinces of East & West Bengal. – We board the steam ferry (dinner, see above). The crossing takes place by searchlight. The landing-place on the l. bank lies, because the curving course followed by the current makes the water too shallow directly opposite, 12km downstream, and is changed from time to time, when the bank is undermined by the water. The construction of a large bridge between both shores is in progress.

132M. *Sara Ghat*, on the l. bank, point of departure for the narrow-gauge N. section of the Eastern Bengal Rly (for berths, see above). Before and after *Nator* (156M) the railway crosses the *River Jamuna* (not to be confused with the arm of the Brahmaputra bearing the same name), and then follows its E. bank. 184M. *Santahar*, junct. for a line to Kaunia; 244M. *Parbatipur*, junc. for another line to Kaunia, and W. to Barsoi-Katihar (p.251); 305M. *Jalpaiguri*, on the r. bank of the *Tista*, a tributary of the Brahamaputra, the last town in the province of Bengal. – The line reaches the frontier area of Darjeeling, the S.

third of the small protectorate of *Sikkim*, occupied by the English in 1849, on the S. slopes of the Himalayas between the two independent states of *Nepal* (p.72) to the W., and *Bhutan* to the E. In clear weather, some snow-capped peaks are visible in the distance.

328M. *Silliguri* (120m), terminus of the Eastern Bengal Rly and point of departure for the mountain railway to Darjeeling. One should reserve a seat on the waiting train, preferably on the l., because of the view, and facing the rear because of the coal smuts; in fine weather one should choose an open carriage, otherwise a closed one. Then one should take one's warmer clothing out of the case (cf.p.230) and breakfast on the sta.

The Darjeeling Himalayan Railway, built in 1879-81, and of only 2-foot gauge, almost toy-like in size, mostly follows the government carriage road, whose steeper gradients it overcomes by numerous loops, in 4 places by a spiral crossing over the lower track, and at 4 others by using the reversing system (cf.p.104). The loops are often barely 20m in radius. The steepest gradient is 1:29. Cog traction is not used anywhere. Numerous water-stops, since the capacity of the locomotives (only 25cwt) is limited.

Immediately after its departure from Silliguri, the train crosses the *Mahanadi* (flowing to the Ganges) by an iron bridge, 750m in length, and then traverses the marshy jungle district (*Tarai*) which skirts the S. slopes of the Himalayas; reeds and bushes, later also primeval forest with tall, slender trees, parasitical plants and orchids. Despite its fertility, the area is almost uninhabited because of the risk of fever. Nonetheless, tea plantations begin to crowd in along the line. Beyond (7M) *Sookna* (162m), the ascent begins. As we rise in altitude, the vegetation changes, and there is a more open view into the plain. Of the rivers, which we look down upon, the Tista to the E. is the largest; then, to the W., the Mahanadi, and the Balasan which joins it. Up to Tindharia, we count 3 spiral loops and a reversing sta. 19½M. *Tindharia* (860m; sta. rest. 11mins stop). Then come the last spiral loop and two reversing stations and, immediately after (23½M) *Gayabari* (1071m), the last reversing station. Onwards, following the carriage road. There are steep rock formations and a fine view of the plain and the Tarai jungle. On this portion of the journey, the train takes as long to descend as it does to ascend: reasonably good walkers can leave it at Kurseong and, by taking a short-cut along footpaths, easily pick it up again at Tindharia (a rewarding detour: 1-1¼hrs.) - 31½M. *Kurseong* or Karsiang (1482m; sta. rest. ½hr's stop), only 16M from Silliguri as the crow flies, and 11M from Darjeeling, a small town of 4500 inhab., with vigorous tea trade, also frequented as a mountain resort, with a hotel, Dak bungalow, English church and schools. Fine view. The terrain all around is covered with European tea plantations. - 41½M. *Sonada* (1977m), where a carriage road to Senchal (p.235) branches off the main road. – 47M.

Ghoom (2275m), the highest point on the railway (it can be bitterly cold here). The houses in the native village are mostly roofed in sheet metal taken from old containers. On a hill above, a Buddhist shrine, on which prayer flags may be seen. – The line now descends quite sharply, with fine views of Darjeeling and the snow-covered mountains in the background. 51M. *Darjeeling;* the sta. is 2077m above sea-level.

Darjeeling.

HOTELS: *Woodland's Hot., P.10-12R, with magnificent view; belonging to it, Drum Druid Hot., P.10R.; Gr.-H. Rockville (Mrs Monk), also good, same prices; Boscolo's Hot., 11 Rm., P.7-8R., praised. – Several boarding-houses and many apartments to rent.

TRANSPORT: rickshaws, dandees and ponies; horses at *Johns.* Excursions are best made by pony, accompanied by a *syce* (horse boy).

DOCTORS: the Civil surgeon; the doctor at the Sanatarium [*sic*]; *Dr Seal;* dentists, *Smith brothers.* – CHEMISTS: *Smith Stanisstreet & Co., Partridge & Co., Robert & Co.* – SANATARIUM: *Eden Sanatarium* (p.234) for convalescents (8, 6, 4 or 2R. per day, incl. food & medical treatment). – BANK: Alliance Bank of Simla.

POST & TELEGRAPH, central.

SHOPS. Equipment from *Francis Harrison Hathaway & Co.; Whiteaway, Laidlaw & Co.* – Tailors: *Hinguen & Bes.* – Photographers: *Burlington & Smith; Smith Stanisstreet & Co.; Paar* (Austrian). – Curiosities, Chinese porcelain, turquoise, coral & amber jewellery, objects in jade and agate and kukris (p.234) from *Möwis & Petri,* and at the native bazaar (p.234), where one can however scarcely make purchases without knowledge of the prices.

CLIMATE. The best time to visit is from the end of October through to January, the mean temperature during this time being 10°C; in January, it sometimes drops below 2°C, when one will spend the evenings by the fireside. During this time, the sky is generally clear and the air refreshing in its purity; snow seldom falls. February is likewise cold, but windy and misty. In May, the thermometer rises rapidly to 15°, in June to 16°, in July and August to 18°; in September it eases and then drops rapidly. Darjeeling is one of the rainiest areas in the Himalayas (annual precipitation 315cm). the summer months are the wettest. But one is never free from rain and mist. Often downpours, storms and thunder will result in a particularly fine day.

Darjeeling or Darjiling (1900-2300m; in Tibetan "Rdo-rja-gling", i.e. land of the thunderbolt or sceptre of Lama), the best-known and most beautifully situated hill station in the Himalayas, with marvellous views of the latters' snow-covered high peaks, stretches out over about 5km along the undulating terrain of a narrow mountain ridge, running N-S. This ridge branches at its N. end, descending precipitously to the *Ranjit*, a tributary of the Tista. The widely scattered houses, framed in, and half hidden among, noble pines, oaks, chestnuts and maples, are most attractive to the eye, also at night because of the large number of electric lights. Despite the high altitude, roses, geraniums, violets and fuchsias are in bloom almost all through the winter. The establishment of the health resort dates from the year 1835, after the English government bought the territory from the Maharaja of Sikkim. The place developed rapidly after the opening of the railway, and it now numbers 17,000 inhab., of whom about 10,300 are Hindu, 4500 Buddhists, 1150 Christians and 1050 Mohammedans. During the summer months, the Governor of Calcutta resides here with his officials, the pop. then rising to 24,000. A European regt. is based here. The town is constantly developing also as the centre for tea-growing, and trade with Sikkim, Tibet, Nepal and Bhutan. In recent years it has been the base for the English campaigns against Tibet, esp. the one in 1904 under Colonel Younghusband, which led to the capture of Lhasa.

The chief tourist attraction of Darjeeling is its proximity to the main range of the eastern Himalayas ("home of the snow"; Sanskr. *hima,* "winter, snow" and *alaya,* "dwelling"), which surpasses in altitude all other mountain ranges on Earth. The total area of the Himalayas, from the Indus gorge (73° 21' E.; p.206) to the gorges of the Brahmaputra (95° 23'), is about 650,000 sq.km, i.e. more than Austria-Hungary. In the E. section, which commences with *Dhaulagiri* (8167m) in W. Nepal, and then throws out 2 branches S., to the NW & NE of Darjeeling, there are 8 peaks of 8000m or more, and another 40 or so which surpass 7600m. From Darjeeling, there is a magnificent view of *Kangchenjunga* (or Kinchinjinga, Kinchinjanga) with its 2 peaks, 8580 & 8474m), which, after K2 in the Karakoram Range in Kashmir, counts as the third highest mountain on Earth. The highest point on this Earth is *Mount Everest* (8840m), whose topmost summit is visible from Tiger Hill (p.235); it was named in 1856 after the director of surveying and is not identical, as was earlier thought, with its spur *Gaurisankar* (7251m). Forming part of the Everest group is also the fifth highest mountain, *Makalu* (8470m), not visible from Darjeeling. The snow-line is at 4940m on the S. slopes of the Himalayas, as opposed to 2700m in our Alps, cf. also p.68.

The charm of the scenery at Darjeeling is increased by the fascination of the inhabitants, whose colourful variety may be observed esp. in the Bazaar (p.234). The majority are Lepchas, a Mongol race which emigrated from Tibet. They live in family units, scattered across the wooded mountains, and practising the most primitive forms of agriculture. They are stocky, with legs well developed from mountain-climbing. Men and women dress almost identically, and can be differentiated (since the men also are beardless) often only by the fact that men wear one pigtail and women two. They carry heavy loads by using a headband. The women like to adorn themselves with ear-rings, necklaces, and little boxes containing amulets, commonly of silver, decorated with turquoise, amber etc. Their uninhibited gaiety, esp. among the girls and children, makes a welcome contrast to the deep seriousness and servility of the Hindus on the plains. The imaginative mythology of the Lepchas has been recorded in literature. Since the 15th c., the land has had Tibetan overlords and Buddhism as its religion, in the form of Lamaism (cf.p.LVII). The monasteries and temples which lie in the mountains, often romantically set in protective forests, give the traveller the opportunity to become acquainted with the prayer-wheels, prayer banners (both with the votive formula *om mani padme hum,* i.e. "O thou jewel in the lotus flower, amen" repeated thousand-fold), rosaries, portraits of holy men and other accessories for divine service in the priest-state of Tibet (barred to the outside world). – Bhutanis (Bhotias or Bhots), a rough and dirty mountain race from Bhutan, are often met with as litter-bearers and coolies. – The lively, adroit Nepalese, slight of stature, are sought after as settlers on the tea plantations, craftsmen and servants; the curved knife, which they wear in their belts, is called the *kukri.* – Apart from representatives of smaller mountain tribes, dealers come in winter from Tibet to Darjeeling, where they live in tents. The Tibetans are of muscular build, like the Lepchas in their hair-style and jewellery; in their leather belts hang knives, chopsticks, wooden bowls, pipes, tobacco pouches etc. They bring ponies, yaks, sheep, goats, salt and musk, which they exchange for tobacco and manufactured articles.

The main street is Auckland Road, on which are situated the hotels and European shops. To the N., below the rly sta., are the *Bazaar* with the native stalls and the *Market Place* (2076m). To the W. of the sta. is the *Lowis Jubilee Sanatarium*, opened in 1887 for natives. To the NW, our eye is caught by the imposing *Eden Sanitarium* [sic, tr.], set up high, for Europeans. It was opened in 1883 and named after Lieut.-Governor Sir Ashley Eden, who was responsible for developing Darjeeling. Further W., *Lloyd's Botanical Gardens* and the *District Jail.* – The S. continuation of Auckland Rd. runs (rising to 2300m) to the military cantonment of *Jalapahar*, with a large convalescent home.

The N. end of Auckland Rd. passes the *Darjeeling Club* and comes out into Chaurasta Square (2136m), where the military band plays in summer. Walks branch off from here to E. and W. of Observatory Hill. The main walk, on the W. side, is called *The Mall* (p.235). Footpaths wind upwards to ***Observatory Hill* (2185m). The view over the valleys and ridges of Sikkim to the Himalayan peaks, which enclose the Tista basin in a horseshoe, is of overwhelming splendour in clear weather. The distance (75-50km) is roughly the same as that separating the Rigi from the Bernese Alps, but the tremendous height of the Himalayan summits, rising clear above their lower spurs, precludes all comparison with Alpine views. Kangchenjunga (p.233) is pre-eminent to the NNW. To the l. of it, rather nearer, stand Kabru (7321m) and, even further forward, the fine Jannu (7714m). To the r. of Kangchenjunga is Pandim (6712m) and the splendid Siniolchum (6894m). The glaciers can be made out with the help of binoculars. The passes stand out clearly, e.g., to the NE, the indentation of the Chola Pass (4419m), leading to the Chumbi valley in Tibet. The pavilion, which the attendant will open, contains a good photographic panorama (though the diagram at the bottom of the glass drum is wrongly orientated). There is also a fine view into the deeply-cut valleys of the Rangit and the Tista, and of the wooded mountain landscape; on a mountain ridge to the N., we can make out the monastery of Pemiongchi (p.236).

The Mall (p.234) runs to the NW of Observatory Hill, past *St Andrew's Church*, built in 1871, and the new park, *Victoria Pleasance*, then the *Town Hall* and the *Amusement Club*. Further to the NW, the Governor's Residence, called the *Shrubbery*, built in 1879. Birch Hill Road, 5km long and offering several views, encompasses *Birch Hill* (2095m), the low NW outlier of the Darjeeling ridge. Walks lead to the top. On the N. side stands *St Joseph's College* (R.C., renovated in 1892), which has more than 200 pupils. – The NE outlier, which branches off at Observatory Hill, is called *Labong*; next to it is a British infantry cantonment.

EXCURSIONS. – Tiger Hill, about 5km SE and accessible in 1¼hrs. by pony, is frequented at sunrise, on account of the prospect it offers of Mount Everest (not visible from Darjeeling). One should set off early. The path goes via Jalapahar (p.234) and Ghoom (p.232), then past the abandoned cantonment *Senchal,* of which virtually only the chimneys still stand, covered in moss, like strange columns. **Tiger Hill* (2595m) has a shelter on the summit. The panorama is more extensive than that from Observatory Hill. Mount Everest is on the NW horizon at a distance of 172km, being the middle and second-highest of three snowy peaks visible to the l. of Phallut (3596m), which is nearer, and part of the Kangchenjunga range. Only his illumination by the first rays of the sun distinguishes him as the king of mountains (cf.p.233).

The excursion to Bhutia Basti Gompa, i.e. the temple of Bhutia village, situated below Darjeeling to the NE, requires 1½hrs. of walking, there and back. On the way, a white enclosed stupa with a low dome and a gilded spire. The temple, recognisable from afar by the poles with prayer flags, is an inferior structure, but a good example of its kind of the Tibetan-Lamaist layout. In the forecourt, we see several prayer-wheels 1½-2m tall, which are filled with written prayers and rotated: this is believed to be as effective as reciting the prayers. Within, the typical altar arrangement with vessels for alms and musical instruments; holy books on both sides. One may attend the services.

The visit to the former Botanic Gardens at *Rangarun* (1800m), SE of Darjeeling, takes about 4hrs. The route goes through Ghoom (p.232) and downhill to the l. from there. The gardens, laid out in 1875 and abandoned because of their unprotected situation, have become a picturesque wilderness. – There is also an attractive descent on the road via Ghoom to *Kurseong;* 3-4hrs' ride), which one can add to one's return journey and even extend on foot to Tindharia (cf.p.231).

Day trips: NE via Bhutia Basti (p.235) and Badamkam, 12-14km on a good bridle path down to the iron *suspension bridge over the Rangit* (300m above sea-level), which forms the frontier between British territory and that of the Maharaja of Sikkim; - N. to the hamlet *Singla Bazaar* at the confluence of the Small and Great Rangit; same distance.

The trip to the Tista bridge, about 30km to the E., takes 2 days. 1st day: we follow the signpost "Pashok Teesta" at Ghoom (p.232), keep to the N. slopes of Tiger Hill and then ascend to the ridge, along which we have about 12km of level path for galloping. Passing the Dak bungalow at *Pashok*, we descend to the Dak bungalow by the suspension bridge over the Tista, where the night is spent. The bridge carries all the trading traffic over the Jelep Pass to Tibet. On the 2nd day, we ride 2-3km up the Tista to its confluence with the Rangit where, from a pavilion about 400m above the river, there is a fine view into both valleys; we continue about 10km up the Rangit to the suspension bridge mentioned above, to which one should have a fresh pony sent, for the uphill return route.

Longer trips must be carefully prepared: one can obtain information and help from one's hotel landlord. Riding animals are needed (incl. a change of mount), coolies and provisions (best brought up from Calcutta). To use the Dak bungalows, one must seek permission from the Government Commissioner at Darjeeling. Provisions should be sent on ahead to the night quarters. The traveller is recommended to follow the ridge of the W. outlier of the mountain range in the direction of Kangchenjunga, which brings him closer to the region of snows and esp. gives more splendid views of Mount Everest: 1st day, approx. 35km up- and downhill to *Tonglu* (3070m); 2nd day, 20km to *Sandakpho* (3634m); 3rd day, 18km to *Phallut* (3600m), in the NW corner of the British territory. Instead of returning by the same route, one can pass through the Maharaja's territory, thus becoming acquainted with the natural world and the life of the people in Sikkim; 4th day: *Dentam*; 5th day, *Pemiongchi*, the principal monastery in the land; 6th day, *Rinchimpong*; 7th day: return to Darjeeling.

The first scientific work about the Himalayas was publ. by the German *Hermann v. Schlaginweit*, who explored them with his brother in 1855-6. In recent times, the range has annually been the objective of larger expeditions, either for scientific purposes, or for the pleasure of the most splendid mountaineering in the world. Up to the present time, few of the conquered peaks exceed 7600m. The following have particularly distinguished themselves: the American couple, Mr & Mrs *W.H.Workman* (almost annually since 1898), the Englishmen *Freshfield* (1899), *Conway* (1892) and *Dr Longstaff* (1907), the Norwegian *Rubenson* (1907) and others. Most of the reports are to be found in the English "Alpine Journal". Cf. also *Waddell's* "Among the Himalayas" (London, 1899; 22s.6d.) and *Freshfield's* "Round Kangchenjunga" (London, 1903; 22s.6d.)

Route 31. Calcutta.

STATIONS. The main sta .is at *Howrah*, where the main lines of the East Indian Rly arrive (Routes 17, 29). The East Bengal Rly has two stations: *Sealdah Sta.,* for Barrackpur-Damukdia-Darjeeling (Route 30), Naihati-Lalgola-Katihar (pp.250-1) etc.; and *Beliaghata Sta.* for Diamond Harbour (p.251) etc. – STEAMER PIERS along Strand Rd. (p.241).

Hotels (not commensurate with the city's importance): Great Eastern Hotel, 1-3 Old Court House St., P. about 12R.; Grand Hotel, 15-17 Chowringhee Rd., 400 Rm., P.10-12R., out of season 8-10R.; Continental Hotel, 9-12 Chowringhee Rd., 66 Rm., P.8R., out of season 6-7R.; Spence's Hotel, 4 Wellesley Place. – For longish stays, there are several good *boarding houses* run by ladies.

Restaurants: Bristol Restaurant, corner of Chowringhee Rd. and Dharamtolla St., good; Bristol Grill, 5 New China Bazaar, near the Exchange, frequented at lunchtime by business people, good; Federigo Peliti, 11 Government Place, E. side, Castellazzo Bros., 18 Chowringhee Rd., both also pastry cooks; Palace Rest., Esplanade Rd.

Hackney carriages: 1st cl. 8a, per mile, 2nd cl. 6a., each succ. hr. 8a., 6a.; all day (9hrs.) 5R., 3R.8a. – *Motor Taxis* may be found in the inner city near the hotels.

Trams (cf.p.XXII): running along the main roads of the city, S. to N. (past the hotels in Chowringhee Rd. and Old Court House St.), and along the more important lateral roads.

Shipping lines & agencies: *Peninsular & Oriental Steam Navigation Co.,* R.A.A.Jenkins, 19 Strand Rd., main connection to Europe via (10¼hrs. by train) Bombay (cf.p.121), also twice a month via Colombo; *Austrian Lloyd,* C.Schmidtmann, 80 Dalhousie Square, SW corner (twice monthly to Madras-Colombo); *British India Steam Navigation Co.,* Mackinnon, Mackenzie & Co., 16 Strand Rd., every fortnight to Madras-Colombo, 3 times a week to Rangoon. – Agency for *North German Lloyd,* Schröder, Smit & Co., 6-7 Old Court House St. (cf.pp.25-6).

Post & Telegraph: *General Post Office,* Dalhousie Square; *Central Telegraph Office*, Old Court House St.

Travel agents: *Thos. Cook & Son*, 9 Old Court House St. (also bank & exchange office).

Banks: *National Bank of India,* 104 Clive St.; *Bank of Bengal*, 3 Strand Rd.; *Chartered Bank of India, Australia & China,* Clive St.; *Hongkong & Shanghai Banking Corporation,* Dalhousie Square, S.; *Deutsch-Asiatische Bank,* 32 Dalhousie Square, S. side.

Consulates. Germany: *Count Karl Luxburg*, consul-general, 16 Ballygunge Store Rd., at Simla in the summer (p.194); *H.R.Schuler*, consul, 9 Clive Row. – Austro-Hungary: *J.J.Czerwenka,* consul-general, 36 Theatre Rd.

Clubs: *Bengal Club,* 33 Chowringhee Rd., Esplanade, the most select club; *United Service Club,* 31 Chowringhee Rd. – *Deutscher Verein,* 13 Elysium Row.

Shops etc. – Bookseller: *Thacker, Spink & Co.,* the largest in India, 5-6 Government Place, N. side; branch in Park St. – Photographers: *Johnston & Hoffmann,* 22 Chowringhee Rd.; *Bourne & Shepherd*, 8 Chowringhee Rd. - Gold and silverware: *Hamilton & Co.,* 8 Old Court House St.; *Cooke & Kelvey*, in the same road. – European & tropical clothing: *Whiteaway, Laidlaw & Co.,* Chowringhee Rd.; *Hall & Andersen*, Chowringhee Rd. and Park St.; tailors: *Clarke, Ranken, Phelps & Co.,* all three in Old Court House St. – Provisions: *F.Schonert,* 4 Government Place, near Thacker's bookshop, esp. for kitting-out for major trips; also, the restaurants mentioned above.

Daily newspapers: *The Englishman, The Statesman* (the premier paper in Bengal); *Indian Daily News; The Hindu Patriot* (a native paper in English).

Scientific & educational establishments. – The university is merely an examining body, with its HQ in the *University Senate House,* College Square. Of the institutions affiliated to it, the nearer ones are: *Presidency College* for Engl. literature, history and philosophy (720 students), the *Sanskrit College* (120 stud.), the *Medical College of Bengal* (550 stud.) etc.; the *City College,* 13 Mirzapur St., teaches English, mathematics, physics, chemistry, philosophy, history, Sanskrit, Bengali, Persian etc. (over 1000 stud.) In other parts of the city, *Doveton College*, for Engl. literature, maths and sciences, Sanskrit, Persian and Arabic (200 stud.). *St Xavier's College* (R.C.) has 350 students. The educational institute *La Martinière* is supported by the same means as the establishment of the same name at Lucknow (p.220). The *Civil Engineering College* (350 stud.) also forms part of the University. – Learned societies: *Asiatic Society of Bengal,* 57 Park St., with a valuable library; *Indian Research Society,* 32 Greek Row. – Libraries: *Imperial Library* (p.241; 100,000 vols) and the libraries in the above-named colleges, and of the Indian Museum (p.245).

Theatres: *Empire Theatre,* Corporation St.; *Royal Theatre,* Chowringhee Rd., near the Grand Hotel; *Opera House*, Lindsay St.

Churches: *St Paul's Cathedral* (p.243), *St John's* (p.241); *St Andrew's* (Scottish Presbyterian); *Old Mission Church; St Thomas's* and the Portuguese church, the *cathedral* of the archbishopric since 1886, both R.C.; *Armenian Church, Greek Church.* – Jewish *synagogue.*

Climate: dry and cool during the time from Nov. to the end of Feb., otherwise hot and humid. The mean annual temperature is 26·1°C. The hottest month is May, with 38·9° as the maximum, the coldest January with 8·9° as the minimum temp. On average there are 188 days of rain per annum, almost exclusively during the summer. The annual precipitation is approx. 2m. The drinking water is regarded as particularly unwholesome. – Hospitals: *Medical College Hosp.* with 600 beds; *Presidency General Hosp.*, for Europeans only;

Eden Hosp., for women. – Chemist: *Bathgate & Co.,* 17 Old Court House St., obliquely opp. the Great Eastern Hotel.

For a limited visit: 1st day: visit *Government House* (p.241; always open, conducted tour) and walk through the business quarter (pp.240-1); in the afternoon, drive through the Maidan (park, p.242; sunset by the Hooghly). – 2nd day: *Indian Museum* (p.245; open 10-5, Sat., Sun., Mon., Tue., Wed.free, Fri.4a; Thu a.m. for students, Thu. p.m. for women only); in the afternoon, the *Botanical Gdns* (pp.244-5). – If the traveller is not acquainted with the Hathi Sing Temple at Ahmedabad, he should visit the *Jain Temple* also (p.244).

Calcutta, the most populous city and the most important trading centre in India, capital of the province of Bengal and, until 1912, of the Indian Empire, seat of a high court and many educational establishments, lies at lat. 22° 33' N., long. 88° 19' E., about 140km from the sea, but only 6m above sea-level, on the l. bank of the *Hooghly,* the westernmost estuarial arm of the Ganges which at high tide permits ships up to 8·5m draught to enter. The city covers an area of 85 sq.km and, with its 1,222,300 inhab., stands second in Asia only to Tokyo (though the latter admittedly has a pop. twice the size). Calcutta proper, lying E. of Upper Circular Rd., and bounded to the S. by Lower Circular Rd., numbers 890,000 inhab. The rest is contained in the surrounding suburbs and the sister town of *Howrah* on the r. bank (179,000 inhab.), to which a 450m pontoon bridge leads across. Only one third of the population was born in Calcutta; two thirds are immigrants, chiefly from Bengal, then from the rest of India and other parts of Asia; the men outnumber the women by 50%. Hindus make up 65% of the pop., Mohammedans 29·4% and Christians 4%. Among the 13,000 Europeans, barely 1/7th are non-English (Germans, few Austrians, French, Italians, many Greeks). The garrison consists of a battalion of infantry, an artillery battery, a company of the Submarine Mining Corps of British troops, and a regt. of native infantry in Fort William; also, an infantry regt. and a half-squadron of native troops at Alipur (p.244).

The name of the fishing village *Kalikata,* where Job Charnock, at the behest of the British East India Co., founded a settlement in 1696, and built Fort William to protect it, is said to be cult centre of the goddess Kali (cf.p.244). Its favourable position at the head of the section of the Ganges navigable for sea-going ships, soon made the town mistress of all trade on the Ganges. Despite hostility from the Nawab of Bengal, it developed so quickly that is territory was made a presidency as early as 1707, and its pop. was estimated at 400,000 in 1752. The capture of the town and destruction of the Fort (p.241) by the Nawab Siraj-ud-Daula in the summer of 1756 interrupted its boom only briefly. Already in January 1757, Lord Clive won the town back and finally conquered the Nawab in June (cf.p.250). In 1773-81, the present *Fort William* was built on the model of Vauban, and made impregnable by the razing of the native villages around it. Simultaneously, the Governor of

Bengal, Warren Hastings, was made Governor-general, to whom the governors of Bombay and Madras were subordinated.

Calcutta is the natural gateway for trade with the whole of N. India, and it still maintains its superiority over Bombay, despite the latter's better position for trade with Europe (cf.p.123). Its share of India's total trade is more than 38%. Just as Bombay is the cotton centre, Calcutta is the jute centre, where it comprises almost 3/8th of the total export, both raw and processed. The same is true of tea, of which almost 72% of the Indian product passes through Calcutta. Other exported goods are opium, skins and hides, oil-seed, wheat and legumes, raw cotton, shellac, coal, raw silk, saltpetre, oils etc. The once thriving export of indigo has been constantly on the decrease since the intervention of artificial dyeing substances. More than half of Calcutta's total exports go to Europe, firstly to England (⅓ of the total), then Germany, which buys more than all the other European countries put together. North America (United States) stands between England and Germany, and immediately after the latter comes China. The most important imports are: cotton goods, gold and silver, metals, oil, sugar, salt, machinery, woollen goods, hardware, tallow, drinks, clothes, drugs and railway materials. – Recently, industries have been springing up, employing more than ⅓ of the pop., jute-spinning in particular. The factories lie mostly in the suburbs and in Howrah where, apart from jute- and cotton-spinning mills, there are foundries and ropeworks.

The interest of the traveller to Calcutta is attracted almost exclusively to the European quarters of the city, which display in an impressive and splendid fashion the brilliant development of the British-Indian colonial empire. The centre-piece is undoubtedly Government House, the Viceroy's palace. It divides the business quarter with its lively traffic (reminiscent almost of London), from the broad grassy expanse of the Maidan. Noble public buildings rise all around, the older ones dating from the early 19th c., their classical style sharply emphasising their European origins, the later ones in Gothic or Renaissance style, with some small concession to Indian forms. Monuments to governors-general and war heroes proclaim the glory of British power and rule. The river teems with sea-going ships of all nations, and with numerous smaller craft. The image of a city that trades with the whole world is completed by shipyards, warehouses, and tall factory chimneys.

The most important business streets meet at Dalhousie Square, the main square and park of the city in the 17th c., with gardens and a large pond in the middle. To the SE., on the corner of Old Court House St. (p.241), is the *Central Telegraph Office,* a brick building of 1873-78. To the W. of this, the *Deutsch-Asiatische Bank* [German-Asian Bank, p.237] and, on the square, the *Dalhousie Institute*, a hall of honour built in 1865, with the marble statues and busts of distinguished men (incl. a statue of Lord Hastings by John Flaxman, 1826) which are to be transferred later to the Victoria Memorial Hall (p.244). The imposing *General Post Office*, on the W. side of the square, completed in 1870, with a 16m-high Corinthian portico and 67m-high dome, stands on part of the site of the old Fort William (p.239); at its NE corner, a tablet and an obelisk, restored in 1902, remind us of the 146 men and women who, at the behest of the Nawab, after the capture of the Fort on the 20th of June 1756, were incarcerated in the dark prison, barely 24 sq.m in size, the so-called "Black Hole", the majority suffocating during the burning hot night. Along the N. side of the square runs the *Bengal Secretariat;* in front of this, a statue to *Sir Ashley Eden* (Lieut-governor of Bengal, 1877-82). The E. continuation of the street, the busy Bow Bazaar where, among other races, many Chinese and Mohammedan dealers offer their wares, leads to Sealdah Sta. (p.237). – The streets issuing from the W. side of the square join Strand Rd, which runs along the entire river face of the city. On Strand Rd. is *Metcalfe Hall* (built in 1840-44), in which the Imperial Library (p.238) has been housed since 1903; no.13 is the *Sailors' Home;* also, many shipping offices, storehouses and the piers for the large liners. Beyond the pontoon bridge between Strand Rd. and Clive St. (running N. past the General Post Office), is the *Mint,* built in 1824-30, where the Indian coinage is minted.

Three roads lead S. from Dalhousie Square to Government House: to the W., Council House Street, running past St John's Church (consecrated in 1781), the oldest public building in modern Calcutta; in the centre, the road called Wellesley Place; and, to the E., the busy Old Court House St., one of the most important business streets for the foreigner (Gr. Eastern Hotel, see p.237).

Government House, an impressive structure and worthy of the King's representative, was built in 1797-1804 on the pattern of the English stately mansion Kedleston Hall (18th c.) at a cost of almost £1 mill. It is completely white, with a dome over the central portion, and possesses four corner wings radiating outwards, colonnades and a magnificent open staircase on the entrance side (N.), surrounded by the lawns and palm-clusters of a garden 2.5ha. in area. The usual carriage entry to the garden is on the W. side (for admission times, see p.238). The central building contains, on its first floor, reception rooms, the throne-room with Tippoo Sahib's throne (p.97), the Council Chamber, where the judiciary council meets, and the large official banqueting hall, with stucco columns (chunam, p.86) and Chinese marble floor. The sumptuous ballroom is on the second floor. The wings contain the apartments of the Viceroy and his family. Rooms, corridors and staircases are adorned with numerous portraits of former viceroys and other historical figures. The windows to the S. offer fine views out over the Maidan.

Esplanade Rd. passes along the S. front of Government House, cutting through the gardens. For this reason, it is closed to traffic. On it, to the W.: the *Town Hall,* built in 1804, with a fine Doric portico; in front, a statue to the Governor-general *Lord Bentinck* (1828-35); then the High Court, built in 1872 in the Early Gothic style, with a tower 50m high, and a fine inner courtyard. To the E., the new building of the *Foreign & Military Dept.*

The **Maidan,* with its enormous expanses of lawn and numerous monuments, is Calcutta's pride: in its area (5 sq.km) and character, it is equalled by no other park within a city, anywhere in the world. *Fort William,* of which it was laid out as the glacis (p.239), obtrudes but little. Two roads, Ellenborough Course and Red Road, cut through the main part of the Maidan, length-wise. At the end of the former, opp. the portal of the Viceroy's Palace, is a bronze statue of the Governor-general *Lord Lawrence* (1864-69) by Thomas Woolmer; to W. and E. of this, equestrian statues: W., *Lord Canning* (1856-62) by J.H.Foley & Th. Brock; E., *Lord* Hardinge (1844-48) by J.H.Foley. To the S., where Red Rd. begins, the jubilee monument to *Queen Victoria* by G.Frampton (1902), which is to be set up later on the steps leading up to the Memorial Hall (p.244). On the E. lawn is the *Ochterlony Monument,* a column rising to a height of 50m, in honour of Sir David Ochterlony, for his outstanding services to the East India Co. in war and peace, 1777-1828. (One can ascend the column, inside; key at the police station, Lall Bazaar St.; from the top, a fine view over Calcutta and its surroundings). E. of Red Rd., at the intersection of two side-roads, a bronze statue of the Governor-general *Lord Mayo* (1869-72), who was assassinated while on a visit to the Andaman Islands. Further on along Red Rd., two equestrian statues: Governor-general *Lord Lansdowne* (1888-94) and Field Marshal *Lord Roberts* (born 1832), who was with the Indian Army from 1851 to 1892, distinguishing himself both in 1857 at Delhi and then in 1878-80 as a colonel in the Afghan war;

further S., a statue of *Lord Dufferin* (1884-88). The eastern side-roads pass the statue of *Lord Curzon* (1898-1905, erected in 1913) and continue to Chowringhee Rd. (equestrian statue of Lord Outram, see p.243).

The NW corner of the Maidan is occupied by Eden Gardens, a bequest by the sisters of Governor-general *Lord Auckland* (1836-42), whose statue stands outside the N. entrance. Within, a cricket ground and a pagoda from Prome (p.264), set up here in 1856. A military band plays at 6 p.m. – The W. edge of the Maidan is bordered by the Strand, the S. continuation of the shore road mentioned on p.241: in the evenings, it provides the spectacle of elegant society driving past in smart carriages with superb horses. Particularly fascinating are the views of the river and port, busy with shipping, esp. at *sunset. In the SW corner of Eden Gdns is a marble statue (1858) of the captain, *Sir William Peel,* who succumbed to the injuries received during the defence of Lucknow. To the r., by the river and outside the gate of Fort William, the *Gwalior Monument*, to the soldiers who fell in the Gwalior rebellion of 1843-44. To the l., an equestrian statue of Field Marshal *Lord Napier of Magdala* (†1870). To the r., *Prinsep's Ghat,* an arch erected to honour the epigraphist James Prinsep (†1840), the meritorious decipherer of Indian inscriptions.

Chowringhee Rd., after Dalhousie Square one of the liveliest business districts in the city, and esp. rich in elegant shops, runs down the E. side of the Maidan. In the N. part of the road are the *Royal Theatre,* the hotels mentioned on p.237 and the *Indian Museum* (p.245) and *Economic Museum*, with a collection of India's economic products, and the *Government School of Arts,* altered in 1910, an establishment for the promotion of native arts and crafts, with collections (excellent miniatures; Tibetan products). Park St. branches off to the SE, leading to the villa suburb Ballygunge (p.244). Opposite its starting-point, a fine *equestrian statue of General Outram,* the hero of Lucknow (p.216) by J.H.Foley, depicting the general leading the sttack with passionate commitment, sword in hand. On the l., no.31 is the *United Service Club*, and no.33 the *Bengal Club*.

Passing the large *Army & Navy Stores* we reach, r., the main English church, St Paul's Cathedral, built in 1839-47 in Gothic style to plans by W.M.Forbes, with a tower 61m high; within, many tombs and inscr. of historical interest, and the great W. window to the memory of Lord Mayo (p.242), after the drawing by Burne Jones (1880). – To the

W. of the Cathedral, the *Victoria Memorial Hall,* begun in 1908 to W.Emerson's designs, has only so far risen a little above its foundations; it is to be executed entirely in white marble, with a colonnade all round, a large outside flight of steps and a high dome, and is intended to house mementoes of the Queen-Empress Victoria, statues and busts of Britons who have distinguished themselves in India, historical paintings, etc., which for the time being are kept in the Belvedere (see p.244).

The *race-course*, with several fine club-houses, occupies the S. end of the Maidan.

The suburbs *Kidderpur* and *Alipur* stretch out beyond the canal called *Tolly's Nala.* The *Zoological Gardens* are worthy of note for their attractive layout. Close by, to the SE, the noble *Belvedere* palace, until 1912 the residence of the Lieut-governor of Bengal, at present containing the above-mentioned collection of mementoes. – Kidderpur is lined on its W. edge by magnificent *docks*, adjacent to which is the suburb *Garden Reach,* stretching along the Hooghly, once the most elegant villa quarters in Calcutta, now partly taken up by industrial plants. Near the spacious estate, which was inhabited from 1854 to 1887 by the last King of Oudh (p.215), there is a ferry, by means of which one can cross to the Botanical Gardens (see below).

The suburb *Ballygunge*, with its European villas set in gardens, is also worth a visit.

In the S. part of the city, the ancient Hindu temple *Kalighat* is notable, though architecturally inferior and dirty, by a bathing-place dedicated to the goddess Kali (p.LX) and much frequented by pilgrims, a favourite religious and patriotic rallying-point for the Bengalis.

The native quarters of the city, esp. the whole N. and NE half of Calcutta ("Black Town"), where a muddle of dirty winding alleys stretches between several broad main and transverse streets, have nothing to show us which might be compared with the country's ancient cultural centres. The picturesque *Jain Temple* in the Halsi Bagan quarter, founded by the jeweller Rai Buddree, is one of the richest examples of the strangely and frivolously overloaded modern style of Jain architecture, with its colourful marble halls, pools and gardens.

On the r. shore of the Hooghly, best arrived at from Chandpal Ghat by steam-boat (½hr.; 8a. return),also from Garden Reach by the ferry (see above), lie the **Botanical Gardens*, founded in 1786, 100ha. in area, for their beauty among the finest in the entire Orient, laid out like an English park with wide expanses of lawn, splendid avenues of palms and groups of trees, flower-beds, pools and cascades, hothouses and an important herbarium All the characteristic tropical plants are represented here. Famous is the *Banyan fig-tree (Ficus bengalensis), about 140yrs old, the largest tree on earth, looking from a distance like a leafy hill, 26m tall, with a main trunk 18m thick and 562 aerial roots, the ends of which grow into the ground, being propagated by protective contrivances; its upper foliage is over 300m in circumference and, at noon, shades an area of almost 7000 sq.m.

The ***Indian Museum* in Chowringhee Rd. contains the most important collections of antiquities, crafts and scientific objects in the country, and is worth several visits. Nowhere else can we enjoy such a complete view of the whole history of Indian art, whose development may here be pursued in all its many directions. Since 1909, the Museum has been altered and a wing added. The re-arrangement of the exhibits is not yet complete. Superintendent: Dr N.Annadale. For visiting times, see p.238.

On the ground floor, to the l. of the main entrance: the *Geological Collection;* in the palaeontological section, the fossils from the Siwalik layers by the Himalayas are of particular interest. – Beyond the courtyard is the *Zoological Collection,* which continues on the upper floor. Connected with this is the anthropological dept., with models of Indian ethnic types and their dwellings.

On the ground floor, r., the *collection of antiquities, the richest assemblage of ancient Indian carvings in existence. Forming its nucleus are the finds of the "Asiatic Society", which originate from excavations undertaken by the Archaeological Survey of India; to these were later added the finds from Bharhut, Gandhara and Buddha Gaya. The chronological arrangement of objects has been since 1870 the responsibility of the Superintendent, Dr John Anderson, with the advice of the General Director, Alex Cunningham. The former also published the first catalogue (1883; in two parts, the first out of print; supplement by Dr Th.Bloch, 1R.) There is no more recent catalogue than this. The rich collection of coins is shown only to specialists (catalogues by Vinc. Smith for the Hindu dynasties, and by Nelson Wright for the Mohammedan dynasties).

I. Vestibule: two *capitals from Ashoka columns* (p.LIV) from Rampurwa in Tirhut (Bihar), one representing a lion, the other surmounted by a bull (the columns themselves, of which the first bears the text of Ashoka's edicts, were left where they were discovered).

II. Bharhut Gallery: stone enclosure from the *stupa at Bharhut* or *Barahat* in Central India. After the stupa at Sanchi (p.157), this is the most important Buddhist monument of the 2nd c. B.C., described by Cunningham in detail, with rich carvings which, because of the explanatory inscr. in Brahmi, are esp. significant. Of particular interest: on the gate pillars, the figures of demi-gods (usually seen standing on animals), which are taken to be the guards of the shrine, incl. the snake king Chakavaka (with 5-fold snake-hood); Kubera the god of wealth (upon a goblin); Sri, the goddess of good fortune; and the nymph Chanda. The cross-beams are decorated with stylised lotus flowers and other motifs. The reliefs on the pillars mainly depict scenes from the Buddha's life, in which the person of the master, just as in the most ancient Chinese art, is always signified by a symbol only (e.g. the holy fig-tree): the dream of Maya, Buddha's mother; Buddha's enlightenment ("Bodhi"; 29th pillar); Buddha being presented by the merchant Anathapindada with the famous (at that time, in the legend) pleasure garden Jetavana (14th pillar). On the architraves and pillars, pictures of the *Jatakas*, i.e. scenes of Buddha's former lives, where he distinguishes himself by devoted love, either as god, man or animal (cf. A.Foucher's explanations to the Musée Guimet in Paris). – In a glass cabinet: *Buddhist reliquary vases,* unearthed in 1898 near Piprahva, not far from the Nepalese border (the remains of bones inside them, attributed by a Brahmi inscr. to the Buddha, were presented by the Indian Government to the Buddhists of Siam). – *Female statue* from Besnagar in the State of Gwalior. Two statues of *Yakshahs* (?), from the ancient Maurya capital Pataliputra (p.228). Parts of a stone enclosure from the temple at *Buddha Gaya* (p.229). Casts of friezes from the cave temples near *Orissa* (p.90).

Room III is devoted to the *Graeco-Buddhist art of Gandhara* (p.207), which announces the far-reaching effects of late classical, Hellenic art (at its peak in the 1st c. B.C.) Here, for the first time, Buddha is depicted as a person, idealised in the manner of antique idols, in single statues and on countless reliefs. The treatment of the garments and the harmonious grouping of the composition clearly point to classical models. The reliefs depict the master's life in a regular series: incl. the story of his birth (often repeated); leaving his parents' house; Buddha and the white dog (G34; according to Bloch the finest piece in the collection); his Nirvana (5147), the visit by the divine King Indra to Buddha in the grotto at Indrasaila, both from Loriyan Tangai in the region of Swat (cf. Bloch's catalogue supplement, p.38). The decorative elements also owe their origins to classical art: depictions of Atlas, giants (G89), hippocamps, Tritons, cupids bearing garlands; we see small pillars of the late Corinthian order along with Persian-Indian ones with small zebu figures on bell capitals. – In the centre of the hall, a restored *miniature stupa* (Bloch, p.5), on which can be seen the manner in which the reliefs were used to adorn such sumptuous buildings.

IV, the so-called Gupta Gallery, a hall with side-rooms like alcoves, where Indian art of the following centuries is displayed, the Mathura school, the Gupta era and the later medieval period up to the Mohammedan conquest, around 1200 A.D. The Buddhist (chiefly the older) carvings are contained in the alcoves on the r. (S. side), the younger (Brahman) carvings are in those on the l. (N. side).

Buddhist section. – 1st alcove: *sculptures from Mathura* (Muttra, p.173). The art of Mathura, which reached its summit during the Indo-Scythian dynasty of the Kushans (1st-2nd c. A.D.), is still under the influence of antiquity which, however, is less marked here than at Gandhara; basically, it turns more to the ancient art of central India, seen esp. in the peculiarities of structure and ornament of the stone enclosures of the stupas. There are examples of classical influence in (among other exhibits) M1, a Bacchanalian double group, and M17, Heracles fighting the Nemean lion. M14, the abacus with its four winged creatures with human faces, shows Iranian influences. Essentially Indian are M15 a, b & c, three pillars of the stone enclosure of Bhutesar near Mathura; on the front, fully-developed and richly adorned female figures standing on dwarfs; the reliefs on the reverse side show scenes from the Buddha's life and previous existences (p.246): *a.* Buddha taming the wild elephant, Nalagiri, which was set upon him at the instigation of his nephew Devadatta; *b.* Buddha, born as a winged horse, rescues 500 merchants stranded on the island of man-eating giantesses (the other 500 being devoured); *c.* Buddha, born as Raja of Sivi, offers a pound of his flesh, to save a dove from a hawk. The great importance of Mathura in Indo-Buddhist art is shown by two finds from more remote provinces: the colossal statue of a Bodhisattva (headless), in red Mathuran sandstone, with the fragment of a stone parasol belonging to it (both bearing dated Brahmi inscr.), from the ruins of the town Sravasti (p.220), and a very similar statue from Sarnath (p.226), from the time of King Kanishka.

2nd alcove: 2 reliefs from the stupa of *Amaravati* (p.88), whose origins coincide with the blossoming of Mathura: A1 (l.), the future Buddha in the Tushita heaven decides to descend to earth; his descent in the form of a white elephant, (r.) Maya's dream, the mother of Buddha; A2. portrayal of a Dharmachakra or wheel of justice.

3rd alcove: sculptures from *Sarnath* (p.226), from the era of the *Gupta Dynasty* (300-600 A.D.); they show pure Indian art at its apogee. The statues of Buddha have discarded their Hellenistic origins, the classical treatment of raiment has gone, and the halo is used for decorative purposes. In their composition the reliefs still hark back to Graeco-Buddhist models, but in their execution they freeze into more and more lifeless formalism. They generally depict (e.g. nos. S2,3) the 4 main events in the master's life: *a.* his birth, *b.* his enlightenment or Bodhi, *c.* his first sermon in the gazelle grove art Benares (Sarnath), *d.* his death or Nirvana. Four other scenes are also displayed (e.g. no. S1): *e.* Buddha's descent from the heaven of 33 gods, *f.* the miracle of Sravasti, *g.* the taming of the elephant Nalagiri, *h.* Buddha being fed by a monkey. Occasionally minor scenes are added, such as Maya's dream, Buddha's first bath, etc., but always united within the frame with the major scene, just as was the case in the old school of central India.

The following alcoves are devoted to the later Indian medieval period and contain, in particular, finds from *Magadha* (Bihar, p.228), principally Buddha statues with the various postures and gestures, the so-called *Mudras*, according to which they are classified. The commonest is the Bhumisparsa Mudra (the "earth-touching" Mudra), which signifies the moment of illumination. Next to the figure of Buddha, only the 4 or 8 main events of his life are portrayed, but in a very concise and formalistic condensaton. Other legendary scenes are no longer present. Apart from Buddha, there are numerous stone figures of Bodhisattvas (beings standing on the threshold of enlightenment), such as (7th alcove) Avalokitesvara or Padmapani, (8th alcove) Manjusri and Buddhist goddesses, such as (9th alc.) Jara, Marici etc. They are partly deities belonging to popular belief, whose veneration becomes more and more prominent during this period.

The Brahman section is on the l. side of the hall. The various gods and goddesses are placed together in groups. The majority belong to the later Indian medieval era.

20th alcove: *Surya*, god of the sun, already praised in the oldest Vedan hymns, standing or sitting on a chariot drawn by seven horses. He usually wears a cuirass and tall boots. His charioteer is Aruna.

19th-17th alcoves: *Vishnu*, originally a Vedan sun-god, later the principal god of the Indians with Shiva and forming, with the latter and Brahma, the so-called trinity of Hinduism, in which he appears as the preserver. He is generally portrayed with 4 arms; his attributes are the discus (chakra), the club (gada), the conch (sankha) and the lotus flower (padma). His spouse is Lakshmi or Sri, the Indian goddess of fate. His steed (vahana) is the mythical sun-bird Garuda. Vishnu is also portrayed esp. in each of his ten incarnations or *avatars*, as fish, turtle, boar, man-lion, dwarf, Parasurama ("Rama with the axe"), Rama (hero of the ancient Indian epic Ramayana, p.LVIII), Krishna, Buddha and Kalkin (the future saviour).

16th alcove: *Shiva* or *Isvara* ("the lord"), a storm-god in the oldest Veda, later the chief god of the Indians alongside Vishnu, and the third person of the trinity, in which he takes the part of the destroyer. Sometimes he is portrayed as united with Vishnu into one person under the name Harihara. His typical attribute is the trident (Sanskr. Trisula); sometimes he also carries a snake and a kind of tambourine (Damaru). His spouse is Durga or Parvati, with whom he often appears, usually sitting on Shiva's steed, the bull Nandi. There is also a form of Shiva in which he appears half female (Ardhanarisvara).

15th alcove. The goddess *Durga* is also honoured on her own account. She usually has 8 arms, with which she wields various kinds of weapons, esp. the trident, and is accompanied by a tiger or lion. She most often appears as conqueror of the devil-buffalo Mahishasura. A fine example is the relief of Mukhed at Hyderabad (Deccan), in which the 8-armed goddess pierces the breast of the buffalo-headed demon with her trident. The latter is usually portrayed, however, entirely in animal form.

The next alcoves are devoted to the lesser gods. Important are Shiva's two sons: *Ganesa* or *Ganapati*, who is set up above temple doors as the god of wisdom; and the warrior god *Kartikeya* or *Skanda*, who has 6 faces and is armed with a lance. The former's mount is a mouse, the latter's a peacock. The love-god *Kama* rides on the fish-elephant Makara, his wives being *Priti* (joy) and *Rati* (desire). 3811, 12. Almost every god has a *Sakti* or "energy", which is equipped with his attributes and his steed, and is portrayed as a woman. The Saktis often form a group of 8, which is then called "the 8 mothers" (ashta Makaras); occasionally, they are given Ganesa as their master. Worthy of note among the images of the lesser gods are: 4220, 4148, 4216, so-called *Nagas*, with human torso (in each case, a man and a woman united as a pair) and long, artificially entwined snake bodies.

12th alcove: *Jain art*, not to be compared with Buddhist art, either in compass or in charm, is in fact sadly monotonous. The Jinas or *Tirthankars* (p.LVIII) are always portrayed naked, either sitting or standing, and are distinguished only by their symbols.

The last alcoves contain *ancient Javanese art,* a daughter of Indian art (cf.p.307), which developed in Java along its own path, so that it cannot be denied a certain national character of its own. The sculptures are hewn from volcanic rock. The deities portrayed belong (r.) to the Buddhist and (l.) to the Brahman sphere. The elephant-headed Ganesa and the demon-slaying Durga occur particularly often.

V. Hall of inscriptions: an important collection of Sanskrit and other inscr. on stone tablets, mostly in Devanagari characters; note a stone tablet from Java with a bilingual inscr. in Sanskr. and Kauri (old Javanese). – Some glass cases contain specimens of the minor arts of ancient India; terra-cottas (Bhitargaun); clay pastes and clay seals, some with inscr., from Basarh (Vaisali), Kasia (Kusinagara) etc.; stone reliquaries from Taxila and Manikyala (both in the Punjab), and Mathura.

We return to the Graeco-Buddhist hall and then pass into the new wing, opened in 1912, which contains, for the present, on the ground-floor, the sculptures and paintings intended for the Victoria Memorial (p.244): pieces pertaining to the history of British rule in India. – In the gallery are smaller antiquities from central Asia (Sir M.A.Stein), Indian Tibet (Dr A.H.Francke) and Bhita near Allahabad (Dr J.H.Marshall); also a few fine Tibetan paintings.

The rich *collection of arts and crafts* is housed on the upper floor of the new wing: Indian fabrics, embroidery, carvings; among the latter, the Burmese section is esp. fine (gold throne from Mandalay, p.272). There is also a very valuable collection of Indian miniatures, put together by Havell.

Eastern Bengal State Railway.

The *Eastern Bengal State Rly*, apart from the line to Goalundo-Silliguri (Darjeeling, see Route 30), has little to interest the tourist.

From Calcutta *(Sealdah Sta.*, p.237) to Katihar, 268M, in approx. 16hrs.; to (46M) *Ranaghat*, see p.230; 62M. *Krishnagar*, a town with 24,000 inhab.; 94M. *Palasy* or *Plassey*, known for Lord Clive's decisive victory, with 3150 men, over the army of Nawab Siraj-ud-Daula on the 23rd of June, 1757, which laid the foundations for the English domination of Bengal; 116M. *Berhampore*, chief town in the Murshidabad district, with 24,000 inhab.; 123M. *Murshidabad*, in the 18th c. capital of the Nawab of Bengal, now numbering only 15,000 inhab., with the large palace of the Nawab (built in 1837) and a mosque situated outside the town, containing the tomb of Nawab Murshid Kali Kahn (†1728); - 144M. *Lalgola Ghat*, on the Ganges; a steamboat crosses to – 156M. *Godagari Ghat*, where the rly to Katihar connects: 205M. *Malda*, 268M. *Katihar*, junc. for several railways, incl. the one to Lucknow-Cawnpore (pp.220, 213).

From Calcutta *(Sealdah Sta.*, p.234) to Khulna, in 6½hrs. – 5M. *Dum-Dum Junc.,* see p.230; 7M. *Dum-Dum Cantonment*, with the large barracks of a British infantry regt.; 48M. *Bongon* or Bangaon (p.230); 75M. *Jessore*, town of 8000 inhab., seat of the Raja of Jessore; 109M. *Khulna*, with 10,000 inhab.. Fertile region, rice-fields, date-palms.

From Calcutta *(Beliaghata Sta.*, p.237) to Diamond Harbour (p.252), 37M in 2¼hrs. – Intermediate stops: 3M. *Ballygunge Junc.*, for the branch to Budge Budge (13M; see below); 10M. *Sonarpur*, junc. for the branch to (28M) *Port Canning*, a rival port to Calcutta, which was built in 1865, but rapidly declined. It lies on the NW edge of the *Sundarbans*, a malarial swamp covered with thick primeval forest, and criss-crossed by innumerable channels, stretching over almost 17,000 sq.km of the Ganges-Brahmaputra delta, an enormous hiding-place for tigers, buffaloes, wild boar, snakes, crocodiles, etc.

Route 32. From Calcutta to Rangoon.

About 1100 S.M., *British India Steam Navigation Co.* (abbr. to B.I.S.N.C, often only B.I.): Sunday mail-boat (to Penang, Singapore, p.280) in 2 days, Tues. & Fri. in 3 days, for 70R. 1st cl., 37½R. 2nd cl., with meals (3rd cl. for the Boy, 10R., without meals). Return Mon. Thu. Sat., return fare 135R., 75R. The ships are reasonably good, the food mediocre. The company also runs a coastal steamer, Sat., calling at *Chittagong, Akyab, Kyaukpyu & Sandsway;* fare 90R., 45R.

The steamer slowly winds its way through the tangle of shipping. To our l., the green Maidan, surrounded by palaces, Fort William, the docks at Kidderpur; to our r., Howrah and Sibpur, then the Botanical Gardens. Once round the sharp bend, which the Hooghly makes southwards, the city is out of sight. The shores are resplendent in their tropical vegetation. Clusters of palms and bamboo, concealing the small village settlements, alternate with rice-fields. On the l. appears the small town *Budge Budge* or Baj Baj, (railway, see above), then, r., *Ulubaria* (p.155), at the mouth of the High Level Canal.

Navigation on the Hooghly is very tricky. Deposits of mud and the strong tidal currents, which are evident in the dry season as far as 80km above Calcutta, change the course of the channel, making daily soundings and a continual repositioning of booms and buoys necessary. Complete safety is guaranteed by an exemplary team of pilots, the most highly-paid in the world. The most dangerous spot is below the confluence with the *Damodar* (r.), at the 5km-long sand- and mud-bank known as *James & Mary Sands,* named after the ship of the British East India Company which foundered here in 1694. At the confluence with the *Rapnayaran,* the river turns SE. On the l. is *Diamond Harbour* (66km from Calcutta), formerly a port for large ships, now insignificant (railway, see p.251).

At high tide, the shores with their sparse growth of grass stand barely 10cm above the water-level. The estuary broadens towards the SW. To the l., *Sagar Island,* with a much frequented bathing-place for pilgrims since, for the Hindu, this is the point where the Ganges meets the ocean. The S. part of the island is covered with thick jungle. On the SW corner, *Middleton Point* (68km from Diamond Harbour), stands an iron lighthouse 23m high.

Our ship reaches the *Bay of Bengal* and sets course SE. The air has become much cooler but, because of the high humidity, remains sultry and oppressive. The following morning, we approach the SW point of Burma. A tall lighthouse, with light and dark rings, marks the flat *Algnado Reef,* which lies on the continuation of *Cape Negrais* (p.253). The ship skirts the reef and turns E. along the low shore of the *Irrawaddy Delta.* The mud-filled waters of the estuaries colour the sea to a great distance. To the r., the lightships *Baracua & Krishna.* Then, l., the lighthouse *China Bakir.* At *Elephant Point,* the ship turns l. into *Rangoon River.* On the r., low-lying land with some houses and palms becomes visible. The journey up the river (strong current at ebb-tide) is unattractive until, to the N., the pagoda at Syriam appears (p.261) and, to its l., and most impressive, the great golden Shwe Dagon Pagoda (p.259), towering above Rangoon.

Rangoon, see p.257.

BURMA.

Apart from Calcutta, the following main connections are relevant to the journey from India: from Colombo, the well-appointed steamers of the *Bibby Line,* twice a month, in 5-6 days, also *North-German Lloyd,* twice monthly in 5 days to Penang (p.283) where, after a 3-4 day stay, one can continue to Rangoon by the *British India Steam Navigation Co.* (p.251) in 3 days; - from Madras, by the *British Steam Navigation Co.*, weekly, in 4-5 days, for 90R., 50R.

Burma (or Birma), the most easterly and, with an area of 613,126 sq.km, the most extensive province in the British-Indian Empire, bordered to the SE by Siam and to the NE by the Chinese province of Yun-nan, is in fact geographically part of Indo-China. Two long mountain ranges, running from the SE corner of the Tibetan uplands, cross the country from N. to S. under various names. The W. range, beginning at lat. 28½° N. in the *Namkiu Mountains* (5700m), decreases in altitude, as the *Patkoi Range* (3830m), into the upper Irrawaddy basin, continuing as *Arakan Yoma (Mount Victoria*, 3170m, lat. 21° N.), in an arc to Cape Negrais (p.252; lat. 17° N.), where it breaks off, to reappear 3° further S. in the Andaman Islands. Extremely rugged, full of dense forest and devoid of people, it has hitherto proved an obstacle to the building of roads and railways between Bengal and Burma. The E. range, separating the Irrawaddy basin from that of the Salween, forms, E. of Mandalay, the limestone plateau (reaching 2000m in places) of the still semi-independent *Shan States* (cf.p.255), continuing, further S., in the Malayan Peninsula. In between several smaller mountain chains stretch also in a S. direction, such as the uplands between the upper Irrawaddy and its tributary, the Chindwin, and the *Pegu Yoma,* between the lower Irrawaddy and the Sittang. The *Irrawaddy* is the country's chief river and most important traffic artery. It has two feeders which unite, 260m above sea-level, N. of Myitkyina (p.277); it accepts the *Chindwin* about half-way through its course (p.268) and, for the most part, flows through fertile alluvial terrain, which is covered with forests and paddy-fields. At its estuary, it forms a 7-armed delta, 30,000 sq.km in area, which is joined to the E. by the *Sittang.* Its total length is 1800km. The second main river, the *Salween,* rises in Tibet, passing, in its middle course, through the Chinese province Yun-nan, and only rejoining Burmese territory later on. Its deep, narrow valley is sparsely populated, its navigability very limited. It enters the Gulf of Martaban at Moulmein (p.261).

The vegetation is generally richer than in India. One finds mangrove thickets on the coast, and tropical jungle with palms, bamboo and predominantly evergreen trees further inland. In the interior there are forests of deciduous trees which furnish valuable timber for building, such as teak *(Tectona grandis),* which is esp. prevalent in the jungles of the upper Irrawaddy. The most important field crops are rice (paddy), which occupies 5/6th of Lower Burma's arable land, then cassava, sugar cane, cotton and tobacco. In Upper Burma one finds many sub-tropical fruit-trees, and several types of corn. The animal world forms a transition between that of India proper and Malaya. Burma is the home of the elephant, which is to be found from the primeval mountain forests to the plains. Particularly numerous are the tapir (so-called shabrack tapir), tiger and panther. Swarms of monkeys enliven the forests. Among the birds, types of raven and chicken are represented in particular; the wild peacock is noteworthy. Equally well represented and varied are the lower orders, amphibians, fish, insects (superb butterflies).

The population, acccording to the 1911 census, numbered 12,115,217, that is only 20 per sq.km, but constantly on the increase because of immigration from India and China. The vast majority are Burmese, who belong to the Mongol race and speak a monosyllabic language related to Chinese. They are small people, often delicate in build, with brown complexions and straight black hair, of open and cheerful disposition and pleasing manner. They like to wear bright silks; the women's skirts differ from those of the men virtually only in length and brighter colouring. The women wear their hair tied up in a bun, and usually have a coloured shawl and a sunshade. The religion is Buddhism of the southern school, with an underlying basis of popular belief (cf.pp.LV/LVI). The country is strewn with large and small *pagodas,* often gilded all over, i.e. reliquaries on the pattern of the dagabas of Ceylon (p.57), but slimmer and rising to a gilded shade of honour, the so-called *Ti.* The chief pagodas (Shwe Dagon, p.259; Arakan, p.273; Shwe Mawdaw, p.262 and Shwe Tsandaw, p.265) are visited by pilgrims from great distances. There are a large number of monasteries *(Kyaung);* according to religious law, each Burmese is supposed to spend a year of his life in a monastery, but this duty is now often symbolically discharged by entering one for a few days only. At festivals, great spectacles *(Pwe)* from legend and saga are performed with dancing. The Indian caste system is unknown in Burma, and women occupy a freer position vis-à-vis their husbands. Both sexes smoke a good deal the fat, light-coloured cigars of local origin, known as "cheroots". – On the E. upland plateaux live the Shan tribes, which are related to the Siamese. They are culturally less advanced than the Burmese, but they do have a literature of their own. They form a N. and S. group of states with the native rulers *(sabwas)* under British control. The Karen in Lower Burma, between the Irrawaddy and the Salween, regard themselves to be the descendants of Chinese conquerors (p.267). Besides these, in the upper Irrawaddy district on the border with India, there are several other offshoots of Mongol type with a still primitive culture.

Burma plays a subordinate role in history. It acquired its culture from India and, in the 3rd c. A.D., its religion also – Buddhism (p.LVI). Among the ancient native part-empires, the *Talaing* of Pegu (p.262) is especially prominent. The Burmese penetrated from the N. In the 5th c., *Prome* (p.264) appeared as the capital of a Burmese empire. It was supplanted in the 7-12th c. by *Pagan* (p.267) and, after the latter's destruction, for a brief period by *Sagaing* (p.269), then, since 1364, *Ava* (p.269). Wars between the kings of Ava and the kings of Toungoo (p.262) and the Talaings of Pegu occupy the succeeding centuries. More recent history begins with the energetic *Alaungpaya* (usually called Alompra), from the peasant class, who made himself king in 1752, extended his kingdom over all of Burma, after conquering the Talaings, and died in 1760 during a campaign against Siam. His second successor *Sinbyushin* (1764-76), who temporarily conquered Siam, moved the capital back to Ava. King *Bodwpaya* (1781-1819) founded Amarapura (p.269) in 1783, conquered Arakan in 1784 and Assam in 1816-17, and brought the empire to the peak of its power. These glories matured in his successors *Bagyidaw* (1819-37), *Tharrawaddy* (1837-46), *Pagan Min* (1846-53), *Mindon Min* (1853-78) who deposed his brother and made Mandalay the capital in 1857, and *Thibaw* (1878-85) who, much given to Caesarist megalomania, constantly increased in courtly ostentation that knew no bounds, in his despotic rule and his pointlessly haughty attitude towards the English. Frontier disputes in Assam led, in 1824-26, to the first Anglo-Burmese wars, which cost Burma the frontier provinces of Assam, Arakan and Tenasserim. The second war of 1852 also put the lower Irrawaddy basin as far as a point above

Prome under English rule. King Thibaw, who had begun his reign with the horrible butchery of his numerous brothers, sisters, stepbrothers and stepsisters, hoped to rid himself of the English by making approaches to the French Empire of Indo-China. He was however taken prisoner by the English in November 1885, without putting up any resistance (p.273), and has since lived in exile near Bombay. The war of 1887-88 against the rebellious Shan tribes extended British domination to include these also.

At the head of the British administration is a lieutenant-governor, who spends the winter at Rangoon and the summer at Maymyo (p.275). The land is divided into the two parts, established in history as *Upper & Lower Burma.* The impetus which it has gained under English rule from the exploitation of its natural resources is quite extraordinary. The pop. had risen (up to 1901) by 18¼% since the first, presumably inexact, count of 1891; and from 1901 to 1911 by a further 15½%. There is a high level of immigration from India and China.

To cover the main routes requires at least 14 days: *Rangoon*, 2 days; railway to *Prome* and boat trip up the *Irrawaddy* to Mandalay, 5 days; *Mandalay*, 3 days; excursion to *Gokteik*, 2 days; return to Rangoon, 2 days. The traveller is also recommended to make the journey from Mandalay to *Bhamo*: going by steamer, returning by rail, or vice versa (6½-7 days). If time permits, one can do the trip to *Moulmein* from Rangoon: 3 days. – There are hotels only in *Rangoon*, *Mandalay* and *Moulmein*, and even in Rangoon these are only of modest pretensions (except those named, in the first instance, on p.257), despite their high prices; likewise in Mandalay; in Moulmein they are poor. Accommodation and food is however of high quality on the Irrawaddy steamers. Otherwise, one must make do with the often primitive Dak bungalows. – Clothing: a tropical suit is the normal wear but, on the steamer journey on the Irrawaddy and the excursion to Gokteik, warmer clothing will be found necessary for the mornings and evenings. One should not forget to take tinted spectacles, as the light is intense. Bedding is a requisite on night journeys by rail (cf.p.XV). One can dispense with the services of a Boy, even if the latter would be welcome as an interpreter.

The most convenient way to travel is to use *Thos.Cook's* circular tickets (p.257): Rangoon-Mandalay return, 1st cl. 76R.3a. – 85R.3a., 2nd cl. 41R.2a. – 45R.10a.; Rangoon-Mandalay-Bhamo, 1st cl. 140R.5a. – 193R.10a. The price depends on whether one uses the Irrawaddy steamers for a shorter or longer period, compared to one's rail travel.

Literature, see p.LXXIII.

Route 33. Rangoon.

The *steamers* moor, according to the state of the tide, either at the piers or out in the river; in the latter case, tenders convey passengers ashore. – The *station* is a long way from the waterfront; during the main travelling season, the visitor is strongly urged to arrive well before the train departs, in order to assure himself a good seat.

Hotels (cf.p.256; pre-booking advisable): Minto Mansions, in a pleasant situation in the Cantonment, similar to the better hotels at Calcutta, 112 Rm., P.10-15R., or 5-10R. out of season; Strand Hot. (prop. Sarkies Bros., who also own the Great Eastern & Oriental Hotel at Penang and Raffles Hot. in Singapore), Strand Rd., near the steamer piers; Grand Hot., also in Strand Rd.; Allendale, a boarding house run on hotel lines, in the Cantonment.

Post & Telegraph, Strand Rd. Postal link with Europe, once a week; last collection for Europe, 7 p.m. on Mon., 5 p.m. for registered mail or, on payment of a late fee (4a.), 8 & 6 p.m. respectively.

Banks: *Bank of Bengal, Chartered Bank of India, Australia & China,* both in Strand Rd.; *National Bank of India,* Phayre St.; *Hongkong & Shanghai Banking Corp.*, Merchant St. near Fytche Square.

Agencies. *North-German Lloyd,* Krüger & Co., Merchant St; *British India Steamship Co. & Bibby Line,* both 74 Phayre St. – Travel Offices: *Thos.Cook & Son,* 71 Phayre St., opp. the new Chief Court.

Trams (1st cl. used by Europeans also). Main routes: 1. from Strand Rd. to the NW suburb Kemmendine (p.264); 2. along Strand Rd., then China St. and Pagoda Rd. to the Shwe Dagon Pagoda (p.259).

Carriages. Hotel carriages: approx. 3R. per hr., 15R. per day. *Tikka Gharries* (ugly closed carriages, whose drivers generally know only a few of the more important places): 1st cl. 1½R. per hr., each succ. hr. 1R.; 2nd cl. 12a., 8a.

Shops. Bookshop: *Myles, Standish & Co.*, 75 Merchant St. – Photographers, curios: *Klier,* Merchant St., not far from Phayre St.; *Hirst,* near Phayre St. – Burmese wood-carvings (the larger pieces imaginative and beautiful, the smaller ones crudely done), in the bazaars in Strand Rd. and China St. – Gold and silverware: the best items are to be found in Godwin St., but supplies are scarce; one can order from models or drawings, but one needs to go in the company of an interpreter; payment for silver items is by weight, with a supplement for the labour which, in the case of exquisite pieces, can double the price.

German consulate: Consul *Carl Kauffeld,* at the firm of Krüger & Co., Merchant St.

Clubs. *German Club*, Commissioner's Rd., one of the most important German clubs in Asia, and playing its part in the social life of Rangoon. – *Pegu*

Club, Prome Rd., for gentlemen only, exclusive; *Gymkhana Club,* Halpin Rd., also for ladies; *Boat Club*, on Royal Lake (p.259).

For a limited visit (1½ days): one should either walk or, around noon, drive through the business quarters, visiting the bazaars and the Sule Pagoda; the Shwe Dagon Pagoda deserves several visits, morning and evening or by moonlight; circular drive through the Cantonment and Dalhousie Park.

Rangoon, capital of Burma, with its 293,300 inhab. and, after Calcutta, Bombay, Madras and Hyderabad, the most populous city in India, lies on lat. 16° 46' N., long. 96° 10' E., 34km from the sea on the *Rangoon River* (which came into being by uniting an arm of the Irrawaddy with the Hlaing), this being joined also by the *Pazundaung* and, from the NE, the broad Pegu which, too, flows to the Sittang delta. The city's original name, *Dagon*, has been preserved in that of the great pagoda (p.259). Rebuilt and renamed in 1755 by King Alompra *(Yangon*, i.e. end of war, cf.p.255), the place remained nonetheless unimportant until the English came (pp.255-6), but then flourished in an extraordinary fashion. Since 1872, the pop. has almost trebled. As a trading town, Rangoon follows immediately after Madras and Karachi. Imports, of a total value of 189,708,523R. (1907-8), cbiefly comprise foodstuffs, luxury goods, cotton yarn and cotton goods, iron and steel, machinery etc. from Europe, mainly England. As far as exports are concerned, (264,087,164R. in 1907-8), rice and rice-flour are by far the most important items, but teak, skins and hides, cotton and petroleum also play their part (p.266).

Of the inhabitants, more than ⅓ are Buddhists, ⅓ Hindus, 1/6th Mohammedans, 1/11th Christians (half of them Europeans and Eurasians, the other half natives). The male pop. outnumbers the female one by more than ¾. In the everyday life of the business quarters, the immigrant elements are particularly noticeable: Hindus, Madrasis (chiefly coolies), Sinhalese, Sikhs (as policemen) and Chinese, the latter often prosperous merchants, or craftsmen. The Burmese live in separate areas: one meets them usually on the way to, and at, the Shwe Dagon Pagoda, to which they lend atmosphere, in their diverse but correct costume.

The business quarters, 5km long, ¾-1km broad, stretch out along the river, bordered to the S. by the busy Strand Rd., with the *Sailors' Home*, the *Custom House*, the *Court House* and the *Post & Telegraph Office* (p.257); to the W., the large building of the *Municipal Bazaar*, busy with its native market. – The next parallel street, Merchant St., contains the most important European businesses, the third, Dalhousie St., public offices: the imposing *Secretariat & Town Hall.* Between these two streets, roughly in the centre of the city, is Fytche Square, a large garden with a pool, bordered on the E. side by the new

Chief Court. In its NW corner rises the Sule Pagoda on its plinth, a typical structure of its kind, dedicated to the Sule Nat (p.LVI), with a beautiful dome rising to a slender spire, and strange chapels and figures round its base. – The W. transverse streets, Mogul St., with several mosques, and China St., with the *Rangoon & Surati Bazaars,* teem with colourful life. – At the N. end of the business quarter lies Montgomerie St. and its W. continuation, Commissioner Rd. In Montgomerie St. are the *Railway Station,* the *English Cathedral,* the *General Hospital* and, further E., *St Paul's Cathedral* (R.C., built in Gothic style). In Commissioner's Rd.: the *Agri-Horticultural Gardens* with Phayre Museum and, to the W., the large *Central Jail.*

N. of the business quarter extends the Cantonment, more spaciously laid out, among its large gardens, with the villas and clubs of the Europeans, and well-maintained shady streets. On the W. side is the impressive *Government House* in its own grounds, the residence of the Lieut.-Governor of Burma, with 3 storeys, a fine drive-way and covered steps. *Jubilee Hall* in Pagoda Rd. is intended for festive gatherings and other purposes. – The E. side of the Cantonment is occupied by **Dalhousie Park* with the *Royal Lake* and, adjoining it to the S., *Victoria Garden,* a masterpiece of English landscape-gardening. Carriage- and bridle-ways surround the lake with its many bays and promontories. There is an extremely charming view of the Shwe Dagon Pagoda, glittering gold, esp. at sunset, but also in the morning hours.

The ***Shwe Dagon Pagoda*, which towers up from the platform of a hill 50m high, stepped in 2 terraces, among palm-trees and thick deciduous trees, and visible afar, is one of the Buddhists' main shrines. It is said to contain eight hairs from Buddha's head and relics of his predecessors, and it is visited by innumerable pilgrims from Burma, India, Ceylon, Siam, Cambodia, China and Korea. Its foundation dates from the 5th or 6th c. B.C., according to the priests. The present structure was completed by King Sinbyushin in 1768. Of the four flights of entrance steps, the W. one is blocked, since the hill would be required to serve the English as a stronghold in the event of a rebellion. The busiest is the S. entrance, opp. Pagoda Rd., at which two enormous winged lions stand guard, the typical decoration for Burmese pagoda steps; they are constructed from brick with a white plaster coating. The staircase, covered since 1903 by a richly carved roof with religious paintings, rises in several stages. In the stalls on each side, candles, artificial flowers, small flags, gold-leaf, pictures illustrating legends etc. are sold as votive offerings or pilgrim souvenirs. We pass through the iron gate of the English fortress and, continuing, reach the platform, 275

X 208m, always crowded with supplicants and donors. At the centre, on a serriform pediment 413m in circumference, stands the giant pagoda, gilded all over, a massive, bell-shaped structure, tapering up in 12 stages to a slender spire which, at a height of 112m, is crowned with the shade-like *Ti.* The gilding (gold leaf below, gold plate above) is said to be worth 300,000R., and has to be renewed every 20-25 years (the last occasion was the winter of 1910-11). The Ti, a votive gift from King Mindon Min (1871), 4m in diameter and of wrought iron, is covered with gold sheet, hung with 1500 small silver and gold bells, whose delicate sound may be heard in the breeze at night, and set with several thousand rubies, emeralds and diamonds, which are of course quite invisible at such a height. Round the pediment on which the pagoda stands, and all over the platform, there is a confusing jumble of temples, chapels (Tazoungs), figures of Buddha and the most fantastic sculptures imaginable of all shapes and sizes, surrounded by palms and holy bo-trees. The different nations, races, representative councils and other groups within the Buddhist world have special holy places here. In decoration, gilding and garish painting alternate with mirrors and coloured glass. The wood-carvings are remarkably rich and exuberant. Bells of all sizes hang from frames. The 800cwt. giant bell of 1775, in the NE corner of the platform, was to be taken as booty to Calcutta in 1852 (p.256), but fell into the river while being loaded and, after vain attempts by the English to lift it, was left to the natives again, who restored it, intact, to its original position. – However bizarre its details may appear to be, the shrine as a whole (with its hordes of supplicants wandering about with rosaries, crouching before the images of Buddha, making offerings of flowers and candles at the altars or sitting about in calm contemplation), is enveloped in an unforgettable atmosphere of sanctity. It is most crowded in the evenings and during festivals. The views, esp. that from the SE corner of the platform, are beautiful; to the NE we see, among other things, the Sacred Lakes to the N. of Dalhousie Park, with many monasteries, temples, a colossal recumbent Buddha etc.

If staying for several days, the visitor should obtain permission to visit one of the large *rice-mills,* which mainly line both banks of the Pazundaung, and one of the *sawmills,* which process the wood for ships and houses, which is floated down the Irrawaddy; the elephants, which were once used to move the trunks have now, in most cases, had to give way to the cheaper machines.

7km E. of Rangoon, on the l. bank of the River Pegu, and overgrown by jungle, are the ruins of the town of *Syriam*, destroyed by King Alompra (p.255), where the Portuguese had trading-posts from 1519, the Dutch in 1631-77 and the English from 1698. The petroleum refineries of the *Burma Oil Co.* are worth a visit (p.266), for which one must seek permission at the agents, Finlay, Fleming & Co. in Rangoon (Strand Rd., Graham's Buildings).

FROM RANGOON TO MOULMEIN.

3-day excursion. Since the rly journey via Pegu (p.262) takes 12½hrs., without leaving any time to visit the town, one will generally do the return journey by steamer: *British India Steam Navigation Co.,* in both directions, Tue., Thu., Sat.; length of journey 9-10hrs., fares 15R. 1st cl., 8R. 2nd cl., return fare 36R. with Cook's tickets. – At *Moulmein* there is an hotel and a Dak bungalow, both unassuming.

The approach from the Gulf of Martaban into the broad estuary of the *Salween* and thence upstream to Moulmein (28M.; 1¼-1½hrs.) is unusually fine. There are hills and islands on both sides, out of whose thick foliage rise many pagodas and monasteries. Sandstone bluffs in the background.

Moulmein or Mulmen, capital of the Tenasserin division and the Amherst district, with about 60,000 inhab., at the confluence of the *Gyaing* and *Ataran* with the Salween (which here divides into E. and S. delta arms) was founded by the English in 1827 as a fortress against Martaban (p.262), and developed rapidly with the export of teak and with shipbuilding. Far outstripped by Rangoon in the last few decades, it still retains some importance in the rice and timber trade. There are several rice- and saw-mills. Its position by the broad, many-islanded expanse of water, among greenery, and against the N. spurs of a hill-chain, which are joined to the E. by the high banks of the Gyaing, is famous as the most beautiful situation in the whole of Indo-China. A steep flight of steps leads up the hill (90m), which is surmounted by whitewashed or gilded pagodas and richly carved chapels (Tazoungs) amid palm-trees, and ever busy with the faithful, praying and making sacrifices. The *Kyaikthalan Pagoda,* at the N. end of the plateau, is 46m high and 115m in circumference at its base; the bell, cast in 1855, bears an inscr. in English. Near the *Usina Pagoda,* to the S., is a group of extremely realistic life-sized wooden figures. Marvellous view.

If time permits, one can visit the rock caves in the sandstone hills in the vicinity of Moulmein, esp. the *Farm Caves,* 10M SE by the Ataran, the *Damathat Caves,* 18M E. by the Gyaing, and the *Pagat Caves,* 26M to the N. by the Salween, all with figures of Buddha and chapels.

Route 34. From Rangoon by train to Mandalay.

386M, narrow-gauge rly, 2 fast trains daily: express in 18¾, mail-train in 20¼hrs., for 30R.2a.6p. 1st cl., 18R.1a.6p. 2nd cl., and 6R.6p. 3rd cl. The traveller who wishes to include *Pegu* should catch the early slow train and, after a 4hr. stop, continue by express, for which he is however advised to book a seat in advance at Rangoon. It is not worth making other stops en route. In the following description, only the stations usesd by the express are named. For meals in the sta. rests., one buys tickets from the guard.

The railway touches on *Pazundaung* (1M), Rangoon's NE suburb, gradually approaches the *River Pegu* and reaches (express in 1¾, slow train in 3hrs.) 47M. *Pegu* (sta. rest.), town of 14,000 inhab. and chief place in its district, allegedly founded in 573 A.D. For centuries it was the capital of the empire of the same name, under the Talaing dynasty (p.255); it was conquered by the Burmese kings of Ava in 1636 and, after a successful revolt by the Talaings (1740-56), was destroyed by King Alompra (p.255), but rebuilt by his son. The sta. lies on the r. bank, the town on the l. bank of the river, both in- and outside the old ramparts (12m thick), on which the Europeans' houses now stand. In the middle of the ramparts, the mighty **Shwe Mawdaw Pagoda* towers up on a mount rising 9m high in 2 terraces. It is 99m in height, gilded all over, shaped like a bell with a slender spire surmounted by a Ti, like the Shwe Dagon Pagoda, and with similar relics; the base, 120m in circumference, is surrounded by a double row of 128 little pagodas about 8m high. Another sight is the recumbent *Giant Buddha* (Shinbinthalyaung), 1-1½ km W. of the sta., discovered in 1881 in the underwood of the primeval forest. It is 55m long, 14m high, recently restored and provided with a protective roof on an iron frame, which is visible from the sta.

From Pegu, a branch-line goes SE round the Gulf of Martaban to *Martaban* (1215M in 8½hrs.), at the confluence of the Salween and Gyaing, once a considerable town, much fought over, but now only an insignificant village. From Martaban there is a steam ferry in ½hr. to Moulmein (p.261).

The monotonous plain, planted mainly with rice, is sprinkled with pagodas. 88M. *Pyuntaza* (sta. rest.) The line approaches the *Sittang,* continuing up its valley. – 166M. *Toungoo* (sta. rest.), town of 15,800 inhab. and seat of the district office, on the r. bank of the river, in the 14-17th c. capital of a kingdom which persisted until 1612 in alternating battles with the kings of Pegu and Ava (p.269). To the W., the *Pegu Yoma Range* can be seen; to the E., the slopes of the Shan Plateau (p.253). 226M. *Pyinmana* (sta. rest.), a thriving town of 14,500 inhab., with extensive teak forests; 275M. *Yamethin* (sta. rest.), chief town of a district. – 306M. *Thazi Junc.*, for the branch to Myingyan (p.268; 75M), built during the famine of 1897-99.- 342M. *Kume Road*, 347M. *Myittha*; 359M. *Kyaukse* (sta. rest.), on the River Zuwayi, chief town of a district; a Buddhist shrine crowns the hill. – The rly crosses the *Myit-ngé*, near its confluence with the Irrawaddy (p.269) and traverses the utterly overgrown ruined site of Amarapura (p.269); 383M. *Myohaung*, junc. for the lines to Sagaing-Myitkyina (p.277) and to Maymyo (p.275); to the l., the Arakan Pagoda, gleaming gold (p.273).

386M. *Mandalay*, see p.270; the sta. is in the European quarter; carriages (tikka gharries), see p.270.

Route 35. From Rangoon by steamer on The Irrawaddy to Mandalay.

The IRRAWADDY FLOTILLA COMPANY (head offices in Glasgow) possesses over 300 large and small steamships which ply on some tributaries and estuarial waters also. *The express ships* are saloon steamers with covered promenade decks, electric lighting and ventilation; they contain 24-30 1st cl. cabins forward and 2nd cl. cabins aft, and steerage in the middle for natives, whose animation and activity are pleasurable to behold; the steamers make only brief halts at the intermediate stopping-places, so that little more than a cursory walk ashore is possible. The *cargo steamers* are designed for freight traffic, but also contain good passenger cabins, which are fitted out only slightly more modestly; they put in to land more often, giving the passenger sufficient time to look around; also, the native activity is more marked, both ashore and on board, where a kind of market goes on, in which many dealers offer their wares on stalls which they hire permanently. The *ferry-boats* ply on the shorter routes. – Since the river is prone to change its course every year because of floods, there is always a pilot on board ship. The navigation channel is marked by buoys and by small zinc plates hung on poles, which glitter in the sunshine. Soundings are frequently taken, the leadsman calling out the depths in a singsong voice. Ships break their journey at night.

The trip from Rangoon to Mandalay (708M) requirs a full week on the express steamers (leaving Wed. & Sat.), or 4½ days, using the rly as far as Prome, where the steamers continue on Sat. & Wed. mornings, (arr. Mandalay Tue., Fri.; arr. Prome Thu., Sat.; arr. Rangoon Sun., Wed.). When going upstream, the ships are less crowded, and one has the sun in one's back, thereby avoiding the blinding reflection of light from the water, two advantages not to be taken lightly. The cargo steamers, which also leave twice a week (Mon., Thu.) take 5 days to reach Prome; thence (Sat., Tue.) to Mandalay in 7 days (arr. Fri., Mon.); downstream, (dep. Mandalay Sun.,

Wed.), 5 days to Prome (arr. Thu., Sun.), thence to Rangoon in 6 days (arr. Wed., Sat.)

The fares are the same on both types of steamer: from Rangoon to Mandalay, 1st cl. cabin 77R., 2nd cl. 38R., deck-space for the Boy 8R.8a.; from Prome to Mandalay, 40R., 20R., 4R.10a., to Rangoon 66R., 33R., 6R.12a. To avoid the unpleasant heat as far as possible, in the cabins facing into the evening sun, the traveller should seek a cabin on the port side for the journey upstream from Prome, and on the starboard side when coming down from Mandalay. At any halt made at an intermediate stopping-place, it is a rule that one may remain aboard from 5 p.m. until 8.30 a.m. the next mornng, and in the case of an early departure the previous evening, one may go aboard up to 10 a.m. – Food good: 1st cl. 4R., 2nd cl. 3R.8a., Boy 8a. per day; pro rata prices if one does not travel for the whole day: chota-hazri 8a.; breakfast in 1st cl. cabin 1R.8a., in 2nd cl., 1R., tiffin 1R.8a.; dinner 2R., 1R.8a.

Most travellers prefer to take the train from Rangoon to Prome: 161M, night fast train in 9¼hrs., for 12R.9a., 7R.8a.; one should present oneself at the station betimes, during the main travel season! Intermediate stations (unimportant): 4M. *Kemmendine*, Rangoon's NW suburb; 77M. *Letpadan*, junc. for the line to Tharawaw (30M)-Henzada-Bassein, see below. – The sta. at *Prome* is on the high bank of the Irrawaddy above the steamer landing-stage. Porters await one's arrival. The express steamer leaves about ¾hr. after the train arrives.

The steamer journey to Prome through the low-lying lands of the Irrawaddy delta takes 3 days, and is fairly monotonous. About 12M below Rangoon, the ship turns W. up a minor arm of the delta, which joins the *River To* or *China Bakir* 2-3M inland of the lighthouse referred to on p.252. Continuing up the To, it reaches *Dedaye* (53M) with its large pagoda, some 7hrs. after leaving Rangoon. Paddy-fields stretch along both banks. The villages lie among cocoa palms and bananas. Beyond (106M) *Ma-ubin* we reach the main course of the *Irrawaddy*. 136M. *Yandoon*, market for salted fish and Ngapi, a fish-paste very popular in Burma. 152M. *Danubya*, with a small gilded pagoda and old Burmese fort, about 70M from the coast, the highest point at which tidal ebb and flow is perceptible. – 196M. *Henzada*, distr. capital with 25,000 inhab., on the l. bank of the river, linked by steam ferry to *Tharramaw* opp., terminus of the branch-line (see above) from Letpadan. From Henzada, the rly runs SW to (82M) *Bassein*, capital of the Irrawaddy division, with 32,000 inhab. and considerable rice export-trade, accessible from Rangoon by direct steamers also. – At (256M) *Myanoung*, the delta comes to an end. Halfway between there and Prome, on the W. shore, is the rock *Akouktuung* (100m above the river), surmounted by a pagoda; in its slopes are artificial caves and old sculptures of Buddha-Gautama. The steamer reaches Prome and remains there during the 3rd night.

311M. *Prome*, on the E. shore of the 1½-2km-broad river, capital of a Burmese kingdom (p.255) in the 5th c. B.C., now capital of a district, rebuilt after the destruction of 1862, with a pop. of 27,400, broad streets, imposing houses (some of 2 storeys) and much bustle and activity. Not a great deal of trading is done (Ngapi, a fish-paste, see p.264). More important is the manufacture of silk clothes and objects varnished in gold. Rising up from a hill 42m high and thickly wooded, is the *Shwe Sandaw Pagoda,* one of the largest in Lower Burma. 4 flights of steps in brick, between winged lions, lead up to the square platform, whose edge is lined with innumerable shrines and quarters for pilgrims (zeyat), bell frames and flagpoles. In the middle of a circle of Buddhist chapels rises the graceful pagoda, 50m high, last restored and regilded in 1858 by voluntary contributions. At the corners of the square plinth are 4 smaller pagodas. The whole complex, with its wealth of artistic wood-carvings, its colourful adornment in glass and faïence, painting and gilding, framed by the greenery of trees and bushes, and enlivened by supplicants and sacrificers, echoes on a smaller scale the impression made by the great Pagoda at Rangoon.

Upstream from Prome, the voyage offers the traveller an almost continuous succession of delightful scenery. The broad Irrawaddy flows majestically on, in the sunshine. On its waters we see rowing- and sailing-boats with pleasingly curved lines, fishermen throwing out their nets, and enormous rafts of teak trunks with neat little huts on them, also of other kinds of wood, e.g. iron- or Pykiado wood (Xylia dolabriformis) from the forests of the Shan estates, which is kept afloat by being placed on a bed of bamboo. The ranges of hills in the foreground are covered with evergreen bushes, from whose subdued colours the red blossoms of the kapok tree *Bombax malabaricum* shine out in splendour, and which the English are wont to call “Flames of the Forest”. Scattered attractively among all these are various types of palm-tree, notably Palmyra palms (p.18). The more distant heights bear deciduous trees, partly bare in the dry travelling season. To remove the withered undergrowth and fertilise the soil, the natives light fires which do not however harm the tall trees: this makes a fantastic spectacle by night, but towards April, when the fires are more numerous and fill the entire atmosphere with smoke, they become a great nuisance to the traveller. Lining the shores, whose steep sides often permit us to see the floodwater mark, are numerous villages with houses built on piles, and natives bathing, or washing their cattle. There is an astonishing number of pagodas of all sizes, singly and in groups, new or ruinous since, from a religious point of view, only the erecting of a pagoda is meritorious, its maintenance is not. – The steamer’s first stop, 5½hrs. after leaving

Prome, is (355M) *Thayetmyo*, on the W. bank, a district capital with 15,800 inhab., since the incorporation of Lower Burma an important English frontier garrison, now on the decline, since the majority of the troops have been posted elsewhere.

– From here, a 6hr. journey to (403M) *Minhla*, also on the W. bank, with 2550 inhab., formerly a frontier town with an old Burmese fort.

420M. *Magwe,* with 6200 inhab., on the E. bank; 423M. *Minbu* with 5780 inhab., on the W. bank, both chief towns of districts. On the steep, high bank we see rows of pagodas such as are found far and wide in this region. At Minbu the pilgrims go ashore to pay their respects to Buddha's footprint in a rock recognisable by its tall wooden pagoda spire. Numerous ox-carts wait for them on the bank. Occasionally, because of displacements of the river bed during the dry season, the steamers anchor at night 2M below Minbu.

The valley has flattened out into a wide, open plain. The river may sometimes be 3-4km broad, with many sandbanks and, frequently, strong currents. The mountain range to the SW provides a rampart against the monsoon. The lack of rain makes itself evident in the appearance of the land. The vegetation becomes dry and sparser. Palms gradually disappear. The voyage becomes hot and monotonous.

458M. *Yenan-gyaung,* on the E. bank, centre of the Burmese petroleum industry. Of its total output, almost one third (65-70 mill.gallons, 295-318 mill.litres), is obtained here. The petroleum wells have been known to the natives for centuries (the place-name means "stinking stream"), and have been in the possession of the kings of Burma since the middle of the 18th c. Now, four companies are involved in their exploitation, the Twinza, the Aungban, the Yenangyaung and the Burma Oil Company. On the shore and further inland, we see large modern derricks. The yield from the boreholes tends to decrease after lengthy operation.

483M. *Sinbyugyun* (W. bank), hidden away behind the shore vegetation. Not far upriver, a large new pagoda with flights of steps and winged lions appears on the E. bank.

508M. *Salemyo* (E. bank), where the steamer spends the second night after leaving Prome. – The river is very broad and placid. On the E. horizon, 40km away, the silhouette of the extinct volcano *Popa* (1482m) rises out of the plain. To the NW, when conditions are clear, Mount Victoria (p.253) is visible in the Arakan range.

545M. *Yenangyat* (W. bank), with petroleum wells which are however practically exhausted. The derricks, on the jagged and sparsely vegetated heights, remind one, from afar, of pagodas in their appearance. Between them are red iron tanks. A pipe-line on the bank.

The river broadens to 5km and, in the dry season, breaks up into several arms between sandy islands. On the E. bank, in a serrated line, we see the pagodas at Pagan, past which our ship travels for a long time. The landing-place is about 4km upstream, near the large village.

563M. *Nyaungu.* The express steamer stops for only ½hr, The traveller wishing to visit the famous ruined site (admittedly of more interest to the archaeologist than the tourist), must break his journey here. The imposing government Rest-house, visible on the edge of the shore, offers good accommodation.

Pagan was capital of the Burmese empire from the 7th to the 12th c., under the royal house of the same name, and has changed its position often, like Delhi (p.177), during the course of time. It reached its peak during the reign of kings Anawrata and Kyansittha, in the 11th c. After being plundered by a Chinese army in 1281, the town became desolate and, from the beginning of the 17th c., sank into total oblivion. The ruins stretch across a shore plateau (which is furrowed by gullies), amid cacti, tamarisks and jujubes (Sisyphus jujuba, called "wild plum" by the English), the site measuring 25km in length and 1½-3km in width. There are around 1000 shrines, some bell-shaped pagodas, others temples, cruciform in plan, with vaulted chambers and a central tower like a pagoda. In the decoration, Indian influence is everywhere apparent. Some shrines, e.g. the Ananda Temple, are still in a good state of repair, and are visited by the faithful. Here and there, a few Buddhist monasteries have sprung up.

Only three of the most important buildings are mentioned here. From Nyangu, we come firstly to the slender, richly-gilded *Shwe Zigon Pagoda*, built by King Anawrata, in a dominant position on a slight rise. The platform upon which it stands is picturesquely strewn with a number of small pagodas, stone basins for holy water, priests' dwellings and flagpoles. – About 3½km to the SW, the remains are preserved of city walls dating from the latter period of the Pagan kings.

To the E., outside this wall, rises the beautiful *Ananda Temple,* built by Kyansittha and named after Buddha's favourite disciple Ananda. It is 62m square, cruciform, rising in six shallow steps, with a slender central dome running to a spire 51m high. Four gates lead to the interior, which consists of four high corridors lit by windows, each corridor ending in a chamber with a skylight; in the chambers are gilded wooden figures, 9m high, representing the Buddha and his three predecessors; small sacred figures rest in niches. The minor fragments of sculpture are kept in a museum. Inside the old city walls is the *Thatpyinnyu Temple*, 56m square and 61m high, built 50 years later.

583M. *Pakokku*, stretching in a thin line along the W. bank, among tamarinds, is, after Mandalay, the largest town in Upper Burma, with its 19,500 inhab., and chief town of a district. There are important shipyards, silk-weaving, wood-carving and presses for sesame oil. 12M upstream, the *Chindwin*, its largest tributary, joins the Irrawaddy from the NW, used by a weekly steamer fitted out for passengers also, going as far as *Kindat* (274M, 6 days) in the dry season and *Homalin* (330M) in the wet season.

618M. *Myingyan* (74m above sea-level), on the E. shore of the Irrawaddy, centre of a district, with 16,000 inhab. and several brass foundries, which produce idols, bells, gongs, etc. (Railway to Thazi, see p.263). The express steamer generally ties up here for the night but, if the water-level is low, it anchors 3M downstream.

The extensive alluvial basin of the middle Irrawaddy, which begins before Myingyan, while still belonging to the rainless area (p.266), has a more fertile soil and richer vegetation. Palms are more in evidence here, likewise the fine tall peepul (Ficus religiosa), with its peculiar root formation.

The river valley gradually turns eastward. After a journey of 6-8hrs., the hill-chain of Sagaing, liberally sprinkled with pagodas, comes into view. The narrow and constricted navigation channel between Sagaing and Ava (see below) is not without its perils. In 1885, the Burmese tried vainly to block the way of the British flotilla carrying troops for the conquest of Mandalay (p.256).

The express steamers pass by (680M) *Sagaing* without stopping. The town of 9600 inhab., situated on the N. bank, is the administrative centre of a division and a district (steam-ferry to Amarapura and railway to Myitkyina, see p.277). Rising up against the hills to the N. are the ruins of the old town, which was a royal seat in 1315-65, and again in 1733-60. Countless pagodas and monasteries (white in colour or, where the plaster has fallen off, gleaming red, often extremely picturesque in style and position) serve as a reminder of Sagaing's period of glory. The most considerable group of buildings surmounts the height above the river. In the depression, not far from Ywataung (p.277) is the white, bell-shaped *Kaung-hmu-daw Pagoda*, built in 1636.

At the ruined town of *Ava*, opposite Sagaing, the *Myit-ngé* (p.276) flows into the Irrawaddy. Ava was the capital of the Burmese empire from 1364 onwards, which warred continually with the kings of Toungoo (p.262) and the Talaings of Pegu, being destroyed by the latter in 1752. Reconstructed again in 1766 by King Sinbyushin, son of Alompra, it became the residence until 1783 and, once again in 1822-37, under King Bagyidaw. The town was surrounded by a canal, and its double circle of ramparts is still visible. The whole area is covered by ruinous pagodas and vestiges of palaces lying in dense thickets of giant tamarind trees, and covered in undergrowth. There is a well-preserved complex of ruined buildings on a platform jutting out close by the river, with parts of a royal palace, and a magnificent view of Sagaing and towards Amarapura.

The river valley curves round to the N. again. On the r., the railway station *Amarapura Shore* (p.277) and, rising out of the greenery on the bank, the white pagodas of *Amarapura*, the penultimate capital of the kings of Burma (p.255), founded in 1783. Despite its name, which means "town of the immortals" or "immortal town", it endured for barely three-quarters of a century, and has virtually disappeared, apart from innumerable pagodas and their remains. The site is covered by dense undergrowth. The dwellings were of the same flimsy construction as those of present-day Mandalay (p.271), which accounts for the ease with which the capitals could be transferred from one place to another.

Worthy of mention are only: the great *Patodawgyi Pagoda,* built in 1818, close to the railway line to Mandalay, and the *Kyauk-taw-gyi Pagoda,* built in 1850. The lake, which once lapped against the S. side of the town, is now dry. To the W. of this, nearer to the Irrawaddy, lies the present town, which numbers 9100 inhab. In the distance, we see the golden Arakan Pagoda and the rocky Mandalay Hill, with the scarp of the Shan plateau on the horizon (p.275). at about 3 or 4 p.m., our express steamer reaches:-

708M. *Mandalay*, and ties up at one of the projecting pontoons, whence gangways lead to the shore, which is subject to constant changes of profile. The town is remote from the river, and not visible here. Transport is provided by a tram, which however does not pass the hotels. Carriages (Tikka gharries, see below) are usually available. Description of the drive, see p.271.

Because of the awkward landing and embarkation arrangements, one should avoid going on board in darkness, when departing from Mandalay.

Route 36. Mandalay.

HOTELS: Salween House, usually fully booked during the travelling season (cf.p.256), P. 10-12R. Better is the Circuit House, built for English officials, which may be used only with a recommendation from the government; one takes one's own bedding; food may be ordered in advance from the butler. Rm. for non-officials 2R., sweeper and waterman 8a. apiece, tea 4a., breakfast 1R.8a. dinner 2R. Similar to this is the Dak bungalow at the sta.

If need be, one can spend the night on the Irrawaddy steamers (P. 10R.), but this is most inconvenient because of the distance, the problems of returning in darkness and the tricky conditions on the river shore.

TRAM (cf.p.257): from the steamer pier through B road to the Clock Tower (p.271) and S. along Bazaar Rd., which intersects here. Through tickets 3a.

CARRIAGES (Tikka gharries, cf.p.257): first hr. 12a. by day, 1R. at night; each succ. hr. 8a., 12a.; half-day (6hrs.) 3R., whole day 5R.; in the locality, first mile 8a., each succ. mile 4a.

POST OFFICE, to the W. of the Fort, in C road; last collection for Europe Sunday morning at 10.30, but 5 p.m. Saturday for registered items. – TELEGRAPH OFFICE, 25th St.

PHOTOGRAPHERS: *American Photograph Company,* 26th St.; *Samuel*, near the Post Office.

CLIMATE. The mean annual temperature is 27·2°C. The coolest days are in December, when the thermometer can sink to 12·8°. The mean temp. is 21·7° in Jan., and 32·8° in Apr. (Highest daytime temp. 43·9°).

If time is limited, 2-3 days suffice. The most important sights are: the former *Royal Palace* (p.272), open from 6 a.m. to 6 p.m., without charge; the *Queen's Golden Monastery* (p.273), the *Arakan Pagoda* (p.273), the *Kuthodaw* (p.274) and *Mandalay Hill* (p.274). For longer distances it is advisable to take a carriage. One should use the morning and evenng hours to best advantage. Noontide is exhausting because of the heat and blinding light. – It is well worth making the excursion by train to *Sagaing & Ava* (p.269; 1 day), and esp. to *Gokteik* (p.275; 2 days).

Mandalay (96m above sea-level), town of 138,000 inhab., administrative centre of the division and district of the same name, is situated in a 13km-broad plain between the Irrawaddy and the W. scarp of the Shan plateau. It is dominated by a solitary rocky height to the NE (p.274) and was the capital of the kingdom of Burma from its foundation by Mindon Min in 1857 to its occupation by British troops in 1885 (cf.p.256), having during that period a population of about 186,000 inhab. As the last place where native art flourished on a large scale, Mandalay is all the more interesting, because most of its buildings are going to rack and ruin on account of their flimsy construction. The town is protected from flooding from the Irrawaddy by dykes all round, to a distance measuring 10 X 5km. It consists of the Old Town, the present Fort and 60 transverse and 40 longitudinal streets laid out like a chess-board. The streets are all designated by numbers; only a few bear special names as well; thus, 35th St. is called A Road, 30th St. is Court House Rd., 26th is B Rd., the 22nd C Rd. and the 84th Bazaar Rd. Apart from the business streets, the houses are mainly built of plaited bamboo and are surrounded by gardens.

The European Quarter, to the W. and S. of the Fort, with the sta. and hotels, is usually reached by taking B Rd. from the steamer landing. This road passes the *Eindaw-ya Pagoda*, 35m tall and gilded (built in 1847) and crosses the *Shwe-ta-chaung Canal*, which passes through the town from N. to S. At the *Clock Tower*, erected in 1898 for Queen Victoria's Jubilee (60 years of rule), the tram turns S. into 84th or Bazaar St., in which is the large *Zegyo Bazaar*, a modern market-hall, renovated in 1897 after a fire, and centre of native business life. Apart from fruit, vegetables and other foodstuffs, industrial products are on sale: silk materials, lacquer-work, silverware and genuine and imitation rubies etc. The sellers are mainly women. Worth a visit, preferably 6-8 a.m. To the E. of the Clock Tower stands the *R.C. Cathedral*, completed in 1898 at the expense of a native convert.

The *Fort* (Fort Dufferin), a square area 8km in perimeter, with almost 9m-high brick enclosing walls, 12 gates and 48 wooden watch-towers, surrounded by its moat (60m wide and covered with lotus flowers), is the original old city founded by Mindon Min, the king's residence being at its centre. Empty expanses of grass now cover the spot where the natives' bamboo houses were removed after the English occupation of 1887. Apart from the Palace, the Fort now contains only *Government House* (residence of the Brit. Commissioner), the barracks and officers' dwelling for one British and two native regts., a large *Jail,* a *Hospital* (built in 1891) and the pleasant ground of the *Upper Burma Club.*

The **former Palace*, a strange and fantastic wooden building, exuberant in its gilding and artistic carvings, with a seven-storey tower 78m high, the "centre of the world", was moved here from Amarapura by Mindon Min and extended by Thibaw. Since then it fell partly into ruin, but was restored in 1898-1900 and, at an expense of 100,000R., regilded and painted. It is now undergoing further restoration. The area was formerly enclosed by a palisade fence 600m. square, of which only a vestige remains. The main entrance is on the E. side. In the forecourt, r., the pretty bell-tower *Bahosin,* with a wooden roof on a stone substructure, where the hours of the watch were struck; on the l., the temple tower *Shwedaw-zin,* said to enshrine a tooth of the Buddha, and built entirely of stone with a bold, steep staircase. To the N. of the Bahosin is *Mindon Min's Tomb,* well preserved and completely covered with glass mosaic; the graceful wooden pavilions to r. and l. are, alas, visibly destined for extinction. S. of the Shwedaw-zin is **Thibaw's Monastery,* a miniature building erected on the site of an earlier one, in which King Thibaw served the customary novitiate of a Buddhist monk (cf.pp.254-5), before ascending the throne. It is a graceful wooden structure on a platform, with glass mosaics and lavish carvings, very delicate in brown and silver, but unfortunately also going to ruin.

An open flight of steps, between two enormous old cannon, leads from the E. to the wooden platform (3·35m high, 150m wide and 275m long), on which the Royal Palace stands. We enter firstly the *Great Throne-room,* a hall 87m long, its flat roof, gleaming gold, supported by gilded teak pillars; jutting out from the red background (and designated as the most important place in the Palace by the tower rising above it outside, see above) is the dais for the Lion Throne, now in Calcutta (p.250). In the pillared halls to r. and l., the dignitaries of the empire used to foregather. Adjacent to the Great Throne-room is a confusing number of halls and rooms, some gilded all over, some decorated with mirrors and glass mosaics, several *audience chambers* with smaller thrones, the *State Council chamber*, the king's and queen's *bedrooms, tea rooms, theatres* etc. At the W. end of the Palace is the so-called *Ladies' Hall,* entirely gilded, with the "Lily Throne", where the queen received the dignitaries' wives once a year. – We can gain a fine view of the whole complex, and of the town and plain, from the *look-*

out tower at the SE corner of the Palace; a spiral staircase running round the outside of it leads to the platform (24m).

The *Royal Gardens,* along the two main façades of the Palace, with thick arboreal foliage, stone-girt water-courses, pools choked with lotus flowers and rocks piled up in Chinese taste, are neglected. The best maintained is the garden on the S. side, in which a tablet on the former summer-house recalls the capture of King Thibaw. Not far from the S. entrance gate of the Palace is a small *Museum,* with life-size figures in court dress, court insignia and photographs of the royal family.

The SW quarter of the town contains several outstanding buildings. S. of Zegyo Bazaar (p.271) is the *Thetkya-thiha Pagoda*, with a 3·9m-tall figure of Buddha, cast in brass in 1824, and two modern *Chinese temples,* usually called "Chinese Joss Houses"; the N. one, built by a Chinese merchant from the province Yun-nan (p.253), is regarded as the finest of its kind in Burma.

Further S. is the ***Queen's Golden Monastery,* founded by queen Supayalat, Thibaw's wife, and surrounded by smaller subsidiary monasteries founded by courtiers. The whole building (constructed of teak), in which imaginative style and extravagant richness of pictorial carving unite in a harmonious whole, displays Burmese art in Mandalay at its peak. Upon courteous request, one of the monks will show the interior (no remuneration necessary).

On the S. edge of the town rises the **Arakan Pagoda,* built by King Bodaw-Paya to house the 3·8m-tall figure of Buddha plundered from Arakan in 1784. After the Shwe Dagon Pagoda (p.259), to which it is admittedly greatly inferior in beauty and size, it is the most notable pagoda in Burma, and was selected for that reason to be the resting-place of the Buddha relics found in 1909 at Peshawar (p.207). The central structure, rising like a series of steps, was restored and richly gilded after a fire in 1884. The main entrance is on the E. side. Long galleries, partly covered with frightening painted depictions of hell, and in which sacrificial gifts are sold, lead to the large gilded alcove in the interior, which contains the 3·83m-tall sacred structure. In the vaulted arcades, pilgrims throng with votive offerings, esp. candles, which are placed by the statue, and gold-leaf, which is stuck all over the figure. The alcove is closed at sunset. – To the SE of the central building is a pool containing turtles. To the NW, a courtyard, in which a number of remarkable bronzes are set up, also carried off from Arakan, incl. a three-headed elephant.

There are many noteworthy things to see in the NE part of the town. Outside the E. gate of the Fort, the richly carved monastery *Taik-daw,* formerly the residence of the spiritual leader of the Buddhists in Burma. Further N., the ruins of the *Atumashi Pagoda* (i.e. "incomparable pagoda"), which burnt down in 1892 and, to the E. of this, the "Glass Monastery" *Ham Kyaung,* built by Mindon's favourite wife and decorated on the inside with mirrors and gilt. – Then we reach King Mindon's most remarkable piece of architecture, the **Kuthodaw,* a pretty pagoda built in stone, 30m tall, with 729 whitewashed smaller pagodas surrounded by a square retaining wall of side 250m. The entrance is to the S. The small pagodas are open at the front, and each contains a marble slab as tall as a man, with a continuous text from the Buddhist holy scriptures, according to the canonic version which the king caused to be authorised by a council of scholar-priests. It therefore presents a gigantic Burmese bible in stone. At the foot of the central pagoda are remains of one of the ceremonial barges in which King Thibaw undertook trips around the moat (p.271).

To the NW of the Kuthodaw, **Mandalay Hill* (291m above sea-level) rises 195m above the plain. It is a bare island of rock, frequented by pilgrims from all over Burma. At the S. access point are stalls with the usual pilgrim articles and food. To the W. of these, the white-painted *Kyauk Taw Gyi Pagoda,* which since 1864 has enshrined a colossal marble statue of Buddha, richly carved. The ugly brick staircase leading up is roofed with corrugated iron and was, like several other structures on the hill, made only in recent years by the holy man Ukanti ("he who dwells at the top") with donations from pilgrims. Each step is paid for by a believer, whose name is fixed to the roof above it. Just below the summit is a large temple hall with a huge gilded marble Buddha, originally put up by King Mindon, and renovated after a fire in 1892. The figure is 7·8m tall, perhaps the largest marble monolith in the world; it points a finger towards the king's residence; in front of it, the kneeling figure of a monk. Pilgrims from the various ethnic groups in Burma, monks in lemon-yellow and nuns in pale yellow robes (both with shaven heads and therefore often only to be distinguished by the colour of their garb) offer up their prayers. A little higher up is a large hall, Ukanti's dwelling. On the summit are some pagodas and a bell. In clear conditions, there is a panoramic view of Mandalay and the plain with its rice-fields, and the broad course of the Irrawaddy: to the SE, the Kuthodaw, to the SW the race-course; to the S., the Kyauk Taw Gyi Pagoda and the vast terrain occupied by the Fort; in the distance, the golden Arakan Pagoda and, to the SW, the numerous pagodas at Amarapura and Ava, and on the hills at Sagaing. To the E., the plain is bordered by the mountains at Maymyo and Gokteik (p.275).

If we descend on the W. side, which is also provided with a brick staircase, we may visit *Salin Monastery* by the SE corner of the race-course, built by a princess in 1875 and named after her. Fine wood-carvings.

Route 37. From Mandalay to Gokteik.

Two days. The excursion pemits one to gain an insight into the uplands of the Shan states, while brushing against the frontiers of civilisation. The Gokteik gorge counts as one of Asia's natural wonders. The splendid freshness of the forests is doubly beneficial after the dustiness of Mandalay. – Rly to Lashio (originally laid down as the starting-point of a major connecting line to China): return fare to Gokteik (8½hrs.), ticket valid for 3 days: 1st cl. 23R.1a., 2nd cl. 11R.8a., 3rd cl. for the Boy, 5R.1a.6p. Depart on the early train; dining-car as far as Sedaw, but one does better to breakfast at *Maymyo* (pre-order by telegraph, also seats on the train for the next part of the journey). Arrival at *Gokteik* in the afternoon, where one can find good food and accommodation in the Dak bungalow owned by the rly. (It is necessary to warn the station master at Gokteik by telegraph from Mandalay, and a cook will be sent up from Maymyo with provisions). Return the next morning; lunch at Maymyo; arrival in Mandalay approx. 8 p.m.

At (3M) *Myohaung*, the rly branches off E. from the main line to Rangoon and passes firstly through the plain, which is rich in bushes and trees, but very dusty in the dry season. Only the most important stops will be mentioned.

16M. *Sedaw*, where a second locomotive is taken on for the steep ascent (1:25) up the long mountain-face, with reversing stations (p.104) and, in clear weather, a progressively more splendid view. At the top, the journey continues, still ascending, across the undulating limestone plateau, which is covered with deciduous forest and bamboo, and criss-crossed by streams. Numerous villages built on piles; the Shan people in various costumes, with large hats.

42M. *Maymyo* (1061m; sta. rest., see above), during the hot season the summer residence of the Lieut.-governor of Burma, and meeting-place for English society, in the manner of Indian hill stations, but devoid of interest in winter. – At Maymyo, carriages are changed. There is an hour's stop.

The landscape becomes more varied. It takes another 3hrs. to reach Gokteik; long before our arrival, we glimpse, l., the deeply-cut ravine and the viaduct at Gokteik (pron. Go-take), to which the line then descends.

83M. Station *Gokteik Viaduct* (915m), amid magnificent jungle. The Dak bungalow is in an attractive situation, 5min from the sta. (see above). Below the latter, the continuation of the railway line crosses the huge *Gokteik Gorge, which the *Chung-zoun,* a tributary of the Myit-ngé, has cut through the mountains. The lattice bridge, constructed in 1903-4 by the American Pennsylvania Steel Co., to the designs of the English engineers A.M.Rendel & Co., has a total length of 689m, and rests on 15 supports (up to 97m high), which in their turn stand on the natural travertine arch, beneath which flows the river, invisible from the edge of the valley. The height of the track above the river bed is more than 250m. There is a pleasant stroll to be had across the bridge and following the railway along the slope on the other side, with views of the jungle in the ravine and the daringly executed bridge structure.

The visit to the ravine (cave) takes about 2hrs. with a guide (1R.) At the entrance to the bridge, an easy path zigzags down. Splendid vegetation: dense treetops, lianas, ferns and, on the boulders, moss and colourful lichens. The river cavity is uncommonly magnificent, and has been made accessible by means of fixed planks for some distance. The river roars down over the rocks in mighty cataracts. Alongside it, trickling water has deposited sinter terraces and basins with moss-covered stalactites and stalagmites. The floor is slippery in places from the guano left by the numerous swallows which populate the gorge. It is possible to proceed to the point where the other end of the gorge becomes visible. The effects of light at sunset are wonderful. – One is enjoined to exercise caution when taking walks in the surroundings after nightfall, since bears and panthers are by no means uncommon in the jungle.

The extremely rewarding excursion to the waterfalls of the Myit-ngé at Manpwe takes almost a further 3 days from Gokteik, but should not be undertaken without first warning the rly administration at Mandalay concerning food and accommodation: one takes the afternoon train from Gokteik, finally ascending the Myit-ngé valley to *Hsipaw* (57M.; 4½hrs.), where one can spend the night at the Dak bungalow or aboard the train; thence by the early train to *Manpwe* (35M; 4hrs.) The Myit-ngé has formed in the jungle a long series of rapids and falls, the finest being the 15-40m-high falls, 8km below the sta., with a Dak bungalow built nearby by the rly co. – Terminus of the rly, 6M further on and 181M from Mandalay, is *Lashio*, residence of the British Superintendent of the 5 northern Shan states (p.253).

Route 38. From Mandalay to Bhamo.

The outward journey by rail to Katha, and return on the Irrawaddy, takes 5½-6½ days, if one uses the express steamer and spends a day at Bhamo, or 6-7 days if one goes by river and returns by rail; if the cargo steamer is used, the times will increase to 9-10 days and 7-8 days respectively. For this reason, the cargo boat should be chosen only for the journey downstream. Otherwise, the advantage of travelling upriver is that one has the sun at one's back, and the landscape is therefore more favourably illuminated (cf.p.263). Warmer clothing is desirable for the morning and evening hours on board.

Route 38a. By rail to Katha.

227M. (The line Mandalay-Myitkyina), only a through train, which does however stop at every sta.; journey time 20hrs., fares 17R.4a.3p. 1st cl., 10R.5a.9p. for 2nd and 6R.7a.3p. for 3rd (for the Boy). Little comfort, and the service rather slack. Meal tickets are obtained from the guard. – Arrival at *Katha* about 9 a.m.; from there, ½hr. later, the ferry steamer leaves, tying up at night and reaching *Bhamo* the next morning: distance 110M; journey downstream from Bhamo to Katha, 8½hrs.; fares 17R.3a., 6R.14a.,3R.7a.

At (3M) *Myohaung* (p.263), the line branches W. from the main one (Mandalay-Rangoon) and, after (6M) *Amarapura* (p.269), turns towards the Irrawaddy, which it reaches at (9M) *Amarapura Shore*. From here (or, if the water-level is low, from the sta. *Ferry Shore*, a little further on), we cross the river on the steam ferry (½hr.; rest. on board) to:-

13M. *Sagaing* (p;269), where we board the train to Myitkyina.

16M. *Ywataung*, with large rly workshops, junc. for the branch to Alon; in the distance, l., the white Kaung-hmu-daw pagoda (p.269). – Monotonous scenery with paddy-fields. – 56M. *Shwebo* (sta. rest.), a town with 9600 inhab, administrative centre for the district of the same name, birthplace of Alompra, who assumed kingship here in 1752 (p.255). – 166M. *Wuntho* (sta. rest.) – 212M. *Naba Junction* (sta. rest.); change of coaches for the 15M-long branch-line through jungle across the Gangaw Hills to (227M) *Katha*, on the r. bank of the Irrawaddy, see p.279. The sta. is close to the river by the pier for the local steamer to Bhamo (see above).

The main line continues N. from Naba to (334M) *Myitkyina*, district capital, with 3600 inhab. and trade with China, on the r. shore of the Irrawaddy, 30M below the confluence of the *N'maikha* and the *Malikha*, which form the Irrawaddy.

Route 38b. Steamer journey on the Irrawaddy.

The express and cargo steamers of the Irrawaddy Flotilla Co., which ply once a week between Mandalay and Bhamo, are just as well-appointed as those on the lower part of the river (p.263). Express steamers: dep. Mandalay Wed. 8 a.m. (one should go on board early the previous evening, cf.p.270), arr. Bhamo Fri. 6 p.m.; in the other direction, dep. Bhamo Sat. 12 noon, arr. Mandalay Mon. 4 p.m. Cargo steamers: dep. Mandalay Sun., arr. at Bhamo Sat.; in the other direction, dep. Bhamo Mon., arr. Mandalay Thu. Fares for both steamers up- and down-stream are the same: 1st cl. cabin 40R., 2nd cl. 20R., place on deck for the Boy, 5R.10a.; food, see p.264. – When the dry season has set in (March), navigation is often impeded.

The steamer trip at first offers much the same charm as that below Mandalay. In places, the river is as broad as a lake, the scenery idyllically beautiful, the vegetation richer, as the dryness of Upper Burma decreases.

On the E. shore, 1½hrs. after departure, at *Mingun,* are the remains of the huge brick pagoda begun in 1795 by King Bodawpaya, intended to be the largest in the world, but attaining only one third of its planned height (area 137 sq.m; height reached, almost 50m). To its r., by the river, a giant bell of 1600cwt., 3·66m high and 4·95m in diameter at its mouth.

On each bank, villages of no importance: 45M. *Sheinmaga* on the W. bank; 70M. *Singu,* 75M. *Kyaukmyaung,* both on the E. bank. Everywhere, there is lively native bustle at the arrival of the steamer. The express boat takes about 9hrs. from Mandalay to Kyaukmaung.

After 1 hr's journey, the steamer reaches the N. end of the great alluvial plain. The river narrows. The mountains become higher, up to 600m on the E. shore. The red "flames of the forest" (p.265) shine in great beauty out of their thick foliage. We are here in the lowest defile of the Irrawaddy, known as the Third Defile. The few villages (85M. *Ma-u*; 90M. *Kabwet*) are charmingly positioned. Below Thabeikkyin, on an island, is the pagoda of *Thihadaw.*

115M. *Thabeikkyin* (E. bank), at the foot of a wooded promontory crowned with several pagodas, is the stopping-place for the Mogok gem mines.

From Thabeikkyin to Mogok 61M, motor car daily, in 6-7hrs. (30R. per passenger). The road, which winds both up and down, is scenically beautiful. Mogok (1200m above sea-level), where accommodation may be had in a staffed Dak bungalow, consists of several villages, comprising 6000 inhab. in all. The gem fields are worked mainly by the *Ruby Mines Co.,* using modern machinery and employing over 1600 people. In 1904, the yield was 199,238 carats of rubies (to a value of 1,300,000R.), 11,955 carats of sapphires and 16,020 carats of spinels. About ⅔ of the exploited gems go to London.

The steamer passes through the upper end of the defile and then anchors for the night, continuing the next morning at first light.

The river-bed broadens. The number of settlements is small. The cargo steamer calls at (130M) *Malé,* then (140M) *Kyanhnyat* on the W. bank, and (160M) *Tagaung* on the E., which was capital of a kingdom for some centuries before and after Christ. The scanty remains are enveloped by thick vegetation. The two pagodas date from King Alompra's reign (p.255). – The express steamer continues to (190M) *Tigyaing,* on the W. bank, with 1600 inhab., prettily situated among palm-trees by the S. spurs of the *Gangaw Hills,* and surrounded by pagodas; opp., on the E. bank, *Mya-daung,* also with pagodas. There is a picturesque view of the broad expanse of water, busy with fishing boats and enlivened by numerous water-birds. Above Mya-daung, the *Shweli* enters the Irrawaddy. Dense jungle stretches from the shore to the Gangaw Hills, which follow the river for a distance. The fauna is rich here, monkeys, peacocks and eagles often to be seen. At Katha, the Gangaw Hills attain a height of more than 850m.

210M. *Katha,* terminus of the railway mentioned on p.277 and usually the second night-stop for the express steamer. It is the chief place of a district, with 2900 inhab., and stretches out along the W. bank.

The third day's travel is the finest. The river, up to 4km in width, and frequently divided by islands, describes a great arc. The shores are covered with Kaing grass, 3-3½m high. – 240M. *Moda.* – 265M. *Shwegu,* in a charming position on the high S. shore, reached by wooden steps. Above are several gilded pagodas among palm-trees. The place consists of scattered groups of houses, with 2500 inhab. in total. In the river is a large sandy island which is the location, every Spring, of a large religious festival: it is then entirely covered with huts, and all kinds of popular entertainments take place (p.255).

After a journey of ¾hr. from Shwegu, the steamer reaches the **Middle (Second) Defile,* only 8km long, but cut deeply through the mountains. At the narrowest point, a steep rock juts out on the N. side, 180-190m above the river which washes round it, and which at this point is barely more than 100m wide and about 60m deep. The high-water mark can be discerned on the rocks. On a strangely-shaped boulder above the water stands a small gold pagoda. Along the river, we see numerous fishing-nets with mechanical lifting devices, as are used in China.

For a distance beyond the upper end of the defile, the river valley turns NE. A superbly beautiful *view opens up of the broad watery expanses of the Irrawaddy, with its islands and luxuriant vegetation stretching from its shores to the blue mountains in the E., which form the frontier with China. The last stops (not however made by the express boats) are: 277M. *Sinkan* and 290M. *Sawadi* on the S. shore.

320M. **Bhamo**. – At the boat's arrival, there is a sufficient number of porters (Chinese coolies) and carriages (Tikka gharries; tariff as for Mandalay, see p.270) on shore. Since the *Circuit House* (cf.p.270) and the *New Gymkhana Club* admit guests by introduction only, it is usual to spend the night on the ships of the Irrawaddy Flotilla, of which there will always be some moored here. – Curio shop: *Cohn & Co.*, German Jews.

Bhamo (130m above sea-level), distr. capital and occupying a long, narrow site along the E. bank of the Irrawaddy, is a depot for the trade with China, which extends up the valley of the *Taping* (confluence 2M higher up), the frontier lying 58km to the NE. Mule-trains bring hides, silk and Chinese goods, and take back European industrial products. Of the 11,000 inhab., more than ¼ are Chinese, partly well-to-do merchants, partly coolies. The majority are Shan people and Burmese, the latter making, as always, a pleasing spectacle with their silk clothes and their neatness. There are also stocky Kachins from the mountains, the British police force, consisting of Sikhs and Mohammedans, and 30-40 Europeans.

From the landing-stage, a shady shore road leads to the *Bazaar* or *China Street*, the main business quarter, with the more important Chinese shops. Nearby, the **Chinese Temple* (tell the driver "joss house") with various courtyards, carved and painted gables, a theatrical stage etc. – in the "Cantonment", outside the native town, rises a large and very old whitewashed *pagoda*, more like the dagabas of Ceylon (a style not normally found in Burma, p.57). Next to this, a wooden tower-pagoda and, behind that, a small monastery. The caravan road to China begins at the pagoda. – At the N. end of the town, two small forts, with the police barracks.

At Bhamo the normal steamer journey on the Irrawaddy is terminated. The distance by river upstream to Myitkyina (p.277) is about 115M. Between Sinbo and Bhamo, the river flows through the 56km-long Upper (First) Defile, where it narrows to approx. 60m.

Route 39. From Rangoon to Penang.

760 S.M. *Brit. India Steam Navigation Co.,* alternately Thu. or Fri., in 2 days, for 82R., 41R., 10R. (cf.p.251). Return on Sun. or Wed. – The freighter connects in Penang with North-German Lloyd (p.253). For the return journey to Rangoon one has usually a 3-4 day stop in Penang (through tickets).

The journey is generally very hot, but the ship's open upper deck is pleasantly fresh. We follow the coast of S. Burma, in front of which lies a dense mass of islands and islets, inhabited virtually only by nomadic fishing-people: the *Mergui Archipelago,* with mountains up to 1000m. Below lat. 10°N., where the *Malayan Peninsula* (p.281) abuts on to British territory, the mainland shrinks in width to from the *Kra Isthmus*, whose narrowness (45km) prompts the notion of a navigation canal, which would shorten the sea-route from Rangoon to Bangkok by 2200km, and that from Calcutta to Canton by 1100km.

On the second day, we pass the island *Pucket Salang* which, like the opp. part of the Peninsula, belongs to the Federated Malay States (p.282). – *Penang,* see p.283.

THE MALAYAN PENINSULA.

STEAMER CONNECTIONS: from Rangoon, see p.280; from Madras, see p.82 (in 12 days); the best route is from Colombo, where steamers leave for Penang-Singapore approx. twice a week (cf.pp.25-6), incl. *North-German Lloyd,* every other Sun. to Penang (1278M) in 4 days, for 214R.50c., 160R., 66R., and to Singapore (1673M) in 6 days for 247R.50, 181R.50, 77R.; also, fortnightly, the *Peninsular & Oriental S.N.Co.*; once a month, *Austrian Lloyd, Marittima Italiana* etc.; twice a month, the Dutch company *Nederland* (p.2), via Sabang (the island before the N. point of Sumatra) to Singapore.

The voyage from Colombo to Penang crosses the Bay of Bengal, passing to the S. of the *Nicobar Is.* (not visible) which, along with the *Andaman Is.* adjacent to the N., belong to the submerged mountain range that linked the Arakan Mts. (p.253) in a broad arc to Sumatra. Since 1858 they have been in the possession of the English who have set up a penal colony here for criminals. On the 3rd day, the mountainous and densely forested N. end of *Sumatra* comes into view, with the lighthouse Willems Toon. The ship passes between the outer islands *Pulo Weh* (l.) and *Pulo Brass* (r.), then past the N. coast of Sumatra, on which the lighthouse on *Diamant Point* comes into sight, and then crosses the Malacca Straits to Penang (p.283).

The *Malayan Peninsula* is the S. outlier of Indo-China, between the Bay of Bengal and the Malacca Straits to the W., and the Gulf of Siam and the S. China Sea to the E. It is about 1500km in length, being about 100km broad in its N. part, which belongs to Siam, and up to 300km broad in its S. part, which is under British protection. The mountain chains which run through it lengthwise consist of granite and gneiss, primary argillaceous schists, sand- and limestone, attaining heights of up to 3000m. The rock, esp. the detritus, is rich in tin, the exploitation of which accounts for almost half the world's entire tin production. Gold, lead, iron, copper, zinc and tungsten are also found; and coal has recently been discovered. The interior of the country is full of jungle, which provides excellent building-timber, gutta-percha and coconuts; the marshy littorals are covered by mangrove thickets. Among the fruit-trees we mention the civet-tree or durian (Durio cibethinus; p.42) and the mangosteen tree (Garcinia mangostana, p.19). The plains produce rice and sugar; coconut palms are grown, also coffee, tapioca, cocoa, pineapples, gambir (a dye from the Uncaria gambir) and, especially, Para rubber. Among the larger animals frequently found in the interior are the elephant, tapir, rhinoceros and tiger.

The population numbers about 2,700,000, consisting chiefly of Malays, who forced their way here in the Middle Ages, restricting the cultureless primeval tribes, the *Sakai, Semang* etc. to a few places in the wooded mountains; and of Chinese who emigrated here as late as the early 19th c. The *Malays* belong to the race – estimated at 45mill. – which probably results from an ancient intermingling of the yellow-skinned Eastern Asians and the dark-skinned southern Asians. A proficient maritime people, they now inhabit the entire SE insular lands as far as Australia, and Madagascar as well. They are of medium build, well-proportioned, olive-brown of complexion, with smooth black hair, but beardless. They generally dress in baggy trousers, with a long colourful cloth *(sarong)* worn at the hip, and a loose jacket. Their language is Mongolian in origin. Along with Islam, to whose adherents they have belonged since the 18th c., they have adopted Arabic script and possess a literature of their own. Their culture rests upon the growing of rice by means of artificial irrigation. They lack business acumen, however, and passively look on as their country is developed economically by foreigners. Of the latter, the *Chinese,* who were attracted here by the tin, form more than half the total population, partly humble coolies, partly industrialists and partly wholesale merchants, extraordinarily wealthy. The *Europeans*, who first set foot in the town of Malacca in 1511 (p.287) lived, until a few decades ago, only along the coastal strip, but they likewise are now penetrating into the interior. A number of other races follow after them, esp. S. Indian *Tamils* as coolies, *Sikhs* as policemen, and other *N. Indians, Sinhalese, Javanese* and *Japanese.*

Politically, the S. portion of the peninsula is composed of the British crown colony known as Straits Settlements and the Malayan Protectorates. The Straits Settlements on the Straits of Malacca, generally abbreviated to "Straits", consist of the 3 provinces *Wellesley* (to which belong the island of Penang, a strip of the mainland coast opp. and the distr. of Dinding, p.286), *Malacca,* (p.287) and the island of *Singapore,* with a total area of 4140 sq.km and 722,075 inhab. (1000 Europeans). The seat of government is at Singapore. The Governor is assisted by an executive and a legislative council. The Malayan Protectorates include the sultanates of (from N. to S.) *Perlis, Kedah, Kelantan, Tringganu, Perak, Pahang, Selangor, Negri Sembilan* and *Johore,* covering 133,500 sq.km in all, with 1,935,900 inhab. Perak, Selangor, Negri Sembilan, Pahang and, since 1910, Tringganu also, form the *Federated Malay States*, with a British Chief Secretary at their head, which are subject to the Governor of the Straits, and obliged to maintain a contingent of troops. The dependent relationship of the others is similarly disposed.

The local currency is the *Straits Dollar* ($) in silver, divided into 100 cents. In 1906, its value was fixed at the equivalent of $60 to £7. Therefore, $1

= 2s.4d. or, in German money, approx. 2*M*40Pf. (cf. the table before the title page). The coins minted in silver bear the values $1, $½, 20cts., 10cts. and 5 cts.; in copper, 1, ½ and ¼cts. There are also state banknotes to the values of $1, 5, 10, 20, 50, 100, 500 & 1000 (one should dispose of these before travelling on, to avoid incurring a loss on the exchange).

Customs duty payable upon entry applies only to spirits and opium.

Post & Telegraph. The postage for letters up to 1oz. (28gr.) in weight is 8cts. for Germany (allow 21 days) and within the World Postal Union, each additional oz. 5cts.; to England and the English colonies, 4cts.; post-cards 3cts.; printed papers and trade samples, 1ct. per 2oz. – Telegrams: to Europe $1.55 per word, to India 80-85cts., within Malaya 3cts.

Most travellers limit themselves to the voyage and the visit to *Penang* and *Singapore*, where the hotels provide good accommodation and comfort approaching what is to be found in Europe. It is however rewarding to make the rly journey from Penang to Singapore which, with stops at the main towns of *Taiping, Ipoh, Kuala Lumpur & Johore* requires 6-7 days. It passes through a region virtually unknown 30 years ago, and provides an insight into the beautiful tropical landscape and the economic upsurge of a fairly new English colony. There are European hotels in Kuala Lumpur and Ipoh only, but in all the major centres there are good government Rest-houses (cf.p.XXIV; price per day $3.50; it is necesasary to reserve in advance by telegraph, government officials having priority), and rickshaws and hackney carriages with tariff. A Boy is not essential. It is most desirable to have recommendations for introduction to the English clubs, visits to plantations and tin-ore plants. The natives' daily and business language is the so-called coastal Malayan. Knowledge of a few expressions (pp.342 ff) will facilitate the traveller's progress. – One should be equipped with tropical clothing, tropical hat, flannel belt etc., as for India (cf.pp.XIV-XV; these may be acquired at Penang or Singapore). *Literature,* see p.LXXIII.

Route 40. Penang.

ARRIVAL. The steamers of North-German Lloyd and the Brit. India Steam Navigation Co. tie up at Swettenham Pier, those of the P & O and other companies anchor in the channel. One is conveyed ashore in hotel barges or in the peculiar Chinese rowing-boats (sampans), 10-15cts. per person. There is no customs inspection. – At the port is the sta. building of the *Federated Malay States Rly* (p.287), recognisable by its tall clock-tower: ticket office and luggage-handling.

HOTELS: *Eastern & Oriental Hot. (prop. Sarkies Bros., cf.p. 257), *Runnymede Hot., 60 beds, P. $5-7, out of season 4-6, both on North Beach, 10-12min rickshaw ride from the landing-place; the staff are Chinese and Malays, of whom only the Chief Boy understands English. – If the traveller intends to stay for several days, he will do better (to avoid the heat of the low-lying plain) to stay at *Crag Hotel (p.286), situated approx. 650m above sea-level in the Penang Hills, also run by Sarkies Bros. It has 8 bungalows with a communal meeting-house, P. from $6, very busy at holiday times; rooms should be booked by telephone in advance, also chair and luggage porters. The number of coolies, each of whom receives 46cts., depends upon the weight; one should limit one's luggage, ensuring that it is well protected from the wet, and remember to take an umbrella and plaid or waterproof for oneself, since one sits unprotected in the chair.

TRAM: from Swettenham Pier to Ayer Itam (p.285; 5cts.)

HACKNEY CARRIAGES: 2nd cl. up to ½ mile, 3 persons, 15cts., 4 persons 25cts., up to 1 mile, 20, 30cts.; 3rd cl. 10, 20, 15, 25cts.; 1st hr., 2nd cl. 40, 3rd cl. 30cts., each succ.hr. 30, 20cts.; all day (9hrs.) $3, $2.25; excursion to the Botanical Gdns (p.285), $1.20 return. A small tip is always expected. Only few of the drivers understand any English.

RICKSHAWS: mostly drawn by Chinese: up to ½ mile, 1st cl.5cts., 2nd cl.3cts.; the first hr. 40, 20cts.; each succ. ¼hr. 10, 5cts.

GENERAL POST OFFICE by the quay. – GOVERNMENT TELEGRAPH OFFICE, near the pier, for inland traffic; *Eastern Extension & Australian Telegraph Co.,* Beach St., for foreign traffic.

BANKS: *Chartered Bank of India, Australia & China, Hongkong & Shanghai Bank, International Banking Corp, Nederlandsche Handels Maatschappij* ("Netherlands Bank"), all in Beach St. – SHIPPING AGENCIES: most are to be found in Beach St. or by the quay.

TRAVEL AGENCIES: *Thos.Cook & Son; Allan Dennys & Co.*

GERMAN VICE-CONSUL: *R.Schubert*, at the firm of Behn, Meyer & Co. Ltd., repr. North-German Lloyd. – The English *Penang Club* has German members also. – Sea-bathing at the *Penang Swimming Club*, on the pretty bay at Tanjong Bunga, 8km to the NW.

SHOPS, all in Beach St., the main business area. Chemists: *Georgetown Dispensary, Graham & Co.;* book-shops: *Prichard, Straits Echo Office;* general merchants: *Prichard, Whiteaway, Laidlaw & Co;* photographer: *H.Bodom*, Northam Rd. Numerous Chinese and Indo-Chinese dealers for jewellery, Malayan weapons, sarongs, mats, carvings in wood, coconut, etc.

The CLIMATE is uniformly hot, mean annual temp. 26·9°C in the plain, and 21·1° in the hills. The annual precipitation reaches 315cm. The wet season is April-October, during the SW monsoon; wettest months are Sept. and Oct. the NE monsoon is dry; the hottest months are Jan., Feb. and Mar.

Penang or Pinang, officially known as *Georgetown,* is situated at lat. 5° 25' N., long. 100° 20' E., on the flat E. shore of the island *Pulo Penang*, which takes its name from the large number of areca palms grown there ("pinang" in Malay). The island consists of partly decomposed granite, is 278 sq.km in size and, except for the 5-6km-wide coastal strip, is completely covered by wooded mountains. The town, founded in 1786 by the East India Company (p.70), and now the administrative centre of the province Wellesley (p.282), is laid out spaciously and set in a single park with splendid palms and huge tropical trees affording shade. The inhab. number 150,000, of whom 80,000 are Chinese (some of them rich merchants who live in imposing houses in their own grounds, have their own club and keep carriages and race-horses, but have nothing to do socially with the Europeans; some of them are simple dealers, craftsmen and coolies). 10,000 are Malays, almost exclusively in the humbler forms of employment; some Indians (mostly Tamils) and about 1000 Europeans, whose bungalows stand out on account of their beautiful gardens. Penang is the chief exporting centre for tin from the Malayan Peninsula and tobacco and pepper from the coast of Sumatra, opposite. In 1909, 5083 ships used the port, with cargoes totalling 7,016, 616 tons. 3913 flew the British flag, 503 the German and 424 the Dutch.

Since the majority of ships stay for no longer than a day, one generally limits oneself to visiting the *Botanical Gardens* (carriage, see p.284), charmingly laid out in the style of an English park, 6km to the NW at the foot of the Penang Hills. At the far end of the valley basin, the municipal waterworks, with a large reservoir. If we now follow up the stream for 5-7mins, we reach a waterfall. – It is also worth paying a visit to *Ayer Itam* (Malay – black water), 8km SW of the port, terminus of the tram-line, with the largest and richest Chinese temple on the Malayan Peninsula. The modern complex, which climbs the slope in a palm wood, consists of a series of courtyards, gardens (with pool for turtles), staircases and many-storeyed temple buildings, rich carvings and idols in gilded stucco. (Note, among others, the double row of Lohans or disciples of Buddha in a chapel). Fine view out to sea. Priests, robed in white, conduct visitors and serve tea. One makes a contribution to the building fund.

The ascent of the Penang Hills commences at the Botanical Gdns where (by previous arrangement, p.283), a hotel official will meet the carriage and assign chair porters to the traveller (pay at the top). A cable railway is under construction. The path, executed in red laterite, climbs in a zigzag (1¼hrs.; it is walkable in parts, but one should walk it in its entirety only when descending, 1hr.) Halfway up, a shelter. The vegetation is of overpowering beauty and variety. At the bottom we see the fan-shaped Ravenala (p.18), Amherstia nobilis with red grape-like blossom, giant ferns, figs and other deciduous trees, areca and kitul palms (p.17). Higher up are conifers of the cypress variety.

The ***Penang Hills* (630-740m; Crag Hotel, see p.283) are the favourite hill-station for a large portion of Indo-China. Tropical clothing is worn by day, but the nights are refreshingly chilly. The Governor of the Straits Settlements also resides here (Government House). Nearby are post and telegraph offices. The view over the town, the plain and the channel busy with shipping, as well as the mainland opposite with its boldly sculpted mountain-ranges, may be reckoned as one of the finest on earth. The jungle paths offer pleasant walks.

Connecting with the German mail-boat, a steamer of North-German Lloyd departs approx. every 5 days from Penang for Sumatra (16hrs.). One lands at the port of *Belawan* (in a fever-ridden mangrove depression) and immediately takes the train (Deli Spoorweg Maatschappij) through the tropical swamps to Medan (approx. 1hr's journey; Hot. Medan, Hot. Orange), seat of the Malayan prince of Deli, under Dutch sovereignty, and centre of the famous tobacco-growing industry.

Route 41. From Penang to Singapore.

a. By sea.

395 S.M. *North-German Lloyd*, fortnightly in 26-28hrs., for £3.6s., £2.4s., £1.7s.6d., incl. food; *Austrian Lloyd*, once a month; *Peninsular & Oriental S.N.C.*, fortnightly; Royal Dutch *Paketvaart Maatschappij* (Batavia), fortnightly. – Also, on working days, the coastal steamers of the *Straits Steamship Co.,* calling at Telok Anson (p.289), Port Swettenham (see below), Port Dickson (p.287) and Malacca (p.287).

Large steamers avoid the S. part of the channel between Penang and the mainland by leaving port instead in a N. direction and sailing round the island to the W. They then follow the mainland coast. At lat. 4° 5' N., our ship passes Dinding, a district belonging to Wellesley Province; 100km S. of this, at lat. 3° 5', we pass the (r.) lighthouse (with its white flashing light and keeper's dwelling) on One Fathom Bank, rising on stilts above the sandbank lying just 2m below sea-level. L., on shore, lies Port Swettenham, largest in the Malay States, at the mouth of the River Klang, founded in 1901 and named after the general resident Sir Frank Swettenham. It is a major exporting centre for rubber (to a value of £9½mill. in 1909) and even long-distance steamers therefore call here (P & O intermediate steamers, on their return journey to Europe). Railway to *Kuala Lumpur*, see p.290; coastal steamer, see above.

At lat. 2° 30' lies *Port Dickson* and, at 2°, the second province of the "Straits" with the old town of Malacca which, conquered by Albuquerque in 1511, was the strong-point of the Portuguese dominion in SE Asia. It passed to the Dutch in 1641 and was acquired by the English in 1824, in exchange for possessions in Sumatra. It then however lost its importance, compared to Penang and Singapore. (The chief product nowadays is tapioca). – At lat. 1° 30', we see (l.) the lighthouse on *Pisang Is.* Between the (r.) high shore of the island *Karimoen* and the promontory *Bulus*, the southernmost tip of mainland Asia (lat. 1° 15' N.), our steamer turns E. At the lightship at *Ajax Shoals*, the Singapore pilot usually comes aboard. Fine journey: wooded islands and coral reefs on both sides. Passing between Singapore Island (l.), whose SW corner, or *Berlanger Point*, bears a white obelisk ("Lot's Wife"), and the island *Blakang Mati*, our ship reaches the harbour of *Singapore* (p.291).

b. By land, through the Malay States.

480M. *Federated Malay States Rly:* through fast train daily (mail, with dining-car) in 24hrs., also several local trains (food at the sta. rests.); fares: Penang-Singapore $24.65, $14.82, Penang-Taiping $3.15, $1.90, Taiping-Kuala Lumpur $9.20, $5.52; the 1st cl. compartments have 4 single seats; luggage is conveyed in the luggage van only, unlike in India; the ticket inspectors are Tamils; the station masters, here also, are most obliging (cf.p.XXII).

A steam ferry crosses from the port station at Penang (p.283) to the mainland sta. at Prai in 25min; fare incl. in the price of the rail ticket; hand luggage is also conveyed to the train free of charge.

The rly passes through a fertile terrain, partly planted with sugar cane; at (18M) *Nibong Tebal*, it crosses the *River Krian* (lined with nipa palms), with a view E. to the peninsula's wooded principal mountain range, then at (22M) *Parit Buntar,* it reaches the border of the Malay state of *Perak* (pron. pera; 20,500 sq.km, 494,120 inhab.) and continues through an extensive rice-growing area (2700 sq.km), which is artificially irrigated from the River Krian, and cultivated by Malays (harvest in Feb.) The equally important plantations of sugar cane, tapioca and rubber are chiefly owned by Chinese and English. Beyond (40M) *Bukit Merah,* the line crosses the large irrigation reservoir, set amid a now decaying jungle, and then enters the foothills of the granite central chain. Between (51M) *Krian Road* and (54M) *Kamunting,* are large deposits of tin-ore being exploited by Chinese, mainly in open-cast workings.

58M. **Taiping**. – Accommodation at the govt. Rest-house, ¼hr. from the sta., between the European and native quarters of the town. – *Hackney carriages,* $1½-2 per day; *rickshaw* about 50cts. per hr., $2 per day; litter for the ascent of Perak Hill, from the Chinese Taik Ho, Main St. (8 bearers, $1 each). – *Perak Club & New Club* at the Recreation Ground, near the Public Gdns.

Taiping (Chinese = eternal peace), capital of the state Perak, seat of the British Resident, with (in 1901) 13,300 inhab. (more than ½ Chinese, ⅓ Indian, the rest Malays) and a British-Indian garrison of about 700 men (Malay States Guides), is very charmingly situated against the W. slopes of the mountains in the old tin-ore district of Larut. The town is divided into an English (N.) and a native (S.) quarter. Between these, the pretty *Public Gardens*, with an artificial lake. Worthy of a visit is the *Perak Museum,* which houses minerals, plants, animals and an admirable ethnographical collection. We mention also the race-course, the state prison, a hospital, etc. – On an easy, well-defined path, we climb (in 3-4hrs. on foot or by litter, see above) through the jungle to *Perak* or *Larut Hill* (1448m), the chief hill station in the Malay States; at 655m, the so-called Tea Gardens, at 1340m the Coffee Gardens, at 1386m the Brit. General Resident's cottage; below this is the view-point Cass.

From Taiping, branch-line (7M) to *Port Weld.*

Beyond (63M) *Bukit Gankang,* the line crosses the *Gapio Pass.* 4 tunnels. Pretty view into the valley of the *River Perak.* Not far from (68M) *Gunung Pondok*, l., an isolated limestone rock (in Malay, gunung = summit; 600m), one of the many limestone and marble hills, rich in caves, which follow the central range (cf.pp.289-90). Then through rubber plantations.

76M. *Kuala Kangsar* (govt. Rest-house, close to the sta.), with 1100 inhab., situated 5-10min from the sta. at the point where the *River Kangsar* joins the Perak, along whose high river margin a fine carriage road leads through tropical scenery past the Governor of Singapore's imposing residence. 15-20mins drive bring us to the palace (Istana) and park of the *Sultan of Perak.* – Before (74M) *Enggor,* the line crosses the Perak on a long, arched bridge and, further on, reaches the *Kinta valley,* rich in tin-ore, down which it continues.

102M. *Ipoh* (govt. Rest-house near the sta; Station Hot., to be opened in 1914), the most important trading-place in the Peninsula with (in 1901) 12,790 inhab., almost ¾ Chinese. A bell-tower reminds us of the murder of the Brit. Resident Birch (1875). More than ¼ of all the tin mined in the Peninsula comes from the Kinta valley, in whose granitic slaty alluvial bed the Chinese first discovered it. They are still the chief exploiters of tin. They recover the ore by the simplest manual technique of washing the earth in wooden conduits. Recently, Europeans have introduced mining with modern machinery, and are exploiting the ore veins in the uplands. The traveller who is furnished with letter of introduction has the opportunity to study the mining of tin in all its forms. – A second important mining town in the Kinta valley is (110M) *Batu Gajah.* – 124M. *Kampar.*

Our train continues onward through tropical scenery virtually untouched by Man, with views l. of the jungles of the central chain. Picturesque limestone formations, numerous streams, rivers and marshes. After a night's rain, the spectacle is enhanced by cloud and mist.

143M. *Tapah Road,* junc. for a branch-line (15M) to the port *Telok Anson,* near the mouth of the River Perak. – 157M. *Trolak,* centre of the state "Trolak Forest Reserve", where efforts are being made to restore the gutta-percha forest, almost destroyed by Malayan rapacity. – 177M. *Tanjong Malim*, on the River Bernam, the first stop in the state of *Selangor*, the most advanced, culturally, of the Malay States (area 8300 sq.km, 29,000 inhab.) Settlements, mineworkings and plantations visibly increase along the railway line. – 191M. *Kuala Kubu,* whence motor-omnibuses cross the E. mountain chain to (20M) *Raub* and (55M) *Kuala Lipis,* capital of the sultanate *Pahang,* the largest of the Malay States (area 36,200 sq.km, but only 117,595 inhab.)

232M. **Kuala Lumpur**. – HOT.: Empire Hot., good; Grand Oriental Hot.; Station Hot., at the sta. The hotel porters meet the mail train.

RICKSHAWS: 10cts. for short distances, 50cts. per hr., $2 per day. – HACKNEY CARRIAGES, with 2 & 4 wheels: 15cts. or 20cts. per mile, all day (8hrs.) $1.50 or $2. The drive round the town usually takes about 2hrs.

Kuala Lumpur ("muddy estuary"), capital of the state Selangor and, since 1897, federal capital of the Malay States, seat of the central govt., with (in 1901) 32,380 inhab., almost ¾ Chinese, the rest Malays and Indian immigrants, offers, in its European quarters, a splendid example of the creation of a modern colonial city. The most important public buildings are grouped around an extensive lawn: the *Government Offices* with a tall central tower and 2 lateral towers,, the *Municipal Council,* the *Post & Telegraph Offices,* the *State Railways Administration Building* (painted red and white), the *Chartered Bank of India,* the *Selangor Club,* etc. *Selangor Museum,* in Damansara Rd., contains collections similar to those in the Perak Museum (p.288; the section on birds is outstanding; some weapons and silver work also). Following Swettenham Rd., we reach the **Public Gardens*, a park approx. 70 ha. in area, with an artificial lake and a preserved piece of jungle. Standing all around, in their spacious gardens, are the Europeans' bungalows; and, on a height offering fine views, the imposing residence *(Caracosa)* of the British General Resident; further on is the *Lake Club* and, on another hill, the dwelling of the Resident of Selangor. We continue through the Chinese quarter to the *Golf Club's* courses; the long, low building with the tall chimney contains the incinerators for the city's combustible rubbish. We pass the *Jail* and return to our hotel through the Indian quarter.

Kuala Lumpur's prosperity derives largely from the rubber plantations in its vicinity. Most valuable of all is Para rubber (Hevea Brasiliensis). The rubber-trees, raised in nurseries and transplanted to jungle clearings, yield from the time they are 5 years old. The milky juice is obtained by making cuts in the bark, then, while still in a fluid state, its water content (about 50%) is removed in presses, and the result is rolled out in bands and dried.

Excursion to Batu Caves: branch-line, 8M in ½hr. for 48cts.; one should take a guide and refreshments from the hotel, and avoid the heat of the day. At the 2nd stop we see, l., the central workshops of the State Railways. The sta. Batu Caves lies among rubber and coffee estates at the foot of a white marble rock covered in tropical vegetation and containing 2 remarkable *caves, 70-80m high, about ⅔ of the way up (10min steep ascent from the sta.) The first cave is illuminated naturally by a shaft at the rear, choked with giant creepers, and by holes in its roof (remarkable effect; numerous swallows); l., a small rock niche with altar. The second cave is narrower and deeper and only dimly lit by a small shaft; the floor is of a soft muddy consistency on account of the bat droppings.

From Kuala Lumpur to Port Swettenham (p.286), 55M, branch-line via *Sungei Renggam*, the centre of the rubber estates in the Klang distr., and *Klang*, residence of the Sultan, then through the palm plantations to the marshy coastal depression.

From Kuala Lumpur to Singapore (travel time 12hrs.), the railway has less of interest to offer. At (269M) *Gatang Benar,* it crosses the border of the state *Negri Sembilan* (consisting of 9 small princedoms). – 297M. *Seremban,* a town with 4700 inhab., half of them Chinese, surrounded by deposits of tin-ore, and junc. for a branch to Port Dickson (p.287). The ensuing stations lie in the Brit. territory of Malacca (p.287): (308M) *Kendone,* (323M) *Tampin* (branch to Malacca) and (327M) *Batang Malaka.*

At (351M) *Gemas,* the rly reaches the Sultanate of *Johore*, which occupies the entire S. portion of the Peninsula. The state is 22,300 sq.km in size, with a pop. of 180,400, ¾ Chinese, and is mostly covered by jungle, which is gradually giving way to plantations of gambier, pepper, sago and, particularly now, rubber.

465M. **Johore Baru**. – HOT.: Johore Hot., at the landing-stage for the steam ferry, P. $6-7, well spoken of. – Rickshaw: ½M 4cts., per hr. 25cts. – HACKNEY CARRIAGES: ½M 1-2 pers. 20cts., 3-4 pers. 25cts.; per hr. 75cts., $1; half-day $2, $3.

Johore Baru (Malay = New Johore), capital of the state of Johore, lies on the 1220-1500m-broad channel, which divides the island of Singapore from the mainland. The following drive is customary, and well-known to the coolies: from the hotel, l., to the unattractive *Sultan's Palace* (Istana), whose interior is now inaccessible (but, in any case, has nothing notable to offer). Thence to the *Botanical Garden*, then to the *mosque*, situated on a rise near the sea, a 4-towered building of 1901, in the European Renaissance style (entry permitted only without shoes); thence to the Sultan's *tiger cages.* One is advised to omit the visit to the Chinese *gambling halls,* where games of chance are played with dice, counting heaps of beans, etc., since not only the games but even entry to the halls are now barred to Europeans.

The steam ferry crosses to Singapore Island in 10min, landing at *Woodlands Station,* where the narrow-gauge Singapore-Kranji Rly commences (16M, 8 trains per day), taking 1hr. to reach Singapore via several intermediate stops. The hilly terrain is covered by rubber and other tropical plantations. About halfway is the sta. *Bukit Timah* (hill of tin), near the highest point in the island, bearing the same name (158m). – 472M *Singapore.*

Route 42. Singapore.

ARRIVAL. The German and French steamers tie up at *West Wharf,* the English ones to the W. of this, at the *P & O Wharf.* Hotel servants come on board and see to the transfer of luggage. At the exit from the port area, carriages, rickshaws and trams wait for the ride into town (20min). – Smaller steamers anchor near Johnson's Pier; passengers are conveyed ashore in 'sampans' (p.283): with 1 rower 10-15cts. for 1-4 pers. from the nearer anchorages, 25cts. from the further ones. – The *main station* (Tank Rd. Sta.) is linked by rly to the port.

HOT.: (among the best in the Orient): *Raffles Hot. ("Hotel Bahru" in Malayan; prop. Sarkies Bros., cf.p.257), Beach Rd., by Raffles Reclamation (p.295), built in the style of the Galle Face Hotel at Colombo (p.25); *Gr.H.de l'Europe (limited co. hotel), on the Esplanade, corner of High St., recently fitted out, 120 Rm., P. $6-10, both hotels offering every comfort, baths, etc. and concerts with tiffin and dinner; Adelphi Hot. ("Hotel German" in Malayan), 1-2 Coleman St., close to the Esplanade, 100 Rm. (the best overlook the Cathedral), with baths etc., rather simpler, but clean and good, P. $5-7; H.de la Paix, 3 Coleman St.; Hot.van Wijk, Stamford Rd., 50 Rm., P. $5, simpler but popular, Dutch cooking.

Transport – *Hackney carriages:* ½M. 15cts., 1M 25cts; outside the town up to 4M, 75cts. per hr., all day (9hrs.) $3. – AUTOMOBILES for excursions from *Abram's Straits Motor Garage Syndicate,* 5 Orchard Rd., *Straits Rickshaw Co.,* 75 Bras Basah Rd., and *Wearne Bros.Ltd.,* Orchard Rd.: 5-seater $3, 7-seater $5 per hr.

Rickshaws, 1st & 2nd cl.: per ½M 5cts., 3cts., per hr. 40, 20, per day $1.50, 80cts. The rickshaw coolies are almost exclusively Chinese; since it is virtually impossible to make oneself understood to them (they answer every time with "yes"), one should indicate the required direction to them (established previously from studying the plan), by touching their r. or l. shoulder or the ricksaw shaft with a small stick.

Trams (cf.p.XXII); fares, 1st cl. 5-20cts.): 1. *Keppel Harbour*, Tanjong Pagar, General Post Office, Anderson Bridge, High St., *Station* (p.291; 20cts.); - 2. *Tanjong Pagar* (Boustead Inst.), South Bridge Rd., North Bridge Rd., *Gelang* (see p.296; 20cts.); - 3. *Raffles Hotel* (p.291), Bras Basah Rd., Serangoon Rd., Paya Lebar (15cts.).

Shipping lines & agencies: *North-German Lloyd*, repr. by Behn, Meyer & Co., Collyer Quay, corner of De Souza St.: fortnightly (mail-boat) Mon. to Europe (cf.p.1), Fri. or Sat. to China & Japan; weekly to Bangkok (p.299), to Deli (Sumatra, p.286), to Brit.Borneo etc.; 5 times a year via Batavia etc. to German New Guinea. – *Austrian Lloyd*, repr. by Rautenberg, Schmidt & Co., 4 Cecil St. (monthly to Europe, cf.p.1, also to China). – *P & O Steam Navigation Co.,* agency in the Arcade, Collyer Quay: fortnightly, Thurs. to Europe, Sat. to China. – *British India Steam Navigation Co.*, repr. by Boustead & Co., Collyer Quay: weekly via Penang-Rangoon to Calcutta (p.253); fortnightly via Penang and Negapatam to Madras (p.82); fortnightly (alternating with P & O) to China. – *Messageries Maritimes*, agency on Collyer Quay, weekly to Saigon; fortnightly to Europe and to China & Japan. – *Stoomvaart Maatschappij Nederland*, repr. by the Ships Agency Ltd., Collyer Quay: fortnightly to Europe and Java (p.311). – *Konkl.Paketvaart Maaschappij*, several times a week to Java (p.311). – *Apcar Line,* repr. by Paterson, Simons & Co., Prince St., near Collyer Quay: monthly to Calcutta and to China. – *East Asiatic Co.*, agency at 7 Telegraph St.: weekly via the E. coast ports of the peninsula to Bangkok. – Japanese *Nippon Yusen Kaisha,* repr. by Paterson, Simons & Co., Prince St., to Europe and Japan. - Apart from these, a large number of less important lines.

Post & Telegraph: General Post Office, near Johnston's Pier; Telegraph Office, 3 Raffles Quay.

Banks: *Deutsch-Asiatische Bank,* corner of De Souza St. and Prince St., near Collyer Quay; *Hongkong & Shanghai Banking Corp,* Collyer Quay; *Chartered Bank of India, Australia & China*, Battery Rd.; *Mercantile Bank of India,* 31 Raffles Place (S. end); *Nederlands Indische Handelsbank,* 193 Cecil St.; *Nederlands Handels-Maatschappij,* corner of Cecil St. & d'Almaida St.; *Banque de l'Indo-Chine*, Raffles Place.

Consulates. Germany: consul-general *Feindal*, trade specialist *Krieg;* offices at the N-German Lloyd Agency (see above). – Austria-Hungary: *Dr E.von Zach,* at the Hôtel de l'Europe. – Netherlands: *H.Spackler*, 6 Raffles Quay. – France: *Taillepied de Bondy*, 106 Orchard Rd.

Clubs.: *Teutonia* (Malay "Club German"), in the villa suburb Tanglin (p.296), one of the most splendid German club buildings in Asia, with a large domed hall and theatre (1900; the wall-paintings in the bar donated by N-

Ger.Lloyd). – The English *Singapore Club* has its HQ on the upper floor of the Exchange (p.294).

Shops. The European businesses are chiefly found in the area round Raffles Place & Collyer Quay. Malayan goods, gold items, weapons (esp. the long daggers called *Kris,* though the older ones, with good craftsmanship, are rarely found): best purchased in High St. (at the Hôtel de l'Europe) & vicinity. – Chemists: *International Dispensary,* High St., in the Hôtel de l'Europe; *Medical Hall* (German), Battery Rd.

The climate is uniformly hot and humid, with only 2° difference between the mean monthly warmest and coolest temps. (May 27·6°, Jan. 25·6°). It is not regarded as unhealthy, but enervating in the long run. Relief comes with the almost daily brief rain-showers. At night there is a heavy dew. From Nov. to Mar., the NE monsoon prevails, from May to Oct., the less consistent SW monsoon, with which short violent cloudbursts (called sumatras) seem to be associated, mainly between 1 a.m. and 5 a.m.

Newspapers: *Singapore Free Press, Straits Times.* A journal in 4 languages called *The Tourist* is distributed to passengers when their steamers arrive.

If time is limited: drive through the town and the garden suburb Tanglin (p.296); visit the Botanical Gdns (p.296) and perhaps the Museum also (p.295). – Photography of any kind is forbidden within 3km of the fortifications, on pain of severe penalties. Since one will hardly be aware of the defences, except for a few batteries on the neighbouring islands and heights, one should pay careful attention to the warning signs.

Singapore, capital of the Straits Settlements, lies at lat.1° 17' N., long. 103° 51' E. on the S. coast of the island of the same name, just off the mainland of Malaya. By virtue of its position at the gateway to the China Sea, it is one of the most important bases for world traffic, and a first-rate strategic strong-point: hence the massive fortifications. It was founded in 1819 by Sir Stamford Raffles on the site of a Malayan settlement, whose name Sinhapur or "lion town" points to ancient Indian connections (cf.p.22). In 1823 it was handed over to the British Government, along with the rest of the island, by the Sultan of Johore. As a free port, in contrast to the Dutch trading policies, it rapidly grew to become the chief centre of commerce with SE Asia and, after the Suez Canal was opened, it acquired tremendous impetus. In 1822 it already numbered 10,000 inhab., then 40,000 in 1840, 162,000 in 1891 and 228,550 in 1911, of whom 3825 were Europeans & Americans, 4120 Eurasians, 164,040 Chinese, 36,080 Malays and other natives of the archipelago, 17,825 Annamese, Siamese, Burmese, Japanese, etc. There is a garrison of 2050 men, consisting of 1 battalion of British and one of native infantry, 2 companies of British and one of native fortress artillery and half a company of pioneers, also a voluntary corps composed mainly of Eurasians.

Apart from native and other minor seagoing craft, the following entered or left the port of Singapore during 1909: 10,624 merchant ships totalling 14,114,120 tons (5625 overseas, 4999 coastal traffic), of which 5146 were British, 2613 Dutch, 1063 German, 512 Norwegian, 344 Japanese, 327 French (the Japanese lying ahead of the Norwegians in tonnage). Imports, totalling $214,404,964, chiefly comprise foodstuffs, manufactured and semi-manufactured textile goods, metal articles & machinery, coal (almost ½ of Japanese and 1/5 of Australian origin). Exports, totalling $179,185,170, comprise rubber, gutta percha, cane for chairs, spices, copra, gambir (p.280) and tin. The steamers of more than 50 large companies take on coal here as they pass through, and a stock of 200,000 tons is always available. Since world trade is striving to cut out intermediary dealing (for example, the raw products from the Dutch Indies have, for some years, been shipped directly to Europe), the increasing economic development of the Malayan hinterland is of great importance for Singapore.

The harbour *(New* or *Keppel Harbour),* 3-4km SW of the town and opp. Blakang Mati Island, is excellently protected and so deep that the largest steamers can tie up at the piers, although the navigable channel is so narrow that they cannot turn round. The piers stretch along the shore for almost 3km: from W. to E., those of the *P & O Co.,* of the firm *Jardine, Matthesen & Co.* and *West Wharf* (p.291). Then the large *Tanjong Pagar Wharves* with Victoria Dry Dock (122m long, 20m wide, 6m deep) and Albert Dock (148m long, over 18m wide, 6·4m deep). A new dock for large warships *(King's Dock)* is to be opened shortly.

The city is built on land reclaimed from the marshes and sea, and consists of 3 main parts: in the centre, on both sides of the broad *Singapore River,* is the European business quarter; to the S., the Chinese quarters; to the N., the Malayan quarters which, however, are inhabited by other Asians also. Three series of main streets run the length of these urban quarters from SW to NE, roughly parallel to the shore. The Europeans' villas and gardens lie on the hills to the W.

The focus of trade is to be found in Commercial Square or *Raffles Place*, a rectangular square with gardens, and Collyer Quay, which stretches along the waterfront from the fish market Teluk Ayer to the S., to Johnston's Pier to the N. All the more important European and American businesses, banks and agencies have their offices and warehouses in this area. Near Johnston's Pier (cf.p.291) is the *Exchange*, with the Chamber of Commerce and the premises of the Singapore Club (p.292). Next to this, the *General Post Office* with a projecting terrace. The fountain at the centre of the triangular square was endowed by a rich Chinese when the city's water mains were completed.

The bridges which cross the Singapore River *(Cavenagh Bridge,* 1869; suspension bridge, and *Anderson Bridge,* 1910, a strong double bridge) offer fine views of the broad river thronged with native craft, and the blue-painted Chinese houses beyond.

The N. part of the European city contains the administrative offices of the government and municipality. First, the *Government Offices* and the *Town Hall,* to which was added the *Queen Victoria Memorial Hall* in 1887, with its tall tower and assembly rooms. The elephant monument outside the Town Hall is a reminder of the first visit of the King of Siam in 1871. Beyond, to the W., is the *Supreme Court.*

The Esplanade (Malay "Padang Bissar"), an expanse of lawn 500m long and 200m wide, and surrounded by a carriageway shaded by thick foliage, comes to life mainly in the late afternoon, when elegant society goes for a drive to enjoy the sea breeze. The lawn serves the Singapore Cricket Club and Recreation Club as pitches etc. Since 1887, a statue of *Sir Stamford Raffles* (1781-1826) has stood in the middle, who, as lieut.-governor of Benkoelen on Sumatra, was the first to realise the significance of the Malacca Straits for sea traffic (p.293). To the NW, the Prot. *St Andrew's Cathedral,* built in 1856-62 in Gothic style.

The continuation of the Esplanade is the section of beach known as *Raffles Reclamation,* bordered to the W. by *Beach Road,* which proceeds NE to the mouth of the *Rochore River.* – The Malayan quarter, to the W. of Beach Rd., offers us a captivating insight into native life. The nocturnal activity in *Hylam St., Malahar St. & Malay St.* reminds one of Tokyo and Yokohama. It is an amusing experience to visit the Malayan theatre *Wajang Malayu* in North Bridge Rd., where native plays are performed, alongside native adaptations of European pieces.

Stamford Road, running inland from St Andrew's Cathedral, passes the *Raffles Institution,* an elementary school founded in 1823, and the *R.C. Cathedral,* and terminates at the foot of *Fort Canning* (Mal. Bukit Bandera, "banner hill"), formerly the seat of the governor, now an artillery barracks. Up on the height (47m, panoramic views) is the Signal Station, (where salutes are fired and the midday shot is let off at 1 p.m. on Sundays), with lighthouse and flagpole. On the SE slope is the tomb of the Mohammedan holy man *Iskander Khan,* frequented by the faithful, esp. on Fri. & Sun. after sunset.

Stamford Rd. then turns N. into Orchard Rd (Mal. Jalan Bissar). On the l., the noble Raffles Museum (Mal. Tempat Buku; opened in 1887), containing a library on the ground-floor and scientific, ethnographic and archaeological collections on the upper floor, giving a good survey of the Malayan world (open Mon.-Sat., 9.30 a.m. to 6 p.m.; explanatory notes on all exhibits). Obliquely opp., the *Ladies' Lawn Tennis Club.* – 10min to the N., on the height, is *Government House* (Mal. Tuan Gubernor punya Ruma), an effective 2-storeyed building of 1869, with a magnificent park.

Beyond the railway crossing, the villa suburb Tanglin commences, an unbroken green undulating park, in which the imposing dwellings of the

Europeans are almost totally hidden away among the trees and shrubs of their gardens. In Scott's Rd., branching off r., is the German *Teutonia Club* (p.292). To the l. of Orchard Rd., a Chinese cemetery. The road ends, after bending round to the SW, at the Tanglin infantry barracks.

The **Botanical Garden* (Mal. Kebun Bunga), an English park, 25ha. in extent, is best visited early in the morning because of its lack of shade, and the oppressive heat. Carriages and rickshaws are admitted to all of the walks. Equatorial tropical vegetation is seen here in superb development. Characteristic, among others, are the native red-trunked palms (Cyrtostachys Lakka), similar in growth to the areca (p.17), the beautiful ravenala and Amherstia. Now and again we see wild monkeys in the treetops. Flowers are noticeably few and far between in the more exposed places, a result of the heavy downpours of rain. The surroundings of the large lake to the W. near the entrance are scenically outstanding. At the highest point, with its extensive views, in the middle of the gardens, is a band-stand, where a military band plays until 11 p.m. when there is a full moon. In the N. part of the gardens, a large piece of primeval jungle, 4ha. in extent, has been preserved. Adjacent to this, to the N., are the *Experimental* or *Economic Gardens,* where experiments are made with useful tropical plants.

To the W. of the Botanical Garden, on a rise, stands the palace *Tyersall* of the Sultan of Johore, built in 1892.

Visitors making a longer stay may also take the trip to the Waterworks which lie 5M away on a height to the N. of the city. At the Ladies' Lawn Tennis Club (see above) follow, r., Selegie Rd., then NW along Bukit Timah Rd., which runs between the *Race Course* and the hill bearing Government House (see above); to our l., the waterworks filter plant, surrounded by gardens; r., the *Christian Cemetery.* Beyond the latter, r., along New Cemetery Rd. into the long Thomson Rd. as far as the branch to the Waterworks (signboard). The *reservoir* is a dammed-up lake of considerable scenic charm. Pretty view from the dam. 1¼M to the S. of *Gelang* (tram no.2, p.292) is the bathing-place *Tanjong Katong* (Sea View Hotel, well furnished).

The trip to Johore takes ½ day by rail (p.291): return ticket, 1st cl., $2.

SIAM.

The kingdom of *Siam,* the sole remaining independent state in Indo-China, has been, since the last cession of territory to French Indo-China in 1909, approx. 240,000 sq.km in area, with 6,700,000 inhab. The Siamese (1·8mill.) are politically and culturally predominant; the Chinese, recently strongly on the increase because of immigration (1·4mill.), have admittedly taken the upper hand in commerce, but are not concerned with the politics of the country. Lower on the numerical scale are the inhabitants of Laos (1·4mill., related to the Shan tribes, p.255) and the Malays (0·7mill.) The number of white residents was about 1200 in 1910, of whom 250 were German, 248 French, 222 English, 144 Americans, 141 Scandinavians etc. – The most densely populated area is the plain of the *River Menam* (i.e. Mother of Waters) which, 700km long, rises at lat. 19° N. near the Mekong, and whose annual floods, lasting from June to November, determine the fertility of the alluvial soil, which is given over almost exclusively to the cultivation of rice. The climate is hot (mean annual temp. at Bangkok 26·7° C). The rainy season begins in May and ends in October.

The Siamese belong to the so-called Thai peoples, who are closely related to the Chinese. They are slight of build and of dark olive complexion, often tattooed on their legs; their black hair is worn straight; their teeth are red from the chewing of betel or, in the case of elegant ladies, enamelled black. Their clothing, similar in both sexes, consists of a brown or white Panung (apron) which is passed between the legs and fastened in the belt, a jacket, a straw hat or head-scarf, and a cotton Parkana round the shoulders. The elegant wear gold-embroidered jackets, costly silk shawls, calf-length stockings and buckled shoes. The temperament and mores of the Siamese are reminiscent of Burma (p.254). Buddhism is the religion here also, practised in similar fashion. Education is under the direction of the monks, who possess innumerable monasteries, but adhere strictly to the old habit of their morning procession with begging-bowl. They wear yellow togas and shave their heads. Every free Siamese is obliged to spend three months in a monastery, at some stage in his life. The custom of going on pilgrimages is widespread, as is that of endowing holy places, with which the country is liberally sprinkled (cf.p.265).

Siamese art favours bright colours and is distinguished by its elegant forms. The equivalent of the Burmese pagoda are the *Wats*, religious cult centres with rectangular enclosures, several courtyards, reliquary towers called *Phras,* priests' dwellings, pilgrims' houses, gardens and holy pools. In the innermost courtyard, opp. the main entrance, is the *Bot*, a temple hall containing the large image of the Buddha. The Phras are sometimes bell-shaped, like the Burmese pagodas, with a needle spire *(Phra Chedi)*, sometimes polygonal and shaped like a tapering beehive, also rising to a point *(Phra Prang)*. The principal Phra is generally surrounded by several small Phras. The temple roofs rise, one above the other in succession, with curved ridges and richly decorated gables, occasionally crowned also by a Phra. The walls are painted or clad with colourful mosaics. Temples and courtyards are filled with fantastic carvings and votive gifts. There is a colourful throng of people at festival times.

The cultivation of rice forms the basis of the country's entire economy. A good harvest will yield 800,000-900,000 tons (16-18 mill.cwt.) for export; deviations up or down depend upon the punctual or late onset of the wet season. The greater part goes to Hongkong and Singapore, in Europe to the Netherlands, Germany and Great Britain. There is also a considerable export of teak (value 1·8mill. marks in 1910-11). Imports include cotton goods and articles of clothing, mainly from Great Britain, British India, Singapore, the Netherlands and Switzerland; also, all kinds of foodstuffs, metal goods, steam- and other machines from Germany, Gt. Britain, America etc. The number of ocean-going ships entering Bangkok harbour in 1910-11 amounted to 925, with a registered tonnage of 863,669: 926 ships left, with a total reg. tonnage of 865,067; among these, the German flag accounted for 43·6%, the Norwegian 28·7% and the British 10·1%.

Buffaloes and bullocks are reared, along with elephants, and all these are also still found in large numbers in the wild (cf.p.304). The elephant is to be found on Siam's coat of arms.

The country's history remained legendary until the late Middle Ages. One assumes that the Siamese settled here in the 3rd c. A.D. They adopted the Brahman religion and culture prevalent in India, which were replaced in the 12th c. by Buddhism penetrating from Burma and Ceylon. Ancient Indian influences can still be clearly seen today in customs, language, law, literature and art. In 1350, *Phra Uthong* founded the capital Ayuthia (p.304), whose name is entirely Indian. The blossoming realm fought victorious wars against the neighbouring tribes, esp. the once superior Cambodia, but succumbed for a while (1556-79) to the Burmese Pegu (p.262). The skirmishing with Burma recommenced in the 18th c. (cf.p.255), in the course of which Ayuthia was destroyed (1767). Liberated by the half-Chinese *Paya Tack,*the inhab. founded the new town of Bangkok in the following year. In 1782, General *Chow Paya Chakkri* elevated himself to be ruler, and founded the present-day pure Siamese dynasty. More important than the ensuing acts of war, and territorial gains and losses, were the trading treaties signed around 1860 with the seafaring states, which encouraged traffic with the West. *King Chulalongkorn* (1868-1910), himself possessed of considerable intellect, did the most to advance his people culturally by opening up the way to European influence (following the Japanese pattern), encouraging young Siamese to study in

Europe, and visiting Europe himself in 1907. The present king is his son *Wajirawudh* (b.1881).

The army, reorganised in 1907 on European and Japanese lines, has a peacetime strength of 25,000-30,000 men and consists of 10 divisions, each with 2 regts. of infantry, 1 of cavalry, 1 of artillery etc. The naval fleet numbered, in 1911, 1 cruiser, 4 gunboats, 3 torpedo boats etc., along with 75 river and coastal craft, with a total of 5000 men. The merchant navy possessed, in 1912, 29 ships totalling 8725 tons, and 91 sailing ships. The length of the railways (state-owned), which were constructed by German engineers, totalled 1090km in 1911.

Currency is the *tikal*, formerly cube-shaped, now a stamped silver coin to the value of *M*1.50-1.60. The tikal is divided into 4 *salungs*, then 2 *fuangs*, which are struck in silver. The fuang equals 2 *songpai;* 1 songpai=2 *pai*, then 2 *att,* then 2 *lot,* all copper coins. There are gold coins to the value of 10 tikals and government bank-notes for 5, 10, 20 & 100 tikals. Also in currency are *Mexican piastres* or *dollars*, worth about 1⅔ Tikals. (3 dollars=5 tikals).

Tourists tend to limit their visit to *Bangkok* and the excursion to *Ayuthia*, for which 3 days will suffice. The interior of the country is as yet barely equipped for tourism.

Literature, see p.LXXIII.

Route 43. From Singapore to Bangkok.

800 SM.: *North-German Lloyd*, once a week, connecting with the German mail-boat, journey time 3-4 days, return fare, 1st cl. 200*M*; *East Asiatic Co.*, also once weekly, with frequent stops at the E. Malayan ports. – A direct connection between Bangkok and Java is provided once a month by the *Dutch Koninklijke Paketvaart Maatschappij*, cargo steamer with passenger accommodation.

The steamer rounds the SE tip of the Malayan Peninsula and sets course NW across the *South China Sea*, in sight of the coast at first, past the small island of *Tiuman*, towering up to 1050m. From Nov. to Mar. the NE monsoon is prevalent, with a few interruptions in the months immediately outside that period; from the middle of May till Oct., the wet and often violent SW monsoon prevails. The typhoons of the China Sea do not penetrate this far. Our ship continues up the *Gulf of Siam,* which becomes shallower to the N.

In the N. corner of the Gulf, before the estuary of the River Menam, navigation is imperilled by a bar which, at ebb tide, lies barely 1m below the surface. Larger ships can only pass on a flood tide and in daylight. During the NE monsoon, freighters must load and discharge part of their cargo using lighters in the outer roads, about 8 SM. before the bar, where a pilot schooner is anchored, or another 21 SM. to the SE, in the harbour of the island *Kohsitshang.* The light from the lighthouse on the bar is visible for 10 SM.

Our boat steers past three other lighthouses into the broad estuary of the *Menam*, whose depth in the channel here reaches 8 fathoms (14·6m) and suffices for normal shipping all the way up to Bangkok. The low banks of the winding river (1½-2km broad in its lower reaches) are planted with mangroves. Further on, tall trees come into view, with bamboo thickets and clumps of coconut palms, arecas and nipa palms, banana groves and paddy-fields. Fortifications are seen on both sides. At the first harbour, *Paknam,* on the l. (E.) bank, 8km from the sea, ships take the customs officer on board. In the town, a Wat much visited by pilgrims (p.227). Paknam is also linked to Bangkok by a railway, which is more direct than the meandering Menam (20km).

On an island above Paknam, a picturesquely sited white temple with a red-painted dagaba comes into view. Amongst the greenery on the shore we see miniature pagodas and brightly-painted tombstones carved in the shape of boats. The river is a-bustle with native shipping. The Siamese craft have triangular sails, the Chinese junks large rectangular matting sails. Dwellings line the banks, resting on piles or floating in the water. On both sides, *Klongs* (delta arms) branch off.

Bright pagoda towers, golden spires, brightly-coloured roofs, and esp. the tall Wat Cheng (p.303) betray the position of *Bangkok.* Rice-mills with tall chimneys, petroleum tanks and the electric power-station announce the city's modern development. The river, now 500m broad and 6-14m deep, forms a good harbour. The ship moors at the quay or anchors some distance out, the passengers being conveyed ashore in a steam launch. Carriages wait on the quay. Only opium and spirits are dutiable; weapons must be deposited at the customs office until permission to import them is granted.

Route 44. Bangkok.

HOTELS: Oriental Hot., prettily situated by the Menam, Bristol Hot. with restaurant, German manager. Daily rate in both approx. 12 tikals.

CARRIAGES: 1-horse about 2 tikkals per ½ day (5hrs.), 4 tik. all day; 2-horse, double the price. Rickshaws are rarely used. – ELECTRIC TRAM (Danish company): 1. from the European quarter through the main streets; 2. from the sta. to the Wat Phra Keo (p.302).

CONSULATES. Germany: *v.Buri,* Resident Extraordinary & Consul-general; Freiherr *Rüdt v.Collenberg,* vice-consul. Austria-Hungary: Ritter *v.Wilkowski,* Consul. – The social centre for Germans is the DEUTSCHER KLUB.

GENERAL POST OFFICE, by the Menam. – BANKS: *Hongkong & Shanghai B.C., Chartered Bank of India, Australia & China,* both near New Rd.; *Banque de l'Indo-Chine.* – Agency for *North-German Lloyd* : A.Markwald & Co., near the old Fort. – German chemists: *Bangkok Dispensary & Tatien Dispensary,* New Rd.

EXHIBITIONS etc.: theatres, shadow plays, Javanese dancing (p.307). The frequent religious processions and festivals provide charming, colourful spectacles.

Bangkok ("town of olives"), the capital and only settlement of any size in the Kingdom of Siam, with 630,000 inhab. (more than ⅓ Chinese), was founded in 1768 on the site of a fishing village (cf.p.298). It lies at lat. 13° 38' N. and long. 100° 31' E. on both banks of the *Menam*, and covers an area of 40 sq.km. All the major state institutes, the most important temples, places of learning, trades and almost all the foreign commerce are centred here. The main part of the town stretches along the l. bank. In the curve described by the river to the W. lies the old town, surrounded by a wall 10m high and 3m thick, preserved in places, with the Royal Palace area and many holy buildings. To the S., the European quarter stretches downstream, with the legations, consulates, banks etc. The newer native quarters lie to the E. In the suburb on the r. bank, the Wat Cheng dominates the entire town.

There is a characteristic bustle on the Menam and the canals branching off it (*Klongs*), which run through the town on concentric rings and are connected by smaller canals. Some of the inhab. live in house-boats which are anchored or moored up. The houses on the banks, amid their gardens, are built of wood and, as a precaution against flooding, stand on tall pile gratings. The river bears barges offering foodstuffs and other domestic items, and cookshops, all surrounded by the customers' small boats. These sights, together with the views of temple towers and the battlements of the Royal Palace, serve to explain the name "Venice of the East", which Bangkok has acquired – although one must think rather of the poorer quarters, than the glories, of the western city of the lagoons.

The main business street is the long *Cherern Krung* or *New Road*, which crosses the European quarter and part of the outer native town. Most houses are built of brick in the European manner. The businesses are run largely by Chinese. Near the main station, the road turns NW, passing through the lively bazaar quarter of *Sampeng*; here also, the Wat of the same name, with a large crocodile pool. It crosses the *Klong Tapan Han* (bordered by trees) and reaches the Old Town which has also undergone considerable modernisation. The innermost part of this, beyond the stone-lined *Klong Talat*, is occupied by the:-

Royal Palace area, enclosed by a 1300m-long battlemented wall, whitewashed and 4m high, bordered to the W. by the Menam, with the royal residence and other palaces, ministries, offices and law-courts, temples, barracks, stores etc. The courtyards are paved with granite and marble slabs. To enter, one requires a permit, which may be had from one's consulate. There is a guided tour.

The Royal Residence, a 3-storeyed building in the European renaissance style, with an imposing outer staircase and vestibule, is covered by a tall Siamese roof. The same mixture of foreign and native styles predominates within. Only the state-rooms are shown, esp. the throne-room. – The **Wat Phra Keo*, in the NE corner of the palace quarter, within an arcaded walk whose walls are covered in painting depicting scenes from the Ramayana epic, is the richest of all the Siamese Wats. The mass of pagodas, the many-gabled roofs, towers, spires, brilliantly coloured glass mosaics and valuable votive offerings make an impression upon the eye that is both dazzling and strange. In the centre stands the *Bot* whose roof, supported on pillars, tapers up in seven stages, running to a tall spire. A large lion guards the entrance. The doors are of ebony, with ivory and mother-of-pearl inlay. The interior, whose floor is covered with bronze plates, contains, beneath a protective roof richly adorned with gold and pearls, the 60m-high so-called Emerald Buddha (in reality a jade figure). We also see a number of other figures of Buddha and treasures, of gold or gilded, and set with precious stones; glass and porcelain of European origin (two Berlin vases, a present from Emperor William II). Beside the Bot rise two enormous gilded *Phra Chedis*, bell-shaped, and a magnificently ornate *temple*, with a triple saddle-roof and a Phra Prang rising above it; the temple walls are covered with mosaics. In the gardens all around we find a confusing abundance of small dagabas and sculptures of every kind (some, ancient pieces from India and Java; others modern, e.g. strangely realistic attempts to portray Europeans in their dress), lotus pools, grottoes; worthy of mention is the large model of the temple of Angkor Wat in Cambodia. – The stable of the white elephants usually contains 3-4 specimens of this (in fact) rather lighter variation of the customary elephant. They are regarded as holy and enjoy royal status.

From the terrace of the Law Courts we have a good general view over the palace complex.

To the S. of the palace area lies the **Wat Poh*, already falling into disrepair, the most extensive of Bangkok's temple groups. Two giant figures of guards in ancient armour watch over the entrance. The picturesque tree-shaded courtyards enclose innumerable colourful temples and remarkable sculptures; of the latter, two colossal gate-keepers in the form of old Dutchmen in top-hats particularly catch the eye, as does the superb statue of a Chinese sage with a long beard. The main temple is distinguished by its slender proportions; it is surrounded by Chinese pagoda candelabra; an arcaded walk contains a series of stylised seated Buddhas, all gilded. Note also the pillared hall with its ebony doors inlaid with mother-of-pearl, and a recumbent Buddha, 30m long, covered in brick with a varnished and gilded plaster coating; the 5m-long soles of the feet show, in mother-of-pearl work, the master's mystical footprints (cf.p.32).

Not far from the Wat Poh is a ferry, by means of which we may cross to the r. bank of the Menam, where stands the towering **Wat Cheng*, artistically the most effective shrine in Bangkok. The great Phra Prang is 90m high, and surrounded by four smaller ones. The main entrance, with the usual statues of the guards, is on the N. side. One can ascend, by steep flights of steps, the terraces of the central tower from outside to about half its height. All the masonry is clad in glittering coloured mosaic made of Chinese porcelain.

Returning to the l. bank, we go past the Royal Gardens, to the E. of the palace area, and reach the large kite-flying Oval which serves for this favourite Siamese sport, as well as for festivities. The NW side of the oval is bordered by the Royal Museum, a modern building containing the King's private collections: splendid Siamese gold- and silver-work, musical instruments, porcelain; note a 2m-high bronze statue of Shiva wearing Siamese royal robes, from the Hindu era; similarly, a four-armed Vishnu. In a wooden shed, a large ceremonial carriage, fantastic in style.

On the E. side of the Klong Talat, opp. the Royal Gardens, lies the *Wat Rachabopit* with gate towers shaped like bishops' hats, and the tombs of the numberless children of King Chulalongkorn, which are done in a great variety of styles, Siamese and European. – Further NE, the small *Wat Suthat*, whose main temple contains a large gilded Buddha and, at his feet, life-size alabaster figures of a teacher and 42 novices. In the square, the swingboat festival *Lo Ching Cha* takes place annually; the swing is 24m in height; for the prize swing, an object fixed high on a bamboo pole must be retrieved in the teeth.

The finest panorama of town and environs is to be had from the Wat Saket, whose bell pagoda towers up, visible at a great distance, from the wooded artificial mound *Po Kao Tong* ("golden hill"). The enclosed "grove of eternal peace", at the foot of the mound, is the cremation place for the bodies of aristocratic Siamese.

Further N. lies *Dusit Park* with the new race-course and a bronze equestrian statue to King Chulalongkorn by the French sculptors Masson and Saulo (1908).

The modern *Wat Thepsurin*, not far from the sta. for Korat, is the burial place for members of the royal family.

Excursion to Ayuthia.

Railway (line to Korat), approx. 65km in 2hrs.; steamer on the meandering River Menam (approx. 75km) in 7-10hrs.

The rly runs along by the canal *Klong Sompoi* and, about 10km before Ayuthia, passes the large park of the modern royal pleasure-seat *Bang-pa-in*, with water-couses, pools, wooden summerhouses, a stone reception hall, a Buddha temple in Gothic style, etc. The palace was mainly the work of Italian builders.

Ayuthia (the "invincible"), the capital of Siam destroyed in 1767 (p.298), now an insignificant small town, lies on one of the many arms of the Menam, on and by whose waters the lives of the inhab. take their course. The ruined site, with a perimeter of 14km, and overgrown by luxuriant jungle vegetation, extends all around the present town. The importance of the ancient city is proclaimed by the ruins of palaces, temples, columns, dagabas and sculptures of every description, some of huge proportions. A steep flight of steps leads from the shore to the former royal palace, within a battlemented wall, where vestiges of the throne-room are still recognisable; the 4-storeyed tower offers a fine survey of the whole site. About 2km to the NW, on a large platform, is a structure rising in several terraces to a height of 120m, crowned by a cruciform domed building.

Close to Ayuthia, on the l. bank, is the Elephant Kraal where, once a year in the King's presence, wild elephants from the surrounding jungles are caught. Trained animals entice the wild ones across the river into a funnel-shaped tapering compound, through which they pass into the inner kraal. The King, who watches the proceedings with his guests from a dais, decides which animals are to be tamed; the others are set free again. One can usually see, in the stables near the kraal, some of the elephants which have been caught.

JAVA.

Java, one of the four "Great Sunda Islands", lying at lat. 6-9° S. and long. 105-114½° E., approaching 1000km in length and 75-200km in width, 131,508 sq.km in area, with the island *Madoera,* forms part of the enormous curved mountain-range which, though much broken up, runs from Burma via the Andaman and Nicobar Is. and Sumatra, continuing down through the "small Sunda Is." to the Banda Is. and the Moluccas: the largest unified formation of its kind on earth. Geologically, the island of Java grew out of the merging together of several smaller islands, from the tertiary period, when violent volcanic activity almost completely obliterated the older rocks. On Java and in the Sunda Strait between Java and Sumatra, more than 100 separate volcanoes have been counted, of which almost a dozen are still active, including some on the grandest scale, such as Krakatoa, whose violent eruption in 1883 cost almost 40,000 people their lives and surpassed all observed volcanic eruptions in its fearfulness. Western Java consists, in its N. third, of a plain, the remainder being plateaux lying 300-600m above sea-level, with volcanic cones towering above them, stretching in two series from W. to E., the highest being: (N. series), *Salak,* (2211m), *Gedeh* (2958m), *Pangerango* (3019m), *Tangkoeban Prahoe* (2076m) and *Tjareme* (3078m); S. series, *Patoea* (2434m), *Malabar* (2343m), *Papandayan* (2660m), *Goentoer* (2244m), *Tjikoeraj* (2818m) and *Geloengoeng* (2241m). The narrower central Java possesses only one mountain range, with *Slamet* (3432m), *Prahoe* (2565m), rising above the so-called Diëng plateau, and *Soembing* (3371m).

In eastern Java the volcanoes, the highest in the island, rise directly out of the plain or from moderately hilly country, and are therefore particularly striking in appearance. In the main chain, from W. to E.: the double peak *Merbaboe-Merapi* (3145, 2911M), *Lawoe* (3269m), *Wilis* (2400m), *Ardjoeno* (3343m), the *Tengger Mts.* (2690m) with *Bromo, Semeroe* (3676m), the *Ijang-Ijang Mts* (3088m), *Raoeng* (3330m) and the *Idjen Group* (2799m).

As one might expect of its situation in the S. hemisphere, Java's seasons are reversed, compared to those of mainland Asia but, because of its proximity to the Equator in a maritime climate, the differences are trifling. In the plains there is very little variation in temperature during the year. From Oct. to Apr. is the NW monsoon, bringing abundant rain to the lowlands, but effective only up to a height of approx. 1600m. During the remaining months, (and all the year round in the highlands), the island is subject to the influence of the SE monsoon, i.e. the normal trade-wind in the S. hemisphere, also bringing regular downpours.

The flora is even richer than that in Ceylon. To be sure, the original forest has mainly been cleared; but wherever it still remains, it thrives in an extraordinarily luxuriant fashion. Characteristic are the fan palms *Corypha umbraculifera, Corypha gebanga,* the *Nipa palm* whose leaves (called "attap") provide the main source of material for roofing houses; also the *Pandanus* and the *Rotang palm* (which provides the so-called "Spanish cane"). The *Rasamalah tree* (Liquidampar Abtingiana) rises, branchless, to 25-30m, thrusting its crown up to a height of 50m. The *tree-ferns* are magnificent, the *lianas* huge; the *bamboo* grows to a size greater than anywhere else. Of the shady trees lining the roads, the splendid *Waringin* (Ficus benjaminea) is conspicuous, carrying aerial roots like the banyan fig of India. The evergreens peter out at 300m. Above this altitude, temperate vegetation begins to establish itself. At 2100m we find conifers,mosses and lichens, with European plants higher still.

Among the indigenous fauna, the following merit a reference: the *gibbon* or anthropoid ape (the fossil remains of Pithecanthropus, which stands even higher on the scale, were discovered in 1894 in the tertiary deposits of Central Java by the River Bangawa, by the German naturalist Eugen Dubois); the *lemur* or flying monkey, the single-horned *rhinoceros* (Rhinoceros sondaicus), the *tiger* and *Banteng ox* (Bos sondaicus), the two last-mentioned still quite common.

The population numbered 30,098,008 souls in 1905, of whom 64,917 were Europeans and half-castes, the latter enjoying the same status by law as the former, along with the Armenians and Japanese; whereas the Chinese, Arabs and all coloured people are less privileged. The natives belong to the Malayan race (cf.pp.281-2), of yellowish or brown complexion and medium build, often very well proportioned, the women graceful. The upper classes have sophisticated manners. The lower orders are submissive and industrious, and thus provide excellent labour in the plantations. The Islamic religion (p.307) is permeated with vestiges of Hinduism, although the priests are often Arabs, and women have not been banished to the harem. It is possible to distinguish between *Sundanese* in the W., true *Javanese* (who are culturally the most advanced) in Central Java, and the *Madurese* in the E. The men usually wear broad coloured trousers (known as sarong), a long seamless apron, a jacket (kabaie) and a headscarf. The women's attire consists of a stitched sarong, a cape (badju), a jacket resembling a corset (kutang) and a kind of shawl (slendang). Subdued colours, in particular browns, are preferred. The genuine sarong, whose original pattern is achieved by waxing, during the dyeing process, those parts which are not intended to be dyed (batik), is often very splendid, and will cost 50fl. or more.

Popular entertainments are the *Wajang* or shadow-plays performed with stylised leather marionettes behind a transparent screen, and the *Wajan Orang,* pantomimes with human actors in similar get-up (gods and good spirits with gilded masks, princes and ladies with white ones, demons and devils with black ones). The plot is generally taken from the heroic sagas of ancient India, and is unfolded by invisible narrators. There are popular dances also *(tandak)*, which consist of artistic movements, esp. of the hands and fingers. Unique is the *gamelan* music, produced by orchestras of percussion instruments, gongs, cymbals, marimbas, drums and two-stringed instruments. Good recitals of this type of music, such as may be heard at the courts of the princes of Central Java in particular, (pp.323 & 329), possess a charming, dreamy quality.

In the towns one can often see an open guardhouse containing a wooden block which is beaten like a bell in case of fire or a person runing amok. The latter (Mal. *Meng-amok*) is a sudden brainstorm frequently aroused in the Malays by drink, jealousy or anger. Those who fall victim to such attacks, and run through the streets in a bloodthirsty frenzy, are automatically outlawed and may be killed by anyone. They are restrained with long wooden forks.

History. – Java was known to the ancient Indians as *Java dwipa*, and was mentioned by Ptolemy as *Jabadiu.* Hindus, who settled here in the Middle Ages, founded several kingdoms with the Brahman and Buddhist religions, culture and art, the flourishing of which is still attested today by the significant remains that are preserved (pp.331-2). With Islam, introduced in the 15th c. by more recent Malayan tribes from Asia, the sultanates of *Bantam* in the W. and *Mataram* in the E. of the island came into being. The *Portuguese* opened up trade with Europe in 1522. These were followed by the Dutch (cf.pp.22-23), who set up a trading station in Bantam in 1594 and then, in 1602, founded the Dutch East India Trading Co., endowed with great privileges. Governor *J.P.Coen* moved the trading post from Bantam, where the English had also settled in 1602, to Jacatra in 1611 (Batavia, p.313) and established the foundation of the Dutch-Indian colonial empire, after victorious fighting against the local sultans. The English left the island in 1683. In 1742 the sultanate of Bantam was subjugated, with Mataram following in 1749, and in 1755 the princedoms of Jogjakarta and Soerakarta (pp.328, 336) took on the vassal status which still exists today. Mismanagement and the bankruptcy of the East India Co. led to the administration being assumed in 1798 by the Dutch government.

One of the most powerful governors-general was *Herm.Will.Daendals* (1808-11), who built the Weltevreden estates (p.313) and the great military road running the length of the island. During the European wars in the reign of Napoleon I, the Dutch colonies in part became English possessions (Java 1811-14, under Sir Stamford Raffles, p.295), until the present frontiers were drawn in 1824. In 1830, Governor-general *Count Joh.van den Bosch* introduced the so-called cultivation system, whereby the natives were compelled to place 1/5 of their working-time and part of their land at the government's disposal, to plant high-yield useful crops and sell their harvests cheaply to the government. In this way, almost the entire island was transformed into small-scale plantations, and so it remains today. A decline in yield and local protests about the oppression of the natives (descr. in Multatuli's novel "Max Havelaar") led in 1870 to the removal of the system, after it had brought the homeland some 400mill.fl. in all. Since then, the state has farmed on its own estates, admittedly with an annual deficit, and lets out ownerless land on hereditary leases. The rapid increase in population causes famines from time to time, which force many workers to emigrate.

Government. – The *Governor-general*, who is nominated by the crown in agreement with the Dutch parliament, rules in a fairly autocratic manner. The *Raad van Indië*, elected to support him, fulfils a merely advisory function. The executive body is the *Algemeene Secretarie.* The capital is Batavia, but the seat of government is located at the healthier Buitenzorg. The island is divided into 22 residencies *(Residentie)*, each with a "resident" at its head. Each residency comprises several *districts* under "assistant residents", each of whom is assisted by a "regent" from the native aristocracy. The native authorities are drawn into the government in other ways also. The *Wedonos* or district council chairmen, with whom the traveller will occasionally have business, are native village headmen, salaried however by the Dutch government.

Practical tips. – Each person arriving must pay a settlement tax of 25fl. before leaving his ship. This follows a law passed in 1912. One receives a receipt with details of one's registration obligations. The amount is refunded if one leaves again within 6 months, but this payment at the secretariat in Batavia lower town (limited service) can be rather a complex process. Only travellers with return tickets are exempted from paying this fee. Apart from this, the usual proof of identity by passport is sufficient. – The best months to travel are May and June, in which the vegetation in the N. lowlands is at its freshest after the rainy season. In Apr. and Oct. the changing trade-wind brings storms. However, no season is so unfavourable for travel as the summer in British India.

Itinerary (2-3 weeks). Travellers short of time will limit themselves to W. Java, where the contrast between the tropical luxuriance of the plain and the volcanic nature of the uplands is particularly striking: *Batavia & Buitenzorg*, 2 days; journey to *Garoet* and excursions in the vicinity, 3-4 days. In Central Java, one can gain some knowledge of the peculiarities of the native princely courts and the remarkable monuments from the island's medieval past: *Jogjakarta*, with excursion to the *Boroboedoer*, 3 days; via *Soerakarta* to *Surabaya*, 1 day. The volcanoes of E. Java are of incomparable splendour, esp. the *Tengger Mts.*, to which one should allot 4-5 days. The hill station *Tosari* in the Tengger Mts. can be recommended as a place of recuperation for a longish stay. To return from Surabaya to Batavia, the coastal steamer may be used (4 days, cf.p.335).

Money. – Java uses Dutch currency. The *Guilder* or florin (fl., worth 1*M*70Pf.) is divided into 100 cents. 10fl. gold coins are rare. In silver, there are coins for 2½fl. ("Rijksdaalder"), 1fl. (Malay "rupia"), ½fl. (Malay "stanga rupia"), ¼fl. ("kwartje"; Mal. "stalie"), 10cts. ("Dubbeltje"; Mal. "ketip"); in nickel: 5cts. ("Stuiver; Mal. "lima sen"); in copper, 2½cts. (Mal. "gobang"), 1 cent (Mal. "sen"), ½ct. ("stenga sen"). The *Javaasche Bank* issues notes for 5, 10, 25, 50, 100, 200, 500 & 1000fl.

Distances are still often measured with the old *paal* (1506·94m); 1 paal = 400 roeden; 1 roede = 12 voet (0·31m). Otherwise, the metric system applies.

Post & Telegraph. Letters: Java 10cts., Straits Settlements 12½cts., Holland 15cts.; elsewhere in the World Postal Union 25cts.; postcards: Java and Straits Settlements 5, Holland and World Postal Union 7½cts.; printed papers: 2½cts. per 50g. within the World Postal Union. – Telegrams: on Java 25cts. basic fee up to 75km, each word 3cts., up to 335km 50 and 6cts., up to 1200km 75 and 9cts.; to Europe 2½fl. per word, to British India 1½fl.

The railways are partly state-owned *(Staats-Spoorweg,* abbr. to *S.S.),* partly private *(Nederlandsch Indische Spoorweg-Maatschappij,* abbr. *N.I.S.)* and they provide a total network of more than 2250km. Even the 2nd cl. is perfectly usable. One is allowed 30kg of luggage free, and therefore it is forbidden to take larger items into the compartments. The carriages are provided with gauze over the windows as a protection against the smuts caused by the poor-quality coal. Apart from the normal railways there are steam tramways still *(Stoomtramwegs),* covering a similar total distance, but these are of little account to the tourist. – The good high-roads have aided the development of automobile travel. Cf. the little book "Through Java, a guide for car-drivers", publ. by Weltreiseverlag (38 Genthiner Strasse, Berlin W35).

One should equip oneself as for British India, although the Dutch are much less formal than the English. Gentlemen wear a white jacket even at dinner. The tropical helmet is indispensable, even in the upland regions. One should also be accoutred with umbrella and raincoat. Stout footwear is necessary on excursions into the volcanic mountains. It is convenient to have one's own mosquito net; in any case, a supply of safety pins to close up holes in the nets above hotel beds. Servants speaking the European languages are seldom found, and expensive (2½-3fl. per day, plus travelling expenses), and unnecessary if one keeps to the normal routes. Ordinary Boys for one's personal service cost barely half, but are likewise inessential. Both types of attendant can be obtained through one's hotel Mandur or through the tourist office in Batavia (p.312).

The hotels are good and clean (by tropical standards) in the larger tourist centres, and adequate in the smaller ones. Apart from the very best, they are generally managed by a native head waiter or *Mandur*, who often speaks only Malay, and who sees to the transfer of luggage from and to the steamer and the station. It is always wise to book in advance by postcard or telegram. One pays a daily price. In the early morning (6-8 a.m.), the room boy brings *Koffie* (i.e. a strong, cold coffee extract with warm milk; tea if so desired). Between 7 & 9 a.m., one is given *Ontbijt* (breakfast of eggs and cold meat. Between 1 & 2 p.m. is the "rice table" *(Rijsttafel)*: boiled rice (Dutch rijst) with curry and an abundance of other piquant ingredients, such as beefsteak with salad. It is usual to appear punctually at 8 p.m. for the main meal *(dinner),* in the European fashion. It is not easy to get charges waived if one misses meals. Service is performed exclusively by natives. The Mandur arranges the laundering of one's linen (5-10cts. per article). – The Rest-houses or *Pasanggrahans,* which the government sets up for its officials in remote areas, resemble the Indian Dak bungalows (p.XXIV). The traveller may need to resort to their use occasionally, when on an excursion, but must normally secure permission.

Language. Dutch is the official and social language among the resident Europeans, but German and French are widely known, as is English, among the educated Dutch. For Malayan expressions, see p.342.

We have retained the Dutch spellings of place-names in the text. Pronunciation is similar in most cases to that of German. One should pay particular attention to the following: *eu* sounds like the German ö (French eu); *ij* like the Engl. ay; *ie* as in Ger. (Engl. ee); *oe* like the Engl. oo in 'good'; *ou* like the Engl. ow; *u* is pron.like the Fr. 'u'; *s* is always voiced; *v* as in Engl 'father'; *z* is like the 's' in 'rose'.

Literature, see p.LXXIV.

Route 45. From Singapore to Batavia.

532 SM, several steamers per week, direct, in 40-46hrs., or 2½-3 days when calling at intermediate ports: *Koninkl.Paketvaart Maatschappij*, once a week (connecting with North German Lloyd to and from Europe), for 78fl., 42½fl., 15fl.60cts., 10fl., free luggage 150, 75 & 40kg; it is advisable to take a return ticket (cf.p.308) which is valid for 3 months and allows a discount of 30%. Similarly, the *Stoomvaart Maatschappij Nederland*, whose ships, coming via Colombo, depart every fortnight (cf.p.2).

Also, from Colombo to Batavia, the *Rotterdamsche Lloyd,* fortnightly via Padang, and the English lines *Ocean Steamship Co. & Queensland Royal Mail,* monthly.

Singapore, see p.291. The steamer sets course E. of Sumatra through a myriad low green islands. The sea is generally calm, the air hot and humid. The Equator is crossed within the *Lingga Archipelago,* 19-21hrs. after dep. from Singapore. Smaller ships then head through the Bangka Straits between Sumatra and the island *Bangka,* the larger ones pass between the latter and the island *Billiton.* Both islands form the continuation of the Malayan Peninsula and, like this, are famous for their rich tin deposits (p.281). Our ship continues through open sea until *Thousand Islands* (Duizend Eilanden). The coast of Java appears, surmounted by several volcanoes, esp., r., the triple-peaked Salak (p.313) and, l., Gedeh (p.320). On the island *Edam* stands a tall white lighthouse in the form of an obelisk. On the coast to the r., covered in coconut palms, is the old harbour of Batavia, now silted up. On the l., the port of *Tandjong Priok,* built in 1886 at a cost of 26½mill.fl., now being considerably extended. It is protected from the open sea by two low moles, each 1850m in length. In the outer harbour is the large dry dock. The steamers moor at the W. quay.

Route 46. Batavia.

ARRIVAL. The port *Tandjong Priok* lies 9km E. of the town of Batavia, and is linked with it by rly. Near the quay, the *Customs House* (Malayan kantor priksa) and the *station* (kareta api). Hotel-servants *(Mandurs)* take possession of the luggage, for which service 30-35cts. per article are added to the bill. Coolies receive 10-25cts. for conveying items to the Customs Ho. and the sta. Only tobacco and spirits are dutiable; firearms must be deposited until the requisite import licence is secured from the Stadhuis (town-hall) in Batavia. – The rly to Batavia (½-hourly in 17mins, 1st cl. 30cts., 2nd cl. 20cts., luggage 10cts. per 1/10 cubic metre) follows along a canal through marshes rich in game, with mangrove thickets, nipa and cocoa palms. The trains go alternately to each of the 2 stations of the Lower Town (see below), whence one may drive to the Upper Town in the hotel carriage (approx. 2fl.) or sado (p.312; approx. ½fl.), or by steam tramway (see below); 15cts.)

Hotels, all in the Upper Town: *Hôt. des Indes (pron. "desindes" by the natives), Molenvliet West, 125 Rm., P.6¼-15fl., excellently run, with large garden; *H. der Nederlanden, Rijswijk-Koningsplein, 135 Rm., P.7-12½fl.; Grand Hôt. Java, Rijswijk-Koningsplein; H.Central, new, obliquely opp. the Hôt. des Indes, similar prices, good cooking. – For more modest tastes: H.Tramzicht, Molenvliet Oost, P. from 4fl., well spoken of; H. de France, also in Molenvliet.

Restaurants (some with café and pastry shop): Versteegh, Rikkers, Stan & Weyns, Noordwijk; Eerste Bataviasche Bierhalle (Ger. Prop.), Noordwijk; Eerste Nederlandsche Bierbrouwerij, Goenoeng Sari. – The Hotel der Nederlanden runs a breakfast room in the Lower Town opp. the Town Hall.

Carriages. Small 2-wheeled *Sado* (the name derives from "dos-à-dos" or "back-to-back"; one faces the rear), not very comfortable, but cheap and popular: 1ct. per min, thus 30 per ½hr. and 60 per hr. Two-horse *Ebro* approx. 1fl. per hr.; *hotel carriage* 2-3fl. per hr, 4-6 per ½ day (6hrs.) – Motor-cars: at the *Hôt. des Indes*, also at the livery stables of *Fuchs,* Parapatan and Tanah Abang, and *Centrum,* Noordwijk.

Trams. Stoomtram, steam-driven, from Kasteelplein in the Lower Town along Molenvliet to the Upper Town as far as Meester Cornelis (p.316), every 7½min. – Electric tram from the state rly sta. in the Lower Town: 1. by the E. route to Weltevreden; 2. along the streets Kampoeng Lima and Tanah Abang to the Harmonie Club (p.313); 3. from Harmonie via Koningsplein (sta.) to Tjekini; 4. from Koningsplein via Waterlooplein, Vrijmetselaarweg to Goenoeng Sari.

Stations. Close together in the Lower Town: to the S., the *Staats-Spoorweg;* to the N., the *Nederlandsch-Indische Spoorweg Maatschappij.* – In the Upper Town: 1. the *State Station* Sawah-Besar, Noordwijk, Weltevreden-Koningsplein, Kebon Sirih, Pegangsaän (pron. sa-an), Meester Cornelis; 2. the *Nederlandsch-Indische station* Weltevreden-Kemajoran, Pasar Senen, Gang Solitude, Meester Cornelis.

Shipping agencies. *North German Lloyd* (Behn, Meyer & Co.), Lower Town Kali Besar West; *Koninkl.Paketvaart Maatschappij,* Upper Town, Sluisbrug, near Noordwijk Sta.; in the same building are also the offices of the *Stoomvaart Maatschappij Nederland,* the *Rotterdamsche Lloyd* and the Japanese *Nippon Yusen Kaisha* (all 3 Daendals & Co.); *Java-China-Japan-Lijn* (L.J.Lambach; limited passenger-carrying facilities), Sluisbrug; *Messageries Maritimes* (Reyns & Vinja), Lower Town, Kali Besar Oost; *Queensland Royal Mail Line* and *British India S.N.Co.* (both repr. by the Borneo Co.); *P & O & Ocean Steamship Co.* (repr. by Maclaine, Watson & Co.)

At the Tourist Office, corner of Noordwijk-Gang Poole, one may obtain information about travel in Java, timetables, illustr. guides etc.

Post & Telegraph Offices (Kantorpos, Kantor kawat): in the Lower Town between the 2 stations. In the Upper Town is the General Post Office, in Waterloo Square; a branch (Bijkantor) in Noordwijk. Counter service 7 a.m. to 6 p.m. (8 p.m. on mailing days for Europe), Sat. 9-5. The Telegraph Office, Sat. until 8 p.m.

Banks: *Javaasche Bank* (the state issuing bank*), Nederlandsche Handels-Maatschappij, Nederlandsch-Indische Escompto-Maatschappij, Nederl. Ind. Handelsbank, Hongkong & Shanghai B.C., Chartered Bank of India,* all in the Lower Town; the Nederl. Ind. Escompto-Maatschappij and the Nederl. Ind. Handels-Maatschappij with branches in the Upper Town, the former in the building of the Koningl. Paketvaart-Maatschappij (see above), the latter near the Post Office. Banking hours 7.30 a.m. to 12.30 p.m. and 4.30 p.m. to 7 p.m.; Sat., 7.30 a.m. to noon.

Consulates. Germany: *Dr Lettenbaur,* consul-general, Koningsplein, W. side; Austro-Hungary: *E.H.Th.Quellhorst;* Switzerland: *A.E.J.Buss;* Gt. Britain: *J.W.Stewart.*

Clubs (accessible only by introduction): *Societeit Harmonie* (p.314), with elegant premises and copiously stocked reading-room, concerts on Sat. 6-8 p.m.; and the military *Societeit Concordia*, open to civilians also (p.316), with beautiful gardens, concert Wed. eve 6.30. – *Deutscher Turnverein* (German Gym Club), Gang Thibault. – *English Sports Club* in the Koningsplein. – Gentlemen may pay calls on families only between 7 p.m. and 8 p.m.

CHEMIST: *Rathkamp,* not far from the Harmonie. – BOOKSHOPS: *Papyros*, in the Old Town; *G.Kolff & Co.*, Noordwijk, in the Upper Town. – Maps from the *Topographical Bureau* (Kantor gambar), Goenoeng Sari.

Division of time (1 day, if time is limited): 6-9 a.m., drive through the Upper & Lower Town; then visit the Museum (p.315); rice table at 1 p.m. (p.310); rest until 5 p.m.; in the evening, walk through Noordwijk and Rijswijk (p.314). After dinner, one can visit the Javanese Theatre *(Wajang malaju* or *Komedi Stambul)* in Molenvliet, where performances last until late into the night. – One is also recommended to visit one of the hut quarters *(kampoengs),*which are reached by narrow alleys from the main streets; and, if one's stay lasts several days and the weather is dry, to make an approx. 1½ drive through the picturesque kampoengs and woodlands (with horseshoe-shaped Chinese tombs), which stretch out on the W. side of the town, from the Tangerang road to the sta. Kampoeng Lima, returning along Tanah Abang.

Batavia, capital of the Dutch-Indian Colonial Empire, with 138,500 inhab. (9000 Europeans and half-castes, 28,000 Chinese), lies at lat. 6° 5' S., long. 106° 53' E., at the mouth of the muddy and pebbly *Tjiliwoeng,* which is conducted by 4 canals to the sea. Founded in 1611 as a Dutch factory (i.e. trading-station) on the territory of the Sultan of *Jacatra,* the settlement solemnly adopted its present name in 1619 after the local princes (whom the English supported) were bravely driven off. Newly fortified, it stood firm and victorious against repeated attacks by the Javanese and, despite its position in a fever-ridden distr., blossomed rapidly as the premier trading-town in the East, being the depot for the export of products from the Indies, China and Japan. The eruption of the volcano Salak (p.317) in 1669, and the earthquake of 1699, both of which blocked the bed of the Tjiliwoeng and held back its waters, only worsened the unfavourable sanitary conditions; nevertheless, the number of inhab. remained at 150,000 until the end of the 18th c. Since the beginning of the 19th c., the European suburbs *Molenvliet,* Noordwijk, Rijswijk etc. came into being on the higher land to the S., also the settlement *Weltevreden* ("well-being") which was laid out in 1808-11 by Governor H.W.Daendals (and which has tended to lend its name to the entire Upper Town), and the S. suburb *Meester Cornelis.*

The Lower Town *Batavia Benedenstad)* is inhabited today only by natives and other Asians, but it still contains the businesses and warehouses of the Europeans. In its outward appearance as well as in its business life, the commercial quarter is a far cry from the big English colonial centres; outside trading hours (9-4 or 5 p.m.), it is quite deserted. At its centre are the two *stations* (p.312), the Town Hall *(Stadhuis*; Mal. "Ruma bitjara"), built in 1652 in Dutch style, with the Resident's offices and the police station, the *Post & Telegraph Building* and the Law Courts *(Raad van Justitie).* To the N. of these, near the tram terminus, is preserved a gate of the former *harbour fort*, in heavy baroque style, all other fortifications having been dismantled. To the W. of the gate, beneath some trees, is an ancient *Chinese gun-barrel,* 4½m long (Mal. kiai stomi), where women pray to be blessed with children, and offer flowers, scented candles, etc.; the Latin inscr. "Ex me ipsa renata sum" ["I am of the new birth"] is a later addition. – The road *Kali Besar* follows the W. side of the canal, with tall old patrician houses, in which large commercial firms, banks, agencies etc. now have their offices. To the N., by the old harbour, is the fish-market *Pasar Ikan* where, among other fish, golden carp are sold for food, having been bred in paddy-fields nearby. – To the S., the Chinese quarter *(Chineesche Kamp),* with its pretty houses and temples, and a theatre *(Komedi Tjina)* on the Godokplein.

The quarter *Jacatra,* to the E. of the business centre, contains the old Stadskerk, dating from the 17th c. and, opp., the tomb of Governor Zwardecroon, with chased copper decoration. Not far to the S., on a wall, is the skull of a rebel, the half-caste Pieter Erberveld, who tried to topple the Dutch mastery in 1722.

From the Lower Town, the street Molenvliet, shaded by waringin trees, tamarinds, acacias and teak, follows the canalised Tjiliwoeng for 3km in a straight line through the upper parts of the town, where the Europeans reside. The mainly one-storeyed houses, with their pillared halls and marble floors, and surrounded by gdns, are freshly whitewashed after each rainy season and, in their simplicity and cleanliness, are very Dutch to the eye. At the S. end of the street, outside the garden of the Hôtel des Indes is a magnificent waringin tree, the largest in Java. The continuation of the Molenvliet, beyond the elgant building of the *Societeit Harmonie* (p.313), is the street Rijswijk West, with good European shops in which one can buy snake-skin belts, purses & cigar-cases etc., also, on occasion, beautiful silver filigree work from Sumatra. On both sides of the Tjiliwoeng Canal, the elegant streets Noordwijk and Rijswijk Oost branch off E., with villas, hotels, shops and, esp. in the Noordwijk, several restaurants where boulevard-style animation develops in the evenings before the main meal. By the Sluisbrug is the entrance to *Wilhelmina Park,* with its groups of old trees and lotus-covered pools (the former moats). – In a large garden, stretching S. as far as Koningsplein, lies the *Town Residence of the Governor-general* (Mal. Ruma Tuan besar, cf.p.319), with several offices attached to it.

The Koningsplein is a uniform expanse of lawn almost 1 sq.km in extent, surrounded by avenues of tamarinds. In the middle of the W. side of the square is the Museum. In front of this, an elephant monument donated by the King of Siam in memory of his visit in 1871 (cf.p.295).

The *Museum (Mal. Gedong permainan gadja), founded by the *Bataviaasche Genootschap van Kunsten en Wetenschappen,* contains outstanding historical, archaeological, ethnographical and industrial collections, and deserves more than one visit (e.g. before *and* after one has seen the island). Entrance, daily, 8 a.m. to 3 p.m.; the attendant will open up the closed rooms. An extensive rearrangement of the collections is intended.

In the marble vestibule, old stone figures and fine old Dutch carved wall panelling. R., the *archaeological collection* (note the war trophies from the Lombok expedition of 1894: gold jewellery, ornaments & weapons), l. the *coin collection* (exceptionally fine is the section on the Dutch islands); the large central hall lies ahead, with *sculptures from the *Boroboedoer* (p.331; cf. also p.250). In the rooms on the N. side of the central hall is the important *ethnographical collection, with many trophies from the Dutch campaigns and presents from native princes to the Dutch governors-general. Room I: native clothing, jewellery and weapons; to the l. of the entrance, a model of a mosque in Palembang (Sumatra). Room II: musical instruments, incl. fine gamelans (p.307): nos. 1243-56, the large gamelan composed of 60 instruments, which belonged to the imperial insignia of the Sultan of Bantam; a large collection of Wajang figures (p.307). Room III: models of native houses; to the r. of the entrance (no.610), a carved seat of honour; artistic plait-work in the cabinets. Brass objects; by the W. wall, a model of the moated citadel of Jogjakarta (p.328). Room IV: an open hall with primitive wood-carvings and statues of idols. – On the S. side of the central hall is a *collection of Buddhist objects & bronzes.* – Further, the *Library*, and some rooms containing fine old *Dutch furniture.* In the last room beyond the reading-room is a collection of batik patterns (cf.pp.306-7). – Stone sculptures in the garden.

The Museum is much frequented by the natives on Sun., Wed. & Sat., when the visitor has an opportunity to see the attractive garb of the women and children.

On the S. side of Koningsplein lie the *Armenian Church*, the building of the *Koningl.Natuurkundige Vereenigung* and the *Residentiehuis,* the dwelling of the Resident of Batavia. – On the E. side, the sta. *Weltevreden* (see below). Beyond, the *Willemskerk*, a circular domed building with steps up, all around it.

To the E. of the River Tjiliwoeng which, at this point, retains its natural winding course, extends the garden suburb Weltevreden, with its many elegant dwellings. At its centre is Waterlooplein, an expanse of lawn approx. 350m square and named after the *Waterloo Monument,* erected in 1825. On Sun. afternoons, from 5.30 to 6.30, the military band *(Bataviaasche Stabsmuziek)*, whose artistic prowess is well known, plays here. On the W. side of the square, opp. Willemslaan, is a monument to *General Michiels,* who fell during the Bali expedition in 1849. On the E. side stands the *Paleis*, originally the residence of Governor-general Daendels (p.307), now a government building where the Raad van Indië holds its meetings on Fridays. In front of this the fine memorial to *Jan Pieterszon Coen,* founder of the Dutch-Indian colonial empire (cf.p.307), who died in 1629 while defending Batavia against the sultans of Bantam and Mataram. To the S., near the Paleis, is the *Concordia Club* (p.313) with large gdns. – To the N. of Waterlooplein we mention: the imposing *Theatre* (Schouwburg), where European troops occasionally perform, and the *General Post Office.*

N. of Weltevreden is the quarter *Pasar Baroe* (pron. passer baru), where many Chinese dealers live. Outside the town stands a *Chinese temple* (Chineesch kerk), which was the governor-general's residence in the 18th c., and the large *Chinese Cemetery.*

To the S. of Weltevreden, the former *Botanical & Zoological Gdns* (Planten- en Dierentuin), now a pleasure-park with dance hall, roller-skating rink, etc. – Not far to the S., the former residence of the Javanese prince *Raden Saleh* (1816-81), who was active as a painter in Holland over a long period; it contains a few hunting scenes by him.

Route 47. From Batavia to Buitenzorg.

Nederlandsch-Indische Spoorweg Maatschappij, fast train morning & afternoon, also slow trains, in 1-1¼hrs., for 3fl., 2fl. or 75cts. The 2nd class is perfectly usable; even in the 3rd cl. there are special compartments for Europeans.

Sta. in the Lower Town, see p.312. The line passes through the suburb Jacatra then, beyond the Chinese cemetery and Chinese quarter, the European quarters, and reaches (6km) *Weltevreden Sta.* (p.315), the main station of the Upper Town, where most passengers alight.

Through the suburb (12km) *Meester Cornelis* (p.313), and onward across the leafy flood-plain of the winding Tjiliwoeng with its cocoa plantations. At (33km) *Depok,* the gentle climb to the upland region commences.

55km. **Buitenzorg**. Hotel Mandurs and carriages await the arrival of the more important trains at the sta.

HOT., simple but good: *H. Bellevue, ¼hr. from the sta., near the main entrance to the Botanical Gdns, with celebrated mountain views from the rooms at the rear; H. du Chemin de Fer, to the S. of the sta., quite close.

POST & TELEGRAPH in the sta. – BANK: branch of the *Nederl.Indische Escompto-Maatschappij* in the Hôtel du Chemin de Fer (8-12 noon).

CARRIAGES (Sado, cf.p.312) for excursions: to Kota batoe 2fl., to Batoe toelis 1½fl. return; hotel carriage dearer.

The CLIMATE is astonishingly uniform. The warmest month is Sept. with 25·5°, the coolest Feb. with 24·5° mean temp. The precipitation is spread throughout the year (total 4427mm). It rains on 18-24 days in the month, generally between 2 and 4 p.m., and in the night. Before and after the rain there is fine weather as a rule.

If time is limited, one day suffices. The *Botanical Gdns* are open from sunrise to sunset. A rapid visit will take about 2hrs. Because of the rain, the paths are set with round pebbles, thus thick-soled shoes are recommended. – For a longer stay, the visitor will find the small handbook for Buitenzorg and surroundings useful (in Dutch & English; Batavia, G.Kolff & Co.), with maps and illustrations.

Buitenzorg (pron. boytenzorch, i.e. "carefree"; Mal. Bogor), a town of 33,400 inhab. (1700 Europeans, 4000 Chinese) and seat of the governor-general of Dutch-India and many officials, was founded in 1745 by Governor G. W. van Imhoff. It occupies an unusually charming situation on a small plateau enclosed by the gorges of the *Tjiliwoeng* and the *Tjisadana* (265m above sea-level), among paddy-fields and groves of palms and bananas; it lies on the N. slopes of the volcanic cones Salak (p.321) and Gedeh (p.320), both of them covered in thick jungle, and with their heads in the clouds. The fertile volcanic soil, the freshness emanating from the rivers and rushing streams and the abundant rainfall – all these produce a luxuriant vegetation unsurpassed in Asia.

From the sta. we go S. to the Hôt. Du Chemin de Fer then, leaving this on our r., turn E. to the Groote Postwweg, which forms the W. edge of the Governor-general's park and the Botanical Gdns. Along the Groote Postweg stand several institutions connected with the latter: the *Herbarium*, the *Library of the Agricultural Dept*., the *Botanical Museum* (open daily 7 a.m. to noon); further on, the *Museum of Technical and Commercial Botany* (accessible only with the permission of the Gardens administration) and a small *Zoological*

Museum, whose collection of reptiles and insects is most instructive (entry by request). At the Hotel Bellevue the road turns E. On our r. is the *Chinese Quarter* (Chineesche Kamp) with an interesting market (passer), where tropical fruit is sold under open halls, and a pretty little temple. On the l. is the main entrance to the Botanical Gardens.

The ***Botanical Gardens ('s Lands Plantentuin, Hortus Bogoriensis)* stretches across an undulating terrain, some 58 ha. in extent, intersected by water-courses lined with stone, and falls away on the E. side to the deeply-cut Tjiliwoeng. Founded in 1817-22 by the German botanist *Karl Reinwardt*, it has developed into the most famous example of its kind in the tropics, because of its great variety, its systematic arrangement, its excellent laboratories and other places of study – and esp. under Directors *J.E.Teijsmann* (1831-68) and *Melchior Treub* (1880-1909). If it is inferior to Peradeniya (p.42) in scenic attractiveness, it remains nonetheless, as a centre for scientific and practical research, a model so far unsurpassed elsewhere. It is principally a collection of trees divided into sections, uniting the natural species with one another, being labelled with Latin numerals and letters. Two examples of every tree are provided. The Director of the Gardens is *Dr J.C.Koningsberger.*

From the main entrance we follow the Kanarie Laan, an avenue of old Canary trees *(Canarium commune)*, whose trunks are completely covered in fungi and creepers. On our l., we catch glimpses of the offices, laboratories, officials' dwelling etc. To our r., in section I.B, the largest liana in the gardens, an *Entada monostachyca,* which stretches on as far as sect. III.A. Turning r. at the tomb of Stamford Raffles' wife (p.308), we reach the *Pandanus* group (II.D), with screw-shaped leaves on the trunk and aerial roots, and the *ferns* (II.KN), represented in numerous varieties. From the small *pavilion* above the E. slope of the Gardens we have a fine view across the palms and water-plants to the volcanoes of the Gedeh group. To the l., across the way, the orchids, growing in great numbers on plumeria, most bearing only a few blooms. On the r. of the path, a magnificent collection of *palms* (II.F). We turn off r. to the tropical conifers *(Gymnospermae)* and then descend S. to the *marsh- and water-plants,* adjacent to which a piece of jungle has been retained, the so-called *Busch Tuin* (II.PO). – An iron suspension bridge (Hangbrug) crosses to the island enclosed by 2 arms to the Tjiliwoeng, where seed-plants are reared in beds, and experiments made with the extraction of rubber (cf.p.290). Further N., we return to the main gardens across a wide wooden bridge.

From this bridge we turn, passing the *Myrtaceae* and *coconut palms* (V.L), towards the narrow N. part of the gardens, which contains the giant tropical deciduous trees, the *fig* and *bread-fruit trees,* the *casuarinas, laurels, euphorbiaceae, dipterocarpas* etc. On our return, going between sections VIII.D and VIII.C, and passing a *belvedere*, we head towards the large pond. On our r., we look into the *Governor-general's park,* fenced off by railings, but also accessible (apart from the immediate surroundings of the one-storeyed

Residence or Paleis, with lawns and groups of trees and plentiful fallow-deer (Hertenkamp).

The Great Pond *(Groote Vijver)* has a rich covering of aquatic flowers, of which the beautiful South-American *Victoria Regia* occupies the NE arm, and encloses a pretty island with palms. We walk round it and, on its W. side, follow the Canary Avenue northwards. At the NW arm of the pond, filled with long-stemmed white water-lilies, there is an attractive view of the Governor's Residence. – In the W. part of the gardens we follow the curving King's Palm Avenue *(Oreodoxa regia)*, from which side-exits lead to the Herbarium and Museum (p.317), and then past the quiet *family cemetery of the governors-general*, set in a bamboo thicket, to another group of *palms* (XII.E) and the rose garden (XIII.L), where a monument commemorates Director Teijsmann. Passing the Director's dwelling and laboratories, we return to the main entrance.

Part of the Botanical Gardens is the Experimental Garden *(Cultuurtuin)*, 1km N. of the sta. in the suburb Tjikeumenh, with the *Agricultural College* (72 ha.), and the Mountain Garden at Tjibodas (p.320).

Excursions (carriages, see p.317): 4km SW to *Kota batoe*, where one can enjoy a refreshing swim in cool spring-water (15°C, 50cts.); - 2-3km SE through paddy fields to *Batoe toelis* (rly, see p.321), with Hindu antiquities: lingams, a slab with footprints and, beneath a small bamboo shelter, a stone tablet (batoe toelis = inscribed stone) upon which, in ancient Javan writing, the foundation of the town Pakuwan Padjadjaran by King Purana is recorded. Nearby, a pretty bamboo bridge over the Tjiliwoeng (panoramic views).

From Buitenzorg to Sindanglaya: 36km by carriage 6-8hrs.; one is advised not to take a sado (p.312), which would be excruciating on such a long drive, but a 2-wheeled *kareta* instead, in which one faces forwards, with 3 strong horses, since the larger part of the journey ascends sharply. It is prudent to hire the carriage only as far as *Tjirokanie,* in the first instance,and to change there for Sindanglaya (3fl.); relay horses for the latter stage, 1-2fl. per horse.

The road is good and shady, the landscape charming, with its huddled native villages, the vegetation lush, the traffic very busy (burdens are carried on springy bamboo poles on the shoulder). The carriage takes 1hr. to reach *Gadok*, the drive being reasonably level and comfortable. Then the upward gradient commences, with fine views. In 1½-2hrs. we reach *Tjisaroea* and thence, in ½hr., *Tjirokanie*, where one can obtain fresh horses or change carriages.

The road continues in wide curves for 1½hrs. to the top of the pass. About 5min before this, a side path goes off to the l. (bring a coolie guide up from Tjirokanie; 40-50cts.), reaching, in 20min, the beautiful tree-fringed crater lake, *Talaga Warna*, whose fish are held to be holy; thence by a footpath to the pass summit *Poentjak* (1482m), the saddle between Gedeh-Pangerango (see below) and Kantjana (1800m), forming the frontier between the residencies of Batavia and Preanger. At the top, a Javanese inn where one may get tea, and a viewing pavilion. Then downhill in ½-¾hr. to *Sindanglaya* (1044m), founded as a health resort in 1864 for the Dutch-Indian army, with a hotel-sanatorium (the Director is Austrian, very obliging). 15-20min to one side, near the warm spring *Tjipanas,* is the country-seat of the Governor-general. There are pretty walks to the heights in the vicinity (extensive views), best undertaken early in the morning or 1½hrs. before sunset. Following the road NW we come to a dam, whose reservoir is surrounded by splendid tree-ferns; then, r., a small cemetery, and onwards to *Tjimadjan* (interesting weekly market).

2hrs. SW (steep, unshaded footpath: saddlehorse 2½fl.; chair 2fl. and 50cts. for each bearer), on the slopes of Gedeh, lies the botanical mountain garden *Tjibodas* (1290m), next to which is a stretch of jungle 283 ha. in size, with a scientific station. The buildings are accessible only to researchers bearing permission from the authorities at Buitenzorg. Rambles in the jungle should be undertaken only with a guide (tigers are not infrequently met with).

The ascent of the volcanic group Gedeh-Pangerango forms a strenuous 3-day tour, which should be discussed in detail with the hotel manager. Apart from provisions and guides, one must take coolies also, to make a path through the more densely overgrown places; horse for the 1st day, 6fl. - On the 5hr. ride, we pass Tjibodas (see above) and *Tjibeureum*, a clearing in the jungle, where there once was a botanical garden, and where 3 waterfalls, 120m high, cascade down a leafy mountain-wall; and so we come to the so-called *Governor's Hut* or *Kandang Badak* (badak = rhinoceros), set on the ridge (2400m) linking the two summits of the Gedeh itself. We spend the night in the hut which, although primitive, is done up from time to time. On the 2nd day we rise early and, by torchlight, set off on foot on the 2hr. gentle ascent to the summit of **Pangerango*, a now dormant volcano, clad with thick vegetation, in whose enormous crater the youngest cone, *Mandalawangi,* forms the highest point (3019m). Before sunrise, the temp. often drops to freezing-point. There are superb views across Java, N. & S. as far as the sea. More interesting is the still-active volcano **Gedeh* (2958m), which we may climb on the 3rd day, again in 2hrs., from Governor's Hut. As we approach we hear, every 5min, the thundering sound made by a huge piece of rock which lies across the innermost crater vent and is jerked upweards. The crater is divided into 2 parts, between which it is possible to walk, by volcanic debris. Several hundred vents emit steam, some of them with a loud roaring noise. One can descend from here to Sindanglaya or Soekaboemi (p.321).

From Sindanglaya, the road descends to (18km) *Tjiandjoer* (p.321): carriage in 1½hrs. for 3fl.

Route 48. From Buitenzorg or Batavia to Tjibatoe and Garoet.

Both lines belong to the *Staats-Spoorweg;* they meet at *Padalarang* (p.322).

Route 48a. From Buitenzorg to Padalarang.

141km. Fast train in 4hrs., slow train in 6½hrs., for 6fl.75cts., 4fl., 2fl.15cts.

Immediately outside Buitenzorg there is a splendid view r. of the volcano *Salak* (2211m) and the River Tjisadene far below. The line touches (5km) *Batoe toelis* (p.319) and begins to curve upwards. The beauty of the mountainous landscape steadily unfolds. Paddy-fields *(sawahs)*, as everywhere in Java, occupy the valley bottom and climb the slopes in terraces; they resemble a single lake divided up by straight causeways; the mountain streams trickle from step to step and fertilise the fields with their mud. Workers wearing broad-brimmed hats plough with teams of oxen and till the fields. Since there are distinct dry periods in winter-time, we can see all the stages of rice-growing: the light-green seed beds with their tiny plants clustering together, the reflecting pools with the young rice bushes set at regular intervals, the dark-green waving fields of mature rice and the yellow fields ready for harvest. The objects resembling turnstiles set on tall bamboo poles are scarecrows.

At (14km) *Massing* we have, l., a fine view of Gedeh (p.320). There are coffee and tea estates on the slopes of the jungle-covered mountains. The railway crosses the saddle (546m) between Salak and Gedeh and reaches the province of the Preanger Residencies, famed for its beauty.

27km. *Tjitjoerog* (505m). – At (35km) *Paroengkoeda* (410m), the stop for *Tjibodas* (not to be confused with the botanical garden mentioned on p.320), begin the upland plateaux of W. Java (p.305), framed by mountain ranges to N. & S., and separated by low saddles. The line continues its ascent.

58km. *Soekaboemi* (601m; hot.: Gr.H.Selabatoe, 60 Rm., P.6½fl.; Gr.H.Victoria, 53 Rm., P. 5½fl.), a town set among greenery at the S. foot of Gedeh (p.320), a favourite resort of retired officials because of its pleasant climate (24° annual mean temp.) and delightful walks.

A tunnel pierces the mountain saddle which divides the plain of Soekaboemi from the next plain. – 83km. *Tjibeber* (452m) The line turns N. and reaches the small town (96km) *Tjiandjoer* (459m; hotel at the sta.), where the main road from Buitenzorg-Sindanglaya arrives (p.320). – We continue E. through fine scenery. After (105km) *Seladjambé*, the rly crosses the *Tjisokan* (r., a waterfall) and, after (114km) *Tjipeujeum*, the deep-cut bed of the *Tjitaroem,* into which we have a view (l.). The softly-shaped mountains on both sides remind one of the German Mittelgebirge. The plateau, which the old military road to E. Java also crosses, is covered with green fields and clusters of trees and bushes. The rly curves up over the saddle to the W. of *Goenoeng Boeboet* and then descends via (135km) *Tagogapoe* to (141km) *Padalarang*, see below.

Route 48b. From Batavia via Bekasi and Padalarang To Tjibatoe and Garoet.

248km. *Staats-spoorweg,* fast train route between Batavia (Weltevreden) and Surabaya (p.336), the first stage being of less interest to the tourist than the route via Buitenzorg, and therefore better considered for the return journey: fast train (with dining-car) in 6hrs., slow train in 12hrs., for 11fl., 7fl.50, 3fl.71cts.

The train departs from *Weltevreden-Kemajoran* sta., see p.312. – 7km *Meester Cornelis* sta. on the E. side of the suburb. – We continue E. through extensive paddy-fields (sawahs; cf.p.321) which, if properly cultivated, can yield up to 3 harvests per annum. The more important stops: 22km *Bekassi;* at (52km) *Kedoenggedeh* we cross the *Tjitaroem;* 59km *Krawang.* – 80km *Tjikampek,* junc. for the line to *Cheriton,* whose extension (instead of the tram-line) as far as Semarang is being planned. – The main line turns S. and begins to ascend. – 99km *Poerwakarta,* on the r. bank of the Tjitaroem, which is crossed again. With a steeper gradient and in many curves, the line rises to (117km) *Plered* and crosses the border of the Preanger Residencies (p.321). There is a descent, also with many bends, then another ascent. Tunnels.

155km *Padalarang,* junc. for the line from Buitenzorg (see above). The broad plateau of Bandoeng, which the railway crosses, is famous for its setting within a circle of volcanoes: to the N. *Boerangrang* (2064m) and *Tangkoeban Prahoe* (p.323), to the NE *Poelo Sari* (1850m) and *Boekit Toenggoel* (2209m); to the E., *Manglajang* (1812m) and, to the S., *Malabar* (2343m). – 161km *Tjimahi.*

170km **Bandoeng**. – HOT.: Hot.Homann (Dutch owner; manager Treipl, Austrian), Societeitweg, close to Groote Postweg, 60 Rm., P.6-7½fl., good; Hot. Preanger, Groote Postweg, well spoken-of; H. Wilhelmina in Bragaweg (coming from the sta.), 27 Rm., P.5¼fl.; H. Mignon, by the sta.; H. Phoenix.

Bandoeng (715m), a lively small town of 47,490 inhab. and larger railway workshops, is the capital of the Preanger Residencies and a favourite hill station. Near the sta. are the dwellings of the Dutch Resident and Assistant

Resident. In the main square, surrounded by waringin trees and called *Aloen-Aloen* (as in all Javanese towns), stands the Regent's residence, the open hall for his gamelan orchestra (p.307) and a whitewashed mosque (Missingit) with a red tiled roof and Moorish arcades. On the race-course outside the town, horse-racing (many spectators) takes place in July.

Ascent of the volcano Tangkoeban Prahoe: take a carriage in the evening to the village *Lembang* (1240m), situated 13·5km N. of Bandoeng on the S. slopes of the mountain. Good road. At Lembang, accommodation and food are available at a Pasanggrahan (p.310) for 2fl. The cinchona plantation was begun in 1855 by the German explorer of Java Franz Junghuhn (1809-64) at the behest of the Dutch govt., for the purpose of obtaining quinine bark; a white obelisk marks his grave. The following morning, set off betimes on foot (guide 50cts.; pony 5fl.; litter 1fl. and 50cts. per bearer) up an easy gradient, mainly through jungle, for 2½hrs., to the summit of *Tangkoeban Prahoe* (2076m), which owes its name ("upturned boat") to the shape of the mountain. The crater, over 4km wide and 200-300m deep, has, since the last eruption (1896), been divided into 2 basins; the larger, *Kawah Ratoe,* still active, contains a lake with warm sulphurous water and some roaring solfataras; the second basin, *Kawah Oepas,* contains a lake of mud. Nearby, a third, smaller, crater: *Kawah Domas.*

The railway goes in a straight line across the broad Bandoeng plain (marshy to the S.) until (197km) *Tjitjalengka* (715m) then, rising sharply over a mountain saddle (panoramic views), which links the N. volcanic chain with the S. one, continues to (205km) *Nagrek* (892m). Descending in great loops across viaducts, it reaches the plain of Leles, with fine views r. of the volcano *Mandalawangi* (1650m) and, l., of the pointed *Kaledong* (1240m), cultivated to its summit and, behind this, the likewise pyramid-shaped *Haromoen* (1211m), also cultivated and rising like an island out of the plain. To the SW rises the massive dark bulk of *Goentoer* (2244m). – 217km *Leles* (710m), 225km *Leuwigoong.* Then across the deep gorge of the *Tjimanoek.*

228km *Tjibatoe* (600m), junc. for the branch to Garoet (20km; coolies transfer one's luggage between trains), which conveys us through the densely-populated fertile plain via the halts *Pasirdjengkol, Wanaradja* (p.326) and *Tjimoerah* to our destination in ¾hr.

Garoet. – HOT.: *Hot. Papandayan (prop.A.Hacks, German newspapers), clean and pleasantly run, with baths, 50 Rm., P.6½-8½fl., good cooking; *Hot.van Horck, on the bungalow system, with garden, attractive rooms, verandahs, baths, same prices; Hot.Kurhaus; H.Villa Dolce (prop.Ingenhoes), 45 Rm., P.5½-7½fl.; H.Hielkert, H.Goentoer. – CLUB: *Societeit Intra Montes*, easy of access to outsiders. – POST OFF. Near H.Papandayan. – DOCTOR and CHEMIST in the town.

For EXCURSIONS, the hotel landlords make all arrangements and provide carriages or motor-cars, saddle-horses, chairs *(Tandu)* and guides according to a tariff. There are 2 kinds of carriage: 3-horse covered two-wheeled carriages with 2 seats, called *Kalarballon* or *Karretje,* for which the prices given below apply, and *Delemans,* which cost half as much again. It is usual, when undertaking longer trips, to set off in darkness between 4 & 5 a.m., after taking early morning coffee at one's hotel. Food is supplied and the 'rice table' (p.310) postponed until one's return. Light clothing is advisable, but one should not forget a top-coat for the early part of the drive. Tinted spectacles and gloves are a convenience when climbing craters. One should avoid much walking on foot; even when the sky is overcast, it is unwise to over-exert oneself during the hot part of the day. – A printed guide *(Gids voor Bandoeng, Garoet en Omstreken* by S.G.Doorman) may be had at one's hotel, 2fl.

Garoet (712m), the small capital of an administrative distr., set among gardens with its neat, low houses, is the favourite hill resort in West Java, and suitable for longer stays. The climate is relatively dry and very pleasant. It occupies a most charming situation in the fertile plain watered by the meandering *Tjimanoek,* within a circle of extinct and still active volcanoes, of which the wooded Tjikoeraj and the smoking Papandayan to the SW, and the gloomy bare Goentoer to the NW, are particularly prominent.

To one side of the main street, which runs through the town from E. to W., is the municipal square *Aloen-Aloen,* a stretch of lawn with fine waringin trees and a view of Tjikoeraj; a bust commemorates the agriculturist Holle for his services to the area. The square is bordered to the N. by the Assistant Resident's dwelling and, to the S., by that of the Regent (p.308); on the W. side, a mosque, without any hint of Moorish influence, with a high tiled roof rising several storeys. – If we continue W. along the main street and follow the signpost to Panembong S. to a small bridge, and then, beyond the latter, climb, r., down to the steep bank of the Tjimanoek, we have a *view across the paddy-fields (around which the river describes a bend), S. to the thickly-forested Tjikoeraj (p.327), a volcanic formation truly classical in line. We enjoy a similarly fine prospect of Goentoer (see below) if, on leaving the sta., we proceed a few paces W. along an avenue of spathodeae.

The following *round trip is rewarding (3hrs., carriage 5-6fl.): cross the Tjimanoek to the NW by the covered bridge and continue across the densely-populated plain, with views across bamboo groves and fields of rice, maize, tobacco and millet to the chain of volcanoes, but esp. to the bare black bulk of Goentoer straight ahead. Our route brings us to the (3 paals=4½km) little town *Trogong* (728m), where several roads meet. We continue NW for a further 2km between fish-ponds (vischvijvers), in whose green-framed surfaces the cocoa palms reflect, to Tjipanas (770m) at the foot of *Goentoer* (2244m). The warm springs (28-35°), which come to the surface here, are used for bathing; from a bamboo pavilion above the village we obtain a good view of the lava stream on the slopes of Goentoer. We return to Trogong and continue NE for

¾hr. to the small lake Sitoe Bagendit (696m) which takes its name from its resemblance in shape to the handle of a creese or kris (bagendit). One can have oneself rowed about on the ferry (made of dugouts and provided with a protective roof), and can visit the pavilion on the hilly island, which offers an enchanting panorama across the surface of the water, partly overgrown with lotus and other aquatic plants, to the smiling plain and the volcanoes all around. – There is also a pretty drive via Trogong across the Leles plain to *Leles* (p.323; 4½hrs. return, 5½fl.); just before Leles is the small lake *Sitoe Tjangkoewang* with several islands, one of which contains the tomb of Tanoek Raka, beneath waringin trees, a sultan of the old Mataram Empire.

The **excursion to Papandayan*, to the SW of Garoet, requires 9hrs' return journey. We take a carriage (5fl.) along a busy road via *Bajongbong* (966m) in 1½-2hrs. to Tjisoeroepan. On our l., we catch sight of the beautiful Tjikoerai, on whose slopes the light-coloured strips are the tea plantations and, straight on, we see Papandayan with its steaming crater. The small town *Tjisoeroepan* (1220m), at the 11th paal (16.5km) from Garoet, lies at the foot of the volcano. At the hotel Villa Pauline we can order lunch for our return (2fl.) If so instructed from Garoet, a native will meet the traveller by a wooden pavilion and assign ponies to the party (according to a written tariff, 3½fl., ladies advised to use the ordinary saddle), guides (75cts.) and grooms (25cts.) or chairs (4fl. incl. bearers). The ascent on foot is extremely wearisome and not to be recommended.

The path passes through paddy-fields and other plantations, then through jungle, with orchids, tree-ferns, wild bananas etc., crossing gulleys and streams. At the only fork we bear r. The stench of sulphur and the change in vegetation announce the proximity of the crater, which lies 2100-2200m above sea-level on the NE slope of Papandayan (2660m), 500m below the summit. The footpath ends, 2-2½hrs. from Tjisoeroepan, at an open shelter. The present crater, with its abrupt side-walls, sits in a larger, older one more gentle in profile. No devastating eruption has been recorded since 1772, but the floor of the crater depression is full of vents, many of which emit steam and sulphurous vapours with a loud hissing sound (which explains the name of the mountain, signifying "smithy"). We also see pools of water, which heat the stream as it flows through them, bubbling mud-pools, yellow sulphur crusts, hollow columns of sulphur etc. One should negotiate these features with care and, on the NE side, where the crater edge has collapsed, enjoy the fine view of the Garoet plain (with its glittering paddy-fields), and the volcanoes all around; in the far distance to the NE is Tjiremai (3078m), near the N. coast of Java. – The climb to the summit is not normally undertaken, and is supposed to be dangerous, on account of beasts of prey.

The journey to the mud crater Kawah Manoek, W. of Garoet, takes 8-9hrs. return: carriage (5fl.) via Trogong (p.324) and *Samarang* (915m) to *Pasair Kiamis* (1230m, 1¾-2hrs.; at the 12th paal, i.e. 18km, from Garoet), where, as in the case of the previous excursion, ponies (2½fl., attendant for the saddle-horse 50cts., coolies 25cts.) or chairs (3½fl.) will be waiting. We notice, even before reaching the village, that the ground is strewn with dark obsidian splinters, as hard as glass, which are characteristic of Manoek. The ascent (1hr.; also on foot, less toilsome than on Papandayan) commences through large cinchona plantations, then through jungle. The crater Kawah Manoek is smaller than that of Papandayan, but more varied in appearance. The name means "bird crater" (kawah = crater, manoek = bird). Its floor is full of bubbling mudholes, hot jets of water of different hues and solfataras, and it appears to be subject to volcanic undermining. One should therefore only venture on it with the greatest caution, so as not to break through the surface crust and suffer scalding.

Quite different in nature is the excursion to the lake Talaga Bodas, to the NE of Garoet, 8-8½hrs. return: carriage (3½fl.) via *Tjiparaj* and *Sadang* to *Pandaharan* (710m; 7 paals = 10.5km from Garoet), 1km SE of the halt *Wanaradja* on the rly to Tjibatoe. One can therefore take the early train (½hr.) The village Wedono (p.308) of Pandaharan, who is notified by the hotel, holds horses (4½fl., grooms 50cts.) and chairs (5½fl. incl. 8 bearers) in readiness for the onward journey and, on request, sends them to the sta. or on in advance to *Wanaseda*, whither one generally drives in the carriage (¼hr.), the latter being left there. From Wanaseda the path, which is marked at 1½km intervals by white posts (paals 1-9), pursues an unshaded course at first through coffee estates, then bamboo and forest. After ¾hr. it begins to zigzag upwards. There are splendid views behind of the plain, with the volcanoes Tjikoeraj, Papandayan and Goentoer in the background, and *Galoengoeng* straight ahead (2230m; the last disastrous eruption of the crater occurred in 1822). Between paals 6 & 7 is a small Rest-house, where the bearers generally eat. Then comes a steep climb up a pleasantly shady path which, after 2½hrs., suddenly ends at **Talaga Bodas*, a round crater lake 500-600m in diameter, splendidly framed by green slopes. The greenish, milky colour of the water is attributed to deposits of aluminium sulphate. It is possible to walk round the lake, but the shore path is difficult to negotiate in places. At several points one can see the streams which flow into it, seething like the lake itself and exhaling sulphurous vapours or cold steam. The guide takes us also, on the NW side, about 200m below the lake, into a barren valley, called *Padjagalan* ("place of slaughter"), because of the carbonic acid which pours out of the ground and kills small creatures.

Much vaunted is the ascent of *Tjikoeraj* (2818m), the extinct and highest volcano in the vicinity of Garoet, esp. for the view of Papandayan from above, and of the S. sea. It takes 3 days and requires special preparations, since it is necessary to send out coolies to clear the path in places (10-12fl.) We spend the first night at the livery stable at *Tjikadjang* (1240m; 5km S. of Tjisoeroepan, p.325); from here we set off at 2 a.m., ride, in 1½hrs., to the upper limit of the tea plantations, and continue for a good 6hrs. on foot through incomparable jungle to the bald peak, below which we spend the night in a tent brought for the purpose.

Route 49. From Tjibatoe to Jogjakarta.

329km. *Staats-Spoorweg,* belonging to the main line from Batavia (Weltevreden) to Surabaya (cf.pp.322 & 334), fast train twice daily in 6½hrs. for 14fl.75cts., 10fl., 2fl.15cts.; luggage, see p.309.

Tjibatoe, where the branch from Garoet meets the main line from Batavia, see p.323. – The line describes a wide arc around the N. outliers of *Sedakeling* (1667m), cutting through the N-S. cross-bar (beyond the halt *Malangbong*, 605m) between the volcanoes *Tjakraboewana* (1720m) in the NE and *Djoelang* (1620m) to the S. It then descends in many curves after the halt *Tjipeundeuj* (800m), with views of the beautifully-shaped *Sawal* (1763m) to the SE, in the plain of Tasikmalaja. The landscape unfolds all the characteristic charm of Java. – 35km *Tjiawi* (500m). Splendid journey. – The fast train does not stop until:-

57km *Tasikmalaja* (350m), capital of a government distr. – We pass the halt *Bodjong* and cross the Tjitandoei again. 97km *Bandjar* (25m). This completes the descent to the lowlands, which is accompanied by a perceptible rise in temperature. The railway runs through the swampy thickets of the Tjitandoei valley, which belongs among the most splendid jungle regions in the world. Only in a few places has it been cleared by burning. The greenish marshlands are full of 10m-tall reeds and other plants. Royal tigers, rhinoceros, black panthers, banteng oxen, crocodiles and all kinds of water-fowl reside here. Beyond the halt *Langgon* (108km), the line crosses to the l. bank of the Tjitandoei and reaches the residency *Banjoe Mas.* 117km *Meloewoeng.* Grassy plains replace the marshy terrain. – The fast train takes 1¼hrs. from Bandjar to Maos. In the evenings, before one reaches

Maos, the warning lights of *Tjilatjap* are visible in the distance r., the only port on the S. coast, to which there is a branch from Maos (21km). The main line crosses the broad *Tjiserajoe* and reaches 176km *Maos* (Hot. Andreas), an unimportant place on an elevated and therefore healthier terrain, while the plain around it is still relatively marshy. The journey is hot, and rendered unpleasant by the soot and coal-dust.

We pass through a long tunnel before (218km) *Gombong* (18m). 225km *Karengajar* (13m); 237km *Keboemen* (20m); 265km *Kotoardjo* (15m). The landscape is densely populated. The villages lie among bamboo groves. The line crosses the *Progo* and passes through the plain E. of the river, which is planted with sugar-cane. – 329km *Jogjakarta.*

Jogjakarta.

HOT.: Gr.Hot.Djokja, Residentielaan, new and well-managed, good cooking; H.Togoe (German prop.), beyond the rly line, near the sta.; H.Mataram, H.-Rest. Centrum, Residentielaan. – CLUB: *de Vereenigung*, at the S. end of Residentielaan (p.329), well-equipped; German magazines in the reading-room.

BANKS: *Javaasche Bank, Nederlandsche Escompto-Maatschappij.*

The districts of Jogjakarta and Soerakarta (p.334), the "Vorstenlanden" or princely states, still ruled over by native sultans, have lost relatively little of their characteristic quality under European influence. Their people, too, are more handsome than in Batavia and its environs. The Sultan's residence, called the *Kraton* (p.329), is, however, far inferior in splendour to the princely courts of India, and a visit to its interior (permission to be obtained through the Dutch Resident) hardly merits the trouble. The picturesque *Waterkasteel* is freely accessible (½hr. by carriage from the hotel; 3fl. Give the driver exact directions). – In the *Market Halls*, not only fine fruits and vegetables are to be seen, but one can also buy knives, swords, woven cigar-cases, batik articles etc. A permanent *exhibition* of craft products is to be found near the Hot.Togoe. – One should not neglect the excursion to the *Boroboedoer* (p.331, 1 day).

Jogjakarta (113m; the name means "flourishing power"), abbr. to *Jogja,* capital of the Javanese state of the same name, nestling with its diminutive houses in the shade of giant tropical trees, residence of the Sultan, the Dutch Resident subordinate to him, and many members of the feudal aristocracy of the land, possesses 80,000 inhab., of whom about 15,000 belong to the princely court as officials, servants, bodyguards, craftsmen, artisans etc. There are 2000 Europeans and half-castes who, apart from the Dutch officials and the officers and men of the Dutch garrison, are principally owners of sugar, coffee and indigo plantations. The town consists of several streets running its length, notably the *Residentielaan* and *Lodje Kedjil*, intersected at right angles by transverse streets; also the *Kraton*, the Sultan's quarter, shut off like a fortress.

The Residentielaan, with the large hotels and business houses, a splendid avenue of fig, waringin, tamarind and other tropical trees, runs due S. from the sta. and is about 1500m long. The transverse streets lead E. to its parallel street, Lodje Kedjil, which also contains shops. Near the S. end of the Residentielaan: l. the *Residentiehuis* or palace of the Dutch Resident, with a pillared marble vestibule and large garden in front in which, beneath a protective canopy, sculptures from Boroboedoer, Parambanan and other ancient temples of the land are set up; r., the small fort *Vredeburg,* with ramparts from Daendel's time (p.307) and the barracks of the Dutch garrison (½ battalion of infantry and a detachment of artillery). To the S. of the Residentiehuis, on the corner of Kampementstraat, is the white building of the *Vereenigung* (p.328).

The Residentielaan comes out into the walled *Aloen-Aloen*, the square in front of the Kraton, an expanse of grass 300m square and framed by tall waringin trees. It is used for parades and festivals. In the centre, among waringin trees cut in the shape of shades, is the place of execution. To the W., the *mosque*, a simple covered structure in Javanese style, with a forecourt through which runs a stone-lined conduit for the sacred ablutions, and two subsidiary courts, in whose open halls the Sultan's gamelans are played (p.307) at festivals. On the SE side of the square are some cages with tigers and panthers. – To the S., between two sentry boxes, is the main entrance to the Sultan's town proper, the:-

Kraton (entry only with special permission, p.328), a rectangle 1100m long and 750m broad, surrounded by a ditch and rampart, bastions and 4 corner towers; it dates from the middle of the 18th c. We pass through several courtyards, in one of which the Sultan's 50-man "guard of honour" is housed, and so into the innermost court, shaded by waringin trees, the scene of celebrations which mark, with great pomp, the birthdays of the Prophet, the Queen of the Netherlands (Aug.31st), the Sultan and the heir to the throne. (Access to these is to be had only through the Dutch Resident's influence and recommendation; tail-coat and white tie obligatory). In the middle of the court is the Audience

Chamber. To the S. of this is a second hall which serves as a banqueting chamber for festivals. Adjoining this to the W. is the Sultan's long, low palace. All around are dwellings of the princes and the court, courtyards and gardens. Further on, we see the streets and squares containing the houses of the other inhabitants. – In the W. portion of the Kraton is the so-called "water-castle" or **Tamansarie* (i.e. "flower garden"), standing in the middle of a pool. It was built in 1758 for Sultan Amang-Ku Buwono, was abandoned in 1812 and destroyed by an earthquake in 1867, and is now accessible only through a subterranean passage. At the gate, where the carriage stops (p.328), one generally finds a Malayan guide (25-50cts.) The interior, formerly the harem and site of opulent luxury, is now a confusing labyrinth of dilapidated brick walls, halls, vaults and bathing-pools with broad stone steps: all this picturesquely covered with damp moss and overgrown with tropical vegetation. We are told that the daring Marshal Daendals made a surprise forced-entry and compelled the astonished sultan, surrounded by his court, to sign a treaty.

Excursions. – TO THE BOROBOEDOER. – tram of the *Nederl.Indische Spoorweg-Maatschappij* (the line Jogjakarta-Magelang) to Moentilan in 1¾-2hrs., for 60cts. 2nd cl.; from the sta., boys guide visitors to the nearby village, where one can obtain a carriage from the kareta-hirer for the drive to the Boroboedoer (2-horse 2fl., or 3fl. return; 4-horse 4fl., 6fl.) – More pleasant is the direct *coach* journey from Jogjakarta to Boroboedoer (4-horse with change of horses half-way; 3 hrs., 1-4 pers. 16fl.) or the drive by *motor-car.*

At the Boroboedoer is the *Hot.Boroboedoer* (5 Rm., P. 5fl.), where one may purchase a printed guide by Gronemann; on display is Leemans' monumental work (Leiden 1873; with plans & drawings).

The road, mostly accompanied by the tramline, ascends in a N. direction between fields of sugar-cane and bamboo groves, among which the villages lie. To our r., the beautiful volcano *Merapi*, still active, and, to the N. and forming part of the same massif, *Merbaboe* (p.335); to our l., the low jagged limestone chain of *Menoreh*, stretching N. as far as the volcano *Soembing* (3371m). The distance to *Moentilan* (359m) is about 30km.

The carriage road to the Boroboedoer (12km) branches off W. from the road to Magelang and, after 7-8km, takes us past the recently restored *Temple of Mendoet;* the stair notches display the favourite Buddhist decorative motif of a monster, out of whose jaws emerges a protuberance which, as it swings downwards, forms the banister (cf.p.58); humorous reliefs of children (boys clambering up a fruit-tree, banging heads together like young buffaloes, catching turtles etc.); in the interior, whose vaulting is composed of corbels, we see, among other things, a superbly-worked seated Buddha, 3m high. The path crosses the *Elo*, a tributary of the *Progo*, then the latter also. To our l., the pretty little temple *Tjandi Pawon,* also restored, and similar in type to the temple of Mendoet. About 2km further on, we reach the *Hot. Boroboedoer*, at the foot of the hill bearing the shrine, and which rises 50m above the plain. A path lined with sculptures leads upwards.

The ***Boroboedoer,* a Buddhist shrine like the dagabas of Ceylon and the Burmese pagodas, presumably erected in the 8th c. A.D. (cf. p.307), unearthed from a long oblivion beneath debris at the instigation of Sir Stamford Raffles in 1814 and, since 1849, more closely examined on the orders of the Dutch govt., rises like a pyramid in ten terraces, approx. 30m above the hill, whose top is covered by its walls. The material is hard grey trachyte. The hewn stones are fitted together without mortar or clamps. The ground plan is in the form of a square of side 151·5m, extended into a 36-sided polygon by outbuildings. The two lowest terraces are open; the five middle ones are enclosed by massive balustrades, behind which run ambulatories; the three circular upper terraces support small dagabas between which, at the top, a large central dagaba towers up. Narrow staircases lead up on all four sides.

The sculptured decoration of the middle and upper terraces is overpoweringly rich: one counts at least 1504 reliefs (988 well preserved) and 441 statues of Buddha. Only very few details can be given here. On the outside of the *3rd terrace:* on the pediment, depictions of men and women, apparently purely for decoration; up on the balustrades, in niches, statues of the Buddha seated in the various postures and hand positions (mudras, see p.248) as the enlightened one, the thinker, teacher and caller. The inner walls of the ambulatory passage, to which we ascend by 8 steps, are covered with reliefs all round, depicting the entire legend and story of Buddha. Upper series, to the l. of the E. stair-gate: 4th image, 1st one beyond the 1st corner: the still unborn Buddha quits his lotus throne before the eyes of his 3 predecessors, in order to begin his wanderings on earth; 1st image past the 9th corner: after his birth, lotus blossom falls down on him to flower beneath his feet; his mother, near him beneath a tree; W. side, 4th image after the 5th corner: Buddha as a young man stretches the mighty bow and shoots the arrow through 7 cocoa palms, so winning the king's daughter Yasodhara. Next come his encounters with a mortally sick man (6th image from the 7th corner), a corpse (1st image from the 9th corner) and a monk, all of whom inspire him to renounce throne and family, in order to overcome the evil in this world by renunciation; in the 4th image beyond the W. steps, he leaves his palace at night, as is suggested by the sleeping guards. The ensuing images depict his abstinence, penitence and saintly career until, finally, he goes up into Nirvana as a perfect being (3rd image from the 9th corner past the N. stairs). The lower series of images portrays mythological scenes from the Buddha's previous existences (Jatakas, p.246). – The reliefs in the passages of the *4th-7th terraces* glorify Buddha and his followers, each in a series of mainly very attractive portrayals. – The bell-shaped dagabas on the *three upper terraces,* 32 on the 8th, 24 on the 9th and 16 on the 10th terrace, are pierced with latticework, each containing a seated figure of Buddha. The dagaba in the middle of the topmost terrace is 8½m high and 16·5m in diameter, and was originally totally enclosed, so that the large (uncompleted) image of Buddha within remained unseen; as a result of the undermining of the floor by treasure-seekers, it has sunk deeply into the cavity beneath. – There is a magnificent *panorama over the verdant valley, the jagged Menoreh Mts. to W. and SW, and the volcanoes Merapi (E.), Merbaboe (NE) and Soembing (NW); in the middle distance, the spire of the temple of Menoet can be seen rising up out of the tops of the palm trees.

To PARAMBANAN: one does best to take the train (p.334; 25min), for 1fl.75cts., 1fl. (return). If one catches the early train, one has the cooler morning hours to visit the temple ruins (3-4hrs.), and can be back in Jogjakarta before noon. – A carriage, there and back, costs 10fl.; the road is bad in places.

Near the temples is a *Pasanggrahan* (p.310), open to visitors: P.5fl., 2 pers. 7½fl.; Rm., supper and breakfast 3½fl., breakfast only, 1fl. – One can purchase a good English account of the ruins.

The temple ruins of Parambanan lie 15km (main road 17) E. of Jogjakarta at the S. foot of Merapi (p.335). Railway and road touch the village *Kalassan* at 12 and 14km respectively, where, ¼hr. NE of the sta., one should note the ruins of one of the most beautiful pieces of Hindu architecture in Java (p.307); according to a Sanskrit inscr., it was completed in 779 A.D., and was a Buddhist reliquary shrine. The interior, part of the roof and the S. chapel are preserved. Not far to the N. is the ruin *Sari,* a structure of delicate proportions and decoration, which served as a vihara to it (p.LXVI). From here, it is 2½km by the main road to the temples at Parambanan. Most travellers will go directly by rly from Jogjakarta to:-

Parambanan, also called Brambanan. Take a coolie as a guide, at the sta.; in ¼hr. we reach the village bazaar, then r., in a few min, to the famous *temples, cleared from the rubble in 1885-90, and lying on a square platform within a three-fold rampart (mostly destroyed); there are three larger temples on the W. side, 3 smaller on the E., and two even smaller ones (virtually destroyed) between the two rows. They are possibly the tombs of princes and doubtless date from the same period as the temple at Kalassan (see above). The sculptures show motifs from Hindu mythology adapted to Buddhist themes.

The temples on the W. side are in the form of polygonal pyramids with terraces round them. In the *S. temple* is a four-headed depiction of Brahma. – The middle one is the **main temple* of the whole group. Its inner walls are covered with a peculiar surface decoration reminiscent of the sarong patterns. The main chamber contains a figure of Shiva approx. 3m tall; in the side chambers are (S.) Shiva as king of penitents, (W.) the elephant-headed Ganesa and (N.) the eight-armed Durga, whom the natives worship as the "Loro Djonggrang" of their mythology, and who gives the temple its name. Charming reliefs cover, esp., the inner wall of the balustrade which runs round the upper terrace, with scenes from the Ramayana epic (p.LVIII), beginning on the l., near the E. steps, and continuing S. and W.: battles, animal scenes, plant motifs etc., all most expressive and imaginative in execution, with the various ethnic types well characterised; on the last tablet on the E. side, on the r. near the steps, we see the hanuman monkeys hurling, into the straits between India and Ceylon, rocks which are arranged by the fish into Rama (Adam's) Bridge. The outside walls are adorned with Hindu and Buddhist divine figures; underneath these, on the N. side (r.) near the steps, are three comely women, who have been called the three Graces. – The *N. temple* contains an image of Vishnu, over 2m tall.

The temples on the E. side are also polygonal in plan, but on square bases surrounded by pretty medallions in relief, depicting the holy bo-tree and all manner of creatures. On the stairs up to the *middle temple* is an elephant in deep relief; within, a monolithic nandi bull (p.80).

With a coolie from the Pasanggrahan to show the way, we follow the main road (forming the boundary between the princely states of Jogjakarta and Soerakarta) N. to the village *Kloerak* and, beyond this, take the road r. to the temples of *Tjandi Loemboeng* ("Tjandi" means a temple tomb), where 16 small ruined temples crowd around a larger one which is decorated with reliefs. – On the same road, further N., is the even larger *Tjandi Boebrah*, which however has been destroyed down to its base. – Then, in the distance, we see the temples of Tjandi Sewoe, the most extensive group of ruins of its kind in Java, called the "thousand temples" (in fact 241), peculiar rather than beautiful, and much destroyed. They lie on a concentric series of square terraces, formerly separated by ramparts. The centre and highest terrace supports the main temple, shaped like a cross with arms of equal length. It is surrounded, on the next and somewhat lower terrace, by 28 small and 44 very small temples. On the 2nd terrace lie 5 medium-sized temples and, on the lowest, 80 small temples with 88 minuscule ones clustered around them. The relief and figure decoration is everywhere well executed. The entrances open in groups towards the main temple or towards the outside. At the bottom of each of the 4 flights of steps are two colossal monolithic kneeling guards.

If the hour is already late, one may dispense with the visit to the ruins of Pelahosan, which can be reached in another ½hr. on a hot road through the fields of sugar-cane. The 2 temples are, incidentally, former viharas (p.118), with numerous Tjandis around them, which however have now almost totally disappeared. By the S. temple is a colossal figure, of which there are 2 at the N. temple. The large inner chambers, about 20 sq.m in size, contain altars, each formerly having 3 figures of Buddha, well executed (the middle figures have disappeared). – From here, it is 20-25min to the sta. Parambanan.

Route 50. From Jogjakarta to Surabaya.

313km. *Nederl.Indische Spoorweg-Maatschappij* to Soerakarta (Solo), 60km; 2 fast trains in 1hr.24min, normal trains in 1½-2hrs., for 3fl.50, 2fl.50cts.; one of the normal trains is a through train (13hrs.), for 13fl., 8fl.50cts.; fares from Jogjakarta to Surabaya 14fl.50, 9fl.75, 4fl.7cts.

The line passes through the fertile and densely-populated lowland at the SE foot of Merapi (p.335). The fields are cultivated mainly with sugar-cane, but tobacco is also grown. There are numerous clean rly halts where, however, the fast trains do not stop: 12 km *Kalassan*, 15km *Brambanan* or Parambanan, see p.332; r., the temple ruins; 28km *Klaten*.

60km. **Soerakarta**. – STATIONS: main sta. *Solo*, also called *Balapan* (i.e. race-course), sta. for the Dutch Indian Rly (Jogjakarta-Semarang, see p.335) and the State Rly, whose 2nd stop, in the direction of Surabaya, is *Solo-Djebres*. – Hotel carriage 50cts.

HOT.: H.Slier, Residentielaan, near the Dutch Resident's dwelling, ¼hr's drive from the sta., quite good, P.5-7fl.; H.Rusche, opp. the Post & Telegraph Office, 36 Rm., P. 4½-5fl. – PASTRY SHOP: *Hecker*, Voostraat, - CLUB: *Harmonie*, Voorstraat.

CARRIAGES: in the streets, ½hr. about 50cts., short distances 25cts.; hotel carriage by tariff: 2hrs. 2fl., 3hrs. 2½fl. – TRAM, without separate classes, rarely used by Europeans; shortest distance 5cts.

BANKS: *Javaasche Bank* near Hot .Slier; *Nederl.Indische Escompto-Maatschappij*. – BUSINESS HOUSE ("Toko"); *Haye Bros.,* Bloomstraat. – PHOTOGRAPHER: *Johannes*, Heerenstraat; *daily attendant* at the Hot.Rusche.

A drive lasting 1hr. suffices to see the town, during which one passes through the *Kraton* (p.335). Permission to view the inner chambers of the Kraton may be obtained through the Dutch Resident, at whose dwelling one must call (p.335) at 9 a.m.; the permission is normally given on the same day; an officer acts as guide. – Horse-racing in June & November.

Soerakarta (140m), also called Solo, with 118,400 inhab., is the capital of the second Javanese state in Central Java. The Sultan, who bears the title *Susuhunan*, dubbed "Keizer" [emperor] by the Dutch, has a dependent relationship with the Dutch govt. similar to that of the Sultan of Jogjakarta, and is much respected by his people. Subordinate to him is the minor prince *Mangko Negoro*, who even possesses a troop of his own, trained and uniformed in European style (1 battalion of infantry, ½ squadron of cavalry). The native aristocracy has also largely preserved its prestige.

The town is very sprawling and set among greenery. The most important traffic artery is the Residentielaan in which, standing opp. one another, are the *Residentiehuis,* dwelling of the Dutch Resident and set in its own grounds, and *Fort Fastenburg,* occupied by 2 Dutch companies of troops. The road runs into the *Aloen-Aloen*, the square in front of the Kraton. As in Jogjakarta, this has two trees in the middle, cut into the shape of shades, and a small courtyard on the W. side, where there are some panther-, leopard- and tiger-cages. The *Kraton,* the Sultan's residence (cf.p.334), is said to contain around 10,000 inhab.; a five-storeyed tower marks the entrance to the inner courtyards containing the princely quarters and banqueting halls, which are however of no special interest (p.328). One drives on through to the *S. Aloen-Aloen*, where one may visit the elephant stall. Further on, we pass the people's garden, then the house of the Mangko Negoro with sculptures in the front garden, the barracks and the parade ground for its soldiers; also, the race-course.

The ascent of the volcano Merapi (2911m) takes 2 days and is toilsome; permission to use the Pasanggrahan must be obtained from the Dutch Resident. We take the tram (2½hrs.) as far as *Bojolali* (413m) and then ride to *Selo* (approx. 1500m) on the ridge linking Merapi to Merbaboe, where we spend the night at the Pasanggrahan. Here, provisions and guides are to be found for the ascent of the summit (6hrs.) The crater is very active with fumaroles, whereas the higher *Merbaboe* (3145m) is extinct.

From Soerakarta (Solo) to Semarang, 106km, Dutch Indian Rly (continuation of the line from Jogjakarta, cf.p.334), in 1hr.40min-3¼hrs., for 6½fl., 4¼fl.; stops made by fast trains: *Goendih & Kedoeng Djati*. – *Semarang* or *Samarang* (*Hôt. Du Pavillon, over 50 Rm. with bath P.6½-10fl., also provides carriages and motor-cars; H.Jansen), capital of a residency and Java's 3rd port and trading-town with 89,500 inhab. (4800 Europeans & half-castes, 12,400 Chinese), can also be reached from Batavia and Surabaya by the steamers of the Kgl.Paketvaart-Maatschappij. Trams provide the link with the port, and with the garden suburb *Tjandi*, set on a hill where, among others, the Chinese multi-millionaire Oei Tjang Hang has his palace.

The rly to Surabaya (distances below reckoned from Djokja) crosses the *River Solo,* the largest in Java, and passes round the N. foot of the beautifully-shaped volcano *Lawoe* (3269m). Fertile lowlands. The fast train stops at (89km) *Modjosragen*, (113km) *Walikoekoen* and (132km) *Paron*, the express takes 1½hrs. to reach (157km) *Madioen* (67m; Hot.van Beresteyn), at the E. foot of Lawoe. Then we continue along the N. foot of the volcanic *Wilis Range* (2183m). The fast train stops at (204km) *Ngandoek,* the express takes 1hr.5min to reach (226km) *Kertosono*, junc for a branch S. to *Blitar*, which then turns E. to *Kepandjen* and from there N. via *Malang & Lawang* (p.341) to Bangil (p.338; 216km). – The line to Surabaya crosses the navigable *River Brantas*, touching on (242km) *Djombang,* (272km) *Modjokerto,* 282km *Tarik,* where a smaller line branches off to Sidhoardjo (p.338) and (285km) *Krian* and reaches (non-stop express from Kertosono in 1hr.18min):-

Surabaya: 310km. stat. *Goebeng*, for upper town, 313km sta. *Kotta*, for lower town. (Local time 24min ahead of railway time).

HOTELS. In the upper town: Oranje Hot. (prop. L.M.Sarkies), Toendjoengan, built in 1911, 80 Rm. with bath, P. 7-12fl., omnibus at the sta., good; H.Simpang in the Simpang quarter; in the Embong Malang quarter is the good pension *van Vloten.* – In the lower town: Hôt. Des Indes, Werftstraat.

RESTAURANTS & PASTRY SHOPS: *Grimm*, corner of Heerenweg & Oude Heerenweg; *Hellenddorn,* Pasar Besar.

BEER at *Oei Moo Liem,* Bültzingslöwenplein.

CLUBS: *Simpangsche Societeit; Societeit Concordia.* – In both clubs, as also in the restaurants and beer-hall, a concert every evening.

CARRIAGES: 2-horse Kossong, 1fl. per hr.; 1-horse dog-cart 60cts.

TRAM: N. to S. along the main street, running the length of the town; also from the lower town to the port.

BANKS: *Javaasche Bank; Chartered Bank of India; Hongkong & Shanghai Banking Corporation; Nederlandsche Indische Handels-maatschappij; Nederl. Indische Escompto-Maatschappij.* – Business hours until 4.30 p.m.

SHIPPING AGENCIES: *North-German Lloyd,* Behn, Meyer & Co., Societeitstraat; *Kgl. Paketvaart-Maatschappij,* Willemskade; *Stoomvaart Maatschappij Nederland,* Willemskade; *Rotterdamsche Lloyd*, Internationale Crediet- & Handelsvereeniging Rotterdam, Willemsplein; *Messageries Maritimes*, Chineesch Voorstraat.

GERMAN CONSUL: *G. Rademacher.*

CHEMISTS: *Simpang Apotheek*, Toendjoengan; *Nederl. Indische Apotheek,* Societeitstraat. In both of these, information about doctors and hospitals.

HAIRDRESSER: *Baum & Co., Societeitstraat.* - BOOKSELLER: *van Dorp.* - PHOTOGRAPHERS: *Kurdjan,* Toendjoengan; *Karli,* Simpangstraat.

GENERAL OUTFITTERS (and tailors): *Henderson & Co.,* Pasat Besar; *Savelkoul*, likewise.

NATIVE SHOPS (engraved items in brass, basket-work etc.): *Toko Toutoren,* Gemlongan.

The most important newspaper is the *Surabaya Handelsblad.*

Surabaya (or Soerabaja), capital of the Dutch residency of the same name, lies at long. 112° 44' E. and lat. 7° 12' S., not far from the point where the *Kali Mas* flows into the 5km-wide sound which separates Java from the island *Madoera*, providing an excellent roadstead. There are 150,200 inhab., of whom 9000 are Europeans and half-castes, over 14,000 Chinese and 2800 Arabs. Trade is on the upsurge and has already outstripped Batavia. The cramped, hot lower town is the centre for the large business concerns and extremely busy. Nor is it so desolate by night as the main capital. The upper town grows out of it to the S., more as a garden suburb, esp. the quarters *Simpang* (with villas and shops, the Dutch Residence and Scheepmakerpark, where there is music on Thu. evenings) and *Embong Malang.* A long series of streets bisects both the lower and upper towns from N. to S.; at times, it follows the Kali Mas which is covered with native river craft. To the W. of the lower town stretches a labyrinth of fish-ponds (vischvijvers).

The mouth of the Kali Mas has been canalised. To its E., 3-4km N. of the lower town, and connected to the latter both by railway and tram, lies the port of *Oedjoeng*, with marine workshops and two large basins. At the entrance to the port is the viewing tower *Wilhelminatoren.*

Route 51. From Surabaya to the Tengger Mountains.

The Tengger Mts., for the exploring of which the mountain health resort of *Tosari* (p.339) provides an excellent base, make up, along with the *Semeroe* (abutting to the S., p.341), the most splendid volcanic region in all Java. The enormous, ancient Tennger crater with its three newer inner craters rates among the most remarkable volcanic formations on earth, even standing comparison with the ring-shaped mountain ranges on the moon. The inhabitants of the upper slopes, called *Tenggerese*, are descendants of the people who fled into the wilderness before the advance of Islam (p.307), and who have retained their popular form of Hinduism, and worship the subterranean fires of Bromo (p.340; Brahma?) Their villages (kampongs), scattered on the mountain ribs, are linked by good paths (in many places, steps have been made out of lengths of bamboo). The houses are windowless and their open door always faces towards the crater. The natural forest has been cleared over considerable distances and has given way to agriculture, whose products, mainly European vegetables, are marketed in the lowlands. The native flora, spurge, rhododendron, edelweiss, violet, strawberry etc., resembles that of central Europe. The casuarina, planted for firewood and called here Tjemara, reminds one of Australia.

From Surabaya to Pasoeroean, 63km: *Staatsbahn* (Oosterlijn to Probolinggo, Pasoeroean etc.), early fast train in 1½hrs., for 2fl.75, 2fl.5cts. Thence to Toasari, 44km: either *motor omnibus,* for 15fl. per person (25fl. return), incl. 60kg of free luggage; or 2-horse *carriage* in 2½hrs. to Poespo, for 5½fl., thence on *horseback* in 3hrs. to Tosari, for 2fl. (pack-horse, "pikoelpaard" 1fl.), or, on request, chair (tandoe; for sitting, with 6 bearers, 3¼fl.; litter for lying down, 8 bearers 4½fl.; on the way, the bearers will ask for a tip with the word "makan"). It is advisable to send warning of one's arrival by telegraph from Surabaya, esp. in Sept. and Oct., when Tosari is often full. Clothing: European summer suit; a tropical suit can be more comfortable around noon.

The railway follows the coast, 1-2km distant from the sea. 26km *Sidhoardjo*, where the branch from Tarik (see p.326) comes in. Beyond (35km) *Porrong*, we cross the broad *Brantas Canal*. The small horse-shoe-shaped white walls, visible on the grassy slopes, are Chinese graves. To our r., the fine volcano *Penanggoengan* (1652m) and the mighty *Ardjoeno* (3343m) come into view; separated from these by a deep valley, the distant massif of the Tengger Mts. and the ever-active Semeroe. – 47km *Bangil*, junc. for the line (mentioned on p.336) from Kepandjen via Malang and Lawang (cf.p.341).

63km. *Pasoeroean*, capital of a residency, with 35,000 inhab. If warned in advance, the representative of the Tosari hotel will meet the train and see to transport for the next stage (see above). Not far from the sta. is Hot. Morbeck, with a restaurant where one may breakfast.

The journey proceeds along the level high road, shaded by tamarinds, S. to *Badjangan*, then SE to *Gondong Wetan*, then S. again to (17km) *Pasrepan*, at the foot of the range. Travellers by carriage have a brief halt here for the horses to be changed. – The ascent, easy at first, steepens. With some difficulty, carriages reach their destination:-

Poespo (pron. Poozpo), near the sanatorium of the same name (640m), the acclimatisation centre for Tosari, under the same management. – From here onwards, the path climbs one of the ribs that radiate outwards and downwards from the Tengger crater. At first we pass through forest, then through the fields of potatoes, maize, onions and cabbage tilled by the Tenggerese. Higher up, the ribs of the volcanic dome stand out sharply. Above the latter, when Bromo is active, hang thick clouds of smoke.

The **Tosari sanatorium* (1777m), near the Tenggerese village of the same name, is famous throughout SE Asia, in account of its refreshing climate, influenced by the SE trade-wind (annual mean temp. 16°, minimum 3°). People come here to recuperate, not only from the Dutch islands but from Burma also. The sanatorium, subsidised by the Dutch govt., is under the direction of a doctor, and is excellently run. It comprises two hotel buildings and several villas of the bungalow type (50 Rm. in all; P.7½-8½fl., for a fortnight's stay 6½-7½, from one month 6-7fl.) All kinds of playing-fields provide opportunities for sport. The well-equipped library of light reading boasts German books also. The morning hours are the finest time; there is generally mist in the afternoon. The view embraces the slopes of the Tengger range, to the W. the volcanoes Penanggoengan and Ardjoeno mentioned on p.338, and the triple-peaked Kawi mountains (2270m), the plains to the N. and the sea as far as the island Madoera.

Excursions. – Exhausting, if done on foot. Saddle-horses at fixed prices: return, incl. boy, to: Ngadiwono 1fl., Penandjaan 3¼fl., Moenggal Pass 2¾, Moenggal Pass and Bromo 3½fl., Ngadisari 4½, Soekapoera 7fl. Litters are also available. – At the hotel, information is given, everything is arranged, breakfast provided, etc. For longer excursions, it is advisable to set off before sunrise, remembering a coat for the early morning ride. For the ascent of *Bromo*, because of the flying ash, gloves and tinted spectacles are mandatory, and veils for ladies. For travellers wishing to continue to *Probolinggo* (p.341), the hotel will obtain permission for the use of the Pasanggrahan at Soekapoera, and also will order a carriage to Bessi for the last section.

To Ngadiwono, a favourite walk (1hr.): up the mountain ridge and, beyond the upper hotel, descend r., following the telephone wire; then up a steep path with steps to the next W. outlier of the mountain; through the Tenggerese village *Ngadiwono* to the *Tengger Hill Station* (1840m; P. 5fl., cooking simple but good); milk may be had at the dairy.

To Penandjaan (5-6hrs. return): as above, up the ridge but descent to the l. after the hotel; cross a stream and zigzag up again; between fields of maize and vegetables, through a village and a pretty casuarina wood, also a plantation of trees laid out by the govt. for forestry use. In 2½-3hrs. we reach the shelter belonging to the sanatorium, on **Penandjaan* (2780m), the highest point in the Tengger range, on the edge of the old Tengger crater. The view is overpowering: to the S., the giant crater; SE, about 20km away, the noble ash cone of Semeroe, exhaling dark clouds of smoke at short intervals (with glasses, it is possible to discern the fall back to earth of the ejected ash and stones); E. the also active Lamongan (1670m) and the Ijang range (3088m); to the N., the plain and the sea; W., Penanggoengan and Ardjoeno. The Tengger crater is a rhombus-shaped basin, about 8km in diameter, with abrupt walls, 300-600m high, and an almost level floor, the Dasar or "sea of sand", out of which three younger craters rise: Batoq, resembling a ribbed pound-cake, the smoking Bromo in the centre, and Widodaren to the S. of this, which is composed of several craters. In the early morning, the bottom of the Tengger crater is often covered with a milky layer of mist, out of which the three inner craters emerge like islands.

The ascent of Bromo takes 6hrs., there and back (dangerous only during the rare larger eruptions). We follow the well-defined path along narrow mountain-ribs upwards for 2hrs., to the Moenggal Pass, a depression in the NW edge of the Tengger crater. Half-way, there is a magnificent view of Semeroe. At the *Moenggal Pass* (2355m), a steep path branches off l., leading to a hut situated 30-40m higher up, with a view of the crater which is astounding, though perhaps less so than the view from Penandjaan. The main path descends in a very steep zigzag to the *Dasar* (see above). The broad area (2120m) is completely covered in dark-grey pebbles and, in the manner of a desert, quite devoid of vegetation. Passing round the crater *Batoq* (2420m) we reach, in ½-¾hr., the foot of **Bromo*, whose summit towers some 250m above the sea of sand (2390m above sea-level). The flat lower slope is deeply furrowed by torrents; the steeper upper slope is covered with fresh ash and largish lumps of lava. Halfway up, we can already hear the thundering from the active mountain. We ride as far as a long wooden staircase leading up to the crater's edge, renewed by the Tenggerese every year on the occasion of their sacrificial festival in May, which attracts crowds of people. At the top, we look down into the steep-sided crater, 250m deep, whose floor resembles a weathered, greenish layer of ice. Glowing lava is visible through larger and smaller fissures. Steam is emitted with a loud hissing sound. – Climbers free from giddiness may, with adequate care, walk round the crater's edge, at whose highest point it is also possible to look down one of the craters of *Widodaren* (2610m).

The excursion to the crater lakes, between the Tengger Mts. and Semeroe, takes 12hrs. return (horse 6fl.): cross the Moenggal Pass to the foot of Bromo, see above; then through the S. part of the Tengger crater, called *Roedjaq*, which is covered with grass and ferns and serves as pasture for the half-wild horses. Then up the steep wall to the edge of the crater, near *Ider-Ider Peak* (2473m). The lakes lie on the plateau between the latter and Semeroe: in the N.

part, *Ranan Pan, Ranan Regoelo & Ranan Tjringo*; in the S. part, *Ranan Koembala.*

The excursion to Semeroe takes 3 days and, for a party of 4 pers., amounts to about 40fl. each, incl. saddle- and pack-horses, a Mandur as guide, 5-6 porters, provisions and a tent. Semeroe (3676m), which is connected by the above-mentioned plateau with the Tengger range, is the highest volcano in Java and ceaselessly active.

For the return journey, the descent to Probolinggo is recommended: a strenuous day's tour, if combined with the ascent of Bromo, which can be deliberately broken at Soekapoera (cf.p.339). – From Bromo, we ride obliquely across the flat Dasar (p.340), then over the natural rampart, about 100m high, of the *Tjemo Lawang* (i.e. gate of spirits), which is the NE dip in the edge of the Tengger crater, and adjacent to which is a funnel-shaped indentation. In the latter lies the Tenggerese village *Ngadisari* (approx.1900m), surrounded by fields of vegetables. From here there is a delightful descent, soon on a good path through the funnel-shaped valley which gradually narrows, and finally through a magnificent defile, to the village *Soekapoera,* 9-10km distant, where one can find good accommodation for the night in the Pasanggrahan. At this point, the horses and coolies brought from Tosari are dismissed. On a fresh horse (1fl.) provided by the Mandur of the Pasanggrahan, we descend another 5km steeply to *Bessi* (350m), where we are awaited by the cart ordered from Probolinggo (5fl.) The uniformly beautiful road descends gently through coffee estates and fields of rice and sugar-cane. There are numerous villages, and the traffic becomes busier. At *Pilang*, 15-16km from Bessi, we reach the coast road, along which it is a further 4km E. to Probolinggo.

Probolinggo (Hot. Busch) is a stop on the railway line, 39km E. of Pasoeroean: to Surabaya 102km, normal train in 4½-5hrs., fast train in 2hrs.20min, for 4½, 3fl.

The return journey from Tosari may also be done in a W. direction: on horseback (3fl.) to *Nongkodjaja* and on a fresh horse (2½fl.) to *Poerwodadi* (350m); then by carriage (50cts.) to the nearby rly sta. *Lawang* (p.336; Hot.Lawang); - or S. from Moenggal Pass across the Dasar plain (p.340). then up over the W. rim of the Tengger crater to the village *Ngadas*, on through jungle to *Toempang* (600m; saddle-horse from Tosari 9fl.); thence, a steam tram goes to the rly sta. *Malang* (p.336; Hot.Bellevue, Hot.Jansen). – There are Hindu antiquities between Malang & Lawang, near the rly sta. *Singosari,* and near *Pagentan.*

In conclusion, a few notes about the Malayan language, which will meet the traveller's needs. For further study we recommend: *Aug. Seidel,* Grammar of the Malayan Language, 2nd ed., Vienna 1908, 2*M*; *R.Hindorf,* Manual of Colloquial Malayan (coastal Malayan), 3rd ed., Berlin 1904, 2*M.*

The stress unless otherwise indicated, lies on the penultimate syllable whose vowel is usually long (if the syllable finishes with it), or short (if it ends in a consonant, e.g. *tûwan* (master), *kî-ta* (we); - *rám-but* (hair), *tún-ju* (fist). There are no diphthongs, so that double vowels must be pronounced separately: *kain* (coat), pron. ká-in, *taun* (year) pron. tá-un. Short unstressed vowels often disappear in speech, as does the *k* at the end of a word: e.g. *kĕlămarin* or *klămarin,* also (common) *kĕmarin* (yersterday); *anak* (child), pron. *aná.* (Only the spoken forms will be given below). The combination *ng* remains soft at the end of a word (as in Engl. "sing"; *s,* on the other hand, is always unvoiced.

DECLENSION. There is no special form for the plural; instead, the word is often doubled: *tuwan* (sir), *tuwan tuwan* (the gentlemen); or quantitative words are placed in front, such as *segala* (all), *banja* (many) etc.; e.g. *kuda* (horse), *barang kuda* (some horses). – The genitive is indicated merely by juxtaposition of nouns: *negri* (the town), *orang negri* (the people of the town), or placing the genitive word in front, followed by *punja* (i.e. "possess"), e.g. *gébenor* (governor), *gébenor punja ruma* the governor's house or govt building). – The dative is expressed by using the prepositions *akan* (at), *sama* (with), *dengan* (with), *kapadda* (additionally); *sama kuda* (to the horse), *kapadda sáhabat* (to the friend).

PRONOUNS: personal: I *(sahaja,* generally *saja),* you (sing.) *tuwan,* he (she, it) *ia* or *dia,* we *kita,* you (plur.) *kamu,* they *dia orang* (written language uses *marika-itu).* – The possessive adjectives are formed like the genitive, by placing the word *punja* after the personal pronoun: my house, *saja punja ruma.* Instead of *dia punja* (his), the suffix *–nja* is very often added: *anak-nja* = *dia punja aná,* his child.

NUMERALS: *1 satu, sa; 2 dua; 3 tiga; 4 ampat; 5 lima; 6 annam; 7 tuju; 8 delapan, dlapan; 9 sembilan; 10 sa-pulu; 11 sa-blass; 12 dua blass;13 tiga blass; 20 dua pulu; 21 dua pulu satu; 30 tiga pulu; 40 ampat pulu; 100 sa-ratus;200 dua ratus; 1000 sa-ribu; 2000 dua ribu; 10,000 sa-laksa; 100,000 sa-pulu laksa; 1 million sa-juta. ½ sa-tenga;⅓ sa-pertiga; ¼ sa-per-ampat.*

There is no proper CONJUGATION. Present, preterite and future are formed by placing adverbial elements in front: *adda* ("now"; in fact "is"), *habis* ("over, finished") and *nanti* (signifying expectation) or *mau* (in fact "to want"): Present: I eat, *saja adda makan;* Past: we ate, *kita habis makan;* Future: you (plur.) will eat, *nanti kamu makan.*

VOCABULARY.

afternoon, see "evening"
allow *kasi permissi*
and *dan*
anger *murka;* angry, annoyed *mara*
answer (n.) *balas, jawab*
to answer *menjawab*
arm, sleeve *langan*
arrive *datang*
ask *tanja*
at, near *akan, di-* (e.g. at the gate *di-pintu*
bad *jahat*
banana *pisang*
bath *permandian* (hot bath *p.ajer panas,* cold b. *p.ajer sejuk;* to bathe *mandi;* bathroom *kamar mandi*
be able *bulih*
beard *janggut*
beautiful *bagus*
bed *tampat tidor;* bed-cover *kain t.t.*
bill *bajar*
bird *burung*
black *hitam, itam*
blood *darah*
blue *biru*
boat *prahu*
bookseller *orang jual baku*
bottle *botol*
bread *roti*
breakfast *makanan pagi hari*
bridge *jambatan*
bering, fetch *ambil*
brush *sikat;* to brush *menjikat*
bull *sapi, lembu* (cf."meat")
butter *mantega*
buy *beli, bli*
calf *ana lembu*

candle *dian,* (tallow light) *dian lilin*
carriage *kareta, kreta*
cease *berhenti*
cent *sen*
chair *kerussi, krussi*
to change (money) *tukar*
money-changer *tukang tukar wang*
cheap *murah*
cheese *kejo*
chemist *ruma obat*
chicken (cock, hen) *hajam*
cock *jantan,* hen *betina*
child *ana*
Christian *orang meschi*
cigar *roko, cherutu*
clean *bressi;* to clean *bekin bressi*
climb *naik*
clock, o'clock *jam (i.e.*hour); used with *pukul* (to strike) when telling the time: I want to eat at 1 o'clock *saja mau makan pukul satu* (strike one); what time is it? *brapa pukul* (how many strikes?) It is 5 o'clock *adda jam pukul lima;* ¼ to 7 *kurang sa-saku pukul ti*
clothes *pakean*
coat *salimut, kain*
coffee *koppi*
cold *dingin*
collar *leher*
comb *sisir;* to comb *menjisir*
come *datang;* come here! *Mari sini!*
cook *tukang dapur;* to cook *massakkan*

to cost: what does that cost? *Brapa itu?* i.e. how much is this?); it costs 3 guilders *adda harganja tiga rupia;* what does the drive cost? *brapa sewa?*
to count *hitung*
crocodile *buaja*
cup *mangko*
cupboard *lamari*
curtain *tire*
to cut *putung*
dagger *kris*
dark *glap*
day *hari;* by day *hari-hari*
day after tomorrow *lussa*
dear (price) *mahal;* that is too dear *itu terlalu mahal*
deep *dalam*
depart *pergi* (usually pron. *peggi)*
departure *pengankatan*
descend *turun*
diarrhoea *tjirit*
difficult *suka*
dirty *kotor*
doctor (Eur.) *dokter*
dog *anjing*
door *pintu*
to drink *minum*
drive *naik kreta;* drive on! *jalan!*
driver *sais,kusir*
dry (adj.) *kring;* to dry *jadi kring*
ear *telinga*
East *timur*
eat *makan*
egg/s *telor*
elephant *gaja*
empty *kosong*
enough *chukup*
evening *sore;* in the e. *sore sore*
eye *mata*
fan *kipas*
far from *jau*
feather *bulu*
fetch, see "bring"
fever *demam*
finger *jari*
fire *api*
fish *ikan*
flower, blossom *bunga*
foot *kaki*
for *karana (krana, karna)*
forest *utan*
forget *lupa*
fork *garfu*
foul, rotten *busuk*
from *deri;* from where? *deri mana?*
in front of *di-muka* (or *ka-muka)*
fruit *bua*
full *penu*
give *kasi;* give me (us) coffee *kasi koppi!*
glass *glass*
go *pergi (peggi, piggi), jalan* (also = "drive")
gold *amas*
good *baik*
greet *bri tabe, kasi tabe.* The usual greetings are *tabe (tuwan)!* = good day (sir); also = good evening etc.; *slamat datang tuan!* welcome; *slamat* also when leaving = farewell
to guide *hantar;* guide *orang penghantar*
guilder *rupia*
gun *bedil*
hair *rambut*
hand *tangan;* hand-towel *kain menjapu (tangan)*
handkerchief *saputangan*
hard *krass*
hat *topi;* sun-hat *tudung*
to have = *adda* + Dative
to have to *harus*
head *kapala*
healthy *baik;* health *salamat*
hear *dengar*
heavy *brat*
here *sini;* hence *ka-sini*
his, see p.342
horse *kuda;* groom *tukang kuda*

hour *jam;* ½-,¼-, *satenga jam, sa-suku jam*
house *ruma*
how much? *brapa?*
hurry, see "quick"
husband *laki*
ice *ajer batu*
idle *malas*
ill *sakit;* also = "illness"
immediately *sabentar* (i.e. one moment)
in *di-,* (direction) *ka-:* in the town *di-negri;* into town *ka-negri*
ink *tinta*
inn *ruma sopi*
journey *perjalanan;* to journey *berjalan;* traveller *orang perjalanan*
jug *tempajan, bujung* (large pitcher for water)
key *ana kunchi*
knife *pissau, pisso*
to know *tahu*
lake *tasik*
lamp *lampu*
large *besar*
to lay *taruh*
lazy *malas*
left *kiri;* on the left *di-kiri, ka-kiri* (cf. "in")
leg *kaki*
letter *surat* (also "note")
letter paper *kartas surat*
to light *pasang*
light (weight) *ringan*
light (n.) *trang* (see "candle")
linen *kain, kain-kain;* dirty linen *kain kotor*
a little *sadikit*
lock (door etc.) *kunchi*
look after, keep safe *simpat*
luggage *barang-barang*
madam (in polite address to European) *nonja*
to make, do *bekin, buat*
man, person *orang;* this word is used superfluously when counting people: 5 men *laki-laki lima orang;* 1 child *sa-orang ana*
matches *rek*
mattress *kasur*
meal *makanan;* when ordering at a hotel, etc. = "breakfast, lunch, dinner" (the meaning being obvious from the circumstances): Provide breakfast for 4 pers. *sediakan makan krana ampat orang!* Boy, is the lunch ready? *Adaka makan sedia, boy?*
meat *daging;* beef, mutton etc. *daging lembu, daging domba* etc.
medicine *abat*
mend *tampal* middle, half *tenga*
milk *(ajer) sussu*
mirror *chermin*
Mohammedan *orang islam*
money *wang;* small change *wang ketchil*
moon *bulan;* moonlight *chahaja bulan*
more *lebi;* used to form the comparative: *bai* (good), *lebi bai* better
morning *pagi;* in the morning *pagi-pagi*
mosquito, midge *njamuk*
mosquito net *klambu*
mountain *gunung*
mouth *mulut*
much, very *banja;* too much *banja chukup*
mutton, see "sheep" & "meat"
native *pasak*
near *dekat*
necessary *harus*
neck *leher*
to need *berhadjat akam;* see also "want"

new *baharu, bahru*
night *malam;* at night *malam-malam*
no *tida*
noon *tenga hari*
North *utara*
nose *hidung*
not *biada;* with an Imperative *jangan;* do not lie (say not lies) *jangan chakap bohong!*
not yet *belum*
old *tua*
on, see "over"
to open *buka*
orange *djeruk mani*
to order *bertitah, suruh;* order
(call) a carriage *panggil kreta!*
other *lain*
over, above, on *di-atas, ka-atas*
pain *sakit;* headache *sakit kapala;* toothache *sakit gigi* etc.
paper *kartas*
path *simpangan, jalan*
to pay *bajer;* payment *bajaran*
pen *kallam*
pepper *lada*
pig *babi* (cf."meat")
pillow *bantal*
plain (n.) *padang*
plate *piring*
to point, show *tunjuk*
poisonous *upas*
pond *telaga, kulam*
poor, wretched *meskin*
port *pelabuhan*
porter *kuli*
post office *kanturpopss;* in Singapore, the Engl. word may be used: where is the post office? *Di-mana Post Offis?*
potato(es) *kentang*
poultry *hajam*
price (value) *harga;* cf. "cost"
to put, see "to lay"
put on (clothes) *pake*
quick *lekas;* also *sigra:* be quick *ber-sigra*
quiet *berdiam*
railway *jalan besi* (i.e. iron way)
rain *hujan*
ready *sedia;* make ready *bekin sedia;* get (something) ready *sediakan*
to request *minta*
rice *brass;* boiled r. *nassi, nasi*
rich *kaja*
ride *berjalan berkuda* (i.e. journey on horse)
right (side, hand etc.) *kanan;* on/to the r. *di-kanan, ka-kanan*
river *sunge, kali, tji*
to roast *tunu;* roast meat *daging tunu*
room *kamar*
saddle *sella;* saddle the horse *paki kuda!*
salt *garam*
say *bilang;* (report) *kabarkan* see "speak"
scissors *gunting*
sea *laut*
see *lihat*
seldom *djarang*
sell *jual*
servant *budak, boy*
shade *bajang, lindung*; sunshade *pajung* (also = umbrella)
sheep *biri-biri,* (mutton) *domba*
ship *kapal*
shirt *kameja*
shoe *sapatu* (also boot)
shoemaker *tukang sapatu*
shoot *passang*
shop *toko*
to shut *tutup*
silver *perak*
Sir, in addressing a European *tuan, tuwan;* in conversation = you: how are you? = is the gentleman well? *Tuwan adda bai?* – in

addressing a Malay of higher rank, *tuwanka*
sit down *duduk*
to sleep *tidor*
slow(ly) *lambat;* drive (or walk) slowly *jalan plan-plan* (for perlahan-perlahan)
small *ketchil*
smith *tukang bessi*
smoke *assap;* to smoke, see "tobacco"
snake *ular*
soap *sabun*
soft *lembi, lembut*
somewhat, see "a little"
soup *sup*
South *selatan*
speak *bichara, chakap*
spoon *senduk*
station *steschn kreta api* (from Engl. "station" & Port. "carreta": station of the fire-carriage, i.e. locomotive)
steamer *kapal asap*
stocking *sarung kaki*
stop! *brenti!* (for *berhenti!)*
storm *ribut*
street *jalan, lebo*
stupid *bodok*
sugar *gula*
suit *pakean*
sun *matahari*
supervise *djaga*
supper *makanan malam* (cf. "eat")
sweep *sapu*
table *meja*
tailor *tukang menjahit*
take *tarima, bawa;* (to a driver) Take me to A.B.& Co's shop *peggi* (i.e. drive) *ka A.B.& Co. punja gedong!*
take away *angkat;* (clear the table) *angkat makanan*
tea (meal) *te;* (drink) *ajer te*
telegraph (office) *telegrap*
to thank *trima kasi*
there *sana*
thief *orang pentjuri*
thin *nipis*
thirsty *berhaus*
this *ini;* that *itu*
thunder *guntur*
tiger *machan*
tired *lela, paja*
tobacco *tembako,* (pipe tobacco) *roko;* to smoke *minum roko*
today *hari ini, harini*
tomorrow *essuk*
too (big, much, etc.) *keralu* (very)
tooth *gigi*
towards *ka-:* to the forest *ka-uten*
town *nergi, bendar;* quarter of a town, see "vi llage"
trousers *chelana*
turn round (turn the carriage) *pussing (kreta)!*
under *di-bawa* (or *ka-bawa,* cf. "in")
underpants *chelana dalam*
understand *bissa*
village *dusun, kampong* (latter also = quarter of a town: the Chinese quarter: *kampong China*
W.C. *tampat buang ajer* (the place of pouring away)
to wait *tangguh*
to wake: Wake (=call) me tomorrow at 7 o'c.lock *pangil saja pukul tuju*
walking-stick *tungkat*
to want *mau*
warm *panas*
to wash *chuchi;* wash oneself *men chuchi diri-nja*
washerman *tukang minatu*
water *ajer;* drinking-water *ajer minum;* mineral water *ajer blanda;* cold w. ajer dingin; *warm w.* ajer panas
West *barat*
what? *apa?* E.g. what does the

gentleman want? *Apa tuwan minta?*
when? *kapan?*
where? *mana, di-mana;* whence? *derimana;* whither? *ka-mana*
white *puti*
who? *siapa?* who is there? *siapa datang?* i.e. who comes?
wife *bini*
window *jandela*
wine *anggur, ajer anggur;* red wine *anggur merah;* champagne *anggur puf;* white wine *anggur puti*
to wish, see "want"; I wish food & accommodation *saja minta makan sama tidor*
woman *orang perampuan*
word *kata*
wound *luka*
write *tulis*
year *taun*
yellow *kuning*
yes *saja*
yesterday *klamarin*
young *muda*

Register

Register

Register

Register

Register

Register

Register

Register

Register

Register

Register

Register

Register

Register

Register

Register

Register

www.ingramcontent.com/pod-product-compliance
Ingram Content Group UK Ltd.
Pitfield, Milton Keynes, MK11 3LW, UK
UKHW041432210726
13854UKWH00010B/1875

9 780956 528964